NEW PERSPECTIVES

Microsoft® Office 365™ & PowerPoint® 2016

COMPREHENSIVE

Katherine T. Pinard

Australia • Brazil • Mexico • Singapore • United Kingdom • United States

New Perspectives Microsoft® Office 365™ & PowerPoint® 2016, Comprehensive
Katherine T. Pinard

SVP, GM Skills & Global Product Management: Dawn Gerrain

Product Director: Kathleen McMahon

Senior Product Team Manager: Lauren Murphy

Product Team Manager: Andrea Topping

Associate Product Manager: Melissa Stehler

Senior Director, Development: Marah Bellegarde

Product Development Manager: Leigh Hefferon

Senior Content Developer: Kathy Finnegan

Developmental Editor: Kim T. M. Crowley

Product Assistant: Erica Chapman

Marketing Director: Michele McTighe

Marketing Manager: Stephanie Albracht

Senior Production Director: Wendy Troeger

Production Director: Patty Stephan

Senior Content Project Manager: Jennifer Goguen McGrail

Designer: Diana Graham

Composition: GEX Publishing Services

Cover image(s): View Apart/Shutterstock.com

For product information and technology assistance, contact us at
Cengage Learning Customer & Sales Support, 1-800-354-9706

For permission to use material from this text or product, submit all requests online at **www.cengage.com/permissions**.
Further permissions questions can be e-mailed to
permissionrequest@cengage.com

Mac users: If you're working through this product using a Mac, some of the steps may vary. Additional information for Mac users is included with the Data Files for this product.

Library of Congress Control Number: 2016934395
ISBN: 978-1-305-88123-5

Cengage Learning
20 Channel Center Street
Boston, MA 02210
USA

Cengage Learning is a leading provider of customized learning solutions with employees residing in nearly 40 different countries and sales in more than 125 countries around the world. Find your local representative at **www.cengage.com.**

Cengage Learning products are represented in Canada by Nelson Education, Ltd.

To learn more about Cengage Learning, visit **www.cengage.com**

Purchase any of our products at your local college store or at our preferred online store **www.cengagebrain.com**

Printed in the United States of America
Print Number: 02 Print Year: 2016

BRIEF CONTENTS

TABLE OF CONTENTS

Module 4 Advanced Animations and Distributing Presentations

Module 5 Integrating PowerPoint with Other Programs

Productivity Apps for School and Work

OneNote
Sway
Office Mix
Edge

Corinne Hoisington

Being computer literate no longer means mastery of only Word, Excel, PowerPoint, Outlook, and Access. To become technology power users, Hunter, Nori, Zoe, and Lochlan are exploring Microsoft OneNote, Sway, Mix, and Edge in Office 2016 and Windows 10.

In this Module

Learn to use productivity apps!
Links to companion **Sways**, featuring **videos** with hands-on instructions, are located on www.cengagebrain.com.

Introduction to OneNote 2016

notebook | section tab | To Do tag | screen clipping | note | template | Microsoft OneNote Mobile app | sync | drawing canvas | inked handwriting | Ink to Text

Bottom Line

- OneNote is a note-taking app for your academic and professional life.
- Use OneNote to get organized by gathering your ideas, sketches, webpages, photos, videos, and notes in one place.

As you glance around any classroom, you invariably see paper notebooks and notepads on each desk. Because deciphering and sharing handwritten notes can be a challenge, Microsoft OneNote 2016 replaces physical notebooks, binders, and paper notes with a searchable, digital notebook. OneNote captures your ideas and schoolwork on any device so you can stay organized, share notes, and work with others on projects. Whether you are a student taking class notes as shown in **Figure 1** or an employee taking notes in company meetings, OneNote is the one place to keep notes for all of your projects.

Figure 1: OneNote 2016 notebook

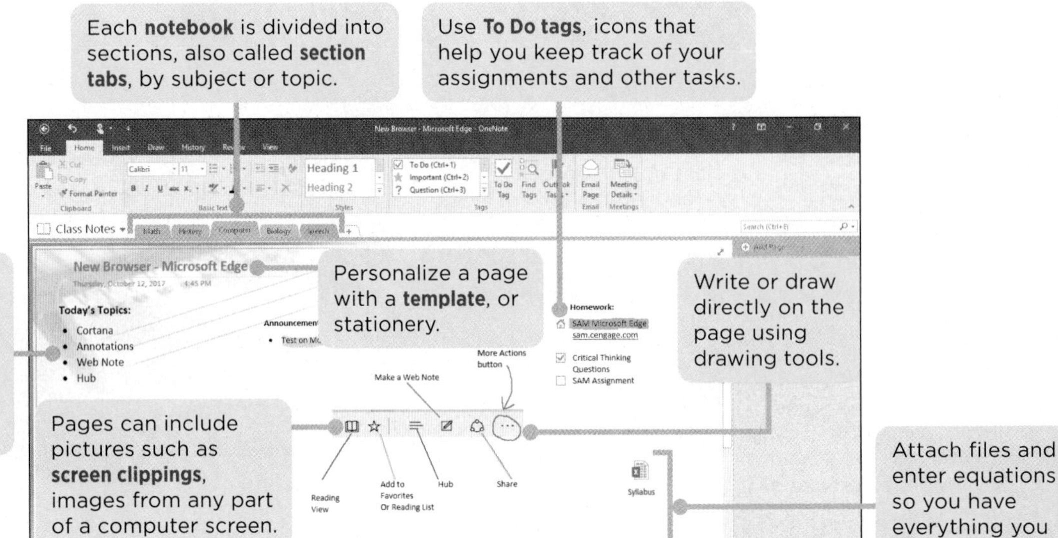

Creating a OneNote Notebook

OneNote is divided into sections similar to those in a spiral-bound notebook. Each OneNote notebook contains sections, pages, and other notebooks. You can use OneNote for school, business, and personal projects. Store information for each type of project in different notebooks to keep your tasks separate, or use any other organization that suits you. OneNote is flexible enough to adapt to the way you want to work.

When you create a notebook, it contains a blank page with a plain white background by default, though you can use templates, or stationery, to apply designs in categories such as Academic, Business, Decorative, and Planners. Start typing or use the buttons on the Insert tab to insert notes, which are small resizable windows that can contain text, equations, tables, on-screen writing, images, audio and video recordings, to-do lists, file attachments, and file printouts. Add as many notes as you need to each page.

Learn to use OneNote!
Links to companion **Sways**, featuring **videos** with hands-on instructions, are located on www.cengagebrain.com.

Syncing a Notebook to the Cloud

OneNote saves your notes every time you make a change in a notebook. To make sure you can access your notebooks with a laptop, tablet, or smartphone wherever you are, OneNote uses cloud-based storage, such as OneDrive or SharePoint. **Microsoft OneNote Mobile app**, a lightweight version of OneNote 2016 shown in **Figure 2**, is available for free in the Windows Store, Google Play for Android devices, and the AppStore for iOS devices.

If you have a Microsoft account, OneNote saves your notes on OneDrive automatically for all your mobile devices and computers, which is called **syncing**. For example, you can use OneNote to take notes on your laptop during class, and then open OneNote on your phone to study later. To use a notebook stored on your computer with your OneNote Mobile app, move the notebook to OneDrive. You can quickly share notebook content with other people using OneDrive.

Figure 2: Microsoft OneNote Mobile app

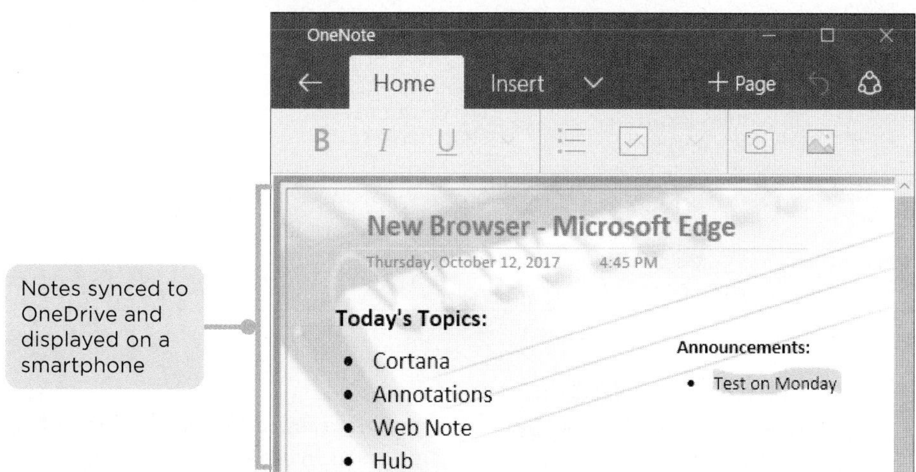

Taking Notes

Use OneNote pages to organize your notes by class and topic or lecture. Beyond simple typed notes, OneNote stores drawings, converts handwriting to searchable text and mathematical sketches to equations, and records audio and video.

OneNote includes drawing tools that let you sketch freehand drawings such as biological cell diagrams and financial supply-and-demand charts. As shown in **Figure 3**, the Draw tab on the ribbon provides these drawing tools along with shapes so you can insert diagrams and other illustrations to represent your ideas. When you draw on a page, OneNote creates a **drawing canvas**, which is a container for shapes and lines.

OneNote is ideal for taking notes during meetings, whether you are recording minutes, documenting a discussion, sketching product diagrams, or listing follow-up items. Use a meeting template to add pages with content appropriate for meetings.

Figure 3: Tools on the Draw tab

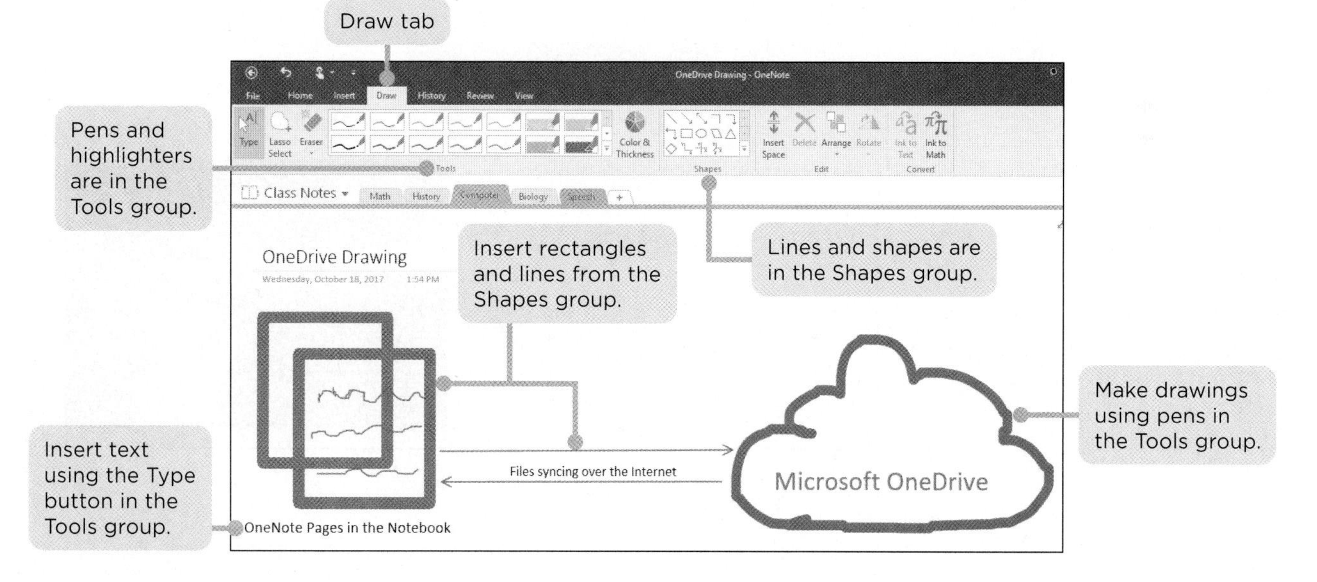

Converting Handwriting to Text

When you use a pen tool to write on a notebook page, the text you enter is called **inked handwriting**. OneNote can convert inked handwriting to typed text when you use the **Ink to Text** button in the Convert group on the Draw tab, as shown in **Figure 4**. After OneNote converts the handwriting to text, you can use the Search box to find terms in the converted text or any other note in your notebooks.

Figure 4: Converting handwriting to text

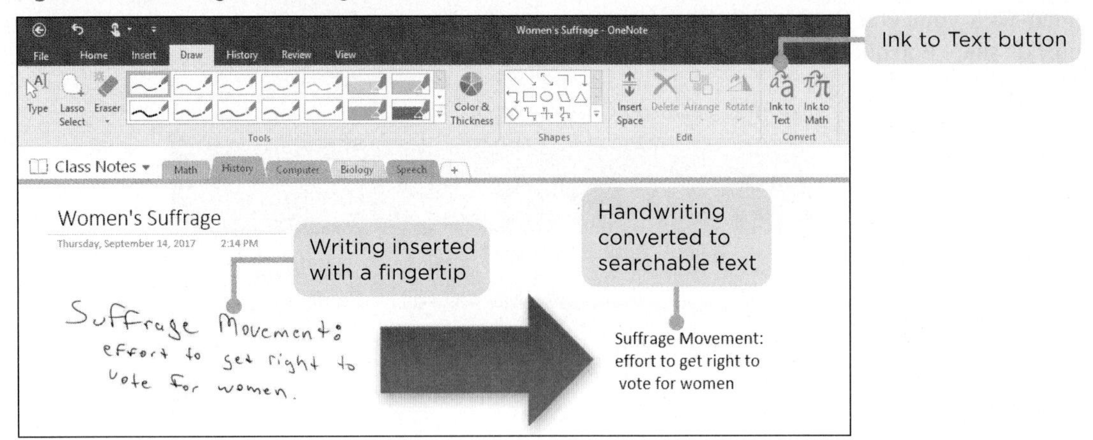

On the Job Now

Use OneNote as a place to brainstorm ongoing work projects. If a notebook contains sensitive material, you can password-protect some or all of the notebook so that only certain people can open it.

Recording a Lecture

If your computer or mobile device has a microphone or camera, OneNote can record the audio or video from a lecture or business meeting as shown in **Figure 5**. When you record a lecture (with your instructor's permission), you can follow along, take regular notes at your own pace, and review the video recording later. You can control the start, pause, and stop motions of the recording when you play back the recording of your notes.

Figure 5: Video inserted in a notebook

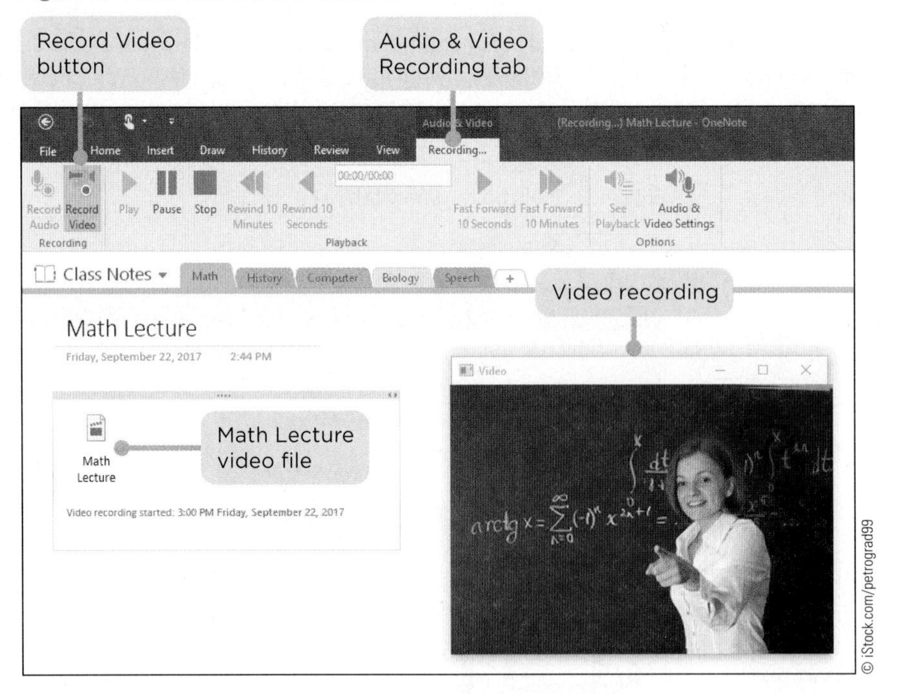

Try This Now

Learn to use OneNote!
Links to companion **Sways**, featuring **videos** with hands-on instructions, are located on www.cengagebrain.com.

1: Taking Notes for a Week

As a student, you can get organized by using OneNote to take detailed notes in your classes. Perform the following tasks:

a. Create a new OneNote notebook on your Microsoft OneDrive account (the default location for new notebooks). Name the notebook with your first name followed by "Notes," as in **Caleb Notes**.
b. Create four section tabs, each with a different class name.
c. Take detailed notes in those classes for one week. Be sure to include notes, drawings, and other types of content.
d. Sync your notes with your OneDrive. Submit your assignment in the format specified by your instructor.

2: Using OneNote to Organize a Research Paper

You have a research paper due on the topic of three habits of successful students. Use OneNote to organize your research. Perform the following tasks:

a. Create a new OneNote notebook on your Microsoft OneDrive account. Name the notebook **Success Research**.
b. Create three section tabs with the following names:
   - **Take Detailed Notes**
   - **Be Respectful in Class**
   - **Come to Class Prepared**
c. On the web, research the topics and find three sources for each section. Copy a sentence from each source and paste the sentence into the appropriate section. When you paste the sentence, OneNote inserts it in a note with a link to the source.
d. Sync your notes with your OneDrive. Submit your assignment in the format specified by your instructor.

3: Planning Your Career

Note: This activity requires a webcam or built-in video camera on any type of device.

Consider an occupation that interests you. Using OneNote, examine the responsibilities, education requirements, potential salary, and employment outlook of a specific career. Perform the following tasks:

a. Create a new OneNote notebook on your Microsoft OneDrive account. Name the notebook with your first name followed by a career title, such as **Kara - App Developer**.
b. Create four section tabs with the names **Responsibilities, Education Requirements, Median Salary**, and **Employment Outlook**.
c. Research the responsibilities of your career path. Using OneNote, record a short video (approximately 30 seconds) of yourself explaining the responsibilities of your career path. Place the video in the Responsibilities section.
d. On the web, research the educational requirements for your career path and find two appropriate sources. Copy a paragraph from each source and paste them into the appropriate section. When you paste a paragraph, OneNote inserts it in a note with a link to the source.
e. Research the median salary for a single year for this career. Create a mathematical equation in the Median Salary section that multiplies the amount of the median salary times 20 years to calculate how much you will possibly earn.
f. For the Employment Outlook section, research the outlook for your career path. Take at least four notes about what you find when researching the topic.
g. Sync your notes with your OneDrive. Submit your assignment in the format specified by your instructor.

Introduction to Sway

Sway site | responsive design | Storyline | card | Creative Commons license | animation emphasis effects | Docs.com

Bottom Line

- Drag photos, videos, and files from your computer and content from Facebook and Twitter directly to your Sway presentation.
- Run Sway in a web browser or as an app on your smartphone, and save presentations as webpages.

Expressing your ideas in a presentation typically means creating PowerPoint slides or a Word document. Microsoft Sway gives you another way to engage an audience. Sway is a free Microsoft tool available at Sway.com or as an app in Office 365. Using Sway, you can combine text, images, videos, and social media in a website called a **Sway site** that you can share and display on any device. To get started, you create a digital story on a web-based canvas without borders, slides, cells, or page breaks. A Sway site organizes the text, images, and video into a **responsive design**, which means your content adapts perfectly to any screen size as shown in **Figure 6**. You store a Sway site in the cloud on OneDrive using a free Microsoft account.

Figure 6: Sway site with responsive design

Creating a Sway Presentation

Learn to use Sway!
Links to companion **Sways**, featuring **videos** with hands-on instructions, are located on www.cengagebrain.com.

You can use Sway to build a digital flyer, a club newsletter, a vacation blog, an informational site, a digital art portfolio, or a new product rollout. After you select your topic and sign into Sway with your Microsoft account, a **Storyline** opens, providing tools and a work area for composing your digital story. See **Figure 7**. Each story can include text, images, and videos. You create a Sway by adding text and media content into a Storyline section, or **card**. To add pictures, videos, or documents, select a card in the left pane and then select the Insert Content button. The first card in a Sway presentation contains a title and background image.

Figure 7: Creating a Sway site

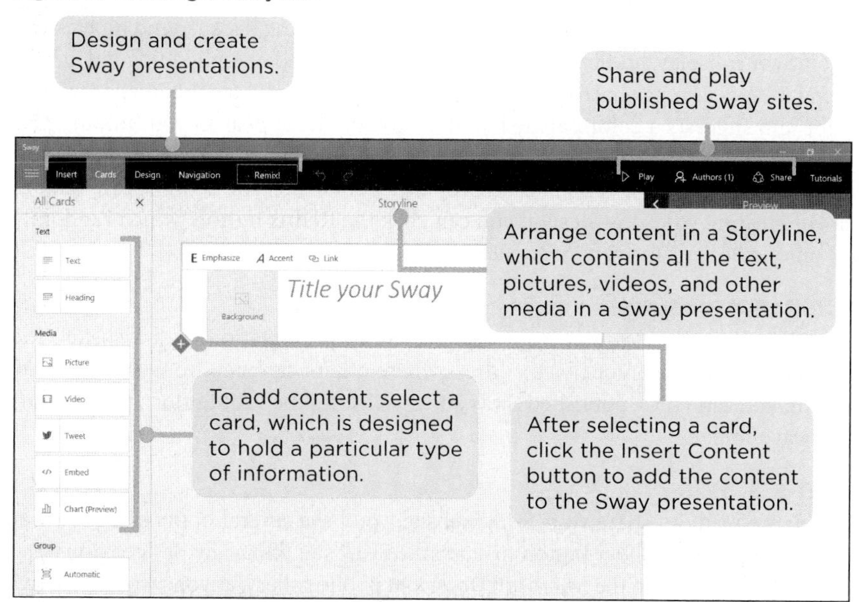

Adding Content to Build a Story

As you work, Sway searches the Internet to help you find relevant images, videos, tweets, and other content from online sources such as Bing, YouTube, Twitter, and Facebook. You can drag content from the search results right into the Storyline. In addition, you can upload your own images and videos directly in the presentation. For example, if you are creating a Sway presentation about the market for commercial drones, Sway suggests content to incorporate into the presentation by displaying it in the left pane as search results. The search results include drone images tagged with a **Creative Commons license** at online sources as shown in **Figure 8**. A Creative Commons license is a public copyright license that allows the free distribution of an otherwise copyrighted work. In addition, you can specify the source of the media. For example, you can add your own Facebook or OneNote pictures and videos in Sway without leaving the app.

On the Job Now

If you have a Microsoft Word document containing an outline of your business content, drag the outline into Sway to create a card for each topic.

Figure 8: Images in Sway search results

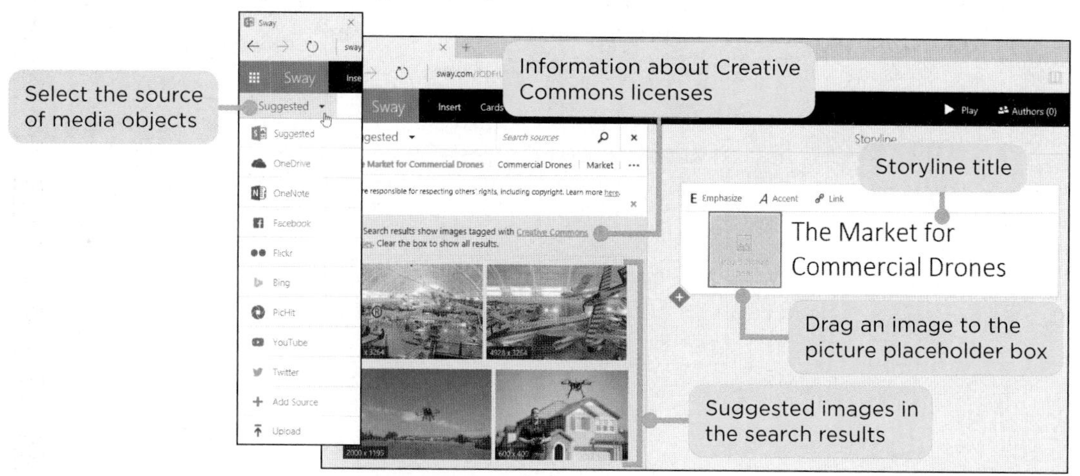

If your project team wants to collaborate on a Sway presentation, click the Authors button on the navigation bar to invite others to edit the presentation.

Designing a Sway

Sway professionally designs your Storyline content by resizing background images and fonts to fit your display, and by floating text, animating media, embedding video, and removing images as a page scrolls out of view. Sway also evaluates the images in your Storyline and suggests a color palette based on colors that appear in your photos. Use the Design button to display tools including color palettes, font choices, **animation emphasis effects**, and style templates to provide a personality for a Sway presentation. Instead of creating your own design, you can click the Remix button, which randomly selects unique designs for your Sway site.

Publishing a Sway

Use the Play button to display your finished Sway presentation as a website. The Address bar includes a unique web address where others can view your Sway site. As the author, you can edit a published Sway site by clicking the Edit button (pencil icon) on the Sway toolbar.

Sharing a Sway

When you are ready to share your Sway website, you have several options as shown in **Figure 9**. Use the Share slider button to share the Sway site publically or keep it private. If you add the Sway site to the Microsoft **Docs.com** public gallery, anyone worldwide can use Bing, Google, or other search engines to find, view, and share your Sway site. You can also share your Sway site using Facebook, Twitter, Google+, Yammer, and other social media sites. Link your presentation to any webpage or email the link to your audience. Sway can also generate a code for embedding the link within another webpage.

Figure 9: Sharing a Sway site

Share button

Play Authors (1) Share

Share Just me

Drag the slider button to Just me to keep the Sway site private

Share with the world

Post the Sway site on Docs.com

Docs.com - Your public gallery

Share with friends

Options differ depending on your Microsoft account

Send friends a link to the Sway site

https://sway.com/JQDFrUaxmg4lEbbk

More options

Viewers can duplicate this Sway

Stop sharing

Try This Now

> **Learn to use Sway!**
> Links to companion **Sways**, featuring **videos** with hands-on instructions, are located on www.cengagebrain.com.

1: Creating a Sway Resume

Sway is a digital storytelling app. Create a Sway resume to share the skills, job experiences, and achievements you have that match the requirements of a future job interest. Perform the following tasks:

a. Create a new presentation in Sway to use as a digital resume. Title the Sway Storyline with your full name and then select a background image.
b. Create three separate sections titled **Academic Background, Work Experience**, and **Skills**, and insert text, a picture, and a paragraph or bulleted points in each section. Be sure to include your own picture.
c. Add a fourth section that includes a video about your school that you find online.
d. Customize the design of your presentation.
e. Submit your assignment link in the format specified by your instructor.

2: Creating an Online Sway Newsletter

Newsletters are designed to capture the attention of their target audience. Using Sway, create a newsletter for a club, organization, or your favorite music group. Perform the following tasks:

a. Create a new presentation in Sway to use as a digital newsletter for a club, organization, or your favorite music group. Provide a title for the Sway Storyline and select an appropriate background image.
b. Select three separate sections with appropriate titles, such as Upcoming Events. In each section, insert text, a picture, and a paragraph or bulleted points.
c. Add a fourth section that includes a video about your selected topic.
d. Customize the design of your presentation.
e. Submit your assignment link in the format specified by your instructor.

3: Creating and Sharing a Technology Presentation

To place a Sway presentation in the hands of your entire audience, you can share a link to the Sway presentation. Create a Sway presentation on a new technology and share it with your class. Perform the following tasks:

a. Create a new presentation in Sway about a cutting-edge technology topic. Provide a title for the Sway Storyline and select a background image.
b. Create four separate sections about your topic, and include text, a picture, and a paragraph in each section.
c. Add a fifth section that includes a video about your topic.
d. Customize the design of your presentation.
e. Share the link to your Sway with your classmates and submit your assignment link in the format specified by your instructor.

Introduction to Office Mix

Bottom Line
- Office Mix is a free PowerPoint add-in from Microsoft that adds features to PowerPoint.
- The Mix tab on the PowerPoint ribbon provides tools for creating screen recordings, videos, interactive quizzes, and live webpages.

add-in | clip | slide recording | Slide Notes | screen recording | free-response quiz

To enliven business meetings and lectures, Microsoft adds a new dimension to presentations with a powerful toolset called Office Mix, a free add-in for PowerPoint. (An **add-in** is software that works with an installed app to extend its features.) Using Office Mix, you can record yourself on video, capture still and moving images on your desktop, and insert interactive elements such as quizzes and live webpages directly into PowerPoint slides. When you post the finished presentation to OneDrive, Office Mix provides a link you can share with friends and colleagues. Anyone with an Internet connection and a web browser can watch a published Office Mix presentation, such as the one in **Figure 10**, on a computer or mobile device.

Figure 10: Office Mix presentation

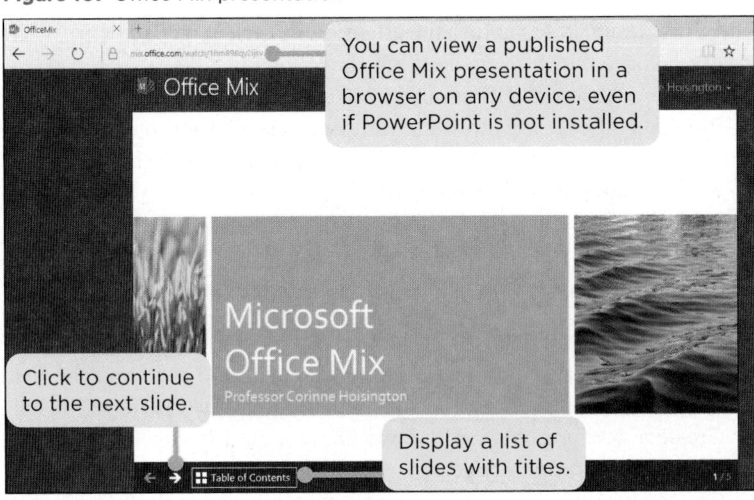

Learn to use Office Mix!
Links to companion **Sways**, featuring **videos** with hands-on instructions, are located on www.cengagebrain.com.

Adding Office Mix to PowerPoint

To get started, you create an Office Mix account at the website mix.office.com using an email address or a Facebook or Google account. Next, you download and install the Office Mix add-in (see **Figure 11**). Office Mix appears as a new tab named Mix on the PowerPoint ribbon in versions of Office 2013 and Office 2016 running on personal computers (PCs).

Figure 11: Getting started with Office Mix

Capturing Video Clips

A **clip** is a short segment of audio, such as music, or video. After finishing the content on a PowerPoint slide, you can use Office Mix to add a video clip to animate or illustrate the content. Office Mix creates video clips in two ways: by recording live action on a webcam and by capturing screen images and movements. If your computer has a webcam, you can record yourself and annotate the slide to create a **slide recording** as shown in **Figure 12**.

Companies are using Office Mix to train employees about new products, to explain benefit packages to new workers, and to educate interns about office procedures.

Figure 12: Making a slide recording

When you are making a slide recording, you can record your spoken narration at the same time. The **Slide Notes** feature works like a teleprompter to help you focus on your presentation content instead of memorizing your narration. Use the Inking tools to make annotations or add highlighting using different pen types and colors. After finishing a recording, edit the video in PowerPoint to trim the length or set playback options.

The second way to create a video is to capture on-screen images and actions with or without a voiceover. This method is ideal if you want to show how to use your favorite website or demonstrate an app such as OneNote. To share your screen with an audience, select the part of the screen you want to show in the video. Office Mix captures everything that happens in that area to create a **screen recording**, as shown in **Figure 13**. Office Mix inserts the screen recording as a video in the slide.

To make your video recordings accessible to people with hearing impairments, use the Office Mix closed-captioning tools. You can also use closed captions to supplement audio that is difficult to understand and to provide an aid for those learning to read.

Figure 13: Making a screen recording

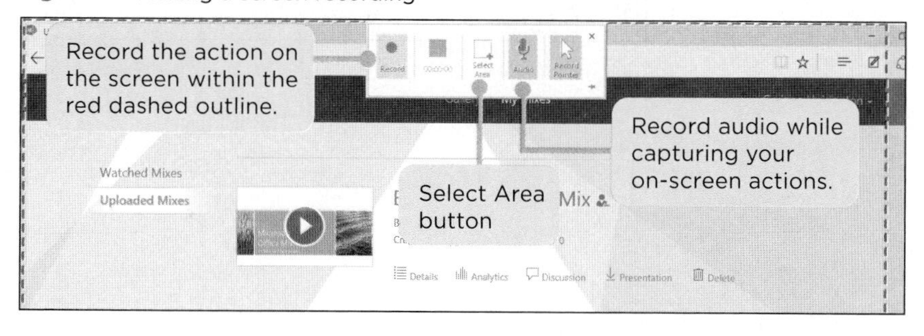

Inserting Quizzes, Live Webpages, and Apps

To enhance and assess audience understanding, make your slides interactive by adding quizzes, live webpages, and apps. Quizzes give immediate feedback to the user as shown in **Figure 14**. Office Mix supports several quiz formats, including a **free-response quiz** similar to a short answer quiz, and true/false, multiple-choice, and multiple-response formats.

Figure 14: Creating an interactive quiz

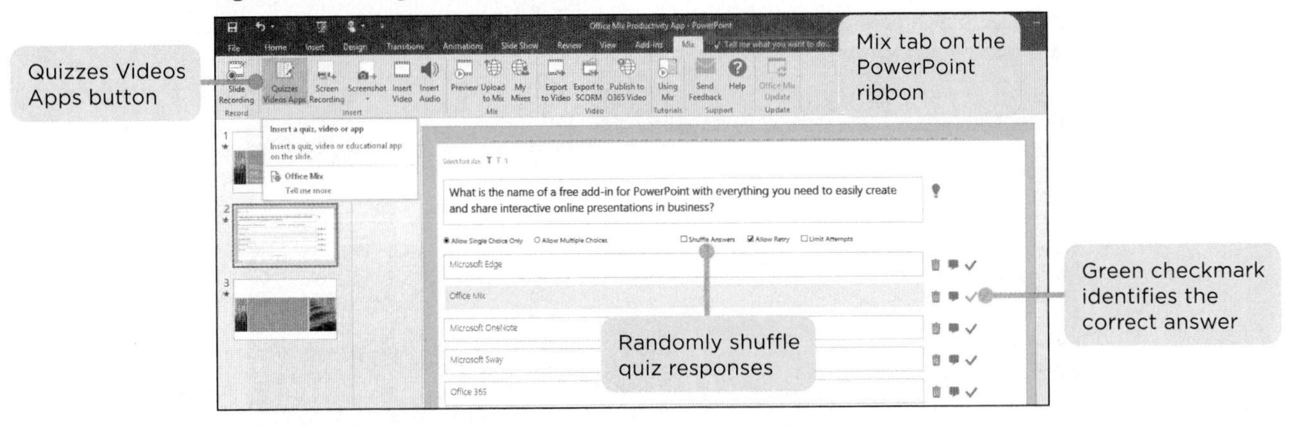

Sharing an Office Mix Presentation

When you complete your work with Office Mix, upload the presentation to your personal Office Mix dashboard as shown in **Figure 15**. Users of PCs, Macs, iOS devices, and Android devices can access and play Office Mix presentations. The Office Mix dashboard displays built-in analytics that include the quiz results and how much time viewers spent on each slide. You can play completed Office Mix presentations online or download them as movies.

Figure 15: Sharing an Office Mix presentation

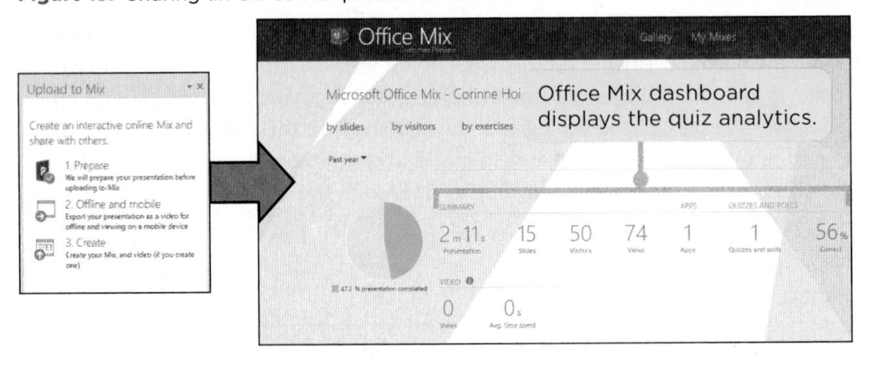

Try This Now

Learn to use Office Mix!
Links to companion **Sways**, featuring **videos** with hands-on instructions, are located on www.cengagebrain.com.

1: Creating an Office Mix Tutorial for OneNote

Note: This activity requires a microphone on your computer.

Office Mix makes it easy to record screens and their contents. Create PowerPoint slides with an Office Mix screen recording to show OneNote 2016 features. Perform the following tasks:

a. Create a PowerPoint presentation with the Ion Boardroom template. Create an opening slide with the title **My Favorite OneNote Features** and enter your name in the subtitle.
b. Create three additional slides, each titled with a new feature of OneNote. Open OneNote and use the Mix tab in PowerPoint to capture three separate screen recordings that teach your favorite features.
c. Add a fifth slide that quizzes the user with a multiple-choice question about OneNote and includes four responses. Be sure to insert a checkmark indicating the correct response.
d. Upload the completed presentation to your Office Mix dashboard and share the link with your instructor.
e. Submit your assignment link in the format specified by your instructor.

2: Teaching Augmented Reality with Office Mix

Note: This activity requires a webcam or built-in video camera on your computer.

A local elementary school has asked you to teach augmented reality to its students using Office Mix. Perform the following tasks:

a. Research augmented reality using your favorite online search tools.
b. Create a PowerPoint presentation with the Frame template. Create an opening slide with the title **Augmented Reality** and enter your name in the subtitle.
c. Create a slide with four bullets summarizing your research of augmented reality. Create a 20-second slide recording of yourself providing a quick overview of augmented reality.
d. Create another slide with a 30-second screen recording of a video about augmented reality from a site such as YouTube or another video-sharing site.
e. Add a final slide that quizzes the user with a true/false question about augmented reality. Be sure to insert a checkmark indicating the correct response.
f. Upload the completed presentation to your Office Mix dashboard and share the link with your instructor.
g. Submit your assignment link in the format specified by your instructor.

3: Marketing a Travel Destination with Office Mix

Note: This activity requires a webcam or built-in video camera on your computer.

To convince your audience to travel to a particular city, create a slide presentation marketing any city in the world using a slide recording, screen recording, and a quiz. Perform the following tasks:

a. Create a PowerPoint presentation with any template. Create an opening slide with the title of the city you are marketing as a travel destination and your name in the subtitle.
b. Create a slide with four bullets about the featured city. Create a 30-second slide recording of yourself explaining why this city is the perfect vacation destination.
c. Create another slide with a 20-second screen recording of a travel video about the city from a site such as YouTube or another video-sharing site.
d. Add a final slide that quizzes the user with a multiple-choice question about the featured city with five responses. Be sure to include a checkmark indicating the correct response.
e. Upload the completed presentation to your Office Mix dashboard and share your link with your instructor.
f. Submit your assignment link in the format specified by your instructor.

Introduction to Microsoft Edge

Reading view | Hub | Cortana | Web Note | Inking | sandbox

Bottom Line

- Microsoft Edge is the name of the new web browser built into Windows 10.
- Microsoft Edge allows you to search the web faster, take web notes, read webpages without distractions, and get instant assistance from Cortana.

Microsoft Edge is the default web browser developed for the Windows 10 operating system as a replacement for Internet Explorer. Unlike its predecessor, Edge lets you write on webpages, read webpages without advertisements and other distractions, and search for information using a virtual personal assistant. The Edge interface is clean and basic, as shown in **Figure 16**, meaning you can pay more attention to the webpage content.

Figure 16: Microsoft Edge tools

Learn to use Edge!
Links to companion **Sways**, featuring **videos** with hands-on instructions, are located on www.cengagebrain.com.

Browsing the Web with Microsoft Edge

One of the fastest browsers available, Edge allows you to type search text directly in the Address bar. As you view the resulting webpage, you can switch to **Reading view**, which is available for most news and research sites, to eliminate distracting advertisements. For example, if you are catching up on technology news online, the webpage might be difficult to read due to a busy layout cluttered with ads. Switch to Reading view to refresh the page and remove the original page formatting, ads, and menu sidebars to read the article distraction-free.

Consider the **Hub** in Microsoft Edge as providing one-stop access to all the things you collect on the web, such as your favorite websites, reading list, surfing history, and downloaded files.

On the Job Now

Businesses started adopting Internet Explorer more than 20 years ago simply to view webpages. Today, Microsoft Edge has a different purpose: to promote interaction with the web and share its contents with colleagues.

Locating Information with Cortana

Cortana, the Windows 10 virtual assistant, plays an important role in Microsoft Edge. After you turn on Cortana, it appears as an animated circle in the Address bar when you might need assistance, as shown in the restaurant website in **Figure 17**. When you click the Cortana icon, a pane slides in from the right of the browser window to display detailed information about the restaurant, including maps and reviews. Cortana can also assist you in defining words, finding the weather, suggesting coupons for shopping, updating stock market information, and calculating math.

Figure 17: Cortana providing restaurant information

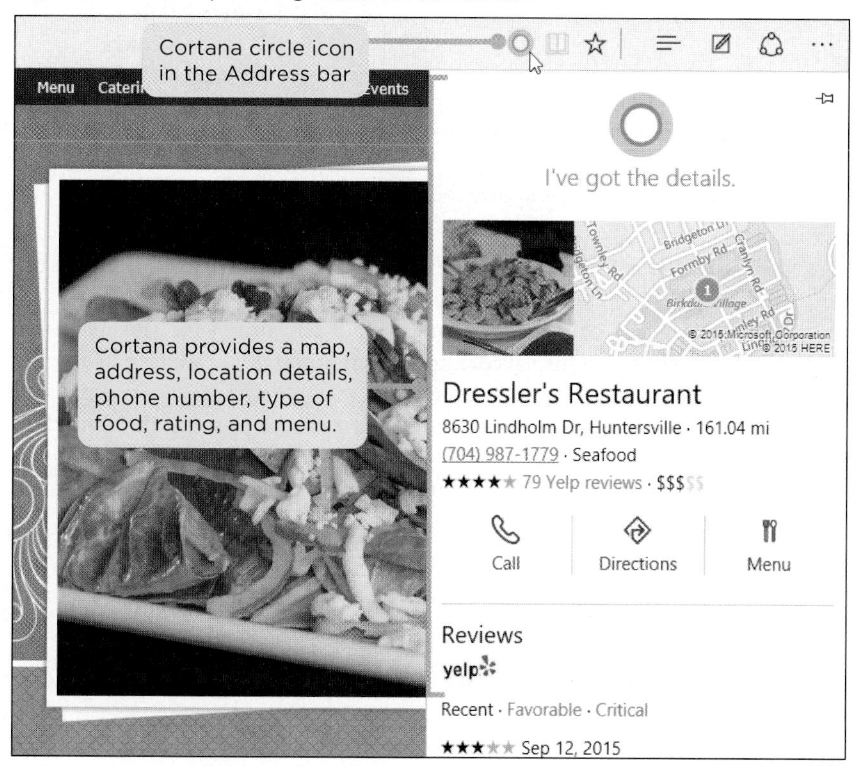

Annotating Webpages

One of the most impressive Microsoft Edge features are the **Web Note** tools, which you use to write on a webpage or to highlight text. When you click the Make a Web Note button, an **Inking** toolbar appears, as shown in **Figure 18**, that provides writing and drawing tools. These tools include an eraser, a pen, and a highlighter with different colors. You can also insert a typed note and copy a screen image (called a screen clipping). You can draw with a pointing device, fingertip, or stylus using different pen colors. Whether you add notes to a recipe, annotate sources for a research paper, or select a product while shopping online, the Web Note tools can enhance your productivity. After you complete your notes, click the Save button to save the annotations to OneNote, your Favorites list, or your Reading list. You can share the inked page with others using the Share Web Note button.

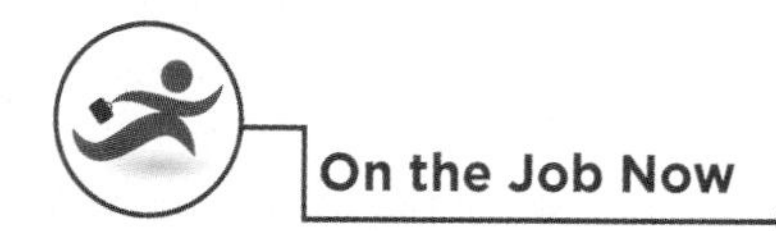

To enhance security, Microsoft Edge runs in a partial sandbox, an arrangement that prevents attackers from gaining control of your computer. Browsing within the **sandbox** protects computer resources and information from hackers.

Figure 18: Web Note tools in Microsoft Edge

Try This Now

> **Learn to use Edge!**
> Links to companion **Sways**, featuring **videos** with hands-on instructions, are located on www.cengagebrain.com.

1: Using Cortana in Microsoft Edge

Note: This activity requires using Microsoft Edge on a Windows 10 computer.

Cortana can assist you in finding information on a webpage in Microsoft Edge. Perform the following tasks:

a. Create a Word document using the Word Screen Clipping tool to capture the following screenshots.
   - Screenshot A—Using Microsoft Edge, open a webpage with a technology news article. Right-click a term in the article and ask Cortana to define it.
   - Screenshot B—Using Microsoft Edge, open the website of a fancy restaurant in a city near you. Make sure the Cortana circle icon is displayed in the Address bar. (If it's not displayed, find a different restaurant website.) Click the Cortana circle icon to display a pane with information about the restaurant.
   - Screenshot C—Using Microsoft Edge, type **10 USD to Euros** in the Address bar without pressing the Enter key. Cortana converts the U.S. dollars to Euros.
   - Screenshot D—Using Microsoft Edge, type **Apple stock** in the Address bar without pressing the Enter key. Cortana displays the current stock quote.

b. Submit your assignment in the format specified by your instructor.

2: Viewing Online News with Reading View

Note: This activity requires using Microsoft Edge on a Windows 10 computer.

Reading view in Microsoft Edge can make a webpage less cluttered with ads and other distractions. Perform the following tasks:

a. Create a Word document using the Word Screen Clipping tool to capture the following screenshots.
   - Screenshot A—Using Microsoft Edge, open the website **mashable.com**. Open a technology article. Click the Reading view button to display an ad-free page that uses only basic text formatting.
   - Screenshot B—Using Microsoft Edge, open the website **bbc.com**. Open any news article. Click the Reading view button to display an ad-free page that uses only basic text formatting.
   - Screenshot C—Make three types of annotations (Pen, Highlighter, and Add a typed note) on the BBC article page displayed in Reading view.

b. Submit your assignment in the format specified by your instructor.

3: Inking with Microsoft Edge

Note: This activity requires using Microsoft Edge on a Windows 10 computer.

Microsoft Edge provides many annotation options to record your ideas. Perform the following tasks:

a. Open the website **wolframalpha.com** in the Microsoft Edge browser. Wolfram Alpha is a well-respected academic search engine. Type **US$100 1965 dollars in 2015** in the Wolfram Alpha search text box and press the Enter key.

b. Click the Make a Web Note button to display the Web Note tools. Using the Pen tool, draw a circle around the result on the webpage. Save the page to OneNote.

c. In the Wolfram Alpha search text box, type the name of the city closest to where you live and press the Enter key. Using the Highlighter tool, highlight at least three interesting results. Add a note and then type a sentence about what you learned about this city. Save the page to OneNote. Share your OneNote notebook with your instructor.

d. Submit your assignment link in the format specified by your instructor.

CONCEPTS

Planning, Developing, and Giving a Presentation

Preparing a Presentation for a Nonprofit Dog Rescue Center

OBJECTIVES

Session 1
- Understand presentations and presentation media
- Learn about common forms of presentations
- Understand how to identify a presentation's purposes and desired outcomes
- Identify an audience's demographics and the audience's relationship to the presenter
- Learn how to recognize the needs and expectations of an audience

Session 2
- Understand the importance of determining the focus for a presentation
- Learn how to identify the key points of a presentation
- Understand how to develop an effective introduction, body, and conclusion
- Explore types of visuals and handouts

Session 3
- Identify the ways to deliver a presentation
- Learn how to prepare for audience questions and participation
- Understand what to focus on when rehearsing a presentation
- Consider aspects of your appearance
- Consider the steps for setting up for a presentation
- Learn how to evaluate your performance

Case | *Ruff Streets*

In 2014, Ben Singh founded Ruff Streets, a nonprofit dog rescue center located in Tampa, Florida. People call the rescue center when they see stray dogs that appear abandoned or are malnourished. He and his staff gently capture the dogs and bring them back to the rescue center, where the dogs are bathed and treated by a veterinarian. After the dogs are deemed healthy, they are put up for adoption. Ben wants to expand his rescue services to other cities on the east coast. He needs to create a presentation to convince businesses and individuals to donate to help him do this.

In this module, you'll learn how to plan presentations by determining their purposes and outcomes and by analyzing the needs and expectations of your audience. You'll also understand the importance of identifying a clear focus for the presentations and outlining your key points, and how to apply this information as you develop an introduction, organized body, and conclusion for presentations. You'll also learn about the types of visuals and handouts you can use to support the content of a presentation and about the criteria for assessing the situation and facilities for giving the presentation. Finally, you will learn the value of rehearsing your delivery and preparing your appearance, and how to evaluate your performance.

STARTING DATA FILES

There are no starting Data Files needed for this module.

Session 1 Visual Overview:

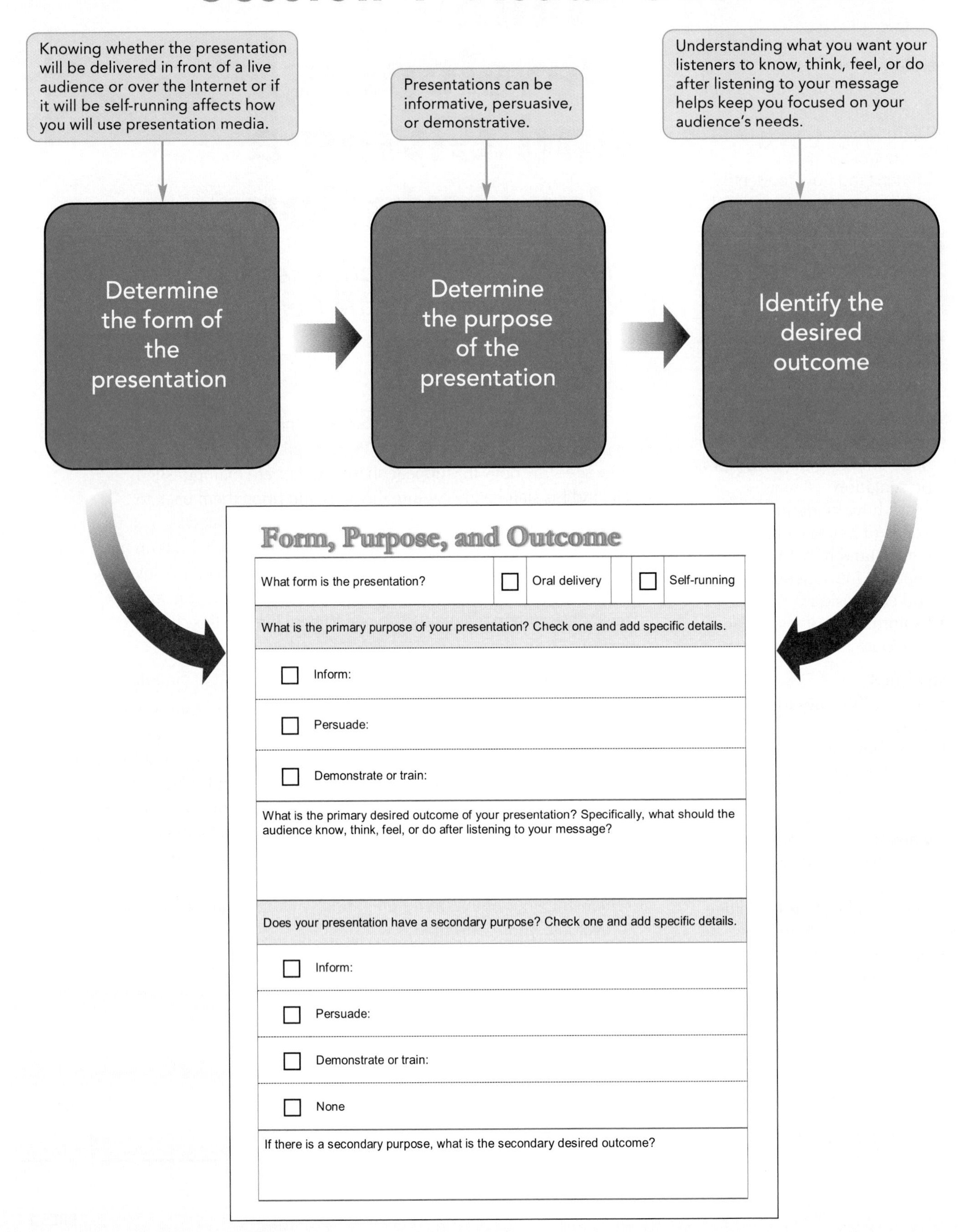

Planning a Presentation

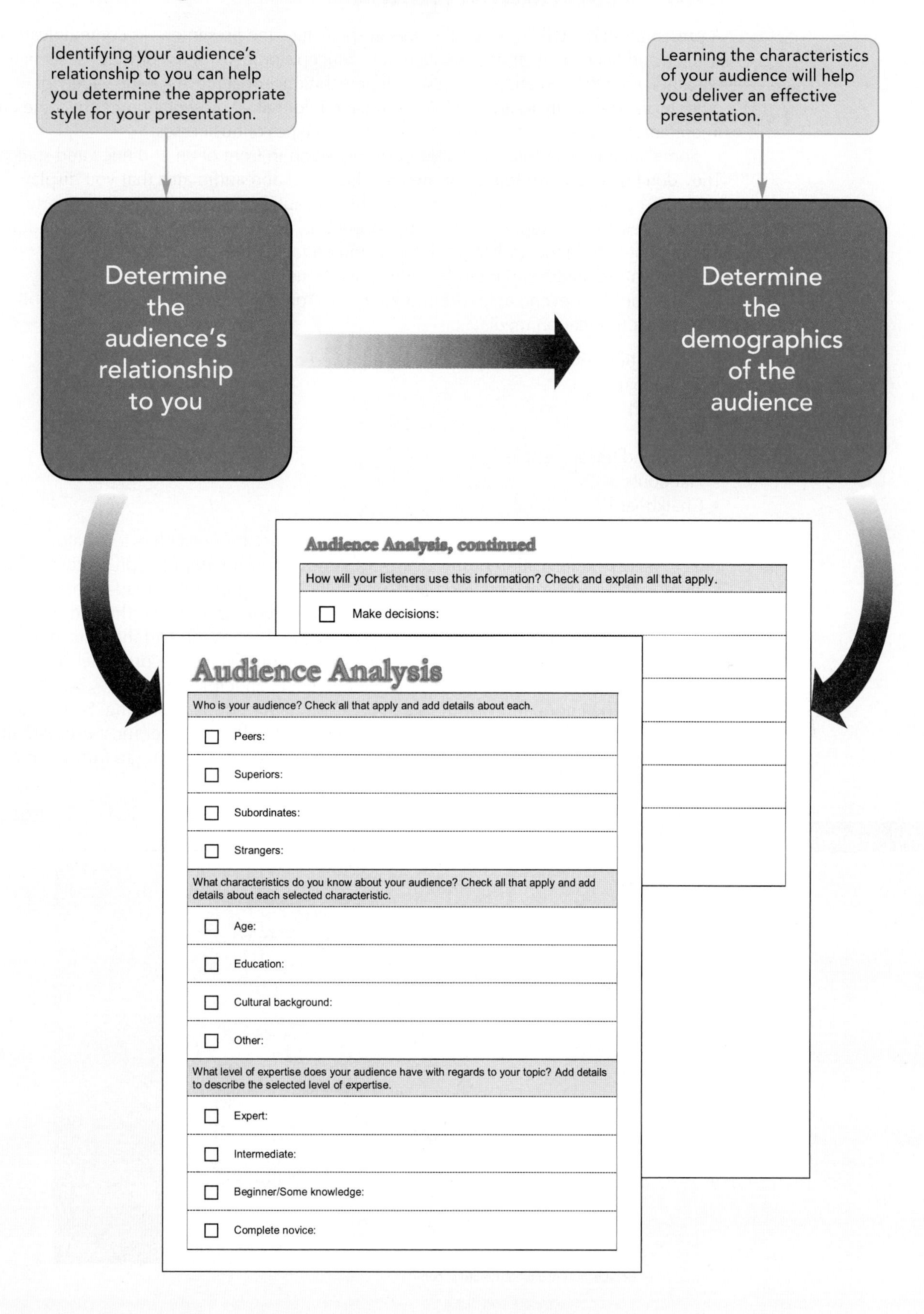

Understanding Presentations and Presentation Media

A **presentation** is a talk in which the person speaking—the **presenter**—is communicating with an audience in an effort to explain new concepts or ideas, sell a product or service, entertain, train the audience in a new skill or technique, or achieve a wide variety of other goals. The ability to give an interesting and informative presentation has become an important skill for students and professionals in all types of businesses.

Some talented presenters are able to simply stand in front of an audience and speak. They don't need any **presentation media**—the visual and audio aids that you display to support your points—because they are able to captivate the audience and clearly explain their topics simply by speaking. Most of us, however, want to use presentation media to help hold the audience's interest and enhance their understanding.

Presentation media can include photos, lists, music, video, and objects that the presenter holds or even passes around the room. You can also use the following tools to display presentation media:

- Presentation software, such as Microsoft PowerPoint
- Whiteboard
- Flip chart
- Posters
- Overhead transparencies
- Handouts
- Chalkboard

Presentation software like PowerPoint makes it very easy for presenters to create bulleted lists of information points. This sometimes results in all of the presenter's content listed on a screen behind them, which they then proceed to read to their audience. Since most people can read faster than someone can speak, the audience finishes reading the words before the presenter finishes speaking, and then sits, bored, waiting for the presenter to move on to new information. Even if the presenter has additional information to communicate, the audience, anticipating that they will be able to read the information on the screen, has probably stopped listening. Sometimes visuals contain so many words that to make them all fit, the presenter must use a small font, making it difficult or impossible for the audience to read, leading to frustration as well as boredom.

Figure 1 **A bored audience member**

Source: Yuri Acurs/Shutterstock.com

Although brief bulleted lists can be very helpful when the presenter is explaining facts, people attend presentations to hear the speaker and perhaps to see diagrams or other illustrations that will help them understand and retain the information. When you give a presentation, you should take advantage of this opportunity to thoroughly engage your audience. For example, if you display a graphic that supports your statements, your presentation will be more interesting, and the audience will pay attention to you and what you are saying, rather than tuning you out while trying to read words on the screen.

Figure 2 **An interested, engaged audience**

Source: Kzenon/Shutterstock.com

In order to deliver a successful presentation, you need to spend time developing it. There are three stages to developing a presentation: planning, creating, and preparing your delivery. In this session, you will focus on the planning stage.

Planning a Presentation

When you plan a presentation, you need to consider some of the same factors you consider when planning a written document—your purpose, audience, and situation. Planning a presentation in advance will improve the quality of your presentation, make it more effective and enjoyable for your audience, and, in the long run, save you time and effort.

As you plan your presentation, you should ask yourself the following questions:

- Will I deliver the presentation in front of a live audience or over the Internet, or will it be a self-running presentation?
- What are the purposes and desired outcomes of this presentation?
- Who is the audience for my presentation, and what do they need and expect?

The following sections will help you answer these questions so that you can create a more effective presentation, and enable you to feel confident in presenting your ideas.

Determining the Form of the Presentation

Usually when someone refers to a presentation, they mean an oral presentation given by a presenter to a live audience. When giving an oral presentation, a person might present to a small audience in a room the size of a classroom, to an audience in a hall large enough to require using a microphone, or over the Internet in webinar format. A **webinar** is a presentation in which the audience signs in to a shared view of the presenter's computer screen and calls in to a conference call to hear the presenter over the telephone line. If the presenter is using video technology, such as a webcam, the webinar audience will be able to see the presenter as well.

With PowerPoint and other presentation software, you can also create a presentation that is self-running or that is controlled by the person viewing it. Sometimes, this type of presentation includes recorded audio, but often it includes only the presentation content. This type of presentation can be challenging to create because the person who prepares the content needs to avoid making it simply a wordy substitute for a written document.

If you are presenting in front of a live audience, you can rely on facial expressions and body language to help convey your points. You can also see your audience's facial expressions and body language, which can help to indicate how they are feeling about your presentation. For example, if you see confused expressions, you might decide to pause for questions. If you are presenting via a webinar you need to make sure all the visuals that you use to help explain your points are very clear, and you need to figure out how to interact with your audience in a way that won't disrupt the flow of your presentation. If the presentation will be self-running, the content will need to be compelling enough on its own to make the audience want to watch the entire presentation. For this reason, the content of a self-running presentation must be even more visually interesting then if it were appearing on a screen behind a speaker because the presenter will not have the opportunity to directly engage the audience.

Determining the Presentation's Purposes and Desired Outcomes

When you are planning a presentation, you need to know what the purpose of the presentation is. Most presentations have one of three purposes: to inform, to persuade, or to demonstrate.

Determining the Purposes

Informative presentations are designed to inform or educate. This type of presentation provides the audience with background information, knowledge, and specific details about a topic that will enable them to gain understanding, make informed decisions, or increase their expertise on a topic. Examples of informative presentations include:

- Summary of research findings at an academic conference
- Briefings on the status of projects
- Overview, reviews, or evaluations of products and services
- Reports at company meetings

Persuasive presentations are designed to persuade or sell. They have the specific purpose of influencing how an audience feels or acts regarding a particular position or plan, or trying to convince the audience to buy something. Persuasive presentations are usually designed as balanced arguments involving logical as well as emotional reasons for supporting an action or viewpoint. Examples of persuasive presentations include:

- Recommendations of specific steps to take to achieve goals
- Sales presentations to sell a product or service
- Motivational presentations

Demonstrative (or **training**) **presentations** show an audience how something works, educate them on how to perform a task, or help them to understand a process or procedure. Sometimes you will provide listeners with hands-on experience, practice, and feedback so they can correct their mistakes and improve their performances. Examples of demonstrative presentations include:

- Software demonstrations
- Process explanations
- Employee training
- Seminars and workshops
- Educational classes and courses

You should always identify the primary purpose of your presentation. However, presenters often have more than one goal, which means your presentation might have additional, secondary purposes. For example, the primary purpose of a presentation might be to inform an audience about a wildlife preserve and describe it to them. But the secondary purpose might be to raise funds for that preserve. Identifying the primary purpose of a presentation helps you focus the content; however, by acknowledging secondary purposes, you can be prepared to answer or deflect questions until after the presentation so that the primary purpose remains the focus of the presentation.

Figure 3 summarizes the three categories of presentation purposes and their goals.

Figure 3 **Purposes for giving presentations**

Purpose	Goal	Examples
Informative	Present facts and details	Summary of research findings, status reports, briefings, discussions of products and services
Persuasive	Influence feelings or actions	Recommendation reports, sales presentations, motivational presentations
Demonstrative (Training)	Show how something works and provide practice and feedback	Software demos, process explanations, employee training, seminars and workshops, educational courses

When Ben gives his presentation about Ruff Streets, his primary purpose will be to persuade the people in his audience to contribute money towards his goal of opening new rescue centers. His secondary purpose will be to publicize several of the dogs currently available for adoption.

Identifying Desired Outcomes

In addition to determining the purpose of a presentation, you should also consider what you hope to achieve in giving your presentation. That means you need to determine the desired outcomes of your presentation—what you want your listeners to know, think, feel, or do after listening to the message. Focusing on the desired outcomes of your presentation forces you to make it more audience-oriented. Just as when you determined the purpose of your presentation, you might find that although you have a primary desired outcome, secondary outcomes might be acceptable as well.

You should be able to concisely express the purpose and desired outcomes of your presentation. Writing down the purpose and desired outcomes helps you decide what to include in the presentation, enabling you to create a more effective presentation. A good statement of your purpose and desired outcomes will also help when you write the introduction and conclusion for your presentation. Consider the following examples of specific purpose statements with specific outcomes:

- **Purpose:** To demonstrate to staff members a newly purchased projector that can be used for giving presentations to small groups.
  Outcome: Staff members will understand how to use the new equipment.

- **Purpose:** To inform department heads at a college about the benefits of a new website where students can receive tutoring.
  Outcome: Audience will understand the benefits of the program.
  Secondary Purpose: To persuade department heads to recruit tutors for the program.
  Secondary Outcome: Department heads will ask their faculty to identify potential tutors.

The desired outcome of Ben's presentation is that individuals and businesses will donate money so that he can open additional rescue centers.

Figure 4 shows a basic worksheet for helping determine the form, purpose, and outcome of a presentation. This worksheet is filled out with Ben's information.

Figure 4 **Form, Purpose, and Outcome worksheet for Ruff Streets presentation**

Form, Purpose, and Outcome

What form is the presentation?	☒	Oral delivery	☐	Self-running

What is the primary purpose of your presentation? Check one and add specific details.

☐ Inform:

☒ Persuade: Persuade individuals and corporations to donate money to be used to open more dog rescue centers.

☐ Demonstrate or train:

What is the primary desired outcome of your presentation? Specifically, what should the audience know, think, feel, or do after listening to your message?

The audience will know about the various services that Ruff Streets offers, how many dogs are helped every year, and how many dogs need help every year along the east coast. As a result, they will want to donate to help create more rescue centers.

Does your presentation have a secondary purpose? Check one and add specific details.

☐ Inform:

☒ Persuade: Persuade individuals to adopt a rescue dog.

☐ Demonstrate or train:

☐ None

If there is a secondary purpose, what is the secondary desired outcome?

Audience members will want to adopt a rescued dog.

Analyzing Your Audience's Needs and Expectations

The more you know about your listeners, the more you'll be able to adapt your presentation to their needs. By putting yourself in your listeners' shoes, you'll be able to visualize your audience as more than just a group of passive listeners, and you can anticipate what they need and expect from your presentation. Anticipating the needs of your audience also increases the chances that your audience will react favorably to your presentation.

The first step in analyzing your audience is to determine their relationship to you. If you are speaking to your peers, you could adopt a less formal style than if you are speaking to your superiors or people who report to you. Also, if you are speaking to a room full of people who know you and your credentials, you might be able to present in a more informal, familiar manner than if you are speaking to people who have never met you.

The second step in analyzing your audience is to find out about their demographics. **Demographics** are characteristics that describe your audience. Some of the demographics that affect your presentations are:

- **Age**—People of different age groups vary in terms of attention span and the way they absorb information. For example, young children have shorter attention spans and generally can't sit still as long as adults, so presentations to young children should be divided into short sessions interspersed with physical activity.
- **Education**—Audiences with more education expect a higher level of technicality than audiences with less education.
- **Cultural background**—Each culture has its own expectations for how to write, speak, and communicate, including nonverbal conventions such as gestures and body movement. It is important to remember that cultural differences can occur even in the same country.
- **Expertise**—Audiences with specialized training expect examples that use terms and concepts from their field. Audiences who are unfamiliar with a topic will require more definitions and explanation to understand the presentation.

INSIGHT

Understanding the Needs of an International Audience

If you're presenting to an international audience, whether over the Internet or in person, it is important to understand the different cultural expectations that international audiences may have for your presentation, including expectations for nonverbal communication. These cultural expectations are subtle but powerful, and you can immediately create a negative impression if you don't understand them. For example, audiences from cultures outside the United States may expect you to speak and dress more formally than you are used to in the United States. In addition, some cultures are hesitant to debate an issue or present disagreement towards popular views.

There are no universal guidelines that would enable you to characterize the needs of all international audiences; however, there are some commonsense recommendations. You should analyze the hand gestures and symbols you use routinely to see if they have different meaning for other cultures. Be cautious about using humor because it is easy to misinterpret. And take special care to avoid using cultural stereotypes.

Understanding who your audience is and their needs and expectations helps you adapt the content of your presentation to a particular audience. Figure 5 shows a worksheet that Ben used to analyze the needs and expectations of his audience.

Figure 5 Audience Analysis worksheet for Ruff Streets presentation

Audience Analysis

Who is your audience? Check all that apply and add details about each.
☐ Peers:
☐ Superiors:
☐ Subordinates:
☒ Strangers: Individuals interested in animal welfare and corporate audiences looking for a charity whose goals align with the corporate identity.
What characteristics do you know about your audience? Check all that apply and add details about each selected characteristic.
☒ Age: Adults of all ages
☒ Education: Probably most will have at least some college education; corporate audiences will be somewhat more educated.
☒ Cultural background: Varied
☒ Other: Most will have high enough income levels to allow them to comfortably donate to causes.
What level of expertise does your audience have with regards to your topic? Add details to describe the selected level of expertise.
☐ Expert:
☒ Intermediate: Most will have some understanding of dog rescue centers, but won't fully grasp the high numbers of abandoned or stray dogs.
☐ Beginner/Some knowledge:
☐ Complete novice:

Audience Analysis, continued

How will your listeners use this information? Check and explain all that apply.
☒ Make decisions: Decide whether to donate and/or adopt a rescued dog
☐ Perform a task:
☒ Form an opinion: Form an opinion about Ruff Streets
☒ Increase understanding: Learn about the services Ruff Streets provides and learn about the scope of the problem of abandoned and stray dogs.
☐ Follow a process:
☐ Other:

PROSKILLS

Teamwork: Planning Collaborative Presentations

Because much of the work in business and industry is collaborative, it's only natural that presentations in these settings often are created and presented by a team of people. These types of presentations are referred to as collaborative presentations and they provide many benefits, including:

- Sharing a greater range of expertise and ideas
- Provoking more discussion due to different presentation styles and a wider range of information being shared
- Providing more people with exposure and the rewards of a task accomplished
- Allowing more people to gain valuable experience in communicating ideas

In addition to creating compelling content, a successful collaborative presentation depends on your group's ability to plan thoroughly and practice together. To ensure a successful group presentation, consider the following as you plan your presentation:

- Involve the whole team in the planning.
- Show respect for the ideas of all team members, and be sensitive to personality and cultural differences among the team members.
- Convey clear time constraints to each speaker and ensure that all speakers are prepared to limit themselves to the time allotted.
- Plan for the transitions between speakers.

In this session you learned how to plan a presentation and to consider the needs and expectations of your audience. In the next session, you will learn about the steps for creating the content of a presentation.

REVIEW

Session 1 Quick Check

1. Describe the difference between a presentation and presentation media.
2. What are the three stages of developing a presentation?
3. List the three categories of presentation purposes.
4. Give an example of each category of presentation purpose.
5. Why is it important to focus on the desired outcomes of a presentation?
6. List three examples of audience demographics.

Session 2 Visual Overview:

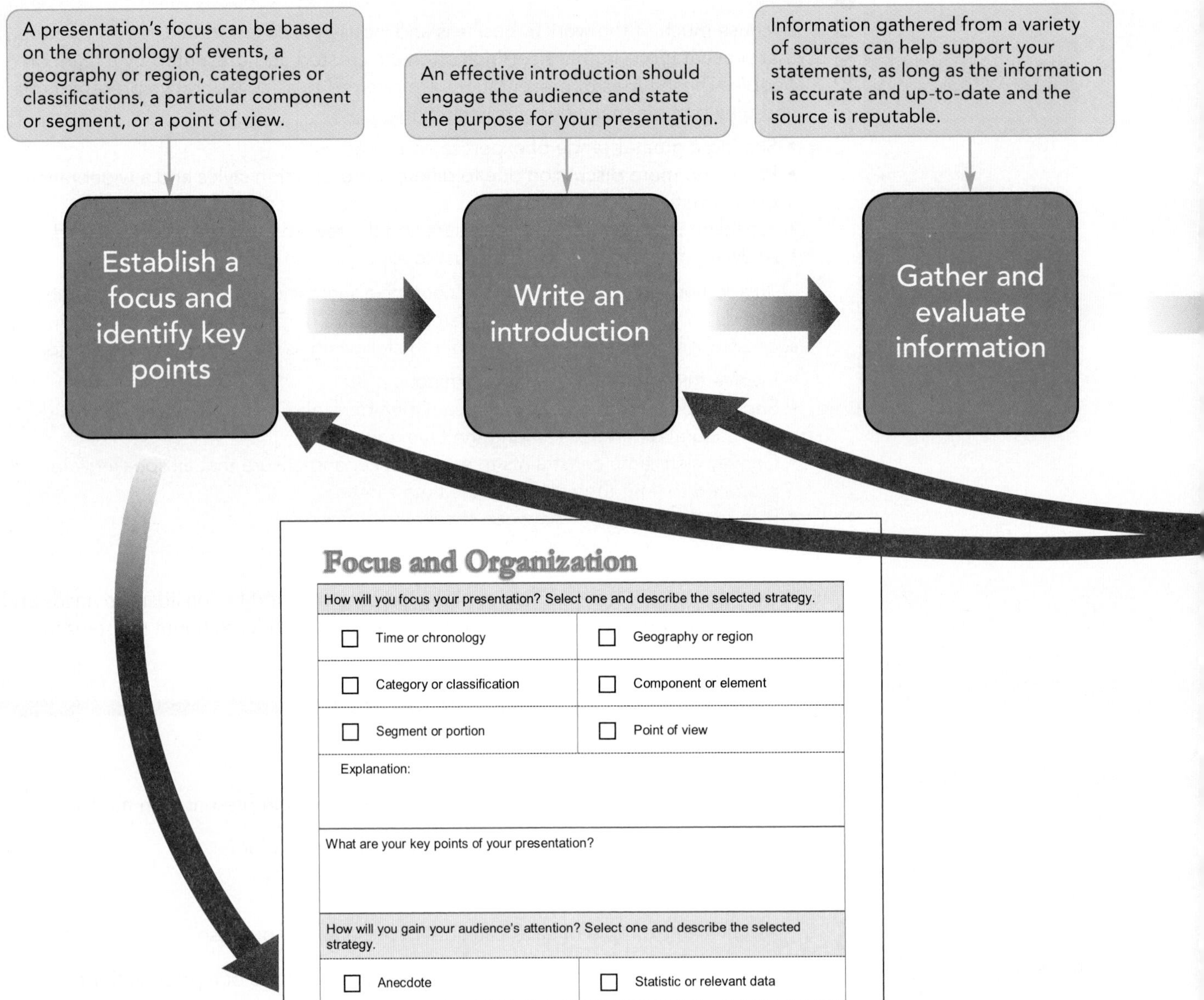

A presentation's focus can be based on the chronology of events, a geography or region, categories or classifications, a particular component or segment, or a point of view.

An effective introduction should engage the audience and state the purpose for your presentation.

Information gathered from a variety of sources can help support your statements, as long as the information is accurate and up-to-date and the source is reputable.

Establish a focus and identify key points

Write an introduction

Gather and evaluate information

Focus and Organization

How will you focus your presentation? Select one and describe the selected strategy.	
☐ Time or chronology	☐ Geography or region
☐ Category or classification	☐ Component or element
☐ Segment or portion	☐ Point of view
Explanation:	
What are your key points of your presentation?	
How will you gain your audience's attention? Select one and describe the selected strategy.	
☐ Anecdote	☐ Statistic or relevant data
☐ Quotation, familiar phrase, or definition	☐ Question(s)
☐ Current problem or issue	☐ Comment about audience or occasion
☐ State purpose	
Explanation:	
Will you provide an overview of your presentation?	☐ Yes ☐ No
If so, how?	

Creating a Presentation

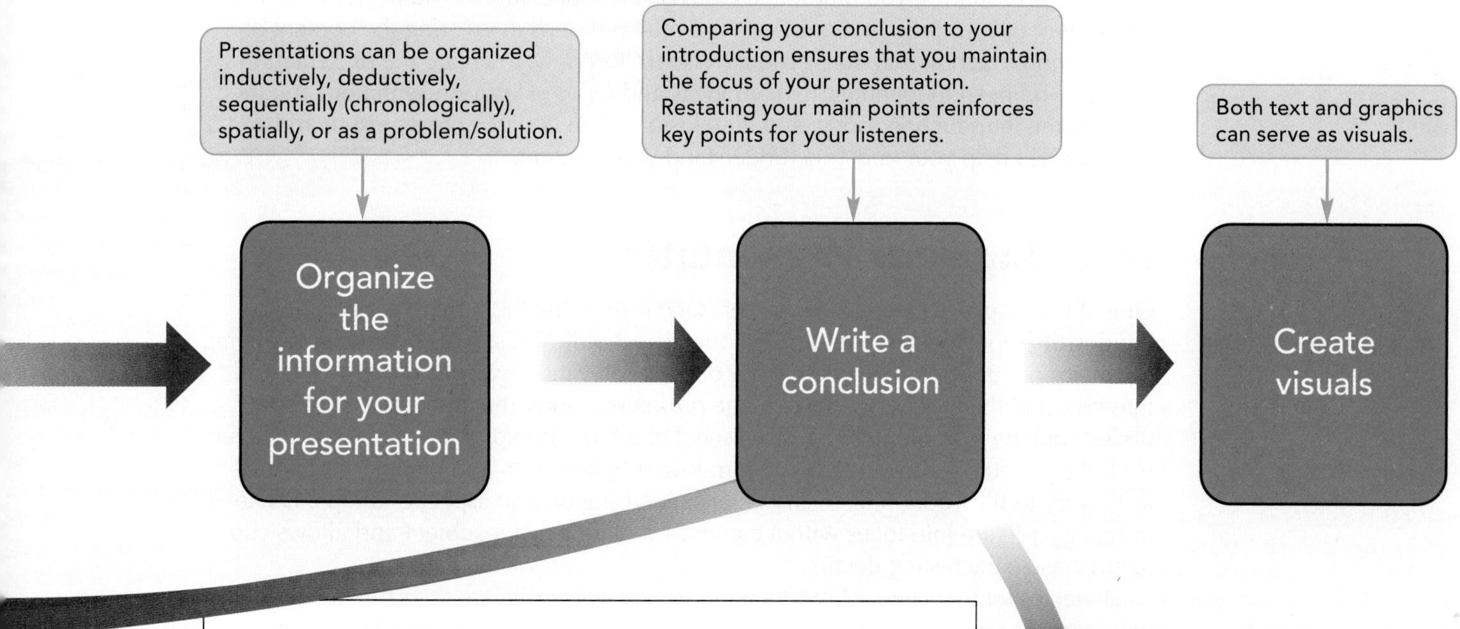

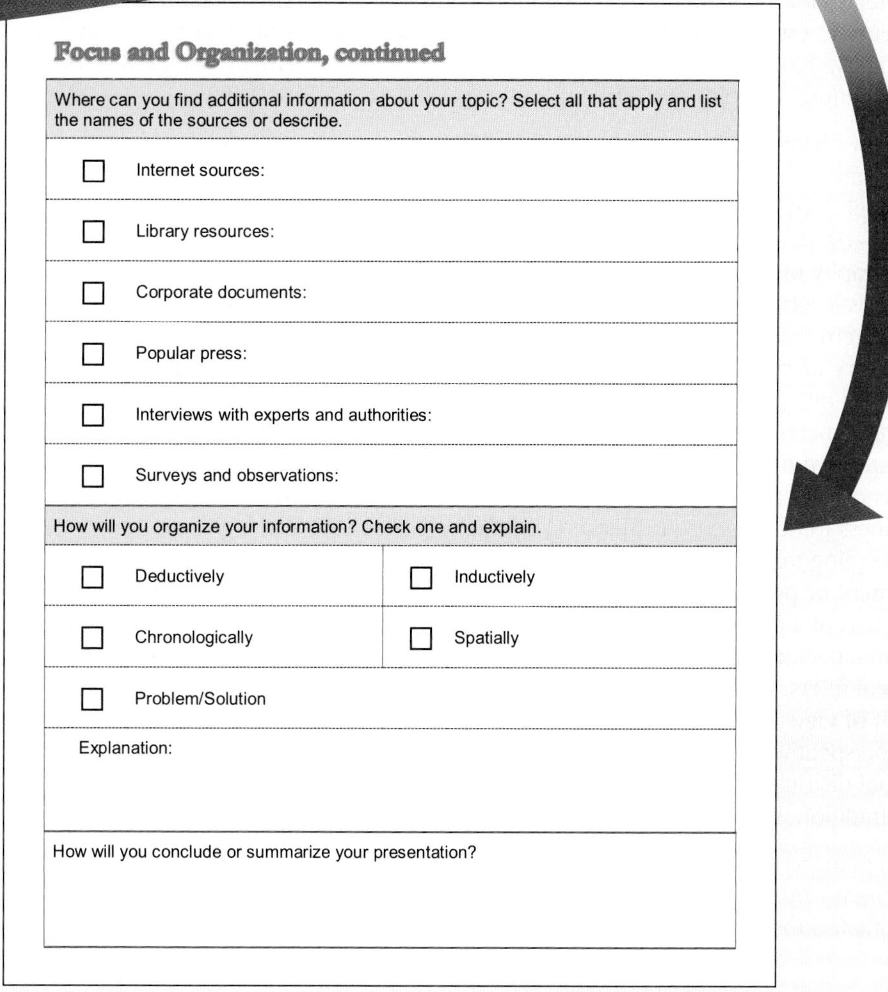

Presentations can be organized inductively, deductively, sequentially (chronologically), spatially, or as a problem/solution.

Organize the information for your presentation

Comparing your conclusion to your introduction ensures that you maintain the focus of your presentation. Restating your main points reinforces key points for your listeners.

Write a conclusion

Both text and graphics can serve as visuals.

Create visuals

Focus and Organization, continued

Where can you find additional information about your topic? Select all that apply and list the names of the sources or describe.
☐ Internet sources:
☐ Library resources:
☐ Corporate documents:
☐ Popular press:
☐ Interviews with experts and authorities:
☐ Surveys and observations:

How will you organize your information? Check one and explain.	
☐ Deductively	☐ Inductively
☐ Chronologically	☐ Spatially
☐ Problem/Solution	
Explanation:	
How will you conclude or summarize your presentation?	

Creating the Presentation

Once you determine the form of the presentation, determine your purpose and outcome, and analyze your audience's needs and expectations, you need to create the content of your presentation. There are multiple steps to creating the content of a presentation. As shown in the Session 2 Visual Overview, to create the presentation's content, you need to identify the main ideas and focus of your presentation, and then develop the introduction, body, and conclusion. Then you can create visual and audio aids that will help your audience understand your content.

Focusing Your Presentation

One of the biggest challenges presenters face is focusing their presentations, that is, limiting the topic by concentrating on one aspect of it. You should begin by identifying the major points or main ideas that are directly relevant to your listeners' needs and interests, and then focus on those. Some presenters worry that audiences will not understand the material unless every aspect of a topic is explained. If you try to cover everything, you'll give your audience irrelevant information and they'll lose interest as they try to filter out unnecessary details. Focusing on one aspect of a topic is like bringing a picture into focus with a camera—it clarifies your subject and allows you to emphasize interesting details.

Strategies for focusing or limiting your presentation topic are the same as those you would use to create a focus for any written document—focus on a particular time or chronology, geography or region, category, component or element, segment or portion of a procedure, or point of view.

- **Time or chronology**—Limiting a topic by time means you focus on a segment of time, rather than trying to cover the entire history of a topic. *Unfocused:* The history of Egypt from 640 to 2000. *Focused:* The history of Egypt during the Nasser years (1952–1970).
- **Geography or region**—Limiting a topic by geography or region means you look at a topic as it relates to a specific location. *Unfocused:* Fly fishing. *Focused:* Fly fishing in western Colorado.
- **Category or classification**—Limiting a topic by category means you focus on one member of a group or on a limited function. *Unfocused:* Thermometers. *Focused:* Using bimetallic-coil thermometers to control bacteria in restaurant-prepared foods.
- **Component or element**—Limiting a topic by component or element means you focus on one small aspect or part of an organization or problem. *Unfocused:* Business trends. *Focused:* Blending accounting practices and legal services, a converging trend in large businesses.
- **Segment or portion**—Limiting a topic by segment or portion means you focus on one part of a process or procedure. *Unfocused:* Designing, manufacturing, handling, storing, packaging, and transporting of optical filters. *Focused:* Acceptance testing of optical filters.
- **Point of view**—Limiting a topic by point of view means you look at a topic from the perspective of a single group. *Unfocused:* Employee benefits. *Focused:* How school districts can retain their teachers by providing child-care assistance and other nontraditional benefits.

Ben plans to focus his presentation by limiting the topic—focusing on a component or element—by stressing the improved welfare of the dogs that he rescues, and not spending too much time on how he finds and captures the dogs.

Identifying Your Key Points

Once you have determined your focus, you need to identify the key points of your presentation. To help you continue to design your presentation with the listener in mind, phrase the key points as the conclusions you want your audience to draw from the presentation.

As you identify the key points, order them in a numbered list with the most important idea listed first and the least important point listed last. This will help you maintain the focus and ensure that the most important points receive the most attention. For example, the key points for Ben's presentation about the Ruff Street center are:

1. There are many abandoned dogs that desperately need food, medical treatment, and homes.
2. Most major cities have a measurable population of homeless dogs and would benefit from additional rescue centers.
3. Rescued dogs returned to good health make great pets.

Once you've established a focus and identified your key points, you need to create the introduction, body, and conclusion of your presentation. Good presentations start with an effective introduction, continue with a well-organized body, and end with a strong conclusion.

Developing an Introduction

The introduction, or opening statement, of a presentation enables you to gain your listeners' attention, establish a relationship with your audience, and preview your key points. The introduction sets the tone for the entire presentation. An inadequate introduction can ruin the rest of your presentation no matter how well you've prepared. Consider these guidelines to avoid common mistakes:

- Don't begin by apologizing about any aspect of your presentation, such as how nervous you are or your lack of preparation. Apologies destroy your credibility and guarantee that your audience will react negatively to what you present.
- Don't use gimmicks to begin your presentation, such as making a funny face, singing a song, or ringing a bell. Members of your audience won't know how to respond and will feel uncomfortable.
- Avoid trite, flattering, or phony statements, such as, "Ladies and gentlemen, it is an unfathomable honor to be in your presence." Gaining respect requires treating your audience as your equal.
- Be cautious when using humor. It's difficult to predict how audiences will respond to jokes and other forms of humor. Also, what one person or group finds humorous might offend another person or group.

Gaining Your Audience's Attention

The purpose of the introduction is to provide the listeners with an organizational overview of your presentation; however, it is also important to remember that the introduction provides the audience with their first impression of you and your presentation. Even if your audience is interested in your topic, they can be easily distracted, so it's important to create an effective introduction that will immediately grab their attention. A truly effective introduction captures the attention of your audience and establishes a rapport with them. Some effective ways to gain your audience's attention are:

- Share anecdotes.
- Discuss statistics or relevant data.
- Mention a quotation, familiar phrase, or definition.
- Ask questions.
- Raise a current problem or issue.
- Comment about the audience or occasion.
- State the purpose of the presentation.

Share Anecdotes

Sharing anecdotes (short stories or personal experiences that demonstrate a specific point) is a very effective method of gaining your audience's attention. Anecdotes allow your audience to relate to you as a person and make your topic more relevant. For example, Ben could begin his presentation relating his story about how he first thought of founding the Ruff Streets center:

"I used to walk to work almost every day. On my walk, I noticed a scraggly-looking dog creeping between two buildings. He looked miserable. He didn't let me get close enough to pat him or check his collar for tags. I started carrying doggy treats with me and would toss a few to him each time I passed. After several days of doing this, he perked up when he saw me, and eventually, I was able to get close enough to pat him and check his collar. It turned out his owner had died, and no one else in the family wanted him, so when he ran away, no one looked for him. I brought him home, bathed him, and took him to a vet. And I've never looked back."

Discuss Statistics and Quantitative Data

Another way to engage your audience is to discuss interesting statistics and quantitative data relating to the needs of your audience. To be effective, make sure that the statistics and data you use are current, accurate, and easily understood.

In Ben's presentation, he could share statistics and data about the number of abandoned dogs nationwide.

Mention a Quotation, Familiar Phrase, or Definition

Short quotes, familiar phrases, or definitions are another way to gain your audience's attention. This strategy works because your audience wants to know how the quote, phrase, or definition relates to your topic, and this leads naturally into the rest of your talk. Ben could use a quotation such as the following one by Albert Schweitzer to introduce his presentation:

"Think occasionally of the suffering of which you spare yourself the sight."

Ask Questions

TIP

Be aware that an audience member might call out humorous or otherwise unwanted answers to your questions, which can detract from the effectiveness of your introduction.

Asking questions to introduce your topic can be effective if the questions are thought-provoking and the issues are important. This can be especially effective in small group settings or situations where you're attempting to find new ways to approach ideas. Asking audience members to give tentative answers to an informal quiz or questionnaire allows you to adjust your presentation to accommodate their responses.

Rhetorical questions (questions you don't expect the audience to answer) are especially effective. Rhetorical questions engage the audience right away because the audience members instinctively reply to the question internally.

In his presentation, Ben could ask "How many of you have pets?" and then pause so audience members could raise their hands. He could then follow up with a rhetorical question asking, "And how many of you love your pets?"

Raise a Current Problem or Issue

Another way to grab the attention of your audience is to raise a current problem or unresolved issue. This provides you with an opportunity to suggest a change or a solution to the problem. By defining a problem for your audience, you develop a common ground upon which you can provide insight, examine alternatives, and make recommendations.

In Ben's presentation, he could describe the current problem such as "In cities all over the country, there are millions of abandoned or stray dogs that need help and a home."

Comment About the Audience or Occasion

To show your enthusiasm about the group you're addressing, as well as about your topic, you can make comments about the audience or occasion. If you do this, your comments should be brief and sincere. Referring to the occasion can be as simple as Ben saying:

- "I'm happy that you're giving me this opportunity to tell you about my vision for expanding the reach of Ruff Streets."
- "Thanks for letting me tell you about Ruff Streets. I think you'll find that we provide a wide range of valuable and humane services in our quest to rescue dogs."

State the Purpose of the Presentation

Simply announcing your purpose works well as an introduction if your audience is already interested in your topic or if your time is limited. Most audiences, however, will appreciate a more creative approach than simply stating, "I'm going to try to convince you that Ruff Streets is worthy of your donation." For example, in Ben's presentation, he might say something like, "My purpose is to describe heartbreaking stories that end well because of Ruff Streets and our rescue program."

Figure 6 summarizes the ways to gain your audience's attention.

Figure 6 **Ways to gain your audience's attention**

Method	Result
Share anecdotes	Helps audience relate to you as a real person
Discuss statistics and quantitative data	Increases audience interest in topic
Mention a quotation, familiar phrase, or definition	Leads in well to remainder of presentation
Ask questions	Gets audience thinking about topic
Raise a current problem or issue	Prepares audience to consider solutions or recommendations for change
Comment about the audience or occasion	Enables you to show your enthusiasm
State the purpose of the presentation	Works well if audience is already interested

Providing an Overview of Your Presentation

TIP

You can choose to show a visual overview or you can simply explain your plan or structure.

After you have gained the attention of your audience, you might choose to provide them with an overview of your presentation. Overviews, sometimes called advance organizers or previews, prepare your audience for the points that will follow. They can be very effective for longer presentations or for presentations that cover complex or technical information. Overviews help your audience remember your presentation by providing a road map of how it is organized. Overviews should be brief and simple, stating what you plan to do and in what order. After you've given your audience an overview of your presentation, it's important that you follow that same order.

Once you've created your introduction, you're ready to develop the body of your presentation.

Developing the Body of Your Presentation

TIP

Always consider whether your content is helping you achieve the desired outcome of the presentation. If it doesn't, revise accordingly.

The body of your presentation is where you present pertinent information, supporting evidence, and important details. To develop the body, you need to gather information on your key points, determine the organizational approach, add supporting details and other pertinent information, and provide transitions from one point to the next.

Gathering Information

Most of the time, you'll give presentations on topics about which you're knowledgeable and comfortable. Other times, you might have to give presentations on topics that are new to you. In either case, you'll need to explain the reasoning behind your statements, provide support for claims, present sensible recommendations, and anticipate objections to your statements or conclusions. This means you need to go beyond your personal experience and do in-depth research to provide relevant and up-to-date information, verifiable facts, truthful statistics, and expert testimony.

You can find additional information on your topic by consulting the following:

- Internet sources—The Internet is an excellent place to find information on any topic.
- Library resources—You can access library resources, such as books, encyclopedias, academic journals, government publications, and other reference materials, using the library's computerized catalog, indexes, and professional database services.
- Corporate documents and office correspondence—Since using these materials might violate your company's nondisclosure policy, you might need to obtain your company's permission or get legal clearance to use the information.
- Popular press items from newspapers, radio, TV, the web, and magazines—This information, geared for general audiences, provides large-scale details and personal opinions that may need to be supplemented by additional research.
- Interviews with experts and authorities in the field or other members of your organization—Talking to other people who are knowledgeable about your topic will give you additional insight.
- Surveys and observations—If you do your own interviews, surveys, and observations, be prepared with a list of specific questions, and always be respectful of other people's time.

Figure 7 Gathering information from a variety of sources

Source: Jaimie Duplass/Shutterstock.com

Evaluating Information

TIP

Some sources have the look and feel of authoritative, research-based information, but are skewed by politics, profits, or personal opinions.

Not all of the information you gather will be of equal value. You must evaluate the information you gather by asking whether it is accurate, up-to-date, and reputable. When evaluating Internet sources in particular, it's important that you ascertain whether the websites you use as sources contain a bias or viewpoint that influences the information, such as a sales pitch.

You should also evaluate whether the information is pertinent to your particular topic. The scope of some topics is so broad, you will need to whittle down the information to only that which serves to clarify or enhance the specific key points of your presentation. Consider whether the information supports your purpose and focus.

For his presentation, Ben collected the following additional information: a book from the library titled *City Dogs: An Unromantic, Urban Tale*; the latest data on the numbers of stray dogs on the east coast from the Seaboard Animal Rescue Society; an article from the *West Coast Times* titled "The Importance of Neutering Pets," and an informal survey of 25 families who adopted dogs from Ruff Streets. Although all of the information is accurate, current, and interesting, the article about neutering pets is not directly relevant to Ben's purpose of convincing people to donate to Ruff Streets.

Organizing Your Information

After you have fully researched your topic and evaluated the information you've gathered, you're ready to organize the information in an understandable and logical manner so that your listeners can easily follow your ideas. You should choose an organizational approach for your information based upon the purpose, audience, and situation of each presentation. Sometimes your company or supervisor might ask you to follow a specific organizational pattern or format in giving your presentations. Other times you might be able to choose your own organizational approach. Some common organizational options include deductive, inductive, chronological, spatial, and problem-solution.

Deductive organization means that you present your conclusions or solutions first, and then explain the information that led you to your conclusions. See Figure 8. Deductive organization is the most common pattern used in business because it presents the most important or bottom-line information first.

Figure 8 **Deductive organization**

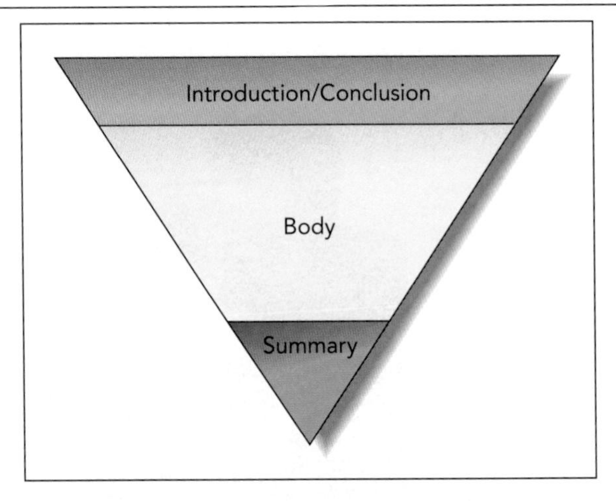

Organizing Ben's presentation in a deductive manner would mean that Ben would begin by describing his rescue center and its successes and then describe how critical the need is in other areas on the east coast.

When you begin with the individual facts and save your conclusions until the end of your presentation, you are using **inductive organization**. See Figure 9. Inductive organization is useful when your purpose is to persuade your audience to follow an unusual plan of action, or you feel your audience might resist your conclusions. However, inductively organized presentations can be more difficult to follow because the most important information may come at the end of the presentation.

Figure 9 **Inductive organization**

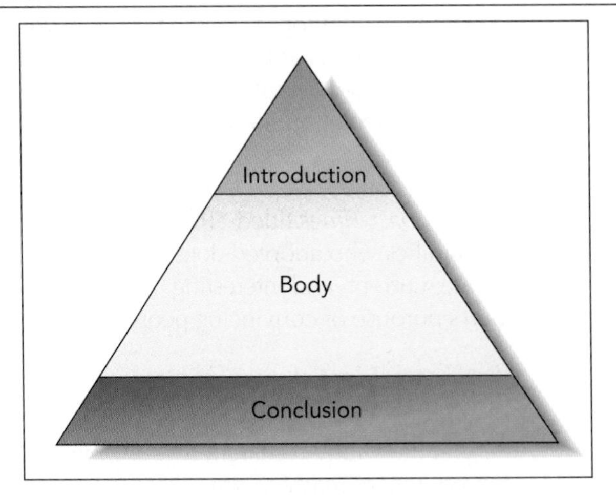

If Ben is concerned that his audience might not think that rescue centers are needed, he could organize his presentation inductively by presenting facts about the numbers of strays in cities across the United States, and then provide his rescue centers as a solution to this problem.

When you use **sequential** or **chronological organization**, you organize information in a step-by-step fashion or according to a time sequence. See Figure 10. Sequential organization works best when you must demonstrate a procedure, train someone to use a piece of equipment, or explain the evolution of a concept. Failing to present sequential information in the proper order can leave your listeners confused and might result in wasting time and resources.

Figure 10 Sequential (chronological) organization

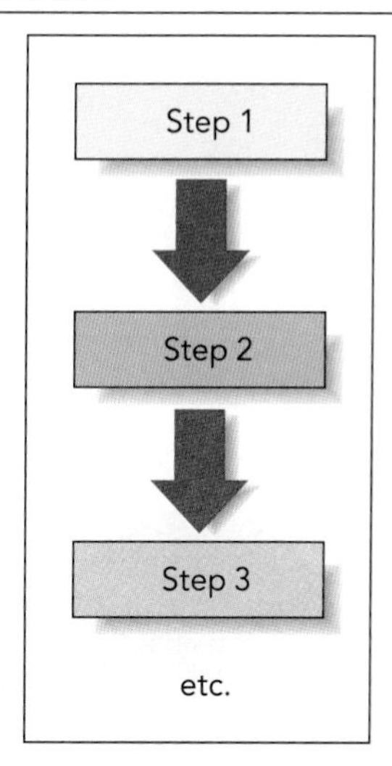

If Ben is confident that his audience wants to donate money for expanding Ruff Streets, he could organize his presentation sequentially by explaining the details of his plans for building the new centers.

Spatial organization is used to provide a logical and effective order for describing the physical layout of an item or system. See Figure 11.

Figure 11 Spatial organization

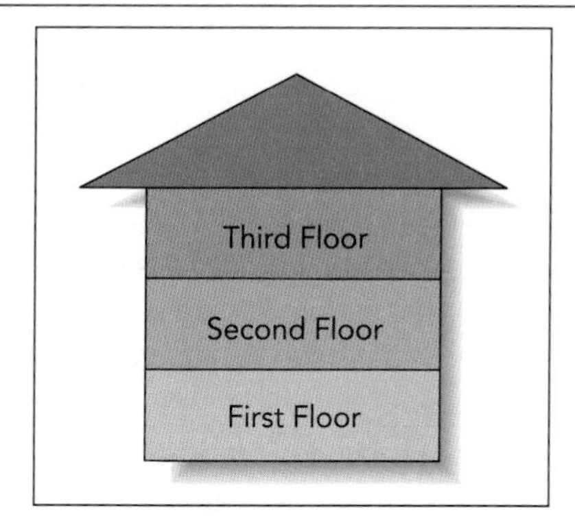

If Ben thinks it is important to describe the building his rescue center occupies or the plans for the new centers, he could describe each room and its purpose. If he has architectural plans or drawings for the new centers, he could show those.

Problem-solution organization consists of presenting a problem, outlining various solutions to the problem, and then explaining the solution you recommend. See Figure 12. Problem-solution presentations work best for recommending a specific action or solution.

Figure 12 Problem-solving organization

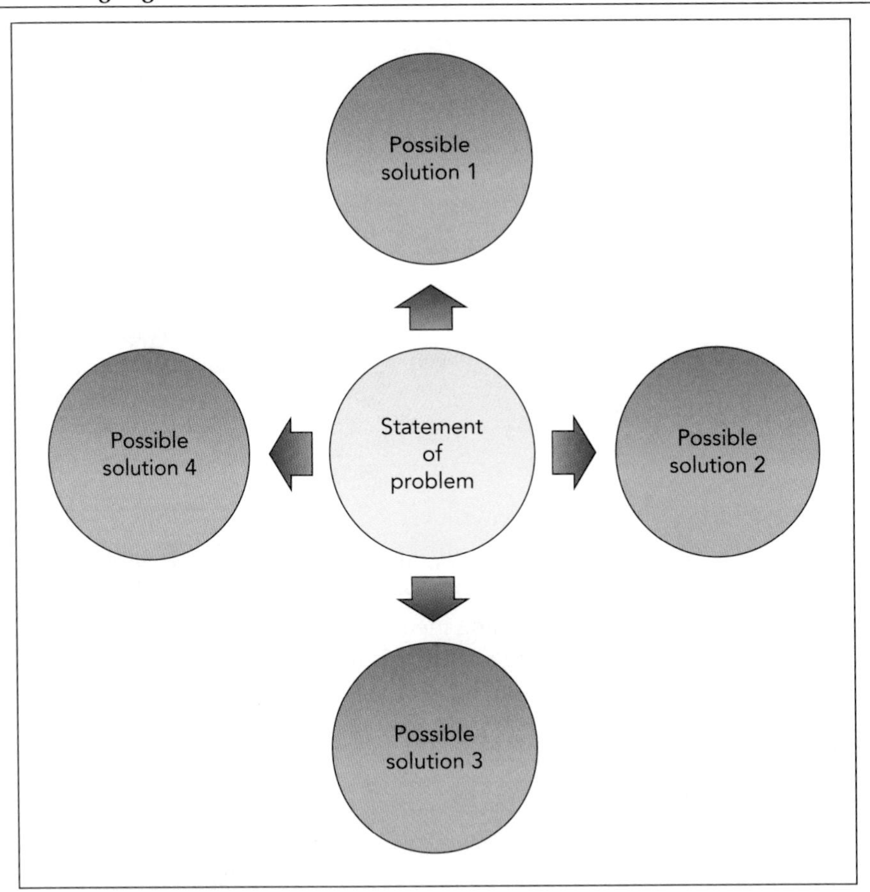

If Ben uses problem-solving organization in his presentation, he would present the problem—the large number of strays in cities along the east coast—and then recommend his solution—that people donate so that he can build more rescue centers.

Figure 13 summarizes the ways you can organize a presentation.

Figure 13 Ways to organize a presentation

Organizational Pattern	Explanation of Pattern
Deductive	Present conclusions or solutions first
Inductive	Present conclusions or solutions last
Sequential (Chronological)	Order by sequence or time
Spatial	Order by space or position
Problem/Solution	Present problem and various solutions, then recommend solution

Developing Your Conclusion

Conclusions are valuable because they allow you to restate your key points, thus helping your listeners remember important information from your presentation. You can also suggest appropriate actions and recommend further resources. The conclusion is the last thing your audience hears and sees, and will likely stay with them longer than individual points you made—if it's effective. Therefore, you should give the same amount of attention and effort to developing the conclusion as you did to your introduction.

The following suggestions will help you create an effective conclusion:

- Use a clear transition to move into your conclusion. This will signal your audience that you're moving from the body of your presentation to the closing statements. Avoid ending with a trite statement like "I see my time is up, so I'll stop here," which sends a general message to your audience that you did not develop a conclusion or prepare adequately to present all the relevant information in the amount of time available.
- Keep your conclusion short and simple. Audiences appreciate speakers who keep their presentations within the allotted time limit.
- Make sure the conclusion reiterates only the central points or essential message of your presentation. Don't introduce new ideas; simply remind your audience why they should care about your topic. Audiences won't appreciate a rehash of your entire presentation.
- Relate your conclusion to your introduction. Consider writing your conclusion at the same time you write your introduction to make sure that they both provide the same focus. Whenever you write your conclusion, compare it to your introduction to make sure they are complementary.
- If your purpose was to persuade your audience to take a specific action, use your conclusion to suggest what the audience should do now.
- If possible, suggest where your audience can find additional resources by providing web addresses, email addresses, phone numbers, or physical addresses.

Ben could conclude his presentation by stating, "Now that you've seen the benefits of the Ruff Streets center, I'd like to briefly summarize the main points I've made today. A significant number of stray dogs live in cities all along the east coast. Ruff Streets has created a successful model for rescuing, treating, and finding homes for these dogs. We need your help to expand to other cities."

Figure 14 shows a worksheet Ben used to determine the focus and organization for his presentation.

Figure 14 Focus and Organization worksheet for Ruff Streets presentation

Focus and Organization

How will you focus your presentation? Select one and describe the selected strategy.	
☐ Time or chronology	☒ Geography or region
☐ Category or classification	☐ Component or element
☐ Segment or portion	☐ Point of view
Explanation: Stress the need for Ruff Streets centers in cities along the east coast.	

What are your key points of your presentation?
Explain the desperate need and the plight of stray dogs, and describe how happy the dogs are after being rescued and adopted.

How will you gain your audience's attention? Select one and describe the selected strategy.	
☐ Anecdote	☒ Statistic or relevant data
☐ Quotation, familiar phrase, or definition	☐ Question(s)
☐ Current problem or issue	☐ Comment about audience or occasion
☐ State purpose	
Explanation: Use statistics from the Humane Society to highlight the problem.	

Will you provide an overview of your presentation?	☐ Yes	☒ No
If so, how?		

Focus and Organization, continued

Where can you find additional information about your topic? Select all that apply and list the names of the sources or describe.
☒ Internet sources: collect data and anecdotes from other rescue centers and organizations
☒ Library resources: books about adopting pets
☐ Corporate documents:
☒ Popular press: national stories and stories from cities all over the east coast about rescuing animals
☐ Interviews with experts and authorities:
☒ Surveys and observations: informal surveys from people who have adopted rescue animals

How will you organize your information? Check one and explain.	
☐ Deductively	☐ Inductively
☐ Chronologically	☐ Spatially
☒ Problem/Solution	
Explanation: Describe problem (large numbers of strays), present solution of creating more Ruff Streets centers.	

How will you conclude or summarize your presentation?
Emphasize how happy rescued pets and their adoptive owners are.

Creating Visuals

Once you have written the content of your presentation, you can create your visuals. As you create your visuals, remember that they are intended to clarify your points, not contain the full content of your presentation. The exception to this is when you are creating a self-running presentation that users can view on their own. Even then, you need to remember that you are creating a presentation, not a document, so the information should be communicated in a creative manner, not just via long bulleted lists.

Using visuals to supplement your presentation does the following:

- Increases the listeners' understanding—Visuals are especially helpful in explaining a difficult concept, displaying data, and illustrating the steps in a process.
- Helps listeners remember information—Audiences will remember information longer when visuals highlight or exemplify the main points, review conclusions, and explain recommendations.
- Adds credibility to the presentation—Speakers who use visuals in their presentation are judged by their audiences as more professional and better prepared.
- Stimulates and maintains the listeners' attention—It's much more interesting to see how something functions, rather than just hear about it.

The primary thing to remember is that the visuals are supposed to enhance the audience's understanding and help keep their attention. Visuals shouldn't draw attention to themselves in such a way as to distract from your main points.

Using Text as Visuals

When you use text as visuals, you allow your audience to absorb the information you are conveying by reading as well as listening. This can help audience members retain the information presented. Text can be formatted as bulleted lists or treated like a graphic.

A common pitfall for presenters is to use too much text. You don't want your presentation to turn into a bedtime story with you reading all the words on your visual as the audience falls asleep. Therefore, if you use bulleted lists, keep the bullet points short. Bullet points should be brief descriptions of your main points, giving your audience a broad overview of what you will be discussing and serving as reminders to help you remember what you want to say.

Instead of creating a bulleted list, one alternative is to display key words in a decorative, large font. You could also use relevant images as the bullets, or use a photo of a person accompanied by dialog balloons, like those in a drawn comic, that contain the text you want to display. Compare the four visuals shown in Figure 15. The text in the first visual is clear enough, but the second is visually more interesting. The third visual uses graphical bullets that relate to the text in each bullet point, and the fourth eliminates text completely and just uses images.

TIP

Text size can indicate relative importance. Show more important ideas or larger numbers in a larger size than less important ideas or smaller numbers.

Figure 15 **A simple bulleted list and alternatives**

Hybrid Automobiles

- Better gas mileage
- Reduced emissions
- Possible tax breaks

Hybrid Automobiles

Better gas mileage

Reduced emissions

Possible tax breaks

Hybrid Automobiles

Better gas mileage

Reduced emissions

Possible tax breaks

Hybrid Automobiles

Source: images used with permission from Microsoft.

When you use text as a visual, keep in mind the following:

- Follow the 7x7 Rule, which says that when you display bulleted lists, use no more than seven bullet points per visual, with no more than seven words per bullet. Some presenters restrict themselves to 4x4—no more than four bullet points per visual or page with no more than four words per bullet.
- Keep phrases parallel. For example, if one bulleted item starts with a verb (such as "Summarize"), the other bulleted items should also start with a verb (such as "Include," "List," or "Review").
- Use basic, plain fonts in a size large enough to be read from the back of the room. Only use decorative fonts for a single word or a few related words for maximum impact.
- Use dark-colored text on a light or white background to make it easy for the audience to quickly read the content. Do not layer text on top of a busy background graphic because the text will be difficult to read and the graphic will compete with the text for the audience's attention.
- Proofread your presentations. One sure way to reduce your credibility as a presenter is to have typographical errors in your presentation. It is especially important to double-check the spelling of proper names.

In his presentation, Ben could list facts about the number of strays, number rescued, number in shelters, and number adopted in a bulleted list.

Using Graphics as Visuals

You can help your listeners comprehend and retain the ideas from your presentation by supplementing it with effective graphics. A **graphic** is a picture, shape, design, graph or chart, diagram, or video. The old adage "A picture is worth a thousand words" especially applies to presentations because listeners understand ideas more quickly when they can see and hear what you're talking about.

You can choose from many types of visuals for your presentations: tables (text and numerical), graphs and charts (bar, line, pie, organizational, flow), illustrations (drawings, diagrams, maps, and photographs), and video. Selecting appropriate visuals for your purpose is a matter of knowing the strengths and weaknesses of the types of visuals. For example, if you want your audience to know facts and figures, a table might be sufficient; however, if you want your audience to make a particular judgment about the data, then a bar graph, line graph, or pie chart might be better. If you want to show processes and procedures, diagrams are better than photographs.

In Ben's presentation, he might want to present data describing the number of dogs put in shelters each year and what happens to them. He could read a summary of the numbers, as shown in Figure 16.

Figure 16 Shelter data as a presenter would read it

"According to the Seaboard Animal Rescue Society, approximately 1.9 million dogs enter shelters along the east coast each year. Of that number, approximately 665 thousand (about 35%) are adopted, 570 thousand (about 30%) are euthanized, and 475 thousand (about 25%) are lucky enough to be returned to their owners."

However, this is not the most interesting way of communicating the data, and Ben's audience might find it difficult to understand or compare this series of numbers if he just speaks them. By using visuals, he can present the same data in a format that's easier to understand, and more interesting. For example, he could present the data in tabular format, as shown in Figure 17.

Figure 17 Shelter data in tabular format

What Happens to Shelter Dogs	Number Each Year
Adopted	665,000
Euthanized	570,000
Returned to owners	475,000
Other	19,000

Although presenting the data in this manner does allow the audience members to read and absorb the numbers as he is speaking, some people can't visualize what this means. Tables are good for showing exact numbers (such as, how many shelter dogs are adopted each year), but they are not as good for showing trends (for instance, the increase or decrease over the past five years in the number of shelter dogs adopted each year) or for illustrating how one number compares to another. To do this, Ben could create a pie chart instead, as shown in Figure 18.

Figure 18 **Shelter data in a pie chart**

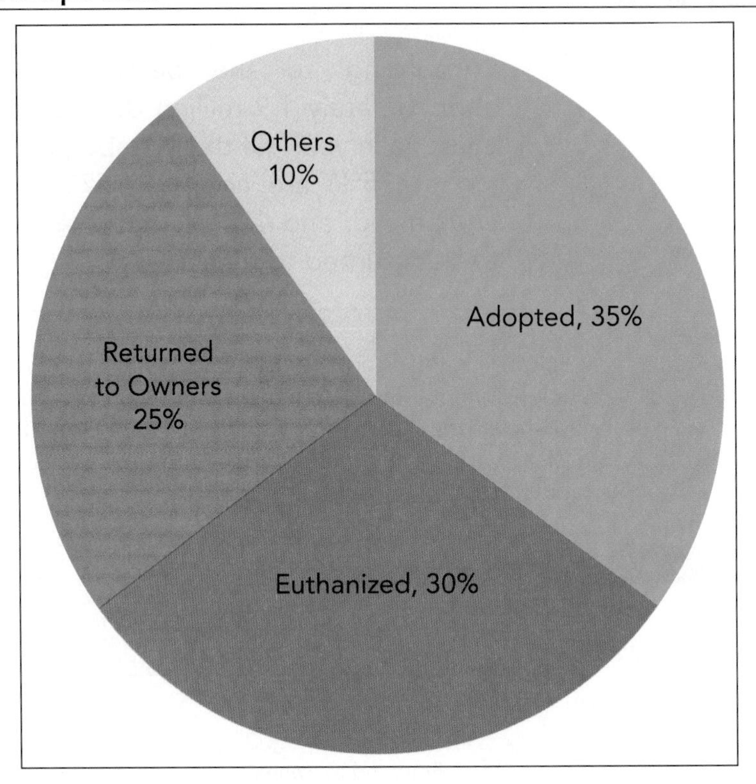

Pie charts are best for showing percentages or proportions of the parts that make up a whole. Pie charts allow your audience to compare the sections to each other, as well as to the whole. Pie charts can be created to display either the percentage relationship or the amount relationship.

Ben wants to highlight the differences in the numbers of each outcome. The pie chart doesn't show this very well because the numbers are relatively close together so the three large pie slices look like they are the same size. Ben decides this information would be better presented in a column chart. Column and bar graphs (graphs that use horizontal or vertical bars to represent specific values) are useful in comparing the value of one item to another over a period of time or a range of dates or values. See Figure 19.

Figure 19 **Shelter data in a column chart**

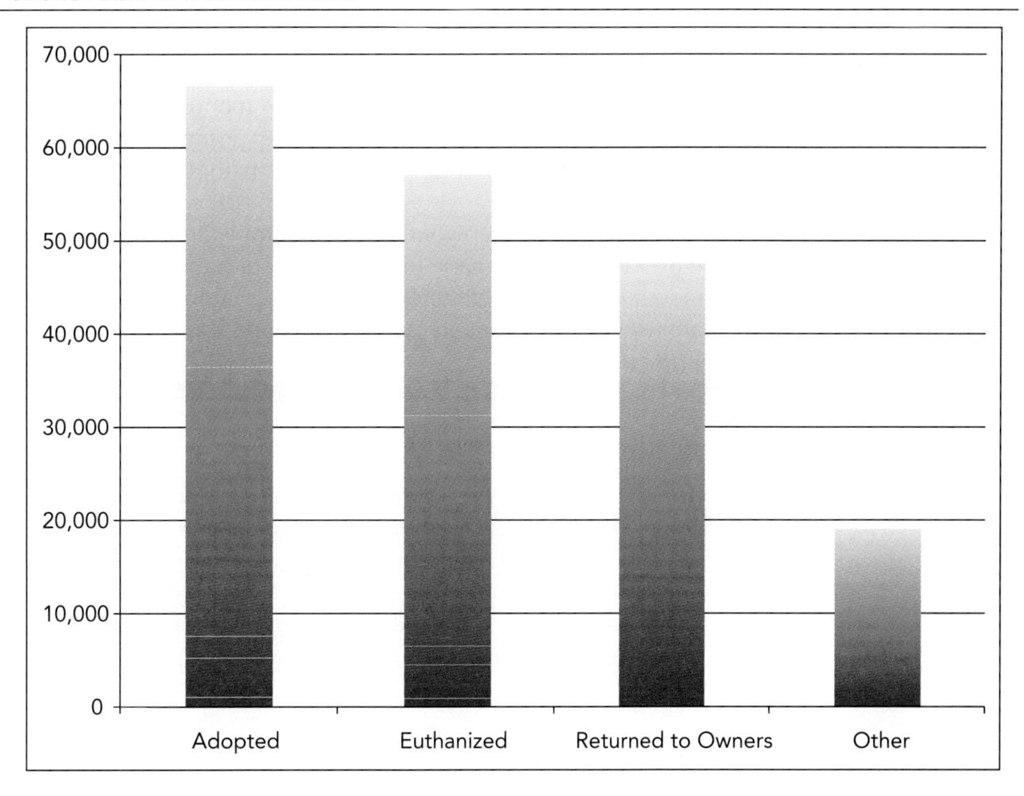

The column chart that illustrates what happens to dogs in shelters each year gives Ben's audience a clear visual comparison of the different outcomes.

Ben plans to use the chart shown in Figure 19 in his presentation. He also plans to include photos showing a couple of dogs just after they were rescued and before they were bathed and medically treated, as well as several photos of obviously happy dogs and a few with adopted families. He is considering showing video of a rescue to showcase how much a dog's life can change.

Decision Making: Text, Graphics, or Both?

Some people think that presentation visuals should consist exclusively of graphics; that is, they should not contain any bulleted or numbered lists at all. Using graphics without any bulleted lists can help keep your audience's attention on you and your message. The audience sees the graphic and then focuses on you as you explain your point and the relevance of the graphic. However, this is not necessarily the best choice if you are presenting facts, summarizing a process, or presenting in an academic setting. Some business and academic audiences expect to see bullet points in a presentation. In these cases, you should give your audience what they expect. Self-running presentations also usually require more text than visuals compared to an oral presentation.

If you decide to use bulleted lists, re-evaluate the content after you create it to see if the list is necessary or if you can use a graphic or series of graphics instead. Whether you decide to use all bulleted lists, all graphics, or a combination, always review your content to make sure it supplements your oral presentation to make it clearer or that your self-running presentation is interesting enough to make someone want to watch it to the end.

Creating Handouts

Handouts are printed documents you give to your audience before, during, or after your presentation. Handouts can be a printed version of your presentation, but they can also be brochures, an instruction manual, booklets, or anything you think will help the audience remember your key points. The information in handouts should complement, rather than compete with, the information contained in your presentation.

It's important to keep your handouts simple and easy to read. Begin by considering the overall design or shape of the page. Your audience is more apt to read your handout if it looks uncluttered and approachable. You can do this by providing ample margins, creating adequate white space, and using prominent headings.

INSIGHT

Distributing Handouts

The decision of when to distribute handouts depends on how you want the audience to use them. If you are presenting complex information about which the audience will probably need to take notes, you should distribute the handouts at the start of your presentation. If you want the audience's undivided attention while you are speaking and your handouts will serve simply as a reminder of your key points, distribute them after your presentation.

Ben has fliers for Ruff Streets that describe the center and its benefits, and he has donation forms. He feels these will be more beneficial handouts than a printed version of his presentation. He will distribute them at the end of his presentation.

After developing the content of a presentation and creating supporting visuals, you can begin to prepare to deliver your presentation. You will learn how to prepare for delivering a presentation in the next session.

REVIEW

Session 2 Quick Check

1. List at least three methods for focusing your topic.
2. Why is it a good idea to order your key points in a numbered list with the most important idea listed first and the least important point listed last?
3. List at least three ways to gain your audience's attention.
4. What is the difference between organizing your presentation deductively and inductively?
5. Why are conclusions important?
6. If you use bulleted lists as visuals, what is a good rule of thumb for how much text should be shown at one time?
7. What is a graphic?
8. What is a handout?

Session 3 Visual Overview:

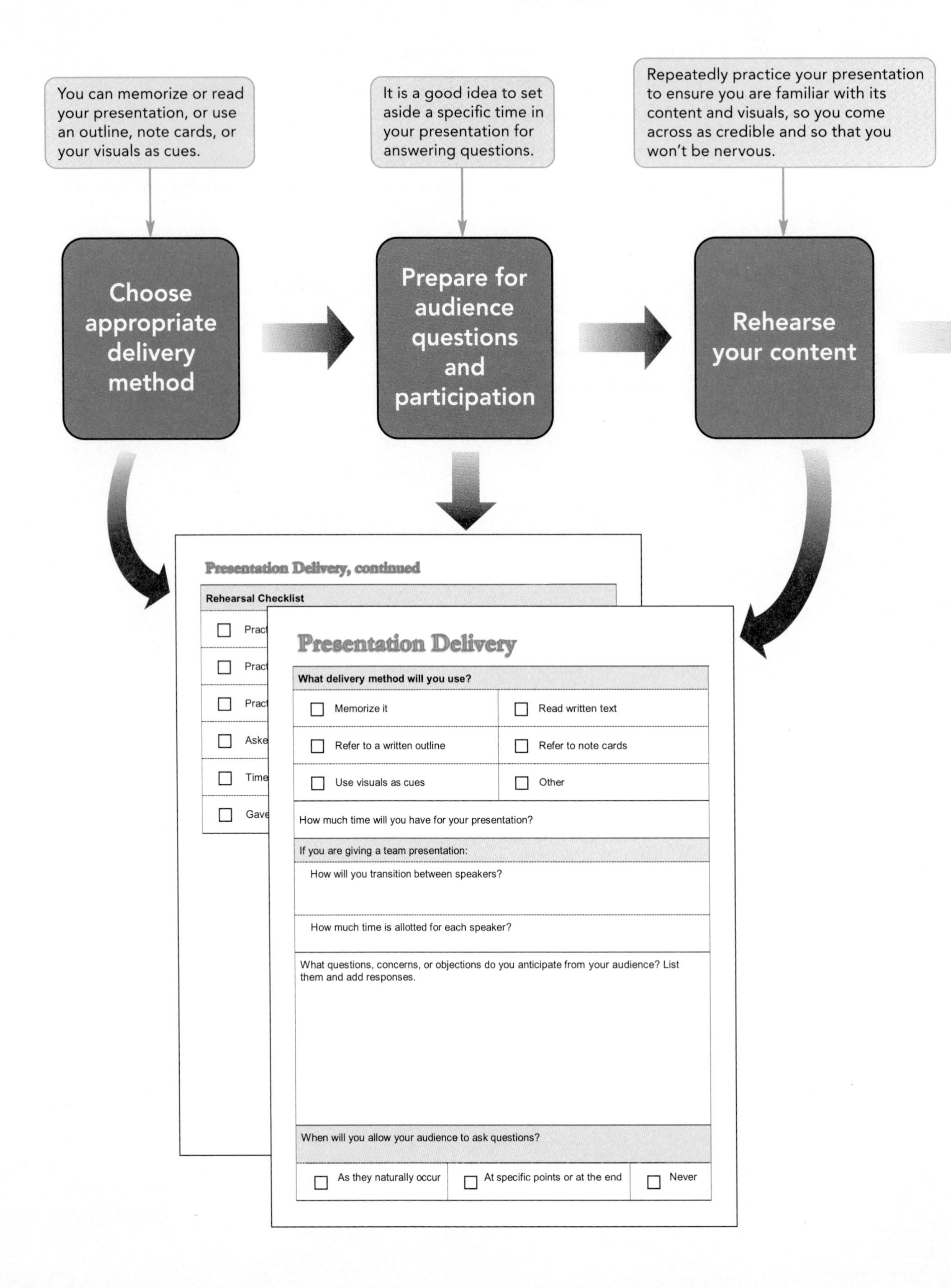

Delivering a Presentation

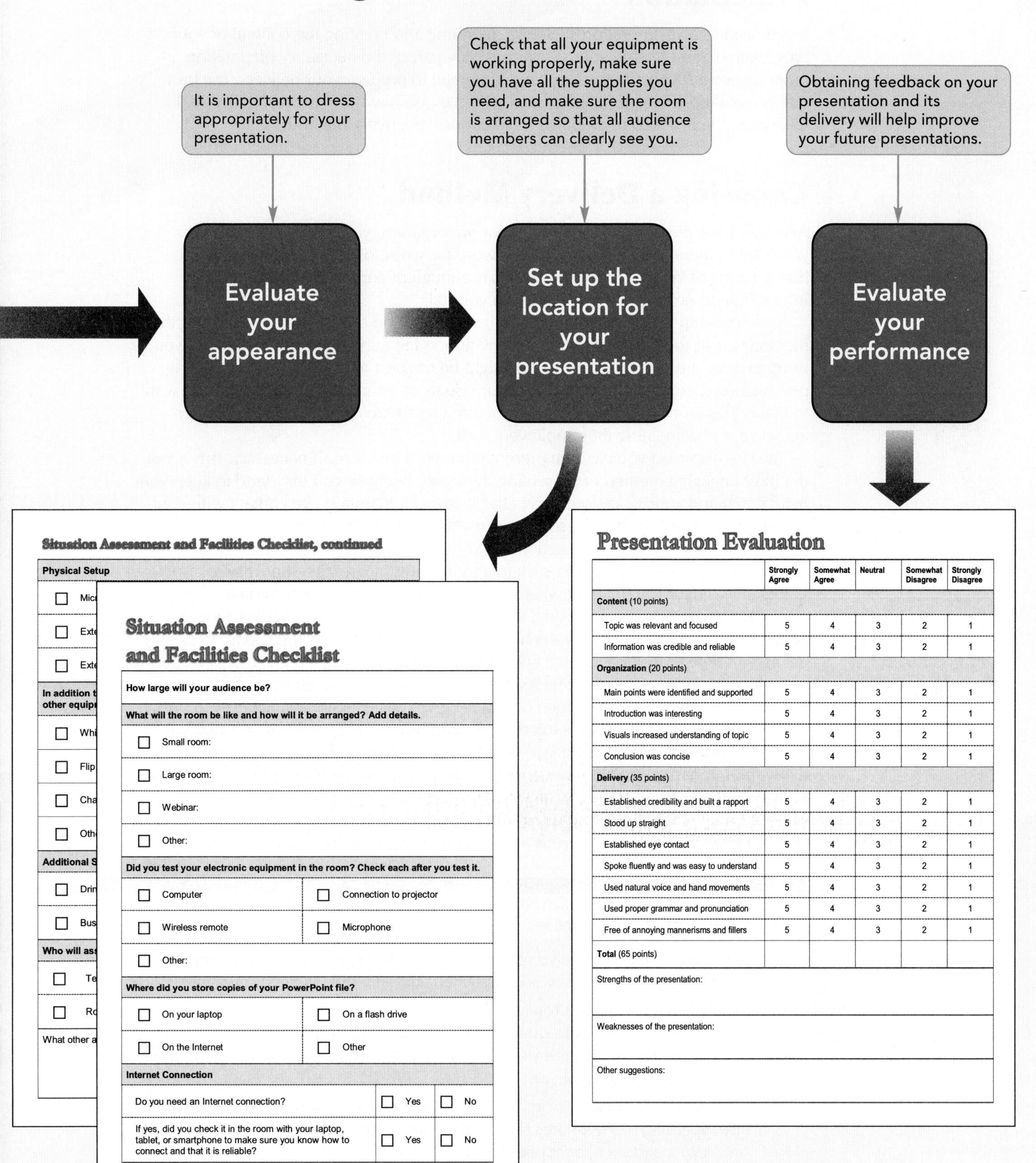

Situation Assessment and Facilities Checklist

How large will your audience be?	
What will the room be like and how will it be arranged? Add details.	
☐ Small room:	
☐ Large room:	
☐ Webinar:	
☐ Other:	
Did you test your electronic equipment in the room? Check each after you test it.	
☐ Computer	☐ Connection to projector
☐ Wireless remote	☐ Microphone
☐ Other:	
Where did you store copies of your PowerPoint file?	
☐ On your laptop	☐ On a flash drive
☐ On the Internet	☐ Other
Internet Connection	
Do you need an Internet connection?	☐ Yes ☐ No
If yes, did you check it in the room with your laptop, tablet, or smartphone to make sure you know how to connect and that it is reliable?	☐ Yes ☐ No

Presentation Evaluation

	Strongly Agree	Somewhat Agree	Neutral	Somewhat Disagree	Strongly Disagree
Content (10 points)					
Topic was relevant and focused	5	4	3	2	1
Information was credible and reliable	5	4	3	2	1
Organization (20 points)					
Main points were identified and supported	5	4	3	2	1
Introduction was interesting	5	4	3	2	1
Visuals increased understanding of topic	5	4	3	2	1
Conclusion was concise	5	4	3	2	1
Delivery (35 points)					
Established credibility and built a rapport	5	4	3	2	1
Stood up straight	5	4	3	2	1
Established eye contact	5	4	3	2	1
Spoke fluently and was easy to understand	5	4	3	2	1
Used natural voice and hand movements	5	4	3	2	1
Used proper grammar and pronunciation	5	4	3	2	1
Free of annoying mannerisms and fillers	5	4	3	2	1
Total (65 points)					

Strengths of the presentation:

Weaknesses of the presentation:

Other suggestions:

Preparing for the Delivery of an Oral Presentation

If you need to give an oral presentation, planning and creating the content of your presentation and creating your visuals are only part of the necessary preparation. In order to give a successful presentation, you need to prepare your delivery. The best oral presentations are prepared well in advance. As shown in the Session 3 Visual Overview, the first step in preparing is to choose a delivery method.

Choosing a Delivery Method

After you have created the content of your presentation, you need to decide if you want to memorize it exactly, read it word for word, or review it thoroughly so that glancing at keywords or your visuals is enough of a trigger to indicate which information to present at a given point in your talk.

Some presenters like to write their entire presentation out, word for word, and then memorize it so they can recite the presentation to the audience from memory. If you've never given a presentation before, this might be the best approach. If you are using presentation media, you can also use your visuals as reminders of the points you want to make. This works well for speakers who are comfortable speaking in front of an audience and who know their topic very well.

You can also read your written presentation word for word, if necessary. This is not the most engaging method of presenting, however, because you may tend to keep your head down and your voice low. It is better if you can maintain eye contact with your audience and stand up straight so that your voice is loud and clear.

Written or memorized presentations don't leave a lot to chance, so they work well in formal settings when you must stick to a topic and stay on schedule. They're also helpful if you think you'll forget what you prepared, or become nervous and tongue-tied as a result of your inexperience with the topic or with giving presentations. However, once you've memorized your presentation, it's not easy to alter it in response to changes in time limits or audience questions. Perhaps the biggest drawback to written or memorized presentations is that it's difficult to sound natural while reading your presentation or reciting it from memory, causing your listeners to lose interest.

Another delivery approach is to create an outline on paper or notecards that you can use to deliver your presentation without memorization. This type of delivery allows you to have a more natural-sounding presentation and the ability to adapt it for audience questions or participation. You still need to thoroughly review your notes to avoid leaving out crucial information, lacking precision when explaining your ideas, or stumbling because you are nervous and unfamiliar with the material.

INSIGHT

Giving an Impromptu Presentation

Impromptu presentations involve speaking without notes, an outline, or memorized text. Impromptu presentations work best when you're in the following situations:

- Extremely familiar with your topic and audience
- Speaking to a small, intimate group, or in your office setting
- More interested in getting the views of your audience than in persuading them or giving them specific information

Generally, you should be wary of impromptu presentations because they leave too much to chance. Speaking without notes may result in taking too much time, saying something that offends your audience, or appearing unorganized. If you think you might be asked to give an impromptu presentation, jot down some notes beforehand so you'll be prepared.

Ben will prepare his oral delivery and memorize it. He knows his material well, so he plans to use his visuals as cues rather than written notes.

Preparing for Audience Interaction

Allowing your audience to ask questions or actively participate in your presentation by offering their own ideas makes the presentation more personal for your audience. This also helps to keep them interested.

Anticipating Audience Questions

You need to decide whether you want your audience to have an opportunity to ask questions or actively participate in your presentation. You should welcome the idea of questions from the audience, rather than trying to avoid them. The absence of questions may indicate that your audience had no interest in what you said or that you spoke for too long. Adopting the attitude that interested listeners will have questions enables you to anticipate and prepare for the questions your audience will ask.

Figure 20 **Interested listeners have questions**

Source: Andrey_Popov/Shutterstock.com

If you plan to invite your audience to ask questions, you need to decide when you want this to happen. The size of your audience and the formality of the presentation might affect this decision. For example, four or five co-workers in a small conference room would probably expect to be able to interrupt your presentation and ask questions or express their own views, whereas a large audience in a lecture hall would not.

Allowing people to ask questions freely during your presentation means that the questions will be relevant and the answers will make sense to all members of the audience. If you allow this, keep an eye on the time and be prepared to halt questions if you need to. To allow you a little more control, you can build time for questions into your presentation as you transition from one section to another.

You can also ask your audience to hold all questions until the end of your presentation. If you do this, you will have more control over the time. However, people might forget their questions by the end of the presentation, and other audience members might not pay any attention at all to a question about something you discussed 30 minutes earlier.

If you decide to open the presentation to questions, you should prepare a few that you can pose in case no one responds when you invite questions. You can start with "I've often been asked…" or "A question that comes up frequently is…" This can be especially helpful if you build in time at the end of your presentation for answering questions, but no one has any.

When preparing for questions, keep in mind the following:

- Announce your plan for handling questions at the beginning of your presentation. If you don't plan to allow questions during your presentation, perhaps let people know they can approach you later.
- Repeat questions to make sure everyone in the audience hears them.
- If you don't understand a question, ask the questioner to rephrase it.
- Be prepared to answer questions about information in your presentation that is new, controversial, or unexpected.
- If you can't answer a question, admit it, indicate you will find out the answer and report back to the group, and then move on.
- If one person is completely confused and asks too many questions, especially questions that most of the audience already knows the answer to, ask this person to talk to you after the presentation so that the focus of your presentation doesn't get derailed.
- Don't be defensive about hostile questions. Treat every person's question as important, and respond courteously.
- Keep your answers brief. If you need additional time to respond to a question, arrange for it after your presentation.
- Be prepared to end a question-and-answer session; for example, state, "We have time for one more question."
- Consider offering to answer questions after the session, or provide your contact information and invite people to send you questions.

Ben anticipates that during his presentation audience members might have questions such as, "How do you capture the dogs without stressing them more than they already are?", "How much does it cost to rescue one dog?", and "Why don't you rescue cats as well?"

Preparing for Audience Participation

TIP

Don't coerce people into participating. Always ask for volunteers. Putting reluctant members of your audience on the spot embarrasses everyone.

If you involve your audience in your presentation, they will pay closer attention to what you have to say. For example, an easy way to get the audience to participate is to start with a question and invite responses, or to stop partway through to discuss a particularly important point. You can also allow audience members to answer others' questions, contribute their own ideas, or ask for volunteers to help with a demonstration. Alternatively, you could ask audience members to give answers to an informal quiz or questionnaire, and then adjust your presentation to accommodate their responses. Allowing the audience to actively participate in your presentation can be especially effective in small group settings or situations where you're attempting to find new ways to approach ideas.

If you decide to allow your audience to participate in your presentation, you need to take extra precautions to avoid losing control of your presentation. Here are some tips to help you handle audience participation:

- Be prepared with tactful ways to interrupt a participant who monopolizes the time. If necessary, you can simply state, "You have some interesting points, but I want to give others a chance to comment before we move on."
- State a limit on the length of each response (such as 30 seconds) or the number of responses.
- Be prepared to halt comments that are taking too much time by saying something such as "These are great comments, but I'm afraid I need to move on as we have a limited amount of time."
- If you are inexperienced with handling audience participation, consider allowing it only at the end of your presentation.

During his presentation, Ben wants to ask members of the audience to relate their experiences adopting rescued dogs.

Now that you've determined how you want to deliver your presentation and you're prepared to interact with your audience, it's time to practice delivering the presentation.

Rehearsing the Presentation

Once the presentation content has been created, enhanced, and perfected, and you have determined your delivery method, it is time to prepare you, the presenter. Even the most knowledgeable speakers rehearse to ensure they know how the topics flow, what the main points are, how much time to spend on each point, and where to place emphasis. Presenters who try to stand up and "wing it" in front of a crowd usually reveal this amateur approach the moment they start speaking—by looking down at their notes, rambling off topic, losing track of what they are saying, or turning their backs on the audience frequently to read information displayed on-screen. To avoid this, you need to rehearse your presentation.

Figure 21 **Confidence comes with practice**

Source: Stephen Coburn/Shutterstock.com

TIP

Consider rehearsing for job interviews using the same techniques as you use for rehearsing for a presentation.

Begin by simply going over the key points of the presentation in your mind. Then rehearse your presentation in private until you are comfortable with the content. Next, practice in front of a few close friends so that they can offer critiques and you can get a feel for what it will be like speaking to an audience. Pay special attention to what your friends say about key aspects of your presentation, such as your introduction, main points, and conclusion. Then, rehearse your presentation again.

During your rehearsals, practice using your visuals to support your points. Know when to pause for a moment to let your audience absorb a visual, and know when to switch to the next visual. Also, time your presentation to make sure it is the correct length. Pay attention to the timing as you are speaking so that you know approximately how much time you have left by where you are in the presentation.

Finally, if you have a video camera, you can record yourself and then review the video. Watching video evidence of your performance often reveals weaknesses that you don't want your audience to see or that your friends or family may be unwilling or unable to identify.

As you rehearse, you should remember to focus on the following areas:

- Connecting to your audience
- Being aware of your body language
- Establishing eye contact
- Speaking in a pleasant, natural, confident voice
- Using proper grammar and pronunciation
- Avoiding fillers

INSIGHT

Overcoming Nervousness

Just thinking about speaking in front of other people may cause your heart to beat faster and your palms to sweat. You aren't alone. Feeling nervous about giving a presentation is a natural reaction. But you don't need to let nervousness interfere with your giving a successful presentation. Being nervous is not all bad. It means your adrenalin is flowing, and you'll have more energy and vitality for your presentation. In most instances, your nervousness will pass once you begin speaking. Sometimes, however, nervousness arises from feelings of inadequacy or from worrying about problems that could occur during a presentation. The most effective way to overcome your nervousness and deliver a smooth presentation is to carefully plan and prepare your presentation, and then to practice, practice, practice.

Experienced public speakers have learned several means of overcoming nervousness:

- Think positively about your presentation. Be optimistic and enthusiastic about your opportunity to gain experience. Visualize yourself as calm and confident.
- Work with your nervousness. Realize that some nervousness is normal and will help make your presentation better. Remember, your audience isn't nearly as concerned about your nervousness as you are.
- Give yourself plenty of time before your presentation. Arrive early to avoid rushing around before your presentation. Devote a few minutes beforehand to relax and review your presentation notes.
- When you first stand up, look at your audience and smile. Then take a few slow breaths to calm yourself before you begin to speak.
- Don't expect everything to be perfect. Have backup plans in case something goes wrong, and be prepared to handle problems with grace and a sense of humor.
- Think about why your audience is there—to learn something from you. When you focus your mind on meeting the needs of your audience, you begin to forget about yourself and how the audience might respond to you.
- Observe other presenters. Make a list of the things they do that you like, and try to implement them in your own presentations. Likewise, note any annoying mannerisms or speech patterns so that you don't duplicate them in your presentation.

Connecting to Your Audience

How an audience perceives a speaker can sometimes be more important than what the speaker says; therefore, it is important to establish a connection with your audience. Begin by introducing yourself and describing your credentials for speaking on your topic. Being aware of your demeanor—your body language, how often you make eye contact, and how you speak—will help you build a rapport with the audience. You often know if you have made a connection with your audience by their behavior and expressions. If your message is getting across, they will instinctively affirm what you're saying by returning your gaze, nodding their heads, or smiling. In Figure 22, the audience is smiling, nodding, and appears engaged with the presenter. If your message is not getting across and you see confused, puzzled, or frustrated expressions, you can make adjustments accordingly.

Figure 22 **Establish a connection with your audience**

Source: ©iStock.com/kupicoo

Being Aware of Your Body Language

Nonverbal communication is the way you convey a message without saying a word. Most nonverbal communication deals with how you use your body when interacting with people—how you look, stand, and move—in other words, your body language. In your everyday life, your body language is unconscious. However, by becoming aware of your body language, you can use it consciously to help you communicate more effectively.

Start by becoming aware of your posture. Stand up straight to signal confidence. Refrain from slouching, as your audience may interpret this to mean that you don't care or you're insecure.

Be aware of your hand movements as you speak. The best position for your hands is to place them comfortably by your side, in a relaxed position. As you talk, it's fine to use hand gestures to help make a point, but be careful not to overdo it. Informal presentations lend themselves to more gestures and movement than do formal presentations where you're standing in front of a microphone on a podium. But giving a formal presentation doesn't mean you should hide behind the lectern, or behave like a robot. Even formal presentations allow for gestures that are purposeful, spontaneous, and natural.

It is important to recognize your unique mannerisms (recurring or unnatural movements of your voice or body) that can be annoying, such as raising your voice and eyebrows as if you are talking to children; playing with your car keys, a pen, or equipment; or fidgeting, rocking, and pacing. All of these mannerisms can communicate nervousness. If they are pervasive, they will detract from your presentation because your audience will start paying attention to your mannerisms instead of to your topic. Consider asking a friend whether your gestures are distracting, and then practice speaking without them.

Resist the temptation to glance at your watch or cell phone; you don't want to send a signal that you'd rather be someplace else or that you are anxious to have the presentation completed.

Establishing Eye Contact

One of the most common mistakes presenters make is failing to establish eye contact with their audience. Speakers who keep their eyes on their notes, stare at their visuals, or look out over the heads of their audience create an emotional distance between themselves and their listeners. A better method is to look directly at your listeners, even if you have to pause to look up. Smiling and looking directly at your audience members, making eye contact, sends the message that you want to connect and that you can be trusted.

Figure 23 **Establish eye contact**

Source: ©iStock.com/kupicoo

To establish eye contact, look at individuals; do not just scan the audience. Focus on a particular member of the audience for just a second or two, then move on to someone else until you eventually get to most of the people in the audience or, if the audience is large, to most parts of the presentation room.

Speaking in a Pleasant, Natural, Confident Voice

TIP

Make sure you speak loudly enough and enunciate clearly so that your audience can hear you; consider using a microphone in a large room.

The best presentations are those in which the presenter appears confident and speaks naturally in a conversational manner. No one enjoys a presentation when the speaker drones on endlessly in a monotone voice. So when delivering your presentation, speak with enthusiasm, with authority, and with a smile. When you project your voice with energy, passion, and confidence, your audience will automatically pay more attention to you. However, be careful not to overdo it. Speaking too loudly or using an overly confident or arrogant tone will quickly turn off an audience and make them stop listening altogether.

Also, try to avoid raising the tone of your voice at the end of statements as if you were asking a question. This is sometimes referred to as uptalking or upspeaking. If you make statements that sound as if you are asking a question, you will sound less confident and knowledgeable.

Using Proper Grammar and Pronunciation

One of the best ways to be seen as a credible speaker is to use proper grammar and pronunciation. To assure you're pronouncing a word correctly, check its pronunciation in a dictionary.

Here are some common pronunciation problems:

- Mispronunciations caused by dropping a letter, such as "liberry" instead of "library," or "satistics" instead of "statistics"
- Mispronunciations caused by adding a letter or inserting the wrong letter, such as "acrost" instead of "across" or "learnt" instead of "learned"
- Colloquial expressions, such as "crick" instead of "creek," or "ain't" instead of "isn't" or "aren't"
- Lazy pronunciation caused by dropping the final consonant, such as "speakin" rather than "speaking"

Avoiding Fillers

Fillers consist of sounds, words, and phrases such as *um, ah, like,* and other breaks in speech that dilute a speaker's message. Fillers don't add any value, yet add length to sentences. At best, they can make you sound unprofessional. At worst, they can distract your audience and make your message incomprehensible.

Ben used the worksheet shown in Figure 24 to help him when practicing the delivery of his presentation. Note that he still needs to practice in front of others to get their feedback.

Figure 24 **Presentation Delivery worksheet for the Ruff Streets presentation**

Presentation Delivery

What delivery method will you use?	
☐ Memorize it	☐ Read written text
☐ Refer to a written outline	☐ Refer to note cards
☒ Use visuals as cues	☐ Other

How much time will you have for your presentation? 30 minutes

If you are giving a team presentation: N/A

How will you transition between speakers?

How much time is allotted for each speaker?

What questions, concerns, or objections do you anticipate from your audience? List them and add responses.

How do you capture dogs without stressing them further? We approach slowly and try to entice the dog with ground beef. When the dog lets us get close enough, we try to pet it, and while petting it, we slip a soft restraint over its head.

How much does it cost to rescue one dog? For dogs without serious medical issues, it costs approximately $150. For dogs that need more intensive medical treatment, the costs can rise to anywhere between $500 and $1,000.

Why don't you also rescue cats? We decided to focus on dogs because the number of dogs that enter shelters each year is larger than the number of cats. If we see cats in need of help, we contact a shelter in the next county that takes in cats.

When will you allow your audience to ask questions?		
☒ As they naturally occur	☐ At specific points or at the end	☐ Never

Presentation Delivery, continued

Rehearsal Checklist
☒ Practiced presentation in private
☐ Practiced presentation in front of friends or sample audience
☒ Practiced with presentation tools (PowerPoint file, props, etc.)
☐ Asked friends for suggestions and feedback on presentation
☒ Timed your presentation. Time in minutes: ___25______
☒ Gave particular attention to introduction, main points, and conclusion

Aa PROSKILLS

Verbal Communication: Avoiding Business Jargon

Business jargon has crept into our everyday language more and more over the past several years, to the point that many expressions are cliché. As you prepare your delivery, avoid using business jargon. For example, avoid saying things like "maximize our growth potential," "leverage our content," "using all our available bandwidth," "productivity solution," and "we need a hard stop here." Think about what you're trying to say and break it down into its simplest, most direct terms. If your audience is used to hearing business jargon, they'll tune out your message because they've heard it all before. If your audience is not used to hearing business jargon, they'll spend most of their time trying to figure out what exactly you're trying to tell them. And if your audience is spending time figuring out what you just said, they are no longer listening to what you are currently saying. After you prepare your oral delivery, go back through and replace any jargon with simple direct language that anyone could understand.

Referring to Visuals During Your Presentation

As you rehearse your presentation, you'll need to plan how to manage and present your visuals so they effectively support your content. Follow these simple guidelines for effectively using visuals when giving your presentation:

- Introduce and interpret the visual. Explain to your audience what they should be looking at in the visual and point to what is important.
- If the visual is text, don't read it word for word; use it as a cue for what you want to say next.
- Stand to the side, not in front, of the visuals. Avoid turning your back on your audience as you refer to a visual. Talk directly to your audience, rather than turning toward or talking at the visual.
- Display the visual as you discuss it and remove the visual after you're through discussing it. Don't let your visuals get ahead of or behind your verbal presentation.

Evaluating Your Appearance

Before a single word is spoken in a presentation, the audience sizes up the way the presenter looks. Your appearance creates your audience's first impression of you, so make sure your dress and grooming contribute to the total impression you want to convey to your audience. You want to make sure you look professional and competent. Dress appropriately for the situation, and in a manner that doesn't detract from your presentation. For example, for a formal presentation, you should wear business attire, such as a suit and tie for a man and a suit or tailored dress for a woman. Consider your audience and situation, but always make sure your appearance is neat, clean, and well-coordinated, and that you choose appropriate clothing. For example, the presenters shown in Figure 25 are appropriately dressed to speak in a professional setting.

Figure 25 Dress appropriately

Source: Serg Zastavkin/Shutterstock.com

Setting Up for Your Presentation

TIP

Don't bend over or stretch up to speak into a microphone; adjust the microphone for your height.

It's important to include the setup, or physical arrangements, for your presentation as a critical element of preparation. Even the best-planned and practiced presentation can fail if your audience can't see or hear your presentation, or if they're uncomfortable. You've probably attended a presentation where the speaker stepped up to the microphone only to find that it wasn't turned on. Or, the speaker tried to start a PowerPoint presentation but nothing appeared on the screen or it was displayed incorrectly.

Much of the embarrassment and lost time can be prevented if you plan ahead. Make sure the equipment works and make sure you know how to use it, especially if it works differently from equipment with which you are familiar. Of course, there are some things over which you have no control. For example, if you're giving your presentation as part of a professional conference, you can't control whether the room you're assigned is the right size for your audience. You often can't control what projection systems are available, the thermostat setting in the room, or the quality of the sound system. But you can control many of the factors that could interfere with or enhance the success of your presentation, if you consider them in advance.

Preparing Copies of Your Content

Usually, the original copy of visuals for a presentation is sufficient and will be available to you when you give your presentation. However, electronic storage can be damaged or files erased, and physical handouts and posters can be accidentally destroyed, for example, by getting wet. Therefore, it's always a good idea to have backups or copies of your visuals.

If you prepared a presentation file, you should make backups of the file on a portable storage device, such as a flash drive. If you are traveling on a plane, consider carrying a copy of your presentation in your carry-on bag and another copy in your checked bags. In addition, send a copy of the presentation via email to yourself on an email service that you can access via the web, or store a copy of the presentation file in the cloud, such as on Microsoft OneDrive, where you can easily retrieve it if necessary.

If you have handouts or posters, consider making extra copies of them and storing them separately from the original versions. This might not be possible in the case of posters, but you could take photos of the posters and bring your camera or storage card with you so that you could recreate the posters if something happens to the originals.

Assessing the Technology and Staff Available

TIP

A wireless remote for advancing a PowerPoint presentation is useful because it allows you to move away from the podium if you want.

You need to think about the technology you will be using. Check with your host or the presentation organizer ahead of time to make sure you know the type of equipment that will be available in the presentation room. If you are planning to use presentation software such as PowerPoint, you need a computer and either a projector and a screen or a large screen monitor and a way to connect to it. If you need to access the Internet during your presentation, obtain the password, if needed, and make sure you test the connection. If you have posters that need to be displayed, make sure an easel or place to mount the posters is available as well as thumbtacks or adhesive. If you want to take notes that people can see, make sure there is a whiteboard and markers or a chalkboard and chalk.

When you arrive at the location where you will be giving the presentation, verify that the presentation tools you need are physically in the room. If you will be using presentation software, connect the computer with the presentation on it to the projector device or to the large screen monitor in the room, making sure you have adequate space for your equipment and access to electrical outlets. Then open the presentation file and start the presentation to make sure that it will be displayed correctly. Make sure that each visual is displayed as you expect it to be. Do this well in advance of the time you are scheduled to give your presentation.

Figure 26 **Setting up for the presentation**

Source: Matej Kastelic/Shutterstock.com

If the venue is going to be providing you with the computer, rather than you using your own, take the time to familiarize yourself with that computer and make sure you know exactly which folder your presentation is stored in. Consider bringing your own computer as a backup just in in case the one provided to you doesn't display the presentation file correctly.

Even with the most carefully laid plans, unexpected problems can come up. If you are giving a presentation at a large facility, such as in a conference room at a hotel, make sure you know how to contact the appropriate staff in case you have technical or other problems.

Becoming Familiar with the Room

It's helpful to know the size and shape of the room where your presentation will occur and the seating arrangement. The setting for a presentation can affect audience expectations and, therefore, will dictate the appropriate level of formality. A small conference room with a round table and moveable chairs would call for a much more informal presentation than a large lecture hall with fixed seating.

Examine the room in which you'll give your presentation. You'll want to check whether the room is properly ventilated, has adequate lighting, and is free from distracting noises, such as clanking of dishes in the kitchen, hammering and sawing by work crews, or interference from the speakers in adjacent rooms. You might not be authorized to change things like temperature settings or the arrangement of chairs, so you may need to adjust your presentation somewhat.

In considering the layout of the room, you'll want to make sure the chairs are arranged so that everyone in the audience can see and hear your presentation. You'll also want to make sure a podium or table provides enough room for your notes, or that the equipment, such as the computer, is close enough so that you won't have to walk back and forth to your notes.

Identifying Other Needed Supplies

In addition to your presentation visuals, you should make sure that you have any other supplies that you need. For example, if you are using technology, make sure you have extension cords. If you need them, make sure a whiteboard or flip chart is available. You should also have pen and paper in case you need to take notes.

If you are going to have handouts, make sure you have enough copies for all your audience members. Even if you don't plan to pass out business cards to everyone in the room, make sure you have some with you in case someone asks for one.

Finally, it's also a good idea to have a glass of water or water bottle available in case your throat or lips get dry.

Figure 27 shows a worksheet Ben used to assess the situation and facilities for this and other presentations.

Figure 27 Situation Assessment and Facilities Checklist worksheet for the Ruff Streets presentation

Situation Assessment and Facilities Checklist

How large will your audience be? 35-50 people	
What will the room be like and how will it be arranged? Add details.	
☐ Small room:	
☒ Large room: Hall at Civic Center	
☐ Webinar:	
☐ Other:	
Did you test your electronic equipment in the room? Check each after you test it.	
☒ Computer	☒ Connection to projector
☒ Wireless remote	☒ Microphone
☒ Other: Lighting	
Where did you store copies of your PowerPoint file?	
☒ On your laptop	☒ On a flash drive
☒ On cloud storage	☐ Other

Internet Connection		
Do you need an Internet connection?	☐ Yes	☒ No
If yes, did you check it in the room with your laptop, tablet, or smartphone to make sure you know how to connect and that it is reliable?	☐ Yes	☐ No

Situation Assessment and Facilities Checklist, continued

Physical Setup	
☒ Microphone height OK	
☒ Extension cords available if you need them	
☒ Extension cords and other wires out of the way	
In addition to your PowerPoint file, laptop, and projection equipment, do you have other equipment available to use?	
☐ Whiteboard	☐ White board markers and eraser
☐ Flip chart	☐ Permanent marker
☐ Chalkboard	☐ Chalk and eraser
☐ Other	
Additional Supplies	
☒ Drinking water	☐ Paper and pen
☐ Business cards	☒ Other—pledge forms
Who will assist you with the equipment and other situational aspects?	
☒ Technical support staff	☒ Friend or colleague
☐ Room monitor	☐ Other
What other aspects must you consider for your presentation? Arrange for drinks and hors d'oeuvres	

For his presentation, Ben will have both technical support staff provided by the Civic Center and a colleague available to help him with technical details, and he will be able to change the arrangement of chairs so that his audience will be seated close to the stage. He will not, however, be able to adjust the room temperature. He plans to access the room in which he will be speaking a day ahead of time so he can become familiar with its setup. When he visits, he will connect his laptop to the projector provided by the facility to make sure that his PowerPoint presentation file will be displayed correctly. He decides that he doesn't need a whiteboard, chalkboard, or flip chart.

Ben feels confident that he has done everything possible to prepare for his presentation.

Evaluating Your Performance

TIP

If you ask someone to critique your presentation, be prepared to take criticism. Even if you think the criticism is unjustified, ask yourself, "How can I use this criticism to improve my presentation?"

An important step in any presentation (and the step that is most often left out) is to review your performance after it is over to determine how you can improve your next presentation. Evaluating your performance and setting goals for improvement ensures that your next presentation will be even better than your last one. After you give your oral presentation, you can also ask your audience to evaluate your presentation. Having written feedback or a numerical score for each aspect of your presentation can be especially helpful in highlighting where you have room for improvement.

You can evaluate your own performance or ask friends or audience members to evaluate your presentation. Ben plans to ask colleagues to evaluate his presentation using the Presentation Evaluation sheet shown in Figure 28.

Figure 28 **Presentation Evaluation worksheet**

Presentation Evaluation

	Strongly Agree	Somewhat Agree	Neutral	Somewhat Disagree	Strongly Disagree
Content (10 points)					
Topic was relevant and focused	5	4	3	2	1
Information was credible and reliable	5	4	3	2	1
Organization (20 points)					
Main points were identified and supported	5	4	3	2	1
Introduction was interesting	5	4	3	2	1
Visuals increased understanding of topic	5	4	3	2	1
Conclusion was concise	5	4	3	2	1
Delivery (35 points)					
Established credibility and built a rapport	5	4	3	2	1
Stood up straight	5	4	3	2	1
Established eye contact	5	4	3	2	1
Spoke fluently and was easy to understand	5	4	3	2	1
Used natural voice and hand movements	5	4	3	2	1
Used proper grammar and pronunciation	5	4	3	2	1
Free of annoying mannerisms and fillers	5	4	3	2	1
Total (65 points)					

Strengths of the presentation:

Weaknesses of the presentation:

Other suggestions:

REVIEW

Session 3 Quick Check

1. What is a good approach for delivering a presentation if you are not used to giving them?
2. What is one benefit of allowing audience members to ask questions during a presentation at the point when questions occur to them?
3. Name three reasons why you should rehearse your presentation.
4. Why is being aware of your body language helpful when giving presentations?
5. What are fillers and why should you avoid them?
6. Why should you create backups or copies of your visuals?
7. If you will be using a computer and projector or large screen monitor to display a presentation file, what should you do when you arrive at the facility where you will be giving your presentation?
8. Why is it useful to evaluate your performance?

PRACTICE

Review Assignments

One of the executives who attended Ben's first presentation asked Ben if he would be willing to present to the board of the directors for the executive's company. Ben will have 20 minutes to present, with another 10 minutes for questions. The presentation will be given to 15 to 20 people in a private dining room at a local yacht club.

Complete the following steps (note that your instructor may provide you with files containing the different worksheets you need to complete):

1. Complete a Purposes and Outcomes worksheet for Ben's presentation.
2. Complete an Audience Analysis worksheet for Ben's presentation.
3. Complete a Focus and Organization worksheet for Ben's presentation, using the following information:
   a. Keep in mind that the audience is composed of members of a corporate board of directors. This type of audience is used to professional presentations that are highly focused on the topic so as not to waste their time.
   b. Prepare an introduction for the presentation using a fictional story or anecdote describing a successful dog rescue and adoption.
   c. Prepare a conclusion for the presentation that includes a fictional quote from a family that recently adopted a rescued dog.
4. Complete a Presentation Delivery worksheet for Ben's presentation (skip the Rehearsal Checklist). Include at least three questions (and fictional responses) that you think the audience will have.
5. Describe what Ben should wear for his presentation. (Remember, his audience consists of corporate professionals.)
6. Complete a Situation and Media Assessment Worksheet for Ben's presentation. Assume the following:
   a. Ben will have access to a large screen monitor to which he can connect his laptop with a cable provided by the yacht club.
   b. A microphone will not be available.
   c. Ben has a wireless remote to switch from one visual to another.
   d. Ben does not need a connection to the Internet.
   e. An employee of the yacht club will be available to assist.
7. Divide into groups of two and deliver a one-minute presentation to your partner. Present a topic that Ben would cover or any topic of your choice. Have your partner fill out a Presentation Evaluation worksheet for you. Then have your partner present, and you fill out a Presentation Evaluation worksheet for him or her.

MODULE 1

Creating a Presentation

Presenting Information About an Event Venue

POWERPOINT

OBJECTIVES

Session 1.1

- Plan and create a new presentation
- Create a title slide and slides with lists
- Edit and format text
- Move and copy text
- Convert a list to a SmartArt diagram
- Duplicate, rearrange, and delete slides
- Close a presentation

Session 1.2

- Open an existing presentation
- Change the theme and theme variant
- Insert and crop photos
- Modify photo compression options
- Resize and move objects
- Create speaker notes
- Check the spelling
- Run a slide show
- Print slides, handouts, speaker notes, and the outline

Case | *Lakeside Event Center*

Lakeside Event Center is a venue in Lake Havasu City, Arizona, that opened in 1981 and is available for functions of all types, including birthdays, bar mitzvahs, corporate events, and weddings. The event center, located on the shore of Lake Havasu, has rooms that can host from 50 to 900 people. The center underwent a recent renovation including planting new gardens and updating the décor inside. Caitlin Keough-Barton was recently hired as the events manager. One of Caitlin's responsibilities is to attract new bookings. Caitlin wants to advertise the hall at upcoming wedding and event-planning conventions.

Microsoft PowerPoint 2016 (or simply **PowerPoint**) is a computer program you use to create a collection of slides that can contain text, charts, pictures, sounds, movies, multimedia, and so on. In this module, you'll use PowerPoint to create a presentation that Caitlin can use to showcase everything Lakeside Event Center has to offer when she attends the Event Planners Association annual convention. After Caitlin reviews it, you'll add graphics and speaker notes to the presentation. Finally, you'll check the spelling, run the slide show to evaluate it, and print the presentation.

STARTING DATA FILES

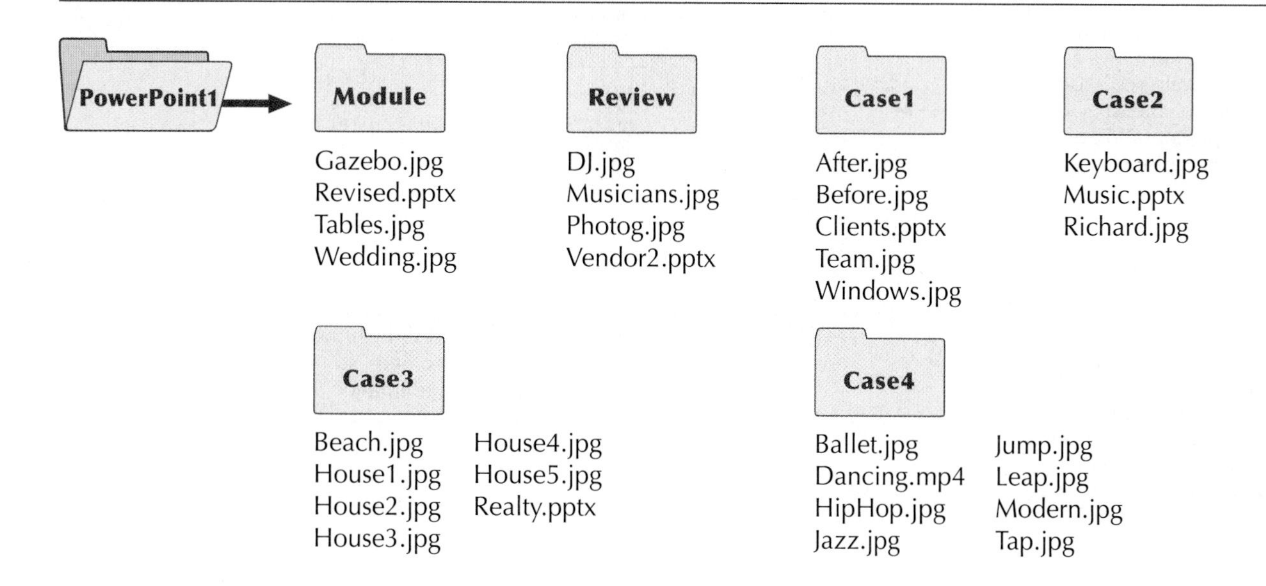

Session 1.1 Visual Overview:

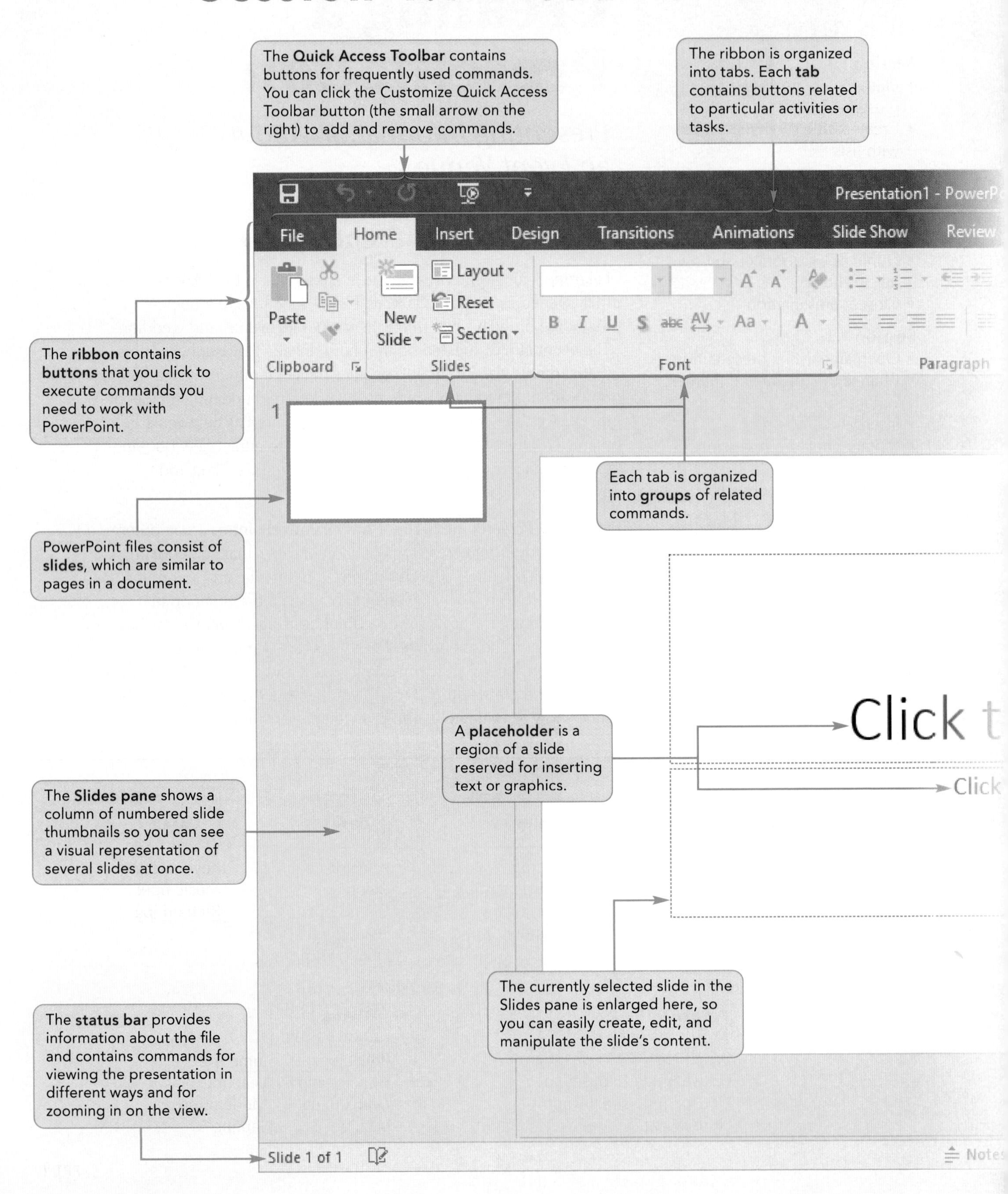

The PowerPoint Window

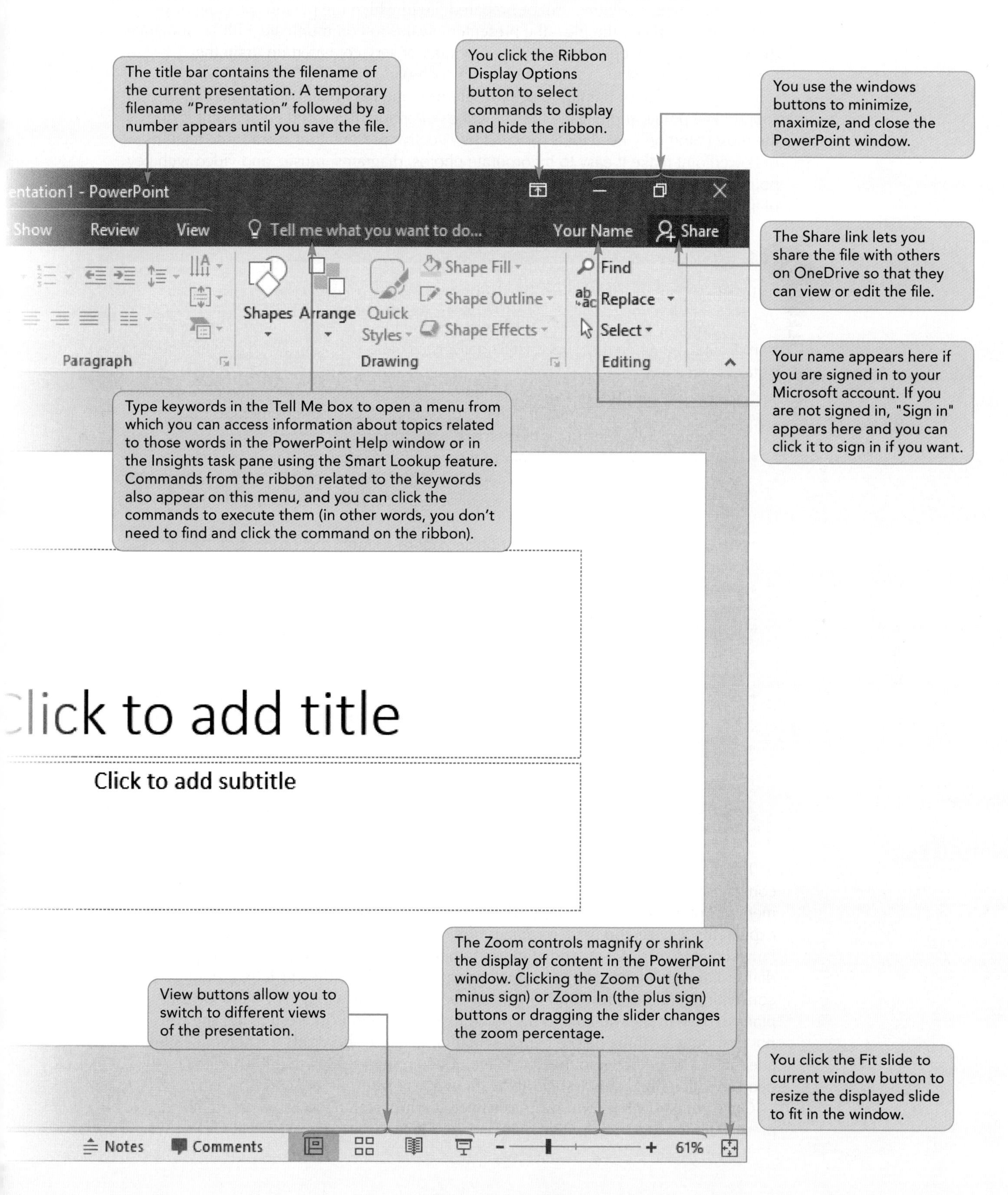

Planning a Presentation

A **presentation** is a talk (lecture) or prepared file in which the person speaking or the person who prepared the file—the presenter—wants to communicate with an audience to explain new concepts or ideas, sell a product or service, entertain, train the audience in a new skill or technique, or any of a wide variety of other topics.

Most people find it helpful to use **presentation media**—visual and audio aids to support key points and engage the audience's attention. Microsoft PowerPoint is one of the most commonly used tools for creating effective presentation media. The features of PowerPoint make it easy to incorporate photos, diagrams, music, and video with key points of a presentation. Before you create a presentation, you should spend some time planning its content.

PROSKILLS

Verbal Communication: Planning a Presentation

Answering a few key questions will help you create a presentation using appropriate presentation media that successfully delivers its message or motivates the audience to take an action.

- What is the purpose of your presentation? In other words, what action or response do you want your audience to have? For example, do you want them to buy something, follow instructions, or make a decision?
- Who is your audience? Think about the needs and interests of your audience as well as any decisions they'll make as a result of what you have to say. What you choose to say to your audience must be relevant to their needs, interests, and decisions or it will be forgotten.
- What are the main points of your presentation? Identify the information that is directly relevant to your audience.
- What presentation media will help your audience absorb the information and remember it later? Do you need lists, photos, charts, or tables?
- What is the format for your presentation? Will you deliver the presentation orally or will you create a presentation file that your audience members will view on their own, without you present?
- How much time do you have for the presentation? Keep that in mind as you prepare the presentation content so that you have enough time to present all of your key points.
- Consider whether handouts will help your audience follow along with your presentation or steal your audience's attention when you want them to be focused on you, the presenter.

The purpose of Caitlin's presentation is to convince people attending wedding conventions to book their weddings at Lakeside Event Center. Her audience will be members of the local community who are planning a wedding. She also plans to explain the service and price packages from which people can choose. Caitlin will use PowerPoint to display lists and graphics to help make her message clear. She plans to deliver her presentation orally to small groups of people as they visit her booth at the convention, and her presentation will be about 10 minutes long. For handouts, she plans to have flyers available to distribute to anyone who is interested, but she will not distribute anything before her presentation because she wants the audience's full attention to be on her, and the details are not complex enough that the audience will need a written document to refer to as she is speaking.

Once you know what you want to say or communicate, you can prepare the presentation media to help communicate your ideas.

Starting PowerPoint and Creating a New Presentation

Microsoft PowerPoint 2016 is a tool you can use to create and display visual and audio aids on slides to help clarify the points you want to make in your presentation or to create a presentation that people view on their own without you being present.

When PowerPoint starts, the Recent screen in Backstage view is displayed. **Backstage view** contains commands that allow you to manage your presentation files and PowerPoint options. When you first start PowerPoint, the only actions available to you in Backstage view are to open an existing PowerPoint file or create a new file. You'll start PowerPoint now.

To start PowerPoint:

1. On the Windows taskbar, click the **Start** button. The Start menu opens.
2. Click **All apps** on the Start menu, scroll the list, and then click **PowerPoint 2016.** PowerPoint starts and displays the Recent screen in Backstage view. See Figure 1-1. In the orange bar on the left is a list of recently opened presentations, and on the right are options for creating new presentations.

Figure 1-1 **Recent screen in Backstage view**

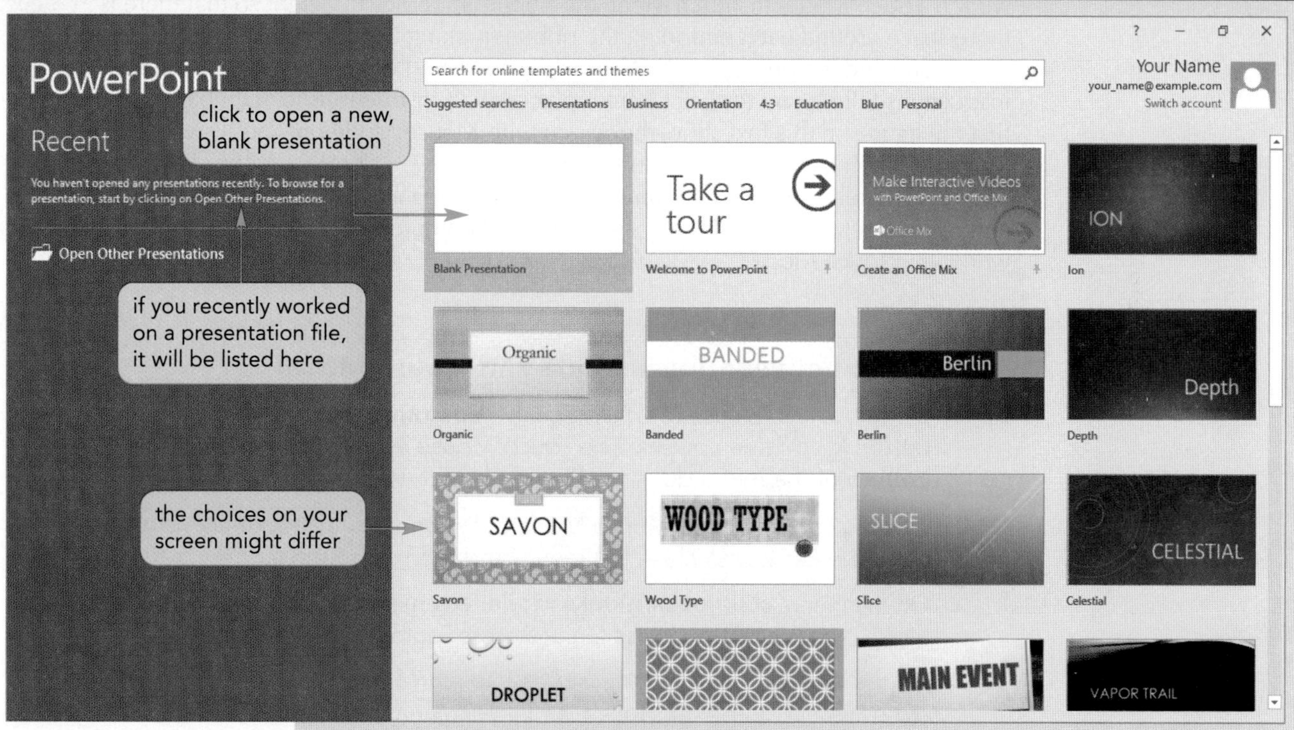

TIP

To create a new blank presentation when PowerPoint is already running, click the File tab on the ribbon, click New in the navigation bar, and then click Blank Presentation.

3. Click **Blank Presentation**. Backstage view closes and a new presentation window appears. The temporary filename "Presentation1" appears in the title bar. There is only one slide in the new presentation—Slide 1.

   Trouble? If you do not see the area on the ribbon that contains buttons and you see only the ribbon tab names, click the Home tab to expand the ribbon and display the commands, and then in the bottom-right corner of the ribbon, click the Pin the ribbon button that appears.

   Trouble? If the window is not maximized, click the Maximize button in the upper-right corner.

When you create a new presentation, it is displayed in Normal view. **Normal view** displays the selected slide enlarged so you can add and manipulate objects on the slide. The Slides pane on the left side of the program window displays **thumbnails**—miniature images—of all the slides in the presentation. The Home tab on the ribbon is selected when you first open or create a presentation. The Session 1.1 Visual Overview identifies elements of the PowerPoint window.

Working in Touch Mode

In Office 2016, you can work with a mouse or, if you have a touch screen, you can work in Touch Mode. In **Touch Mode** the ribbon increases in height so that there is more space around each button on the ribbon, making it easier to use your finger to tap the specific button you need. Also, in the main part of the PowerPoint window, the instructions telling you to "Click" are replaced with instructions to "Double tap." Note that the figures in this text show the screen with Mouse Mode on. You'll switch to Touch Mode and then back to Mouse Mode now.

Note: The following steps assume that you are using a mouse. If you are instead using a touch device, please read these steps but don't complete them, so that you remain working in Touch Mode.

To switch between Touch Mode and Mouse Mode:

1. On the Quick Access Toolbar, click the **Customize Quick Access Toolbar** button. A menu opens. The Touch/Mouse Mode command near the bottom of the menu does not have a checkmark next to it.

   Trouble? If the Touch/Mouse Mode command has a checkmark next to it, press the Esc key to close the menu, and then skip Step 2.

2. On the menu, click **Touch/Mouse Mode**. The menu closes and the Touch/Mouse Mode button appears on the Quick Access Toolbar.

3. On the Quick Access Toolbar, click the **Touch/Mouse Mode** button. A menu opens listing Mouse and Touch, and the icon next to Mouse is shaded orange to indicate it is selected.

   Trouble? If the icon next to Touch is shaded orange, press the Esc key to close the menu and skip Step 4.

4. On the menu, click **Touch**. The menu closes and the ribbon increases in height so that there is more space around each button on the ribbon. Notice that the instructions in the main part of the PowerPoint window changed by replacing the instruction to "Click" with the instruction to "Double tap." See Figure 1-2. Now you'll change back to Mouse Mode.

Figure 1-2 PowerPoint window with Touch mode active

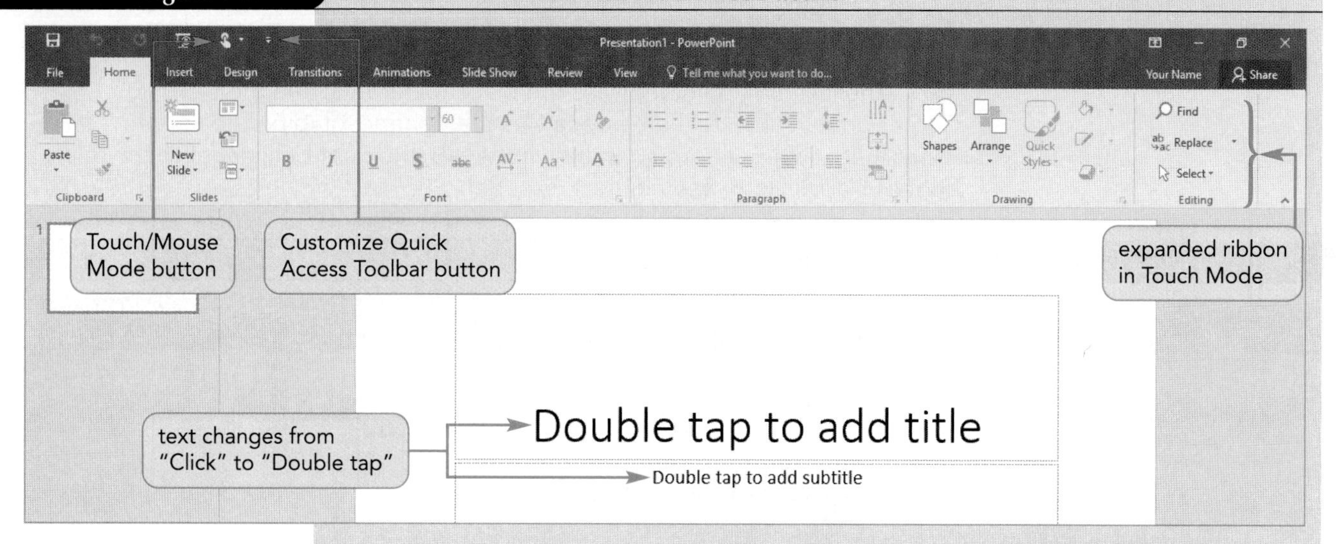

Trouble? If you are working with a touch screen and want to use Touch Mode, skip Steps 5 and 6.

5. Click the **Touch/Mouse Mode** button, and then click **Mouse**. The ribbon and the instructions change back to Mouse Mode defaults as shown in the Session 1.1 Visual Overview.
6. Click the **Customize Quick Access Toolbar** button, and then click **Touch/Mouse Mode** to deselect this option and remove the checkmark. The Touch/Mouse Mode button is removed from the Quick Access Toolbar.

Creating a Title Slide

The **title slide** is the first slide in a presentation. It generally contains the title of the presentation plus any other identifying information you want to include, such as a company's slogan, the presenter's name, or a company name. The **font**—a set of characters with the same design—used in the title and subtitle may be the same or may be different fonts that complement each other.

The title slide contains two objects called text placeholders. A **text placeholder** is a placeholder designed to contain text. Text placeholders usually display text that describes the purpose of the placeholder and instructs you to click so that you can start typing in the placeholder. The larger text placeholder on the title slide is designed to hold the presentation title, and the smaller text placeholder is designed to contain a subtitle. Once you enter text into a text placeholder, it is no longer a placeholder and becomes an object called a **text box**.

When you click in the placeholder, the **insertion point**, which indicates where text will appear when you start typing, appears as a blinking line in the center of the placeholder. In addition, a contextual tab, the Drawing Tools Format tab, appears on the ribbon. A **contextual tab** appears only in context—that is, when a particular type of object is selected or active—and contains commands for modifying that object.

You'll add a title and subtitle for Caitlin's presentation now. Caitlin wants the title slide to contain the company name and slogan.

To add the company name and slogan to the title slide:

1. On **Slide 1**, move the pointer to position it in the title text placeholder (where it says "Click to add title") so that the pointer changes to I, and then click. The insertion point replaces the placeholder text, and the Drawing Tools Format contextual tab appears as the rightmost tab on the ribbon. Note that in the Font group on the Home tab, the Font box identifies the title font as Calibri Light. See Figure 1-3.

Figure 1-3 Title text placeholder after clicking in it

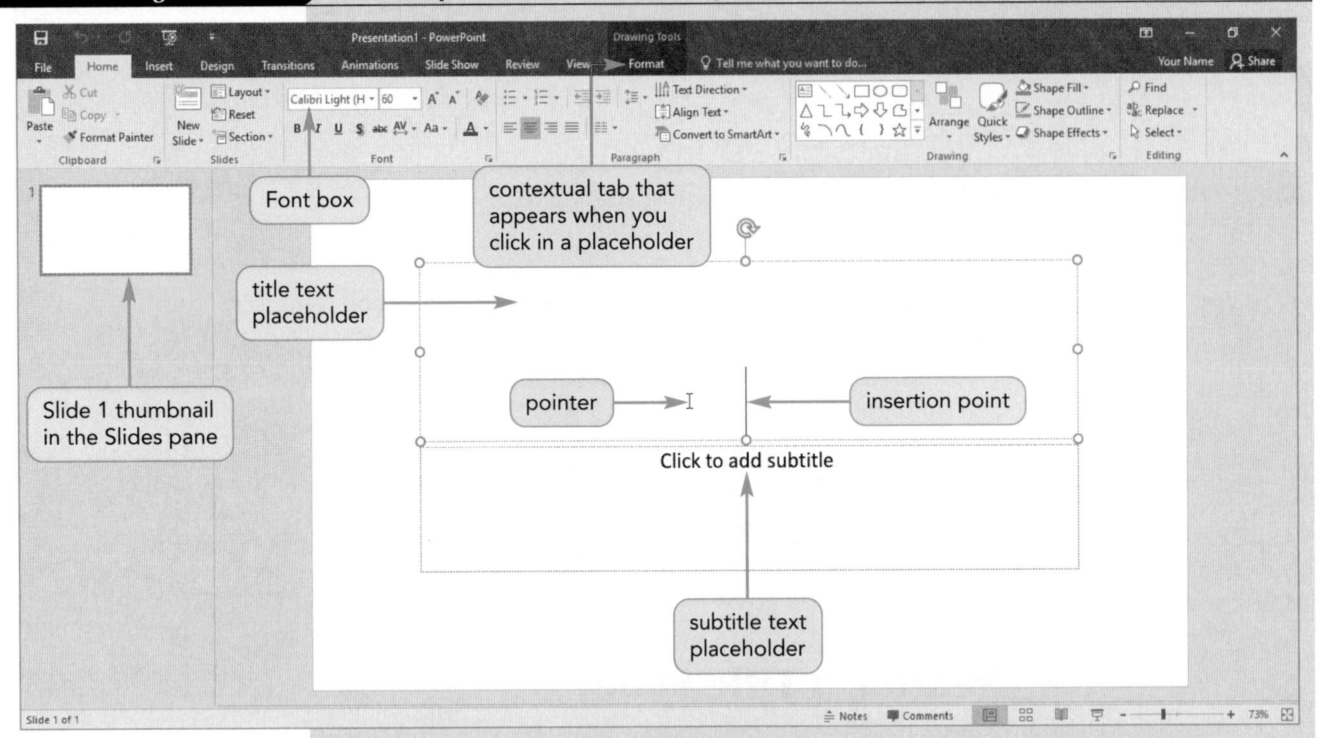

2. Type **Lakeside Event Hall**. The placeholder is now a text box.
3. Click a blank area of the slide. The border of the text box disappears, and the Drawing Tools Format tab no longer appears on the ribbon.
4. Click in the **subtitle text placeholder** (where it says "Click to add subtitle"), and then type **Perfect venue for all occasions!**. Notice in the Font group that the subtitle font is Calibri, a font which works well with the Calibri Light font used in the title text.
5. Click a blank area of the slide.

Saving and Editing a Presentation

Once you have created a presentation, you should name and save the presentation file. You can save the file on a hard drive or a network drive, on an external drive such as a USB drive, or to your account on OneDrive, Microsoft's free online storage area.

To save the presentation for the first time:

1. On the Quick Access Toolbar, point to the **Save** button. A box called a **ScreenTip** appears, identifying the button.
2. Click the **Save** button. The Save As screen in Backstage view appears. See Figure 1-4. The **navigation bar** on the left contains commands for working with the file and program options. Recently used folders on the selected drive appear in a list on the right.

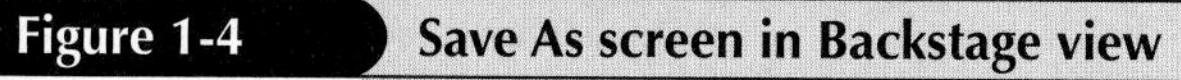

Figure 1-4 Save As screen in Backstage view

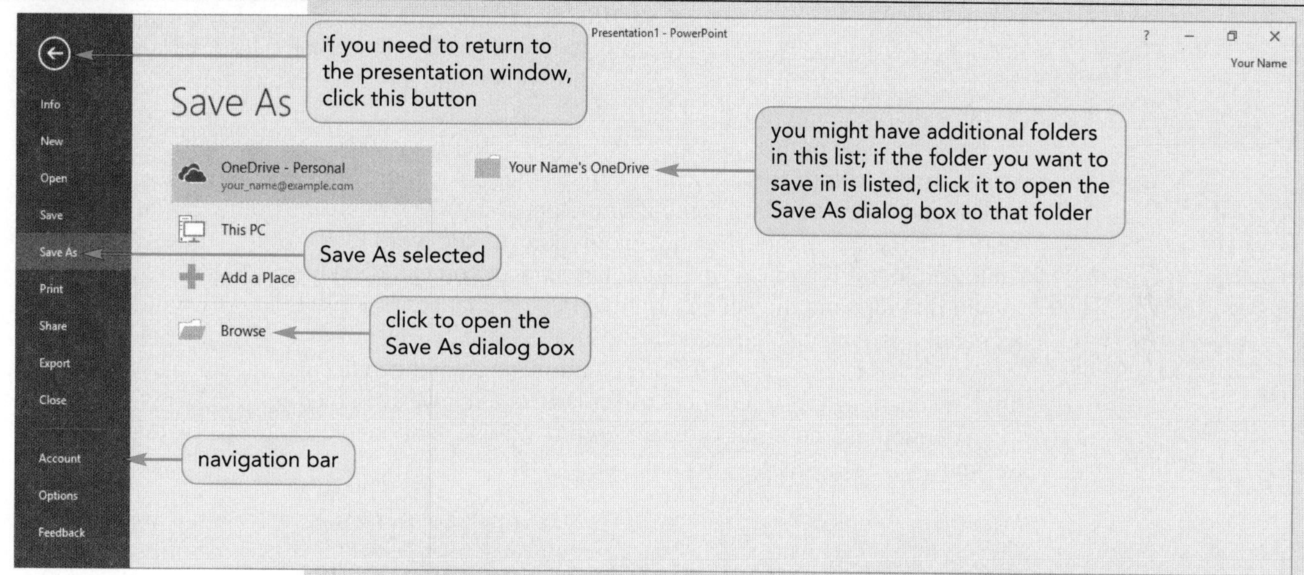

3. Click **Browse**. The Save As dialog box opens, similar to the one shown in Figure 1-5.

Figure 1-5 Save As dialog box

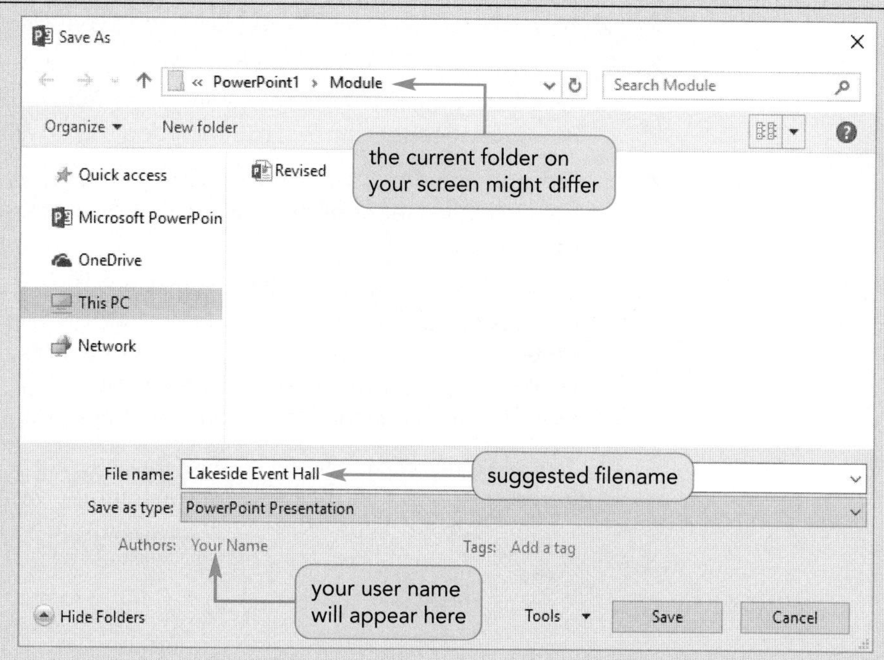

4. Navigate to the drive and folder where you are storing your Data Files, and then click in the **File name** box. The suggested filename, Lakeside Event Hall, is selected.
5. Type **Convention Presentation**. The text you type replaces the selected text in the File name box.
6. Click the **Save** button. The file is saved, the dialog box and Backstage view close, and the presentation window appears again with the new filename in the title bar.

Once you have created a presentation, you can make changes to it. For example, if you need to change text in a text box, you can easily edit it. The Backspace key deletes characters to the left of the insertion point, and the Delete key deletes characters to the right of the insertion point.

If you mistype or misspell a word, you might not need to correct it because the **AutoCorrect** feature automatically corrects many commonly mistyped and misspelled words after you press the spacebar or the Enter key. For instance, if you type "cna" and then press the spacebar, PowerPoint corrects the word to "can." If you want AutoCorrect to stop making a particular change, you can display the AutoCorrect Options menu, and then click Stop making the change. (The exact wording will differ depending on the change made.)

After you make changes to a presentation, you will need to save the file again so that the changes are stored. Because you have already saved the presentation with a permanent filename, using the Save command does not open the Save As dialog box; it simply saves the changes you made to the file.

To edit the text on Slide 1 and save your changes:

1. On Slide 1, click the **title**, and then use the ← and → keys as needed to position the insertion point to the right of the word "Hall."
2. Press the **Backspace** key four times. The four characters to the left of the insertion point, "Hall," are deleted.
3. Type **Center**. The title is now "Lakeside Event Center."
4. Click to the left of the word "Perfect" in the subtitle text box to position the insertion point in front of that word, type **Teh**, and then press the **spacebar**. PowerPoint corrects the word you typed to "The."
5. Move the pointer over the word **The**. A small, very faint rectangle appears below the first letter of the word. This indicates that an AutoCorrection has been made.
6. Move the pointer on top of the faint rectangle that appears under the "T" so that it changes to the AutoCorrect Options button, and then click the **AutoCorrect Options** button. A menu opens, as shown in Figure 1-6. You can change the word back to what you originally typed, instruct PowerPoint to stop making this type of correction in this file, or open the AutoCorrect dialog box.

   Trouble? If you can't see the AutoCorrection indicator box, point to the letter "T," and then slowly move the pointer down until it is over the box and changes it to the AutoCorrect Options button.

Figure 1-6 AutoCorrect Options button menu

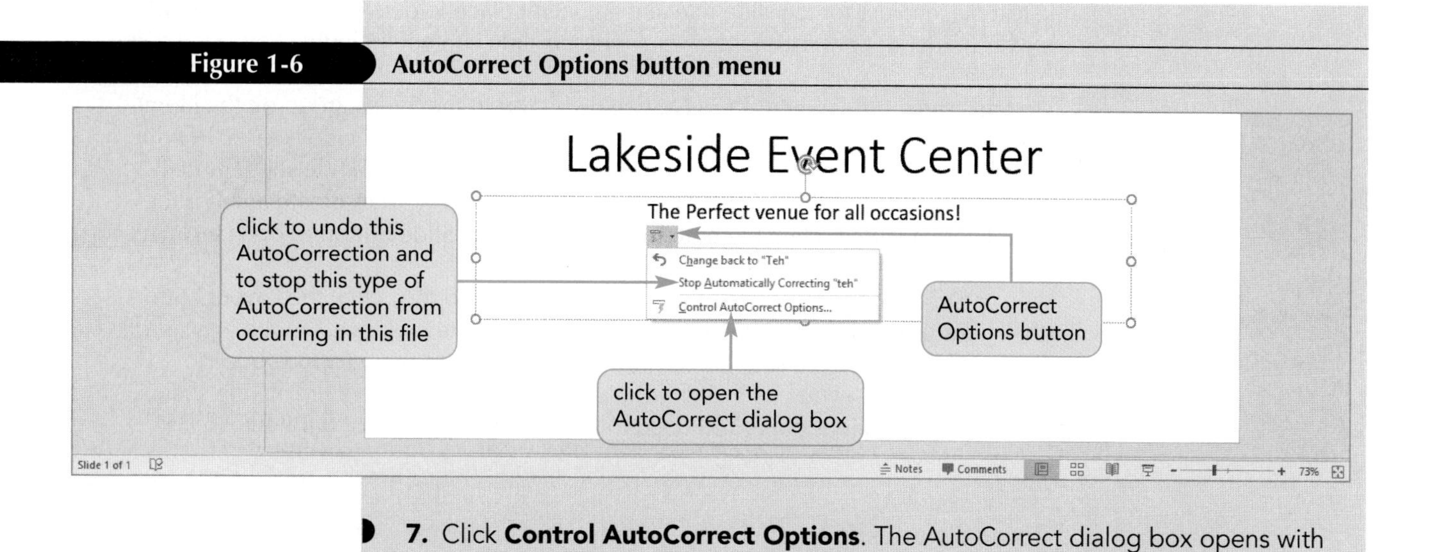

7. Click **Control AutoCorrect Options**. The AutoCorrect dialog box opens with the AutoCorrect tab selected. See Figure 1-7.

Figure 1-7 AutoCorrect tab in the AutoCorrect dialog box

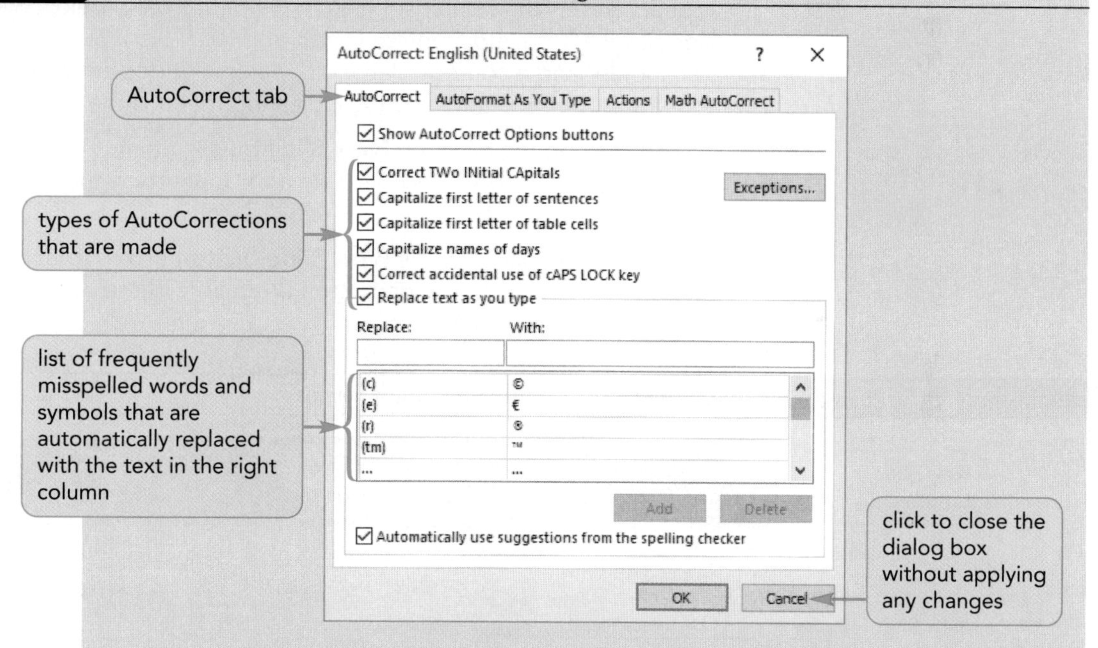

8. Examine the types of changes the AutoCorrect feature makes, and then click the **Cancel** button.
9. Click to the left of the "P" in "Perfect," if necessary, press the **Delete** key, and then type **p**. The subtitle now is "The perfect venue for all occasions!" Now that you have modified the presentation, you need to save your changes.
10. On the Quick Access Toolbar, click the **Save** button. The changes you made are saved to the Convention Presentation file.

Adding New Slides

Now that you've created the title slide, you need to add more slides. Every slide has a **layout**, which is the arrangement of placeholders on the slide. The title slide uses the Title Slide layout. A commonly used layout is the Title and Content layout, which contains a title text placeholder for the slide title and a content placeholder. A **content placeholder** is a placeholder designed to hold several types of slide content including text, a table, a chart, a picture, or a video.

To add a new slide, you use the New Slide button in the Slides group on the Home tab. When you click the top part of the New Slide button, a new slide is inserted with the same layout as the current slide, unless the current slide is the title slide; in that case the new slide has the Title and Content layout. If you want to create a new slide with a different layout, click the bottom part of the New Slide button to open a gallery of layouts, and then click the layout you want to use.

You can change the layout of a slide at any time. To do this, click the Layout button in the Slides group to display the same gallery of layouts that appears in the New Slide gallery, and then click the slide layout you want to apply to the selected slide.

As you add slides, you can switch from one slide to another by clicking the slide thumbnails in the Slides pane. You need to add several new slides to the file.

To add new slides and apply different layouts:

1. Make sure the Home tab is displayed on the ribbon.
2. In the Slides group, click the top part of the **New Slide** button. A new slide appears and its thumbnail appears in the Slides pane below Slide 1. The new slide has the Title and Content layout applied. This layout contains a title text placeholder and a content placeholder. In the Slides pane, an orange border appears around the new Slide 2, indicating that it is the current slide.
3. In the Slides group, click the **New Slide** button again. A new Slide 3 is added. Because Slide 2 had the Title and Content layout applied, Slide 3 also has that layout applied.
4. In the Slides group, click the **New Slide button arrow** (that is, click the bottom part of the New Slide button). A gallery of the available layouts appears. See Figure 1-8.

Figure 1-8 Gallery of layouts on the New Slide menu

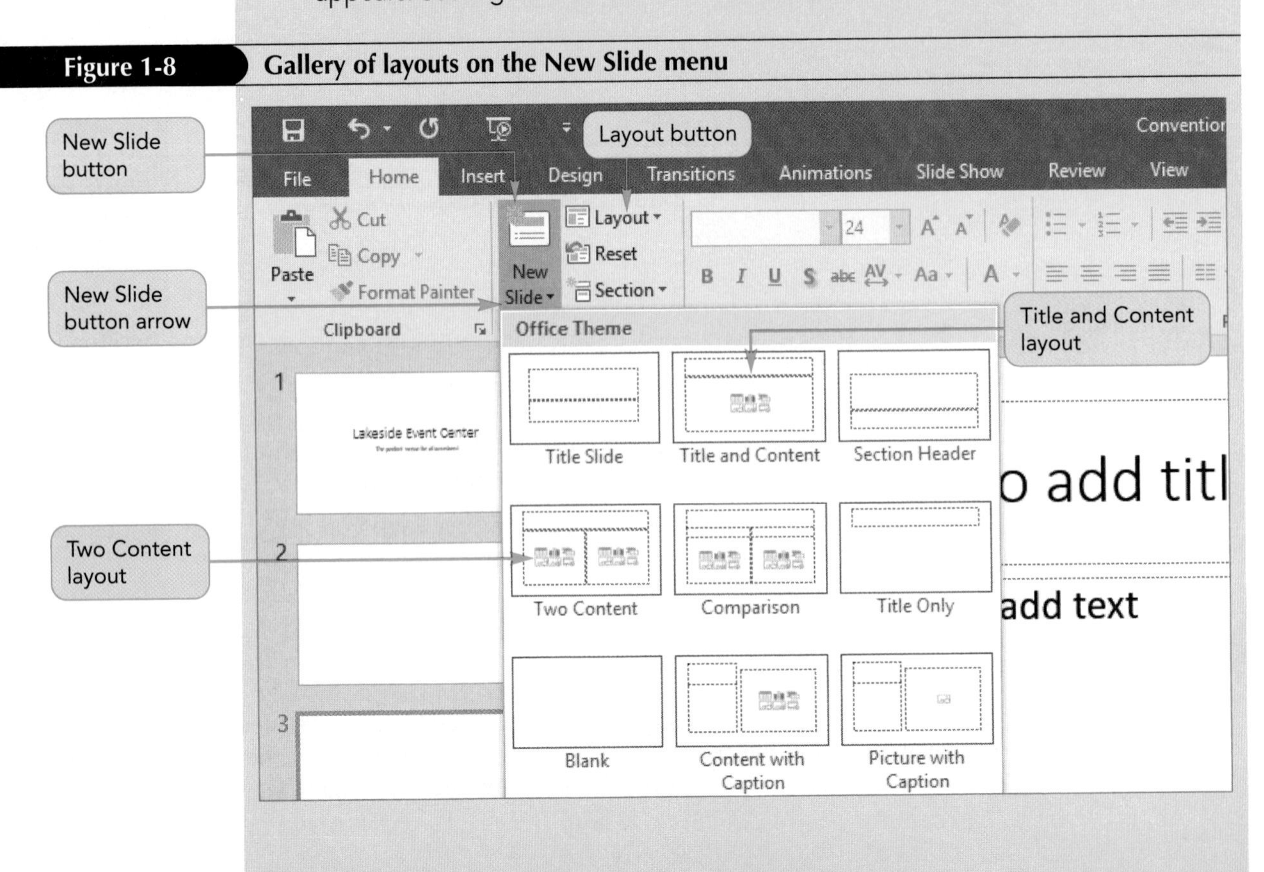

5. In the gallery, click the **Two Content** layout. The gallery closes and a new Slide 4 is inserted with the Two Content layout applied. This layout includes three objects: a title text placeholder and two content placeholders.
6. In the Slides group, click the **New Slide** button. A new Slide 5 is added to the presentation. Because Slide 4 had the Two Content layout applied, that layout is also applied to the new slide. You need to change the layout of Slide 5.
7. In the Slides group, click the **Layout** button. The same gallery of layouts that appeared when you clicked the New Slide button arrow appears. The Two Content layout is selected, as indicated by the shading behind it, showing you that this is the layout applied to the current slide, Slide 5.
8. Click the **Title and Content** layout. The layout of Slide 5 is changed to Title and Content.
9. In the Slides group, click the **New Slide** button twice to add two more slides with the Title and Content layout.
10. Add a new slide with the Two Content layout. There are now eight slides in the presentation. In the Slides pane, Slides 1 through 3 have scrolled up out of view, and vertical scroll bars are now visible in both the Slides pane and along the right side of the program window.
11. In the Slides pane, drag the **scroll box** to the top of the vertical scroll bar, and then click the **Slide 2** thumbnail. Slide 2 appears in the program window and is selected in the Slides pane. See Figure 1-9.

Figure 1-9 Slide 2 with the Title and Content layout

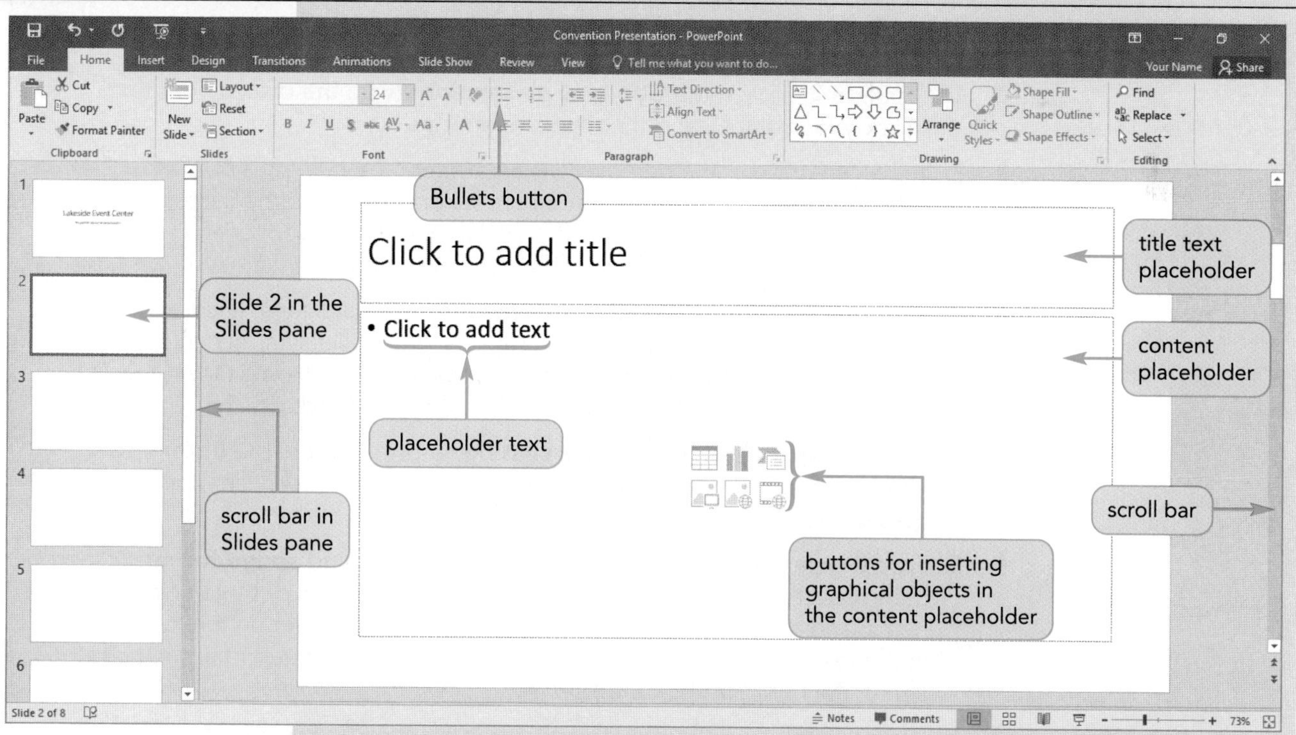

12. On the Quick Access Toolbar, click the **Save** button. The changes you made are saved in the file.

If you accidentally close a presentation without saving changes and need to recover it, you can do so by clicking the File tab, clicking Open in the navigation bar, and then clicking the Recover Unsaved Presentations button.

Creating Lists

One way to help explain the topic or concept you are describing in your presentation is to use lists. For oral presentations, the intent of lists is to enhance the oral presentation, not replace it. In self-running presentations, items in lists might need to be longer and more descriptive. However, keep in mind that PowerPoint is a presentation graphics program intended to help you present information in a visual, graphical manner, not create a written document in an alternate form.

Items in a list can appear at different levels. A **first-level item** is a main item in a list; a **second-level item**—sometimes called a **subitem**—is an item beneath and indented from a first-level item. Usually, the font size—the size of the text—in subitems is smaller than the size used for text in the level above. Text is measured in **points**, which is a unit of measurement. Text in a book is typically printed in 10- or 12-point type; text on a slide needs to be much larger so the audience can easily read it.

Creating a Bulleted List

A **bulleted list** is a list of items with some type of bullet symbol in front of each item or paragraph. When you create a subitem in the list, a different or smaller symbol is often used. You need to create a bulleted list that describes the amenities of the Lakeside Event Center and one that describes the catering packages available.

To create bulleted lists on Slides 2 and 3:

1. On **Slide 2**, click in the **title text placeholder** (with the placeholder text "Click to add title"), and then type **Amenities**.
2. In the content placeholder, click any area where the pointer is shaped as I—in other words, anywhere except on one of the buttons in the center of the placeholder. The placeholder text "Click to add text" disappears, the insertion point appears, and a light gray bullet symbol appears.
3. Type **Comfortable**. As soon as you type the first character, the icons in the center of the content placeholder disappear, the bullet symbol darkens, and the content placeholder changes to a text box. On the Home tab, in the Paragraph group, the Bullets button is shaded to indicate that it is selected.
4. Press the **spacebar**, type **indoor seating**, and then press the **Enter** key. The insertion point moves to a new line, and a light gray bullet appears on the new line.
5. Type **Dance floor**, press the **Enter** key, type **Surround sound for music**, and then press the **Enter** key. The bulleted list now consists of three first-level items, and the insertion point is next to a light gray bullet on the fourth line in the text box. Notice on the Home tab, in the Font group, that the point size in the Font Size box is 28 points.
6. Press the **Tab** key. The bullet symbol and the insertion point indent one-half inch to the right, the bullet symbol changes to a smaller size, and the number in the Font Size box changes to 24. See Figure 1-10.

Figure 1-10 Subitem created on Slide 2

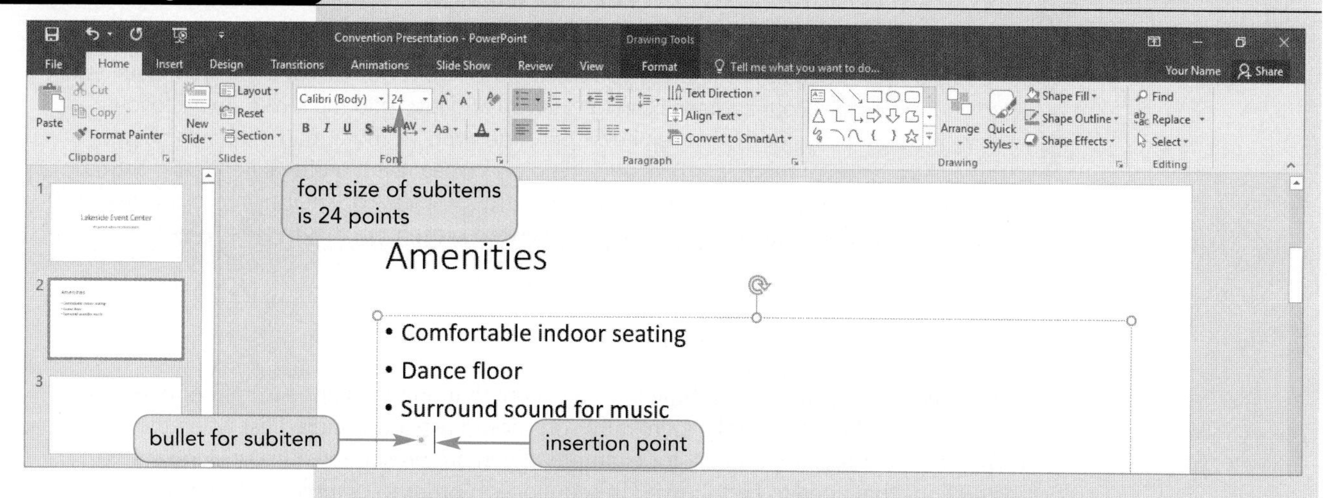

7. Type **DJs can easily plug in** and then press the **Enter** key.
8. Type **Live bands have plenty of room** and then press the **Enter** key. A third subitem is created. You will change it to a first-level item using a key combination. In this book, when you need to press two keys together, the keys will be listed separated by a plus sign.
9. Press the **Shift+Tab** keys. The bullet symbol and the insertion point shift back to the left margin of the text box, the bullet symbol changes back to the larger size, and 28 again appears in the Font Size box because this line is now a first-level bulleted item.
10. Type **Optional outdoor seating on patio**, press the **Enter** key, and then type **Additional appetizers and pasta stations available as add-ons**.
11. In the Slides pane, click the **Slide 3** thumbnail to display Slide 3, click in the **title text placeholder**, and then type **Packages**.
12. In the content placeholder, click the **placeholder text**, type **Basic--5 hours, standard catering package**, press the **Enter** key, and then type **Special--5 hours, deluxe catering package**. When you pressed the spacebar after typing 5, AutoCorrect changed the two dashes to an em-dash, a typographical character longer than a hyphen.

TIP

You don't need to press the keys at exactly the same time—press and hold the first key, press and release the second key, and then release the first key.

If you add more text than will fit in the text box with the default font sizes and line spacing, **AutoFit** adjusts these features to make the text fit. When AutoFit is activated, the AutoFit Options button appears below the text box. You can click this button and then select from among several options, including turning off AutoFit for this text box and splitting the text between two slides. Although AutoFit can be helpful, be aware that it also allows you to crowd text on a slide, making the slide less effective.

PROSKILLS

Written Communication: How Much Text Should I Include?

Text can help audiences retain the information you are presenting by allowing them to read the main points while hearing you discuss them. But be wary of adding so much text to your slides that your audience can ignore you and just read the slides. Try to follow the 7x7 rule—no more than seven items per slide, with no more than seven words per item. A variation of this rule is 6x6, and some presenters even prefer 4x4. If you create a self-running presentation (a presentation file others will view on their own), you will usually need to add more text than you would if you were presenting the material in person.

Creating a Numbered List

A **numbered list** is similar to a bulleted list except that numbers appear in front of each item instead of bullet symbols. Generally you should use a numbered list when the order of the items is important—for example, if you are presenting a list of step-by-step instructions that need to be followed in sequence in order to complete a task successfully. You need to create a numbered list on Slide 5 to explain how clients can reserve the event center for a function.

To create a numbered list on Slide 5:

1. In the Slides pane, click the **Slide 5** thumbnail to display Slide 5, and then type **Reserve Lakeside Event Center for Your Function!** in the title text placeholder.
2. In the content placeholder, click the **placeholder text**.
3. On the Home tab, in the Paragraph group, click the **Numbering** button. The Numbering button is selected, the Bullets button is deselected, and in the content placeholder, the bullet symbol is replaced with the number 1 followed by a period.

   Trouble? If a menu containing a gallery of numbering styles appears, you clicked the Numbering button arrow on the right side of the button. Click the Numbering button arrow again to close the menu, and then click the left part of the Numbering button.
4. Type **Specify date of function**, and then press the **Enter** key. As soon as you start typing, the number 1 darkens to black. After you press the Enter key, the insertion point moves to the next line, next to the light gray number 2.
5. Type **Choose package**, press the **Enter** key, type **Submit deposit**, and then press the **Enter** key. The number 4 appears on the next line.
6. In the Paragraph group, click the **Increase List Level** button. The fourth line is indented to be a subitem under the third item, and the number 4 changes to a number 1 in a smaller font size than the first-level items. Clicking the Increase List Level button is an alternative to pressing the Tab key to create a subitem.
7. Type **Credit card**, press the **Enter** key, type **Debit from checking account**, and then press the **Enter** key.
8. In the Paragraph group, click the **Decrease List Level** button. The sixth line is now a first-level item, and the number 4 appears next to it. Clicking the Decrease List Level button is an alternative to pressing the Shift+Tab keys to promote a subitem.

9. Type **Confirm**. The list now consists of four first-level numbered items and two subitems under number 3.
10. In the second item, click before the word "Choose," and then press the **Enter** key. A blank line is inserted above the second item.
11. Press the ↑ key. A light-gray number 2 appears in the blank line. The item on the third line in the list is still numbered 2.
12. Type **Specify number of guests**. As soon as you start typing, the new number 2 darkens in the second line, and the third item in the list is numbered 3. Compare your screen to Figure 1-11.

Figure 1-11 **Numbered list on Slide 5**

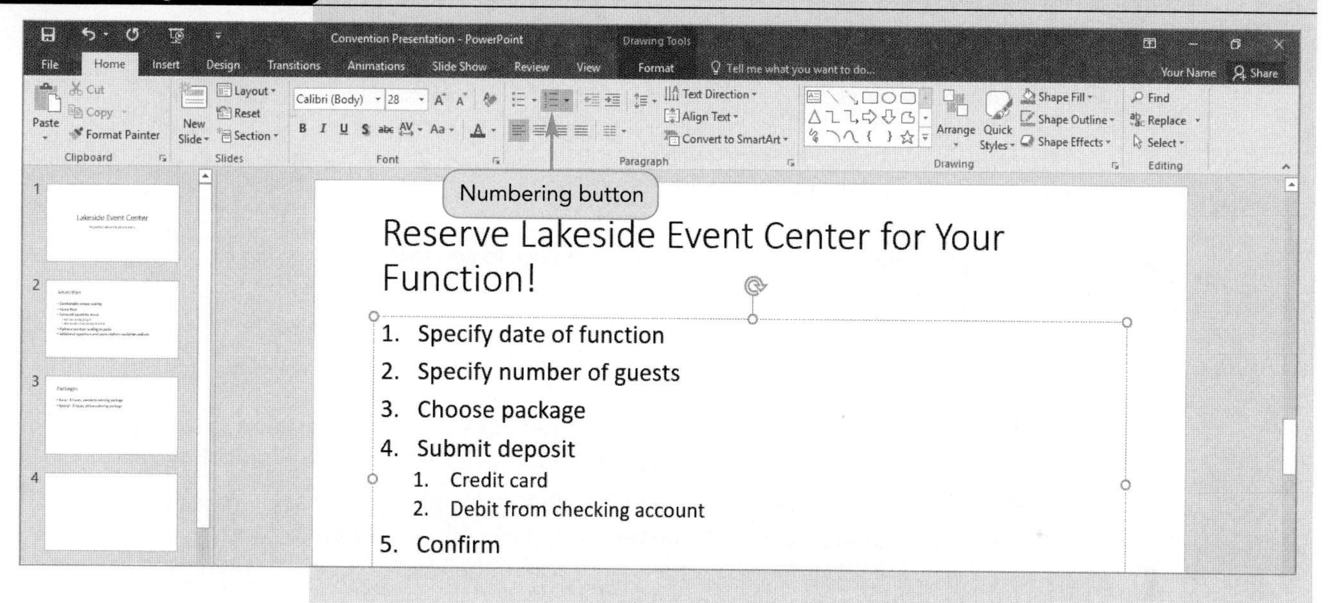

Creating an Unnumbered List

An **unnumbered list** is a list that does not have bullets or numbers preceding each item. Unnumbered lists are useful in slides when you want to present information on multiple lines without actually itemizing the information. For example, contact information for the presenter, including his or her email address, street address, city, and so on, would be clearer if it were in an unnumbered list.

As you have seen, items in a list have a little extra space between each item to visually separate bulleted items. Sometimes, you don't want the extra space between lines. If you press the Shift+Enter keys instead of just the Enter key, a new line is created, but it is still considered to be part of the item above it. Therefore, there is no extra space between the lines. Note that this also means that if you do this in a bulleted or numbered list, the new line will not have a bullet or number next to it because it is not a new item.

You need to create a slide that explains the event center's name. Also, Caitlin asks you to create a slide containing contact information.

To create unnumbered lists on Slides 4 and 7:

1. In the Slides pane, click the **Slide 4** thumbnail to display Slide 4. Slide 4 has the Two Content layout applied.

2. Type **About Us** in the title content placeholder, and then in the left content placeholder, click the **placeholder text**.
3. On the Home tab, in the Paragraph group, click the **Bullets** button. The button is no longer selected, and the bullet symbol disappears from the content placeholder.
4. Type **Lakeside**, press the **Enter** key, type **Event**, press the **Enter** key, and then type **Center**. Compare your screen to Figure 1-12.

Figure 1-12 Unnumbered list on Slide 4

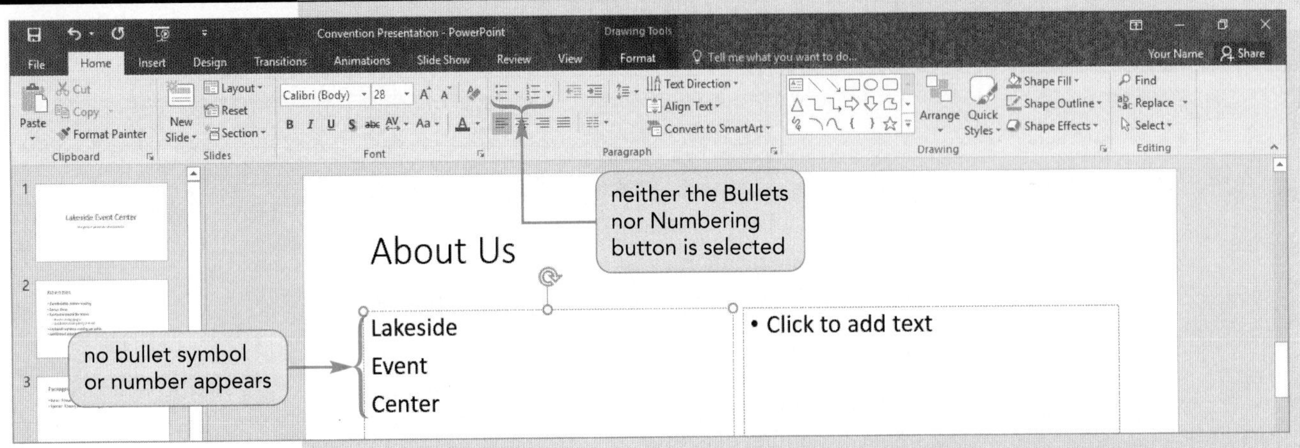

5. Display **Slide 7** in the Slide pane, type **For More Information** in the title text placeholder, and then in the content placeholder, click the **placeholder text**.
6. In the Paragraph group, click the **Bullets** button to remove the bullets, type **Lakeside Event Center**, and then press the **Enter** key. A new line is created, but there is extra space above the insertion point. This is not how addresses usually appear.
7. Press the **Backspace** key to delete the new line and move the insertion point back to the end of the first line, and then press the **Shift+Enter** keys. The insertion point moves to the next line, and, this time, there is no extra space above it.
8. Type **15680 Shore Drive**, press the **Shift+Enter** keys, and then type **Lake Havasu City, AZ 86403**. You need to insert the phone number on the next line, the general email address for the group on the line after that, and the website address on the last line. The extra space above these lines will set this information apart from the address and make it easier to read.
9. Press the **Enter** key to create a new line with extra space above it, type **(928) 555-HALL**, press the **Enter** key, type **info@lec.example.com**, and then press the **Enter** key. The insertion point moves to a new line with extra space above it, and the email address you typed changes color to blue and is underlined.

   When you type text that PowerPoint recognizes as an email or website address and then press the spacebar or Enter key, the text is automatically formatted as a link that can be clicked during a slide show. To indicate this, the color of the text is changed and the text is underlined. Links are active only during a slide show.

10. Type **www.lec.example.com**, and then press the **spacebar**. The text is formatted as a link. Caitlin plans to click the link during her presentation to show the audience the website, so she wants it to stay formatted as a link. However, there is no need to have the email address formatted as a link because no one will click it during the presentation.
11. Right-click **info@lec.example.com**. A shortcut menu opens.
12. On the shortcut menu, click **Remove Hyperlink**. The email address is no longer formatted as a hyperlink. Compare your screen to Figure 1-13.

Figure 1-13 List on Slide 7

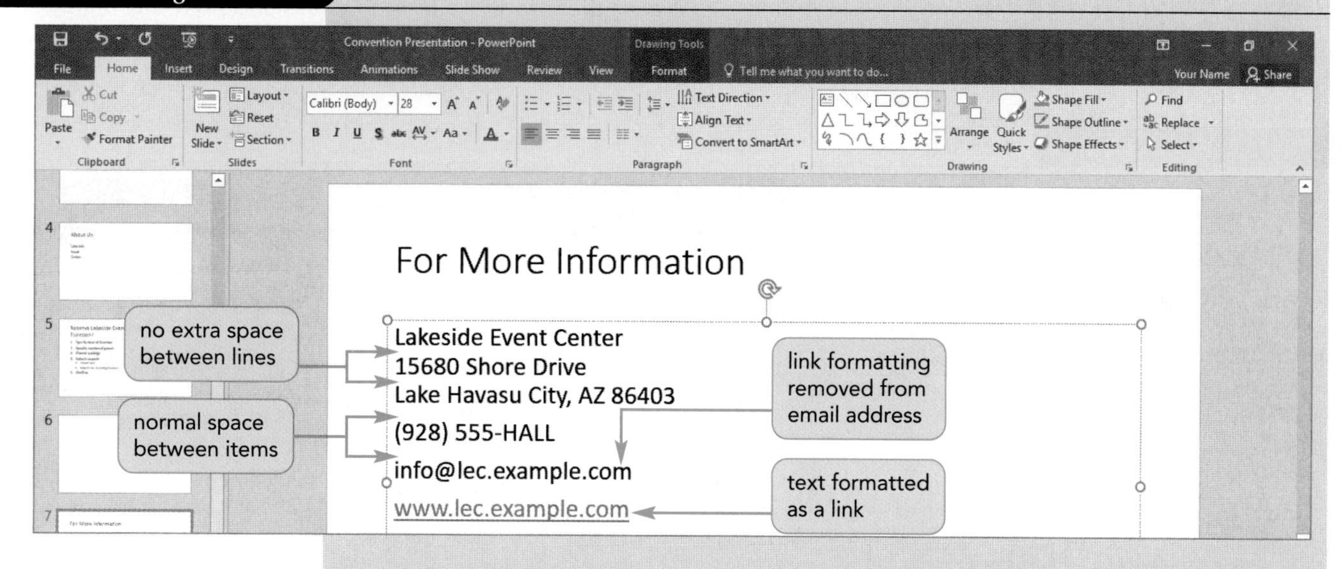

13. On the Quick Access Toolbar, click the **Save** button to save the changes.

Formatting Text

Slides in a presentation should have a cohesive look and feel. For example, the slide titles and the text in content placeholders should be in complementary fonts. However, there are times when you need to change the format of text. For instance, you might want to make specific words bold to make them stand out more.

To apply a format to text, either the text or the text box must be selected. If you want to apply the same formatting to all the text in a text box, you can click the border of the text box. When you do this, the dotted line border changes to a solid line to indicate that the contents of the entire text box are selected.

TIP

To remove all formatting from selected text, click the Clear All Formatting button in the Font group.

The commands in the Font group on the Home tab are used to apply formatting to text. Some of these commands are also available on the Mini toolbar, which appears when you select text with the mouse. The **Mini toolbar** contains commonly used buttons for formatting text. If the Mini toolbar appears, you can use the buttons on it instead of those in the Font group.

Some of the commands in the Font group use the Microsoft Office **Live Preview** feature, which previews the change on the slide so you can instantly see what the text will look like if you apply that format.

Caitlin wants the contact information on Slide 7 ("For More Information") to be larger. She also wants the first letter of each item in the unnumbered list on Slide 4 ("About Us") formatted so they are more prominent.

To format the text on Slides 4 and 7:

1. On **Slide 7** ("For More Information"), position the pointer on the border of the text box containing the contact information so that it changes to ⇳, and then click the border of the text box. The border changes to a solid line to indicate that the entire text box is selected.
2. On the Home tab, in the Font group, click the **Increase Font Size** button A twice. All the text in the text box increases in size with each click, and all the text in the text box is now 36 points.
3. Display **Slide 4** ("About Us").
4. In the unnumbered list, click to the left of "Lakeside," press and hold the **Shift** key, press the → key, and then release the **Shift** key. The letter "L" is selected. See Figure 1-14.

Figure 1-14 Text selected to be formatted

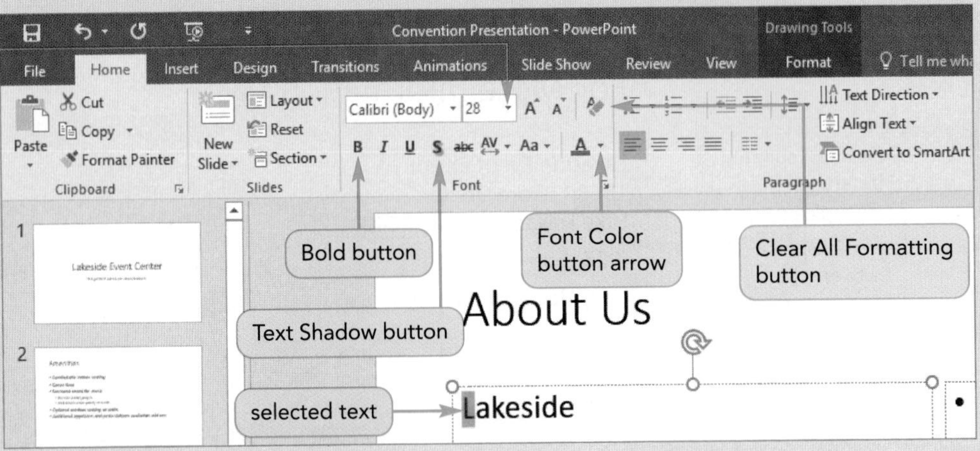

5. In the Font group, click the **Bold** button B. The Bold button becomes selected, and the selected text is formatted as bold.
6. Make sure the letter "L" is still selected, and then in the Font group, click the **Text Shadow** button S. The selected text is now bold with a slight drop shadow.
7. In the Font group, click the **Font Size arrow** to open the Font Size menu, and then click **48**. The selected text is now 48 points.
8. In the Font group, click the **Font Color button arrow** A ▾. A menu containing colors opens.
9. Under Theme Colors, move the pointer over each color, noting the ScreenTips that appear and watching as Live Preview changes the color of the selected text as you point to each color. Figure 1-15 shows the pointer pointing to the Orange, Accent 2, Darker 25% color.

Figure 1-15 Font Color menu

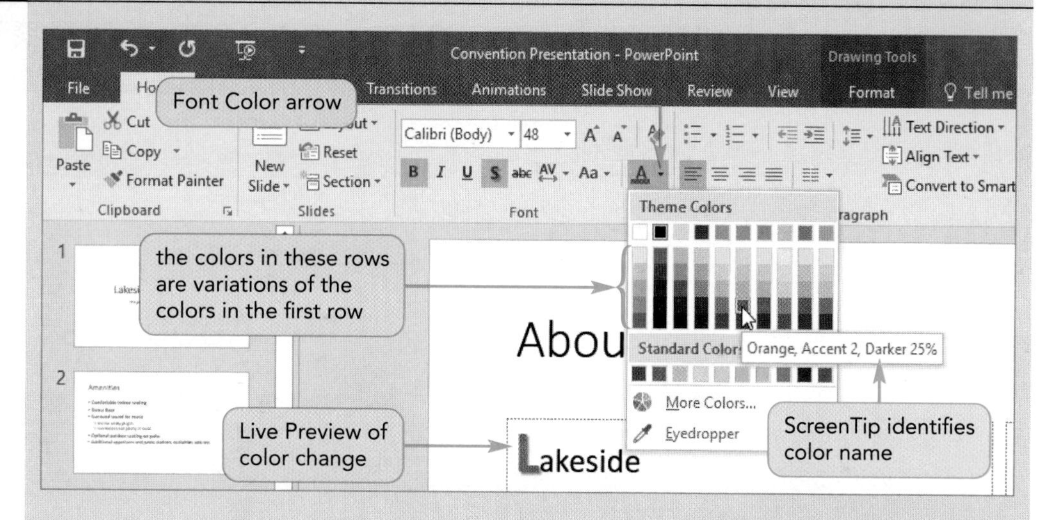

10. Using the ScreenTips, locate the **Orange, Accent 2, Darker 25%** color, and then click it. The selected text changes to the orange color you clicked.

Now you need to format the first letters in the other words in the list to match the letter "L." You can repeat the steps you did when you formatted the letter "L," or you can use the Format Painter to copy all the formatting of the letter "L" to the other letters you need to format.

Also, Caitlin wants the text in the unnumbered list to be as large as possible. Because the first letters of each word are larger than the rest of the letters, the easiest way to do this is to select all of the text, and then use the Increase Font Size button. All of the letters will increase in size by four points with each click.

To use the Format Painter to copy and apply formatting on Slide 4:

1. Make sure the letter "L" is still selected.
2. On the Home tab, in the Clipboard group, click the **Format Painter** button, and then move the pointer on top of the slide. The button is selected, and the pointer changes to [pointer icon].
3. Position the pointer before the letter "E" in "Event," press and hold the mouse button, drag over the letter **E**, and then release the mouse button. The formatting you applied to the letter "L" is copied to the letter "E," and the Mini toolbar appears. See Figure 1-16. The Mini toolbar appears whenever you drag over text to select it.

Figure 1-16 The Mini toolbar

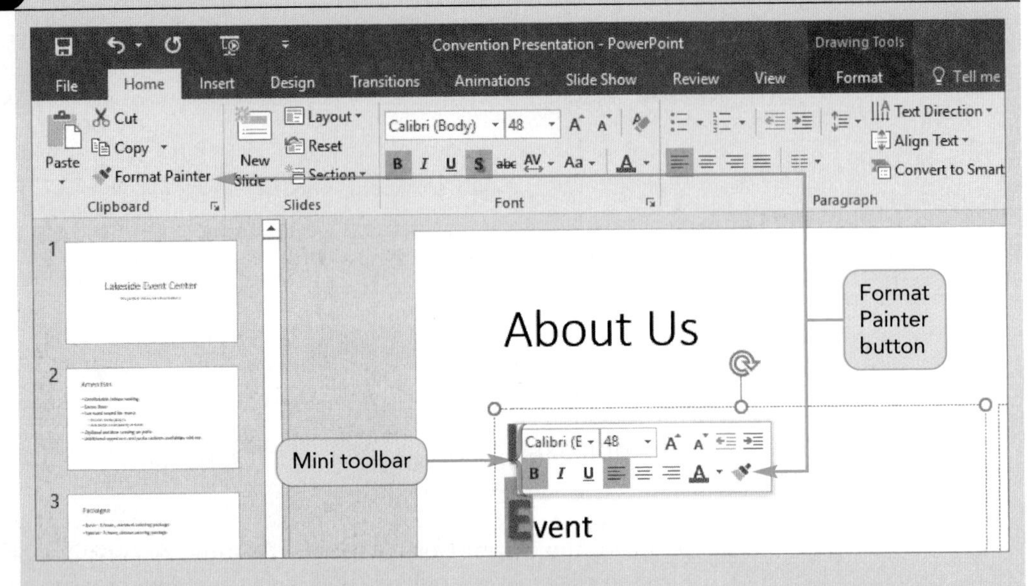

TIP

If you need to copy formatting to more than one location, double-click the Format Painter button to keep it selected until you deselect it.

4. On the Mini toolbar, click the **Format Painter** button, and then drag across the letter **C** in "Center."
5. Click the border of the text box to select the entire text box, and then in the Font group, click the **Increase Font Size** button five times. In the Font group, the Font Size button indicates that the text is 48+ points. This means that in the selected text box, the text that is the smallest is 48 points and there is some text that is a larger point size.
6. On the Quick Access Toolbar, click the **Save** button to save the changes.

INSIGHT

Undoing and Redoing Actions

If you make a mistake or change your mind about an action as you are working, you can reverse the action by clicking the Undo button on the Quick Access Toolbar. You can undo up to the most recent 20 actions by continuing to click the Undo button or by clicking the Undo button arrow and then selecting as many actions in the list as you want. You can also Redo an action that you undid by clicking the Redo button on the Quick Access Toolbar.

When there are no actions that can be redone, the Redo button changes to the Repeat button. You can use the Repeat button to repeat an action, such as formatting text as bold. If the Repeat button is light gray, this means it is unavailable because there is no action to repeat (or to redo).

Moving and Copying Text

You can move or copy text and objects in a presentation using the Clipboard. The **Clipboard** is a temporary storage area available to all Windows programs on which text or objects are stored when you cut or copy them. To **cut** text or objects—that is, remove the selected text or objects from one location so that you can place it somewhere else—you select the text or object, and then use the Cut button in the Clipboard group on the Home tab to remove the selected text or object and place it on the Clipboard. To **copy** selected text or objects, you use the Copy button in the Clipboard group on the Home tab, which leaves the original text or object on the slide and places a copy of it on the Clipboard. You can then **paste** the text or object stored on the Clipboard anywhere in the presentation or, in fact, in any file in any Windows program.

You can paste an item on the Clipboard as many times and in as many locations as you like. However, the Clipboard can hold only the most recently cut or copied item. As soon as you cut or copy another item, it replaces the previously cut or copied item on the Clipboard.

Note that cutting text or an object is different from using the Delete or Backspace key to delete it. Deleted text and objects are not placed on the Clipboard; this means they cannot be pasted.

Caitlin wants a few changes made to Slides 5 and 3. You'll use the Clipboard as you make these edits.

To copy and paste text using the Clipboard:

1. Display **Slide 5** ("Reserve Lakeside Event Center for Your Function!"), and then double-click the word **Reserve** in the title text. The word "Reserve" is selected.
2. On the Home tab, in the Clipboard group, click the **Copy** button. The selected word is copied to the Clipboard.
3. In the last item in the numbered list, click after the word "Confirm," and then press the **spacebar**.
4. In the Clipboard group, click the **Paste** button. The text is pasted and picks up the formatting of its destination; that is, the pasted text is the 28-point Calibri font, the same font and size as the rest of the first-level items in the list, instead of 44-point Calibri Light as in the title. The Paste Options button appears below the pasted text.
5. Click the **Paste Options** button. A menu opens with four buttons on it. See Figure 1-17.

Figure 1-17 Buttons on the Paste Options menu when text is on the Clipboard

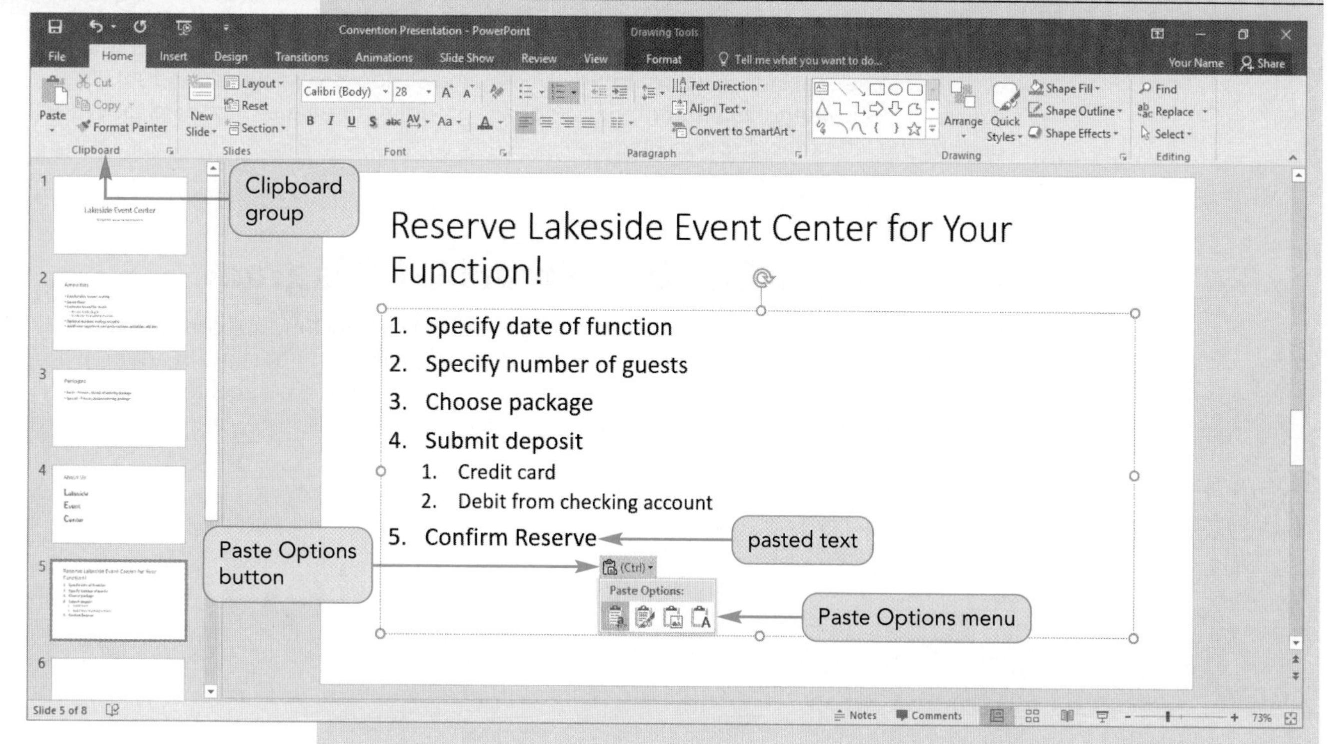

6. Point to each button on the menu, reading the ScreenTips and watching to see how the pasted text changes in appearance. The first button is the Use Destination Theme button, and this is the default choice when you paste text.
7. Click a blank area of the slide to close the menu without making a selection, press the **Backspace** key, type **ation**, click to the left of "Reservation," press the **Delete** key, and then type **r**. The word "reservation" in the numbered list is now all lowercase.
8. Display **Slide 2** ("Amenities"). The last bulleted item (starts with "Additional appetizers") belongs on Slide 3.
9. In the last bulleted item, position the pointer on top of the bullet symbol so that the pointer changes to ✥, and then click. The entire bulleted item is selected.
10. In the Clipboard group, click the **Cut** button. The last bulleted item is removed from the slide and placed on the Clipboard.
11. Display **Slide 3** ("Packages"), click after the second bulleted item, and then press the **Enter** key to create a third bulleted item.
12. In the Clipboard group, click the **Paste** button. The bulleted item you cut is pasted as the third bulleted item on Slide 3 using the default paste option of Use Destination Theme. The insertion point appears next to a fourth bulleted item.
13. Press the **Backspace** key twice to delete the extra line, and then on the Quick Access Toolbar, click the **Save** button to save the changes.

TIP

To cut text or an object, you can press the Ctrl+X keys; to copy text or an object, press the Ctrl+C keys; and to paste the item on the Clipboard, press the Ctrl+V keys.

INSIGHT

Using the Office Clipboard

The **Office Clipboard** is a special Clipboard available only to Microsoft Office applications. Once you activate the Office Clipboard, you can store up to 24 items on it and then select the item or items you want to paste. To activate the Office Clipboard, click the Home tab. In the Clipboard group, click the Dialog Box Launcher (the small square in the lower-right corner of the Clipboard group) to open the Clipboard task pane to the left of the displayed slide.

Converting a List to a SmartArt Diagram

A **diagram** visually depicts information or ideas and shows how they are connected. **SmartArt** is a feature that allows you to create diagrams easily and quickly. In addition to shapes, SmartArt diagrams usually include text to help describe or label the shapes. You can create the following types of diagrams using SmartArt:

- **List**—Shows a list of items in a graphical representation
- **Process**—Shows a sequence of steps in a process
- **Cycle**—Shows a process that is a continuous cycle
- **Hierarchy** (including organization charts)—Shows the relationship between individuals or units
- **Relationship** (including Venn diagrams, radial diagrams, and target diagrams)—Shows the relationship between two or more elements
- **Matrix**—Shows information in a grid
- **Pyramid**—Shows foundation-based relationships
- **Picture**—Provides a location for a picture or pictures that you insert

There is also an Office.com category of SmartArt, which, if you are connected to the Internet, displays additional SmartArt diagrams available in various categories on Office.com, a Microsoft website that contains tools for use with Office programs.

A quick way to create a SmartArt diagram is to convert an existing list. When you select an existing list and then click the Convert to SmartArt Graphic button in the Paragraph group on the Home tab, a gallery of SmartArt layouts appears. For SmartArt, a **layout** is the arrangement of the shapes in the diagram. Each first-level item in the list is converted to a shape in the SmartArt diagram. If the list contains subitems, you might need to experiment with different layouts to find one that best suits the information in your list.

REFERENCE

Converting a Bulleted List into a SmartArt Diagram

- Click anywhere in the bulleted list.
- In the Paragraph group on the Home tab, click the Convert to SmartArt Graphic button, and then click More SmartArt Graphics.
- In the Choose a SmartArt Graphic dialog box, select the desired SmartArt type in the list on the left.
- In the center pane, click the SmartArt diagram you want to use.
- Click the OK button.

Caitlin wants the numbered list on Slide 5 changed into a SmartArt diagram.

To convert the list on Slide 5 into a SmartArt diagram:

1. Display **Slide 5** ("Reserve Lakeside Event Center for Your Function!"), and then click anywhere in the numbered list to display the text box border.
2. On the Home tab, in the Paragraph group, click the **Convert to SmartArt** button. A gallery of SmartArt layouts appears.
3. Point to the first layout. The ScreenTip identifies this layout as the Vertical Bullet List layout, and Live Preview shows you what the numbered list will look like with that layout applied. See Figure 1-18. Notice that the subitems are not included in a shape in this diagram.

Figure 1-18 Live Preview of the Vertical Bullet List SmartArt layout

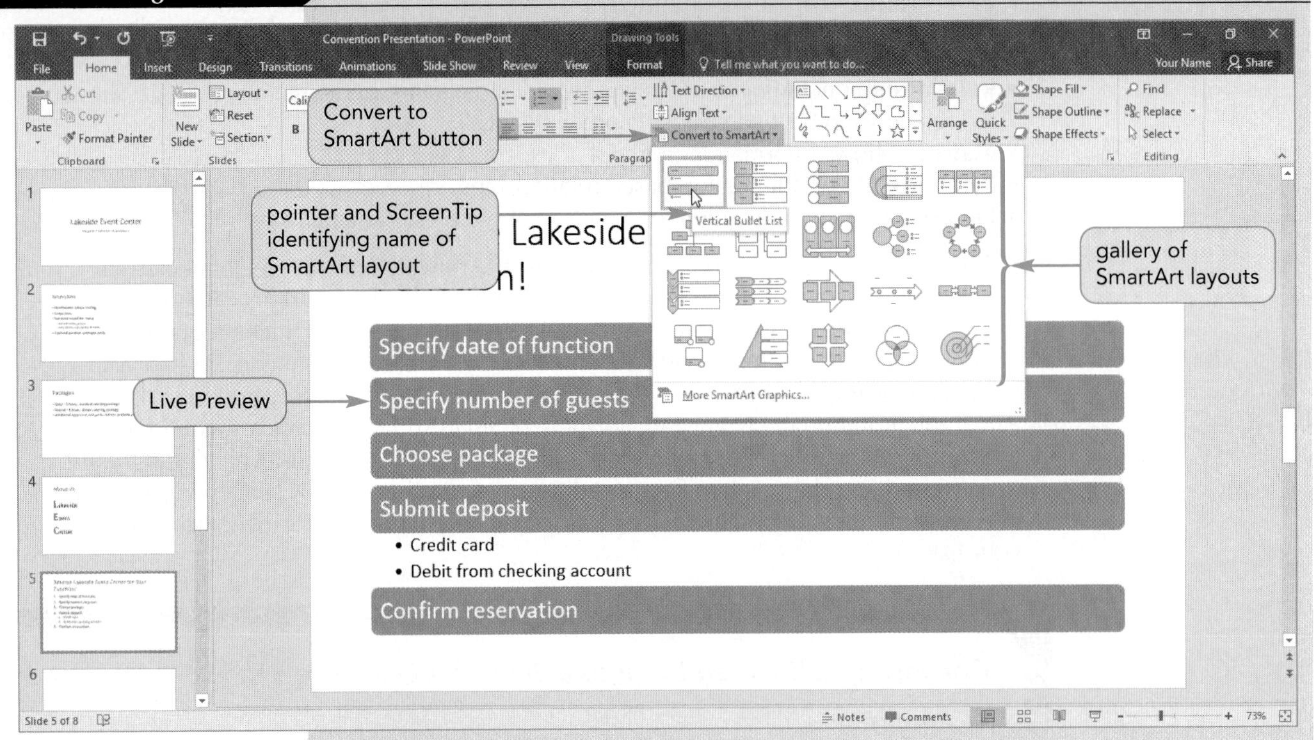

4. Point to several other layouts in the gallery, observing the Live Preview of each one. In some of the layouts, the subitems are included in a shape.
5. At the bottom of the gallery, click **More SmartArt Graphics**. The Choose a SmartArt Graphic dialog box opens. See Figure 1-19. You can click a type in the left pane to filter the middle pane to show only that type of layout.

Figure 1-19 Choose a SmartArt Graphic dialog box

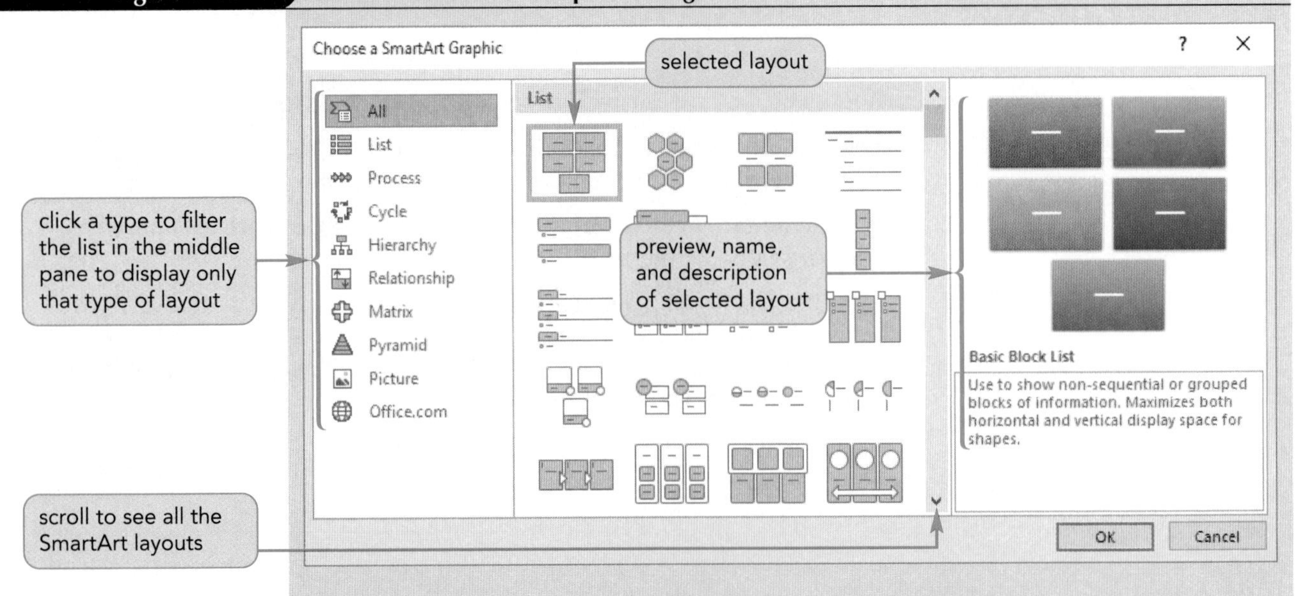

6. In the left pane, click **Process**, and then in the middle pane, click the **Step Up Process** layout, using the ScreenTips to identify it (it's the second layout in the first row). The right pane changes to show a description of that layout.
7. Click the **OK** button. The dialog box closes, and each of the first level items in the list appears in the square shapes in the diagram. The items also appear as a bulleted list in the Text pane, which is open to the left of the diagram. The SmartArt Tools contextual tabs appear on the ribbon. See Figure 1-20.

Figure 1-20 SmartArt diagram with the Step Up Process layout

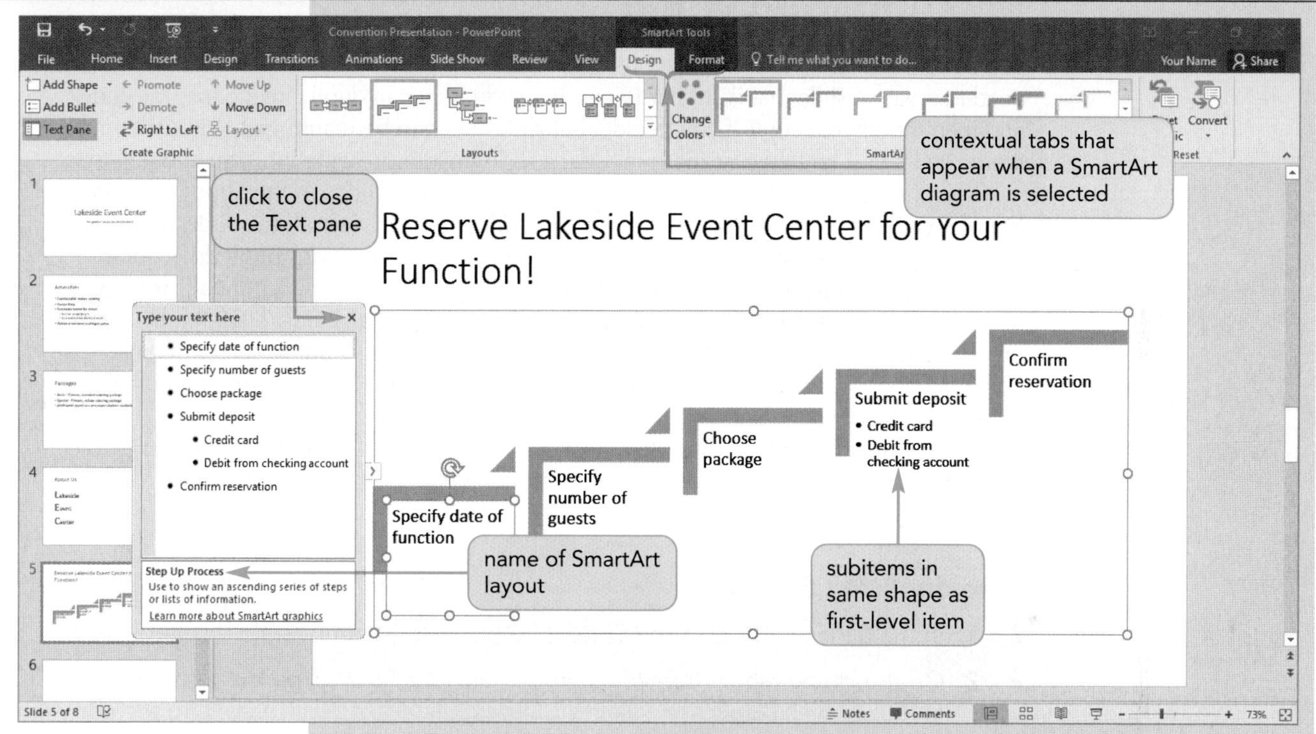

Trouble? If you do not see the Text pane, click the Text pane button on the left border of the selected SmartArt diagram.

In this layout, the subitems below "Submit deposit" are included in the fourth step shape; they are not placed in their own shapes in the diagram. Caitlin decides the information in the subitems does not need to be on the slide because people will see those options on the website when they submit their deposit.

8. In the "Submit deposit" shape, select **Debit from checking account**, and then press the **Delete** key. The text is deleted from the shape and from the Text pane.
9. In the Text pane, click to the right of the word "card," press the **Backspace** key as many times as necessary to delete all of the bullet text, and then press the **Backspace** key once more. The bullet changes to a first-level bullet and a new square shape is inserted in the diagram.
10. Press the **Backspace** key one more time. The empty bullet and the blank line are deleted in the Text pane, and the newly added shape is removed from the diagram. The "Submit deposit" shape now contains only the first-level item. Notice that AutoFit increased the size of the text in all the shapes so that the text still fills the shapes and is as large as possible. The "Submit deposit" shape is still selected. This shape should appear after the "Confirm reservation" shape.

11. On the SmartArt Tools Design tab, in the Create Graphic group, click the **Move Down** button. The selected "Submit deposit" shape moves down one spot in the bulleted list in the text pane and one shape to the right in the SmartArt graphic on the slide.
12. Click a blank area of the slide to deselect the diagram, and then on the Quick Access Toolbar, click the **Save** button to save your changes.

Manipulating Slides

You can manipulate the slides in a presentation to suit your needs. For instance, if you need to create a slide that is similar to another slide, you can duplicate the existing slide and then modify the copy. If you decide that slides need to be rearranged, you can reorder them. And if you no longer want to include a slide in your presentation, you can delete it.

To duplicate, rearrange, or delete slides, you select the slides in the Slides pane in Normal view or switch to Slide Sorter view. In **Slide Sorter view** all the slides in the presentation are displayed as thumbnails in the window; the Slides pane does not appear. You already know that to select a single slide you click its thumbnail. You can also select more than one slide at a time. To select sequential slides, click the first slide, press and hold the Shift key, and then click the last slide you want to select. To select nonsequential slides, click the first slide, press and hold the Ctrl key, and then click any other slides you want to select.

Caitlin wants to display the slide that shows the name of the center at the end of the presentation. To create this slide, you will duplicate Slide 4 ("About Us").

To duplicate Slide 4:

1. In the Slides pane, click the **Slide 4** ("About Us") thumbnail to display Slide 4.
2. On the Home tab, in the Slides group, click the **New Slide button arrow**, and then click **Duplicate Selected Slides**. Slide 4 is duplicated, and the copy is inserted as a new Slide 5 in the Slides pane. Slide 5 is now the current slide. If more than one slide were selected, they would all be duplicated. The duplicate slide doesn't need the title; Caitlin just wants to reinforce the center's name.
3. On Slide 5, click anywhere on the title **About Us**, click the **text box border** to select the text box, and then press the **Delete** key. The title and the title text box are deleted and the title text placeholder reappears.

You could delete the title text placeholder, but it is not necessary. When you display the presentation to an audience as a slide show, any unused placeholders will not appear.

Next you need to rearrange the slides. You need to move the duplicate of the "About Us" slide so it is the last slide in the presentation because Caitlin wants to leave it displayed after the presentation is over. She hopes this visual will reinforce the company's name for the audience. Caitlin also wants the "Packages" slide (Slide 3) moved so it appears before the "Amenities" slide (Slide 2), and she wants the original "About Us" slide (Slide 4) to be the second slide in the presentation.

To rearrange the slides in the presentation:

1. In the Slides pane, scroll up, if necessary, so that you can see Slides 2 and 3, and then drag the **Slide 3** ("Packages") thumbnail above the Slide 2 ("Amenities") thumbnail. As you drag, the Slide 3 thumbnail follows the pointer and Slide 2 moves down. The "Packages" slide is now Slide 2 and "Amenities" is now Slide 3. You'll move the other two slides in Slide Sorter view.
2. On the status bar, click the **Slide Sorter** button. The view switches to Slide Sorter view. Slide 2 appears with an orange border, indicating that it is selected.
3. On the status bar, click the **Zoom Out** button as many times as necessary until you can see all nine slides in the presentation. See Figure 1-21.

TIP

You can also use the buttons in the Presentation Views group on the View tab to switch views.

Figure 1-21 Slide Sorter view

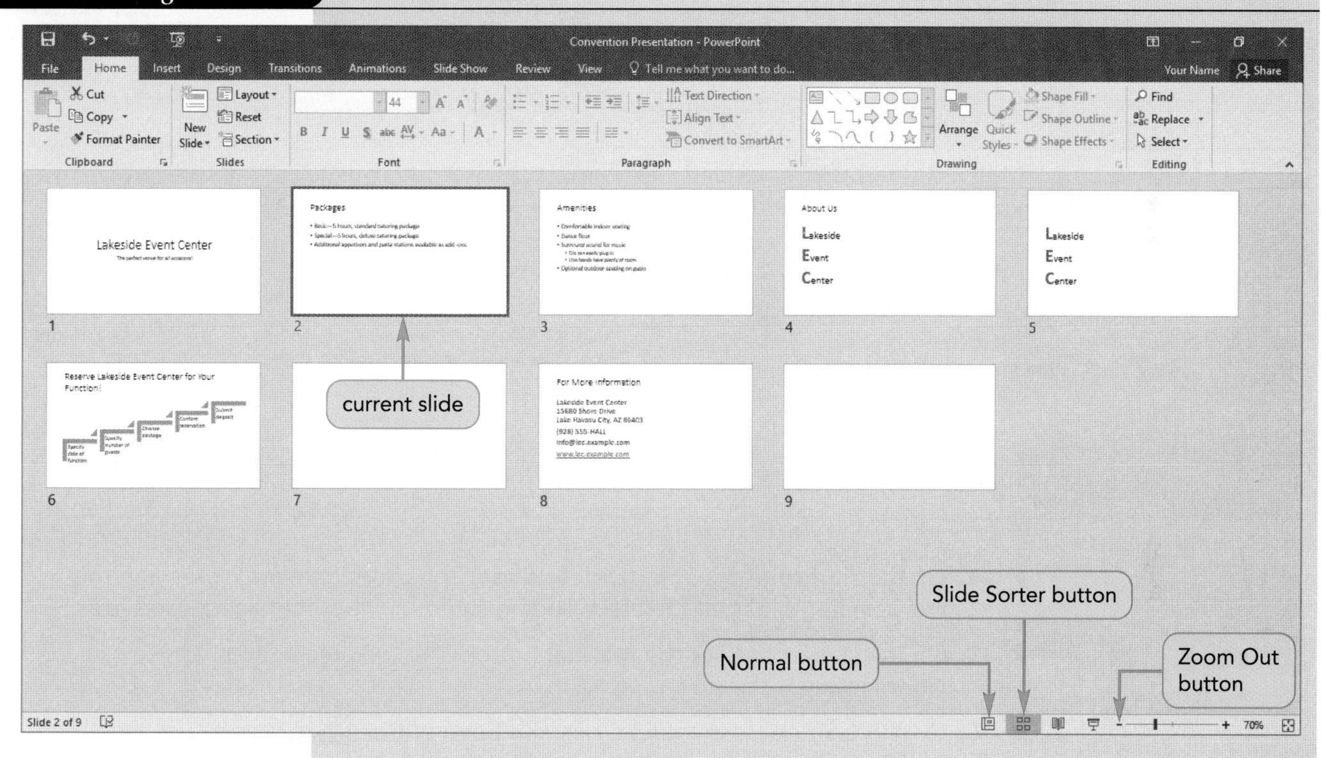

4. Drag the **Slide 4** ("About Us") thumbnail to between Slides 1 and 2. As you drag, the other slides move out of the way. The slide is repositioned, and the slides are renumbered so that the "About Us" slide is now Slide 2.
5. Drag the **Slide 5** thumbnail (the slide containing just the name of the company) so it becomes the last slide in the presentation (Slide 9).

Now you need to delete the two blank slides. To delete a slide, you can right-click its thumbnail to display a shortcut menu.

To delete the blank slides:

1. Click **Slide 6** (a blank slide), press and hold the **Shift** key, and then click **Slide 8** (the other blank slide), and then release the **Shift** key. The two slides you clicked are selected, as well as the slide between them. You want to delete only the two blank slides.

2. Click a blank area of the window to deselect the slides, click **Slide 6**, press and hold the **Ctrl** key, click **Slide 8**, and then release the **Ctrl** key. Only the two slides you clicked are selected.
3. Right-click either selected slide. A shortcut menu appears. See Figure 1-22.

Figure 1-22 Shortcut menu for selected slides

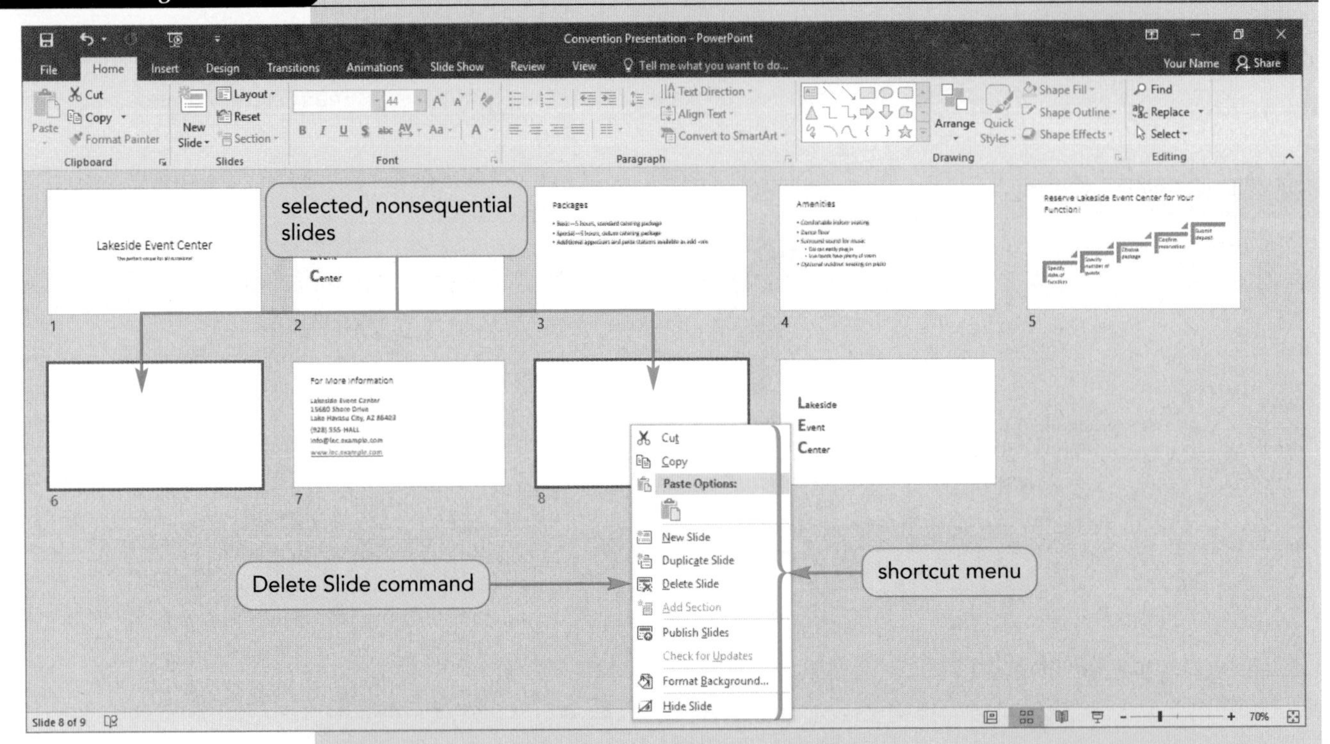

4. On the shortcut menu, click **Delete Slide**. The shortcut menu closes and the two selected slides are deleted. The presentation now contains seven slides.
5. On the status bar, click the **Normal** button. The presentation appears in Normal view.
6. On the Quick Access Toolbar, click the **Save** button to save the changes to the presentation.

TIP

You can also double-click a slide thumbnail in Slide Sorter view to display that slide in Normal view.

Closing a Presentation

When you are finished working with a presentation, you can close it and leave PowerPoint open. To do this, you click the File tab to open Backstage view, and then click the Close command. If you click the Close button in the upper-right corner of the PowerPoint window and only one presentation is open, you will not only close the presentation, you will exit PowerPoint as well.

You're finished working with the presentation for now, so you will close it. First you will add your name to the title slide.

To add your name to Slide 1 and close the presentation:

1. Display **Slide 1** (the title slide), click the **subtitle**, position the insertion point after "occasions!," press the **Enter** key, and then type your full name.

2. Click the **File** tab. Backstage view appears with the Info screen displayed. See Figure 1-23.

Figure 1-23 **Info screen in Backstage view**

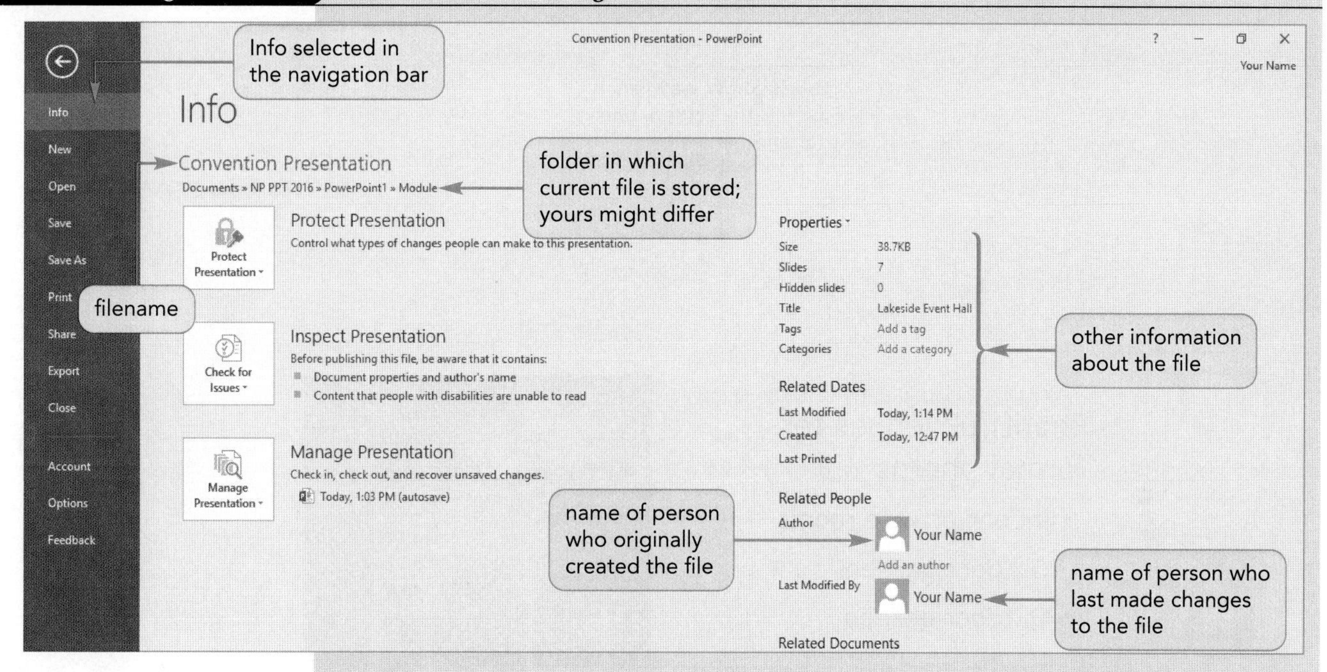

3. In the navigation bar, click **Close**. Backstage view closes, and a dialog box opens, asking if you want to save your changes.

4. In the dialog box, click the **Save** button. The dialog box and the presentation close, and the empty presentation window appears.

Trouble? If you want to take a break, you can exit PowerPoint by clicking the Close button in the upper-right corner of the PowerPoint window.

You've created a presentation that includes slides to which you added bulleted, numbered, and unnumbered lists. You also formatted text, converted a list to SmartArt, and manipulated slides. You are ready to give the presentation draft to Caitlin to review.

REVIEW

Session 1.1 Quick Check

1. Define "presentation."
2. How do you display Backstage view?
3. What is a layout?
4. In addition to a title text placeholder, what other type of placeholder do most layouts contain?
5. What is the term for an object that contains text?
6. What is the difference between the Clipboard and the Office Clipboard?
7. How do you convert a list to a SmartArt diagram?

Session 1.2 Visual Overview:

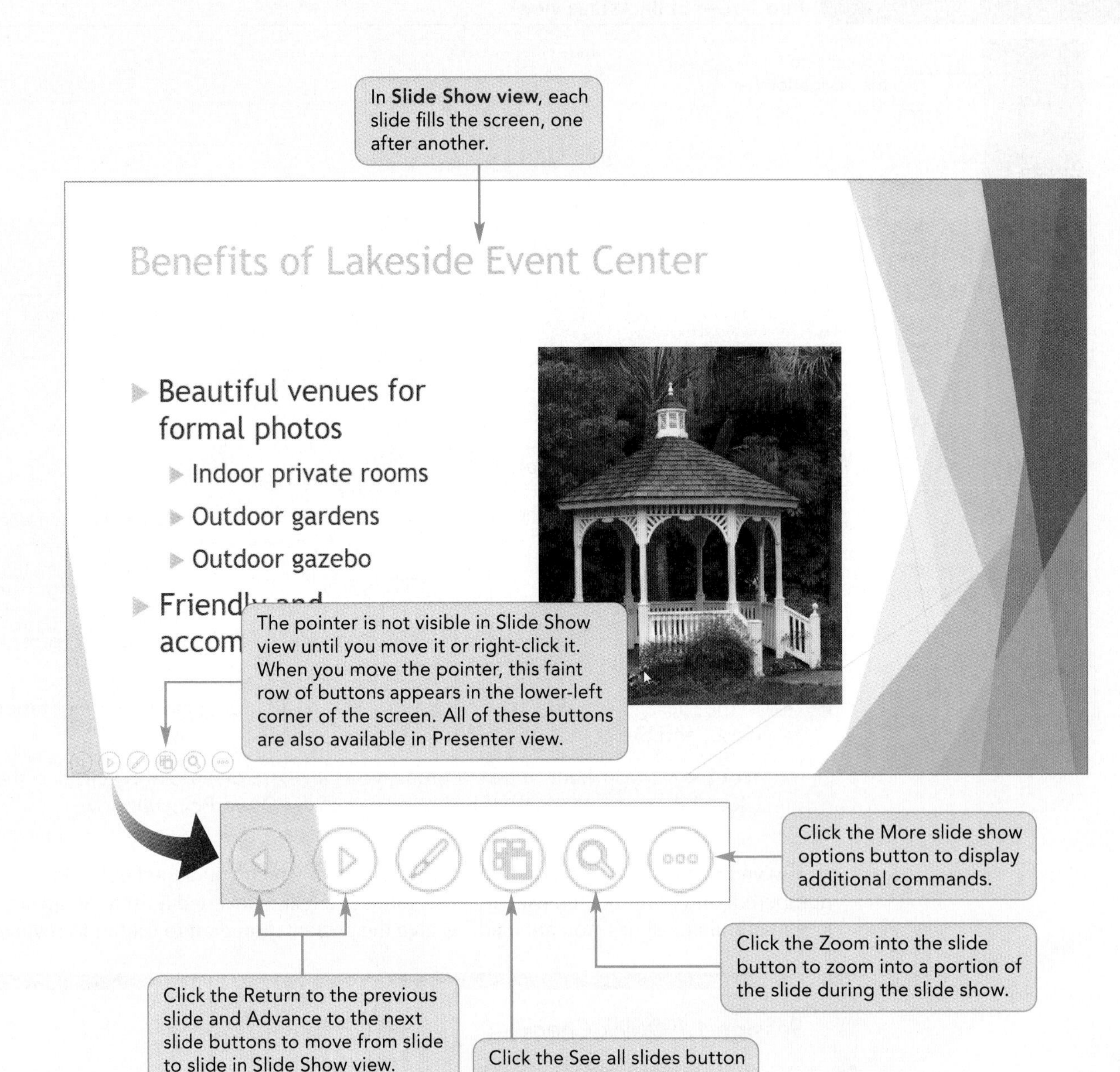

Slide Show and Presenter Views

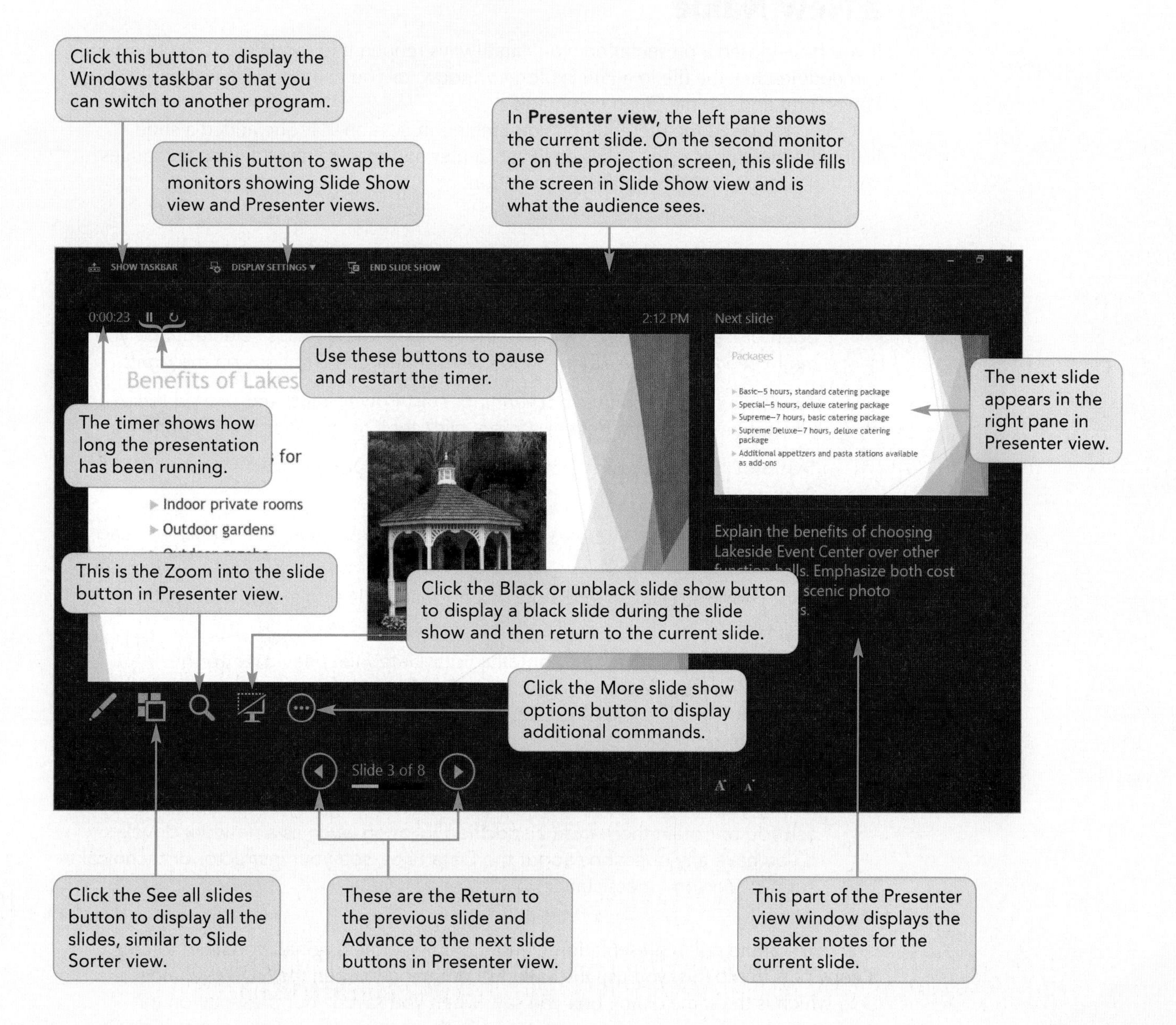

Opening a Presentation and Saving It with a New Name

If you have closed a presentation, you can always reopen it to modify it. To do this, you can double-click the file in a File Explorer window, or you can open Backstage view in PowerPoint and use the Open command.

Caitlin reviewed the presentation you created in Session 1.1. She added a slide listing the benefits of using Lakeside Event Center and made a few additional changes. You will continue modifying this presentation.

To open the revised presentation:

1. Click the **File** tab on the ribbon to display Backstage view. Because there is no open presentation, the Open screen is displayed. Recent is selected, and you might see a list of the 25 most recently opened presentations on the right.

   Trouble? If PowerPoint is not running, start PowerPoint, and then in the navigation bar on the Recent screen, click the Open Other Presentations link.

   Trouble? If another presentation is open, click Open in the navigation bar in Backstage view.

   Trouble? If you are storing your files on your OneDrive, click OneDrive, and then log in if necessary.

2. Click **Browse**. The Open dialog box appears. It is similar to the Save As dialog box.
3. Navigate to the drive that contains your Data Files, navigate to the **PowerPoint1 > Module** folder, click **Revised** to select it, and then click the **Open** button. The Open dialog box closes and the Revised presentation opens in the PowerPoint window, with Slide 1 displayed.

   Trouble? If you don't have the starting Data Files, you need to get them before you can proceed. Your instructor will either give you the Data Files or ask you to obtain them from a specified location (such as a network drive). If you have any questions about the Data Files, see your instructor or technical support person for assistance.

If you want to edit a presentation without changing the original, you need to create a copy of it. To do this, you use the Save As command to open the Save As dialog box, which is the same dialog box you saw when you saved your presentation for the first time. When you save a presentation with a new name, a copy of the original presentation is created, the original presentation is closed, and the newly named copy remains open in the PowerPoint window.

To save the Revised presentation with a new name:

1. Click the **File** tab, and then in the navigation bar, click **Save As**. The Save As screen in Backstage view appears.
2. Click **Browse** to open the Save As dialog box.

3. If necessary, navigate to the drive and folder where you are storing your Data Files.

4. In the File name box, change the filename to **Convention Final**, and then click the **Save** button. The Save As dialog box closes, a copy of the file is saved with the new name Convention Final, and the Convention Final presentation appears in the PowerPoint window.

Changing the Theme and the Theme Variant

A **theme** is a coordinated set of colors, fonts, backgrounds, and effects. All presentations have a theme. If you don't choose one, the default Office theme is applied; that is the theme currently applied to the Convention Final presentation.

You saw the Office theme set of colors when you changed the color of the text on the "About Us" slide. You have also seen the Office theme fonts in use on the slides. In the Office theme, the font of the slide titles is Calibri Light, and the font of the text in content text boxes is Calibri. In themes, the font used for slide titles is the Headings font, and the font used for the content text boxes is the Body font.

In PowerPoint, each theme has several variants with different coordinating colors and sometimes slightly different backgrounds. A theme and its variants are called a **theme family**. PowerPoint comes with several installed themes, and many more themes are available online at Office.com. In addition, you can use a custom theme stored on your computer or network.

You can select a different installed theme when you create a new presentation by clicking one of the themes on the New or Recent screen in Backstage view instead of clicking Blank Presentation, and then clicking one of the variants. If you want to change the theme of an open presentation, you can choose an installed theme on the Design tab, or you can apply a theme applied to another presentation or a theme stored on your computer or network. When you change the theme, the colors, fonts, and slide backgrounds change to those used in the new theme.

Caitlin wants the theme of the Convention Final presentation changed to one that has more color in the background. First you'll display Slide 2 so you can see the effect a different theme has on the text formatted with a theme color.

To examine the current theme and then change the theme and theme variant:

1. Display **Slide 2** ("About Us"), and then, in the unnumbered list select the orange letter **L**.

2. On the Home tab, in the Font group, click the **Font Color button arrow** A. Look at the colors under Theme Colors, and note the second to last color is selected in the sixth column, which contains shades of orange. Notice also the row of Standard Colors below the theme colors.

3. In the Font group, click the **Font arrow**. A menu of fonts installed on the computer opens. At the top under Theme Fonts, Calibri (Body) is selected because the letter L that you selected is in a content text box. See Figure 1-24.

Figure 1-24 Theme fonts on the Font menu

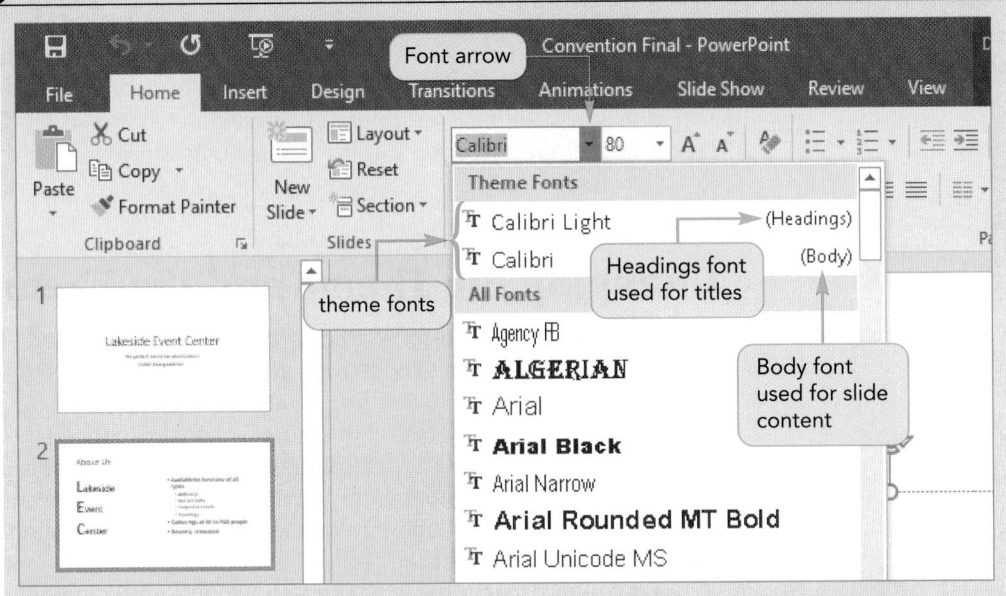

4. On the ribbon, click the **Design** tab. The Font menu closes and the installed themes appear in the Themes gallery on the Design tab. See Figure 1-25. The current theme is the first theme listed in the Themes group on the Design tab. The next theme is the Office theme, which, in this case, is also the current theme.

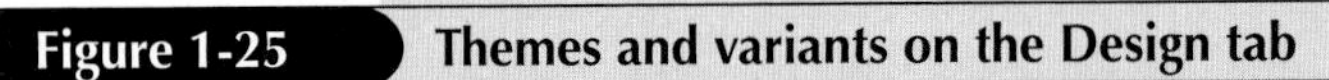

Figure 1-25 Themes and variants on the Design tab

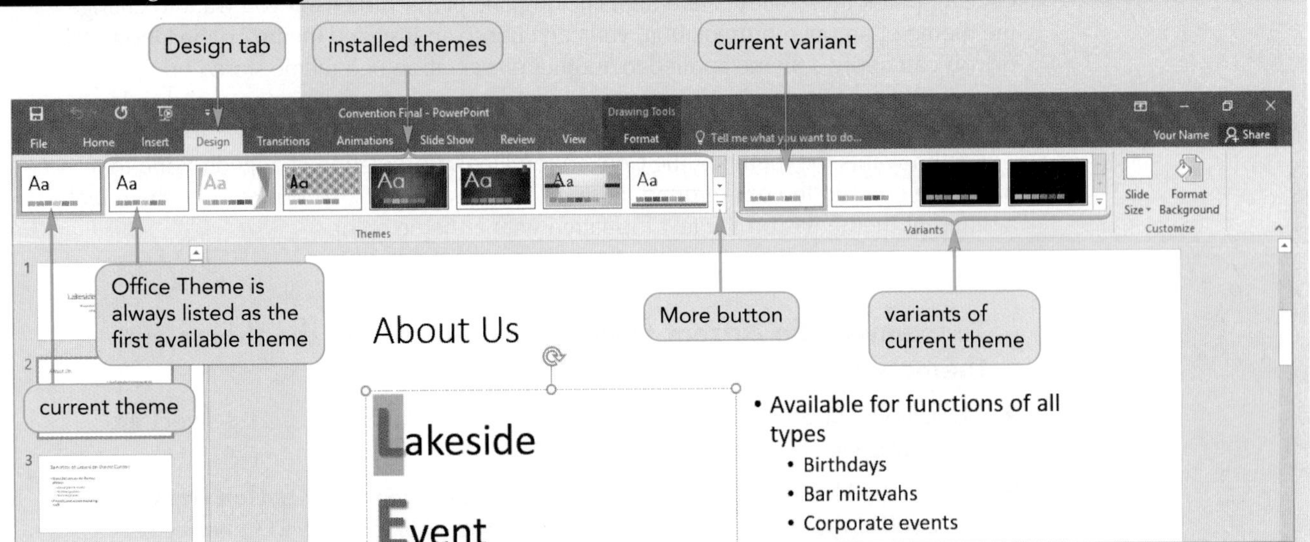

To see all of the installed themes, you need to scroll through the gallery by clicking the up and down scroll buttons on the right end of the gallery or clicking the More button to expand the gallery to see all of the themes at once. The **More button** appears on all galleries that contain additional items or commands that don't fit in the group on the ribbon.

5. In the Themes group, click the **More** button. The gallery of themes opens. See Figure 1-26. When the gallery is open, the theme applied to the current presentation appears in the first row. In the next row, the first theme is the Office theme, and then the rest of the installed themes appear. Some of these themes also appear on the Recent and New screens in Backstage view.

Figure 1-26 Themes gallery expanded

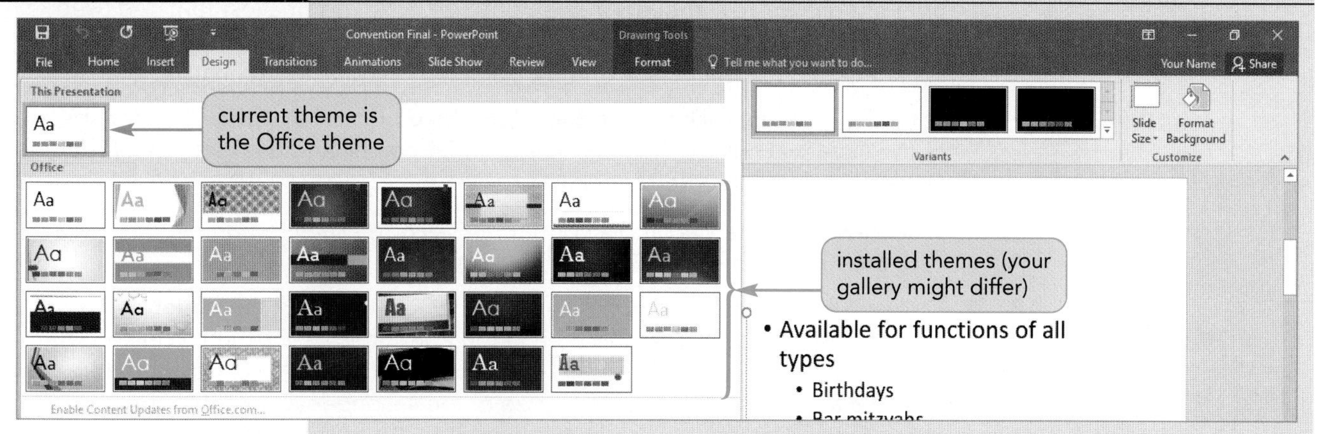

TIP

If the content of a slide is no longer positioned correctly or changes size when you apply a different theme, click the Reset button in the Slides group on the Home tab.

6. Point to several of the themes in the gallery to display their ScreenTips and to see a Live Preview of the theme applied to the current slide.
7. In the first row of the Office section of the gallery, click the **Facet** theme. The gallery closes, and the Facet theme is applied to all the slides with the default variant (the first variant in the Variants group). The title text on each slide changes from black to green, the letters that you had colored orange on Slide 2 are dark green, the bullet symbols change from black circles to green triangles, and in the Slides pane, you can see on the Slide 6 thumbnail that the SmartArt shapes are now green as well.
8. In the Variants group, point to the other three variants to see a Live Preview of each of them, and then click the **second variant** (the blue one).

   Trouble? If there are no variants, your installation of Office might have an extra version of the Facet theme installed. In the Themes group, click the More button, and then make sure you click the Facet theme in the first row.
9. Click the **Home** tab, and then in the Font group, click the **Font Color button arrow** A. The selected color—the color of the selected letter "L"—is now a shade of blue in the Theme Colors of the Facet theme. Notice also that the row of Standard Colors is the same as it was when the Office theme was applied.
10. In the Font group, click the **Font arrow**. You can see that the Theme Fonts are now Trebuchet MS for both Headings (slide titles) and the Body (content text boxes).
11. Press the **Esc** key. The Font menu closes.

After you apply a new theme, you should examine your slides to make sure that they look the way you expect them to. The font sizes used for the text in lists in the Facet theme are considerably smaller than those used in the Office theme. You know that Caitlin wants the slides to be legible and clearly visible, so you will increase the font sizes on some of the slides. The title slide is fine, but you need to examine the rest of the slides.

To examine the slides with the new theme and adjust font sizes:

1. On **Slide 2** ("About Us"), in the bulleted list, click the **first bulleted item**. In the Font group, the font size is 18 points, quite a bit smaller than the font size of first-level bulleted items in the Office theme, which is 28 points. You can see that the font size of the subitems is also fairly small.

2. In the bulleted list, click the **text box border** to select the entire text box. In the Font group, 16+ appears in the Font Size box. The smallest font size used in the selected text box—the font size of the subitems—is 16, and the plus sign indicates that there is text in the selected text box larger than 16 points.
3. In the Font group, click the **Increase Font Size** button twice. The font size of the first-level bulleted items changes to 24 points, and the font size of the second-level bulleted items changes to 20 points.

   Trouble? If the Drawing Tools Format tab becomes selected on the ribbon, click the Home tab.
4. Display **Slide 3** ("Benefits of Lakeside Event Center"), click the **bulleted list**, click the **text box border**, and then in the Font group, click the **Increase Font Size** button three times. The font size of the first-level bulleted items changes to 28 points, and the font size of the second-level bulleted items changes to 24 points.
5. On **Slide 4** ("Packages") and **Slide 5** ("Amenities"), increase the size of the text in the bulleted lists so that the font size of the first-level items is 28 points and of the subitems is 24 points.
6. Display **Slides 6, 7, 8,** and then **Slide 1** in the Slide pane. These remaining slides look fine.
7. On the Quick Access Toolbar, click the **Save** button. The changes to the presentation are saved.

INSIGHT

Understanding the Difference Between Themes and Templates

As explained earlier, a theme is a coordinated set of colors, fonts, backgrounds, and effects. A **template** has a theme applied, but it also contains text, graphics, and placeholders to help direct you in creating content for a presentation. You can create and save your own custom templates or find everything from calendars to marketing templates among the thousands of templates available on Office.com. To find a template on Office.com, display the Recent or New screen in Backstage view, type keywords in the "Search for online templates and themes" box, and then click the Search button in the box to display templates related to the search terms. To create a new presentation based on the template you find, click the template and then click Create.

If a template is stored on your computer, you can apply the theme used in the template to an existing presentation. If you want to apply the theme used in a template on Office.com to an existing presentation, you need to download the template to your computer first, and then you can apply it to an existing presentation.

Working with Photos

Most people are exposed to multimedia daily and expect to have information conveyed visually as well as verbally. In many cases, graphics are more effective than words for communicating an important point. For example, if a sales force has reached its sales goals for the year, including a photo in your presentation of a person reaching the top of a mountain can convey a sense of exhilaration to your audience.

Inserting Photos Stored on Your Computer or Network

Content placeholders contain buttons that you can use to insert things other than a list, including photos stored on your hard drive, a network drive, a USB drive, an SD card from a digital camera, or any other medium to which you have access. You can also use the Pictures button in the Images group on the Insert tab to add photos to slides.

Caitlin has photos that she wants inserted on three of the slides in the presentation. She asks you to add the photos to the presentation.

To insert photos on Slides 3, 5, and 8:

1. Display **Slide 3** ("Benefits of Lakeside Event Center"), and then in the content placeholder on the right, click the **Pictures** button. The Insert Picture dialog box opens. This dialog box is similar to the Open dialog box.
2. Navigate to the **PowerPoint1 > Module** folder included with your Data Files, click **Gazebo**, and then click the **Insert** button. The dialog box closes, and a picture of a gazebo appears in the placeholder and is selected. The contextual Picture Tools Format tab appears on the ribbon to the right of the View tab and is the active tab. See Figure 1-27.

Figure 1-27 Picture inserted on Slide 3

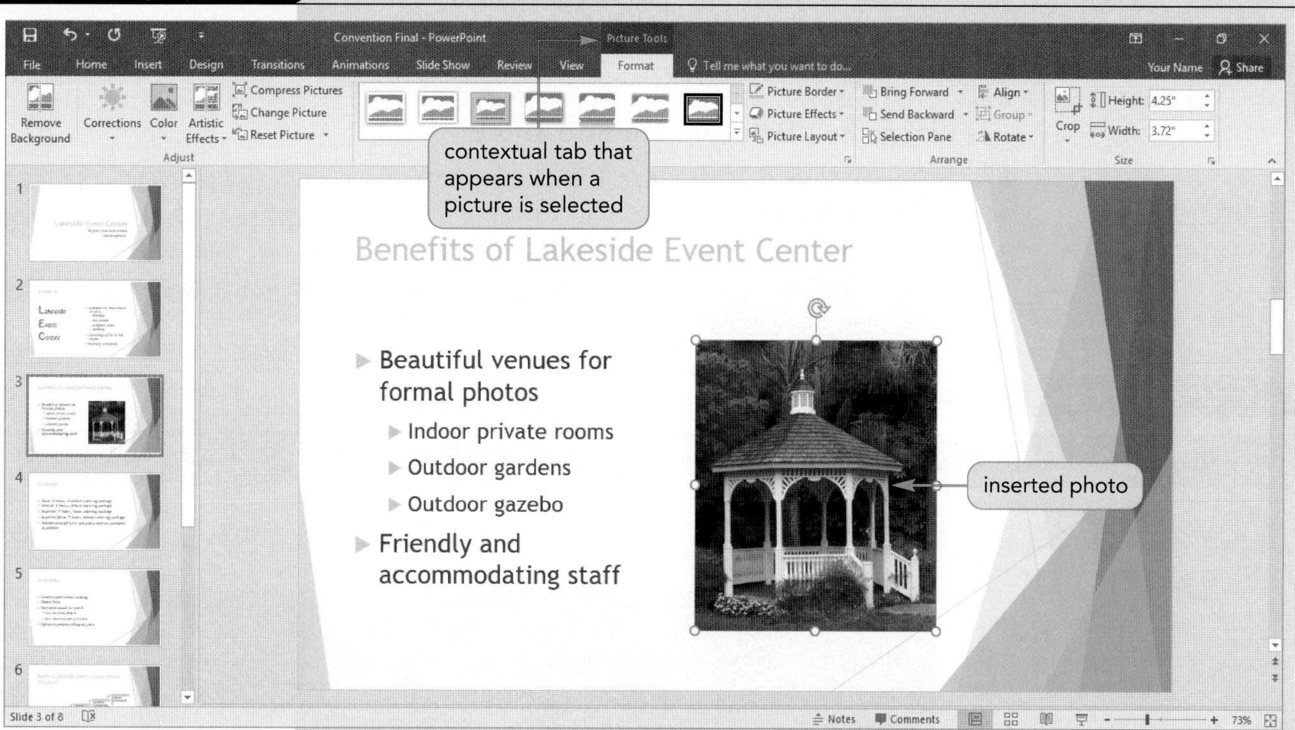

©iStock.com/bloggityblog

3. Display **Slide 5** ("Amenities"). This slide uses the Title and Content layout and does not have a second content placeholder. You can change the layout to include a second content placeholder, or you can use a command on the ribbon to insert a photo.
4. Click the **Insert** tab, and then in the Images group, click the **Pictures** button. The Insert Picture dialog box opens.

5. In the PowerPoint1 > Module folder, click **Tables**, and then click the **Insert** button. The dialog box closes and the picture is added to the slide, covering the bulleted list. You will fix this later.
6. Display **Slide 8** (the last slide). This slide has the Two Content layout applied, but you can still use the Pictures command on the Insert tab.
7. Click the **Insert** tab on the ribbon.
8. In the Images group, click the **Pictures** button, click **Wedding** in the PowerPoint1 > Module folder, and then click the **Insert** button. The picture replaces the content placeholder on the slide.

Cropping Photos

Sometimes you want to display only part of a photo. For example, if you insert a photo of a party scene that includes a bouquet of colorful balloons, you might want to show only the balloons. To do this, you can **crop** the photo—cut out the parts you don't want to include. In PowerPoint, you can crop it manually to any size you want, crop it to a preset ratio, or crop it to a shape.

Caitlin wants you to crop the photo on Slide 5 ("Amenities") to make the dimensions of the final photo smaller without making the images in the photo smaller. She also wants you to crop the photo on Slide 8 (the last slide) to an interesting shape.

To crop the photos on Slides 5 and 8:

1. Display **Slide 5** ("Amenities"), click the **photo** to select it, and then click the **Picture Tools Format** tab, if necessary.
2. In the Size group, click the **Crop** button. The Crop button is selected, and crop handles appear around the edges of the photo just inside the sizing handles. See Figure 1-28.

Figure 1-28 **Photo with crop handles**

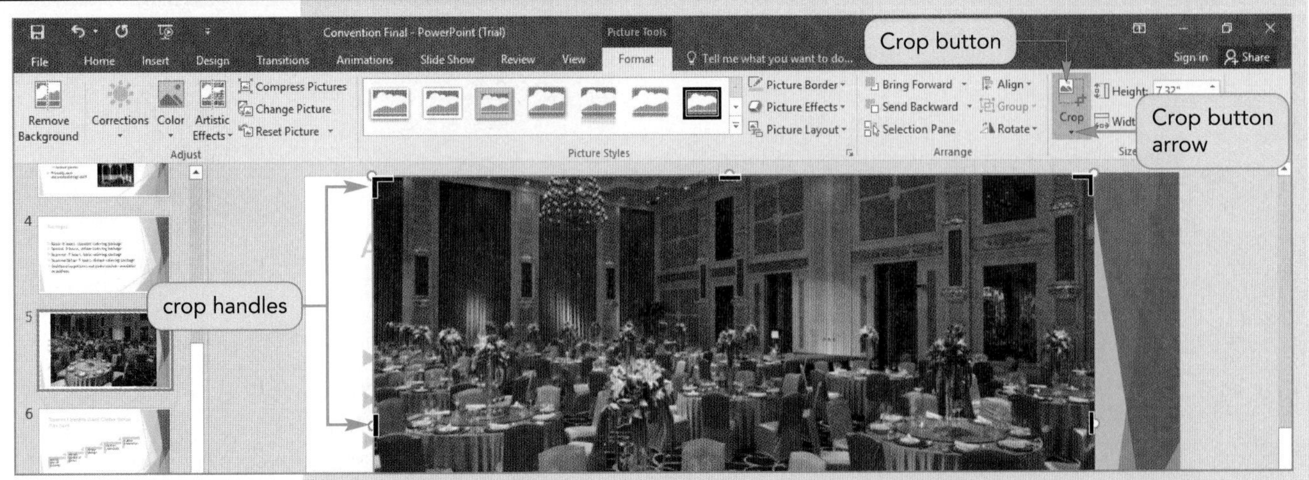

©iStock.com/kai zhang; ©iStock.com/bloggityblog

3. Position the pointer directly on top of the right-middle crop handle so that it changes to ⊢, press and hold the mouse button, and then drag the crop handle to the left approximately two inches. See Figure 1-29.

Figure 1-29 Cropped photo

©iStock.com/kai zhang; ©iStock.com/bloggityblog; Courtesy of Dina White

4. Click the **Crop** button again. The Crop feature is turned off, but the photo is still selected and the Format tab is still the active tab.
5. Display **Slide 8** (the last slide), click the **photo** to select it, and then click the **Picture Tools Format** tab, if necessary.
6. In the Size group, click the **Crop button arrow**. The Crop button menu opens. See Figure 1-30.

Figure 1-30 Crop button menu

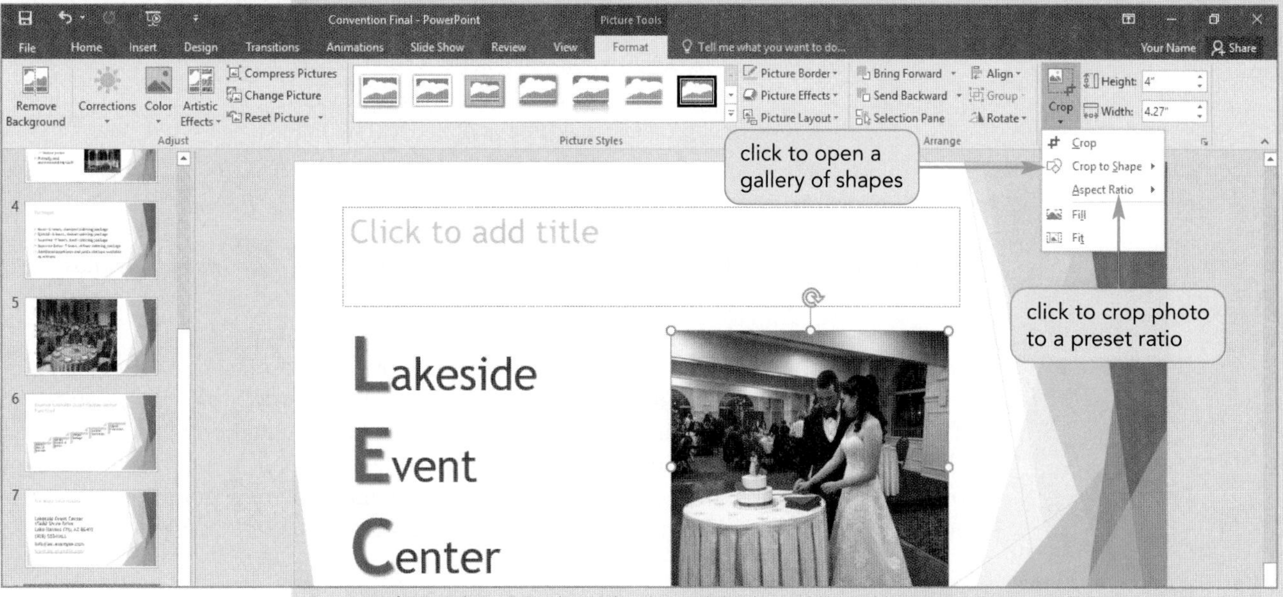

Courtesy of Dina White; ©iStock.com/kai zhang; ©iStock.com/bloggityblog

7. Point to **Crop to Shape** to open a gallery of shapes, and then in the second row under Basic Shapes, click the **Plaque** shape. The photo is cropped to a plaque shape. Notice that the rectangular selection border of the original photo is still showing.
8. In the Size group, click the **Crop** button. You can now see the cropped portions of the original, rectangle photo that are shaded gray.
9. Click a blank area of the slide. The picture is no longer selected, and the Home tab is the active tab on the ribbon.

Modifying Photo Compression Options

When you save a presentation that contains photos, PowerPoint automatically compresses the photos to a resolution of 220 pixels per inch (ppi). (For comparison, photos printed in magazines are typically 300 ppi.) Compressing photos reduces the size of the presentation file, but it also reduces the quality of the photos. See Figure 1-31 for a description of the compression options available. If an option in the dialog box is gray, the photo is a lower resolution than that setting. Note that many monitors and projectors are capable of displaying resolutions only a little higher (98 ppi) than the resolution designated for email (96 ppi).

Figure 1-31 Photo compression settings

Compression Setting	Description
330 ppi	Photos are compressed to 330 pixels per inch; use when slides need to maintain the quality of the photograph when displayed on high-definition (HD) displays. Use when photograph quality is of the highest concern and file size is not an issue.
220 ppi	Photos are compressed to 220 pixels per inch; use when slides need to maintain the quality of the photograph when printed. This is the default setting for PowerPoint presentations. (Note that although this is minimal compression, it is still compressed, and if photograph quality is the most important concern, do not compress photos at all.)
150 ppi	Photos are compressed to 150 pixels per inch; use when the presentation will be viewed on a monitor or screen projector.
96 ppi	Photos are compressed to 96 pixels per inch; use for presentations that need to be emailed or uploaded to a webpage or when it is important to keep the overall file size small.
Document resolution	Photos are compressed to the resolution specified on the Advanced tab in the PowerPoint Options dialog box. The default setting is 220 ppi.
No compression	Photos are not compressed at all; used when it is critical that photos remain at their original resolution.

You can change the compression setting for each photo that you insert, or you can change the settings for all the photos in the presentation. If you cropped photos, you also can discard the cropped areas of the photo to make the presentation file size smaller. (Note that when you crop to a shape, the cropped portions are not discarded.) If you insert additional photos or crop a photo after you apply the new compression settings to all the slides, you will need to apply the new settings to the new photos.

REFERENCE

Modifying Photo Compression Settings and Removing Cropped Areas

- After all photos have been added to the presentation file, click any photo in the presentation to select it.
- Click the Picture Tools Format tab. In the Adjust group, click the Compress Pictures button.
- In the Compress Pictures dialog box, click the option button next to the resolution you want to use.
- To apply the new compression settings to all the photos in the presentation, click the Apply only to this picture check box to deselect it.
- To keep cropped areas of photos, click the Delete cropped areas of pictures check box to deselect it.
- Click the OK button.

You will adjust the compression settings to make the file size of the presentation as small as possible so that Caitlin can easily send it or post it for others without worrying about file size limitations on the receiving server.

To modify photo compression settings and remove cropped areas from photos:

1. On **Slide 8** (the last slide), click the **photo**, and then click the **Picture Tools Format** tab, if necessary.
2. In the Adjust group, click the **Compress Pictures** button. The Compress Pictures dialog box opens. See Figure 1-32. Under Target output, the Use document resolution option button is selected. Other than that option button, only the E-mail (96 ppi) option button is selected. This is because the currently selected photo's resolution is higher than 96 ppi but lower than the next largest photo size, Web (150 ppi).

Figure 1-32 **Compress Pictures dialog box**

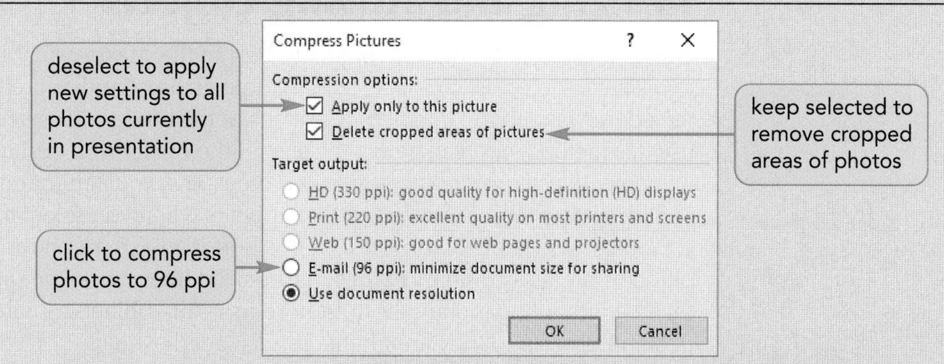

3. Click the **E-mail (96 ppi)** option button. This setting compresses the photos to the smallest possible size. At the top of the dialog box under Compression options, the Delete cropped areas of pictures check box is already selected. This option is not applied to cropped photos until you open this dialog box and then click the OK button to apply it. Because you want the presentation file size to be as small as possible, you do want cropped portions of photos to be deleted, so you'll leave this selected. The Apply only to this picture check box is also selected; however, you want the settings applied to all the photos in the file.

Be sure you deselect the Apply only to this picture check box, and be sure you are satisfied with the way you cropped the photo on Slide 5 before you click OK to close the dialog box.

4. Click the **Apply only to this picture** check box to deselect it.
5. Click the **OK** button.

   The dialog box closes and the compression settings are applied to all the photos in the presentation. You can confirm that the cropped areas of photos were removed by examining the photo on Slide 5. (The photo on Slide 8 was cropped to a shape, so the cropped areas on it were not removed.)
6. Display **Slide 5** ("Amenities"), click the **photo**, and then click the **Picture Tools Format** tab, if necessary.
7. In the Size group, click the **Crop** button. The Crop handles appear around the photo, but the portions of the photo that you cropped out no longer appear.
8. Click the **Crop** button again to deselect it, and then save the changes to the presentation.

INSIGHT

Keeping Photos Uncompressed

Suppose you are a photographer and want to create a presentation to show your photos. In that case, you would want to display them at their original, uncompressed resolution. To do this, you need to change a setting in the PowerPoint Options dialog box before you add photos to slides. Click the File tab to open Backstage view, click Options in the navigation bar to open the PowerPoint Options dialog box, click Advanced in the navigation bar, and then locate the Image Size and Quality section. To keep images at their original resolution, click the Do not compress images in file check box to select it. Note that you can also change the default compression setting for photos in this dialog box—you can increase the compression or choose to automatically discard cropped portions of photos and other editing data. Note that these changes affect only the current presentation.

Resizing and Moving Objects

You can resize and move any object to best fit the space available on a slide. One way to resize an object is to drag a sizing handle. **Sizing handles** are the circles that appear in the corners and in the middle of the sides of the border of a selected object. When you use this method, you can adjust the size of the object so it best fits the space visually. If you need to size an object to exact dimensions, you can modify the measurements in the Size group on the Format tab that appears when you select the object.

You can also drag an object to reposition it anywhere on the slide. If more than one object is on a slide, **smart guides**, dashed red lines, appear as you drag to indicate the center and the top and bottom borders of the objects. Smart guides can help you position objects so they are aligned and spaced evenly.

In addition to using the smart guides, it can be helpful to display rulers and gridlines in the window. The rulers appear along the top and left sides of the displayed slide. Gridlines are one-inch squares made up of dots one-sixth of an inch apart. As you drag an object, it snaps to the grid, even if the grid is not visible.

Resizing and Moving Pictures

Pictures and other objects that cause the Picture Tools Format tab to appear when selected have their aspect ratios locked by default. The **aspect ratio** is the ratio of the object's height to its width. When the aspect ratio is locked, if you resize the photo by dragging a corner sizing handle or if you change one dimension in the Size group on the Picture Tools Format tab, the other dimension will change by the same percentage. However, if you drag one of the sizing handles in the middle of an object's border, you will override the locked aspect ratio setting and resize the object only in the direction you drag. Generally you do not want to do this with photos because the images will become distorted.

You need to resize and move the photos you inserted on Slides 3, 5, and 8 so the slides are more attractive. You'll display the rulers and gridlines to help you as you do this.

To move and resize the photos on Slides 3, 5, and 8:

1. Click the **View** tab, and then in the Show group, click the **Ruler** and the **Gridlines** check boxes. Rulers appear above and to the left of the displayed slide, and the gridlines appear on the slide.
2. On **Slide 5** ("Amenities"), click the **photo**, if necessary, and then position the pointer on the top-middle sizing handle so that the pointer changes to ⇕.
3. Press and hold the mouse button so that the pointer changes to +, drag the top-middle sizing handle down approximately two inches, and then release the mouse button. The photo is two inches shorter, but the image is distorted.
4. On the Quick Access Toolbar, click the **Undo** button. You need to resize the photo by dragging a corner sizing handle to maintain the aspect ratio.
5. Click the **Picture Tools Format** tab, and then note the measurements in the Size group. The photo is 7.32 inches high and about 8.4 inches wide. (The exact width on your screen might differ depending on how much you cropped.)
6. Position the pointer on the bottom-left corner sizing handle so that it changes to ⤢, press and hold the mouse button so that the pointer changes to +, and then drag the bottom-left sizing handle up. Even though you are dragging in only one direction, because you are dragging a corner sizing handle, both the width and height are changing proportionately to maintain the aspect ratio.
7. When the photo is approximately 4.5 inches high and approximately 5 inches wide, release the mouse button. Note that the measurements in the Height and Width boxes changed to reflect the picture's new size.
8. Drag the photo to the right so that the right edge of the photo aligns with the 6-inch mark on the horizontal ruler above the slide, and drag it down so that smart guides appear indicating that the bottom and top of the photo is aligned with the bottom and top of the text box that contains the unnumbered list as shown in Figure 1-33.

TIP

If you don't want objects you are moving to snap to the grid, press and hold the Alt key while you are dragging.

Figure 1-33 Repositioning photo on Slide 5 using smart guides and gridlines

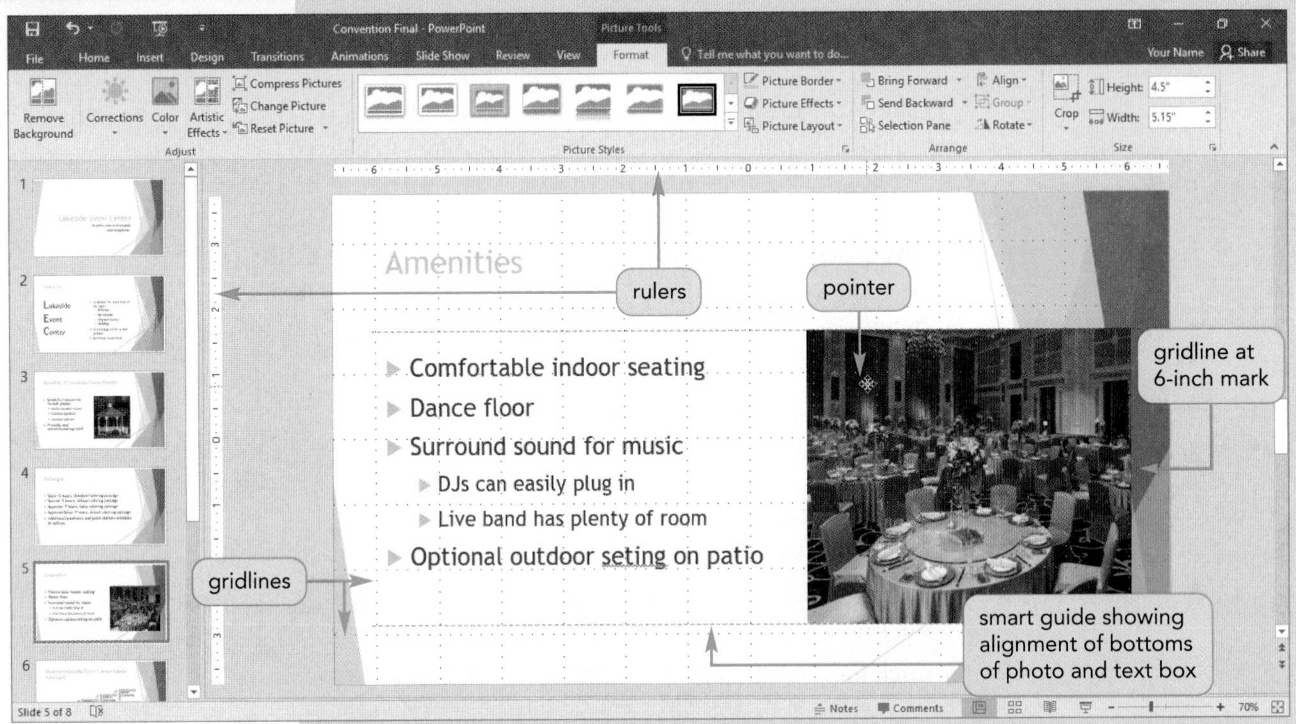

©iStock.com/kai zhang; ©iStock.com/bloggityblog

9. Release the mouse button. The photo is repositioned.
10. Display **Slide 3** ("Benefits of Lakeside Event Center"), click the **photo** to select it, and then click the **Picture Tools Format** tab if necessary.
11. In the Size group, click in the **Height** box to select the current measurement, type **4.5**, and then press the **Enter** key. The measurement in the Width box in the Size group changes proportionately to maintain the aspect ratio, and the new measurements are applied to the photo.
12. Drag the photo up and to the right until horizontal smart guides appear above and below the photo indicating that the top and bottom of the photo and the top and bottom of the text box containing the bulleted list are aligned, and so that the right edge of the photo aligns with the right edge of the title text box (at the 3.5-inch mark on the ruler), as shown in Figure 1-34.

Figure 1-34 Moving resized photo on Slide 3

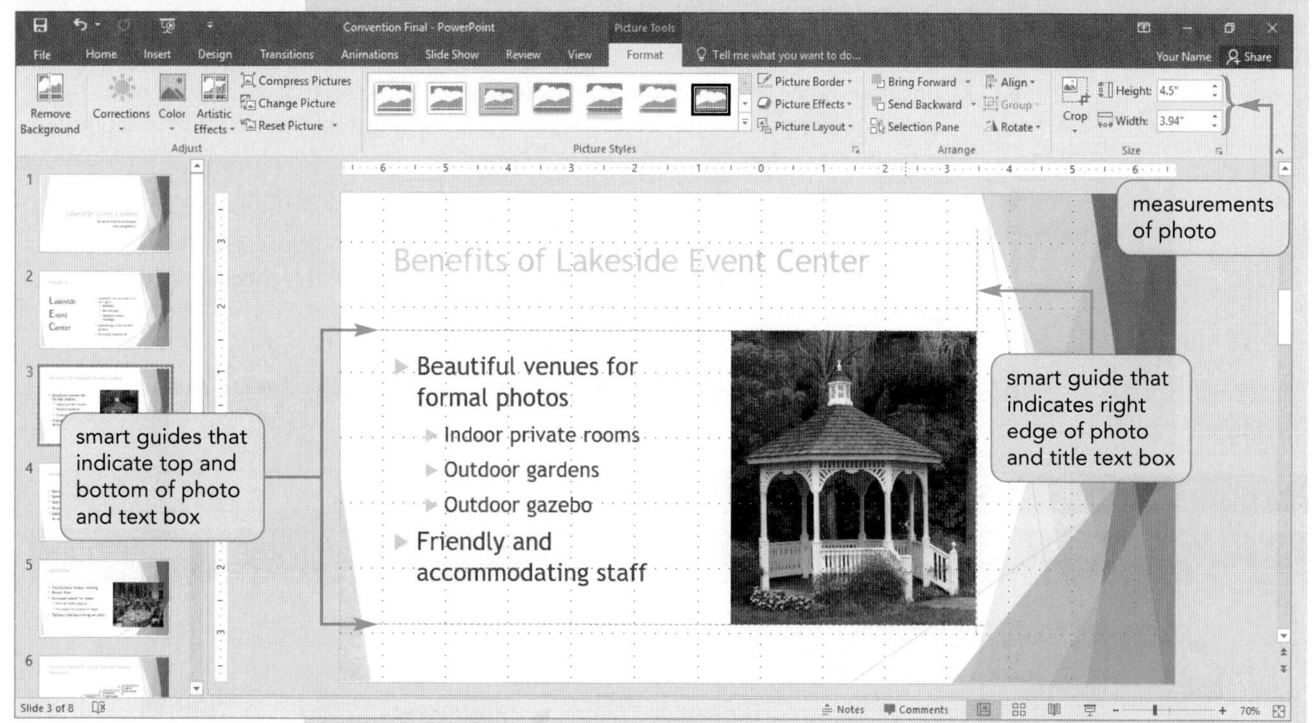

©iStock.com/bloggityblog; ©iStock.com/kai zhang

13. When the photo is aligned as shown in Figure 1-34, release the mouse button.
14. Display **Slide 8** (the last slide), resize the photo so it is 5.9 inches high and 6.3 inches wide, and then position it so that its bottom edge is aligned with the gridline at the 3-inch mark on the vertical ruler, and its right edge is aligned with the gridline at the 6-inch mark on the horizontal ruler.
15. Click the **View** tab, and then click the **Ruler** and **Gridlines** check boxes to deselect them.

Resizing and Moving Text Boxes

The themes and layouts installed with PowerPoint are designed by professionals, so much of the time it's a good idea to use the layouts as provided to be assured of a cohesive look among the slides. However, occasionally there will be a compelling reason to adjust the layout of objects on a slide, by either resizing or repositioning them.

Text boxes, like other objects that cause the Drawing Tools Format tab to appear when selected, do not have their aspect ratios locked by default. This means that when you resize a text box by dragging a corner sizing handle or changing one dimension in the Size group, the other dimension is not affected.

Like any other object on a slide, you can reposition text boxes. To do this, you must position the pointer on the text box border, anywhere except on a sizing handle, to drag it to its new location.

To improve the appearance of Slide 8, you will resize the text box containing the unnumbered list so it vertically fills the slide.

To resize the text box on Slide 8 and increase the font size:

1. On **Slide 8** (the last slide in the presentation), click the unnumbered list to display the text box border.
2. Position the pointer on the top-middle sizing handle so that it changes to ↕, and then drag the sizing handle up until the top edge of the text box is aligned with the top edge of the title text placeholder.
3. Drag the right-middle sizing handle to the right until the right edge of the text box is aligned with the left edge of the photo.
4. Click the **Home** tab, and then in the Font group, click the **Increase Font Size** button [A^] three times. Even though the title text placeholder will not appear during a slide show, you will delete it to see how the final slide will look.
5. Click the **title text placeholder border**, and then press the **Delete** key. See Figure 1-35.

Figure 1-35 Slide 8 with resized text box

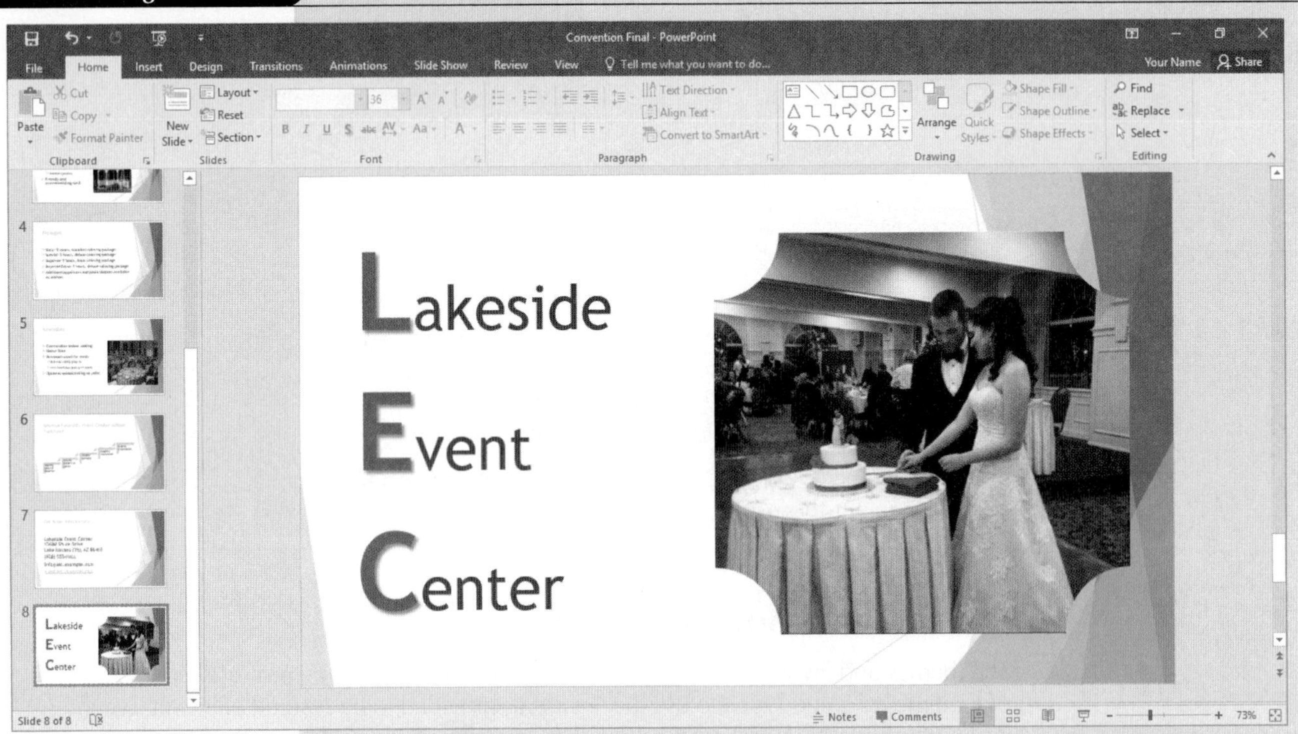

Courtesy of Dina White; ©iStock.com/bloggityblog; ©iStock.com/kai zhang

6. Save the changes to the presentation.

Adding Speaker Notes

Speaker notes, or simply **notes**, are information you add about slide content to help you remember to bring up specific points during the presentation. Speaker notes should not contain all the information you plan to say during your presentation, but they can be a useful tool for reminding you about facts and details related to the content on specific slides. You add notes in the **Notes pane**, which you can display below the displayed slide in Normal view, or you can switch to **Notes Page view**, in which an image of the slide appears in the top half of the presentation window and the notes for that slide appear in the bottom half.

To add notes to Slides 3 and 7:

1. Display **Slide 7** ("For More Information"), and then, on the status bar, click the **Notes** button. The Notes pane appears below Slide 7 with "Click to add notes" as placeholder text. See Figure 1-36.

Figure 1-36 Notes pane below Slide 7

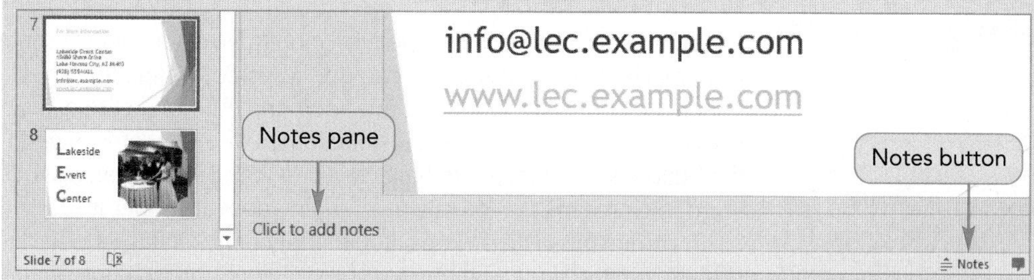

Courtesy of Dina White

2. Click in the **Notes** pane. The placeholder text disappears, and the insertion point is in the Notes pane.
3. Type **Hand out contact information to audience. Use the link to demonstrate how to use the website**.
4. Display **Slide 3** ("Benefits of Lakeside Event Center"), click in the **Notes** pane, and then type **Explain the benefits of choosing Lakeside Event Center over other function halls**.
5. Click the **View** tab on the ribbon, and then in the Presentation Views group, click the **Notes Page** button. Slide 3 is displayed in Notes Page view. See Figure 1-37.

Figure 1-37 Slide 3 in Notes Page view

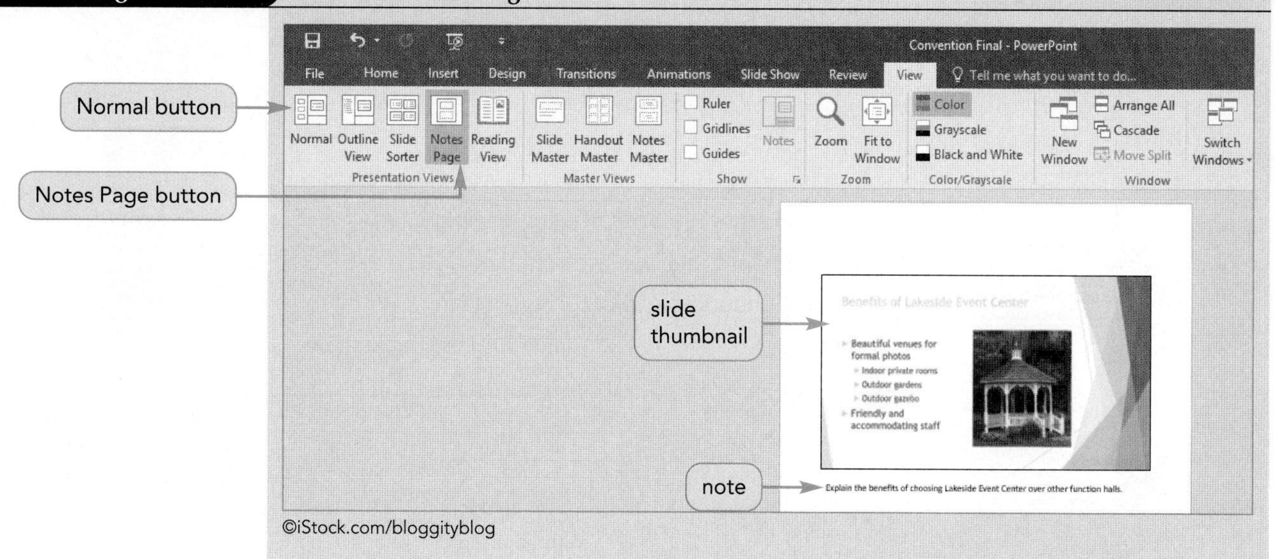

©iStock.com/bloggityblog

TIP

Use the Zoom in button on the status bar to magnify the text to make it easier to edit the note.

6. In the note, click after the period at the end of the sentence, press the **spacebar**, and then type **Emphasize both cost benefits and scenic photo opportunities**.
7. In the Presentation Views group, click the **Normal** button to return to Normal view. The Notes pane stays displayed until you close it again.
8. On the status bar, click the **Notes** button to close the Notes pane, and then save the changes to the presentation.

Checking Spelling

TIP

You can click the Thesaurus button in the Proofing group on the Review tab to look up synonyms of a selected word, or you can click the Smart Lookup button in the Insights group to open the Insights task pane listing search results from the web.

You should always check the spelling and grammar in your presentation before you finalize it. To make this task easier, you can use PowerPoint's spelling checker. You can quickly tell if there are words on slides that are not in the built-in dictionary by looking at the Spelling button at the left end of the status bar. If there are no words flagged as possibly misspelled, the button is [icon]; if there are flagged words, the button changes to [icon]. To indicate that a word might be misspelled, a wavy red line appears under it.

To correct misspelled words, you can right-click a flagged word to see a list of suggested spellings on the shortcut menu, or you can check the spelling of all the words in the presentation. To check the spelling of all the words in the presentation, you click the Spelling button in the Proofing group on the Review tab. This opens the Spelling task pane to the right of the displayed slide and starts the spell check from the current slide. A **task pane** is a pane that opens to the right or left of the displayed slide and contains commands and options related to the task you are doing. When a possible misspelled word is found, suggestions are displayed for the correct spelling. Synonyms for the selected correct spelling are also listed.

To check the spelling of words in the presentation:

1. Display **Slide 4** ("Packages"), and then right-click the misspelled word **Delux** in the fourth item in the list. A shortcut menu opens listing spelling options. See Figure 1-38.

Figure 1-38 **Shortcut menu for a misspelled word**

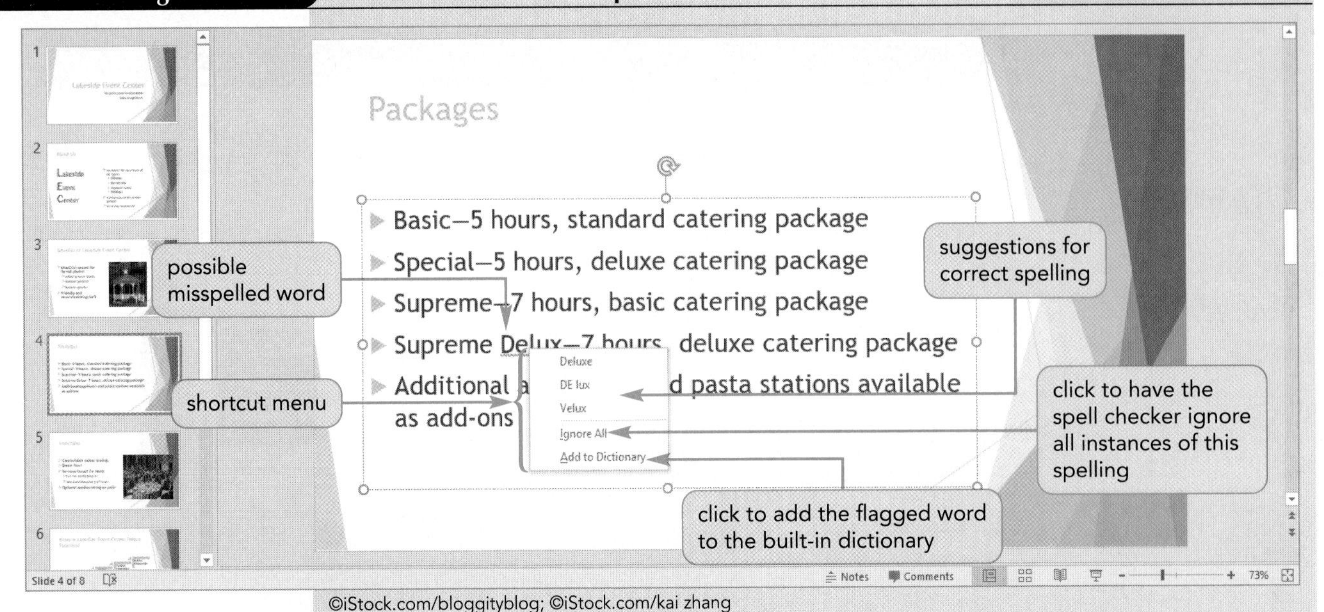

©iStock.com/bloggityblog; ©iStock.com/kai zhang

2. On the shortcut menu, click **Deluxe**. The menu closes and the spelling is corrected.

3. Click the **Review** tab, and then in the Proofing group, click the **Spelling** button. The Spelling task pane opens to the right of the displayed slide, and the next possible misspelled word on Slide 5 ("Amenities") appears with the flagged word, "seting," highlighted. See Figure 1-39. In the Spelling task pane, the first suggested correct spelling is selected. The selected correct spelling also appears at the bottom of the task pane with synonyms for the word listed below it and a speaker icon next to it.

Figure 1-39 **Spelling task pane displaying a misspelled word**

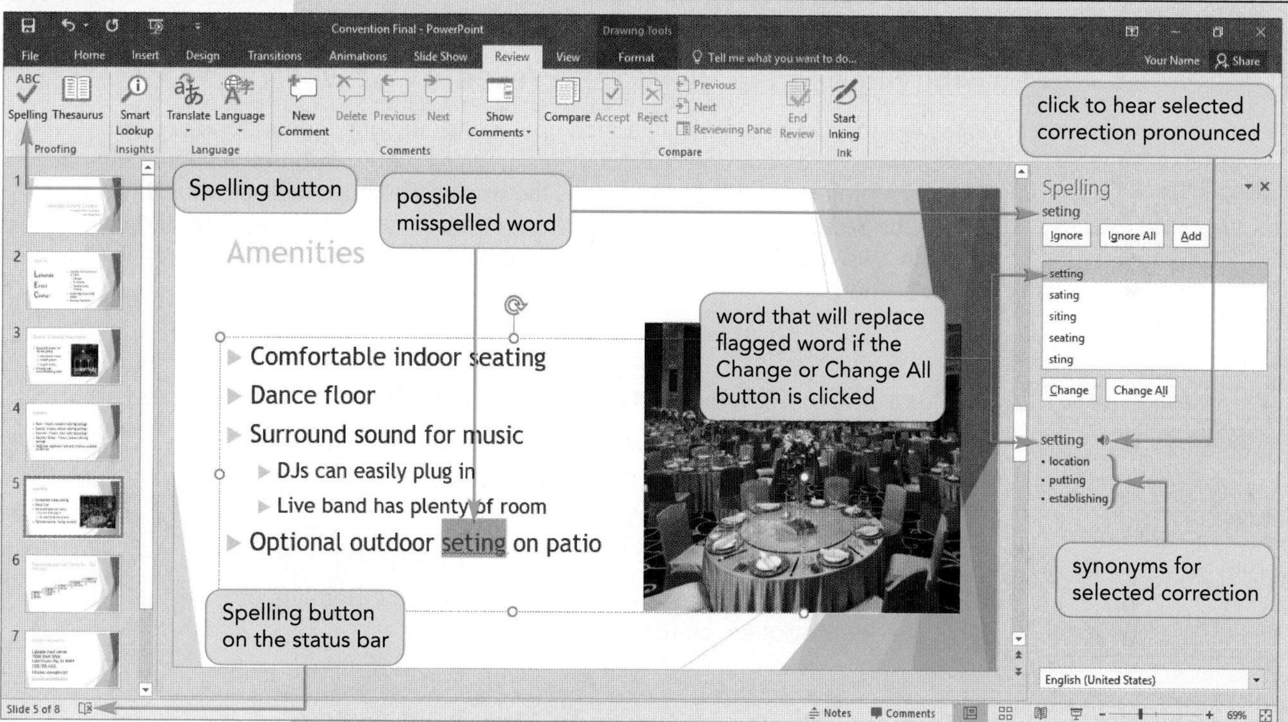

©iStock.com/kai zhang; ©iStock.com/bloggityblog

4. In the Spelling task pane, click the **speaker** icon. A male voice says the word "setting."

5. In the list of suggested corrections, click **sting**. The word at the bottom of the task pane changes to "sting," and the synonyms change also.

6. In the list of suggested corrections, click **setting**, and then click the **Change** button. The word is corrected, and the next slide containing a possible misspelled word, Slide 1, appears with the flagged word, "Keough," highlighted and listed in the Spelling task pane. This is part of Caitlin's last name so you want the spell checker to ignore this.

7. In the task pane, click the **Ignore All** button. Because that was the last flagged word in the presentation, the Spelling task pane closes, and a dialog box opens telling you that the spell check is complete.

Trouble? If the spell checker finds any other misspelled words, correct them.

8. Click the **OK** button. The dialog box closes. The last flagged word, "Keough," is still selected on Slide 1.
9. Click a blank area of the slide to deselect the text, and then save the changes to the presentation.

Running a Slide Show

After you have created and proofed your presentation, you should view it as a slide show to see how it will appear to your audience. There are several ways to do this—Slide Show view, Presenter view, and Reading view.

Using Slide Show View and Presenter View

You can use Slide Show view if your computer has only one monitor and you don't have access to a screen projector. If your computer is connected to a second monitor or a screen projector, Slide Show view is the way an audience will see your slides. Refer to the Session 1.2 Visual Overview for more information about Slide Show view.

Caitlin asks you to review the slide show in Slide Show view to make sure the slides look professional.

TIP

To start the slide show from the current slide, click the Slide Show button on the status bar.

To use Slide Show view to view the Convention Final presentation:

1. On the Quick Access Toolbar, click the **Start From Beginning** button. Slide 1 appears on the screen in Slide Show view. Now you need to advance the slide show.
2. Press the **spacebar**. Slide 2 ("About Us") appears on the screen.
3. Click the mouse button. The next slide, Slide 3 ("Benefits of Lakeside Event Center"), appears on the screen.
4. Press the **Backspace** key. The previous slide, Slide 2, appears again.
5. Press the **7** key, and then press the **Enter** key. Slide 7 ("For More Information") appears on the screen.
6. Move the mouse to display the pointer, and then position the pointer on the website address **www.lec.example.com**. The pointer changes to to indicate that this is a link, and the ScreenTip that appears shows the full website address including "http://". If this were a real website, you could click the link to open your web browser and display the website to your audience. Because you moved the pointer, a very faint row of buttons appears in the lower-left corner. The buttons provide access to commands you need in order to run the slide show. See Figure 1-40.

Figure 1-40 Link and row of buttons in Slide Show view

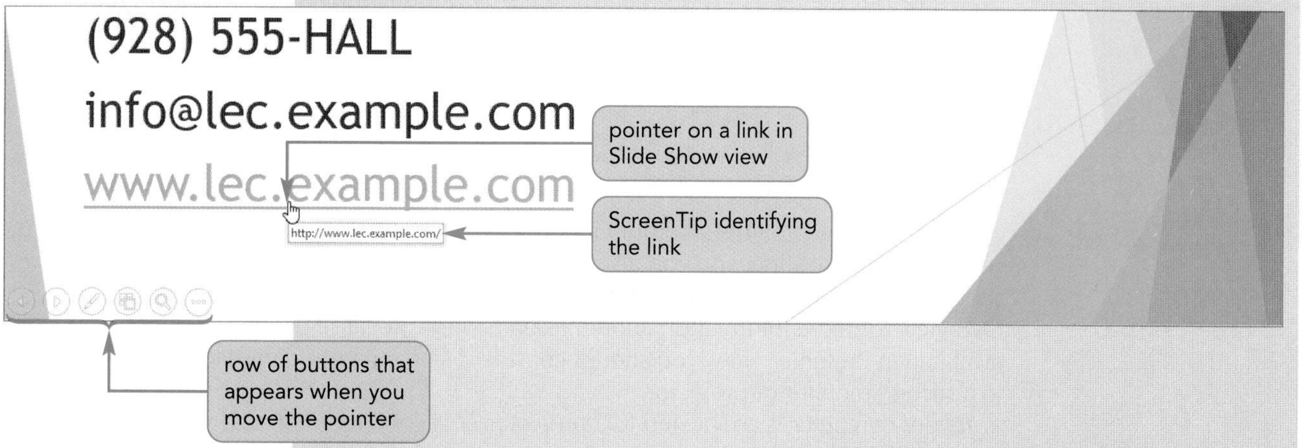

(928) 555-HALL
info@lec.example.com
www.lec.example.com
http://www.lec.example.com/

pointer on a link in Slide Show view
ScreenTip identifying the link
row of buttons that appears when you move the pointer

7. Move the pointer again, if necessary, to display the buttons that appear in the lower-left corner of the screen, and then click the **Return to the previous slide** button four times to return to Slide 3 ("Benefits of Lakeside Event Center").

   Trouble? If you can't see the buttons at the bottom of the screen, move the pointer to the lower-left corner so it is on top of the first button to darken that button, and then move the pointer to the right to see the rest of the buttons.

8. Display the buttons at the bottom of the screen again, and then click the **Zoom into the slide** button. The pointer changes to , and three-quarters of the slide is darkened. See Figure 1-41.

Figure 1-41 Zoom feature activated in Slide Show view

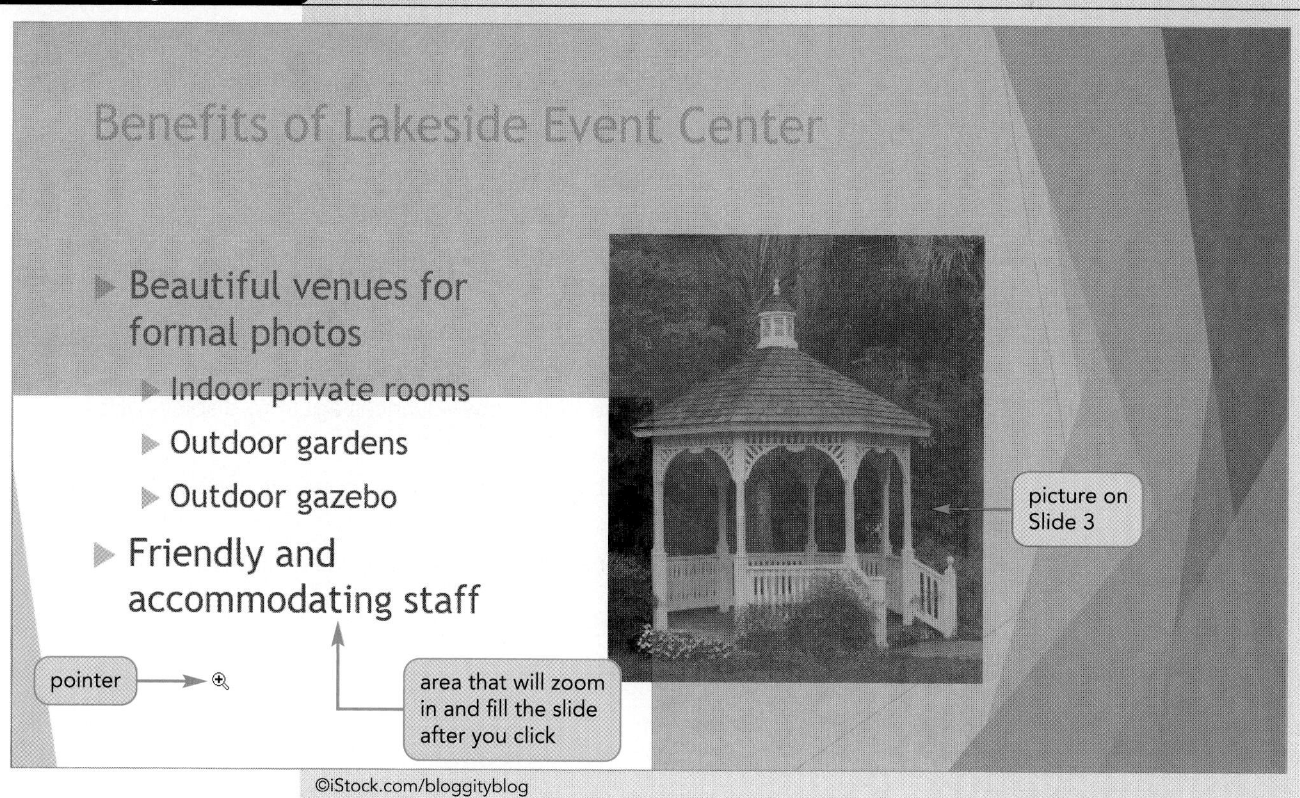

©iStock.com/bloggityblog

9. Move the pointer to the picture, and then click the **picture**. The view zooms so that the part of the slide inside the bright rectangle fills the screen, and the pointer changes to .

10. Press and hold the mouse button to change the pointer to , and then drag to the right to pull another part of the zoomed in slide into view.

11. Press the **Esc** key to zoom back out to see the whole slide.

Presenter view provides additional tools for running a slide show. In addition to seeing the current slide, you can also see the next slide, speaker notes, and a timer showing you how long the slide show has been running. Refer to the Session 1.2 Visual Overview for more information about Presenter view. Because of the additional tools available in Presenter view, you should consider using it if your computer is connected to a second monitor or projector.

If your computer is connected to a projector or second monitor, and you start a slide show in Slide Show view, Presenter view starts on the computer and Slide Show view appears on the second monitor or projection screen. If, for some reason, you don't want to use Presenter view in that circumstance, you can switch to Slide Show view. If you want to practice using Presenter view when your computer is not connected to a second monitor or projector, you can switch to Presenter view from Slide Show view.

Caitlin wants you to switch to Presenter view and familiarize yourself with the tools available there.

To use Presenter view to review the slide show:

1. Move the pointer to display the buttons in the lower-left corner of the screen, click the **More slide show options** button to open a menu of commands, and then click **Show Presenter View**. The screen changes to show the presentation in Presenter view.

2. Below the current slide, click the **See all slides** button . The screen changes to show thumbnails of all the slides in the presentation, similar to Slide Sorter view.

3. Click the **Slide 4** thumbnail. Presenter view reappears, displaying Slide 4 ("Packages") as the current slide.

4. Click anywhere on Slide 4. The slide show advances to display Slide 5 ("Amenities").

5. At the bottom of the screen, click the **Advance to the next slide** button . Slide 6 ("Reserve Lakeside Event Center for Your Function!") appears.

6. Press the **spacebar** twice. The slide show advances again to display Slides 7 and then 8.

7. Press the **spacebar** again. A black slide appears displaying the text "End of slide show, click to exit."

8. Press the **spacebar** once more. Presentation view closes, and you return to Normal view.

PROSKILLS

Decision Making: Displaying a Blank Slide During a Presentation

Sometimes during a presentation, the audience has questions about the material and you want to pause the slide show to respond. Or you might want to refocus the audience's attention on you instead of on the visuals on the screen. In these cases, you can display a blank slide (either black or white). When you do this, the audience, with nothing else to look at, will shift all of their attention to you. Some presenters plan to use blank slides and insert them at specific points during their slide shows. Planning to use a blank slide can help you keep your presentation focused and remind you that the purpose of the PowerPoint slides is to provide visual aids to enhance your presentation; the slides themselves are not the presentation.

If you did not create blank slides in your presentation file, but during your presentation you feel you need to display a blank slide, you can easily do this in Slide Show or Presenter view by pressing the B key to display a blank black slide or the W key to display a blank white slide. You can also click the More button—in Slide Show view, in Presenter view—or right-click the screen, point to Screen on the menu, and then click Black Screen or White Screen. To remove the black or white slide and redisplay the slide that had been on the screen before you displayed the blank slide, press any key on the keyboard or click anywhere on the screen. In Presenter view, you can also use the Black or unblack slide show button to toggle a blank slide on or off.

An alternative to redisplaying the slide that had been displayed prior to the blank slide is to click the Advance to the next slide button. This can be more effective than redisplaying the slide that was onscreen before the blank slide because, after you have grabbed the audience's attention and prepared them to move on, you won't lose their focus by displaying a slide they have already seen.

Using Reading View

Reading view displays the slides so that they almost fill the screen, similar to Slide Show view; however, in Reading view, a status bar appears, identifying the number of the current slide and providing buttons to advance the slide show. You can also resize the window in Reading view to allow you to work in another window on the desktop.

To use Reading view to review the presentation:

1. Display **Slide 2** ("About Us"), and then on the status bar, click the **Reading View** button. The presentation changes to Reading view with Slide 2 displayed. See Figure 1-42.

Figure 1-42 Slide 2 in Reading view

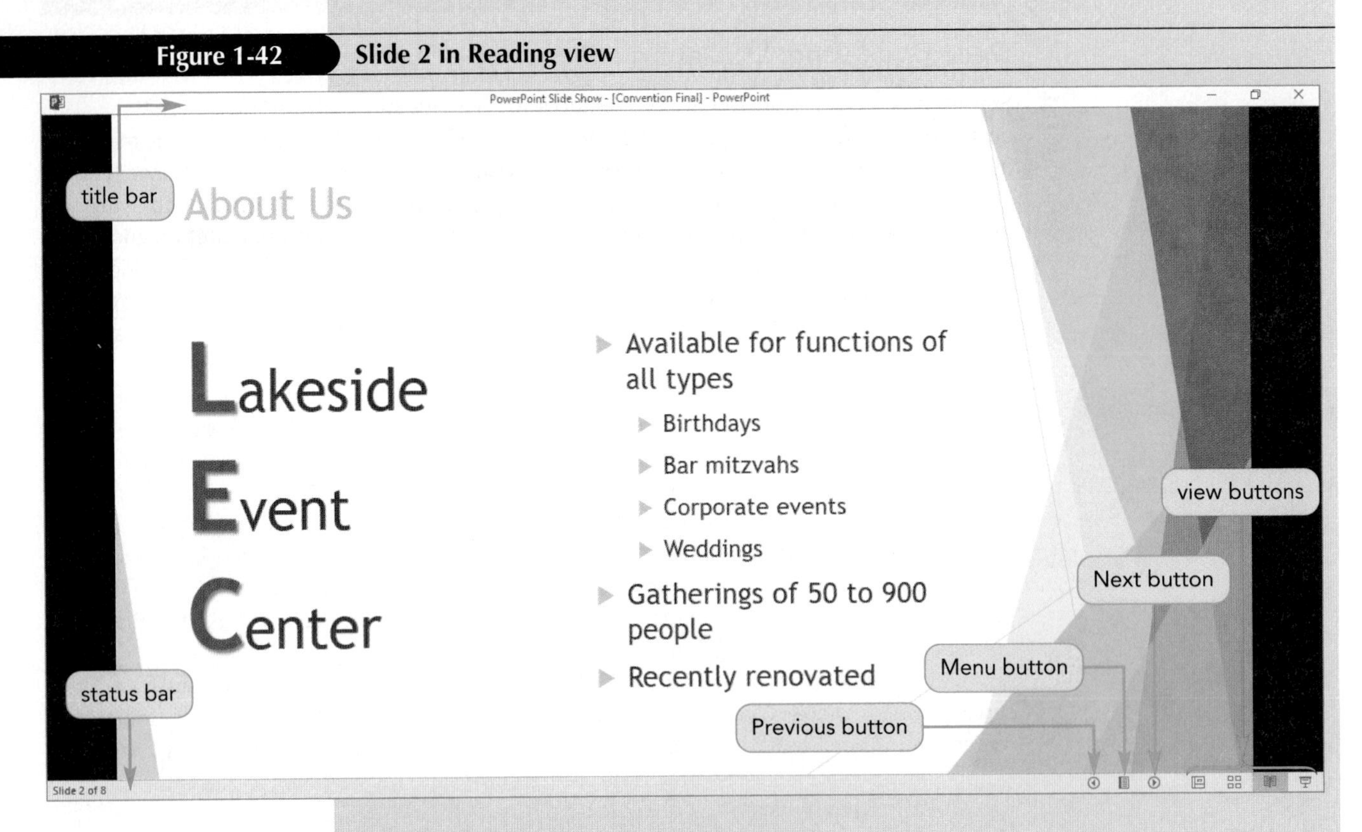

2. On the status bar, click the **Menu** button . A menu appears with commands for working in Reading view, some of which are also available in Slide Show and Presenter views.
3. Click **Full Screen**. The presentation switches to Slide Show view displaying the current slide, Slide 2.
4. Press the **Esc** key. Slide Show view closes, and you return to Reading view.
5. On the status bar, click the **Next** button . The next slide, Slide 3 ("Benefits of Lakeside Event Center"), appears on the screen.
6. On the status bar, click the **Normal** button to return to Normal view with Slide 1 displayed in the Slide pane.

Printing a Presentation

Before you deliver your presentation, you might want to print it. PowerPoint provides several printing options. For example, you can print the slides in color, grayscale (white and shades of gray), or pure black and white, and you can print one, some, or all of the slides in several formats.

You use the Print screen in Backstage view to set print options such as specifying a printer and color options. First, you will add your name to the title slide.

To add your name to the title slide and choose a printer and color options:

1. Display **Slide 1**, click after Keough-Barton in the subtitle, press the **Enter** key, and then type your full name.

2. Click the **File** tab to display Backstage view, and then click **Print** in the navigation bar. Backstage view changes to display the Print screen. The Print screen contains options for printing your presentation, and a preview of the first slide as it will print with the current options. See Figure 1-43.

Figure 1-43 **Print screen in Backstage view**

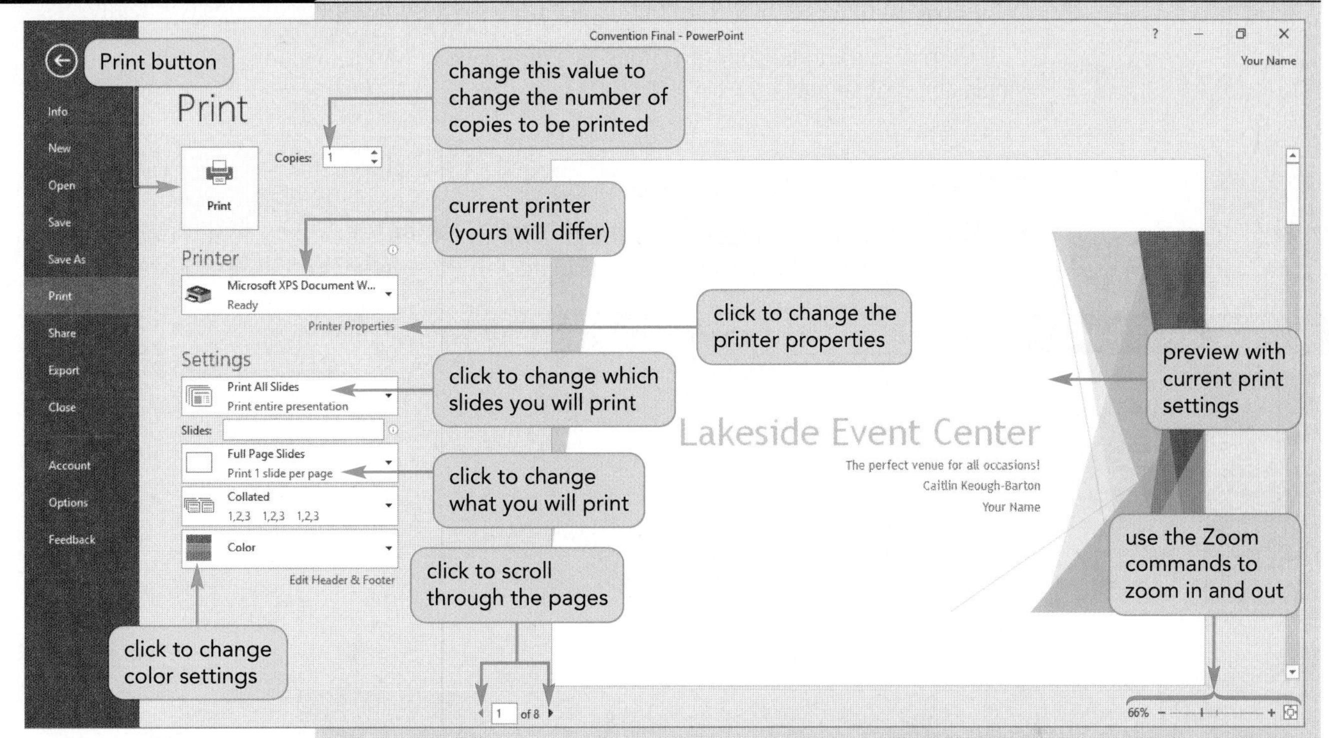

Trouble? If your screen does not match Figure 1-43, click the first button below Settings, and then click Print All Slides, and then click the second button below Settings and then click Full Page Slides.

3. If you are connected to a network or to more than one printer, make sure the printer listed in the Printer box is the one you want to use; if it is not, click the **Printer** button, and then click the correct printer in the list.
4. Click the **Printer Properties** link to open the Properties dialog box for your printer. Usually, the default options are correct, but you can change any printer settings, such as print quality or the paper source, in this dialog box.
5. Click the **Cancel** button to close the Properties dialog box. Now you can choose whether to print the presentation in color, black and white, or grayscale. If you plan to print in black and white or grayscale, you should change this setting so you can see what your slides will look like without color and to make sure they are legible.
6. Click the **Color** button, and then click **Grayscale**. The preview changes to grayscale.
7. At the bottom of the preview pane, click the **Next Page** button ▶ twice to display Slide 3 ("Benefits of Lakeside Event Center"). The slides are legible in grayscale.
8. If you will be printing in color, click the **Grayscale** button, and then click **Color**.

In the Settings section on the Print screen, you can click the Full Page Slides button to choose from among several choices for printing the presentation, as described below:

- **Full Page Slides**—Prints each slide full size on a separate piece of paper.
- **Notes Pages**—Prints each slide as a notes page.
- **Outline**—Prints the text of the presentation as an outline.
- **Handouts**—Prints the presentation with one or more slides on each piece of paper. When printing four, six, or nine slides, you can choose whether to order the slides from left to right in rows (horizontally) or from top to bottom in columns (vertically).

Caitlin wants you to print the slides as a one-page handout, with all eight slides on a single sheet of paper.

To print the slides as a handout:

1. In the Settings section, click the **Full Page Slides** button. A menu opens listing the various ways you can print the slides. See Figure 1-44.

Figure 1-44 **Print screen in Backstage view with print options menu open**

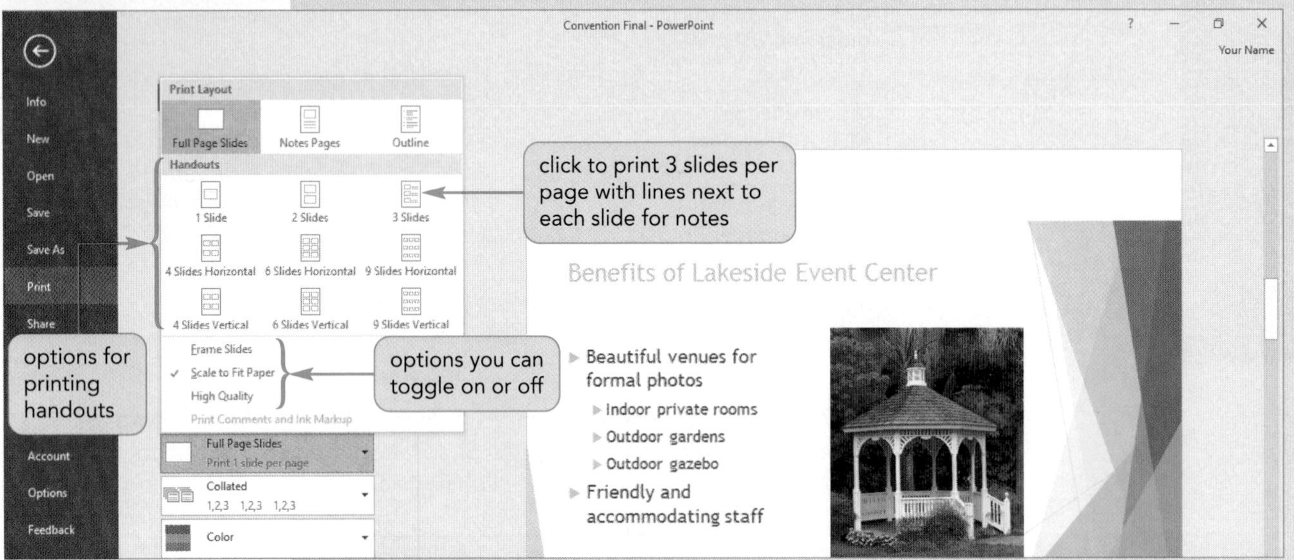

©iStock.com/bloggityblog

2. In the Handouts section, click **9 Slides Horizontal**. The preview changes to show all eight slides in the preview pane, arranged in order horizontally, that is, in three rows from left to right. The current date appears in the top-right corner, and a page number appears in the bottom-right corner.
3. At the top of the Print section, click the **Print** button. Backstage view closes and the handout prints.

Next, Caitlin wants you to print the title slide as a full-page slide so that she can use it as a cover page for her handouts.

To print the title slide as a full-page slide:

1. Click the **File** tab, and then click **Print** in the navigation bar. The Print screen appears in Backstage view. The preview still shows all eight slides on one page. "9 Slides Horizontal" appears on the second button in the Settings section because that was the last printing option you chose.

2. In the Settings section, click **9 Slides Horizontal**, and then click **Full Page Slides**. Slide 1 (the title slide) appears as the preview. Below the preview of Slide 1, it indicates that you are viewing Slide 1 of eight slides to print.
3. In the Settings section, click the **Print All Slides** button. Note on the menu that opens that you can print all the slides, selected slides, the current slide, or a custom range. You want to print just the title slide as a full-page slide.
4. Click **Print Current Slide**. Slide 1 appears in the preview pane, and at the bottom, it now indicates that you will print only one slide.
5. Click the **Print** button. Backstage view closes and Slide 1 prints.

Recall that you created speaker notes on Slides 3 and 7. Caitlin would like you to print these slides as notes pages.

To print the nonsequential slides containing speaker notes:

1. Open the Print screen in Backstage view again, and then click the **Full Page Slides** button. The menu opens.
2. In the Print Layout section of the menu, click **Notes Pages**. The menu closes, and the preview displays Slide 1 as a Notes Page.
3. In the Settings section, click in the **Slides** box, type **3,7** and then click a blank area of the Print screen.
4. Scroll through the preview to confirm that Slides 3 ("Benefits of Lakeside Event Center") and 7 ("For More Information") will print, and then click the **Print** button. Backstage view closes, and Slides 3 and 7 print as notes pages.

Finally, Caitlin would like you to print the outline of the presentation. Recall that Slide 8 is designed to be a visual Caitlin can leave displayed at the end of the presentation, so you don't need to include it in the outline.

To print Slides 1 through 7 as an outline:

1. Open the Print tab in Backstage view, click the **Notes Pages** button, and then in the Print Layout section, click **Outline**. The text on Slides 3 and 7 appears as an outline in the preview pane.
2. Click in the **Slides** box, type **1-7** and then click a blank area of the Print screen. See Figure 1-45.

Figure 1-45 Print screen in Backstage view with Slides 1–7 previewed as an outline

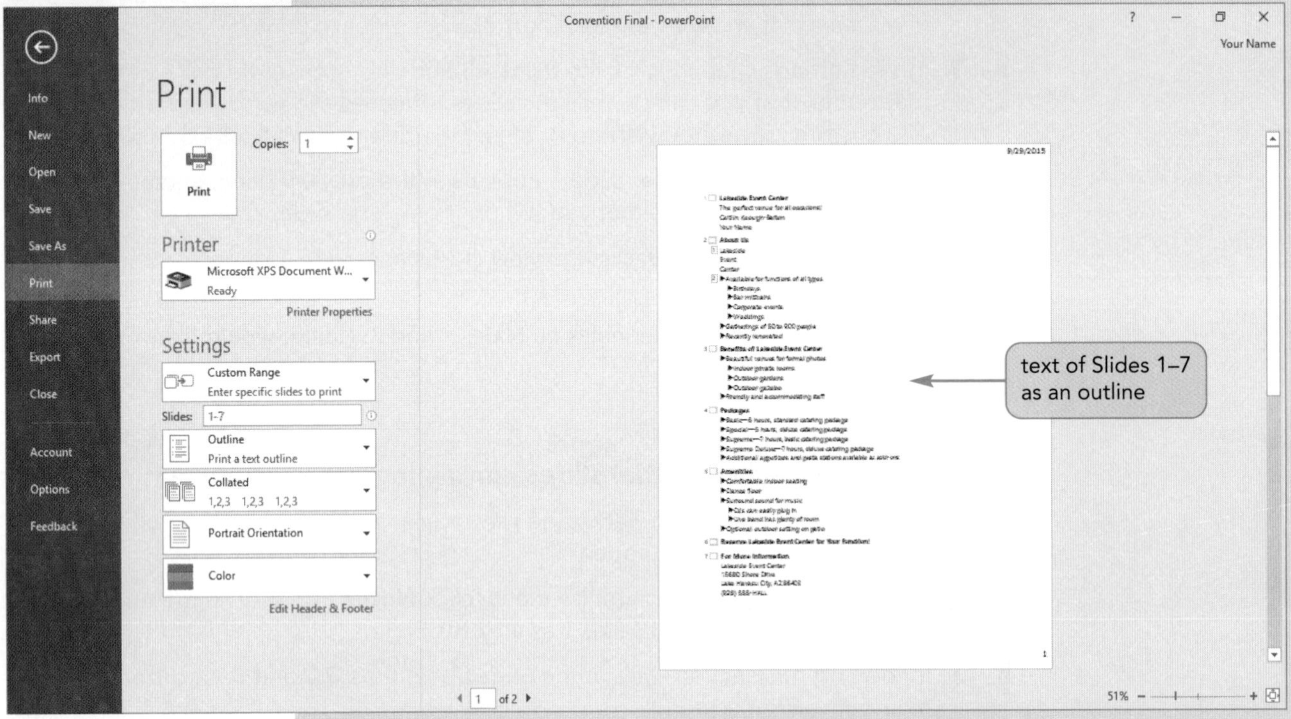

3. At the top of the Print section, click the **Print** button. Backstage view closes, and the text of Slides 1–7 prints on two sheets of paper.

Exiting PowerPoint

When you are finished working with your presentation, you can exit PowerPoint. If there is only one presentation open, you click the Close button in the upper-right corner of the program window to exit the program. If more than one presentation is open, clicking this button will only close the current presentation; to exit PowerPoint, you need to click the Close button in each of the open presentation's windows.

To exit PowerPoint:

1. In the upper-right corner of the program window, click the **Close** button. A dialog box opens, asking if you want to save your changes. This is because you did not save the file after you added your name to the title slide.
2. In the dialog box, click the **Save** button. The dialog box closes, the changes are saved, and PowerPoint exits.

   Trouble? If any other PowerPoint presentations are still open, click the Close button on each open presentation's program window until no more presentations are open to exit PowerPoint.

In this session, you opened an existing presentation and saved it with a new name, changed the theme, added and cropped photos and adjusted the photo compression, and resized and moved objects. You have also added speaker notes and checked the spelling. Finally, you printed the presentation in several forms and exited PowerPoint. Your work will help Caitlin give an effective presentation to potential clients of Lakeside Event Center.

REVIEW

Session 1.2 Quick Check

1. Explain what a theme is and what changes with each variant.
2. Describe what happens when you crop photos.
3. Describe sizing handles.
4. Describe smart guides.
5. Why is it important to maintain the aspect ratio of photos?
6. What is the difference between Slide Show view and Presenter view?
7. List the four formats for printing a presentation.

PRACTICE

Review Assignments

Data Files needed for the Review Assignments: DJ.jpg, Musicians.jpg, Photog.jpg, Vendor2.pptx

In addition to booking new clients, Caitlin Keough-Barton, the event manager at Lakeside Event Center, maintains a preferred vendors list for providing additional services of entertainment, music, photography, and so on that clients might want. If clients who book the hall use a preferred vendor, they receive a discount on the price of the vendor's services. Caitlin wants to create a presentation that she can use when she meets with new vendors to describe their responsibilities to both the function hall and to the clients. She asks you to begin creating the presentation.

1. Start PowerPoint and create a new, blank presentation. On the title slide, type **Information for Vendors** as the title, and then type your name as the subtitle. Save the presentation as **Vendor Info** to the drive and folder where you are storing your files.
2. Edit the slide title by adding **Lakeside Event Center** before the word "Vendors."
3. Add a new Slide 2 with the Title and Content layout, type **Types of Vendors We Partner With** as the slide title, and then in the content placeholder type the following:
   - **Photographers**
   - **Videographers**
   - **Florists**
   - **Music**
     - **DJs**
     - **Bands**
4. Create a new Slide 3 with the Title and Content layout. Add **Requirements for Vendors** as the slide title, and then type the following as a numbered list on the slide:
   1) **Supply advertisement for brochure**
   2) **Pay annual fee by January 15**
   3) **Submit availability schedule for clients**
   4) **Contact Caitlin Keough-Barton**
5. Create a new Slide 4 using the Two Content layout. Add **Questions?** as the slide title.
6. Use the Cut and Paste commands to move the last bulleted item on Slide 3 ("Contact Caitlin Keough-Barton") to the left content placeholder on Slide 4.
7. On Slide 4, remove the bullet symbol from the text you pasted, and then add the following as the next two items in the unnumbered list:

   Email: c.keoughbarton@example.com

   Cell: 602-555-8723
8. Click after "Keough-Barton" in the first item in the list, and then create a new line below it without creating a new item in the list and so that there is no extra space above the new line. On the new line, type **Events Manager**.
9. Remove the hyperlink formatting from the email address.
10. Create a new Slide 5 using the Title and Content layout. Delete the title text placeholder. In the content placeholder, type **Thank You!** as a single item in an unnumbered list. Increase the size of the text "Thank You!" to 96 points, and then change the color of this text to Blue, Accent 1.
11. On Slide 3 ("Requirements for Vendors"), change the numbered list to a SmartArt graphic. Use the Vertical Circle List layout, which is a List type of diagram.
12. Save your changes, and then close the presentation.
13. Open the file **Vendor2**, located in the PowerPoint1 > Review folder included with your Data Files, add your name as the subtitle on the title slide, and then save it as **LEC Vendor Information** to the drive and folder where you are storing your files.

14. Change the theme to Basis and choose the third variant. On Slide 2, change the size of the text in the bulleted list so that the size of the text of the first-level items is 28 points and the size of the text of the second-level items is 24 points.
15. Change the layout of Slide 4 ("Photographers") to Title and Content, and then duplicate Slide 4. In the title of Slide 5 (the duplicate slide), replace the slide title with **Music Vendors**.
16. On Slide 4, insert the photo **Photog**, located in the PowerPoint1 > Review folder. Resize the photo so it is five inches high, maintaining the aspect ratio, and reposition it so its top and right edges are aligned with the top and right edges of the slide title text box.
17. On Slide 5, change the layout to Two Content, and then in the content placeholder on the left, insert the photo **DJ**. Crop the photo from the right about one-half inch and from the top about one-quarter inch. Resize the cropped photo so it is 2.4 inches high, maintaining the aspect ratio, and then reposition the photo so its left edge is aligned with the left edge of the slide title text box and its middle is aligned with the middle of the content placeholder on the right.
18. On Slide 5, in the content placeholder on the right, insert the photo **Musicians**. Resize it so that it is 2.5 inches tall. Position it so that its right edge is aligned with the right edge of the slide title text box and its middle is aligned with the middle of the photo on the left.
19. Move Slide 5 ("Music Vendors") so it becomes Slide 7.
20. On Slide 9 ("Questions?"), crop the photo to the Oval shape. Increase the size of the text in the unnumbered list to 20 points, and then resize the text box to make it wide enough so that the line containing the email address fits on one line. Remove the hyperlink formatting from the email address.
21. Compress all the photos in the slides to 96 ppi and delete cropped areas of pictures.
22. On Slide 4 ("Photographers"), add **Must be available for the entire event. Should be able to take both formal portraits and candids.** in the Notes pane. On Slide 7 ("Music Vendors"), add **Must be available for the entire time during the event. Should be versatile and be able to play music for all audiences.** as a note on this slide.
23. Delete Slide 3 ("Vendor Requirements") and the last slide (the blank slide).
24. Check the spelling in the presentation. Correct the two spelling errors on Slide 7, ignore all instances of Caitlin's last name, and ignore the flagged instance of "candids" in the Notes pane on Slide 3 ("Photographers"). If you made any additional spelling errors, correct them as well. Save the changes to the presentation.
25. Review the slide show in Slide Show, Presenter, and Reading views.
26. View the slides in grayscale, and then print the following in color or in grayscale depending on your printer: the title slide as a full-page-sized slide; Slides 1–9 as a handout on a single piece of paper with the slides in order horizontally; Slides 3 and 6 as notes pages; and Slides 1–8 as an outline. Save and close the presentation when you are finished.

APPLY

Case Problem 1

Data Files needed for this Case Problem: After.jpg, Before.jpg, Clients.pptx, Team.jpg, Windows.jpg

Cleaning Essentials Suzanne Yang owns Cleaning Essentials, a home cleaning company in New Rochelle, New York. She markets her company at home shows in Westchester County and in New York City. She asks you to help her create PowerPoint slides that she will use at the home shows. Complete the following steps:

1. Open the presentation named **Clients**, located in the PowerPoint1 > Case1 folder included with your Data Files, and then save it as **New Clients** to the drive and folder where you are storing your files.
2. Insert a new Slide 1 that has the Title Slide layout. Add **Cleaning Essentials** as the presentation title on the title slide. In the subtitle text placeholder, type your name.

3. Create a new Slide 2 with the Title and Content layout. Add **What Is Cleaning Essentials?** as the slide title, and **An affordable door-to-door cleaning service designed to make a homeowner's life easier.** as the only item in the content placeholder. Change this to an unnumbered list.
4. Apply the Savon theme, and then apply its second variant. (If the Savon theme is not listed in the Themes gallery, choose any other theme and variant that uses a white or solid color background, places the slide titles at the top of the slides, uses bullet symbols for first-level bulleted items, and positions the content in the bulleted lists so it aligns to the top of the content text box, not the middle.)
5. On Slide 2 ("What Is Cleaning Essentials?"), increase the size of the text in the text box below the slide titles to 28 points.
6. On Slide 3 ("What Services Do We Provide?"), Slide 7 ("Extra Services Offered"), and Slide 9 ("Book Us Now!"), increase the size of the text in the bulleted list so it is 28 points.
7. On Slide 4 ("Why Choose Cleaning Essentials?"), increase the size of the text in the bulleted list so that the first-level items are 24 points.
8. On Slide 2 ("What Is Cleaning Essentials?"), insert the photo **Team**, located in the PowerPoint1 > Case1 folder. Resize the photo, maintaining the aspect ratio, so that it is 3.6 inches wide, and then use the smart guides to position it so that its center is aligned with the center of the text box above it and its bottom is aligned with the bottom border of the text box.
9. On Slide 3 ("What Services Do We Provide?"), add the speaker note **All clients are welcome to request extra services needed to completely clean their homes.**
10. On Slide 6 ("Picture Proof"), change the layout to the Comparison layout, which includes two content placeholders and a small text placeholder above each content placeholder. In the small text placeholder on the left, add **Before**, and then in the small text placeholder on the right, add **After**. Change the font size in both text boxes to 24 points.
11. In the left content placeholder, insert the photo **Before**, and in the right content placeholder, insert the photo **After**.
12. On Slide 5 ("Polish wood floors"), cut the slide title, and then paste it in on Slide 3 ("What Services Do We Provide?") as the fifth bulleted item. If a blank line is added below the pasted text, delete it.
13. On Slide 7 ("Extra Services Offered"), add **Laundry** as a third bulleted item in the list, and then add **Use in-home machines** and **Send out and pick up dry cleaning** as subitems under the "Laundry" first-level item. Change the layout to Two Content.
14. On Slide 7, in the content placeholder, insert the photo **Windows**, located in the PowerPoint1 > Case1 folder. Resize the photo so it is 5 inches high, maintaining the aspect ratio, and then reposition it so that the top of the photo and the top of the title text box are aligned and the right edge of the photo is aligned with the right edge of the title text box.
15. Compress all the photos in the presentation to 96 ppi.
16. On Slide 8 ("Cleaning Visit Options"), add **Once a week** as the second item in the list, and then add **Most popular option** and **Visit is the same day each week** as subitems below "Once a week."
17. On Slide 8, convert the bulleted list to a SmartArt diagram using the Vertical Bullet List layout, which is a List type of diagram. In the Text pane, click before "Still produces a clean and uncluttered home," and then press the Tab key to make it the second subitem under "Once a month."
18. Delete Slide 5 (a blank slide). Move Slide 4 ("Why Choose Cleaning Essentials?") so it becomes Slide 6, and then move Slide 5 ("Extra Services Offered") so it becomes Slide 4.
19. Check the spelling in the presentation and correct all misspelled words.
20. Save the changes to the presentation, view the slide show in Presenter view, and then print the title slide as a full-page slide, print Slides 2–8 as a handout using the 9 Slides Horizontal arrangement, and print Slide 3 as a notes page.

TROUBLESHOOT

Case Problem 2

Data Files needed for this Case Problem: Keyboard.jpg, Music.pptx, Richard.jpg

Dillaire Music Richard Dillaire has owned Dillaire Music in Easton, Pennsylvania, since 1991. He sells, rents, and repairs musical instruments, and he teaches students how to play instruments. He wants to expand his business and attract new students, so he asks you to help him create a presentation. He created slides containing text and a few photos that he wants to include, and he wants you to finish the presentation by inserting additional photos and formatting the presentation. Complete the following steps:

1. Open the file named **Music**, located in the PowerPoint1 > Case2 folder included with your Data Files, and then save it as **Music School** to the drive and folder where you are storing your files. Add your name as the subtitle on Slide 1.
2. **Troubleshoot** Review the presentation to identify the two slides that contain information that is repeated on another slide in the presentation, and delete those slides.
3. Display Slide 1 (the title slide), and then apply the Headlines theme to the presentation. Change the variant to the second variant.
4. **Troubleshoot** Evaluate the problem that the theme change caused on Slide 1 and fix it.
5. **Troubleshoot** Consider how changing the theme affected the readability of the lists on the slides and the size of the photos in the file. Make the appropriate changes to the slides. (*Hint:* On the slides that have pictures of a child playing an instrument on them, the first-level items should not be larger than 24 points.)
6. On Slide 8 ("Contact Info"), in the first item in the bulleted list, move "Easton, PA 18042" to a new line below the street address without creating a new bulleted item.
7. Move Slide 7 ("Lessons") so it becomes Slide 4.
8. On Slide 7 ("How to register online"), change the bulleted list to a numbered list. Add as a new item 2 **Click the green Apply button**.
9. Change the layout of Slide 8 ("Contact Info") to Two Content, and then insert the photo **Richard**, located in the PowerPoint1 > Case2 folder, in the content placeholder. Crop off about one-half inch from the top of the photo, and then increase the size of the picture, maintaining the aspect ratio, so that it is 3 inches wide. Reposition the photo so it is vertically centered below the slide title and bottom aligned with the bottom of the slide title text box.
10. On Slide 1 (the title slide), insert the photo **Keyboard** located in the PowerPoint1 > Case2 folder. Resize the photo so it is 5.25 inches square, and then position it so it is aligned with the right and bottom edges of the slide.
11. Compress all the photos in the presentation to 96 ppi and delete cropped portions of photos.
12. Check the spelling in the presentation, and then save the changes.
13. View the slide show in Presenter view, zooming in on the pictures in the presentation.
14. Print the title slide as a full-page slide in grayscale, and then print the entire presentation as an outline.

CREATE

Case Problem 3

Data Files needed for this Case Problem: Beach.jpg, House1.jpg, House2.jpg, House3.jpg, House4.jpg, House5.jpg, Realty.pptx

Shoreside Realty Karen Bridges owns Shoreside Realty, a real estate company in Scarborough, Maine, that specializes in selling and renting homes in local beach communities. As part of her marketing, she attends local events, such as the farmers' market, weekly summer concerts, and chamber of commerce events, and shows photos of houses near beaches for sale or rent. She created a presentation with slides containing the addresses and brief descriptions of newly listed properties. She asks you to finish the presentation. The completed presentation is shown in Figure 1-46. Refer to Figure 1-46 as you complete the following steps:

Figure 1-46 Shoreside Realty presentation

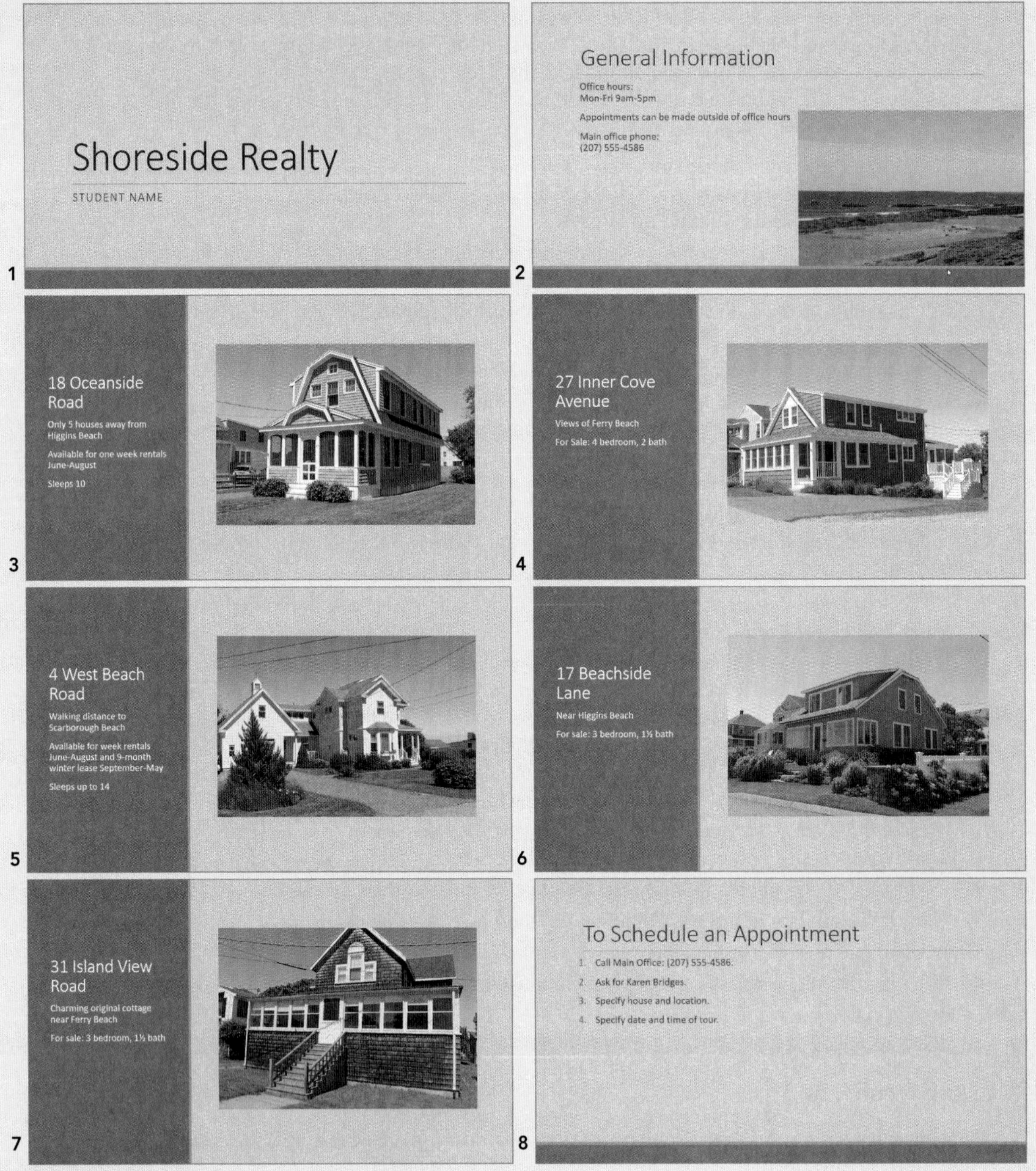

Courtesy of Helen M. Pinard

1. Open the file named **Realty**, located in the PowerPoint1 > Case3 folder included with your Data Files, and then save it as **Shoreside Realty** to the drive and folder where you are storing your files.
2. Add a new slide with the Title Slide layout, and move it so it is Slide 1. Type **Shoreside Realty** as the title and your name as the subtitle.
3. Move Slide 8 ("General Information") so it becomes Slide 2, and then delete Slide 3 ("Newest Homes on the Market").
4. Change the theme to Retrospect, and the variant of the Retrospect theme to the seventh variant. (Note that in this theme, bulleted lists do not have any bullet symbols before each item.)
5. On Slide 2 ("General Information"), in the first item in the list, move the phone number so it appears on the next line, without any additional line space above the phone number. Then move the text "Mon–Fri 9am–5pm" so it appears on the next line, without any additional line space above it.
6. On Slide 2, move the "Main office phone" list item and the phone number so these appear as the last list items on the slide.
7. On Slide 2, insert the photo **Beach**, located in the PowerPoint1 > Case3 folder. Crop two inches from the top of the photo, and then resize the photo so that it is 3.4 inches high.
8. On Slide 2, position the photo so that its right edge is flush with the right edge of the slide and so that its bottom edge is slightly on top of the lighter blue line at the bottom of the slide.
9. Change the layout of Slides 3 through 7 to Content with Caption. On all five slides, move the unnumbered list from the content placeholder on the right to the text placeholders on the left, as shown in Figure 1-46, and then change the font size of the text in the unnumbered lists you moved to 16 points. Then insert the photos named **House1** through **House5** provided in the PowerPoint1 > Case3 folder on Slides 3 through 7, using Figure 1-46 as a guide.
10. Compress all the photos in the presentation to 96 ppi.
11. On Slide 8 ("To Schedule an Appointment"), change the list to a numbered list, and then add **Specify house and location.** as a new item 3.
12. Save the changes to the presentation, and then view the presentation in Reading view.

CHALLENGE

Case Problem 4

Data Files needed for this Case Problem: Ballet.jpg, Dancing.mp4, HipHop.jpg, Jazz.jpg, Jump.jpg, Leap.jpg, Modern.jpg, and Tap.jpg

Greater Dayton Dance Academy Paul LaCroix owns Greater Dayton Dance Academy, a dance studio that teaches students ages two through adult. He has an open house every September to attract new students. He asks you to help him create a presentation that includes photos and video that he can show at the open house. Complete the following steps:

Explore 1. Create a new presentation using the Striped black border presentation template from Office.com. (*Hint:* Use "striped black border" as the search term. If you get no results, type **white** as the search term, and then choose a template with a simple theme.)

2. Replace the title text on the title slide with **Greater Dayton Dance Academy**, and replace the subtitle text with your name. Save the presentation as **New Students** to the drive and folder where you are storing your files.
3. Delete all the slides except the title slide.
4. Add a new Slide 2 with the Two Content layout. Add **About Us** as the title, and then type the following as a bulleted list in the left content placeholder:
    - **Recreational classes meet once a week**
    - **Competitive classes meet 3 to 5 times a week**
    - **Private lessons available**
    - **Annual winter and spring productions**

5. On Slide 2, in the right content placeholder, insert the photo **Leap**, located in the PowerPoint1 > Case4 folder included with your Data Files. Resize it, maintaining the aspect ratio, so it is 3.8 inches high, and then reposition it so that the top edge of the photo is aligned with the top edge of the text box and the left edge of the photo is aligned with the right edge of the text box.
6. Add a new Slide 3 with the Title and Content layout. Add **Styles Offered** as the title, and then type the following as a bulleted list in the content placeholder:
   - **Ballet**
   - **Modern**
   - **Jazz**
   - **Tap**
   - **Hip Hop**
7. On Slide 3, convert the bulleted list to a SmartArt diagram with the Bending Picture Semi-Transparent Text layout, which is a Picture type of diagram.

Explore 8. Change the colors of the diagram to Colorful Range – Accent Colors 3 to 4 by using the Change Colors button in the SmartArt Styles group on the SmartArt Tools Design tab.

Explore 9. Insert the following pictures, located in the PowerPoint1 > Case4 folder, in the appropriate picture placeholders in the SmartArt diagram: **Ballet**, **Modern**, **Jazz**, **Tap**, and **HipHop**.

10. Add a new Slide 4 with the Two Content layout. Add **Call Today!** as the title. In the content placeholder on the left, type the following as an unnumbered list (no bullets) without extra space between the lines:

    Greater Dayton Dance Academy

    1158 North St.

    Dayton, OH 45417
11. On Slide 4, add the phone number **(937) 555-1254** and the website address **www.daytondance.example.com** as new items in the unnumbered list. Press the spacebar after typing the website address to format it as a link.
12. On Slide 4, change the size of the text in the unnumbered list to 22 point. (*Hint:* Click in the Font Size box, type **22**, and then press the **Enter** key.)
13. On Slide 4, add the photo **Jump**, located in the PowerPoint1 > Case4 folder, to the content placeholder on the right. Resize it so it is 3.6 inches high, maintaining the aspect ratio, and then position it so the top edge aligns with the top edge of the text box on the left and there is approximately one inch of space between the right side of the photo and the right edge of the slide.
14. Compress all the photos in the presentation to 96 ppi, and then save the changes.
15. Add a new Slide 5 with the Two Content layout. Add **Classic Ballet Technique Emphasized** as the title. In the content placeholder on the right, add **Because ballet is the foundation of all dance, all students are required to take ballet technique classes.** Remove the bullet from this item.
16. Move this slide so it becomes Slide 4.

Explore 17. On Slide 4 ("Classic Ballet Technique Emphasized"), insert the video **Dancing**, located in the PowerPoint1 > Case4 folder, in the content placeholder.

Explore 18. Open the Info tab in Backstage view. Use the Compress Media command to compress the videos to the lowest quality possible. Use the Back button at the top of the navigation bar in Backstage view to return to Normal view.

19. Save the changes to the presentation, and then run the slide show in Slide Show view. When Slide 4 ("Classic Ballet Technique Emphasized") appears, point to the video to make a Play button appear, and then click the Play button to play the 20-second video. (*Hint:* Point to the video as it plays to display the play bar again.)

MODULE 2

Adding Media and Special Effects

Using Media in a Presentation for a Nonprofit River Cleaning Organization

POWERPOINT

OBJECTIVES

Session 2.1
- Apply a theme used in another presentation
- Insert shapes
- Format shapes and pictures
- Rotate and flip objects
- Create a table
- Modify and format a table
- Insert symbols
- Add footers and headers

Session 2.2
- Apply and modify transitions
- Animate objects and bulleted lists
- Change how an animation starts
- Add video and modify playback options
- Understand animation effects applied to videos
- Trim video and set a poster frame
- Compress media
- Create a mix

Case | *RiverClean*

José Quiñones is a volunteer for RiverClean™, a nonprofit organization in New England that raises money and supports volunteer efforts to clean riverbanks in the area. José lives in Lowell, Massachusetts, where several intense storms have knocked down tree limbs, some of which block access to the Riverwalk trail next to the Merrimack River. In addition to the storm damage, portions of the trail are overgrown and in disrepair, and many areas along the trail have significant erosion problems. José wants to present this information to the city councilors so that he can get permission to organize a trail cleanup and obtain some funding for the project as well. José prepared the text of a PowerPoint presentation, and he wants you to add photos and other features to make the presentation more interesting and compelling.

In this module, you will modify a presentation that illustrates the poor conditions of the Riverwalk trail and estimates costs for addressing the problems. You will add formatting and special effects to photos and shapes, add transitions and animations to slides, and add and modify video.

STARTING DATA FILES

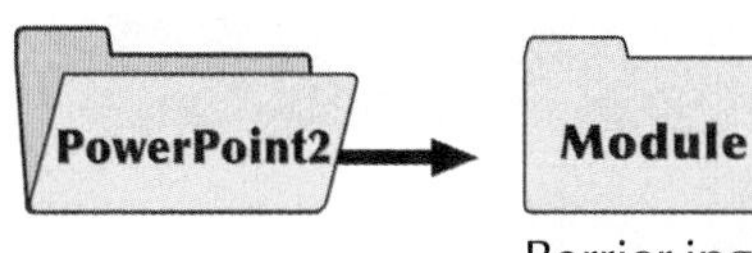

Module

Barrier.jpg
Erosion1.jpg
Erosion2.mp4
Mix.pptx
Riverwalk.pptx
Sign.jpg
Stairs.jpg
Tree.jpg
WalkTheme.pptx

Review

Cleared.jpg
Landscape.jpg
NewSign.jpg
NewStairs.jpg
NewTheme.pptx
NewView.mp4
Railings.jpg
Renewed1.pptx
Renewed2.pptx
Wall.jpg

Case1

Equipment.jpg
Exercise.mp4
FitTheme.pptx
HomeFit.pptx

Case2

Build.jpg
Finish.jpg
Furniture.pptx
Sand.jpg
Sketch.jpg
Trees.jpg

Case3

Paws.pptx
PawsTheme.pptx

Case4

Candy.png
CarePak.pptx
CPTheme.pptx
Games.png
Personal.png
Salty.png

Session 2.1 Visual Overview:

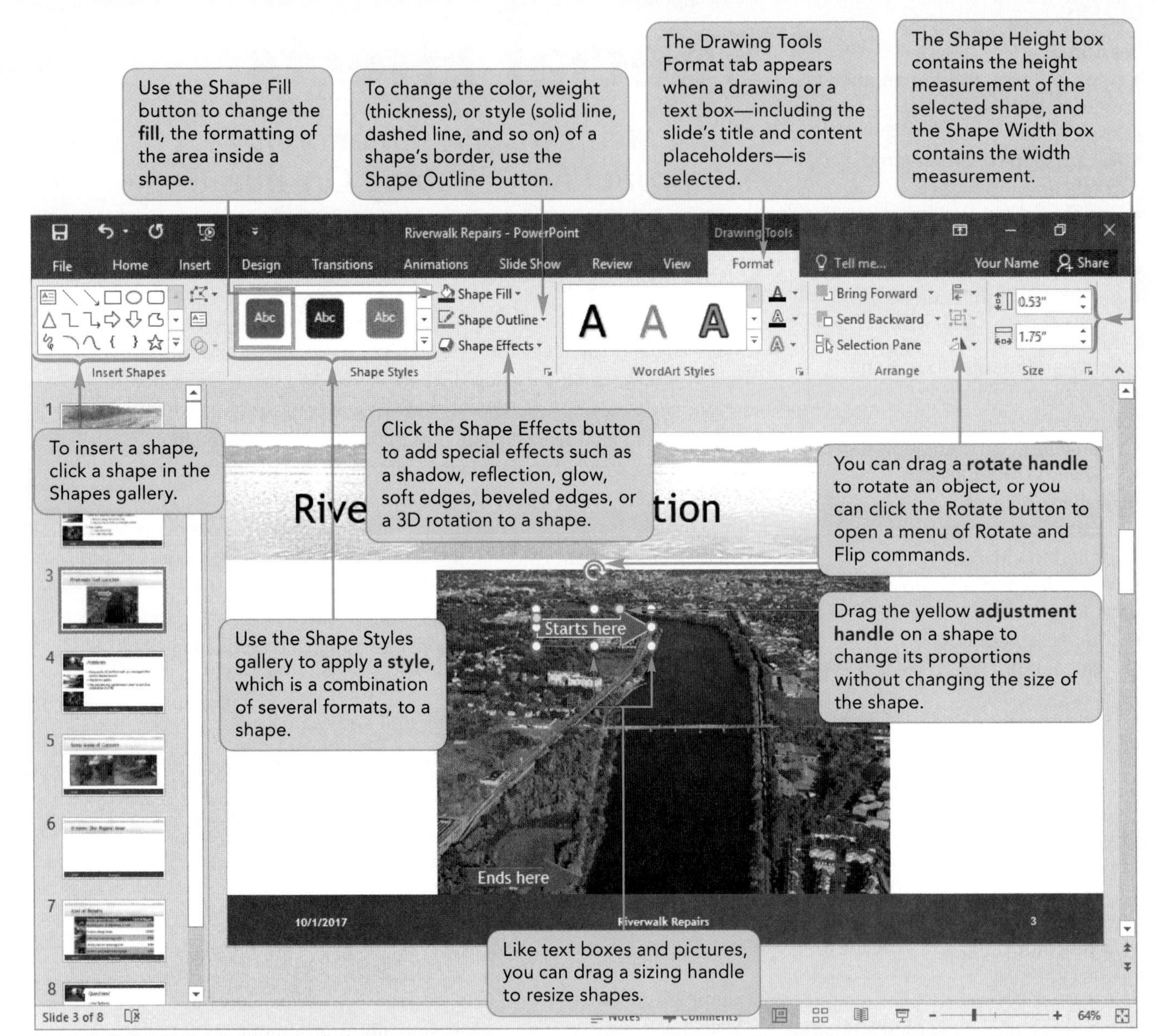

Formatting Graphics

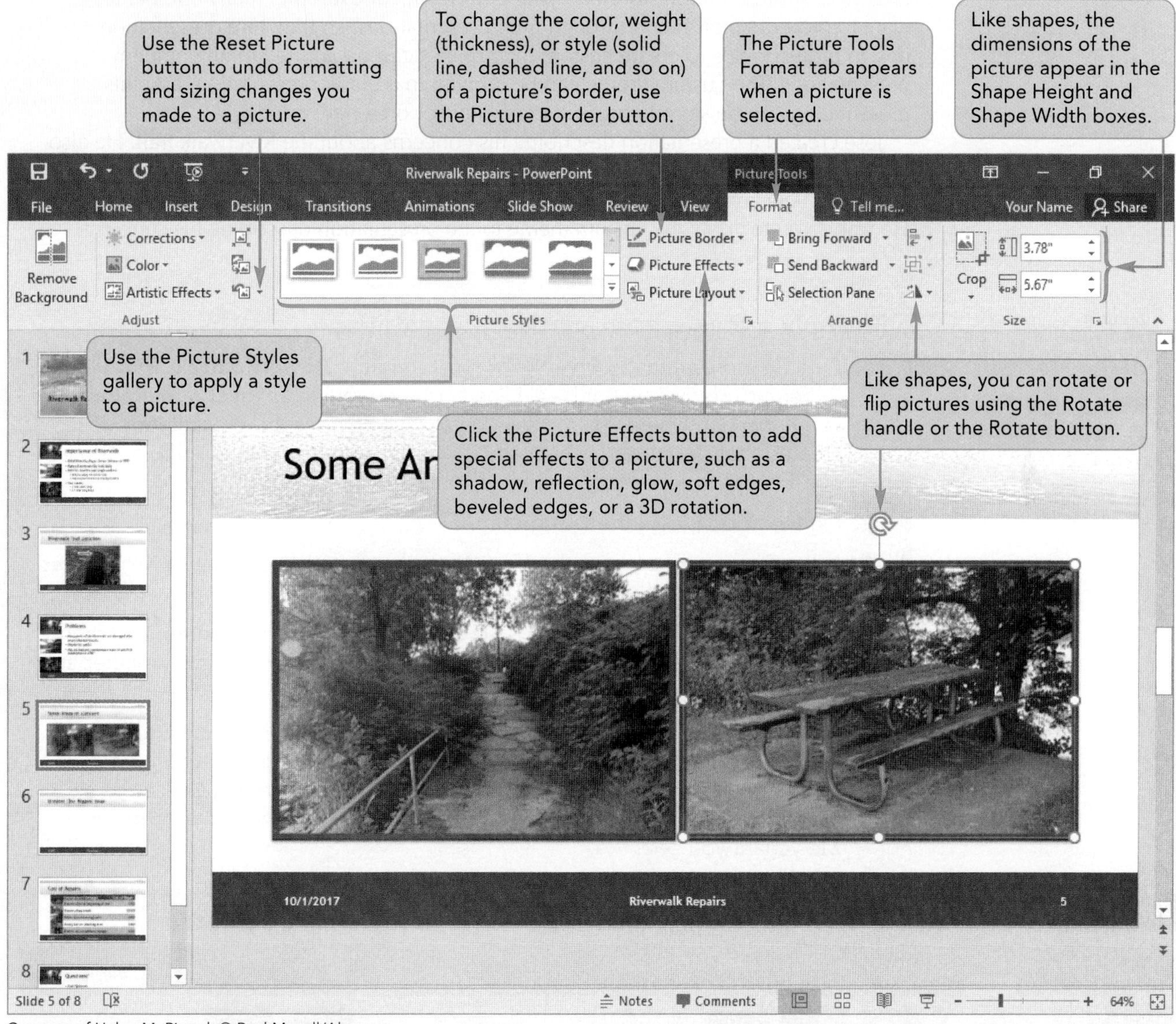

Courtesy of Helen M. Pinard; © Paul Mozell/Alamy

Applying a Theme Used in Another Presentation

As you learned earlier, an installed theme can be applied by clicking one in the Themes group on the Design tab. An installed theme is actually a special type of file that is stored with PowerPoint program files. You can also apply themes that are applied to any other presentation stored on your computer. For example, many companies want to promote their brand through their presentations, so they hire presentation design professionals to create custom themes that can be applied to all company presentations. The custom theme can be applied to a blank presentation, and this presentation can be stored on users' computers or on a network drive.

José created a presentation describing his concerns about the Riverwalk trail. He also created a custom theme by changing the theme fonts and colors, modifying layouts, and creating a new layout. He applied this theme to a blank presentation that he sent to you. He wants you to apply the custom theme to the presentation describing his concerns.

To apply a theme from another presentation:

1. Open the presentation **Riverwalk**, located in the **PowerPoint2** > **Module** folder included with your Data Files, and then save it as **Riverwalk Repairs** in the location where you are saving your files. This is the presentation José created that describes his concerns. The Office theme is applied to it. You need to apply José's custom theme to it.
2. On the ribbon, click the **Design** tab.
3. In the Themes group, click the **More** button, and then click **Browse for Themes**. The Choose Theme or Themed Document dialog box opens.
4. Navigate to the **PowerPoint2** > **Module** folder, click **WalkTheme**, and then click the **Apply** button. The custom theme is applied to the Riverwalk Repairs presentation.
5. In the Themes group, point to the first theme in the gallery, which is the current theme. Its ScreenTip identifies it as the WalkTheme. See Figure 2-1. Although variants appear in the Variants group, these are the Office theme variants, and if you click one of them, you will reapply the Office theme with the variant you selected.

Figure 2-1 **Custom WalkTheme applied**

Courtesy of Helen M. Pinard

6. Click the **Home** tab, and then on Slide 1 (the title slide), click **Riverwalk Repairs**, the title text.

7. In the Font group, click the **Font arrow**. Notice that Trebuchet MS is the theme font for both the headings and the body text. This is different from the Office theme, which uses Calibri for the body text and Calibri Light for the headings.
8. In the Slides group, click the **Layout** button. The Layout gallery appears. The custom layouts that José created are listed in the gallery, as shown in Figure 2-2.

Figure 2-2 **Custom layouts in the WalkTheme custom theme**

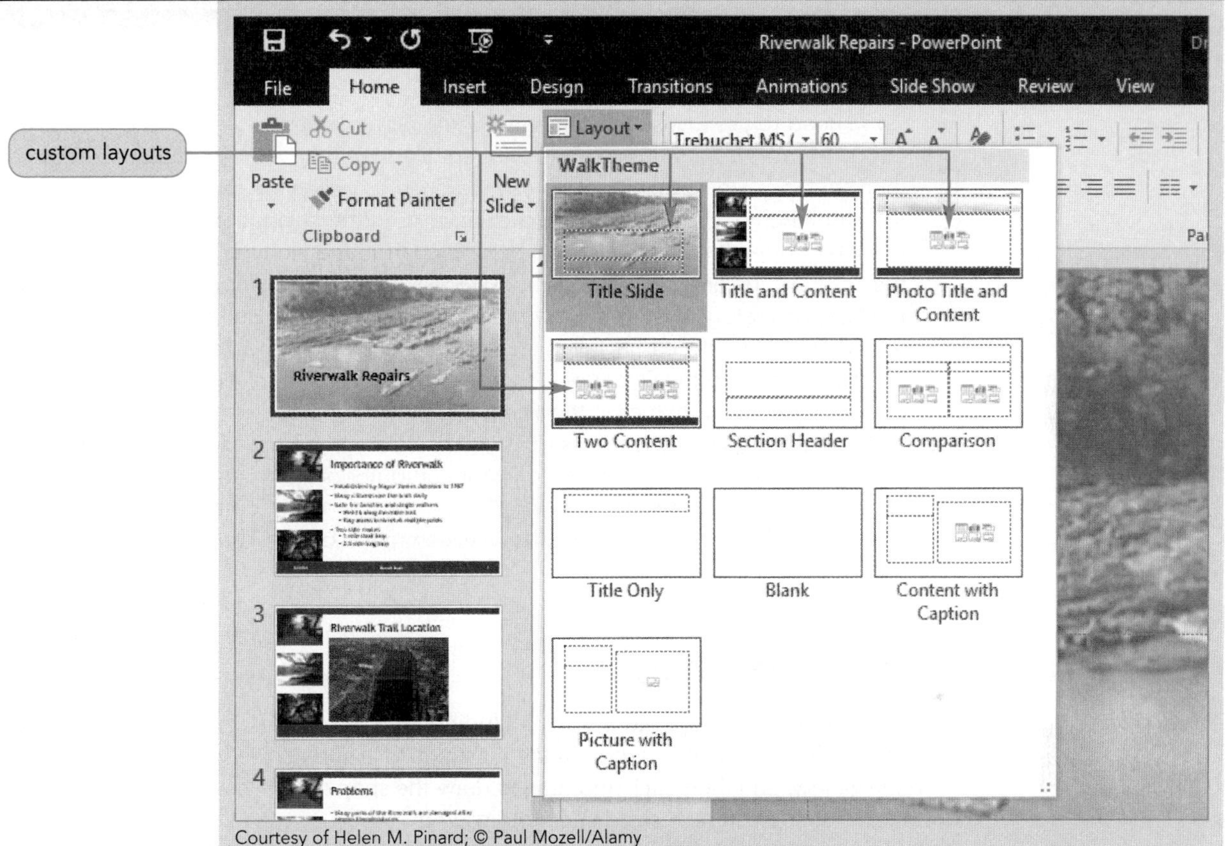

Courtesy of Helen M. Pinard; © Paul Mozell/Alamy

Notice the customized Title Slide layout has a photo as a slide background, the Title and Content customized layout has photos along the left edge of the slide, and the customized Photo Title and Content and the Two Content layouts include a photo under the slide title.

9. Press the **Esc** key to close the Layout gallery.

When you applied the custom theme from the WalkTheme presentation, the title slide and the slides with the Title and Content and Two Content layouts were changed to use the customized versions of these layouts. José wants you to change the layout of Slides 3, 6, and 7 to the custom layout he named Photo Title and Content.

To apply a custom layout to Slides 3, 6, and 7:

1. Display **Slide 3** ("Riverwalk Trail Location").
2. In the Slides group, click the **Layout** button. The Layout gallery appears.

3. Click the **Photo Title and Content** layout. The custom layout is applied to Slide 3.
4. Apply the **Photo Title and Content** layout to Slide 6 ("Erosion: The Biggest Issue") and Slide 7 ("Cost of Repairs").
5. Save your changes.

INSIGHT

Saving a Presentation as a Theme

If you need to use a custom theme frequently, you can save a presentation file as an Office Theme file. A theme file is a different file type than a presentation file. You can then store this file so that it appears in the Themes gallery on the Design tab. To save a custom theme, click the File tab, click Save As in the navigation bar, and then click Browse to open the Save As dialog box. To change the file type to Office Theme, click the Save as type arrow, and then click Office Theme. This changes the current folder in the Save As dialog box to the Document Themes folder, which is a folder created on the hard drive when Office is installed and where the installed themes are stored. If you save a custom theme to the Document Themes folder, that theme will be listed in its own row above the installed themes in the Themes gallery. (You need to click the More button in the Themes gallery to see this row.) You can also change the folder location and save the custom theme to any location on your computer or network or to a folder on your OneDrive. If you do this, the theme will not appear in the Themes gallery, but you can still access it using the Browse for Themes command on the Themes gallery menu.

Inserting Shapes

You can add many shapes to a slide, including lines, rectangles, stars, and more. To draw a shape, click the Shapes button in the Illustrations group on the Insert tab, click a shape in the gallery, and then click and drag to draw the shape in the size you want. Like any object, a shape can be resized after you insert it.

You've already had a little experience with one shape—a text box, which is a shape specifically designed to contain text. You can add additional text boxes to slides using the Text Box shape. You can also add text to any shape you place on a slide.

José wants you to add labels identifying the trail in the aerial photo on Slide 3. You will do this with arrow shapes. First you will add an arrow that points to the start of the trail.

To insert and position an arrow shape with text on Slide 3:

1. Display **Slide 3** ("Riverwalk Trail Location").
2. Click the **Insert** tab, and then in the Illustrations group, click the **Shapes** button. The Shapes gallery opens. See Figure 2-3. In addition to the Recently Used Shapes group at the top, the gallery is organized into nine categories of shapes.

Figure 2-3 Shapes gallery

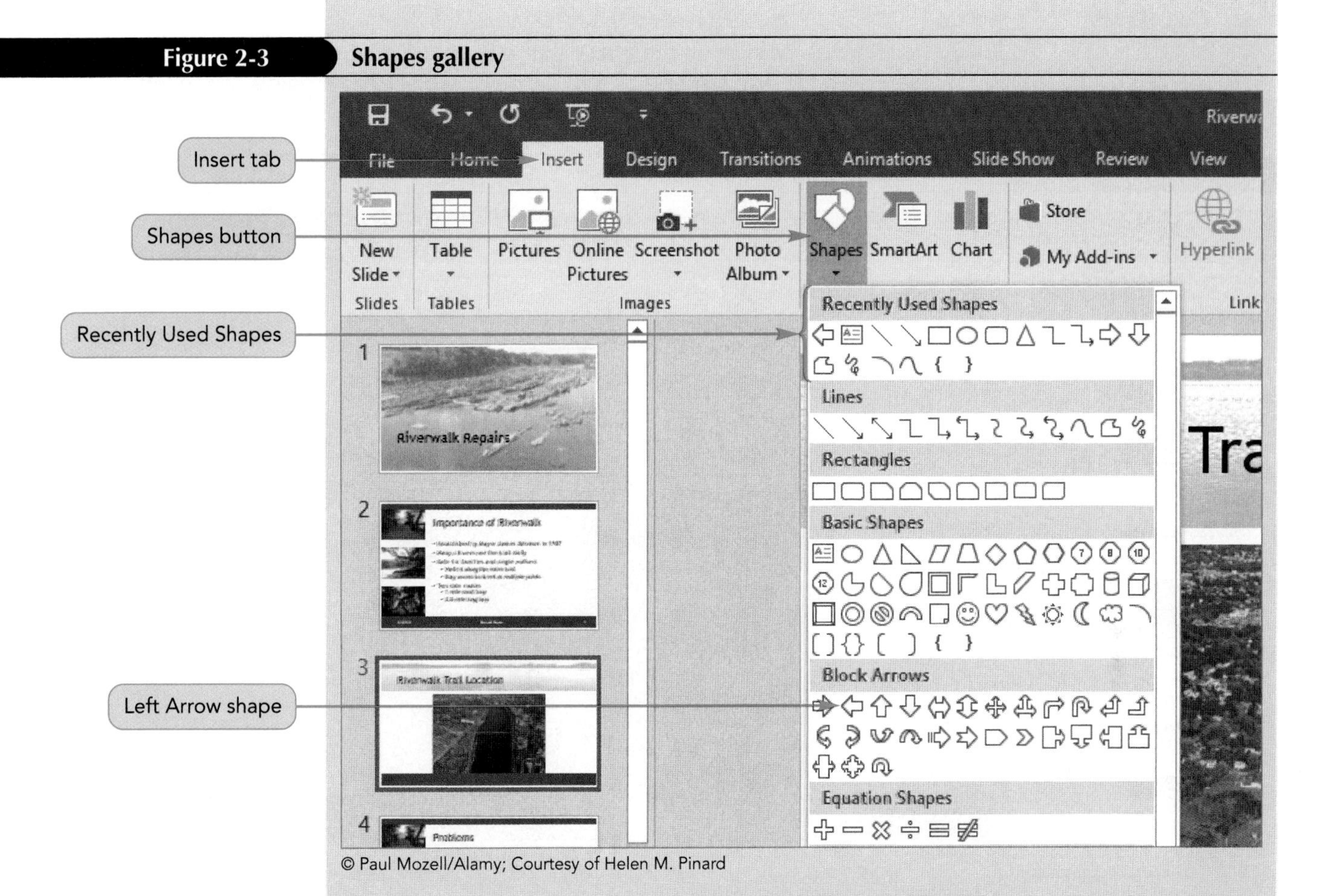

TIP

You can also insert a shape using the Shapes gallery in the Drawing group on the Home tab.

3. Under Block Arrows, click the **Left Arrow** shape. The gallery closes and the pointer changes to +.
4. On the slide, click to the right of the photo. A left-pointing arrow, approximately one inch long, appears. (Don't worry about the exact placement of the arrow; you will move it later.) Note that the Drawing Tools Format tab is the active tab on the ribbon.
5. With the shape selected, type **Starts here**. The text you type appears in the arrow, but it does not all fit.
6. Drag the middle sizing handle on the right end of the arrow to lengthen the arrow until both words fit on one line inside the arrow and the arrow is 1.75" long as indicated in the Shape Width box in the Size group on the Drawing Tools Format tab.

   Now you need to position the arrow shape on the photo. When you drag a shape with text, it is similar to dragging a text box, which means you need to drag a border of the shape or a part of the shape that does not contain text.

7. Position the pointer on the arrow shape so that the pointer changes to ✥, and then drag the arrow shape on top of the photo so that it points to the left of the curve in the river near the top of the photo, as shown in Figure 2-4.

Figure 2-4 Arrow shape with text on Slide 3

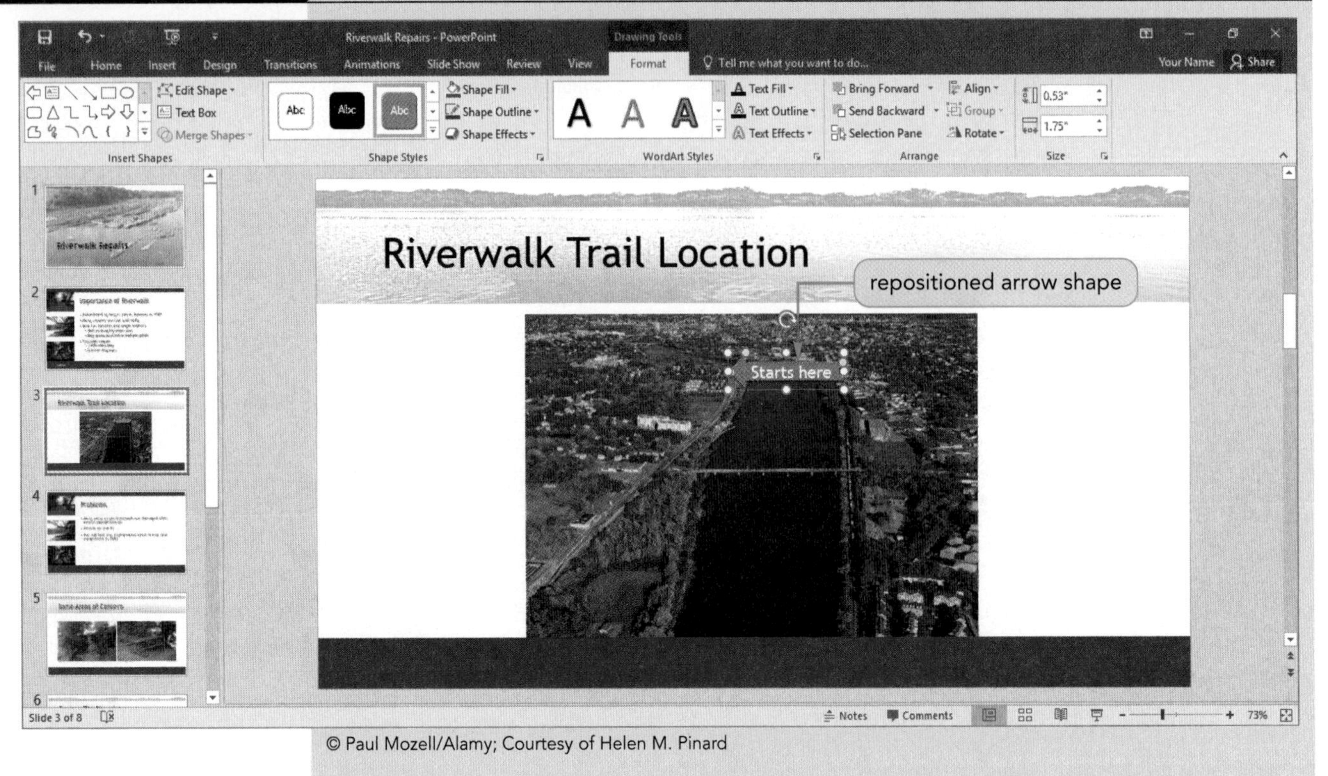

© Paul Mozell/Alamy; Courtesy of Helen M. Pinard

Next, you to need to add an arrow pointing to the end of the trail. You could draw another arrow, but instead, you'll duplicate the arrow you just drew. Duplicating is similar to copying and pasting, but nothing is placed on the Clipboard.

To duplicate the arrow on Slide 3 and edit the text in the shape:

1. On Slide 3 ("Riverwalk Trail Location"), click the **"Starts here"** arrow to select it, if necessary.
2. Click the **Home** tab, and then in the Clipboard group, click the **Copy button arrow**. A menu opens.
3. On the menu, click **Duplicate**. A duplicate of the "Starts here" arrow appears on the slide.
4. Double-click **Starts** in the duplicate arrow, and then type **Ends**.
5. Drag the duplicate of the arrow down so that it points to the left bank of the river at the bottom of the photo as shown in Figure 2-5.

Figure 2-5 Duplicate arrow positioned at the bottom of the photo on Slide 3

© Paul Mozell/Alamy; Courtesy of Helen M. Pinard

6. Save your changes.

Rotating and Flipping Objects

You can rotate and flip any object on a slide. To flip an object, you click the Rotate button in the Arrange group on the Drawing Tools Format tab to access the Flip commands on the Rotate menu. To rotate an object, you can use the Rotate commands on the Rotate menu to rotate objects in 90-degree increments. You can also drag the rotate handle that appears above the top-middle sizing handle when the object is selected to rotate it to any position that you want, using the center of the object as a pivot point.

The arrows you drew on Slide 3 would look better if they were pointing from left to right. To make this change, you need to flip the arrows.

TIP

You can also click the Arrange button in the Drawing group on the Home tab to access the Rotate and Flip commands.

To flip the arrow shapes and reposition them on Slide 3:

1. With Slide 3 ("Riverwalk Trail Location") displayed, click the **Starts here** arrow.
2. Position the pointer on the Rotate handle so that the pointer changes to , and then drag the Rotate handle clockwise until the Starts here arrow is pointing to the right. The arrow is pointing in the correct direction, but the text in the arrow is now upside down.
3. On the Quick Access Toolbar, click the **Undo** button , and then click the **Drawing Tools Format** tab, if necessary.

4. In the Arrange group, click the **Rotate** button. The Rotate menu opens. See Figure 2-6.

Figure 2-6 Rotate menu

© Paul Mozell/Alamy; Courtesy of Helen M. Pinard

5. Click **Flip Horizontal**. The arrow flips horizontally and is now pointing right. Unlike when you rotated the arrow so that it pointed right, the text is still right-side up.
6. Drag the **Starts here** arrow to the left until it is pointing to the riverbank on the left side of the river at the curve at the top of the photo.
7. Click the **Ends here** arrow to select it, and then flip it horizontally. The Ends here arrow now points from the left to the right.
8. Drag the **Ends here** arrow to the left until it is pointing to the riverbank on the left side of the river at the bottom of the photo, and then click a blank area of the slide to deselect the arrow. Compare your screen to Figure 2-7, and then make any adjustments needed for your screen to match the figure.

Figure 2-7 Arrows flipped and repositioned on Slide 3

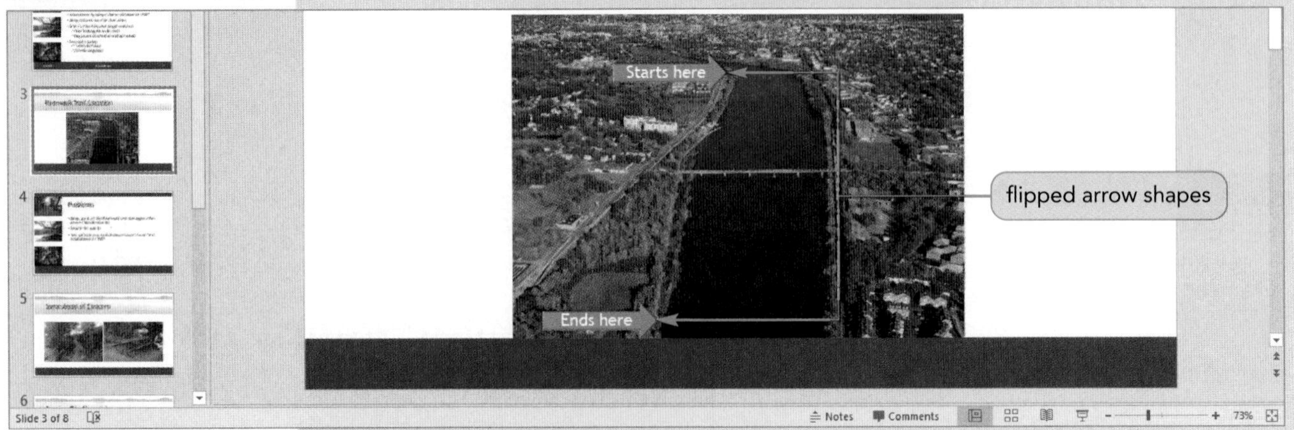

© Paul Mozell/Alamy; Courtesy of Helen M. Pinard

9. Save your changes.

Formatting Objects

Recall that both shapes and pictures, such as photos and clip art, are treated as objects in PowerPoint. The Picture Tools and Drawing Tools Format contextual tabs contain tools for formatting these objects. For both shapes and pictures, you can use these tools to apply borders or outlines, special effects such as drop shadows and reflections, and styles. You can also resize and rotate or flip these objects. Some formatting tools are available only to one or the other type of object. For example, the Remove Background tool is available only to pictures, and the Fill command is available only to shapes. Refer to the Session 2.1 Visual Overview for more information about the commands on the Format contextual tabs.

Formatting Shapes

You can modify the fill of a shape by filling it with a color, a gradient (shading in which one color blends into another or varies from one shade to another), a textured pattern, or a picture. When you add a shape to a slide, the default fill is the Accent 1 color from the set of theme colors, and the default outline is a darker shade of that color.

José wants you to change the default color of the "Starts here" arrow shape to green and the color of the "Ends here" arrow shape to red.

To change the fill and style of the arrow shapes:

1. On Slide 3 ("Riverwalk Trail Location"), click the **Ends here** arrow, and then click the **Drawing Tools Format** tab, if necessary.
2. In the Shape Styles group, click the **Shape Fill button arrow**. The Shape Fill menu opens. See Figure 2-8. You can fill a shape with a color, a picture, a gradient, or a texture, or you can remove the fill by clicking No Fill.

Figure 2-8 **Shape Fill menu**

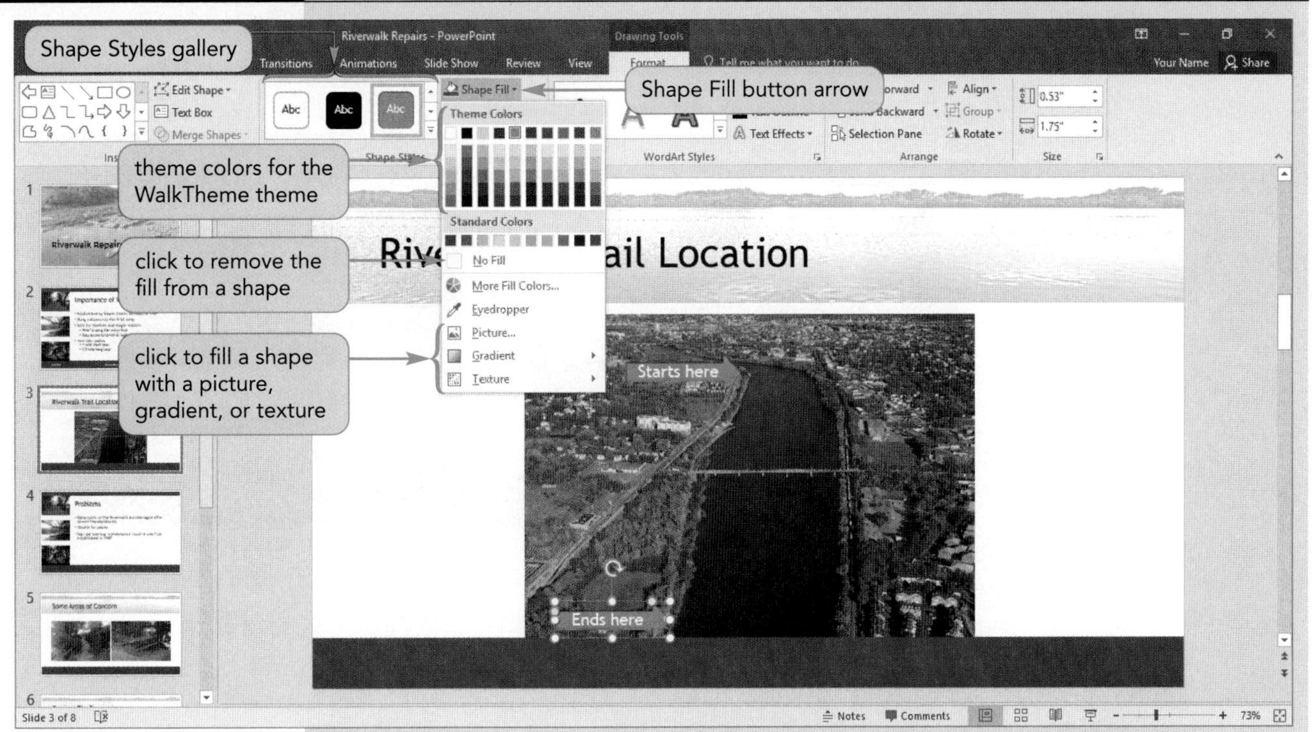

© Paul Mozell/Alamy; Courtesy of Helen M. Pinard

3. Under Standard Colors, click **Red**. The shape fill of the selected arrow changes to red. Next, you'll apply a style to the other arrow shape.
4. Click the **Starts here** arrow, and then in the Shape Styles group, click the **More** button. The Shape Styles gallery opens.
5. Click the **Light 1 Outline, Colored Fill – Dark Green, Accent 4** style. The style, which fills the shape with green and changes the shape outline to white, is applied to the shape.

On some shapes, you can drag the yellow adjustment handle to change the shape's proportions. For instance, if you dragged the adjustment handle on the arrow shape, you would change the size of the arrowhead relative to the size of the arrow.

You need to make the arrowhead larger relative to the size of the arrow shape.

To adjust the arrow shapes:

1. Click the **Starts here** shape, if necessary, to select it.
2. Drag the yellow adjustment handle at the top point on the arrowhead to the left so that the bottom point on the arrowhead aligns with the left side of the second "e" in "here."
3. Click the **Ends here** shape, and then drag the yellow adjustment handle at the top point on the arrowhead to the left so that the bottom point on the arrowhead aligns with the left side of the second "e" in "here." Compare your screen to Figure 2-9.

Figure 2-9 Formatted arrow shapes

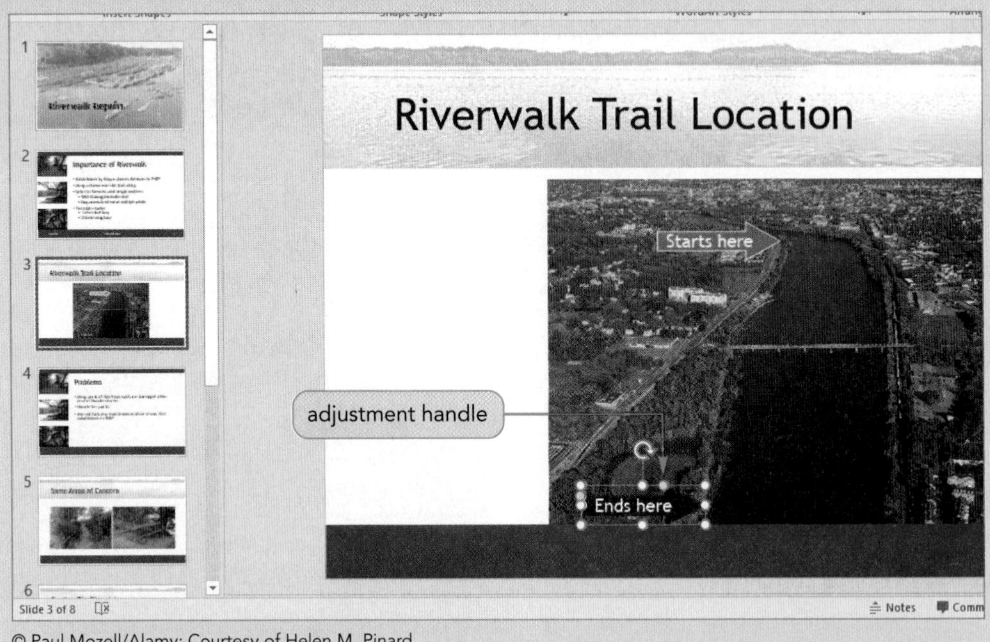

Formatting Pictures

You can format photos as well as shapes. To format photos, you use the tools on the Picture Tools Format tab.

José wants you to format the pictures on Slide 5 by adding a colored border. To create the border, you could apply a thick outline, or you can apply one of the styles that includes a border and then modify it.

To format the photos on Slide 5:

1. Display **Slide 5** ("Some Areas of Concern"), click the photo on the left, and then click the **Picture Tools Format** tab.
2. In the Picture Styles group, click the **Simple Frame, White** style. This style applies a seven-point white border to the photo.
3. In the Picture Styles group, click the **Picture Border button arrow**, and then click the **Dark Blue, Accent 3** color. See Figure 2-10. You need to apply the same formatting to the photo on the right on Slide 5. You can repeat the same formatting steps, or you can copy the formatting.

Figure 2-10 Picture with a style and border color applied

Courtesy of Helen M. Pinard; © Paul Mozell/Alamy

4. With the left photo on Slide 5 still selected, click the **Home** tab.
5. In the Clipboard group, click the **Format Painter** button, and then move the pointer to the slide. The pointer changes to .
6. Click the photo on the right. The style and border color of the photo on the left is copied and applied to the photo on the right.
7. Save your changes.

Creating and Formatting Tables

A **table** is information arranged in horizontal rows and vertical columns. The area where a row and column intersect is called a **cell**. Each cell contains one piece of information. A table's structure is indicated by borders, which are lines that outline the rows and columns.

Creating a Table and Adding Data to It

José wants you to add a table to Slide 7 that itemizes the damages to the trail and associated repair costs. This table will have three columns—one to describe the damages, one to contain the expected costs for the repair, and one to list notes.

REFERENCE

Inserting a Table

- In a content placeholder, click the Insert Table button; or, click the Insert tab on the ribbon, click the Table button in the Tables group, and then click Insert Table.
- Specify the numbers of columns and rows, and then click the OK button.

or

- On the ribbon, click the Insert tab, and then in the Tables group, click the Table button.
- Click a box in the grid to create a table of that size.

José hasn't decided how many examples of trail damages to include in the table, so he asks you to start by creating a table with four rows.

To add a table to Slide 7:

1. Display **Slide 7** ("Cost of Repairs").
2. Click the **Insert** tab, and then in the Tables group, click the **Table** button. A menu opens with a grid of squares above three commands.
3. Point to the grid, and without clicking the mouse button, move the pointer over the grid. The label above the grid indicates how large the table will be, and a preview of the table appears on the slide. See Figure 2-11.

Figure 2-11 **Inserting a 3x4 table on Slide 7**

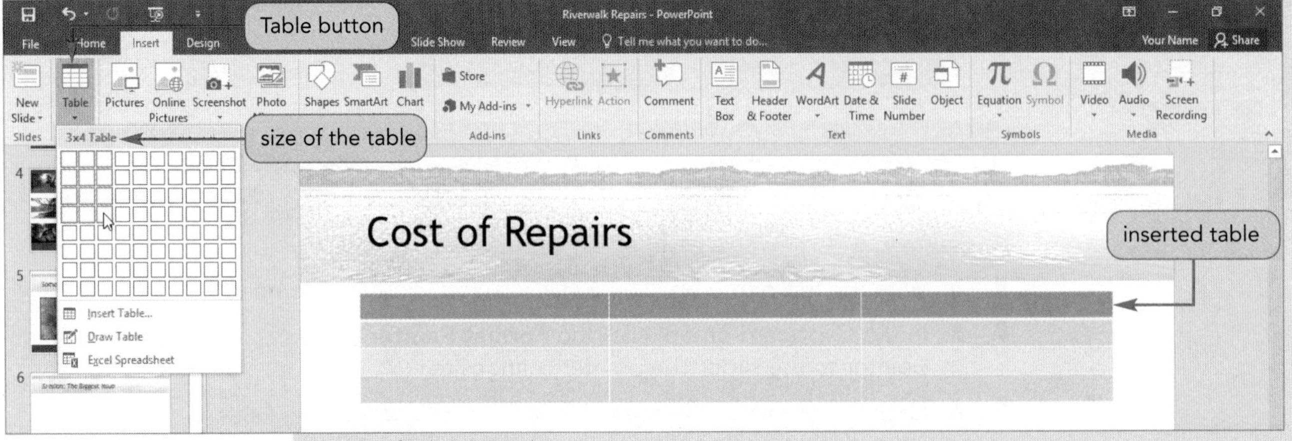

Courtesy of Helen M. Pinard

4. When the label above the grid indicates 3x4 Table, click to insert a table with three columns and four rows. A selection border appears around the table, and the insertion point is in the first cell in the first row.

Now you're ready to fill the blank cells with the information about the trail repairs. To enter data in a table, you click in the cells in which you want to enter data and then start typing. You can also use the Tab and arrow keys to move from one cell to another.

To add data to the table:

1. In the first cell in the first row, type **Description of Damages**. The text you typed appears in the first cell.
2. Press the **Tab** key. The insertion point moves to the second cell in the first row.
3. Type **Cost of Repair**, press the **Tab** key, type **Notes**, and then press the **Tab** key. The insertion point is in the first cell in the second row.
4. In the first cell in the second row, type **Broken stairs at beginning of trail**, press the **Tab** key, and then type **$700**.
5. Click in the first cell in the third row, type **Erosion along banks**, press the **Tab** key, and then type **$2500**.
6. Click in the first cell in the last row, type **Fallen trees blocking trail**, press the **Tab** key, and then type **$350**.

Inserting and Deleting Rows and Columns

You can modify the table by adding or deleting rows and columns. You need to add more rows to the table for additional descriptions of damage to the trail.

To insert rows and a column in the table:

1. Make sure the insertion point is in the last row in the table.
2. Click the **Table Tools Layout** tab, and then in the Rows & Columns group, click the **Insert Below** button. A new row is inserted below the current row. See Figure 2-12.

Figure 2-12 Table with row inserted

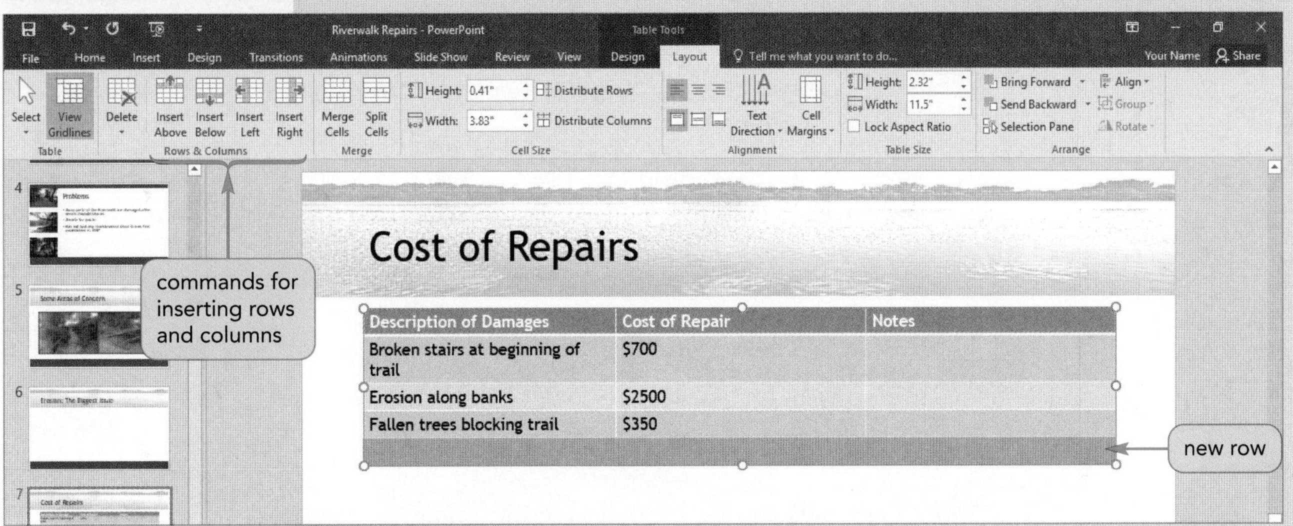

Courtesy of Helen M. Pinard

3. Click in the first cell in the new last row, type **Jersey barrier blocking trail**, and then press the **Tab** key.
4. Type **$300**, and then press the **Tab** key. The insertion point is in the last cell in the last row.
5. Press the **Tab** key. A new row is created, and the insertion point is in the first cell in the new row.
6. Type **Broken and vandalized signage**, press the **Tab** key, and then type **$250**. You need to insert a row above the last row.
7. In the Rows & Columns group, click the **Insert Above** button. A new row is inserted above the current row, and all the cells in the new row are selected.
8. Click any cell in the first column, and then in the Rows & Column group, click the **Insert Left** button.

   A new first column is inserted.

Make sure you click a cell in the first column before you insert the new column. Otherwise, you will insert three new columns.

José decided he doesn't want to add notes to the table, so you'll delete the last column. He also decided that the new row you added as the second to last row in the table isn't needed, so you'll delete that row.

To delete a column and a row in the table:

1. Click in any cell in the last column in the table. This is the column you will delete.
2. On the Table Tools Layout tab, in the Rows & Columns group, click the **Delete** button. The Delete button menu opens.
3. Click **Delete Columns**. The current column is deleted, and the entire table is selected.
4. Click in any cell in the second to last row (the empty row). This is the row you want to delete.
5. In the Rows & Columns group, click the **Delete** button, and then click **Delete Rows**. See Figure 2-13.

Figure 2-13 Table after adding and deleting rows and columns

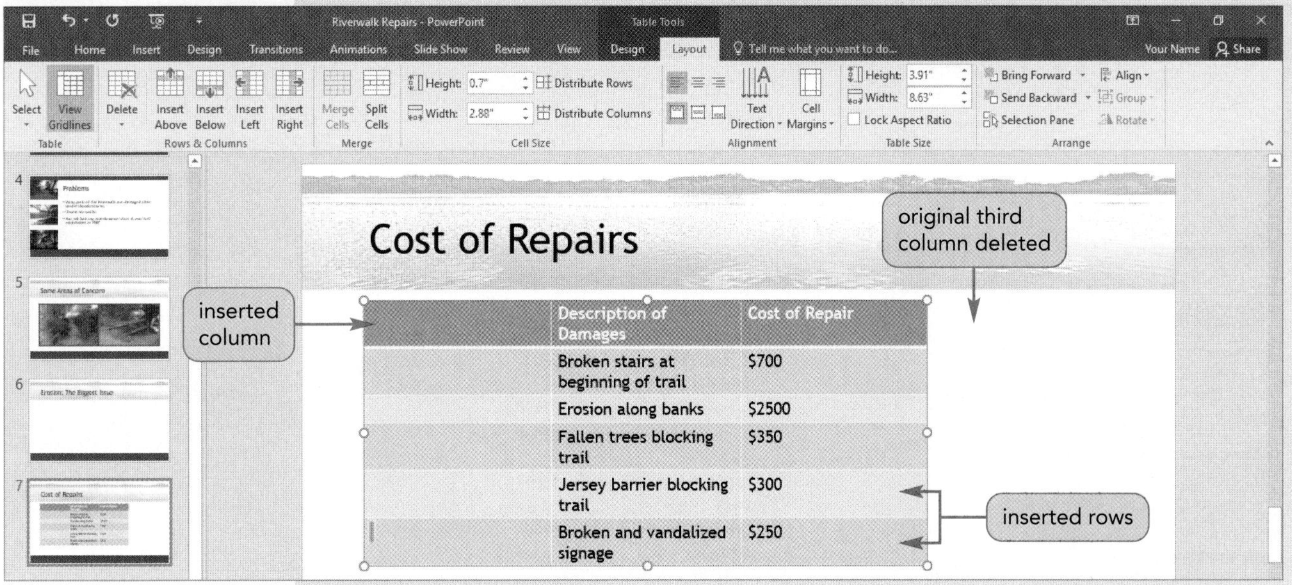

Cost of Repairs

original third column deleted

inserted column

	Description of Damages	Cost of Repair
	Broken stairs at beginning of trail	$700
	Erosion along banks	$2500
	Fallen trees blocking trail	$350
	Jersey barrier blocking trail	$300
	Broken and vandalized signage	$250

inserted rows

Courtesy of Helen M. Pinard

Formatting a Table

After you insert data into a table, you need to think about how the table looks and whether the table will be readable for the audience. As with any text, you can change the font, size, or color, and as with shapes and pictures, you can apply a style to a table. You can also change how the text fits in the table cells by changing the height of rows and the width of columns. You can also customize the formatting of the table by changing the border and fill of table cells.

You need to make the table text larger so that an audience will be able to read it.

To change the font size of text in the table:

1. Click any cell in the table. You want to change the size of all the text in the table, so you will select the entire table. Notice that a selection border appears around the table. This border appears any time the table is active.
2. Click the **Table Tools Layout** tab, if necessary, and then in the Table group, click the **Select** button. The Select menu opens with options to select the entire table, the current column, or the current row.
3. Click **Select Table**. The entire table is selected. Because the selection border appears any time the table is active, the only visual cues you have that it is now selected are that the insertion point is no longer blinking in the cell that you clicked in Step 1 and the Select button is gray and unavailable. See Figure 2-14.

Figure 2-14 Table selected on Slide 7

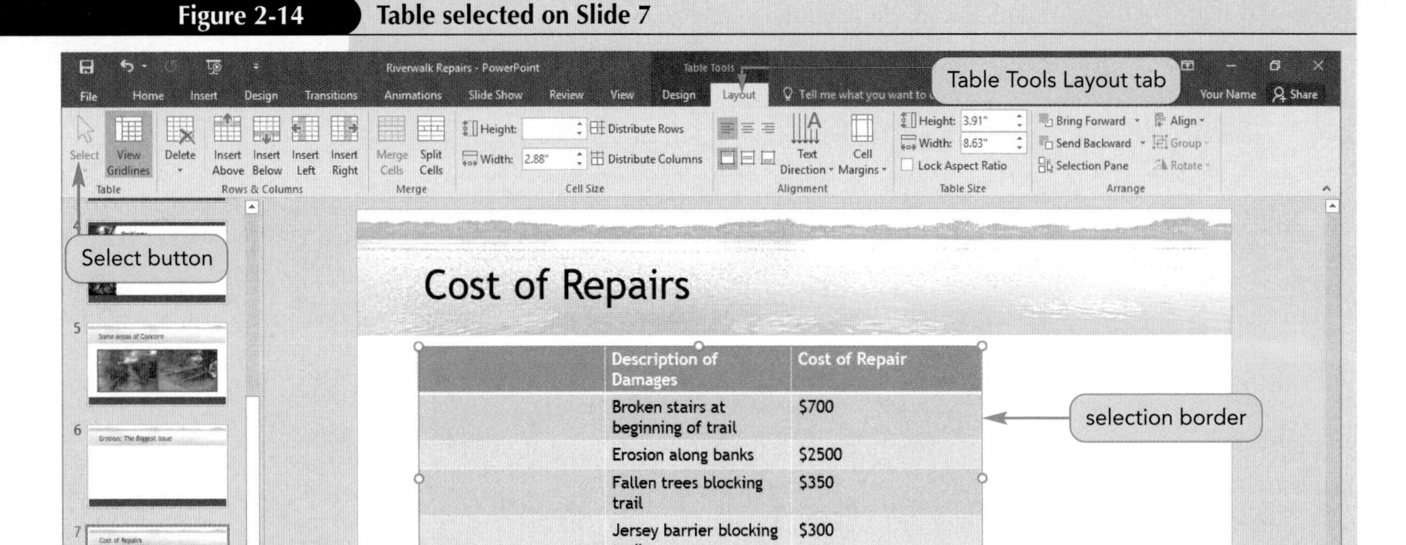

Courtesy of Helen M. Pinard

4. On the ribbon, click the **Home** tab.
5. In the Font group, click the **Font Size arrow**, and then click **28**. Because the entire table is selected, the size of all the text in the table changes to 28 points.

One of the rows is now off of the slide at the bottom. You will adjust the column widths so that all of the rows fit on the slide. To adjust column widths, you can drag a column border or type a number in the Width box in the Cell Size group on the Table Tools Layout tab. You can also automatically adjust a column to fit its widest entry by double-clicking its right border.

To adjust column sizes in the table:

1. Position the pointer on the border between the first and second columns so that the pointer changes to +||+, and then drag the border to the left until it is below the "o" in the word "of" in the slide title.
2. Click the **Table Tools Layout** tab, click any cell in the first column, and then in the Cell Size group, examine the measurement in the Width box.
3. If the measurement in the Width box is not 1.6", click in the **Width** box, type **1.6**, and then press the **Enter** key. The width of the first column is changed to 1.6 inches.
4. Position the pointer on the border between the second and third columns so that it changes to +||+, and then double-click. The second column widens to accommodate the widest entry in the column. See Figure 2-15.

Figure 2-15 Table column widths adjusted

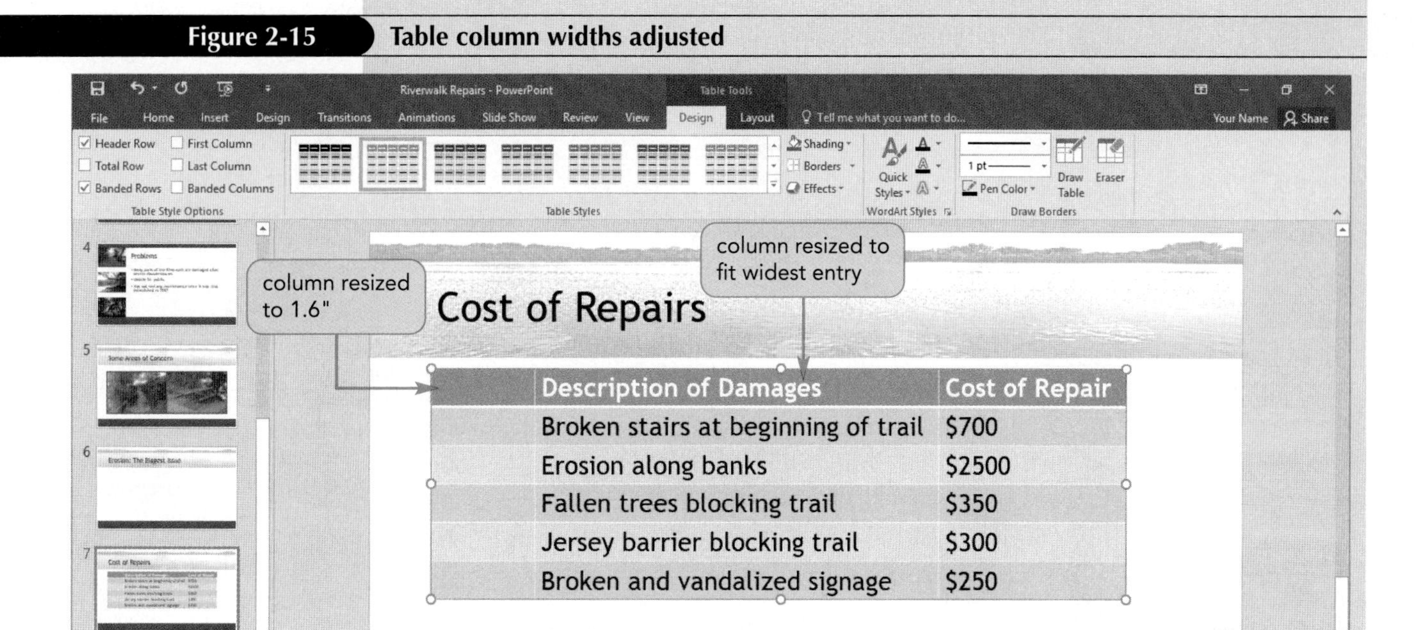

Courtesy of Helen M. Pinard

José wants you to change the format of the table so it looks more attractive and so that its colors complement the photo in the slide's layout. You will do this by applying a style to the table. When you apply a style to a table, you can specify whether the header and total rows and the first and last columns are formatted differently from the other rows and columns in the table. You can also specify whether to use banded rows or columns, that is, whether to fill alternating rows or columns with different shading.

To apply a style to the table:

1. Click the **Table Tools Design** tab on the ribbon, if necessary. In the Table Styles group, the second style, Medium Style 2 – Accent 1, is selected. In the Table Style Options group, the Header Row and Banded Rows check boxes are selected, which means that the header row will be formatted differently than the rest of the rows and that every other row will be filled with shading. See Figure 2-16.

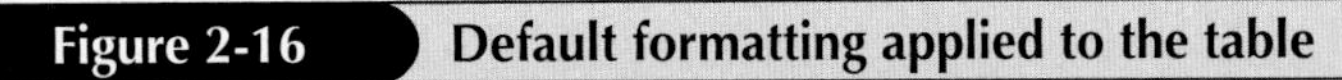

Figure 2-16 Default formatting applied to the table

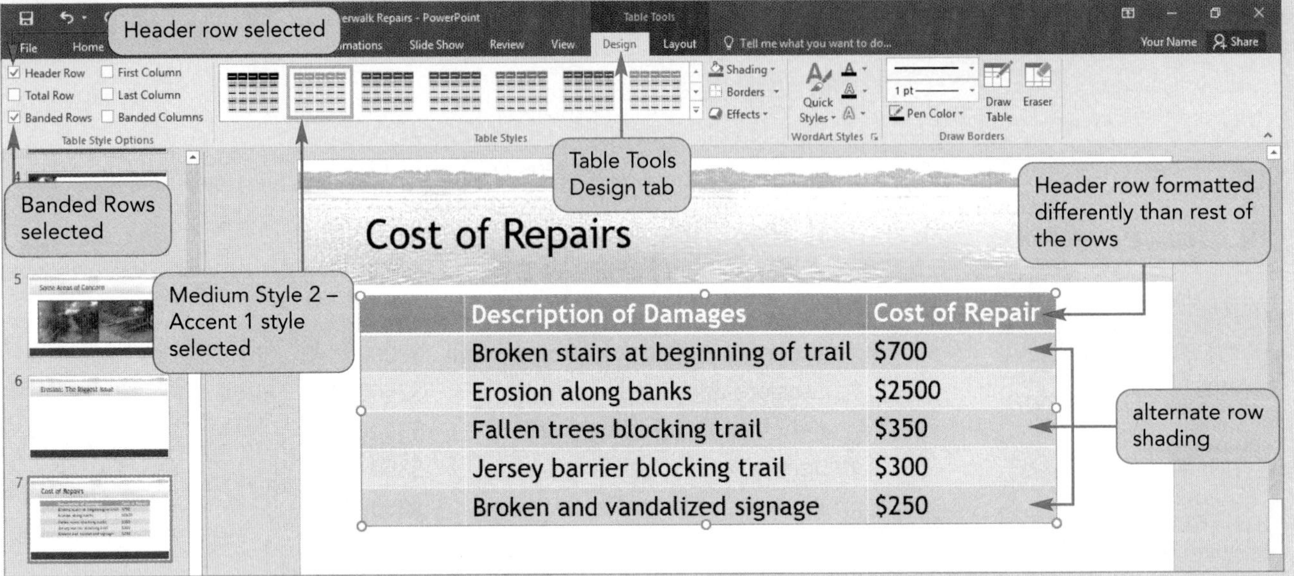

Courtesy of Helen M. Pinard

2. In the Table Styles group, click the **More** button. The Table Styles gallery opens.
3. Click the **Light Style 1** style, and then click a blank area of the slide to deselect the table. This style shades every other row with gray and adds a border above and below the top row and below the bottom row.

You can change the fill of table cells in the same manner that you change the fill of shapes. José wants the first row to be more prominent.

To change the fill of cells in the first row of the table:

1. In the table, click any cell in the first row, and then click the **Table Tools Layout** tab.
2. In the Table group, click the **Select** button, and then click **Select Row**. The first row in the table is selected.
3. Click the **Table Tools Design** tab.
4. In the Table Styles group, click the **Shading button arrow**. The Shading menu is similar to the Shape Fill menu you worked with earlier.
5. Click **Dark Blue, Accent 3**. The menu closes and the cells in the first row are shaded with dark blue. The text is a little hard to read.
6. In the WordArt Styles group, click the **Text Fill button arrow** A, and then click the **White, Background 1, Darker 5%** color. The text in the selected cells changes to the white color you selected.

TIP

You can also change the font color of table text using the Font Color button in the Font group on the Home tab.

In addition, the table might be easier to read if the horizontal borders between the rows were visible. You can add these by using the Borders button arrow and the buttons in the Draw Borders group on the Table Tools Design tab. When you use the Borders button arrow, you can apply borders to all the selected cells at once. The borders will be the style, weight, and color specified by the Pen Style, Pen Weight, and Pen Color buttons in the Draw Borders group. Note that borders are different than gridlines. Gridlines are the lines that form the structure of a table. Borders are drawn on top of the gridlines. Gridlines are always there, but they appear only if the View Gridlines button in the Table group on the Table Tools Layout tab is selected and if the table itself is selected.

You want to see how the table looks without gridlines, then you will remove the top border on the top row in the table and make the bottom border of that row thicker.

To view and hide gridlines and modify the borders of the table:

1. Click the **Table Tools Layout** tab, and then in the Table group, click the **View Gridlines** button to deselect it. The faint vertical lines between the table columns disappear.

   Trouble? If the View Gridlines button was already deselected, click it again to deselect it.

2. In the Table group, click the **View Gridlines** button again to select it. The faint vertical lines between the table columns are visible again.
3. Make sure the first row of the table is still selected. You want to remove the top border on this row.
4. Click the **Table Tools Design** tab, and then in the Table Styles group, click the **Borders button arrow**. A menu opens listing borders that you can apply to the selected cells. Notice that the Top Border and Bottom Border commands are selected on the menu. This is because the selected cells have a top and bottom border. As indicated in the Draw Borders group, the borders are solid-line borders, one point wide, and black. See Figure 2-17. You can change any of these attributes.

Figure 2-17 **Current format of borders for top row of table**

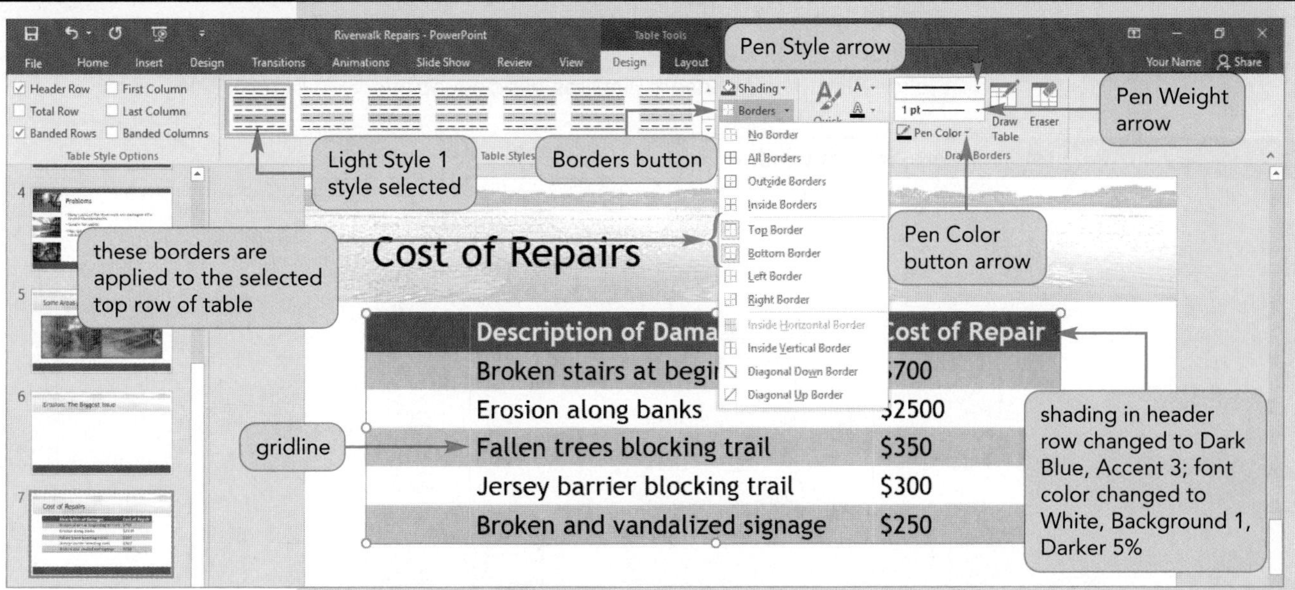

Courtesy of Helen M. Pinard

5. Click **Top Border**. The top border on the selected row is removed.
6. In the Table Styles group, click the **Borders button arrow**. Only the Bottom Border command is selected on the menu now.

   Trouble? If the Top Border command is still selected, click Top Border again, and then repeat Step 6.

Next you will change the first row's bottom border to a three-point line.

7. In the Draw Borders group, click the **Pen Weight arrow**, and then click **3 pt**. The pointer changes to a pencil, and the Draw Table button in the Draw Borders group is selected. You could drag the pointer along the border you want to change, or you can use the Borders menu again.
8. In the Table Styles group, click the **Borders button arrow**. None of the options on the Borders menu is selected because even though the selected row has a bottom border, it is a one-point border, not a three-point border.
9. Click **Bottom Border**. The bottom border of the selected row changes to a three-point line. In the Draw Borders group, the Draw Table button is no longer selected.

Filling Cells with Pictures

Recall that one of the things you can fill a shape with is a picture. You can do the same with cells. Note that most of the table styles include shaded cells as part of the style definition, so if you want to fill table cells with pictures and apply a table style, you need to apply the table style first. Otherwise, the shading that is part of the table style definition will replace the pictures in the cells.

José wants you to add a picture to each row that shows an example of the described damage.

To fill the cells in the first column with pictures:

1. Click in the first cell in the second row in the table, and then click the **Table Tools Design** tab, if necessary.
2. In the Table Styles group, click the **Shading button arrow**, and then click **Picture**. The Insert Pictures window opens. See Figure 2-18.

Figure 2-18 Insert Pictures window

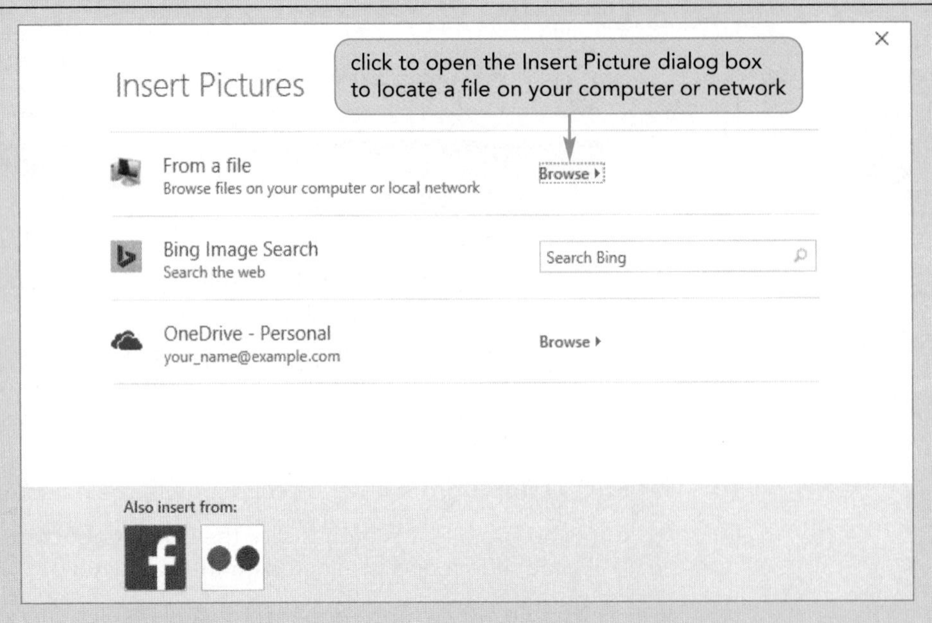

3. Next to From a file, click **Browse**. The Insert Picture dialog box opens.
4. Navigate to the **PowerPoint2** > **Module** folder, click **Stairs**, and then click the **Insert** button. The photo fills the cell.
5. Insert the following photos, all located in the **PowerPoint2** > **Module** folder, in the first cells in the next four rows: **Erosion1**, **Tree**, **Barrier**, and **Sign**.

The text in the table is large enough, but the photos are too small, and some of them are distorted because they were stretched horizontally to fill the cells. To fix both of these problems, you'll increase the height of the rows containing the pictures.

To change row heights in the table:

1. Position the pointer to the left of the second row in the table so that it changes to ➡.
2. Press and hold the mouse button, drag down until the pointer is to the left of the bottom row in the table, and then release the mouse button. All the rows in the table except the first one are selected.
3. Click the **Table Tools Layout** tab.
4. In the Cell Size group, click in the **Height** box, type **.85** (make sure you type a decimal point before "85"), and then press the **Enter** key. The height of the selected rows increases to 0.85 inches.

The text in all cells in the table is horizontally left-aligned and vertically aligned at the top of the cells. The text in all the rows except the heading row would look better vertically aligned in the center of the cells. And because the data in the last column is dollar amounts, it would be better if these numbers were right-aligned. Finally, you also need to reposition the table on the slide to better fill the space. You move a table the same way you move any other object.

To adjust the alignment of text in cells and reposition the table:

1. Make sure all the rows except the heading row are still selected.
2. On the Table Tools Layout tab, in the Alignment group, click the **Center Vertically** button. The text in the selected rows is now centered vertically in the cells.
3. In the third column, click in the cell containing $700.
4. Position the pointer in the last cell in the second row (the cell containing $700), press and hold the mouse button, drag down through the rest of the cells in the third column, and then release the mouse button. The cells you dragged over (all the cells in the third column except the heading cell) are selected.
5. In the Alignment group, click the **Align Right** button. The dollar amounts are now right-aligned in the cells. Now you will adjust the table's placement on the slide.
6. In the Arrange group, click the **Align** button. A menu with commands for aligning the objects on the slide appears. Because only one object—the table—is selected, selecting a command will align the object to the borders of the slide.

7. Click **Align Center**. The table is horizontally aligned so that it is centered between the left and right borders of the slide. The bottom of the table slightly overlaps the blue bar at the bottom of the slide.
8. On the Table Tools Layout tab, in the Table group, click the **Select** button, and then click **Select Table**. The entire table is selected.
9. Press the ↑ key as many times as needed to move the table up slightly so that the bottom of the table no longer overlaps the bar at the bottom of the slide. Compare your screen to Figure 2-19.

TIP

You could also drag the table by its border to reposition it on the slide.

Figure 2-19 Final formatted table

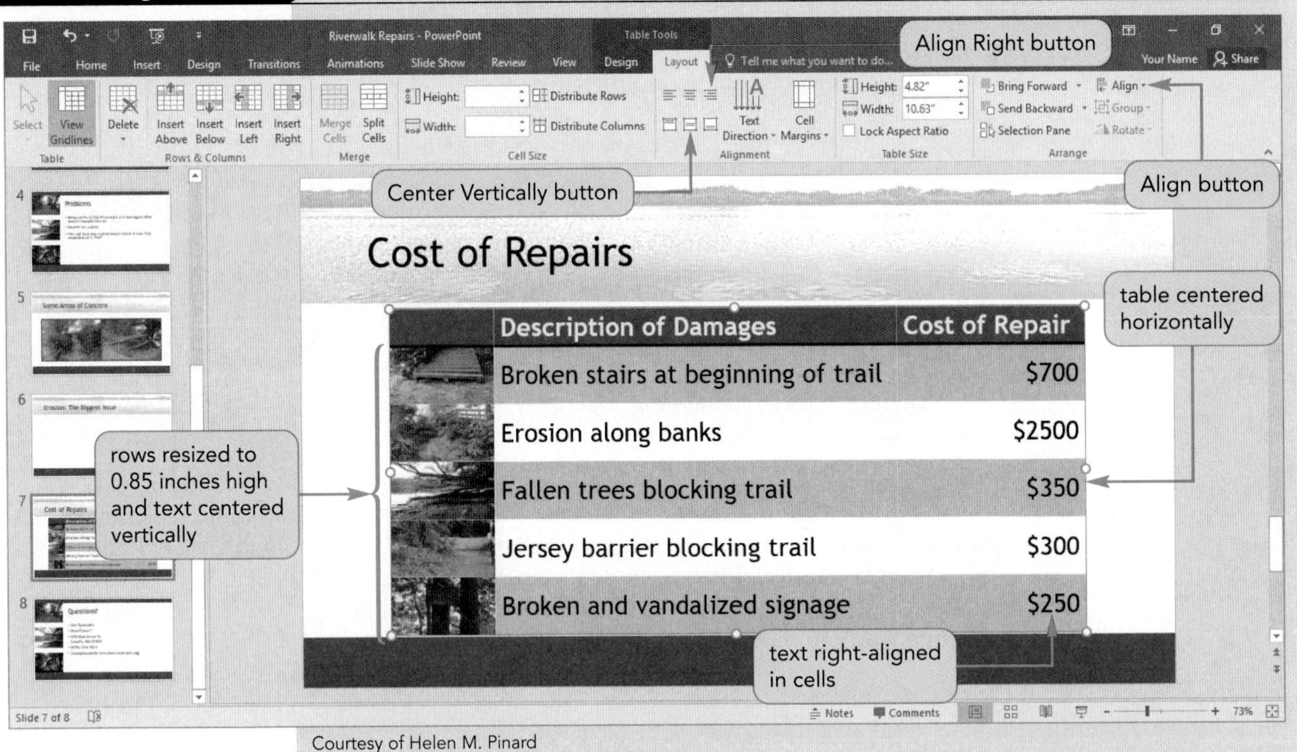

Courtesy of Helen M. Pinard

10. Click a blank area of the slide to deselect the table, and then save your changes.

Inserting Symbols

You can insert some symbols, such as the trademark symbol, the registered trademark symbol, and the copyright symbol, by typing letters between parentheses and letting AutoCorrect change the characters to a symbol. You can insert all symbols, including letters from another alphabet using a keyboard with only English letters, by using the Symbol button in the Symbols group on the Insert tab.

The nonprofit organization's name "RiverClean" is a trademarked name, so it usually appears with the trademark symbol ™ after it. You will add the trademark symbol after the organization's name on the last slide in the presentation.

To insert the trademark symbol by typing:

1. Display **Slide 8** ("Questions?"), and then in the bulleted list, click after "RiverClean" in the second bulleted item.
2. Type **(tm**.
3. Type **)** (close parenthesis). The text "(tm)" changes to the trademark symbol, which is ™.

TIP

To insert the copyright symbol ©, type (c). To insert the registered trademark symbol ®, type (r).

José's name contains two letters that are not in the English alphabet. You need to correct the spelling of José's first and last name. You'll do this using the Symbol dialog box.

To insert special characters:

1. In the first bulleted item, click after "Jose," and then press the **Backspace** key. The "e" is deleted.
2. Click the **Insert** tab, and then in the Symbols group, click the **Symbol** button. The Symbol dialog box opens.
3. Drag the scroll box to the top of the vertical scroll bar, click the **Subset** arrow, and then click **Latin-1 Supplement**.
4. Click the down scroll arrow three times, and then in the bottom row, click **é**. In the bottom-left corner of the Symbol dialog box, the name of the selected character is "Latin Small Letter E With Acute." See Figure 2-20.

Figure 2-20 Symbol dialog box

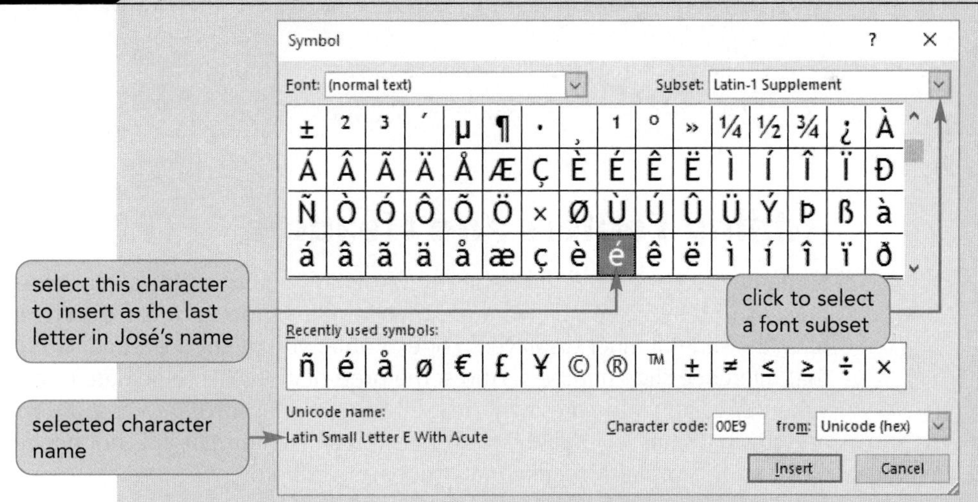

Trouble? If the letter does not appear in the row mentioned in Step 4, someone might have resized the Symbol dialog box. Refer to Figure 2-20 for help locating the symbol.

5. Click the **Insert** button. The letter "é" is inserted in the table, and the Cancel button in the dialog box changes to the Close button.
6. Click the **Close** button. The first word in the first bulleted item is now "José."
7. In the first bulleted item, click after the first "n" in "Quinones," and then press the **Backspace** key to delete the "n."

8. In the Symbols group, click the **Symbol** button to open the Symbols dialog box. The first row contains the é that you just inserted. You need to insert ñ, which appears in the row below the row containing the é.
9. In the second row in the dialog box, click **ñ**, which has the name "Latin Small Letter N With Tilde."
10. Click the **Insert** button, and then click the **Close** button. The first bulleted item is now "José Quiñones." See Figure 2-21.

Figure 2-21 Symbols inserted on Slide 8

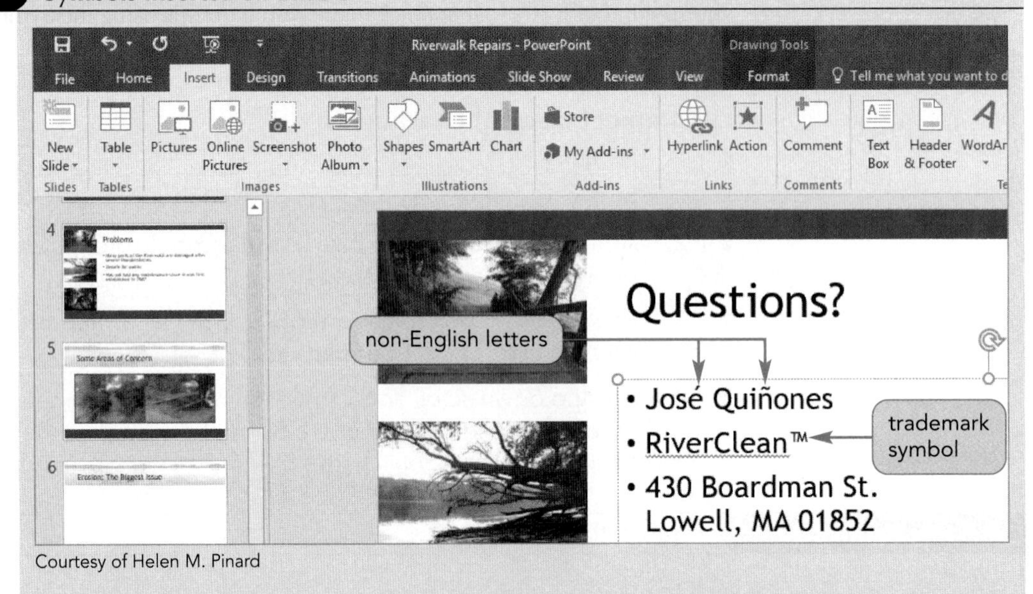

Courtesy of Helen M. Pinard

11. Click a blank area of the slide to deselect the text box, and then save your changes.

Adding Footers and Headers

Sometimes it can be helpful to have information on each slide such as the title of the presentation or the company name. This is called a **footer**. It can also be helpful to have the slide number displayed. For example, you might need to distribute handouts that reference slide numbers. And some presentations need the date to appear on each slide, especially if the presentation contains time-sensitive information. You can easily add this information to all the slides. Usually this information is not needed on the title slide, so you can also specify that it not appear there.

TIP

Clicking the Date & Time button and the Slide Number button also opens the Header and Footer dialog box.

To add a footer, slide numbers, and the date to slides:

1. Click the **Insert** tab on the ribbon if necessary, and then in the Text group, click the **Header & Footer** button. The Header and Footer dialog box opens with the Slide tab selected.
2. Click the **Footer** check box to select it, and then click in the **Footer** box. In the Preview box on the right, the middle placeholder on the bottom is filled with black to indicate where the footer will appear on slides. See Figure 2-22. Note that the position of the footer, slide number, and date changes in different themes.

Figure 2-22 Slide tab in the Header and Footer dialog box

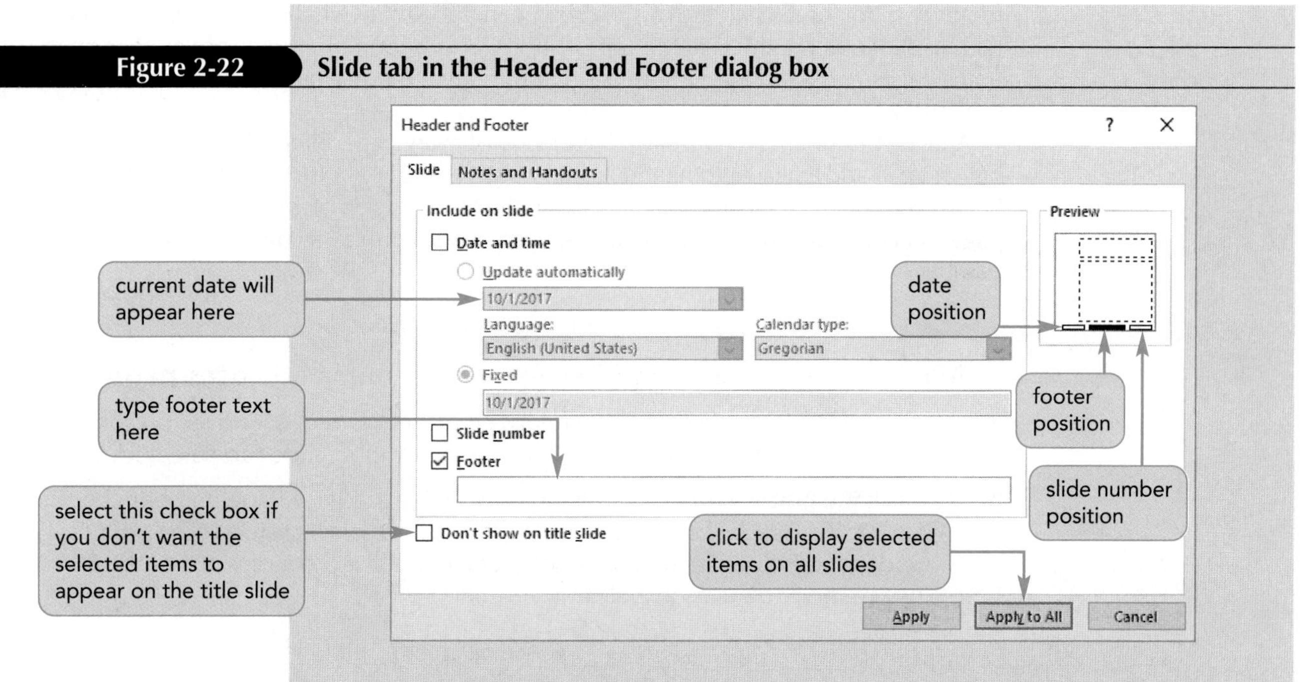

3. Type **Riverwalk Repairs**.
4. Click the **Slide number** check box to select it. In the Preview box, the box in the bottom-right is filled with black.
5. Click the **Date and time** check box to select it. The options under this check box darken to indicate that you can use them, and in the Preview box, the box in the bottom-left is filled with black.

   You don't want the date in the presentation to update automatically each time the presentation is opened. You want it to show today's date so people will know that the information is current as of that date.
6. Click the **Fixed** option button, if necessary. Now you want to prevent the footer, slide number, and date from appearing on the title slide.
7. Click the **Don't show on title slide** check box to select it, and then click the **Apply to All** button. On Slide 8, the footer, date, and slide number are displayed. See Figure 2-23.

Figure 2-23 Date, footer, and slide number on Slide 8

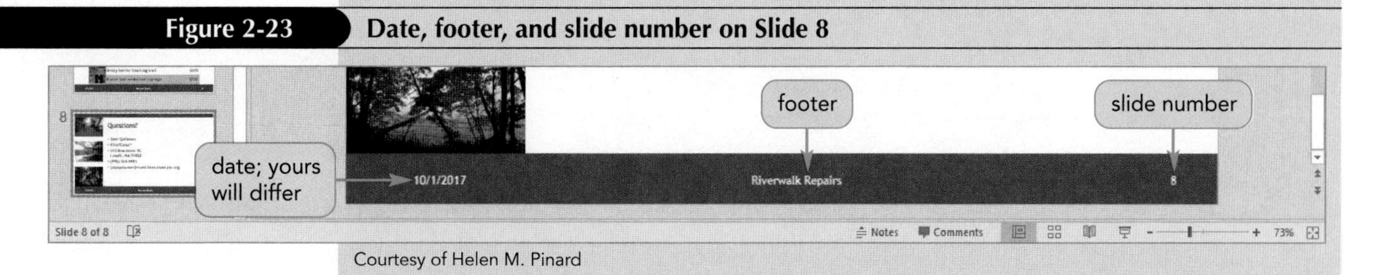

Courtesy of Helen M. Pinard

8. Display **Slide 1** (the title slide). Notice the footer, date, and slide number do not appear on the title slide.

In common usage, a footer is any text that appears at the bottom of every page in a document or every slide in a presentation. However, as you saw when you added the footer in the Header and Footer dialog box, in PowerPoint a footer is specifically the text that appears in the Footer box on the Slide tab in that dialog box and in the footer text box on the slides. This text box can appear anywhere on the slide; in some themes the footer appears at the top of slides. This information does not appear on notes pages and handouts. You need to add footers to notes pages and handouts separately.

A **header** is information displayed at the top of every page. Slides do not have headers, but you can add a header to handouts and notes pages. Like a footer, in PowerPoint a header refers only to the text that appears in the Header text box on handouts and notes pages. In addition to headers and footers, you can also display a date and the page number on handouts and notes pages.

To modify the header and footer on handouts and notes pages:

1. On the Insert tab, in the Text group, click the **Header & Footer** button. The Header and Footer dialog box opens with the Slide tab selected.
2. Click the **Notes and Handouts** tab. This tab includes a Page number check box and a Header box. The Page number check box is selected by default, and in the Preview, the lower-right rectangle is bold to indicate that this is where the page number will appear.
3. Click the **Header** check box to select it, click in the **Header** box, and then type **Riverwalk Repairs**.
4. Click the **Footer** check box to select it, click in the **Footer** box, and then type your name.
5. Click the **Apply to All** button. To see the effect of modifying the handouts and notes pages, you need to look at the print preview.
6. Click the **File** tab to open Backstage view, and then in the navigation bar, click **Print**.
7. Under Settings, click the **Full Page Slides** button, and then click **Notes Pages**. The preview shows Slide 1 as a notes page. The header and footer you typed appear, along with the page number. See Figure 2-24.

Figure 2-24 Header and footer on the Slide 1 notes page

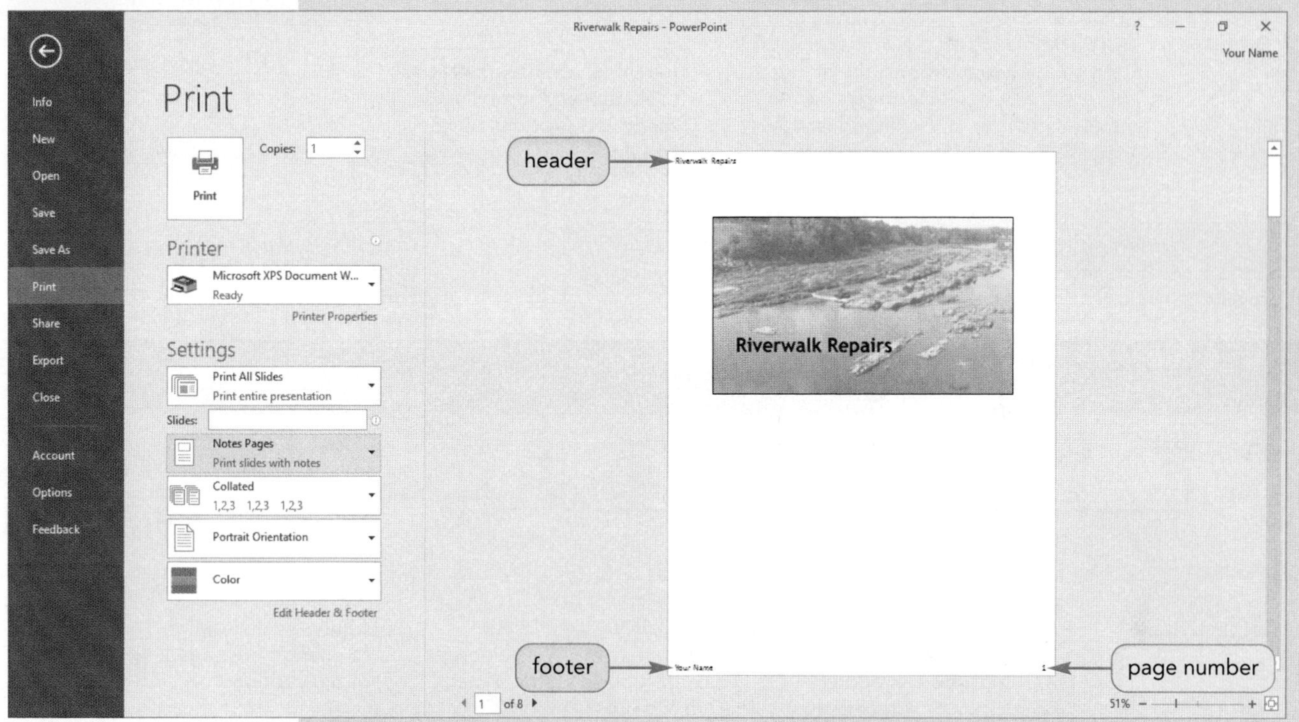

Courtesy of Helen M. Pinard

8. At the top of the navigation bar, click the **Back** button to return to Normal view.
9. Save your changes.

You have modified a presentation by applying a theme used in another presentation, inserting and formatting pictures and shapes, and inserting a table and characters that are not on your keyboard. You also added footer and header information to slides and handouts. In the next session, you will continue modifying the presentation by applying and modifying transitions and animations, adding and modifying videos, and creating an Office mix.

REVIEW

Session 2.1 Quick Check

1. Which contextual tab appears on the ribbon when a shape is selected?
2. What is a style?
3. What is a shape's fill?
4. In a table, what is the intersection of a row and column called?
5. How do you know if an entire table is selected and not just active?
6. How do you insert characters that are not on your keyboard?
7. In PowerPoint, what is a footer?

Session 2.2 Visual Overview:

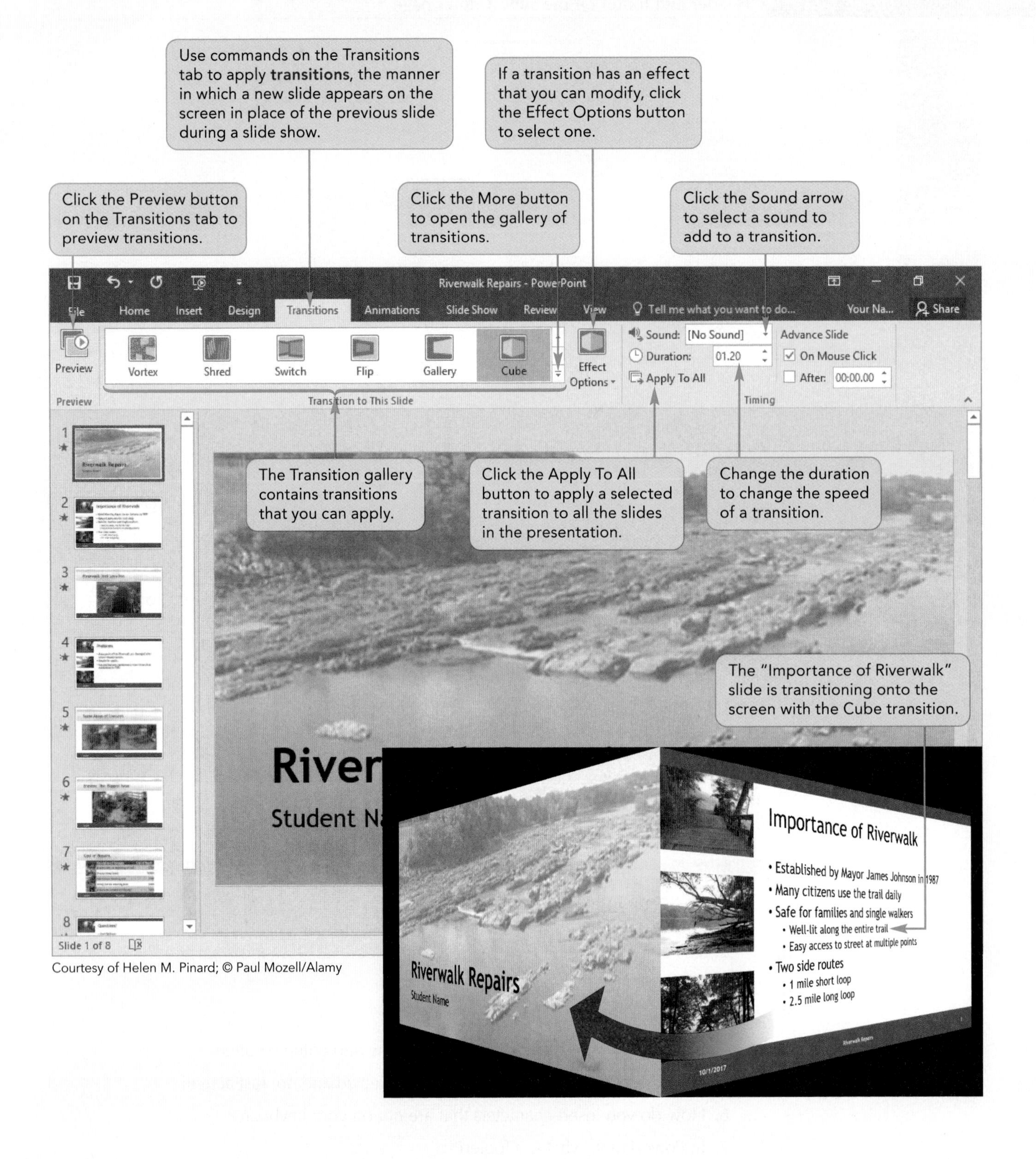

Courtesy of Helen M. Pinard; © Paul Mozell/Alamy

Using Animations and Transitions

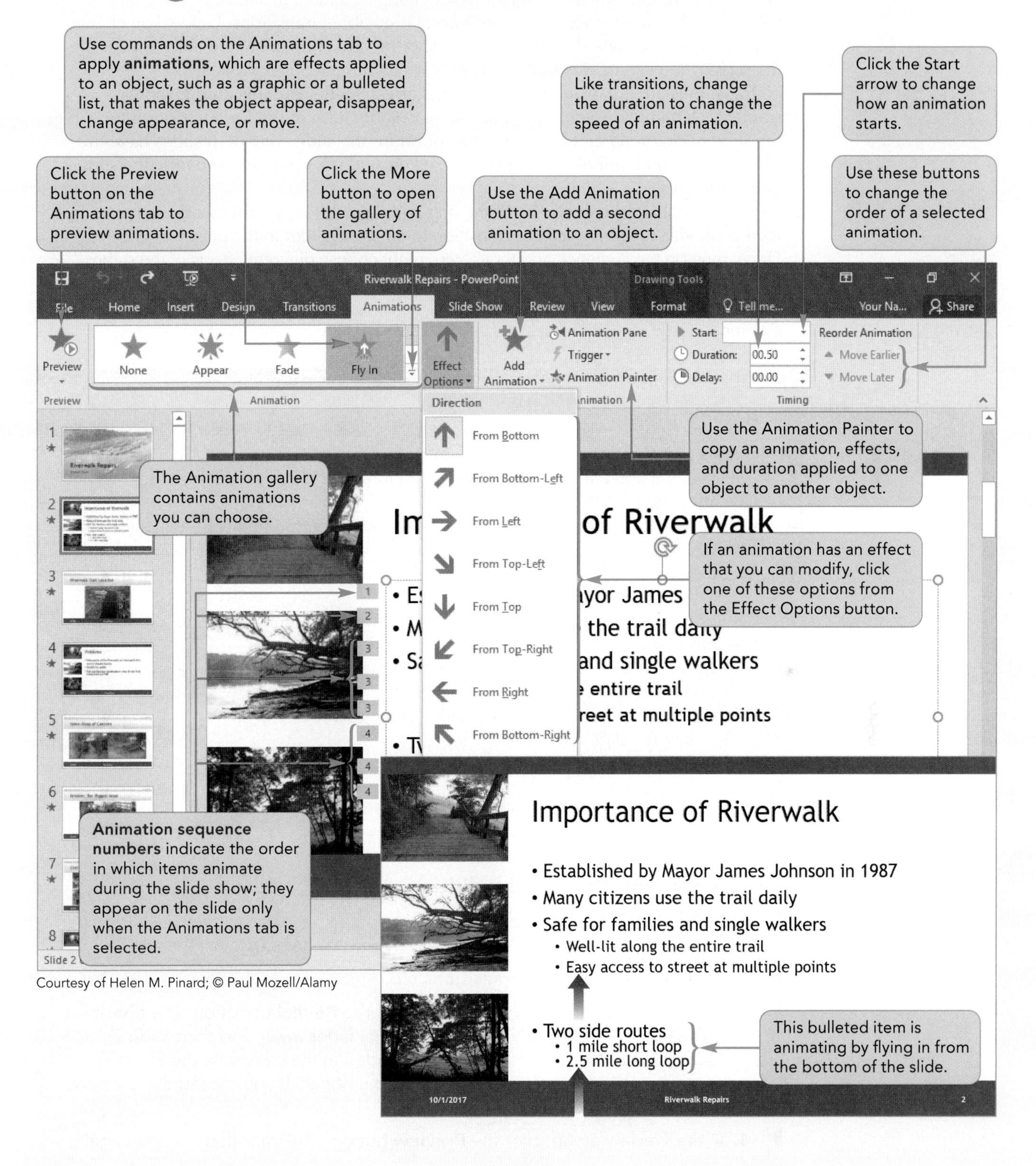

Courtesy of Helen M. Pinard; © Paul Mozell/Alamy

Applying Transitions

The Transitions tab contains commands for changing slide transitions. Refer to the Session 2.2 Visual Overview for more information about transitions. Unless you change it, the default is for one slide to disappear and the next slide to immediately appear on the screen. You can modify transitions in Normal or Slide Sorter view.

Transitions are organized into three categories: Subtle, Exciting, and Dynamic Content. Dynamic Content transitions are a combination of the Fade transition for the slide background and a different transition for the slide content. If slides have the same background, it looks like the slide background stays in place and only the slide content moves.

Inconsistent transitions can be distracting and detract from your message, so generally it's a good idea to apply the same transition to all of the slides in the presentation. Depending on the audience and topic, you might choose different effects of the same transition for different slides, such as changing the direction of a Wipe or Push transition. If there is one slide you want to highlight, for instance, the last slide, you can use a different transition for that slide.

REFERENCE

Adding Transitions

- In the Slides pane in Normal view or in Slide Sorter view, select the slide(s) to which you want to add a transition, or, if applying to all the slides, select any slide.
- On the ribbon, click the Transitions tab.
- In the Transition to This Slide group, click the More button to display the gallery of transitions, and then click a transition in the gallery.
- If desired, in the Transition to This Slide group, click the Effect Options button, and then click an effect.
- If desired, in the Timing group, click the Sound arrow to insert a sound effect to accompany each transition.
- If desired, in the Timing group, modify the time in the Duration box to modify the speed of the transition.
- To apply the transition to all the slides in the presentation, in the Timing group, click the Apply To All button.

José wants to add more interesting transitions between the slides.

To apply transitions to the slides:

1. If you took a break after the previous session, make sure the **Riverwalk Repairs** presentation is open, and then display **Slide 2** ("Importance of Riverwalk").
2. On the ribbon, click the **Transitions** tab.
3. In the Transition to This Slide group, click the **Reveal** transition. The transition previews as Slide 1 (the title slide) appears, fades away, and then Slide 2 fades in. The Reveal transition is now shaded in the gallery. In the Slides pane, a star appears next to the Slide 2 thumbnail. If you missed the preview, you can see it again.
4. In the Preview group, click the **Preview** button. The transition previews again.
5. In the Transition to This Slide group, click the **More** button. The gallery opens listing all the transitions. See Figure 2-25.

Figure 2-25 Transitions gallery

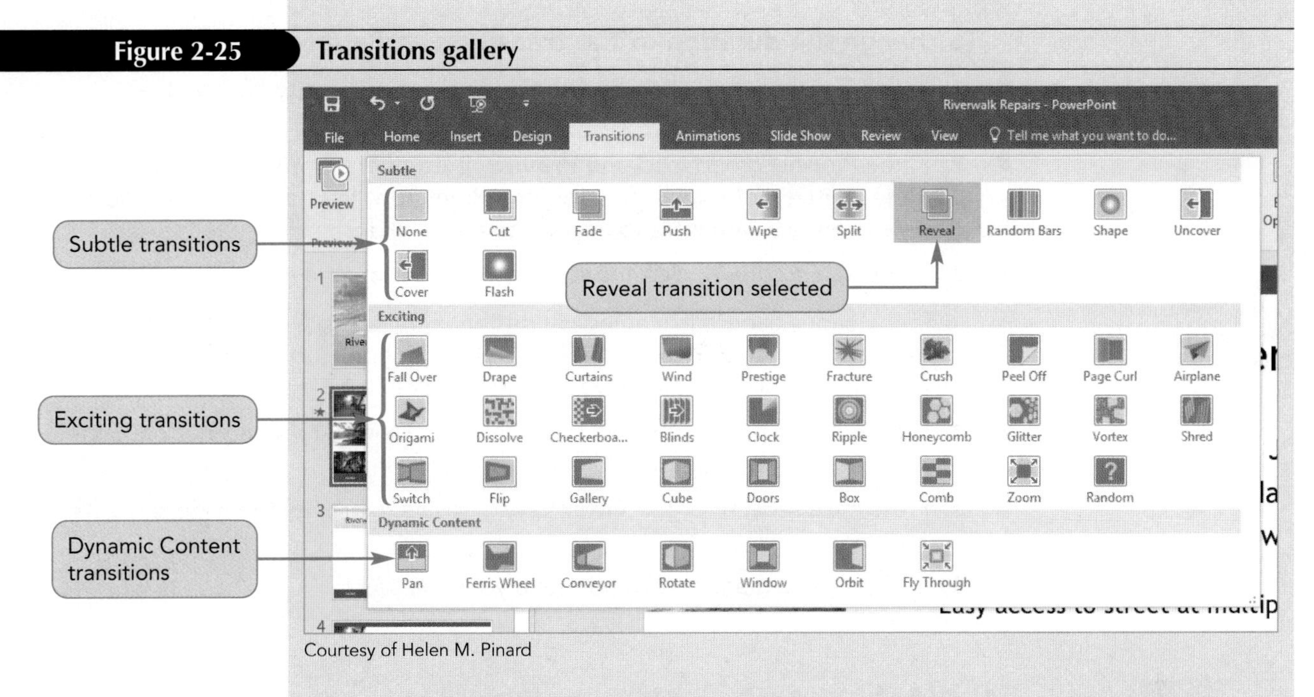

Courtesy of Helen M. Pinard

6. Click the **Push** transition. The preview shows Slide 2 slide up from the bottom and push Slide 1 up and out of view.

Most transitions have effects that you can modify. For example, the Peel Off transition can peel from the bottom-left or the bottom-right corner, and the Wipe transition can wipe from any direction. You'll modify the transition applied to Slide 2.

To modify the transition effect for Slide 2:

1. In the Transition to This Slide group, click the **Effect Options** button. The effects that you can modify for the Push transition are listed on the menu.
2. Click **From Right**. The Push transition previews again, but this time Slide 2 slides from the right to push Slide 1 left. The available effects change depending on the transition selected.
3. In the Transition to This Slide group, click the **Shape** transition. The transition previews with a brief view of Slide 1, before Slide 2 appears in the center of Slide 1 and enlarges in a circular shape to fill the slide.
4. Click the **Effect Options** button. The effects that you can modify for the Shape transition are listed.
5. Click **Out**. The preview of the transition with this effect displays Slide 2 in the center of Slide 1 that grows in a rectangular shape to fill the slide.

Finally, you can also change the duration of a transition. The duration is how long it takes the transition to finish, in other words, the speed of the transition. To make the transition faster, decrease the duration; to slow the transition down, increase the duration. José likes the Shape transition, but he thinks it is a little fast, so you will increase the duration. Then you can apply the modified transition to all the slides.

To change the duration of the transition and apply it to all the slides:

1. In the Timing group, click the **Duration** up arrow twice to change the duration to 1.50.
2. In the Preview group, click the **Preview** button. The transition previews once more, a little more slowly than before. Right now, the transition is applied only to Slide 2. You want to apply it to all the slides.
3. In the Timing group, click the **Apply To All** button.

   In the Slides pane, the star indicating that a transition is applied to the slide appears next to all of the slides in the presentation. You should view the transitions in Slide Show view to make sure you like the final effect.
4. On the Quick Access Toolbar, click the **Start From Beginning** button. Slide 1 (the title slide) appears in Slide Show view.
5. Press the **spacebar** or the **Enter** key to advance through the slide show. The transitions look fine.
6. End the presentation, and then save your changes.

Make sure you click the Apply To All button or the transition is applied only to the currently selected slide or slides.

Applying Animations

Animations add interest to a slide show and draw attention to the text or object being animated. For example, you can animate a slide title to fly in from the side or spin around like a pinwheel to draw the audience's attention to that title. Refer to the Session 2.2 Visual Overview for more information about animations.

Animation effects are grouped into four types:

- **Entrance**—Text and objects are not shown on the slide until the animation occurs; one of the most commonly used animation types.
- **Emphasis**—Text and objects on the slide change in appearance or move.
- **Exit**—Text and objects leave the screen before the slide show advances to the next slide.
- **Motion Paths**—Text and objects follow a path on a slide.

Animating Objects

You can animate any object on a slide, including pictures, shapes, and text boxes. To animate an object you click it, and then select an animation in the Animation group on the Animations tab.

REFERENCE

Applying Animations

- On the slide displayed in Normal view, select the object you want to animate.
- On the ribbon, click the Animations tab.
- In the Animation group, click the More button to display the gallery of animations, and then click an animation in the gallery.
- If desired, in the Animation group, click the Effect Options button, and then click a direction effect; if the object is a text box, click a sequence effect.
- If desired, in the Timing group, modify the time in the Duration box to modify the speed of the animation.
- If desired, in the Timing group, click the Start arrow, and then click a different start timing.

Slide 5 contains two pictures of damaged parts of the trail. José wants you to add an animation to the title text on this slide.

To animate the title on Slide 5:

1. Display **Slide 5** ("Some Areas of Concern"), and then click the **Animations** tab on the ribbon. The animations in the Animation group are grayed out, indicating they are not available. This is because nothing is selected on the slide.
2. Click the **Some Areas of Concern** title text. The animations in the Animation group are green to indicate that they are now available. All of the animations currently visible in the Animation group are entrance animations.
3. In the Animation group, click the **Fly In** animation. This entrance animation previews on the slide—the title text disappears and then flies in from the bottom. In the Timing group, the Start box displays On Click, which indicates that this animation will occur when you advance the slide show by clicking the mouse or pressing the spacebar or the Enter key.

   Notice the animation sequence number 1 in the box to the left of the title text box, which indicates that this is the first animation that will occur on the slide. You can preview the animation again if you missed it.
4. In the Preview group, click the **Preview** button. The animation previews again.
5. In the Animation group, click the **More** button. The Animation gallery opens. The animation commands are listed by category, and each category appears in a different color. At the bottom are four commands, each of which opens a dialog box listing all the effects in that category. See Figure 2-26. You will try an emphasis animation.

Figure 2-26 Animation gallery

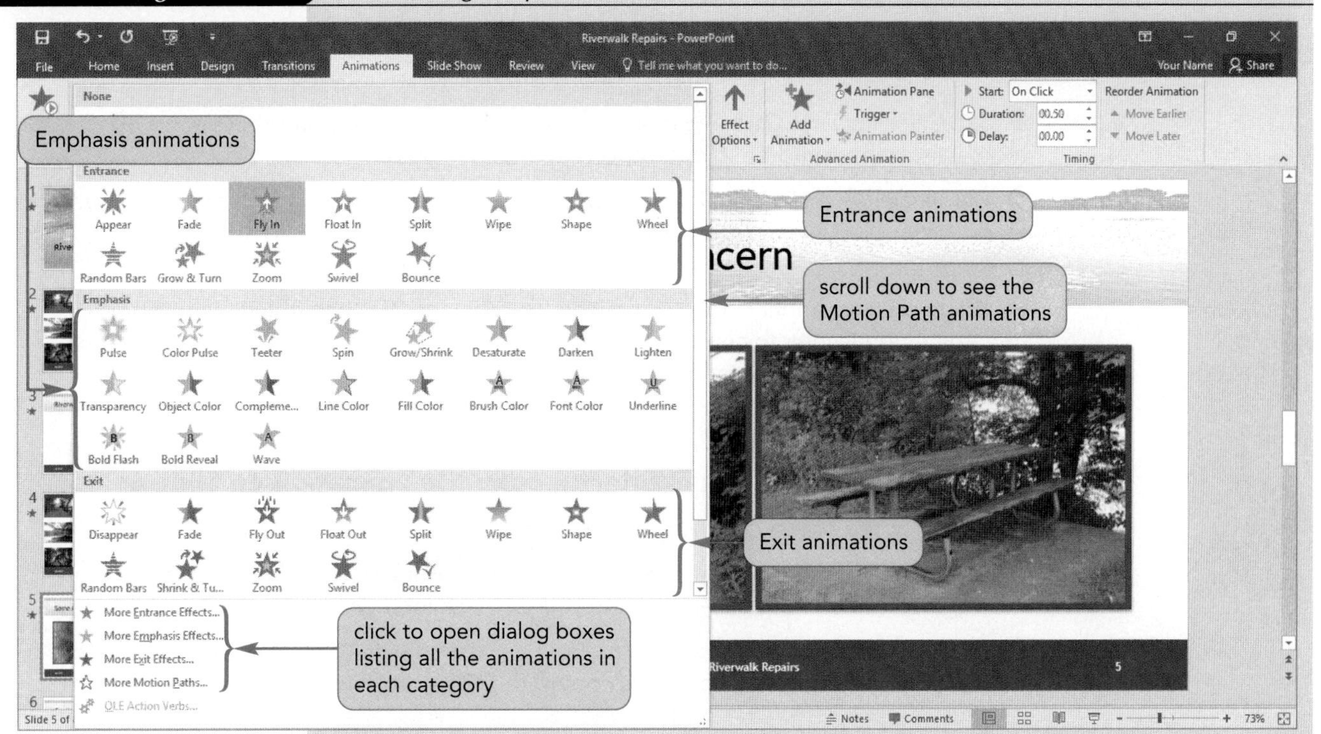

Courtesy of Helen M. Pinard

6. Under Emphasis, click the **Underline** animation. The Underline animation replaces the Fly In animation, and the slide title is underlined in the preview.

The Underline animation you applied to the slide title is an example of an emphasis animation that is available only to text. You cannot apply that animation to objects such as pictures.

Slide 5 contains photos showing some areas of trail damage. To focus the audience's attention on one photo at time, you will apply an entrance animation to the photos so that they appear one at a time during the slide show.

To apply entrance animations to the photos on Slide 5:

1. With Slide 5 ("Some Areas of Concern") displayed, click the picture on the right.
2. In the Animation group, click the **More** button. Notice that in the Emphasis section, six of the animations, including the Underline animation you just applied to the slide title, are gray, which means they are not available for this object. These six animations are available only for text.
3. In the Entrance section, click the **Split** animation. The picture appears starting from the left and right edges. In the Timing group, On Click appears in the Start box, indicating that this animation will occur when you advance the slide show. The animation sequence number to the left of the selected picture is 2, which indicates that this is the second animation that will occur on the slide when you advance the slide show.

You need to change the direction from which this animation appears, and you want to slow it down.

To change the effect and duration of the animation applied to the photo:

1. In the Animation group, click the **Effect Options** button. This menu contains Direction options.
2. Click **Vertical Out**. The preview shows the picture appearing, starting from the center and building out to the left and right edges.
3. In the Timing group, click the **Duration** up arrow once. The duration changes from 0.50 seconds to 0.75 seconds.

After you have applied and customized the animation for one object, you can use the Animation Painter to copy that animation to other objects. You will copy the Split entrance animation to the other photo on Slide 5.

To use the Animation Painter to copy the animation on Slide 5:

1. Click the photo on the right to select it.
2. In the Advanced Animation group, click the **Animation Painter** button, and then move the pointer onto the slide. The pointer changes to .
3. Click the photo on the left. The Split animation with the Vertical Out effect and a duration of 0.75 seconds is copied to the photo on the left and previews.

After you apply animations, you should watch them in Slide Show, Presenter, or Reading view to see what they will look like during a slide show. Remember that On Click appeared in the Start box for each animation that you applied, which means that to see the animation during the slide show, you need to advance the slide show.

To view the animations on Slide 5 in Slide Show view:

1. Make sure Slide 5 ("Some Areas of Concern") is displayed.
2. On the status bar, click the **Slide Show** button. Slide 5 appears in Slide Show view. Only the photo that is part of the layout and the title appear on the slide.
3. Press the **spacebar** to advance the slide show. The first animation, the emphasis animation that underlines the title, occurs.
4. Press the **spacebar** again. The photo on the right appears starting at the center of the photo and building out to the left and right edges.
5. Click anywhere on the screen. The photo on the left appears with the same animation as the photo on the right.
6. Press the **Esc** key. Slide 5 appears in Normal view.

José doesn't like the emphasis animation on the slide title. It's distracting because the title is not the focus of this slide, the photos are. Also, it would be better if the photo on the left appeared before the photo on the right. To fix this, you can remove the animation applied to the title and change the order of the animations applied to the photos.

To remove the title animation and change the order of the photo animations:

1. Click the **slide title**. In the Animation group, the yellow emphasis animation Underline is selected.
2. In the Animation group, click the **More** button, and then at the top of the gallery, click **None**. The animation that was applied to the title is removed, the animation sequence icon no longer appears next to the title text box, and the other two animation sequence icons on the slide are renumbered 1 and 2.

   Now you need to select the animation applied to the photo on the left and change it so that it occurs first. You can select the object or the animation sequence icon to modify an animation.
3. Next to the left photo, click the animation sequence icon **2**. In the Animation group, the green Split entrance animation is selected. See Figure 2-27.

TIP

You can also click the animation sequence icon, and then press the Delete key to remove an animation.

Figure 2-27 Animation selected to change its order

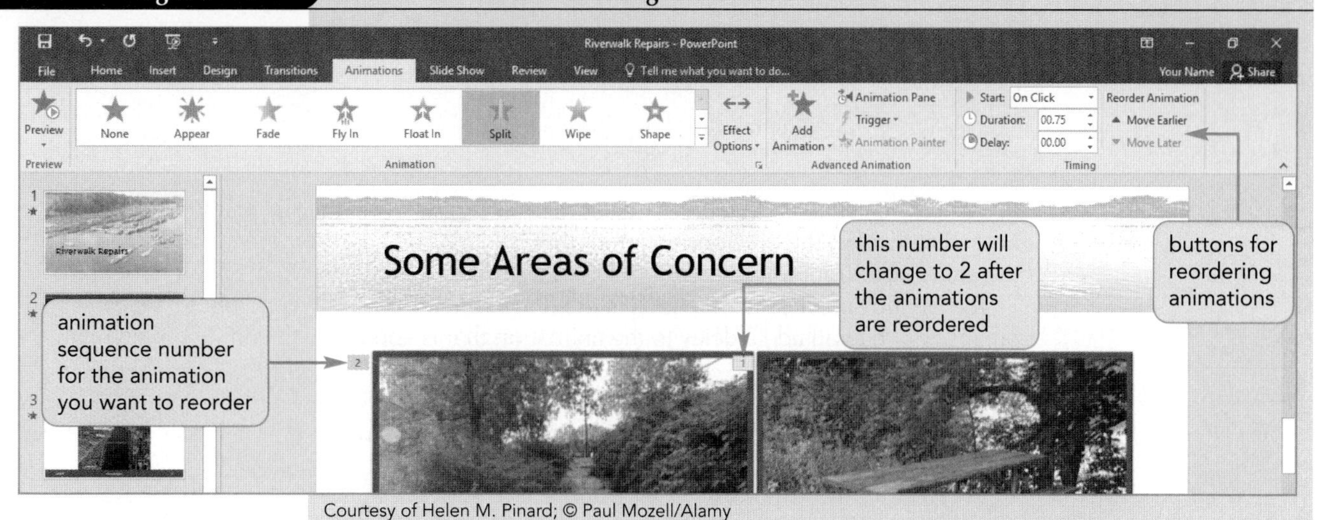

Courtesy of Helen M. Pinard; © Paul Mozell/Alamy

4. In the Timing group, click the **Move Earlier** button. The animation sequence icon next to the photo on the left changes from 2 to 1, and the animation sequence icon next to the photo on the right changes from 1 to 2.
5. In the Preview group, click the **Preview** button. The photo on the left appears, and then the photo on the right appears.

Changing How an Animation Starts

Remember that when you apply an animation, the default is for the object to animate On Click, which means when you advance through the slide show. You can change this so that an animation happens automatically, either at the same time as another animation or when the slide transitions, or after another animation.

José wants the photo on the right to appear automatically, without the presenter needing to advance the slide show.

To change how the animation for the photo on the right starts:

1. With Slide 5 ("Some Areas of Concern") displayed, click the photo on the right. The entrance animation Split is selected in the Animation group, and in the Timing group, On Click appears in the Start box.
2. In the Timing group, click the **Start** arrow. The three choices for starting an animation—On Click, With Previous, and After Previous—are listed on the menu.
3. Click **After Previous**. Now this photo will appear automatically after the photo on the left appears. Notice that the animation sequence number next to this photo changed to 1, the same number as the animation sequence number next to the photo on the left. This is because you will not need to advance the slide show to start this animation.

When you preview an animation, it plays automatically on the slide in Normal view, even if the timing setting for the animation is On Click. To make sure the timing settings are correct, you need to watch the animation in a slide show.

To view and test the animations:

1. On the status bar, click the **Slide Show** button. Slide 5 appears in Slide Show view.
2. Press the **spacebar**. The photo on the left appears, and then the photo on the right appears.
3. Press the **Esc** key to end the slide show.

When you set an animation to occur automatically during the slide show, it happens immediately after the previous action. If that is too soon, you can add a pause before the animation. To do this, you increase the time in the Delay box in the Timing group.

To give the audience time to look at the first photo before the second photo appears on Slide 5, you will add a delay to the animation that is applied to the photo on the right.

To add a delay to the After Previous animation:

1. With Slide 5 ("Some Areas of Concern") displayed, click the photo on the right, if necessary, to select it. In the Timing group, 00.00 appears in the Delay box.

2. In the Timing group, click the **Delay** up arrow four times to change the time to one second. After the photo on the left appears (the previous animation), the photo on the right will appear after a delay of one second.
3. On the status bar, click the **Slide Show** button. Slide 5 appears in Slide Show view.
4. Press the **spacebar**. The photo on the left appears, and then after a one-second delay, the photo on the right appears.
5. Press the **Esc** key to end the slide show, and then save your changes.

Animating Lists

If you animate a list, the default is for each of the first-level items to animate On Click. This type of animation focuses your audience's attention on each item, without the distraction of items that you haven't discussed yet. José wants you to add an Entrance animation to the bulleted list on Slide 2. He wants each first-level bulleted item to appear on the slide one at a time so that the audience won't be able to read ahead while he is discussing each point.

To animate the bulleted lists:

1. Display **Slide 2** ("Importance of Riverwalk"), and then click anywhere in the bulleted list to make the text box active.
2. On the Animations tab, in the Animation group, click the **Fly In** animation. The animation previews on the slide as the bulleted items fly in from the bottom. When the "Safe for families" and "Two routes" items fly in, their subitems fly in with them. After the preview is finished, the numbers 1 through 4 appear next to the bulleted items. Notice that the subitems have the same animation sequence number as their first-level items. This means that the start timing for the subitems is set to With Previous or After Previous. See Figure 2-28.

Figure 2-28 Fly In entrance animation applied to a bulleted list with subitems

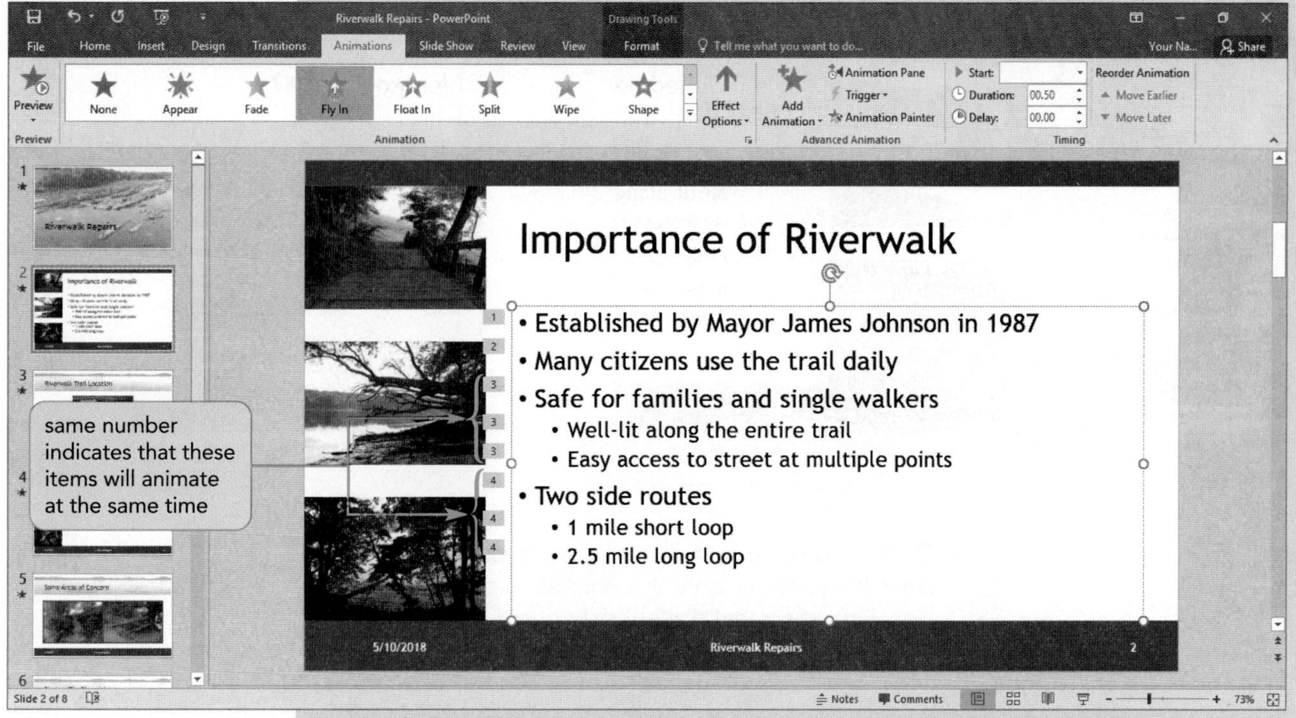

Courtesy of Helen M. Pinard; © Paul Mozell/Alamy

3. Next to the "Safe for families and single walkers" bulleted item, click the animation sequence icon **3** to select it. In the Timing group, On Click appears in the Start box.
4. Next to the subitem "Well-lit along the entire trail," click the animation sequence icon **3**. In the Timing group, With Previous appears in the Start box.

If you wanted to change how the items in the list animate during the slide show, you could change the start timing of each item, or you could change the sequence effect. Sequence effects appear on the Effect Options menu in addition to the Direction options when an animation is applied to a text box. The default is for the items to appear By Paragraph. This means each first-level item animates one at a time—with its subitems, if there are any—when you advance the slide show. You can change this setting so that the entire list animates at once as one object, or so that each first-level item animates at the same time but as separate objects.

To examine the Sequence options for the animated list:

1. Click in the bulleted list, and then in the Animation group, click the **Effect Options** button. The Sequence options appear at the bottom of the menu, below the Direction options, and By Paragraph is selected. See Figure 2-29.

Figure 2-29 Animation effect options for a bulleted list

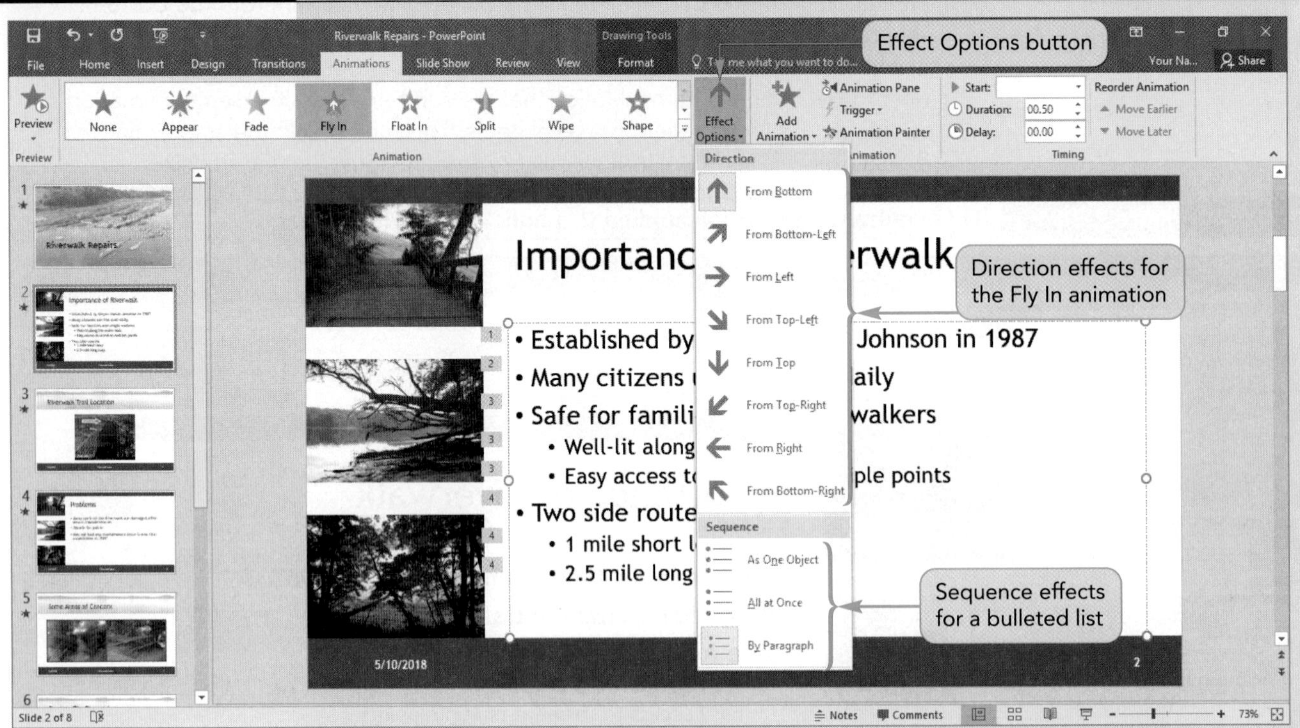

Courtesy of Helen M. Pinard; © Paul Mozell/Alamy

2. Click **As One Object**. The animation preview shows the entire text box fly in. After the preview, only one animation sequence icon appears next to the text box, indicating that the entire text box will animate as a single object. In the Timing group, On Click appears in the Start box.

3. In the Animation group, click the **Effect Options** button, and then under Sequence, click **All at Once**. The animation previews again, but this time each of the first-level items fly in as separate objects, although they all fly in at the same time. After the preview, animation sequence icons, all numbered 1, appear next to each bulleted item, indicating that each item will animate separately but you only need to advance the slide show once.
4. Next to the first bulleted item, click the animation sequence icon **1**. In the Timing group, On Click appears in the Start box.
5. Next to the second bulleted item ("Many citizens use the trail daily"), click the animation sequence icon **1**. In the Timing group, With Previous appears in the Start box.
6. In the Animation group, click the **Effect Options** button, and then click **By Paragraph**. The sequence effect is changed back to its original setting.
7. Save your changes.

PROSKILLS

Decision Making: Just Because You Can Doesn't Mean You Should

PowerPoint provides you with many tools that enable you to create interesting and creative slide shows. However, you need to give careful thought before deciding to use a tool to enhance the content of your presentation. Just because a tool is available doesn't mean you should use it. One example of a tool to use sparingly is sound effects with transitions. Most of the time you do not need to use sound to highlight the fact that one slide is leaving the screen while another appears.

You will also want to avoid using too many or frivolous animations. It is easy to go overboard with animations, and they can quickly become distracting and make your presentation seem less professional. Before you apply an animation, you should know what you want to emphasize and why you want to use an animation. Remember that animations should always enhance your message. When you are finished giving your presentation, you want your audience to remember your message, not your animations.

Adding and Modifying Video

You can add video to slides to play during your presentation. PowerPoint supports various file formats, but the most commonly used are the MPEG-4 format, the Windows Media Audio/Video format, and the Audio Visual Interleave format, which appears in Explorer windows as the Video Clip file type. After you insert a video, you can modify it by changing playback options, changing the length of time the video plays, and applying formats and styles to the video.

Adding Video to Slides

To insert a video stored on your computer or network, click the Insert Video button in a content placeholder, and then in the Insert Video window, in the From a file section, click Browse to open the Insert Video dialog box. You can also click the Video button in the Media group on the Insert tab, and then click Video on My PC to open the same Insert Video dialog box.

REFERENCE

Adding Videos Stored on Your Computer or Network

- In a content placeholder, click the Insert Video button to open the Insert Video window, and then in the From a file section, click Browse to open the Insert Video dialog box; or click the Insert tab on the ribbon, and then in the Media group, click the Video button, and then click Video on My PC to open the Insert Video dialog box.
- Click the video you want to use, and then click the Insert button.
- If desired, click the Video Tools Playback tab, and then in the Video Options group:
  - Click the Start arrow, and then click Automatically to change how the video starts from On Click.
  - Click the Play Full Screen check box to select it to have the video fill the screen.
  - Click the Rewind after Playing check box to select it to have the poster frame display after the video plays.
  - Click the Volume button, and then click a volume level or click Mute.

José gave you a video that he wants you to add to Slide 6. The video shows an eroded bank along the trail.

To add a video to Slide 6 and play it:

1. Display **Slide 6** ("Erosion: The Biggest Issue"), and then in the content placeholder, click the **Insert Video** button. The Insert Video window opens.
2. Next to From a file, click **Browse**. The Insert Video dialog box opens.
3. In the **PowerPoint2 > Module** folder, click **Erosion2**, and then click the **Insert** button. The video is inserted on the slide. The first frame of the video is displayed, and a play bar with controls for playing the video appears below it. See Figure 2-30.

Figure 2-30 **Video added to Slide 6**

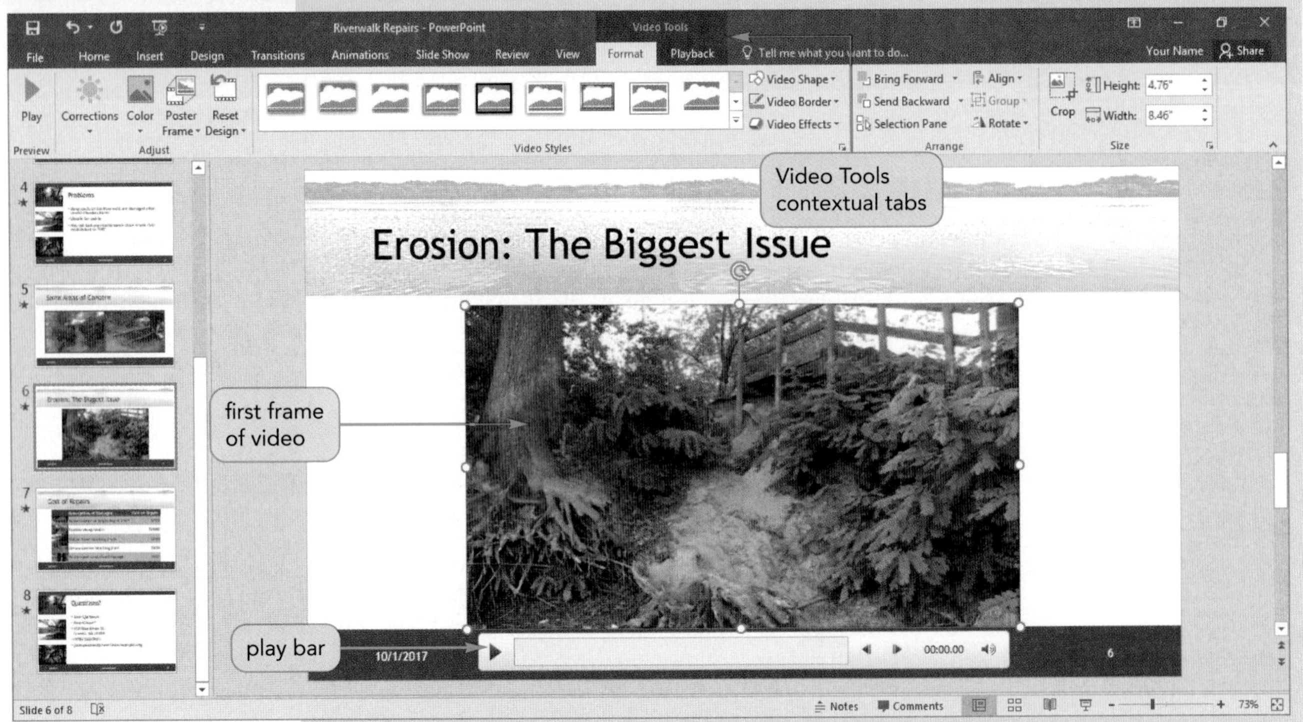

Courtesy of Helen M. Pinard

4. On the play bar, click the **Play** button. The Play button changes to the Pause button and the video plays. Watch the 13-second video (note that this video does not have any sound). Next, you'll watch the video in Slide Show view.
5. On the status bar, click the **Slide Show** button. Slide 6 appears in Slide Show view.
6. Point to the **video**. The play bar appears, and the pointer changes to . You don't need to click the Play button to play the video in Slide Show view; you can click anywhere on the video to play it as long as the pointer is visible. While the video is playing, you can click it again to pause it.
7. Click anywhere on the video. The video plays.

   Trouble? If Slide 7 appeared instead of the video playing, the pointer wasn't visible or you didn't click the video object, so clicking the slide advanced the slide show. Press the Backspace key to return to Slide 6, move the mouse over the video to make the pointer visible, and then click the video.
8. Before the video finishes playing, move the pointer to make it visible, and then click the **video** again. The video pauses.
9. Move the pointer to make it visible, if necessary, click the **video** to finish playing it, and then press the **Esc** key to end the slide show.

INSIGHT

Inserting Pictures and Videos You Find Online

In addition to adding pictures and video stored on your computer or network to slides, you can also add pictures and video stored on websites. To add pictures from a website, you click the Online Pictures button in a content placeholder. When you do this, the Insert Pictures window opens, in which you can use the Bing search engine to search for images stored on the Internet. Your results will be similar to those you would get if you typed keywords in the Search box on the Bing home page in your browser. However, in the Insert Pictures window, only images that are licensed under Creative Commons appear. (When you search using Bing in a browser, you see all results, not just the images licensed under Creative Commons.)

To add a video from a website, you click the Insert Video button in a content placeholder to open the Insert Video window. There, you can type search terms in the Search YouTube box to find a video on YouTube, or, if you have the embed code from a website, you can paste the embed code in the Paste embed code here box. When you search for a video on YouTube, videos that match your search terms appear in the window. You click the video you want to add, and then click Insert. To add a video whose embed code you copied, right-click in the Paste embed code here box, click Paste on the shortcut menu, and then click the Insert button in the box.

Trimming Videos

If a video is too long, or if there are parts at the beginning or end of the video that you don't want to show during the presentation, you can trim it. To do this, click the Trim Video button in the Editing group on the Video Tools Playback tab, and then, in the Trim Video dialog box, drag the green start slider or the red stop slider to a new position to mark where the video will start and stop.

José doesn't think the audience needs to watch all 13 seconds of this video, so he wants you to trim it to 10 seconds.

To trim the video on Slide 6:

1. With Slide 6 ("Erosion: The Biggest Issue") displayed, click the **video** to select it, if necessary, and then click the **Video Tools Playback** tab.
2. In the Editing group, click the **Trim Video** button. The Trim Video dialog box opens. See Figure 2-31.

Figure 2-31 Trim Video dialog box

Courtesy of Helen M. Pinard

3. Drag the red **Stop** tab to the left until the time in the End Time box is approximately 10 seconds, and then click the **OK** button.
4. On the play bar, click the **Play** button ▶. The video plays but stops after playing for 10 seconds.
5. Save your changes.

Setting a Poster Frame

The frame that appears on the slide when the video is not playing is called the **poster frame**. You can set the poster frame to be any frame in the video, or you can set the poster frame to any image stored in a file. The default poster frame for a video is the first frame of the video. You can change this so that any frame from the video or any image stored in a file is the poster frame. If the video is set to rewind, you can make the poster frame appear if you set the video to rewind after playing. José wants you to do this for the video on Slide 6.

To set a poster frame for the video on Slide 6:

1. With Slide 6 ("Erosion: The Biggest Issue") displayed, click the **video** to select it, if necessary, and then click the **Video Tools Format** tab.
2. Point to the **play bar** below the video. A ScreenTip appears identifying the time of the video at that point. See Figure 2-32.

Figure 2-32 **Setting a poster frame**

Courtesy of Helen M. Pinard

3. On the play bar, click at approximately the one-second mark. The video advances to the one-second mark, and the frame at the one-second mark appears in the video object.
4. In the Adjust group, click the **Poster Frame** button. The Poster Frame menu opens.
5. Click **Current Frame**. The message "Poster Frame Set" appears in the video's play bar, and the frame currently visible in the video object is set as the poster frame.

Modifying Video Playback Options

You can change several options for how a video plays. The video playback options are listed in Figure 2-33.

Figure 2-33 Video playback options

Video Option	Function
Volume	Change the volume of the video from high to medium or low or mute it.
Start	Change how the video starts, either when the presenter clicks it or the Play button on the play bar or automatically when the slide appears during the slide show.
Play Full Screen	The video fills the screen during the slide show.
Hide While Not Playing	The video does not appear on the slide when it is not playing; make sure the video is set to play automatically if this option is selected.
Loop until Stopped	The video plays until the next slide appears during the slide show.
Rewind after Playing	The video rewinds after it plays so that the first frame or the poster frame appears again.

One of the playback options you can modify is the start timing so that the video plays automatically when the slide appears during the slide show. When you insert a video, its start timing is set to On Click. This start timing means something different for videos than for animations. For animations, On Click means you can do anything to advance the slide show to cause the animation to start. For videos, On Click means you need to click the video object or the Play button on the play bar. If you click somewhere else on the screen or do anything else to advance the slide show, the video will not play. The start timing setting is on the Video Tools Playback tab.

In addition to changing the start timing, you can set a video to fill the screen when it plays during the slide show. If you set the option to play full screen, the video will fill the screen when it plays, covering the slide title and anything else on the slide. You can also set a video to rewind after it plays.

José wants you to change the start timing of the video on Slide 6 so that it starts automatically when Slide 6 appears during a slide show. He also wants the video to fill the screen when it plays during the slide show, and for the video to rewind after it plays. He asks you to set these options.

To modify the playback options of the video:

1. With Slide 6 ("Erosion: The Biggest Issue") displayed, click the **video** to select it, if necessary.
2. On the ribbon, click the **Video Tools Playback** tab. In the Video Options group, On Click appears in the Start box. See Figure 2-34.

Figure 2-34 Options on the Video Tools Playback tab

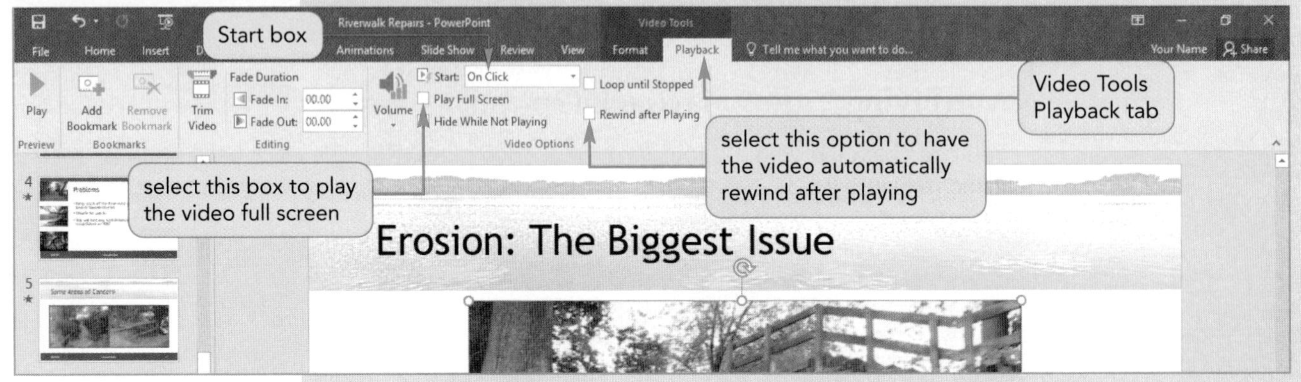

Courtesy of Helen M. Pinard

TIP

You can adjust the volume of a video while it plays, or you can set the default volume by clicking the Volume button in the Video Options group on the Playback tab and then clicking an option on the menu.

3. In the Video Options group, click the **Start** arrow, and then click **Automatically**. Now the video will start automatically when the slide appears during the slide show.
4. In the Video Options group, click the **Play Full Screen** check box to select it. The video will fill the screen when it plays.
5. In the Video Options group, click the **Rewind after Playing** check box to select it. The video will reset to the beginning after it plays and display the poster frame.
6. On the status bar, click the **Slide Show** button. Slide 6 appears briefly in Slide Show view, and then the video fills the screen and plays. After the video finishes playing, Slide 6 reappears displaying the poster frame of the video.
7. Press the **Esc** key to end the slide show, and then save the changes.

Understanding Animation Effects Applied to Videos

When you insert a video (or audio) object, an animation is automatically applied to the video so that you can click anywhere on the video to start and pause it when the slide show is run. This animation is the Pause animation in the Media animation category, and it is set to On Click. The Media animation category appears only when a media object—either video or audio—is selected on a slide. The Pause animation is what makes it possible to start or pause a video during a slide show by clicking anywhere on the video object. (When you click the video to play it, you are actually "unpausing" it.)

When you change the Start setting of a video on the Playback tab to Automatically, a second animation, the Play animation in the Media animation category, is applied to the video as well as the Pause animation, and the start timing of the Play animation is set to After Previous. If there are no other objects on the slide set to animate before the video, the Play animation has an animation sequence number of zero, which means that it will play immediately after the slide transition.

To see these animations, click the Animations tab on the ribbon, and then select a video object on a slide. The Pause and Play animations appear in the Animation gallery in the Media category.

You'll examine the video animations now.

To examine the Media animation effects for the video:

1. With Slide 6 ("Erosion: The Biggest Issue") displayed, click the **video** to select it, if necessary.
2. On the ribbon, click the **Animations** tab. Because you set this video to start automatically, two animation sequence icons appear next to it, one containing a zero and one containing a lightning bolt. In the Animation group, Multiple is selected because two animations are applied to this video. See Figure 2-35.

Figure 2-35 Two animations applied to a video

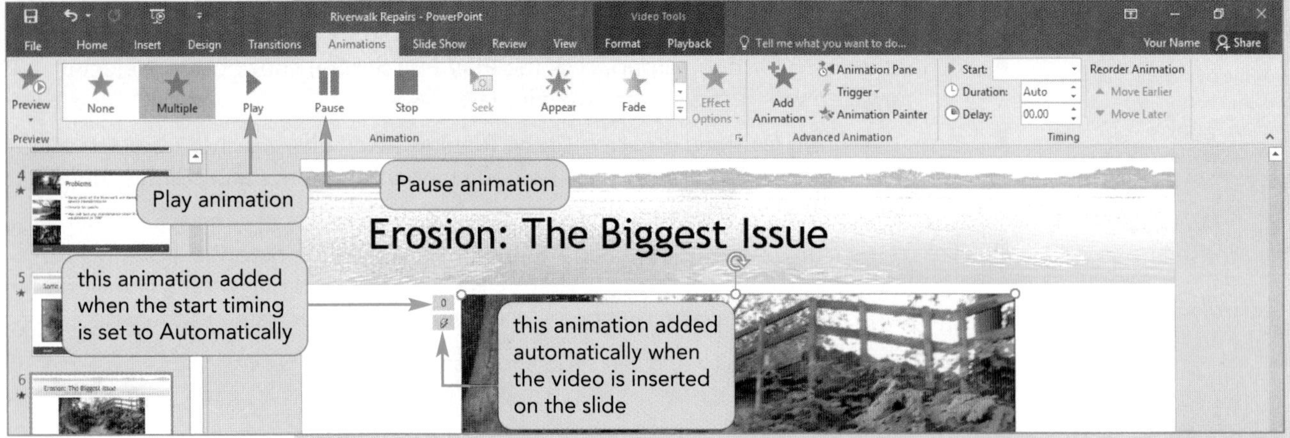

Courtesy of Helen M. Pinard

3. In the Animation group, click the **More** button. The Media category appears at the top of the Animation gallery because a media object is selected.
4. Press the **Esc** key. The gallery closes without you making a selection.

   When more than one animation is applied to any object, you need to click each animation sequence icon to see which animation is associated with each icon.
5. Click the **lightning bolt** animation sequence icon. In the Animation group, the Pause animation is selected, and in the Timing group, On Click appears in the Start box. This animation is applied automatically to all videos when you add them to slides. It is because of this animation that you can click anywhere on the video object during a slide show to play or pause it.
6. Click the **0** animation sequence icon. In the Animation group, Play is selected, and in the Timing group, After Previous appears in the Start box. This Play animation was added to this video when you selected Automatically in the Start box on the Playback tab.

Compressing and Optimizing Media

TIP

If you might want to show the presentation using a projector capable of high-quality display, save a copy of the presentation before you compress the media.

As with pictures, you can compress media files. If you need to send a file via email or you need to upload it, you should compress media files to make the final PowerPoint file smaller. The more you compress files, the smaller the final presentation file will be but also the lower the quality. For videos, you can compress using the following settings:

- **Presentation Quality**—compresses the videos slightly and maintains the quality of the videos
- **Internet Quality**—compresses the videos to a quality suitable for streaming over the Internet
- **Low Quality**—compresses the videos as small as possible

With all of the settings, any parts of videos that you trimmed off will be deleted, similar to deleting the cropped portions of photos.

After you compress media, you should watch the slides containing the videos using the equipment you will be using when giving your presentation to make sure the reduced quality is acceptable. Usually, if the videos were high quality to start with, the compressed quality will be fine. However, if the original video quality was grainy, the compressed quality might be too low, even for evaluation purposes. If you decide that you don't like the compressed quality, you can undo the compression.

You will compress the media files you inserted. You need to send the presentation to José via email, so you will compress the media as much as possible.

To compress the videos in the presentation:

1. With Slide 6 ("Erosion: The Biggest Issue") displayed, click the **File** tab. Backstage view appears displaying the Info screen. See Figure 2-36.

Figure 2-36 Compression options on the Info screen in Backstage view

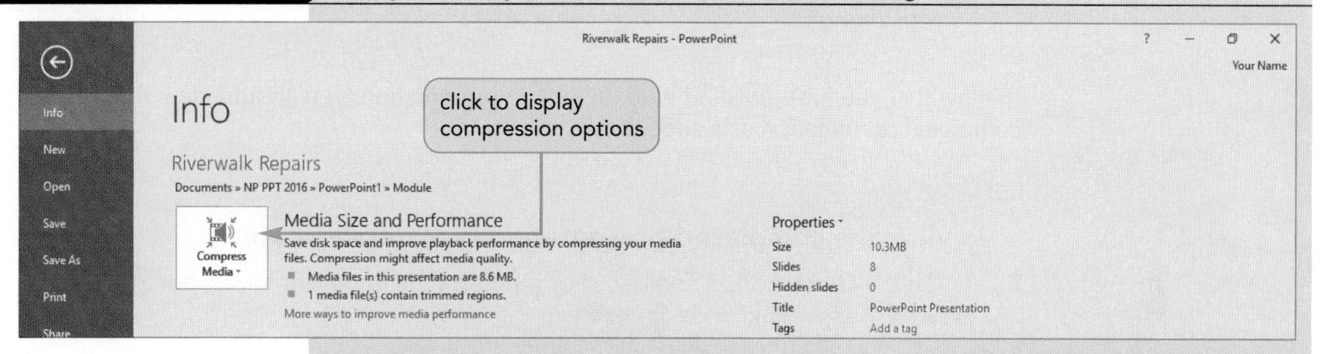

2. Click the **Compress Media** button. A menu opens listing compression choices.
3. Click **Low Quality**. The Compress Media dialog box opens listing the video file in the presentation with a progress bar to show you the progress of the compression. See Figure 2-37.

Figure 2-37 Compress Media dialog box

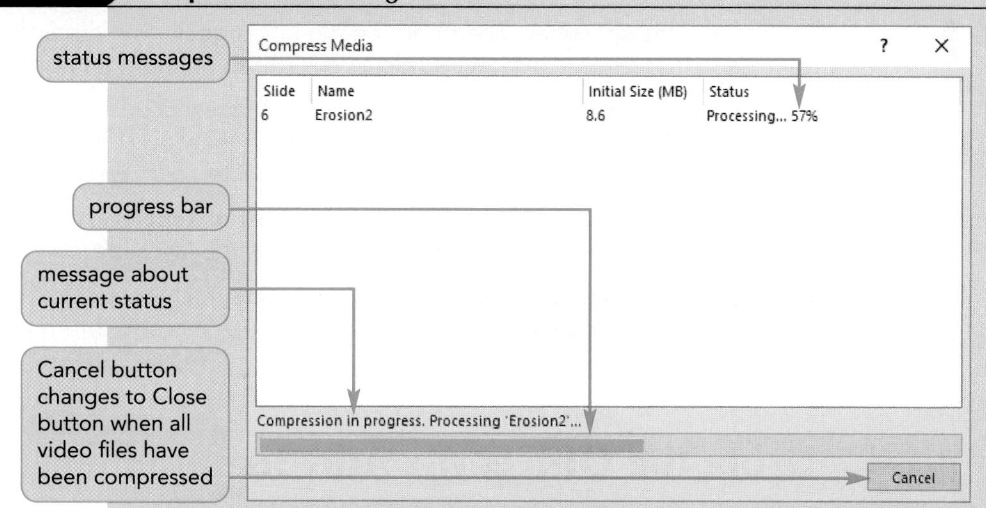

After the file is compressed, a message appears in the Status column indicating that compression for the file is complete and stating how much the video file size was reduced. A message also appears at the bottom of the dialog box stating that the compression is complete and indicating how much the file size of the presentation was reduced. Because there is only one video in this presentation, the amount the video was reduced and the amount the presentation was reduced is the same.

4. Click the **Close** button. Next to the Compress Media button on the Info screen, the bulleted list states that the presentation's media was compressed to Low Quality and that you can undo the compression if the results are unsatisfactory. Now you need to view the compressed videos.
5. At the top of the navigation bar, click the **Back** button to display Slide 6.
6. On the status bar, click the **Slide Show** button to display the slide in Slide Show view, and then watch the video. The quality is lower, but sufficient for José to get the general idea after you send the presentation to him via email.
7. Press the **Esc** key to end the slide show.
8. Display **Slide 1** (the title slide), add your name as the subtitle, and then save your changes.

Now that you have finished working on the presentation, you should view the completed presentation as a slide show.

To view the completed presentation in Slide Show view:

1. On the Quick Access Toolbar, click the **Start From Beginning** button. Slide 1 appears in Slide Show view.
2. Press the **spacebar**. Slide 2 ("Importance of Riverwalk") appears in Slide Show view displaying the photos on the slide layout, the slide title, and the footer, date, and slide number.
3. Press the **spacebar** four times to display all the bulleted items, and then press the **spacebar** again to display Slide 3 ("Riverwalk Trail Location").
4. Press the **spacebar** twice to display Slide 4 ("Problems") and then Slide 5 ("Some Areas of Concern").
5. Press the **spacebar**. The photo on the left appears with the Split animation, and then after a one-second delay, the photo on the right appears.
6. Press the **spacebar**. Slide 6 ("Erosion: The Biggest Issue") appears, the video fills the screen and plays automatically. When the video is finished, Slide 6 appears again with the poster frame you selected displayed in the video object.
7. Press the **spacebar** to display Slide 7 ("Cost of Repairs"), and then press the **spacebar** to display Slide 8 ("Questions?"), the last slide.
8. Press the **spacebar** to display the black slide that appears at the end of a slide show, and then press the **spacebar** once more to return to Normal view.

Using the Office Mix Add-In

The presentation with transitions, animations, and video is interesting and should enhance the presentation José will give to the city councilors. However, José wants to post the presentation to a website so that any city councilors—and any citizens—who do not attend the meeting can see the presentation.

To do this, he will use Office Mix, a PowerPoint add-in to create a mix. An **add-in** is software that you can install to add new commands and features to PowerPoint. A **mix** is an interactive video created from a PowerPoint presentation using Office Mix and posted to a website. When you use Office Mix, you can record your voice as you give your presentation and describe your slides. You can also record video of yourself as you speak; this video becomes part of the mix and appears on each slide as people view the mix. You can also record annotations (notes and drawings) that you add to slides while they are displayed. You can also add links to websites that viewers can click when they watch the mix. In addition, you can add quizzes to your mix that ask viewers questions that test their understanding of the content presented. After you create a mix, you can upload it to a Microsoft website using your Microsoft account, and anyone with the link can view it.

Installing Office Mix

In order to use Office Mix, you need to install the add-in. If the Mix tab does not appear on the ribbon to the right of the View tab, then Office Mix might not be installed.

If Office Mix is not installed as an add-in, you need to download it from Microsoft's website and then install it. You first need to close PowerPoint because you cannot install the Office Mix add-in while PowerPoint is running.

Note: The following steps were accurate at the time of publication. However, the Office Mix webpage is dynamic and might change over time, including the way it is organized and how commands are performed.

Also, if you are working in a lab or on a school-issued computer, get permission from your instructor before installing the Office Mix add-in.

To exit PowerPoint and then download and install the Office Mix add-in:

1. In the upper-right corner of the PowerPoint window, click the **Close** button to close the presentation and exit PowerPoint.

   Trouble? If there is still a PowerPoint button on the taskbar, another presentation is open. Right-click the PowerPoint button on the taskbar, and then click Close window or Close all windows.

2. Start your browser, and then go to mix.office.com.

   Trouble? If the Internet address in Step 2 is not correct, use a search engine to search for Office Mix.

3. On the Office Mix webpage, click the **Get Office Mix button**. The Welcome to Office Mix page opens, asking you to sign in.

   Trouble? If you are already signed in with your Microsoft account, the Office Mix PowerPoint Add-in page appears instead. Skip Steps 4 and 5.

4. If you have a work or school account associated with Microsoft or Office, click the **Sign in with a work or school account button**; if you do not have a work or school account associated with the computer you are using, click the **Sign in with a Microsoft account button**. The sign in page appears.

   Trouble? If you don't have a Microsoft account, click the Sign in with a Microsoft account button, on the Sign in page that appears, click the Sign up now link, fill in the requested information to create a Microsoft account, and then sign in. Skip Step 5.

5. Enter your username and password in the appropriate boxes, and then click the **Sign in** button. The Office Mix PowerPoint Add-in page appears, and the Office Mix installation file starts downloading automatically.

   Trouble? If the software does not start downloading automatically, click the "click here" link next to "If your download doesn't start automatically."

6. After the file has finished downloading, click the **Run** button in the message box that appears at the bottom of the browser window to start installing the add-in. The Office Mix license dialog box appears.

   Trouble? If you are using a browser other than Microsoft Edge, you might see the name of the file—OfficeMix.Setup.exe—in a button at the bottom of the browser window. Click that button to start installing the add-in. If the downloaded file does not appear at the bottom of the window, you need to locate the folder to which the file downloaded, and then double-click the OfficeMix.Setup file. If you can't find the file, ask your technical support person for assistance.

7. Click the **I agree to the license terms and conditions** check box to accept the software license, and then click the **Install** button. The license screen closes and the User Account Control dialog box appears, asking if you want to allow this app to make changes to your PC.

   Trouble? If the dialog box displays "Modify Setup" instead of the license agreement, Office Mix is already installed on your computer. Click the Close button, close your browser, skip the rest of the steps in this section, and continue with the section "Creating a Mix."

8. Click the **Yes** button. The User Account Control dialog box closes and the Office Mix Preview Setup dialog box appears. After the add-in is installed, PowerPoint starts.

9. In the Office Mix Preview Setup dialog box, click the **Close** button.

   Trouble? If you don't see the Office Mix Preview Setup dialog box, click the Office Mix Preview Setup button on the taskbar, and then execute Step 9.

   In the PowerPoint window, a Welcome to Office Mix slide is displayed, the Welcome task pane is open, and the Mix tab now appears on the ribbon to the right of the View tab and is the active tab. See Figure 2-38.

Figure 2-38 Mix tab on the ribbon

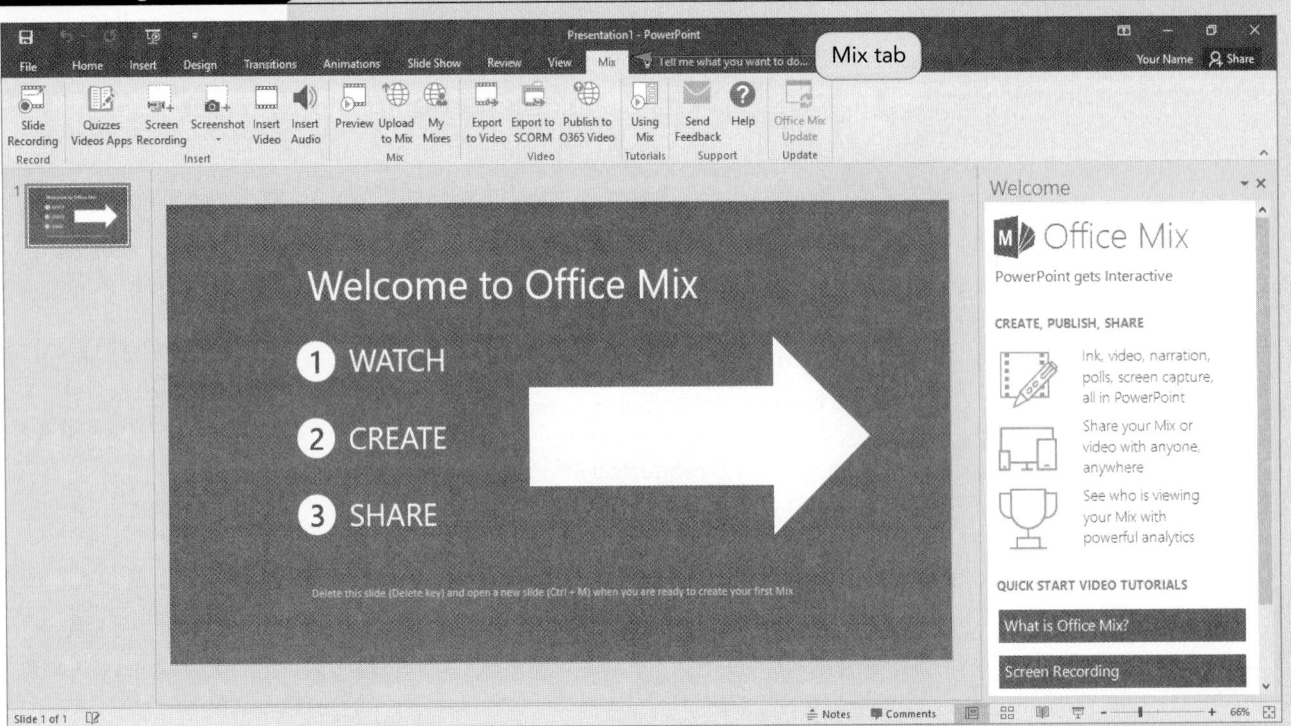

Trouble? If the Mix tab is not the active tab on the ribbon, click the Mix tab on the ribbon.

Trouble? If the Mix tab does not appear on the ribbon, click File, click Options, and then click Customize Ribbon. In the Customize the Ribbon list, click the Mix check box to select it, and then click the OK button.

TIP

If you want to watch video tutorials about Office Mix, on the Mix tab on the ribbon, click the Using Mix button in the Tutorials group to open the Welcome task pane, and then click a button to start a tutorial.

10. In the task pane title bar, click the **Close** button [X]. The Welcome task pane closes.

    Trouble? If the Welcome task pane does not appear on your screen, skip Step 10.

11. On the ribbon, click the **File** tab, and then in the navigation bar, click **Close**. The new presentation with one slide closes.
12. On the taskbar, click your browser's program button, and then close your browser.

Now you are ready to use Office Mix to create an interactive presentation.

Creating a Mix

To create a mix, you basically record the slide show and then post it to a website. In a mix, the recording of each slide is independent of the other slides in the presentation. This means that you can reorder the slides after you have recorded them for the mix, and the timing, annotations, audio, and video that you recorded for each slide will travel with that slide. It also means that you do not need to record all of the slides in one session. You can record each slide individually if you want.

José asked you to practice recording a mix. He wants you to record yourself explaining a few of the slides, but he does not want you to include video of yourself. Because this is just practice, you will use a version of the file that contains only three slides to reduce the file size and make the upload to the Microsoft Mix server faster.

To start recording a mix:

1. Start PowerPoint if necessary, open the file **Mix**, which is located in the **PowerPoint2 > Module** folder, and then save it as **Riverwalk Repairs Mix** to the location where you are storing your files. This file is similar to the file you created in this module, but it contains only three slides.
2. On Slide 1 (the title slide), add your name as the subtitle.
3. On the ribbon, click the **Mix** tab, if necessary. The Mix tab contains commands for recording and working with a mix.

   Trouble? If the Mix tab is not on the ribbon, click File, click Options to open the PowerPoint Options dialog box, and then click Customize Ribbon in the navigation pane. In the Customize the Ribbon list, click the Mix check box to select it, and then click the OK button. If the Mix check box is not listed, click Add-ins in the navigation pane on the left, and then click the Go button at the bottom next to Manage COM Add-ins. In the COM Add-Ins dialog box, click the Office Mix check box to select it. (If it is already selected, do not click it.) Click the OK button. If the Mix tab still doesn't appear on the ribbon, open the Customize Ribbon screen in the PowerPoint Options dialog box again, click the Mix check box to select it, and then click the OK button.

4. In the Record group, click the **Slide Recording** button. The recording window appears with Slide 1 displayed. The ribbon in the recording window contains four groups of commands, and the Audio and Video task pane is open on the right side of the window. See Figure 2-39.

Figure 2-39 Slide recording window in Office Mix

Courtesy of Helen M. Pinard

Before you start recording, you need to set the audio and video options. If you are going to record video of yourself, you need to select a camera. You also need to select a microphone if you are recording yourself speaking.

You can draw on slides while you are recording a mix. When you draw with the pointer, the lines you draw will be the color that is selected at the bottom of the Audio and Video task pane. The default color is black, and the Black color in the task pane has a faint gray border around it to indicate that it is selected. The default weight is medium, and the Medium Pen button is shaded to indicate that it is selected. You can change the pen color and weight during the recording, but it takes several seconds to do this. So in order to have a smooth recording session, you will change these options now.

To set video, audio, and pen options:

1. In the Audio and Video task pane, if the top button below the Thumbnail and Full Screen option buttons is not labeled "No camera," click it, and then click **No camera**.
2. Click the **microphone button** that appears below the No camera button. A menu of microphone options opens.

Trouble? If the only menu option is No microphone, you do not have a microphone built into or connected to your computer. You need to get a microphone and connect it to your computer in order to record yourself speaking. If you do not have a microphone, you can still create the mix, but skip the rest of the steps in this set of steps.

3. Click the microphone you want to use. The menu closes and the bar below the microphone box shows a moving white bar. The moving white bar indicates the volume level that is being detected by the microphone. You can test the microphone.
4. Say **Testing, testing** into the microphone. (If you are using the internal microphone on a laptop, you can speak sitting in front of the laptop and the microphone will pick it up.) When you speak, the white bar increases in size.

   Trouble? If the white bar does not move when you speak, you either selected the wrong option on the microphone menu or the microphone you selected is not enabled in Windows. Repeat Steps 2–4, making sure you select the correct microphone. If the white bar still doesn't move, in the upper-right corner of the window, click the Close button. At the right end of the Windows taskbar, right-click the speaker icon, and then click Recording devices. In the Sound dialog box that opens, on the Recording tab, right-click the microphone you want to use, and then click Enable. (If Enable is not listed on the shortcut menu, the microphone is already enabled.) Click the OK button. In the PowerPoint window, on the Mix tab, click the Slide Recording button to return to the Slide Recording window. Repeat Steps 2–4.
5. In the Audio and Video task pane, in the Inking section, click the **Thick Pen** button.
6. In the Audio and Video task pane, click the **Red** color. When you draw on the slides, the lines you draw will be thick and red.

Now that the recording options are set up, you can record the mix. To do this, you click the Record button on the ribbon.

To record slides with audio for the mix:

1. On the ribbon, in the Record group, click the **Record** button. The Record button changes to the Pause your recording button, and a moving, dashed line appears around the slide.
2. Move the pointer on top of the slide. The pointer changes to a pen. This indicates that you can use the pointer to draw on the slide. This also means that you cannot click to advance the slide show.
3. Say **The Riverwalk trail is badly in need of repairs.** and then press the **spacebar**. Slide 2 ("Importance of Riverwalk") appears. On the ribbon, the Move to your next slide button is no longer available. Instead, the Go to the next animation button is available. This is because the text on Slide 2 has animations applied, and you need to display the bulleted items before you can advance to the next slide.

   Trouble? If you do not have a microphone, skip the part of Step 3 in which you speak.

4. On the ribbon click the **Go to the next animation** button, pause for a moment, click the **Go to the next animation** button again, pause, and then press the **spacebar**. Three first-level bulleted items and associated subitems appear on the slide.
5. In the second bullet, position the pointer below the word "Safe," press and hold the mouse button, drag below the word "Safe," and then release the mouse button. A red line appears along the path you dragged.
6. In the Navigation group, click the **Move to your next slide** button. Slide 3 ("Some Areas of Concern") appears.
7. Press the **spacebar**. The photo on the left appears, and then after a brief delay, the photo on the right appears.
8. On the ribbon, click the **Stop your recording** button.

TIP

If you want to rerecord a slide, display that slide, click the Record button, keep the slide displayed for as long as you want, click the Stop your recording button, and then click Yes in the dialog box that asks if you want to overwrite the recording on the slide.

When you record a mix, a mix media object is placed on each slide that you record. The mix media object contains the slide timing, any drawings you added while recording, and any audio or video you recorded. You can see the mix media object on each slide when the slide is displayed in Normal view.

To close the recording window and view the mix media icons:

1. In the upper-right corner, click the **Close** button. The recording window closes, and Slide 3 ("Some Areas of Concern") appears in Normal view. In the upper-right corner of the slide, a mix media icon appears. This is the mix media icon that appears when a microphone is selected while you record the mix.

   Trouble? If you do not have a microphone, the mix media icon looks like an analog clock showing three o'clock.
2. Display **Slide 1** (the title slide), and then point to the mix media icon. A play bar appears.
3. On the play bar, click the **Play** button. The verbal recording you made plays.

Adding Interactive Content to a Mix

Mixes can include interactive content. If you include a link to a website in a mix, people watching the mix can click the link to open their browsers and display that webpage. You can also add slides containing quiz questions that users can answer as they watch the mix. The questions can be multiple choice, true/false, or free response.

To add a quiz to a mix:

1. Display **Slide 2** ("Importance of Riverwalk"), click the **Home** tab, and then click the **New Slide** button. A new Slide 3 with the Title and Content layout is added and is the current slide.
2. Click in the **title text placeholder**, and then type **Quick Quiz**.
3. Click the **Mix** tab, and then in the Insert group, click the **Quizzes Videos Apps** button. The Lab Office Add-ins window opens with the STORE tab selected. See Figure 2-40. Three types of quizzes and a poll are listed below Quizzes and Polls in the window.

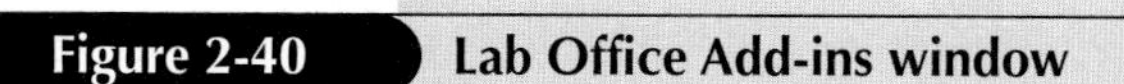

Figure 2-40 **Lab Office Add-ins window**

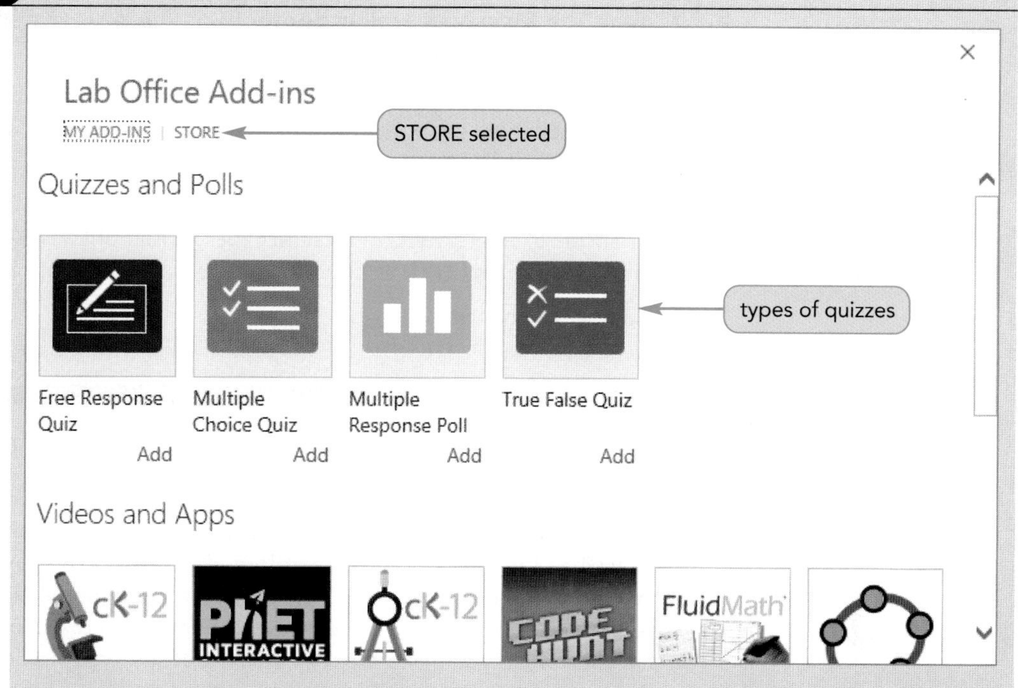

Trouble? If Quizzes and Polls does not appear in the window on your screen, at the top of the window, click STORE.

4. In the Quizzes and Polls section, click **True False Quiz**. The window changes to describe the True False Quiz.
5. Click the **Trust It** button. The window closes, and a True False Quiz object is inserted on Slide 3. See Figure 2-41.

Figure 2-41 **True False Quiz object on Slide 3**

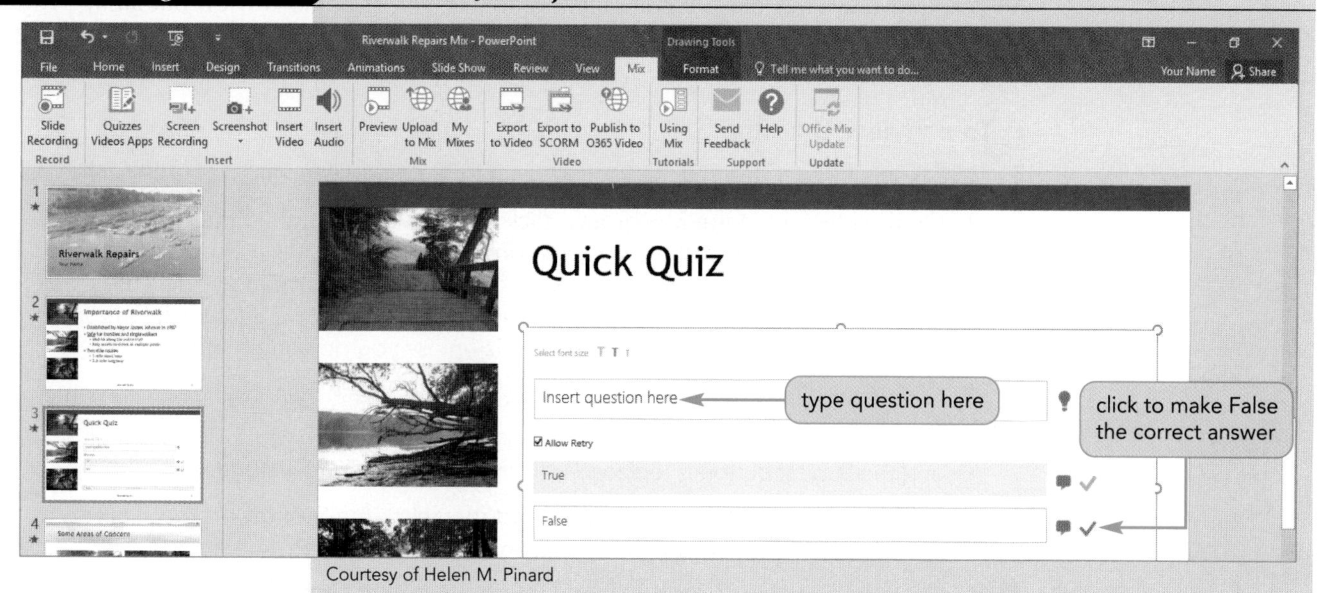

Courtesy of Helen M. Pinard

6. Click in the **Insert question here** box, and then delete all of the text in the box.
7. Type **The Riverwalk trail is poorly lit.** in the box. The answer to this is False, so you need to change the correct answer option.
8. To the right of the False box, click the **Select for correct answer** button ✓. The check mark changes to green to indicate that False is the correct answer.
9. At the bottom of the quiz object, click the **Preview** button. The borders around the question and answers disappear, and the Allow Retry check box changes to an instruction to select the correct answer. Also, the check marks that the user will click to choose True or False are both colored gray.
10. Save your changes.

INSIGHT

Recording a Mix of a Presentation That Includes Audio and Video

In a mix, only one media element—that is, audio or video—on a slide will play. This means that if a slide contains more than one media element, only the first element will play when the mix is viewed. Therefore, if you are going to create a mix of a presentation, do not create slides with more than one media element on them.

If a slide contains a media element, you cannot record audio or video of yourself on that slide when you make the mix. This is because you would be adding a second media element to that slide. If you are recording a mix of a presentation that contains media, the recording will stop when the slide containing media appears. To continue recording the mix, you need to move to the next slide, and then restart the recording. When you upload the mix to a website, the slide with the media on it will be included in the mix, and the media (either a video or recorded audio) will play automatically when that slide appears when someone watches the mix.

Previewing and Uploading a Mix

You can preview a mix on your computer. To do this, you click the Preview button in the Mix group on the Mix tab.

To preview the mix:

1. Display **Slide 1** (the title slide).
2. On the Mix tab, in the Mix group, click the **Preview** button. Slide 1 appears in Slide Show view, and the voice recording you made plays. Then Slide 2 ("Importance of Riverwalk") appears, the bulleted items animate onto the slide, and the word "Safe" is underlined in red. Next, Slide 3 ("Quick Quiz") appears. The mix will not move past this unless you do something.
3. Click **True**. "True" is highlighted in green, and its check mark changes to green.
4. Click the **Submit** button. This is incorrect, so a message appears indicating that, and the Submit button is replaced with the Retry and Continue buttons.
5. Click the **Retry** button, click **False**, and then click the **Submit** button. This is the correct answer, so a message appears indicating that.
6. Click the **Continue** button. Slide 4 ("Some Areas of Concern") appears and the two photos appear.
7. In the bottom-left corner, click the **Close and return to presentation view** button ✖. The mix preview closes and Slide 4 appears in Normal view.

Now that the mix is complete and you have previewed it, you can upload it so that others can view it. Before you upload a mix, you should review any quizzes you added and reset them if you answered them in a preview.

To upload the mix:

1. Display **Slide 3** ("Quick Quiz"), and then at the bottom of the slide, click the **Preview** button. The quiz changes to Preview mode, and the Retry and Continue buttons appear at the bottom-right. The False option is selected. You need to reset this slide.
2. Click the **Retry** button. The quiz resets and neither answer is selected.
3. Save your changes.
4. On the Mix tab, in the Mix group, click the **Upload to Mix** button. The Upload to Mix task pane appears on the right.
5. At the bottom of the task pane, click the **Next** button. After a moment, the task pane changes to list buttons that you can click to sign in to your Microsoft account.

   Trouble? If the task pane indicates that you are signed in, skip Steps 6 and 7 and continue with Step 8.
6. If you have a work or school account associated with Microsoft or Office, click the **Sign in with a work or school account** button; if you do not have a work or school account or are using your own computer, click the **Sign in with a Microsoft account** button. The task pane changes to display boxes for your user name and password.
7. Enter your username and password in the appropriate boxes, and then click the **Sign in** button. The task pane indicates that you are signed in, and the "This is a new Mix" option button is selected.

   Trouble? If a message appears asking you if you want your browser to remember this password, click the Yes or No button depending on your preference. If the computer you are using is a school-issued or lab computer, it is safer to click the No button.
8. In the Upload to Mix task pane, click the **Next** button. The task pane changes to show the progress of the upload and the publishing processes. When the mix is published, a message appears in the task pane indicating this, and the "Show me my Mix" button changes to orange.
9. Click the **Show me my Mix** button. Your browser starts, and the webpage that contains the details for your mix appears. See Figure 2-42. You can edit the title, description, category, and tags (keywords that describe the mix content), and you can edit the permissions level (that is, change who can view the mix).

Figure 2-42 Riverwalk Repairs Mix Details webpage in the Edge browser

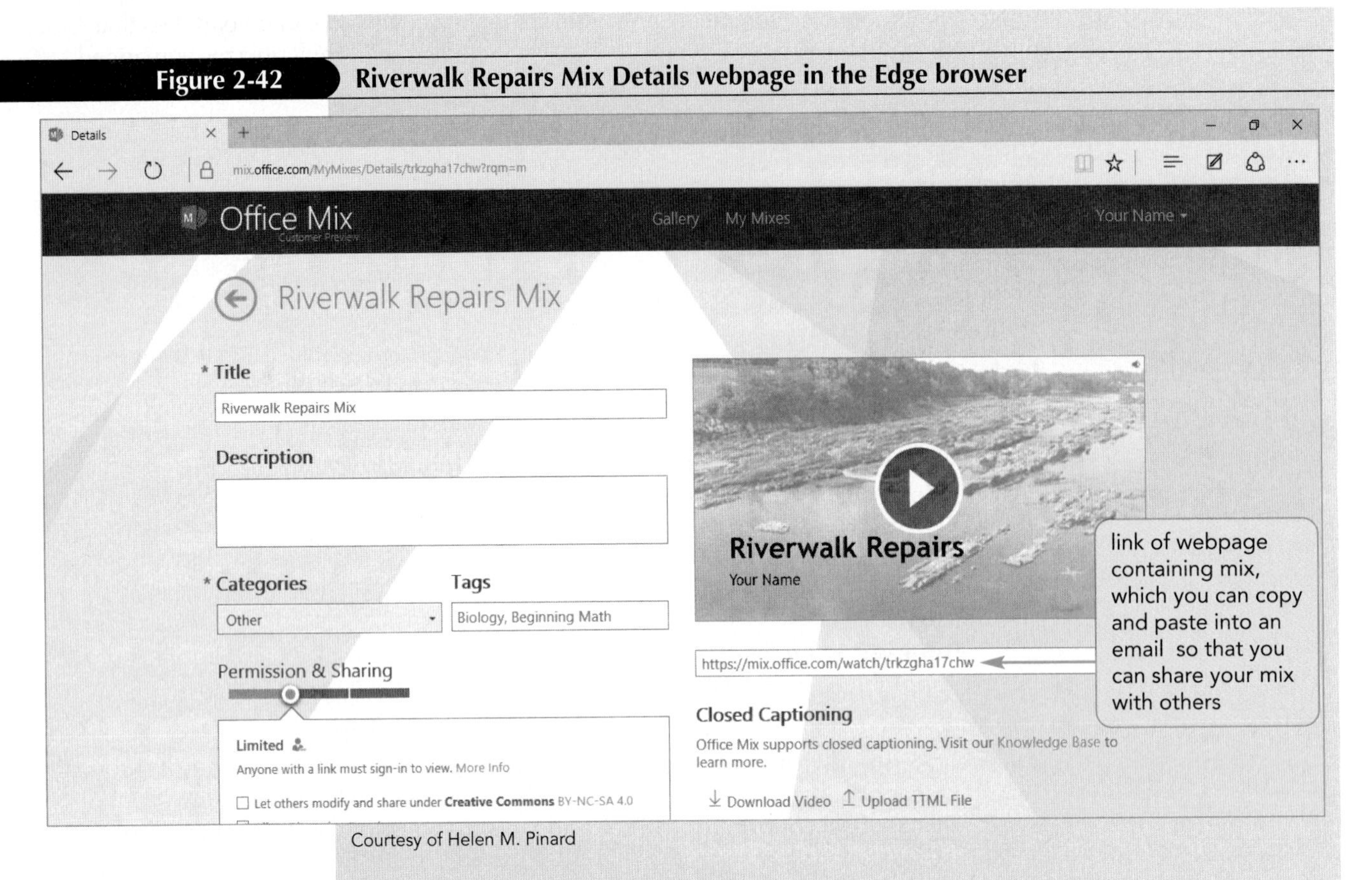

Courtesy of Helen M. Pinard

10. Click the **video**. The webpage containing the mix appears. See Figure 2-43.

Figure 2-43 Riverwalk Repairs Mix webpage

Courtesy of Helen M. Pinard

11. Click the **Play** button. The mix plays until Slide 3 ("Quick Quiz") appears. Notice that the transition between the slides is the Fade transition. The Fade transition is the only transition that is used in mixes. You can either answer the quiz or advance to the next slide without answering the quiz.
12. In the play bar, click the **next** button. Slide 4 ("Some Areas of Concern") appears, and then the photos appear.
13. Click the browser's **Back** button to return to the page containing the details of your mix.
14. If you want to sign out of your Microsoft account, click your username in the upper-right corner, click **Sign out**, and then close your browser.
15. In the PowerPoint window, close the Upload to Mix task pane.

The final presentation file with transitions, animations, and video is interesting and should enhance the presentation that José will give to the city council. José also plans to record his presentation and create a new mix so that he can send the mix link to anyone who misses his presentation.

REVIEW

Session 2.2 Quick Check

1. What is a transition?
2. What are animations?
3. How do you change the speed of a transition or an animation?
4. When you apply an animation to a bulleted list with subitems, how do the first-level items animate? How do the second-level items animate?
5. What is a poster frame?
6. What does "On Click" mean for a video?
7. What animation is applied to every video that you add to a slide?
8. What is a mix created with the PowerPoint add-in Office Mix?

PRACTICE

Review Assignments

Data Files needed for the Review Assignments: Cleared.jpg, Landscape.jpg, NewSign.jpg, NewStairs.jpg, NewTheme.pptx, NewView.mp4, Railings.jpg, Renewed1.pptx, Renewed2.pptx, Wall.jpg

José Quiñones needs to explain the improvements RiverClean™ made to the Riverwalk trail in Lowell, Massachusetts. He decides to create a presentation that will include photos and video of the improved trail. This presentation will show the city council how the money allocated was spent. José also created a new custom theme to highlight the improvements. Complete the following:

1. Open the presentation **Renewed1**, located in the PowerPoint2 > Review folder included with your Data Files, add your name as the subtitle, and then save it as **Renewed Riverwalk** to the drive and folder where you are storing your files.
2. Apply the theme from the presentation **NewTheme**, located in the PowerPoint2 > Review folder.
3. Change the layout of Slide 4 ("Projects") and Slide 6 ("New Views of the River from the Trail") to the Photo Title and Content layout, and change the layout of Slide 5 ("Views of the Trail") to the Four Content layout.
4. On Slide 5 ("Views of the Trail"), in the top, empty content placeholder, insert the photo **Landscape**, located in the PowerPoint2 > Review folder. In the bottom, empty content placeholder, insert the photo **NewStairs**, also located in the PowerPoint2 > Review folder. Apply the Drop Shadow Rectangle style to the four pictures.
5. On Slide 5, add a Right Arrow shape anywhere on the slide. Type **Improved visibility** in the arrow, and then lengthen the arrow until the text you typed just fits on one line.
6. Change the shape style of the arrow to the Subtle Effect – Orange, Accent 1 style. Then change the outline of the arrow to the Red, Accent 2 color.
7. Make three copies of the arrow. Delete the text in one of the copies, and then type **Debris and brush cleared**. Resize this arrow so that the new text just fits on one line. Delete the text in another copy, and then type **Path set back to prevent more erosion**. Resize this copy so that the new text just fits on one line. Delete the text in the last copy, and then type **New stairs**.
8. Flip the "Path set back to prevent more erosion" and the "New stairs" arrows horizontally.
9. Position the "Improved visibility" arrow so it points to the top-left picture about one-half inch from the top of the photo and so its straight end is aligned with the left edge of the slide. Position the "Debris and brush cleared" arrow so it points to the bottom-left picture about one-half inch from the bottom of that photo and so its straight end is aligned with the left edge of the slide.
10. Position the "Path set back to prevent more erosion" arrow so it points to the top-right picture with its straight end aligned with the right edge of the slide and so that it aligns with the "Improved visibility" arrow. Position the "New stairs" arrow so it points to the bottom-right picture with its straight end aligned with the right edge of the slide and so that its middle aligns with the middle of the "Debris and brush cleared" arrow.
11. On Slide 4 ("Projects"), insert a 3x4 table. Refer to Figure 2-44 to add the rest of the data to the table. Add a row if needed.

Figure 2-44 Data for table on Slide 4 in the Renewed Riverwalk presentation

Improvement	Cost	Donated?
New sign	$0	Cushing Landscaping
New stairs	$1000	No
Cleared out debris and brush	$0	Martinez and Sons
Groundcover & retaining walls	$2000	No

12. On Slide 4, add a new row above the last row in the table. Type **New railings** in the new cell in the Improvement column, type **$0** in the new cell in the Cost column, and then type **Cushing Landscaping** in the Donated? column.
13. On Slide 4, apply the Light Style 2 – Accent 4 table style.
14. On Slide 4, insert a new column to the left of the Improvement column. Fill each cell in the new column (except the first cell) with the following pictures, all located in the PowerPoint2 > Review folder, in order from the second row to the bottom row: **NewSign**, **NewStairs**, **Cleared**, **Railings**, and **Wall**.
15. On Slide 4, format the table as follows:
    - Change the font size of all of the text in the table to 20 points.
    - Change the height of rows 2 through 5 to one inch.
    - Change the width of the first column to two inches.
    - Make the second and third columns just wide enough to hold the widest entry on one line.
    - Align the text in all of the rows except the first row so it is centered vertically.
    - Right-align the data in the Cost column (do not right-align the "Cost" column head).
    - Change the borders between rows 2 through 6 to a three-point black border.
16. Reposition the table so it is centered horizontally on the slide, and then move the table up so that the top half of the top row in the table overlaps the photo behind the slide title.
17. Apply the Uncover transition to any slide. Change the Effect Options to From Bottom, and then change the duration to 0.50 seconds. Apply this transition to all of the slides.
18. On Slide 2 ("Improvements Made"), animate the bulleted list using the Wipe animation. Change the Effect Options to From Left and the duration of the animation to 0.75 seconds.
19. On Slide 5 ("Views of the Trail"), apply the Fade entrance animation to each of the photos. Apply the Wipe animation with the From Left effect to each of the two arrows on the left, and then apply the Wipe animation with the From Right effect to each of the two arrows on the right.
20. On Slide 5, reorder the animations so that the arrow associated with each photo appears immediately after the photo with the top-left photo and arrow appearing first, then the top-right objects, then the bottom-right objects, and finally the bottom-left objects.
21. On Slide 5, add a 0.25-second delay to the animations applied to the arrows.
22. On Slide 6 ("New Views of the River from the Trail"), add the video **NewView**, located in the PowerPoint2 > Review folder. Trim three seconds from the beginning of the video. Set the poster frame to the four-second mark. Finally, set the playback options so that the video starts playing automatically, fills the screen, and rewinds after playing.
23. On Slide 7 ("Thank You!"), add the trademark sign after "RiverClean" and replace the "e" in "Jose" with "é" and the first "n" in "Quinones" with "ñ".
24. Add **Renewed Riverwalk** as the footer on all the slides except the title slide, and display the slide number on all the slides except the title slide. On the notes and handouts, add **Renewed Riverwalk** as the header and your name as the footer, and show page numbers.
25. Compress all the photos in the presentation to 96 ppi, and then compress the media to Low Quality.
26. Save your changes, and then close the Renewed Riverwalk presentation.
27. Open the file **Renewed2**, located in the PowerPoint2 > Review folder, and then save it as **Riverwalk Renewed Mix**.
28. Create a mix using this presentation. Make sure the Pen color is set to red. While Slide 1 is displayed, record yourself saying, "We've made many improvements to the Riverwalk trail," and then on Slide 3 draw an exclamation point after Jose's name.
29. After you record the slides, add a new Slide 3 with the Title and Content layout. Type **Do You Know?** as the slide title. Add a True False quiz to the new Slide 3 with the question **Views of the river from the trail have been greatly improved.** and with True as the correct answer.
30. Save the changes, and then upload the mix.

APPLY

Case Problem 1

Data Files needed for this Case Problem: Equipment.jpg, Exercise.mp4, FitTheme.pptx, HomeFit.pptx

HomeFit Sam Kim is the president of HomeFit, a company in Modesto, California, that sells exercise DVDs and subscriptions to online workout videos. To help advertise his videos, he created a PowerPoint presentation that he will use when he visits local colleges. He asks you to help him finish the presentation, which will include photos, a video, and a table to provide details his audience might be interested in knowing. Complete the following steps:

1. Open the file named **HomeFit**, located in the PowerPoint2 > Case1 folder included with your Data Files, add your name as the subtitle on Slide 1, and then save it as **HomeFit Videos** to the drive and folder where you are storing your files.
2. Apply the theme from the presentation **FitTheme**, located in the PowerPoint2 > Case1 folder.
3. On Slide 2 ("Videos Include"), apply the picture style Double Frame, Black to the picture on the slide, and then change the border color to the Dark Blue, Text 2, Darker 50% color. Apply this same style to the picture on Slide 3 ("Three Phases").
4. On Slide 2, animate the bulleted list using the Float In animation with the Float Down effect, and change the duration to 0.50 seconds. Animate the bulleted list on Slide 3 using the same animation.
5. On Slide 4 ("Sample Clip from a HomeFit Video"), insert the video **Exercise**, located in the PowerPoint2 > Case1 folder. Set the movie to play automatically, fill the screen when playing, and rewind after playing. Trim about eight seconds from the end of the video so the video ends at about the 16-second mark. Set the poster frame to the frame at approximately the seven-second mark.
6. On Slide 5 ("Packages"), add a new row below the row containing "HomeFit Original" in the first column with the following data: **HomeFit Plus**, **15 hours of online video per week**, **More options for cardio and strength training**, **$45/month**.
7. Change the table style to Light Style 1 – Accent 1. In the header row, change the font to Century Gothic (Headings), change the font size to 20 points, and then align the text so it is centered horizontally. Select the text in the last column, and then center the contents of each cell horizontally.
8. On Slide 6 (the last slide), which has the Blank layout applied, insert the picture **Equipment**, located in the PowerPoint2 > Case1 folder. Crop about an inch off of the bottom of the picture, and then resize it to be the same height as the slide (it will be 7.5 inches high). Position the photo so its left edge aligns with the left edge of the slide.
9. On Slide 6, draw rectangle shape that is 3.5 inches high and 5 inches wide, and then position it so it is centered-aligned with the photo and approximately centered horizontally in the white space on the slide. Type **Subscribe or Order Your DVDs Today!**. Change the font to Century Gothic (Headings), change the font color to Black, make the text bold, and change the font size to 48 points.
10. On Slide 6, remove the fill from the rectangle containing the text, and remove the outline (that is, change the fill to No Fill and change the outline to No Outline).
11. On Slide 6, animate the rectangle containing the text using the entrance animation Grow & Turn. Set its duration to 1.25 seconds, set its start timing to After Previous, and set a delay of one-half second.
12. Compress the all the photos to 96 ppi, deleting cropped areas of pictures, and then compress the media to Low Quality.
13. Apply the Checkerboard transition to all the slides using the default From Left effect and with a duration of 1.25 seconds. Then remove the transition from Slide 1 (the title slide).
14. Save your changes, and then watch the slide show in Slide Show view. Remember, after the transition to Slide 6 (the last slide), wait for the text box to animate automatically.
15. Make sure you saved your changes, and then save a copy of the presentation to the location where you are saving your files as **HomeFit Mix**. Delete Slides 3–5, and then create a mix of the presentation. Change the Inking options to Thick Pen with the Red Color. On Slide 1, record your voice saying, "HomeFit Videos—quality instruction at a fair price." On Slide 2, circle the second subbullet under "Strength Training" after it appears.

16. Insert a new Slide 3 with the Title and Content layout. Type Quiz as the slide title, and then add a True False quiz. Type **HomeFit videos do not include warm-ups or cool-downs.** as the question, and then make False the correct answer.
17. Save your changes, and then upload the mix.

CREATE

Case Problem 2

Data Files needed for this Case Problem: Build.jpg, Finish.jpg, Furniture.pptx, Sand.jpg, Sketch.jpg, Trees.jpg

Cutting Edge Furniture Carl Bertoni is the manager for Cutting Edge Furniture, in Forest Lake, Minnesota. Carl's grandfather founded the business more than 50 years ago, and they now have the resources to expand the company. To advertise this, Carl created a PowerPoint presentation that describes his custom furniture and the painstaking process used to create the pieces. He will use the presentation at home shows around the country. He asks you to help him complete the presentation. Complete the following steps:

1. Open the presentation **Furniture**, located in the PowerPoint2 > Case2 folder included with your Data Files, add your name as the subtitle, and then save the presentation as **Cutting Edge Furniture** to the drive and folder where you are storing your files.
2. On Slide 1 (the title slide), add the trademark symbol after "Furniture."
3. Refer to Figure 2-45 and insert the pictures as shown on Slides 3 through 7, and format the tables on Slide 8. The picture files are located in the PowerPoint2 > Case2 folder.

Figure 2-45 Slides 3 – 8 in the Cutting Edge Furniture presentation

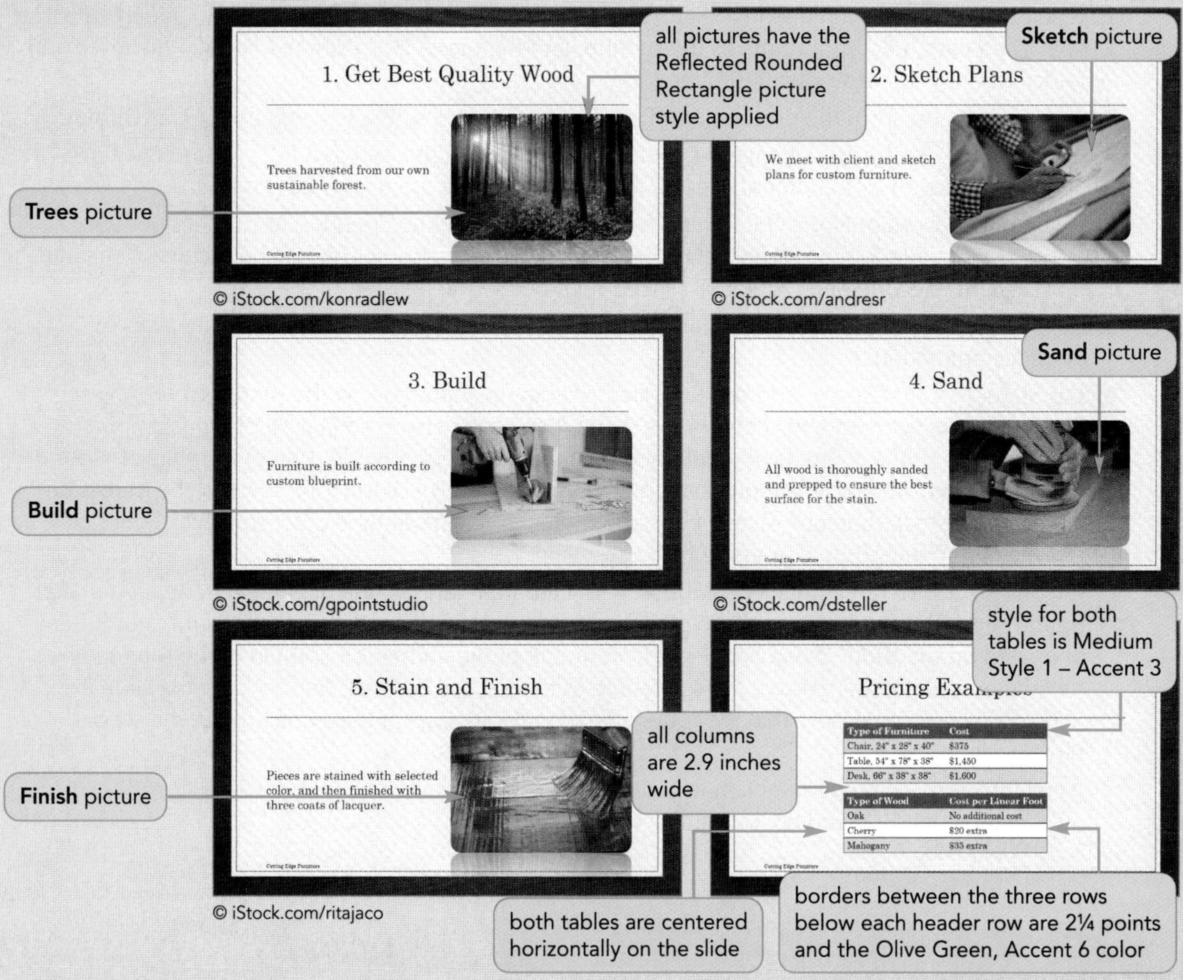

1. Get Best Quality Wood
Trees harvested from our own sustainable forest.
Trees picture
all pictures have the Reflected Rounded Rectangle picture style applied
© iStock.com/konradlew

2. Sketch Plans
We meet with client and sketch plans for custom furniture.
Sketch picture
© iStock.com/andresr

3. Build
Furniture is built according to custom blueprint.
Build picture
© iStock.com/gpointstudio

4. Sand
All wood is thoroughly sanded and prepped to ensure the best surface for the stain.
Sand picture
© iStock.com/dsteller

5. Stain and Finish
Pieces are stained with selected color, and then finished with three coats of lacquer.
Finish picture
© iStock.com/ritajaco

Pricing Examples

Type of Furniture	Cost
Chair, 24" x 28" x 40"	$375
Table, 54" x 78" x 38"	$1,450
Desk, 66" x 38" x 38"	$1,600

Type of Wood	Cost per Linear Foot
Oak	No additional cost
Cherry	$20 extra
Mahogany	$35 extra

style for both tables is Medium Style 1 – Accent 3
all columns are 2.9 inches wide
both tables are centered horizontally on the slide
borders between the three rows below each header row are 2¼ points and the Olive Green, Accent 6 color

4. Compress all the photos to 96 ppi.
5. On Slide 2 ("What We Offer"), animate both bulleted lists so they appear with the Wipe animation with the From Top effect. Keep the start timing of the list on the left set to On Click, and change the start timing of the list on the right to After Previous with a delay of two seconds. Then, set the start timing of the animations applied to each of the three subitems in the list on the right to With Previous.
6. Apply the Fade transition to Slides 1, 2, 8, and 9. Apply the Conveyor transition to Slides 3 through 7.
7. Add **Cutting Edge Furniture** as a footer on all slides except the title slide. On the notes and handouts, display the current date to be updated automatically, and add your name as a header on the notes and handouts.
8. Save your changes, and then view the slide show. Remember to wait for the second bulleted list to appear on Slide 2 two seconds after the first list appears.

APPLY

Case Problem 3

Data Files needed for this Case Problem: PawsTheme.pptx, Paws.pptx

Primped Paws Primped Paws is an animal-grooming service in Parkville, Maryland. Jasmine Feurman, the manager, needs to prepare a PowerPoint presentation that shows the care and attention that the groomers at Primped Paws give to animals. She will show the presentation to animal shelters and pet stores to convince them to recommend Primped Paws to new pet owners. Complete the following steps:

1. Open the presentation named **Paws**, located in the PowerPoint2 > Case3 folder included with your Data Files, add your name as the subtitle, and then save it as **Primped Paws** to the drive and folder where you are storing your files.
2. Apply the theme from the presentation **PawsTheme**, located in the PowerPoint2 > Case3 folder.
3. On Slide 3 ("Our Care"), change the font size of the text in the bulleted list to 24 points. On Slide 7 ("Make an Appointment Today"), change the size of the text to 28 points.
4. Change the layout of Slides 5 ("Canine Friends") and 6 ("Feline Friends") to Content Bottom Caption. On Slide 5, type **Daisy gets a bath** in the text placeholder below the picture. On Slide 6, type **Sam gets brushed** in the text placeholder below the picture.
5. On Slides 2 ("About Us") and 3 ("Our Care"), animate the bulleted lists on with the Appear entrance animation.
6. On Slide 3 ("Our Care"), add the Rounded Rectangle shape below the picture. Type **Two groomers keep animals calm** in the shape. Resize the shape so that all of the text appears on one line and the shape is one-half inch high and four inches wide. Center the shape below the picture and so that its middle is aligned with the top edge of the footer. Apply the Moderate Effect – Dark Teal, Accent 1 shape style, and then change the outline color to White. Animate the shape with the Appear animation.
7. On Slide 3, move the animation of the last bulleted item later so that it is the fifth item animated on the slide. Then move the animation of the third bulleted item later so that it is the fourth item animated on the slide. Then change the start timing of the animation applied to the rounded rectangle so that it animates at the same time as the second bulleted item. Watch the slide in Slide Show view to ensure that the rounded rectangle appears at the same time as the second bulleted item.
8. Apply the Metal Rounded Rectangle picture style to the photos on Slides 3 ("Our Care"), 5 ("Canine Friends"), and 6 ("Feline Friends").

9. On Slide 4 ("Pricing"), insert a 5x4 table. Enter the data shown in Figure 2-46.

Figure 2-46 Data for table on Slide 4 in Primped Paws presentation

Size	Wash and Brush	Trim Fur	Trim Nails	All Three
0-15 lbs.	$15	$10	$10	$35
16-40 lbs.	$20	$15	$10	$45
41-80 lbs.	$25	$20	$10	$55

10. On Slide 4, add a new bottom row to the table. Enter the following data in the new row: **81+ lbs.**, **$30**, **$25**, **$10**, **$65**.
11. On Slide 4, increase the size of all the text in the table to 28 points.
12. On Slide 4, horizontally and vertically center the text in the first row, and then right-align all of the dollar values.
13. On Slide 4, add a three-point border (using the default White color) between all the rows and columns.
14. Add **Primped Paws** as the footer, and display the footer and slide number on all of the slides except the title slide. Add your name as a header on the notes and handouts.
15. Apply the Honeycomb transition to any slide, change the duration of the transition to 1.75 seconds, and then apply that transition to all of the slides except the first one.
16. Save your changes, and then view the slide show.

CHALLENGE

Case Problem 4

Data Files needed for this Case Problem: Candy.png, CarePak.pptx, CPTheme.pptx, Games.png, Personal.png, Salty.png

CarePak CarePak markets care packages containing snacks and games to parents of college students. They are based in Carmel, Indiana, and ship to colleges nationwide. Tim King, a sales representative for CarePak, travels to colleges to convince the colleges to partner with CarePak. In return, CarePak will give a percentage of the sales to the college. He wants to use PowerPoint to give a presentation that describes the packages. He has asked you to help him prepare the presentation. Complete the following steps:

1. Open the presentation **CarePak**, located in the PowerPoint2 > Case4 folder included with your Data Files, add your name as the subtitle, and then save the presentation as **CarePak for Students** to the drive and folder where you are storing your files.
2. Apply the theme from the presentation **CPTheme**, located in the PowerPoint2 > Case4 folder.
3. On Slide 2 ("About Us"), animate the bulleted list using the Random Bars animation with the Vertical effect.
4. On Slide 3 ("Package Options"), insert a 2x4 table. Deselect the Header Row check box on the Table Tools Design tab. In the first column, enter **Sweet Snacks Package**, **Salty Snacks Package**, **Games Package**, and **Personalized Combo Package**. In the second column, fill the cells with the pictures **Candy**, **Salty**, **Games**, **Personal**, all located in the PowerPoint2 > Case4 folder.
5. On Slide 3, change the height of all of the rows in the table to 1.2 inches, and then change the width of the second column to 1.8 inches.
6. Make all of the text in the table bold, change the color of the text to the White, Text 1 color, and then change the font size to 24 points. Center the text in the first column vertically in the cells.
7. Remove the fill from all the cells in the first column, and then remove the table borders. (*Hint*: If the View Gridlines button in the Table group on the Layout tab is selected, you will still see the table gridlines after removing the borders.)
8. On Slide 3, insert a rectangle 1.25 inches high and 7.5 inches wide, and position it on top of the first row in the table so that the text and picture of candy is covered.

9. Apply the Wipe exit animation with the From Left effect to the rectangle. (*Hint*: Make sure you use the Wipe animation in the Exit category, not the Entrance category.)
10. Duplicate the rectangle three times, and then position the three copies on top of the other three rows in the table. (The shapes will slightly overlap.)

Explore 11. Change the fill of each rectangle to the same color as the slide background. (*Hint*: Use the Eyedropper tool on the Shape Fill menu.) Remove the outline from the rectangles.

Explore 12. On Slide 4 ("Customer Reviews"), apply the Appear animation to the bulleted list, and then modify the animation so that the letters appear one by one. (*Hint*: Use the Animation group Dialog Box Launcher, and then change the setting in the Animate text box on the Effect tab.) Speed up the effect by changing the delay between letters to 0.1 seconds.

Explore 13. Add the Typewriter sound to the animation. (*Hint*: Use the Animate text box again.)

14. Apply the Airplane transition to all the slides except Slide 1 (the title slide).
15. Save your changes, and then run the slide show.
16. Make sure you have saved your changes, and then save a copy of the presentation as **CarePak Mix** to the location where you are saving your files, Delete Slides 2 and 4, and then create a mix. Before you record it, change the microphone setting to No microphone and change the pen color to Red. When you record it, remember to advance the slide show to make the rectangles on top of the table disappear, and then after the fourth rectangle disappears, draw a red circle around the Personalized Combo Package on Slide 2.

Explore 17. Add a new Slide 4 titled **Survey** with the Title and Content layout, and insert a Multiple Response Poll. Enter **Which package appeals to you?** as the question, and **Sweet Snacks**, **Salty Snacks**, **Games**, **Combo** as the four options.

18. Save your changes, and upload the mix. Ask a few people to watch the mix and take the survey.
19. Add a new Slide 5 to the CarePak Mix presentation with the Blank layout.

Explore 20. View the responses to your survey by opening your browser, going to www.mix.office.com, and sign in to your Microsoft account if necessary. At the top of the window, click My Mixes. Below the CarePak for Students mix, click Analytics, and then click the slide containing the survey. (It can take up to 10 minutes for the statistics to be updated.)

Explore 21. Switch back to Slide 5 in the CarePak Mix presentation in the PowerPoint window, and then use the Screenshot button in the Insert group on the Mix tab or in the Images group on the Insert tab to take a screenshot of your Analytics screen and paste it on Slide 5. (Note: If you are using Edge as your browser and that window does not appear as an option on the Screenshot menu, switch back to Edge, and then press the Print Screen key (usually labeled PrtScr, PrntScr, or PrtScn on your keyboard). Switch back to Slide 5 in the CarePak Mix presentation, and then on the Home tab, in the Clipboard group, click the Paste button.) With the screenshot selected, on the Picture Tools Format tab, change the height to 7.5 inches and then position the picture on the slide if necessary (the picture will be the same size as the slide).

MODULE 3

Applying Advanced Formatting to Objects

Formatting Objects in a Presentation for a Study Abroad Company

POWERPOINT

OBJECTIVES

Session 3.1
- Create a SmartArt diagram
- Modify a SmartArt diagram
- Add an audio clip to a slide
- Create a chart
- Modify a chart
- Insert and format text boxes
- Apply a WordArt style to text

Session 3.2
- Correct photos using photo editing tools
- Remove the background from a photo
- Apply an artistic effect to a photo
- Create a custom shape
- Fill a shape with a texture and a custom gradient
- Add alt text to graphics
- Use the Selection pane

Case | *International Study Crossroads*

International Study Crossroads (ISC), located in Baltimore, Maryland, arranges semesters abroad for college students. They have partnerships with more than 20 colleges and universities in five countries and will be expanding into three more countries soon. Robert Cloud is a registration councilor for ISC. One of his duties is to attend college fairs and advertise the services ISC offers. He has created a presentation to advertise ISC at these fairs. He asks for your help in enhancing the presentation with some more advanced formatting of the presentation's content.

In this module, you will add interest to the presentation by creating a SmartArt graphic and a chart and by inserting an audio clip. You will also create a text box and use WordArt styles. You will improve the photos in the presentation using PowerPoint's photo editing tools. In addition, you will create a custom shape and apply advanced formatting to the shape. Finally, you will add text to describe some of the graphics to make the presentation more accessible for people who use screen readers.

STARTING DATA FILES

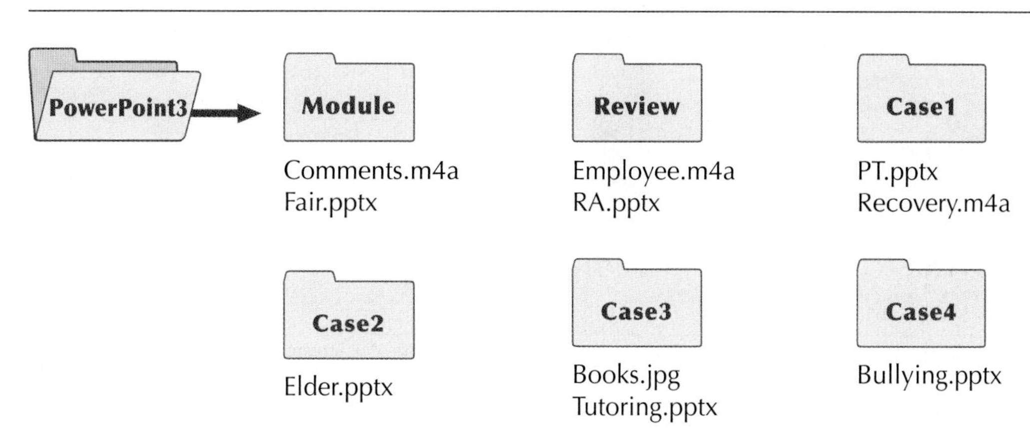

Session 3.1 Visual Overview:

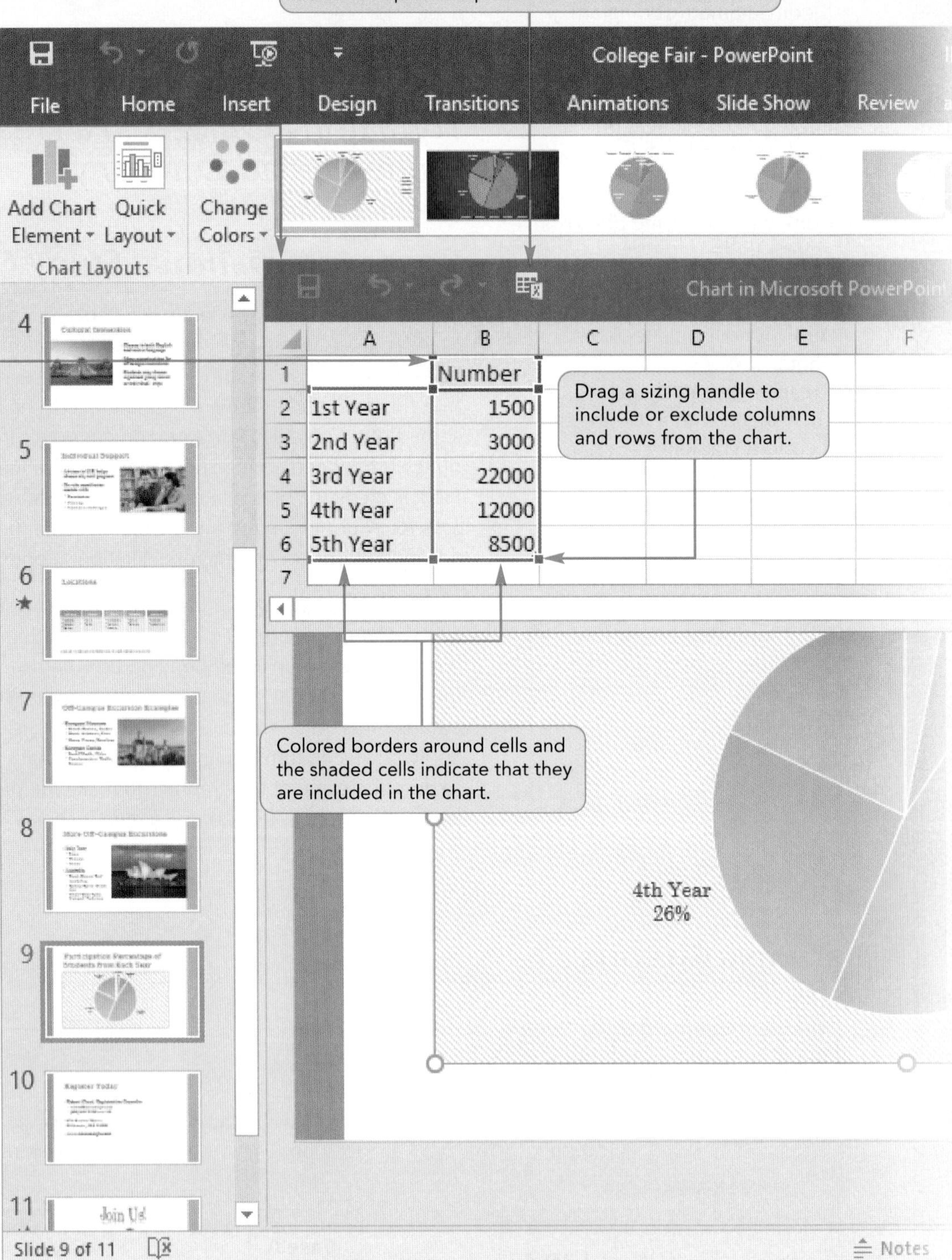

Creating a Chart on a Slide

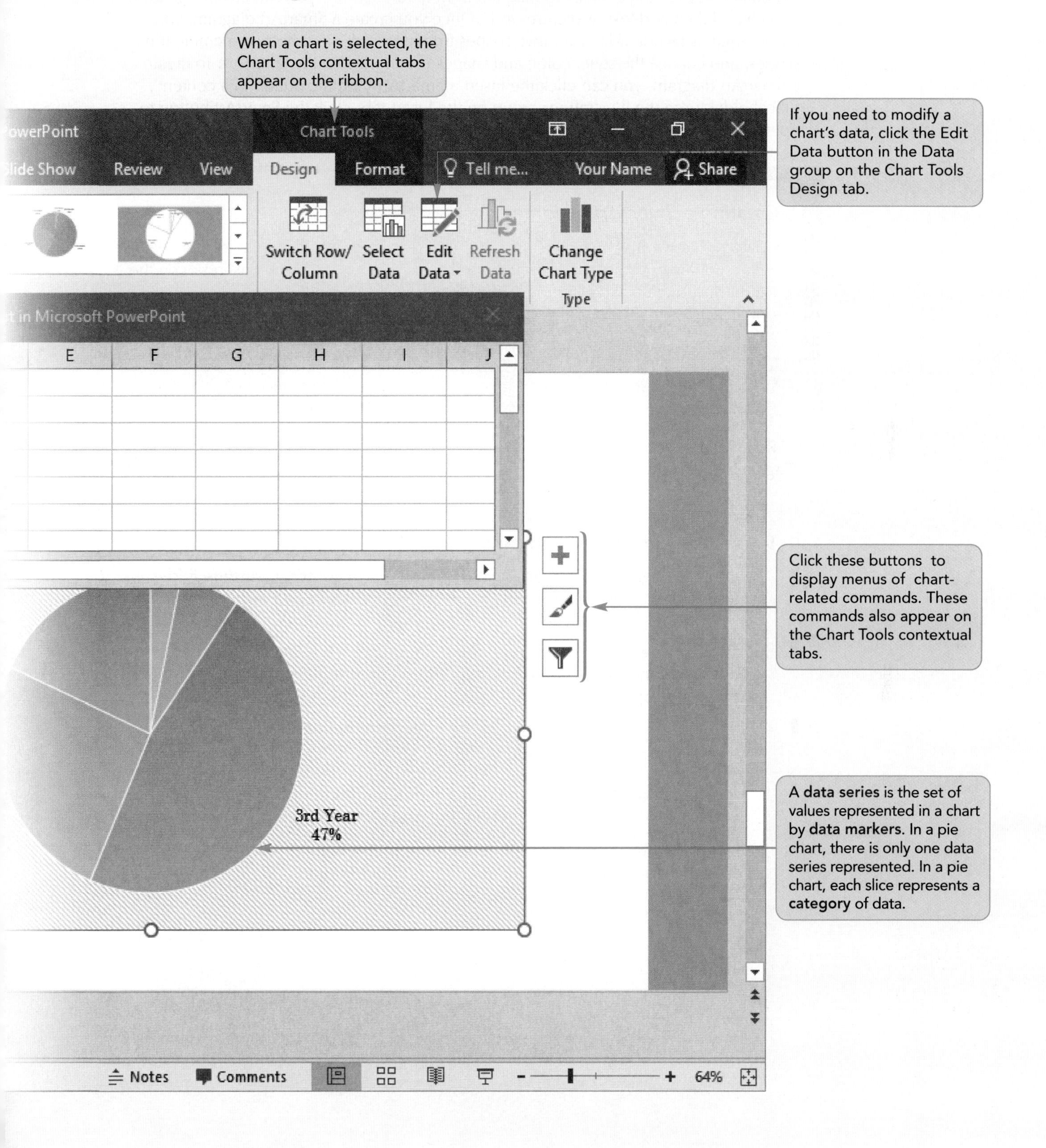

Creating SmartArt Diagrams

In addition to creating a SmartArt diagram from a bulleted list, you can create one from scratch and then add text or pictures to it. Once you create a SmartArt diagram, you can change its layout; add or remove shapes from it; reorder, promote, or demote the shapes; and change the style, color, and shapes used to create the SmartArt. To create a SmartArt diagram, you can click the Insert a SmartArt Graphic button in a content placeholder, or in the Illustrations group on the Insert tab, click the SmartArt button to open the Choose a SmartArt Graphic dialog box.

REFERENCE

Creating a SmartArt Diagram

- Switch to a layout that includes a content placeholder, and then in the content placeholder, click the Insert a SmartArt Graphic button; or click the Insert tab on the ribbon, and then in the Illustrations group, click the SmartArt button.
- In the Choose a SmartArt Graphic dialog box, select the desired SmartArt category in the list on the left.
- In the center pane, click the SmartArt diagram you want to use.
- Click the OK button.

Robert wants you to create a SmartArt diagram on Slide 6 of his presentation. The diagram will list the countries and cities in which ISC has programs.

To create a SmartArt diagram:

1. Open the presentation **Fair**, located in the **PowerPoint3 > Module** folder included with your Data Files, and then save it as **College Fair** to the location where you are saving your files.
2. Display **Slide 6** ("Locations"), and then in the content placeholder, click the **Insert a SmartArt Graphic** button. The Choose a SmartArt Graphic dialog box opens.
3. In the list on the left, click **List**, click the **Vertical Bullet List** layout (in the second row), and then click the **OK** button. A SmartArt diagram containing placeholder text is inserted on the slide with the text pane open next to the diagram, and the SmartArt Tools Design tab is selected on the ribbon. See Figure 3-1. The insertion point is in the first bullet in the text pane.

   Trouble? If the text pane is not displayed, click the Text Pane button in the Create Graphic group on the SmartArt Tools Design tab.

Figure 3-1 SmartArt inserted on Slide 6

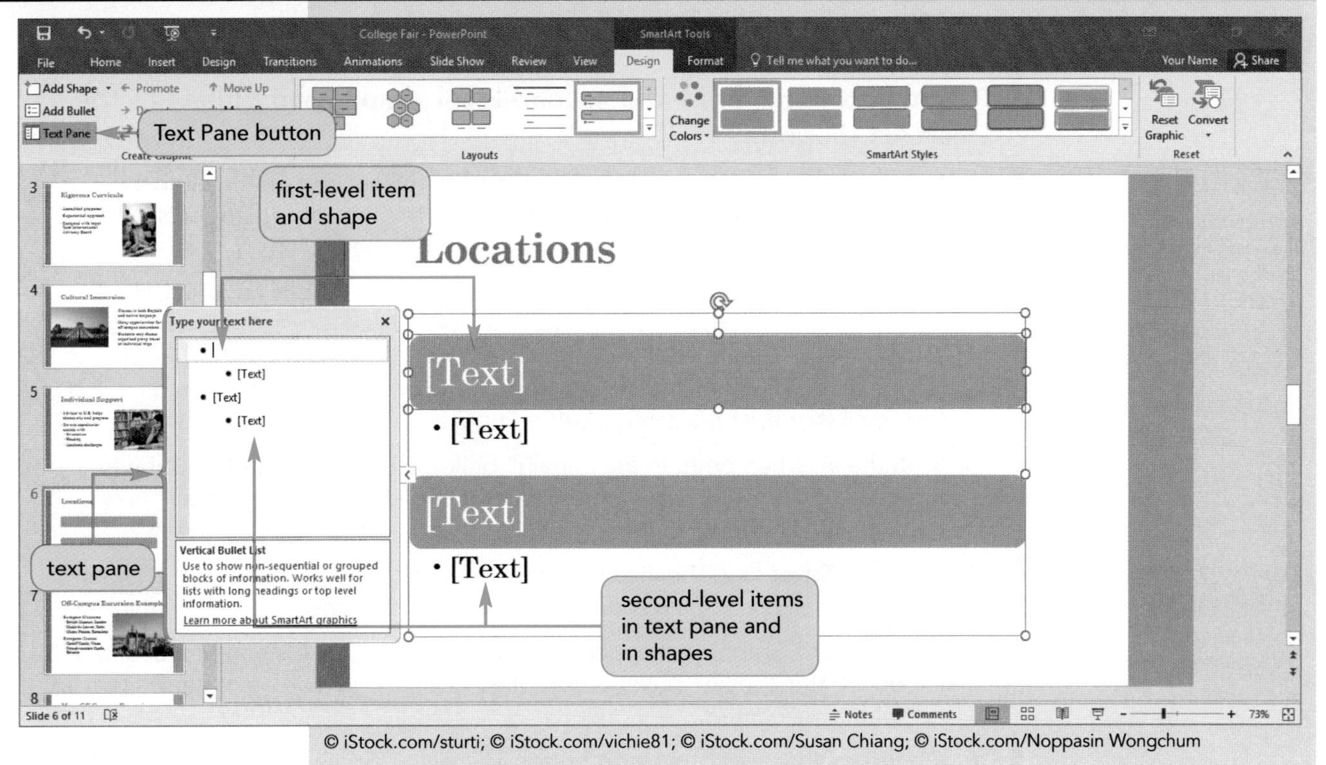

© iStock.com/sturti; © iStock.com/vichie81; © iStock.com/Susan Chiang; © iStock.com/Noppasin Wongchum

Now that you've added the diagram to the slide, you can add content to it. You will first add a first-level item and subitems to the diagram, and then reorder the shapes in the diagram.

To add text to the SmartArt diagram and move shapes:

1. With the insertion point in the first bulleted item in the text pane, type **England**. The text appears in the bulleted list in the text pane and in the top rectangle shape in the diagram.
2. In the text pane, in the first second-level bullet in the bulleted list, click **[Text]**. The placeholder text disappears and the insertion point appears.
3. Type **Oxford**. The text "Oxford" replaces the placeholder text in the second-level bullet.
4. Press the **Enter** key, type **London**, press the **Enter** key, and then type **Leeds**. The "London" bullet needs to be moved so it is the first second-level bullet.
5. In the text pane, click the **London** bullet, and then in the Create Graphic group, click the **Move Up** button. The London bullet moves up to become the first second-level bullet in the bulleted list.

With some SmartArt diagram layouts, you can click the Promote and Demote buttons in the Create Graphic group on the SmartArt Tools Design tab to move shapes up or down a level. But in other SmartArt diagrams, the insertion point must be in the text pane in order for this to work.

You need to add more first-level shapes to the SmartArt diagram. You do this using the Add Shape and Add Bullet buttons in the Create Graphic group on the SmartArt Tools Design tab.

TIP

To change the shapes in the diagram, select all the shapes, and then click the Change Shape button in the Shapes group on the SmartArt Tools Format tab.

To add additional first- and second-level shapes and bullets to the SmartArt diagram:

1. In the graphic, click the placeholder **[Text]** in the second first-level shape (below "Leeds,"), and then type **France**. The text you typed appears in the first-level shape in the diagram and in the text pane.
2. In the graphic, click the placeholder **[Text]** in the second-level item below "France," type **Paris**, press the **Enter** key, type **Nice**, press the **Enter** key, and then type **Spain**. The three items you typed appear as second-level bullets in the diagram and in the text pane. However, "Spain" should be in a first-level shape, at the same level as "England."
3. With the insertion point in the "Spain" bullet, click the **Promote** button in the Create Graphic group on the SmartArt Tools Design tab. "Spain" now appears in a first-level shape.
4. Press the **Enter** key. The insertion point moves to the next line in the "Spain" shape. The cities in Spain should be second-level items.
5. In the Create Graphic group, click the **Demote** button. Instead of creating a subbullet, the "Spain" bullet is demoted to a second-level item again. This is not what you wanted.
6. On the toolbar, click the **Undo** button twice. "Spain" again appears in the first-level shape in the diagram.
7. In the Create Graphic group, click the **Add Bullet** button. A second-level bullet is added below the "Spain" shape.
8. Type **Barcelona**, press the **Enter** key, type **Madrid**, press the **Enter** key, and then type **Seville**.
9. Click in the **Spain** shape, and then in the Create Graphic group, click the **Add Shape** button. A new first-level shape is added to the bottom of the diagram.
10. Type **Germany**, and then add **Berlin** and **Munich** as second-level bullets below Germany.
11. Add **Australia** in a new first-level shape with **Sydney** and **Newcastle** as second-level bullets below it, and then add **Japan** in a new first-level shape. Compare your screen to Figure 3-2.

Figure 3-2 SmartArt with text added

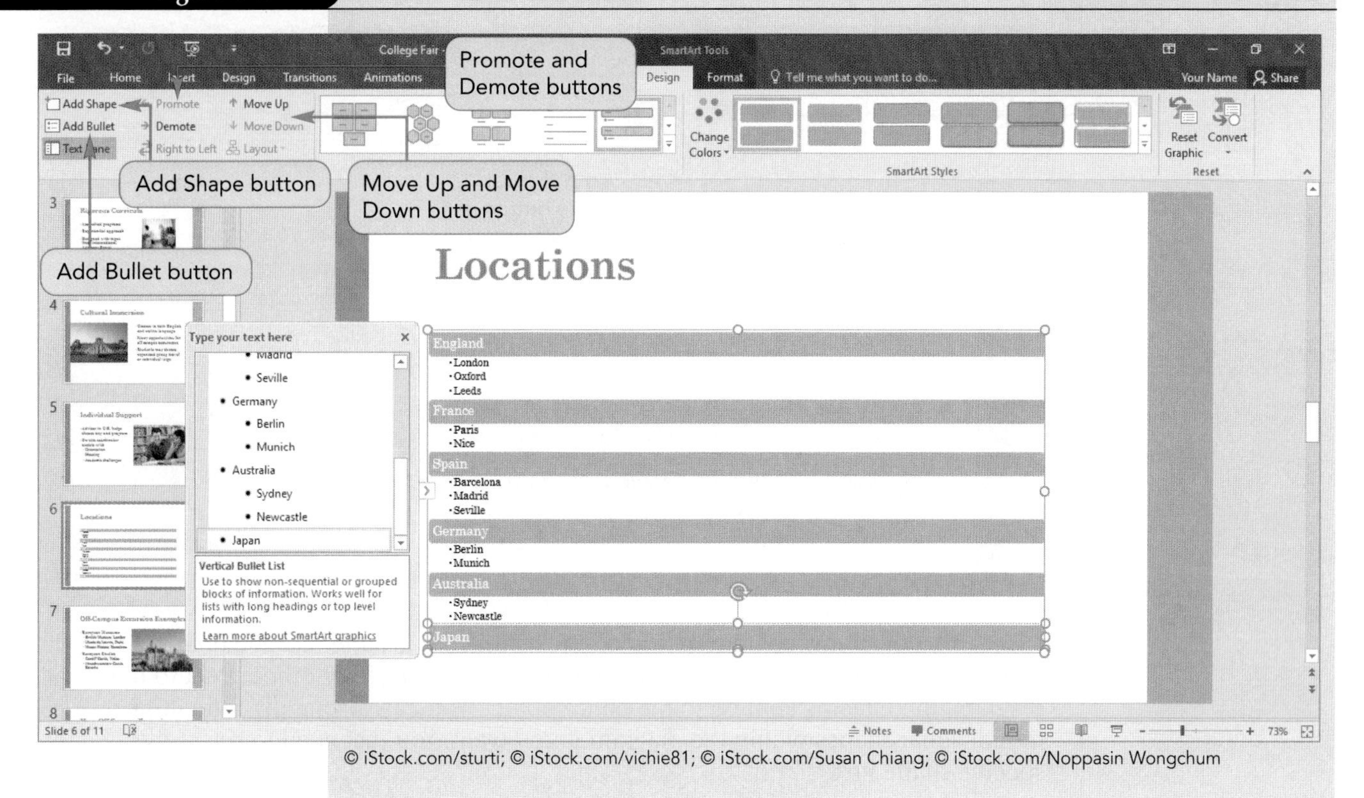

Modifying a SmartArt Diagram

There are many ways to modify a SmartArt diagram. For example, you can change the layout of the diagram so the information is presented differently. You will do this next.

TIP

To switch the order of the shapes, click the Right to Left button in the Create Graphic group on the SmartArt Tools Design tab.

To change the layout of the SmartArt diagram:

1. On the SmartArt Tools Design tab, in the Layouts group, click the **More** button. The gallery of layouts in the List category opens.
2. Click the **Horizontal Bullet List** layout (the fourth layout in the second row). The layout of the diagram changes to the new layout.
3. Click the **Japan** shape, and then press the **Delete** key. The text and the shape are deleted.

   Trouble? If nothing happened when you pressed the Delete key, make sure you clicked the top part of the Japan shape—the part that contains the text "Japan," and then press the Delete key again.

   Trouble? If one of the letters in the word "Japan" was deleted when you pressed the Delete key, click the border of the top part of the Japan shape, and then press the Delete key again.
4. In the text pane, click the **Close** button [X]. See Figure 3-3.

Figure 3-3 SmartArt after changing the layout

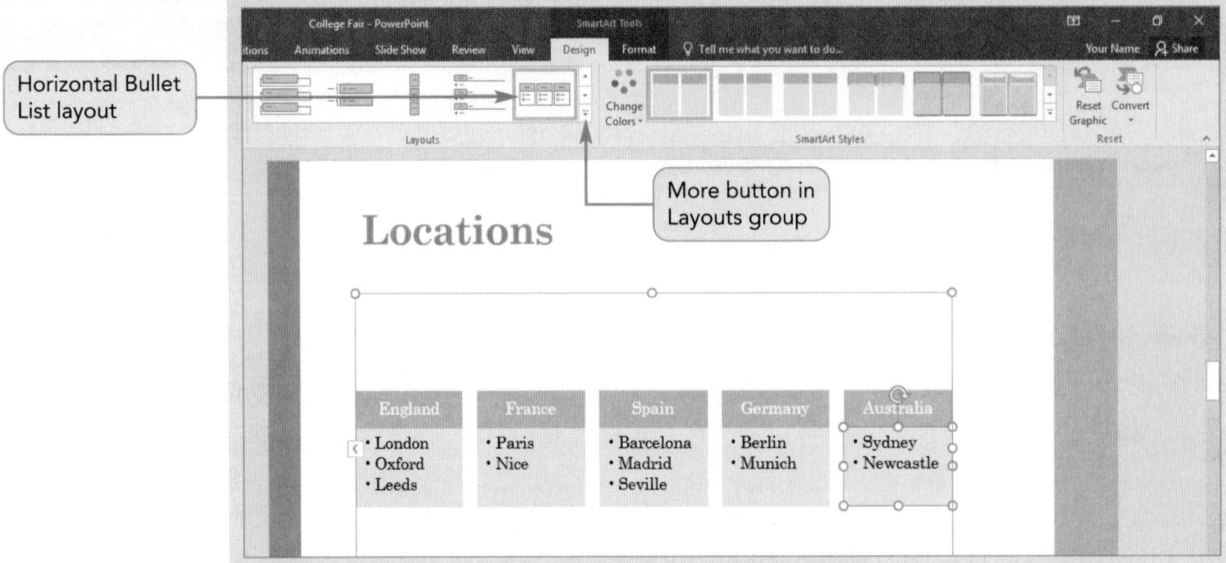

SmartArt diagrams contain multiple objects that are grouped as one object, which is then treated as a whole. So when you apply a style or other effect to the diagram, the effect is applied to the entire object. You can also apply formatting to individual shapes within the diagram if you want. You just need to select the specific shape first.

To apply a style to the SmartArt diagram and change its colors:

1. On the SmartArt Tools Design tab, in the SmartArt Styles group, click the **More** button to open the gallery of styles available for the graphic.
2. In the gallery, click the **Inset** style. The style of the graphic changes to the Inset style.
3. In the SmartArt Styles group, click the **Change Colors** button. A gallery of color styles opens.
4. Under Colorful, click the **Colorful – Accent Colors** style. See Figure 3-4.

Figure 3-4 SmartArt with color and style changed

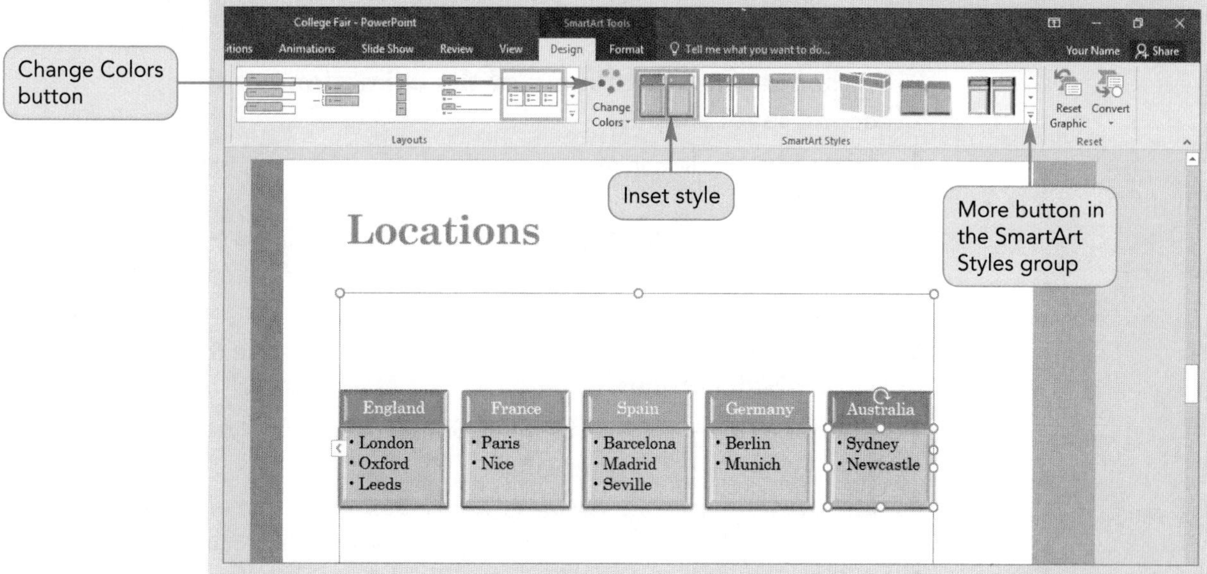

Animating a SmartArt Diagram

You animate a SmartArt diagram in the same way you animate any object. The default is for the entire object to animate as a single object. But similar to a bulleted list, after you apply an animation, you can use the Effect Options button and choose a different sequence effect. For example, you can choose to have each object animate one at a time.

Robert wants the shapes in the SmartArt diagram to appear on the slide one at a time during his presentation.

To animate the SmartArt diagram:

1. With Slide 6 displayed, on the ribbon, click the **Animations** tab.
2. In the Animation group, click the **Appear** animation. The animation previews, and the SmartArt diagram quickly appears on the slide. One animation sequence icon appears above and to the left of the diagram.
3. In the Animation group, click the **Effect Options** button. The selected effect is As One Object.
4. Click **One by One**. The animation previews, and each shape in the diagram appears one at a time. Ten animation sequence icons appear to the left of the diagram.
5. On the status bar, click the **Slide Show** button. Slide 6 appears in Slide Show view.
6. Advance the slide show twice. The first top-level shape, "England," appears, followed by the second-level shape containing the cities in England.
7. Advance the slide show eight more times. Each first-level shape appears, followed by its associated second-level shape.
8. Press the **Esc** key to end the slide show.

Robert wants the second-level shapes containing the cities to appear at the same time as the corresponding first-level shapes containing the countries. To make this happen, you need to change the start timing of each second-level shape to With Previous.

To change the start timing of the animations of the second-level shapes:

1. On Slide 6, click animation sequence icon **2**. The animation for the shape containing the cities in England is selected.
2. Press and hold the **Ctrl** key, click animation sequence icons **4**, **6**, **8**, and **10**, and then release the **Ctrl** key. The animations for the second-level shapes are selected.
3. On the Animations tab, in the Timing group, click the **Start** arrow, and then click **With Previous**.
4. On the status bar, click the **Slide Show** button. Slide 6 appears in Slide Show view.
5. Advance the slide show once. The first top-level shape, "England," and its associated second-level shape containing the cities in England appear.
6. Advance the slide show four more times. Each time the slide show is advanced, a first-level shape appears along with its associated second-level shape.
7. Press the **Esc** key to end the slide show.
8. Save the changes to the presentation.

INSIGHT

Converting a SmartArt Diagram to Text or Shapes

You can convert a SmartArt diagram to a bulleted list or to its individual shapes. To convert a diagram to a bulleted list, select the diagram, and then on the SmartArt Tools Design tab, in the Reset group, click the Convert button, and then click Convert to Text. To convert a group to its individual shapes, click Convert to Shapes on the Convert menu or use the Ungroup command on the Group menu on the Drawing Tools Format tab. In both cases, the shapes are converted from a SmartArt diagram into a set of grouped shapes. To completely ungroup them, you would need to use the Ungroup command a second time. Keep in mind that if you convert the diagram to shapes, you change it from a SmartArt object into ordinary drawn shapes, and you will no longer have access to the commands on the SmartArt Tools contextual tabs.

Adding Audio to Slides

Audio in a presentation can be used for a wide variety of purposes. For example, you might want to add a sound clip of music to a particular portion of the presentation to evoke emotion, or perhaps include a sound clip that is a recording of customers expressing their satisfaction with a product or service. To add a sound clip to a slide, you use the Audio button in the Media group on the Insert tab. When a sound clip is added to a slide, a sound icon and a play bar appear on the slide. Similar to videos, the options for changing how the sound plays during the slide show appear on the Audio Tools Playback tab. For the most part, they are the same options that appear on the Video Tools Playback tab. For example, you can trim an audio clip or set it to rewind after playing. You can also compress audio in the same way that you compress video.

REFERENCE

Inserting an Audio Clip into a Presentation

- Display the slide onto which you want to insert the sound.
- On the ribbon, click the Insert tab, click the Audio button in the Media group, and then click Audio on My PC.
- In the Insert Audio dialog box, navigate to the folder containing the sound clip, click the audio file, and then click the Insert button.
- If desired, click the Audio Tools Playback tab, and then in the Audio Options group:
    - Click the Start arrow, and then click Automatically.
    - Click the Hide During Show check box to select it to hide the icon during a slide show.
    - Click the Volume button, and then click a volume level or click Mute.

Robert wants you to add a sound clip to the presentation—a recording of a student praising the ISC. The recorded message is an MPEG-4 audio file, which is a common file format for short sound clips.

TIP

To record an audio clip, click the Audio button, and then click Record Audio.

To add a sound clip to Slide 11:

1. Display **Slide 11** (the last slide), and then click the **Insert** tab on the ribbon.
2. In the Media group, click the **Audio** button, and then click **Audio on My PC**. The Insert Audio dialog box opens.
3. Navigate to the **PowerPoint3 > Module** folder, click the **Comments** file, and then click the **Insert** button. A sound icon appears in the middle of the slide with a play bar below it, and the Audio Tools Playback tab is selected on the ribbon. See Figure 3-5. As with videos, the default start setting is On Click.

Figure 3-5 **Sound icon on Slide 11**

© iStock.com/Christopher Futcher; © iStock.com/Noppasin Wongchum; Courtesy of S. Scott Zimmerman

4. Drag the sound icon to the lower-right corner of the slide so it is positioned at the bottom of the blue bar.

5. On the play bar, click the **Play** button ▶. The sound clip, which is a comment from a student complimenting the company on its programs, plays. Robert wants the clip to play automatically after the slide appears on the screen.
6. On the Playback tab, in the Audio Options group, click the **Start** arrow, and then click **Automatically**. Because the clip will play automatically, there is no need to have the sound icon visible on the screen during a slide show.
7. In the Audio Options group, click the **Hide During Show** check box to select it.
8. Save the changes to the presentation.

INSIGHT

Playing Music Across Slides

You can add an audio clip to a slide and have it play throughout the slide show. On the Audio Tools Playback tab, in the Audio Styles group, click the Play in Background button. When you select this option, the Start timing in the Audio Options group is changed to Automatically, and the Play Across Slides, Loop until Stopped, and Hide During Show check boxes become selected. Also, the Play in Background command changes the trigger animation automatically applied to media to an After Previous animation set to zero so that the sound will automatically start playing after the slide transitions. These setting changes ensure the audio clip will start playing when the slide appears on the screen during a slide show and will continue playing, starting over if necessary, until the end of the slide show. To change the settings so that the audio no longer plays throughout the slide show, click the No Style button in the Audio Styles group.

Adding a Chart to a Slide

The terms "chart" and "graph" often are used interchangeably; however, they do, in fact, have distinct meanings. **Charts** are visuals that use lines, arrows, and boxes or other shapes to show parts, steps, or processes. **Graphs** show the relationship between variables along two axes or reference lines: the independent variable on the horizontal axis and the dependent variable on the vertical axis.

Despite these differences in the definitions, in PowerPoint a chart is any visual depiction of data in a spreadsheet, even if the result is more properly referred to as a graph (such as a line graph). Refer to the Session 3.1 Visual Overview for more information about creating charts and using spreadsheets in PowerPoint.

Creating a Chart

To create a chart, you click the Insert Chart button in a content placeholder or use the Chart button in the Illustrations group on the Insert tab. Doing so will open a window containing a spreadsheet with sample data, and a sample chart will appear on the slide. You can then edit the sample data in the window to reflect your own data to be represented in the chart on the slide.

REFERENCE

Creating a Chart

- Switch to a layout that includes a content placeholder, and then click the Insert Chart button in the content placeholder to open the Insert Chart dialog box; or click the Insert tab, and then, in the Illustrations group, click the Chart button to open the Insert Chart dialog box.
- In the list on the left, click the desired chart type.
- In the row of styles, click the desired chart style, and then click the OK button.
- In the spreadsheet that opens, enter the data that you want to plot.
- If you need to chart fewer rows or columns than are shaded in the spreadsheet, drag the handle in the lower-right corner of the shaded area up to remove rows or to the left to remove columns.
- In the spreadsheet window, click the Close button.

Robert wants you to create a chart on Slide 9 to illustrate the percentage of students from each grade level that typically make up the total of participating students in a given year. A pie chart is a good choice when you want to show the relative size of one value compared to the other values and compared to the total set of values.

To create a chart on Slide 9:

1. Display **Slide 9** ("Participation Percentage of Students from Each Year"), and then, in the content placeholder, click the **Insert Chart** button. The Insert Chart dialog box opens. Column is selected in the list of chart types on the left, and the Clustered Column style is selected in the row of styles at the top and shown in the preview area. See Figure 3-6.

Figure 3-6 **Insert Chart dialog box**

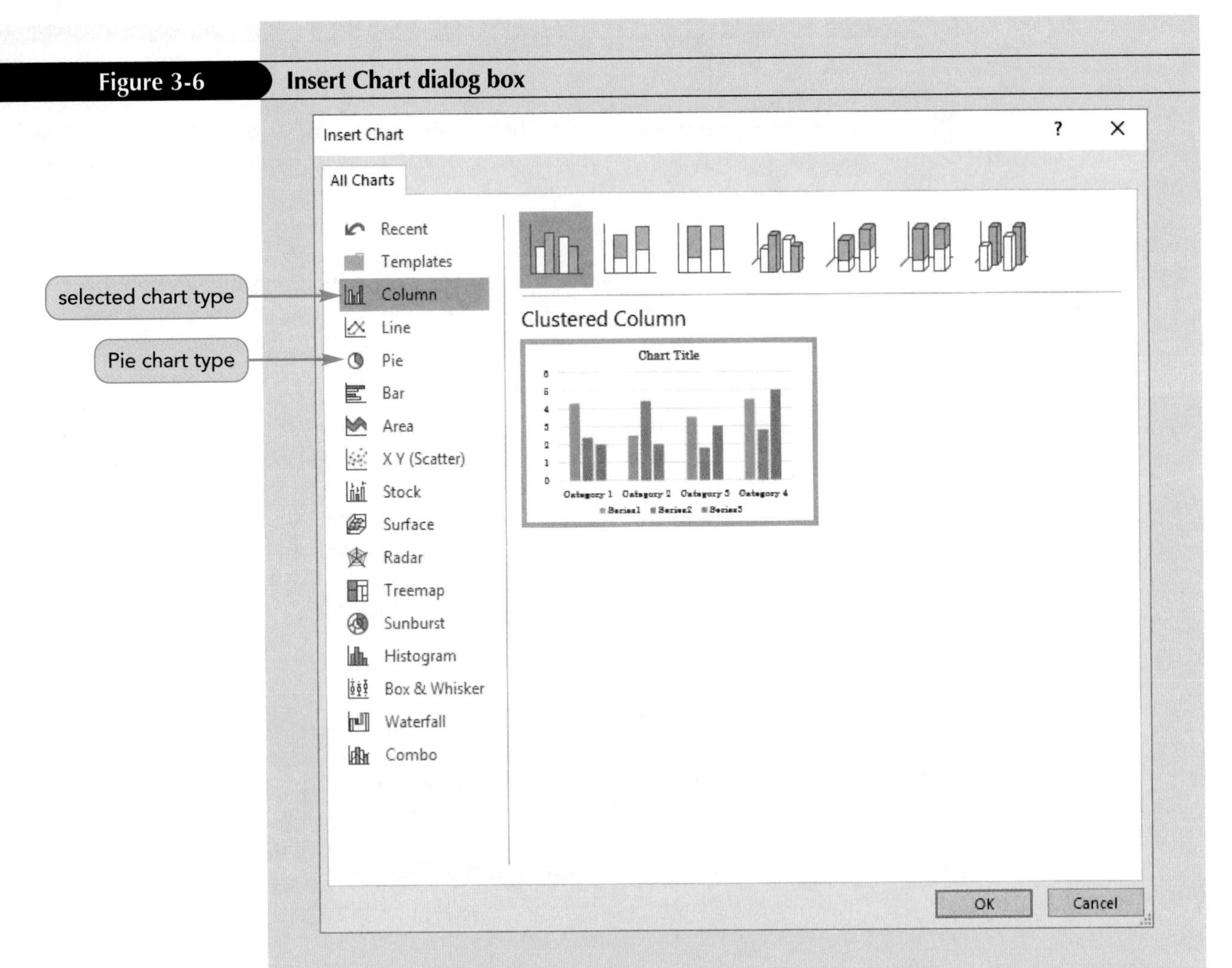

2. In the list of chart types, click **Pie**. The row of chart styles changes to pie chart styles. The Pie style is selected.
3. Click the **OK** button. A sample chart is inserted on Slide 9, and a small spreadsheet (sometimes called a datasheet) opens above the chart, with colored borders around the cells in the spreadsheet indicating which cells of data are included in the chart. See Figure 3-7.

Figure 3-7 Spreadsheet and chart with sample data

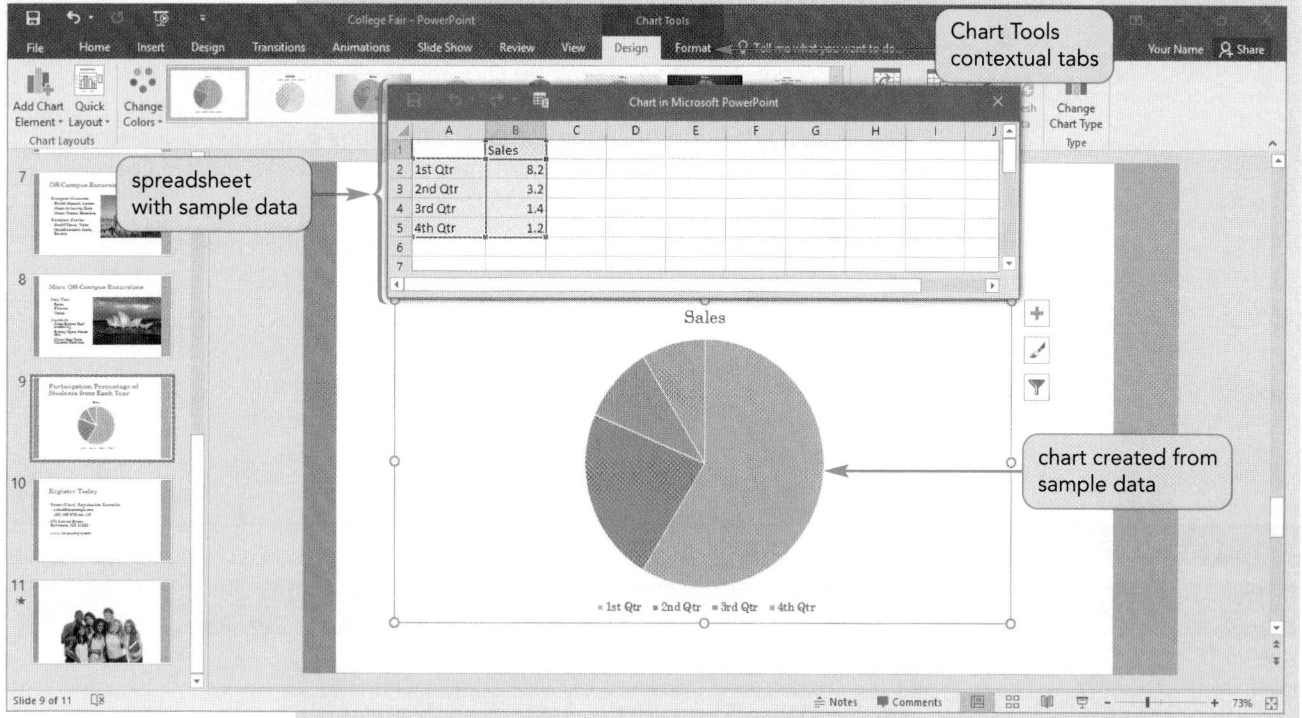

To create the chart for Robert's presentation, you need to edit the sample data in the spreadsheet. When you work with a spreadsheet, the cell in which you are entering data is the **active cell**. The active cell has a green border around it.

To enter the data for the chart:

1. In the spreadsheet, click cell **A2**. A green border surrounds cell A2, indicating it is selected.
2. Type **1st Year**, and then press the **Enter** key. Cell A3 becomes the active cell. In the chart, the category name in the legend for the blue pie slice changes to "1st Year."
3. Enter the following in cells **A3** through **A5**, pressing the **Enter** key after each entry:

   2nd Year

   3rd Year

   4th Year
4. In cell A6, type **5th Year**, and then press the **Enter** key. The active cell is cell A7, and the colored borders around the cells included in the chart expand to include cells A6 and B6. In the chart, a new category name is added to the legend. Because there is no data in cell B6, a corresponding slice was not added to the pie chart.

TIP

To add or remove a row or column from the chart, drag the corner sizing handles on the colored borders.

5. Click in cell **B1** to make it the active cell, type **Number**, and then press the **Enter** key. The active cell is now cell B2.
6. In cell **B2**, type **15000**, and then press the **Enter** key. The slice in the pie chart that represents the percentage showing the numbers of first-year students increases to essentially fill the chart. This is because the value 15000 is so much larger than the sample data values in the rest of the rows in column B. As you continue to enter the data, the slices in the pie chart will adjust as you add each value.
7. In cells **B3** through **B6**, enter the following values, and then compare your screen to Figure 3-8:

   3000

   22000

   12000

   8500

Figure 3-8 Spreadsheet and chart after entering data

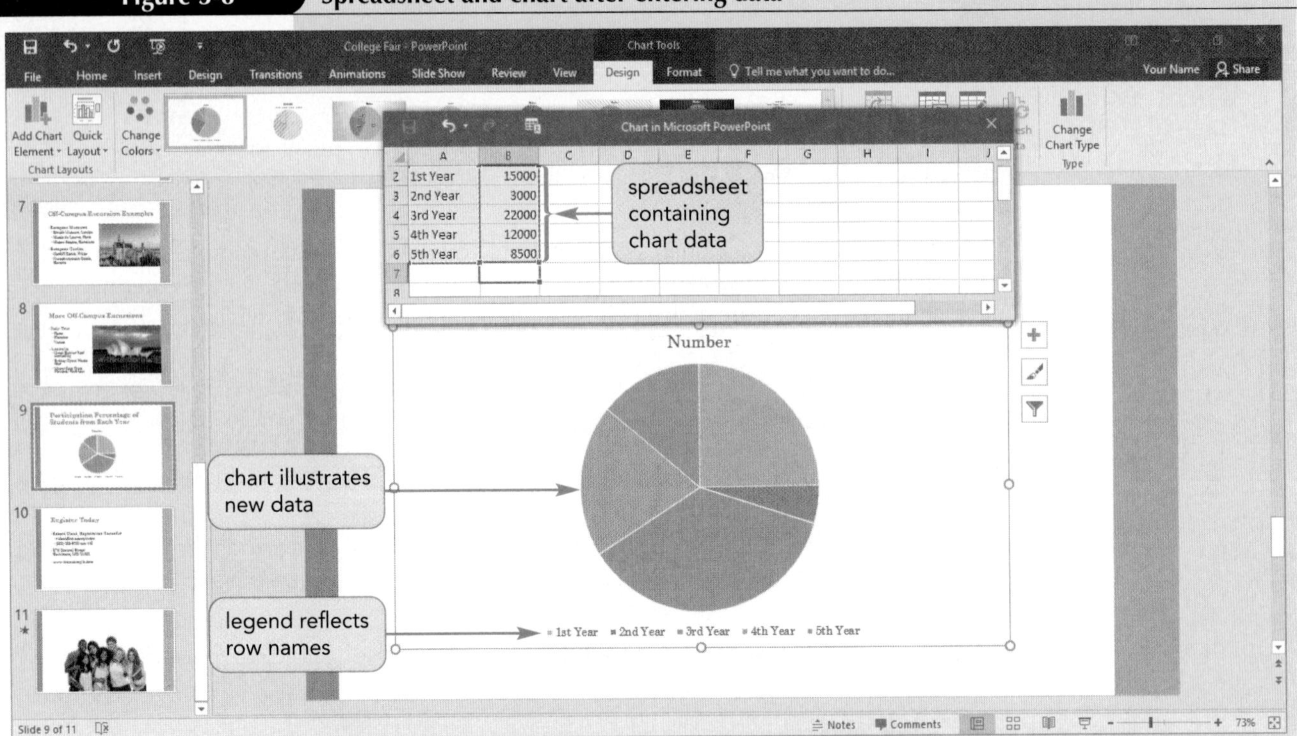

8. In the spreadsheet, click the **Close** button ☒. The spreadsheet closes.
9. Save the changes to the presentation.

PROSKILLS

Decision Making: Selecting the Correct Chart Type

To use charts effectively, you need to consider what you want to illustrate with your data. To represent values, column charts use vertical columns, and bar charts use horizontal bars. These types of charts are useful for comparing the values of items over a period of time or a range of dates or costs. Line charts and area charts use a line to connect points that represent values. They are effective for showing changes over time, and they are particularly useful for illustrating trends. Line and area charts are a better choice than column or bar charts when you need to display large amounts of information and exact quantities that don't require emphasis. Pie charts are used to show percentages or proportions of the parts that make up a whole. Treemap and sunburst charts also show the proportion of parts to a whole, but these chart types also show hierarchies.

Modifying a Chart

Once the chart is on the slide, you can modify it by changing or formatting its various elements. For example, you can edit the data; apply a style; add, remove, or reposition chart elements; add labels to the chart; and modify the formatting of text in the chart.

You need to make several changes to the chart you created on Slide 9. First, Robert informs you that some of the data he provided was incorrect, so you need to edit the data. Remember that a pie chart shows the size of each value relative to the whole. Therefore, if you change the value corresponding to one pie slice, the rest of the slices will change size as well.

TIP

To switch to another type of chart, click the Change Chart Type button in the Type group on the Chart Tools Design tab.

To change the data used to create the chart:

1. On the Chart Tools Design tab, in the Data group, click the **Edit Data** button. The spreadsheet opens again above the chart. You need to change the number of first-year students who participate in the program. The 1st Year slice is the blue slice.
2. Click cell **B2**, type **1500**, and then press the **Enter** key. The blue slice in the pie chart decreases significantly in size, and the other slices in the pie chart adjust to reflect the new relative values.
3. On the spreadsheet, click the **Close** button. The spreadsheet closes.

Robert also wants you to make several formatting changes to the chart. There is no need for a title on the chart because the slide title describes the chart. Robert also wants you to remove the legend and, instead, label the pie slices with the category names and the percentage values. He also would like you to apply a different style to the chart.

To format and modify the chart:

1. On the Chart Tools Design tab, in the Chart Layouts group, click the **Quick Layout** button. A gallery of chart layouts specific to pie charts opens. Each layout includes different chart elements, such as the chart title and legend.
2. Point to several of the layouts to see which elements are added to the chart, and then click **Layout 1**. The category name and percentage of each slice is added as a label on the slices, and the legend is removed. With this layout, there is no need for the legend.

3. To the right of the chart, click the **Chart Styles** button. A gallery opens with the Style tab selected at the top.
4. Point to several of the styles to see the effect on the chart. In addition to changing the colors used, some of the styles include layouts and add or remove chart elements, similar to the Quick Layouts.
5. Click **Style 6**. This style adds the legend and a background of thin, slanted lines. See Figure 3-9.

Figure 3-9 Chart after changing the layout and applying a style

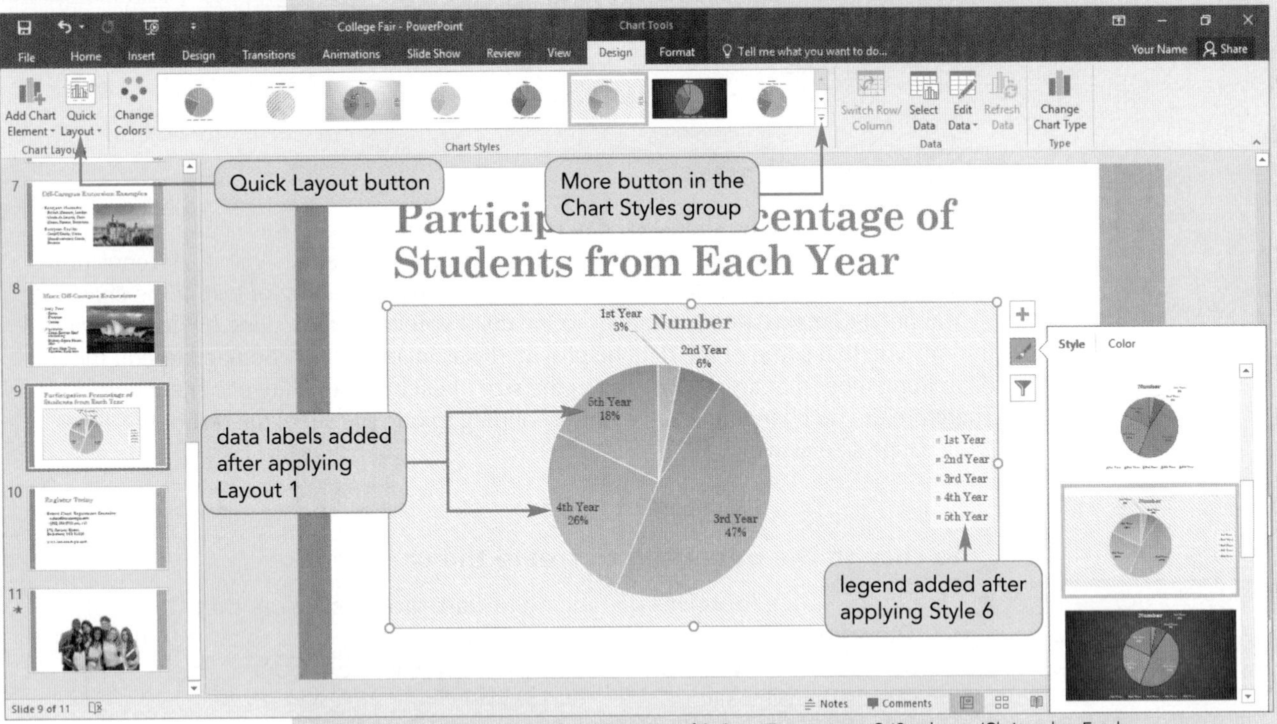

6. To the right of the chart, click the **Chart Elements** button. The CHART ELEMENTS menu opens to the right of the chart. The Chart Title, Data Labels, and Legend check boxes are all selected, which means these elements are shown on the chart.
7. On the CHART ELEMENTS menu, click the **Chart Title** check box, and then click the **Legend** check box to deselect them. The chart title and the legend are removed from the chart.
8. On the CHART ELEMENTS menu, point to **Data Labels**. An arrow appears.
9. Click the **arrow** to open the Data Labels submenu. See Figure 3-10.

TIP

Double-click a chart element to open a task pane containing additional commands for modifying that element.

Figure 3-10 Data Labels submenu on CHART ELEMENTS menu

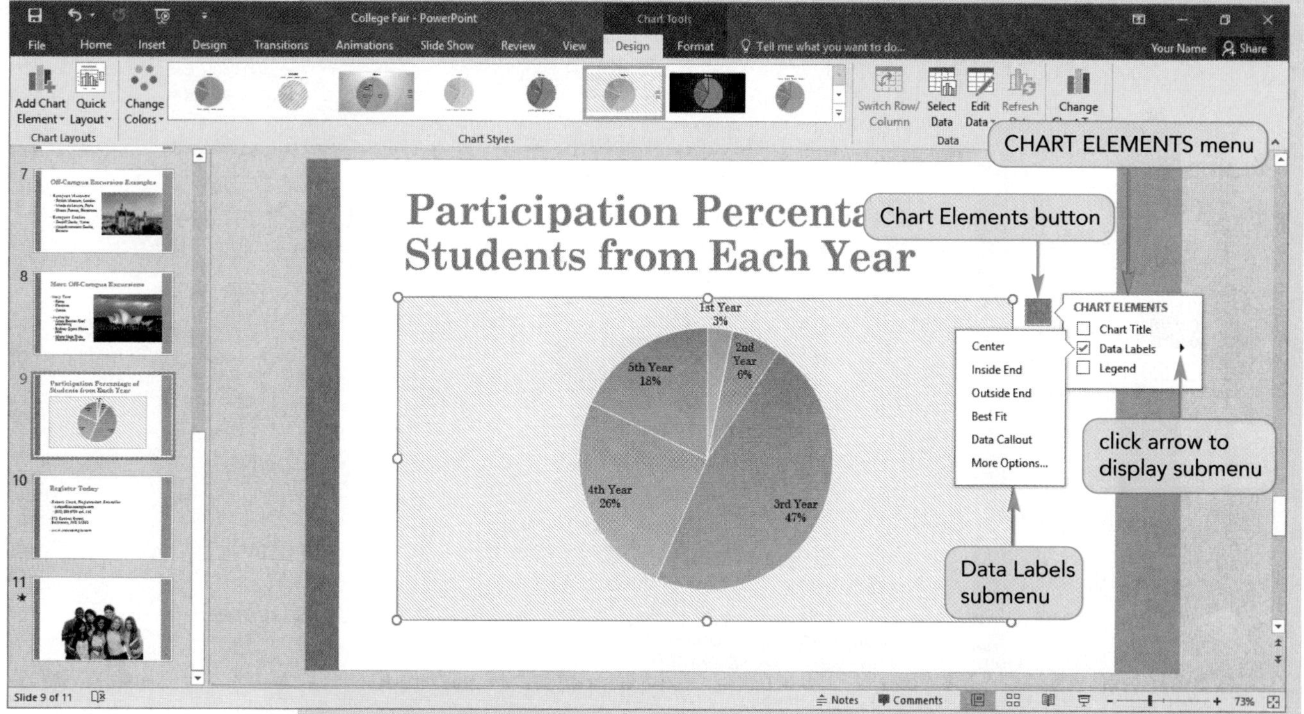

© iStock.com/Noppasin Wongchum; Courtesy of S. Scott Zimmerman; © iStock.com/Christopher Futcher

10. On the submenu, click **Outside End**. The data labels are positioned next to each pie slice.

The data labels are a little bit small, so Robert asks you to increase their font size. When you change the font size of data labels on a pie chart, it is sometimes necessary to move a label so it is better positioned. You'll do this next.

To change the point size of the data labels and adjust their position:

1. To the right of the chart, click the **Chart Elements** button to close the menu, and then in the chart, click one of the data labels. All of the data labels are selected.
2. On the ribbon, click the **Home** tab, and then change the font size of the selected data labels to **14** points. The 1st Year data label is now too close to the 2nd Year data label.
3. Click the **1st Year** data label. Because all the data labels had been selected, now only the 1st Year data label is selected.
4. Position the pointer on the edge of the selected **1st Year** data label so that it changes to , and then drag it to the left a little so that it is not touching the 2nd Year data label and so that the "3" is above the blue pie slice. See Figure 3-11.

Figure 3-11 Final chart on Slide 9

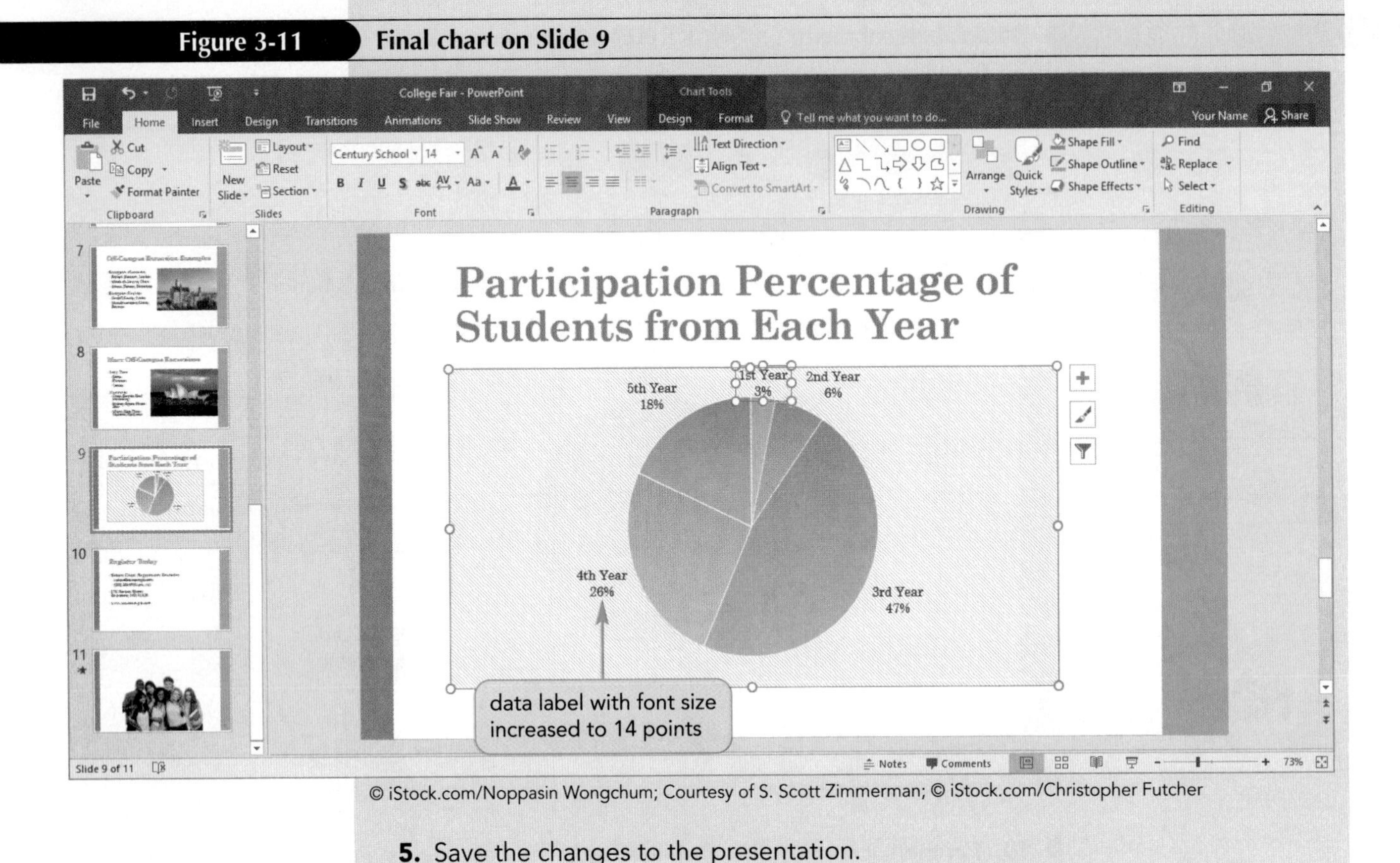

5. Save the changes to the presentation.

Inserting and Formatting Text Boxes

Sometimes you need to add text to a slide in a location other than in one of the text box placeholders included in the slide layout. You could draw any shape and add text to it, or you can add a text box shape. Unlike shapes that are filled with the Accent 1 color by default, text boxes by default do not have a fill. Another difference between the format of text boxes and shapes with text in them is that the text in a text box is left-aligned and text in shapes is center-aligned. Regardless of the differences, after you create a text box, you can format the text and the text box in a variety of ways, including adding a fill, adjusting the internal margins, and rotating and repositioning it.

Robert wants you to add text on Slide 6 that informs the audience of three new countries that will be available study abroad locations next spring. You will add a text box to accomplish this.

To add a text box to Slide 6:

1. Display **Slide 6** ("Locations"), and then click the **Insert** tab.
2. In the Text group, click the **Text Box** button, and then move the pointer to the slide. The pointer changes to ↓.
3. Position ↓ below the left edge of the first shape in the SmartArt, and then click and drag to draw a text box as wide as the England and France shapes and about one-half-inch high. See Figure 3-12.

Figure 3-12 Text box inserted on Slide 6

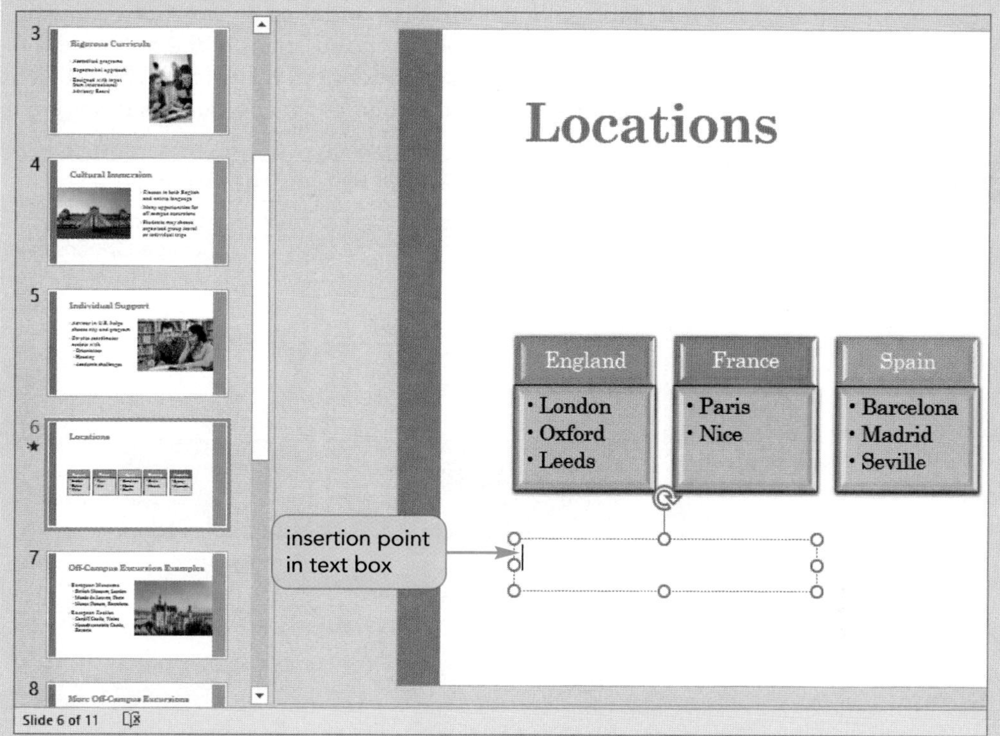

© iStock.com/sturti; © iStock.com/vichie81; © iStock.com/Susan Chiang; © iStock.com/Noppasin Wongchum

Trouble? If your text box is not the same size or is not positioned exactly as shown in Figure 3-12, don't worry. You'll adjust it later.

4. Type **Programs in South Africa, Japan, and Vietnam available next spring.** (including the period). As you type the text in the text box, the height of the text box changes, and the additional text wraps to the next line.

Trouble? If all the text fits on one line, drag the right-middle sizing handle to the left until some words appear on the next line so that you can complete the next sets of steps.

When you drag to create a text box, the default setting is for the text to wrap and for the height of the box to resize to accommodate the text you type. (If you simply click to place the text box, the text box will expand horizontally as wide as necessary to accommodate the text you type, even if it needs to flow off the slide.) This differs from text boxes created from title and content placeholders and shapes with text in them. Recall that text boxes created from placeholders have AutoFit behavior that reduces the font size of the text if you add more text than can fit. When you add text to a shape, if you add more text than can fit in that shape, the text extends outside of the shape.

Robert thinks the text below the SmartArt would look better if it were all on one line and italicized. You can widen the text box, or if you do not want the text to wrap to the next line regardless of how much text is in the text box, you can change the text wrapping option.

To modify and reposition the text box:

1. Right-click the text box, and then on the shortcut menu, click **Format Shape**. The Format Shape task pane opens to the right of the displayed slide. At the top, the Shape Options tab is selected. This tab contains categories of commands for formatting the shape, such as changing the fill. See Figure 3-13.

Figure 3-13 Format Shape task pane and text box with wrapped text

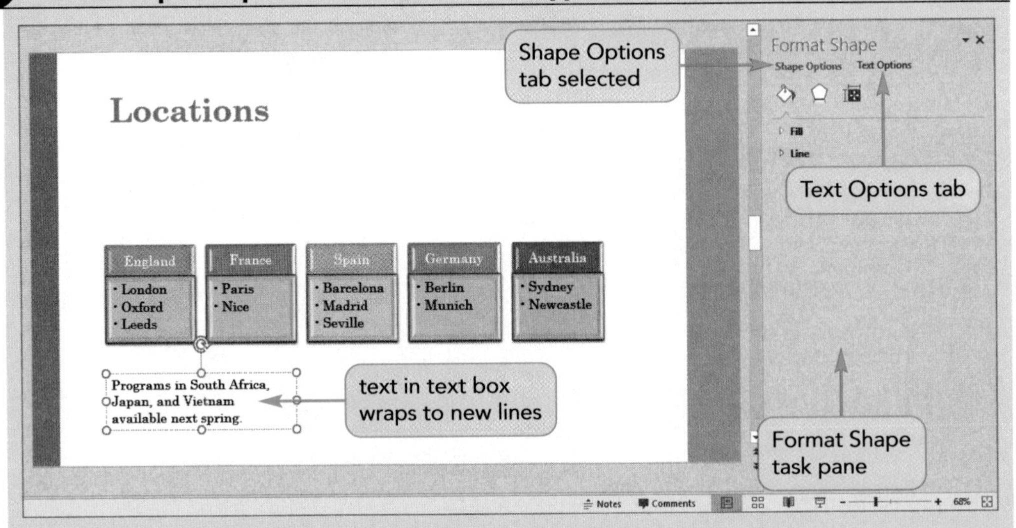

2. In the task pane, click **Text Options** to display the Text Options tab. This tab contains commands for formatting the text and how it is positioned.

TIP

Clicking any of the Dialog Box Launchers on the Drawing Tools Format tab also opens the Format Shape task pane.

3. Click the **Textbox** button. The task pane changes to show the Text Box section, containing options for formatting text in a text box. First you want to change the wrap option so the text does not wrap in the text box.
4. Click the **Wrap text in shape** check box to deselect it. The text in the text box appears all on one line. Next, you want to decrease the space between the first word in the text box and the left border of the box. In other words, you want to change the left margin in the text box.

   Trouble? If the Wrap text in shape check box is not selected, you clicked instead of dragging to create the text box in Step 3 in the previous set of steps. In this case, do not click the check box; leave it unselected.
5. Click the **Left margin down arrow**. The value in the box changes to 0", and the text shifts left in the text box.
6. Click the text box border to select all of the text in the text box, and then, in the Font group on the Home tab, click the **Italic** button *I*. The text in the text box is italicized.
7. Point to the border of the text box so that the pointer changes to the move pointer, press and hold the mouse button, and then drag the text box until its left edge is aligned with the left edge of the SmartArt and its top edge is aligned with the bottom edge of the SmartArt box, as shown in Figure 3-14.

Figure 3-14 Formatted and repositioned text box

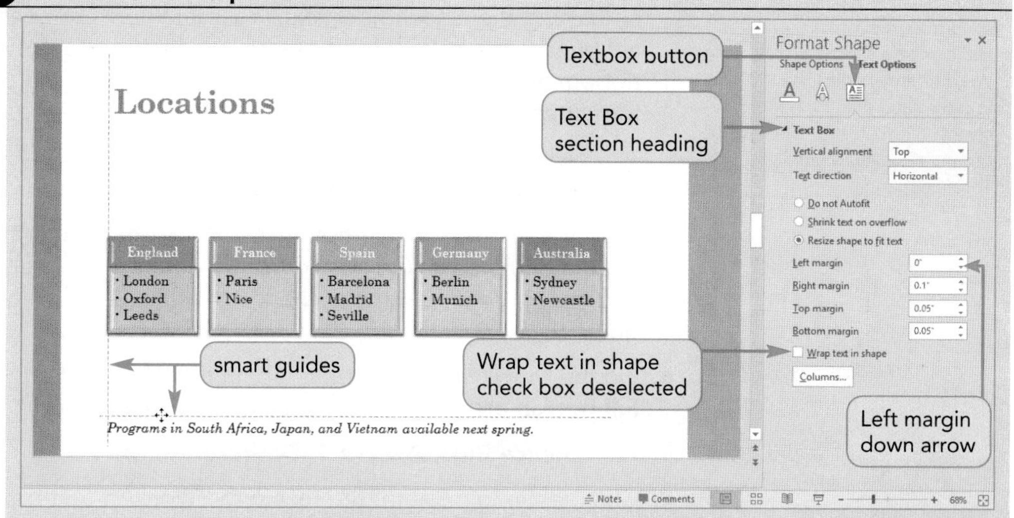

8. Release the mouse button.
9. In the Format Shape task pane, click the **Close** button, and then save the changes to the presentation.

Applying WordArt Styles to Text

WordArt is a term used to describe formatted, decorative text in a text box. WordArt text has a fill color, which is the same as the font color, and an outline color. To create WordArt, you can insert a new text box or format an existing one. You can apply one of the built-in WordArt styles or you can use the Text Fill, Text Outline, and Text Effects buttons in the WordArt Styles group on the Drawing Tools Format tab.

Robert would like you to add a text box that contains WordArt to Slide 11 that reinforces the invitation to register with ISC.

To create a text box containing WordArt on Slide 11:

1. Display **Slide 11** (the last slide), and then click the **Insert** tab.
2. In the Text group, click the **WordArt** button to open the WordArt gallery. See Figure 3-15.

Figure 3-15 WordArt gallery

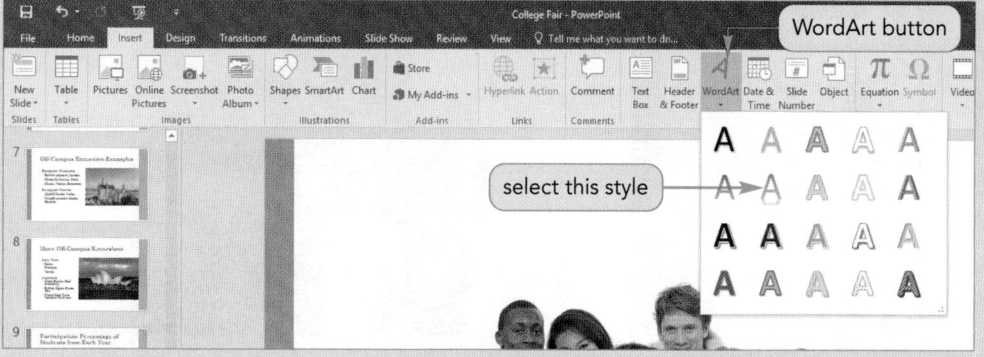

© iStock.com/Christopher Futcher; © iStock.com/Noppasin Wongchum; Courtesy of S. Scott Zimmerman

TIP

To format an existing text box on a slide with a WordArt style, select the text box, and then click a style in the WordArt Styles group on the Drawing Tools Format tab.

3. Click the **Gradient Fill – Green, Accent 1, Reflection** style. A text box containing the placeholder text "Your text here" appears on the slide, although it is a little hard to see because it is on top of the photo. On the ribbon, the Drawing Tools Format tab is selected. The placeholder text is formatted with the style you selected in the WordArt gallery. The placeholder text in the text box is selected.
4. Type **Join Us!**. The text you typed replaces the placeholder text.
5. Drag the text box to position it above the photo so that it is aligned with the middle of the slide and it is vertically centered between the top of the slide and the photo. You want to change the color used in the gradient fill from green to blue.
6. On the Drawing Tools Format tab, in the WordArt Styles group, click the **Text Fill button arrow**. The theme color palette appears.
7. Click the **Ice Blue, Accent 1, Darker 50%** color.
8. Change the font size of the text in the WordArt text box to **72** points.

The shape of text in a text box can be transformed into waves, circles, and other shapes. To do this, you use the options located on the Transform submenu, which is accessed from the Text Effects menu on the Drawing Tools Format tab.

Robert wants you to change the shape of the WordArt on Slide 11.

To change the shape of the WordArt by applying a transform effect:

1. With the WordArt on Slide 11 selected, click the **Drawing Tools Format** tab.
2. In the WordArt styles group, click the **Text Effects** button, and then point to **Transform**. The Transform submenu appears. See Figure 3-16.

Figure 3-16 **Transform submenu on Text Effects menu**

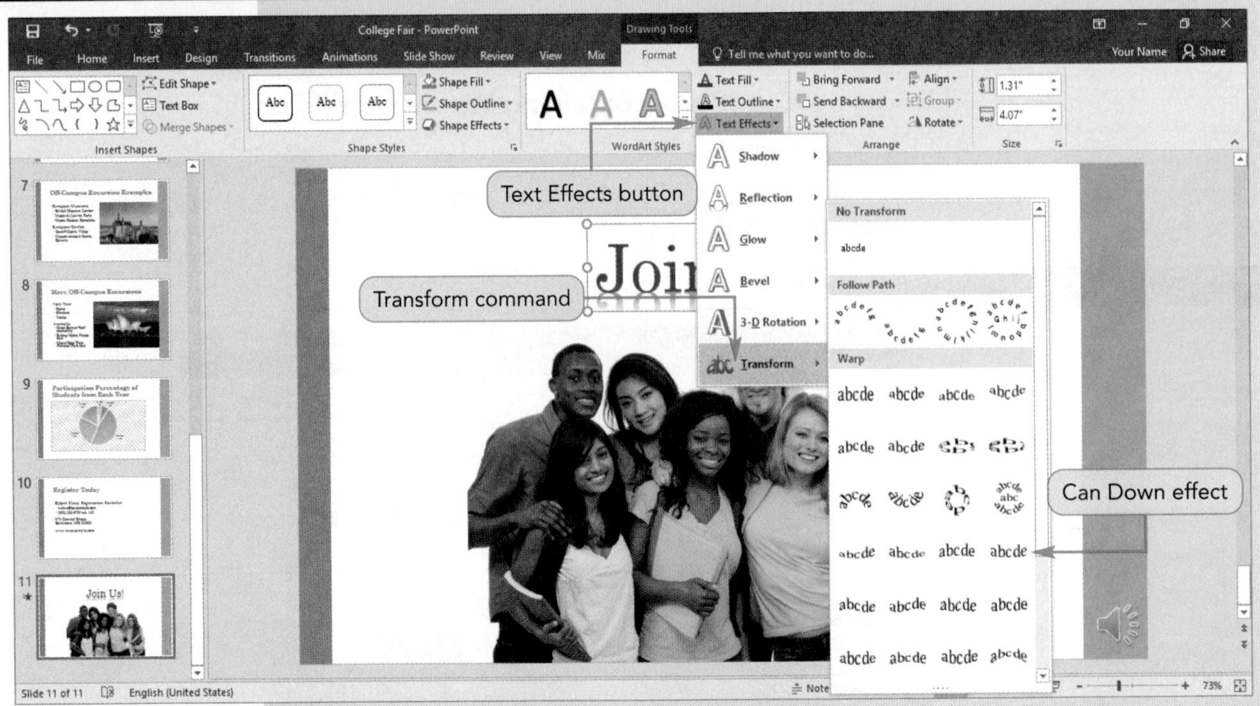

© iStock.com/Christopher Futcher; © iStock.com/Noppasin Wongchum; Courtesy of S. Scott Zimmerman

3. In the fourth row under Warp, click the **Can Down** effect. See Figure 3-17.

Figure 3-17 WordArt after applying Can Down transform effect

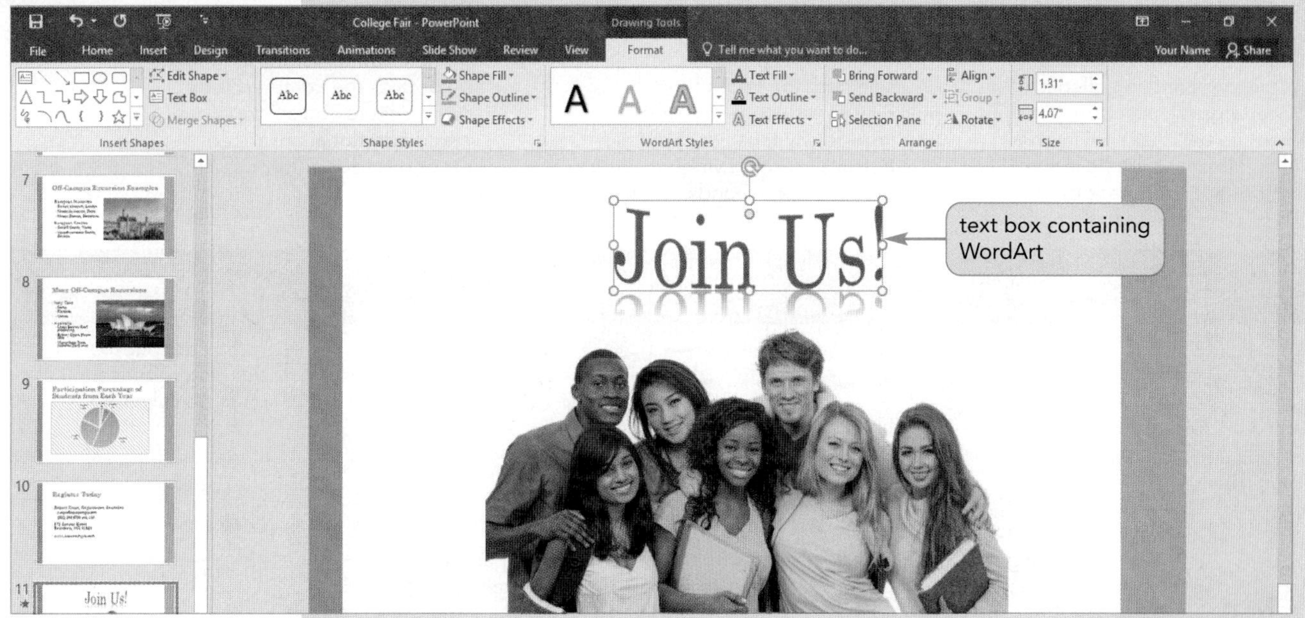

4. Save the changes to the presentation.

PROSKILLS

Decision Making: Selecting Appropriate Font Colors

When you select font colors, make sure your text is easy to read during your slide show. Font colors that work well are dark colors on a light background or light colors on a dark background. Avoid red text on a blue background or blue text on a green background (and vice versa) unless the shades of those colors are in strong contrast. These combinations might look fine on your computer monitor, but they are almost totally illegible to an audience viewing your presentation on a screen in a darkened room. Also avoid using red/green combinations, which color-blind people find illegible.

REVIEW

Session 3.1 Quick Check

1. How do you change the animation applied to a SmartArt diagram so that each shape animates one at a time?
2. What happens when you click the Play in Background button in the Audio Styles group on the Audio Tools Playback tab?
3. What is the difference between a chart and a graph?
4. What is a spreadsheet?
5. How do you identify a specific cell in a spreadsheet?
6. What is WordArt?

Session 3.2 Visual Overview:

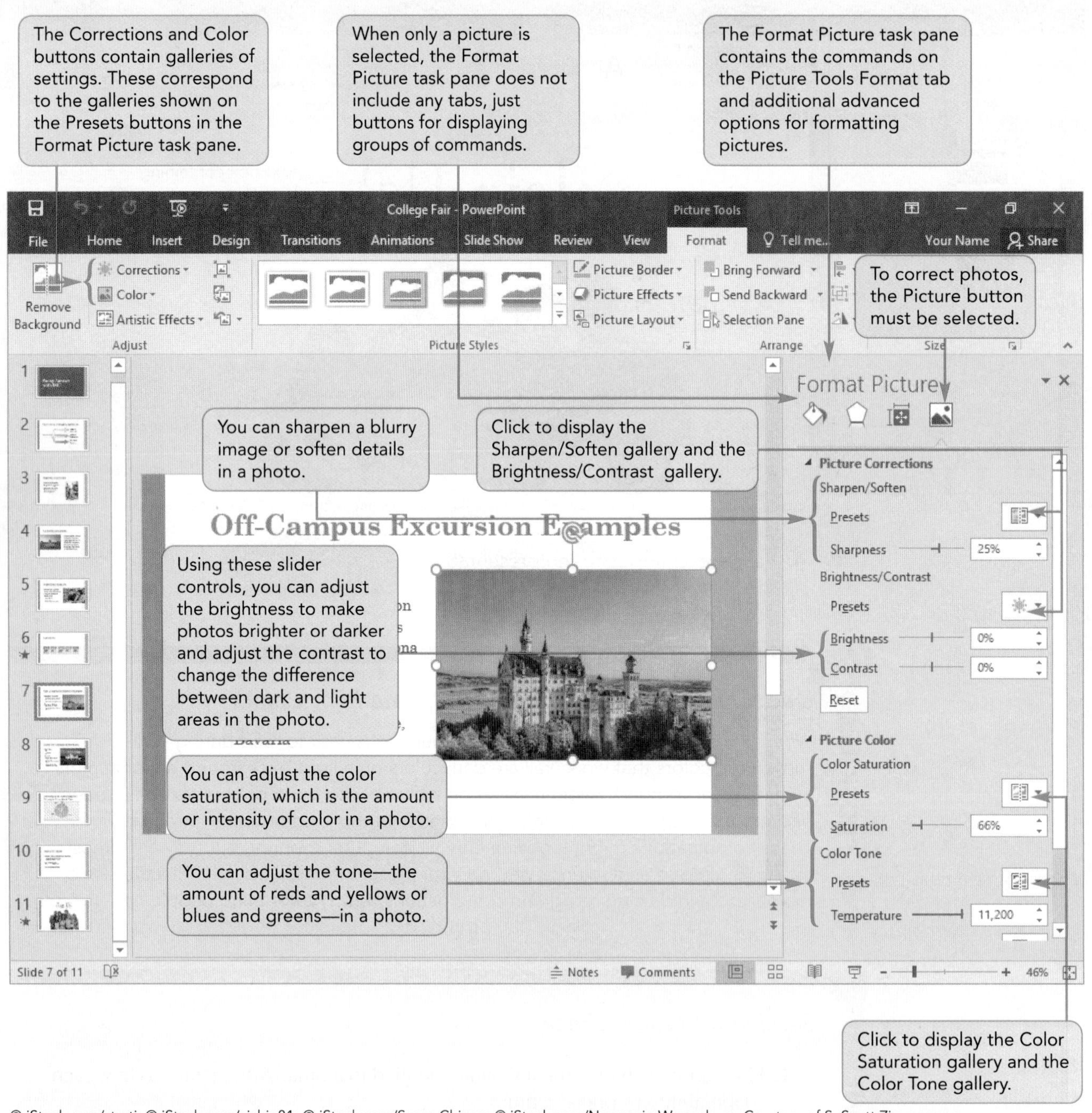

© iStock.com/sturti; © iStock.com/vichie81; © iStock.com/Susan Chiang; © iStock.com/Noppasin Wongchum; Courtesy of S. Scott Zimmerman; © iStock.com/Christopher Futcher

Formatting Shapes and Pictures

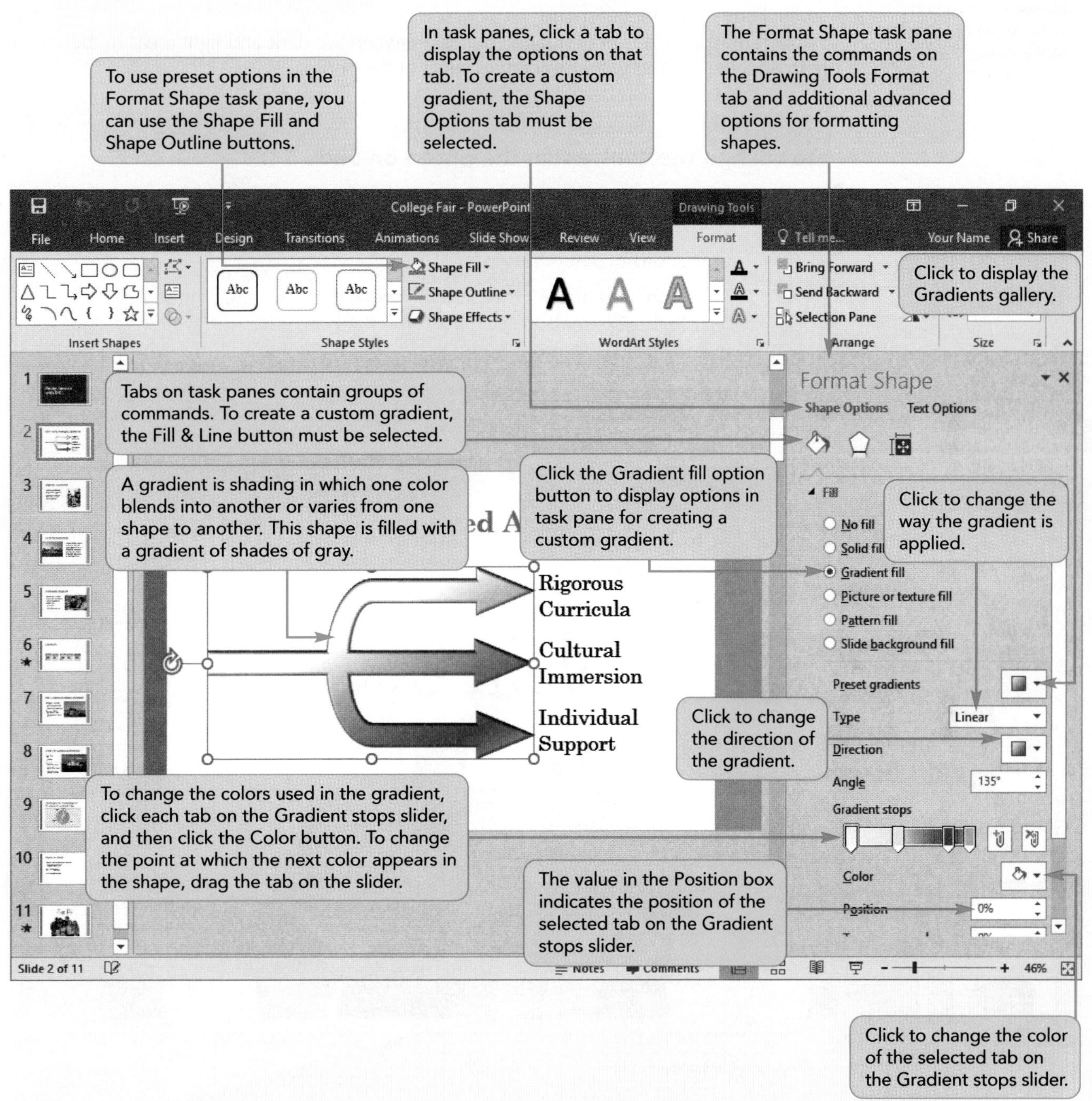

Editing Photos

TIP

If you make changes to photos and then change your mind, you can click the Reset Picture button in the Adjust group on the Picture Tools Format tab.

If photos you want to use in a presentation are too dark or require other fine-tuning, you can use PowerPoint's photo-correction tools to correct the photos. These photo-correction tools appear on the ribbon and in the Format Picture task pane. Refer to the Session 3.2 Visual Overview for more information about correcting photos and the Format Picture task pane.

Robert thinks there is not enough contrast between the dark and light areas in the photo on Slide 11. You will correct this aspect of the photo.

To change the contrast in the photo on Slide 11:

1. If you took a break after the previous session, make sure the **College Fair** presentation is open and **Slide 11** (the last slide) is displayed.
2. Click the photo to select it.
3. On the ribbon, click the **Picture Tools Format** tab, and then in the Adjust group, click the **Corrections** button. A menu opens, showing options for sharpening and softening the photo and adjusting the brightness and the contrast. See Figure 3-18.

Figure 3-18 Corrections menu

© iStock.com/Christopher Futcher

4. In the Brightness/Contrast section, click the **Brightness 0% (Normal) Contrast -20%** style (the third style in the second row). The contrast of the image changes. Because you chose a style with a Brightness percentage of 0%, the brightness of the photo is unchanged.

   You want to decrease the contrast just a little more. However, the gallery provides options that change the contrast in increments of 20 percent, which will be more of an adjustment than you are looking for. For selecting a more precise contrast setting, you need to open the Format Picture task pane.

TIP

You can also right-click the photo, and then click Format Picture on the shortcut menu to open the Format Picture task pane.

5. Click the **Corrections** button again, and then click **Picture Corrections Options**. The Format Picture task pane opens with the Picture button selected and the Picture Corrections section expanded.
6. Drag the **Contrast** slider to the left until the box next to the slider indicates -30%. The contrast increases slightly.

   Trouble? If you can't position the slider exactly, click the up or down arrow in the box containing the percentage as needed, or select the current percentage and then type -30.
7. Close the task pane.

Next, Robert wants you to adjust the photo on Slide 7. He wants you to make the colors in the photo more realistic, by reducing the saturation and the tone.

To change the saturation and tone of the photo on Slide 7:

1. Display **Slide 7** ("Off-Campus Excursion Examples"), click the photo to select it, and then click the **Picture Tools Format** tab on the ribbon, if necessary.
2. In the Adjust group, click the **Color** button. A menu opens with options for adjusting the saturation and tone of the photo's color. See Figure 3-19.

Figure 3-19 Color menu

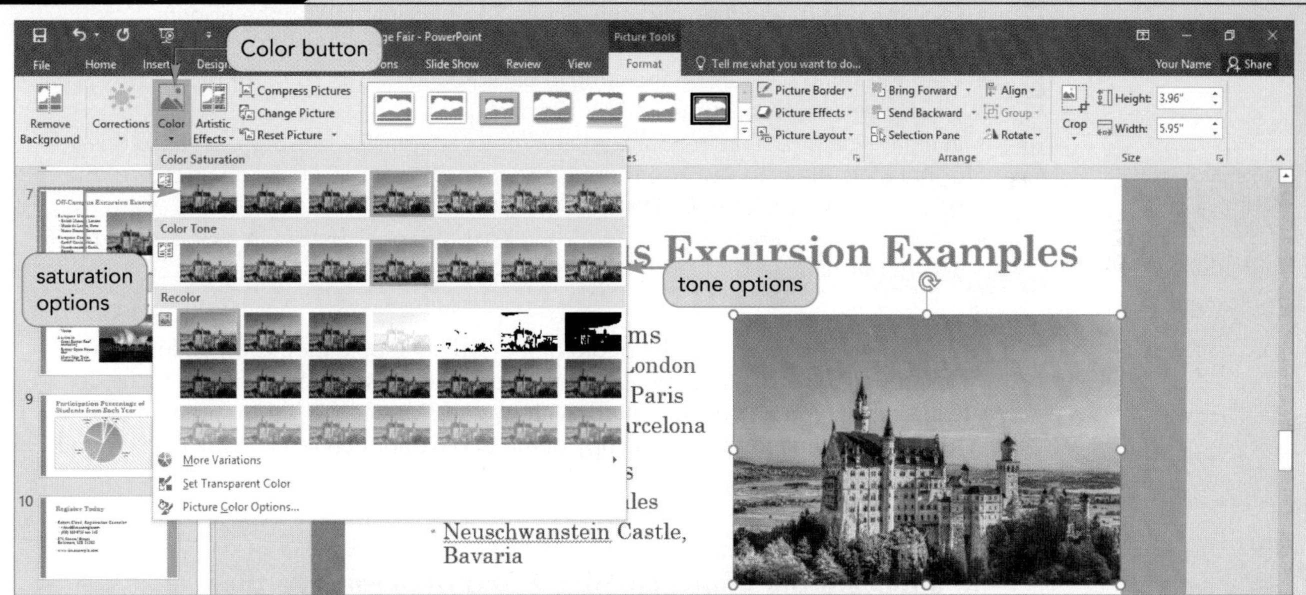

© iStock.com/Noppasin Wongchum; Courtesy of S. Scott Zimmerman

TIP

To recolor a photo so it is all one color, click the Color button in the Adjust group on the Picture Tools Format tab, and then click a Recolor option.

3. Under Color Saturation, click the **Saturation: 66%** option. The colors in the photo are now less intense.
4. Click the **Color** button again.
5. Under Color Tone, click the **Temperature: 11200K** option. More reds and yellows are added to the photo, most noticeably in the skyline on the right side of the image.

Finally, Robert wants you to sharpen the photo on Slide 7 so that the objects in the photo are more in focus.

To sharpen the photo on Slide 7:

1. On Slide 7 ("Off-Campus Excursion Examples"), make sure the photo is still selected, and on the ribbon, the Picture Tools Format tab is the active tab.
2. In the Adjust group, click the **Corrections** button. The options for sharpening and softening photos appear at the top of the menu.
3. Under Sharpen/Soften, click the **Sharpen: 25%** option. The edges of the objects in the picture are sharper and clearer.
4. Save the changes to the presentation.

Removing the Background from Photos

Sometimes a photo is more striking if you remove its background. You can also layer a photo with the background removed on top of another photo to create an interesting effect. To remove the background of a photo, you can use the Remove Background tool. When you click the Remove Background button in the Adjust group on the Picture Tools Format tab, PowerPoint analyzes the photograph and marks parts of it to remove and parts of it to retain. If the analysis removes too little or too much of the photo, you can adjust it.

REFERENCE

Removing the Background of a Photograph

- Click the photo, and then click the Picture Tools Format tab on the ribbon.
- In the Adjust group, click the Remove Background button.
- Drag the sizing handles on the remove background border to make broad adjustments to the area marked for removal.
- In the Refine group on the Background Removal tab, click the Mark Areas to Keep or the Mark Areas to Remove button, and then click or drag through an area of the photo that you want marked to keep or remove.
- Click a blank area of the slide or click the Keep Changes button in the Close group to accept the changes.

Robert wants you to modify the photo of the Sydney Opera House on Slide 8 so that the background looks like a drawing, but the opera house stays sharp and in focus. To create this effect, you will need to work with two versions of the photo. You will use the Duplicate command to make a copy of the photo and then remove the background from the duplicate photo.

To duplicate the photo on Slide 8 and then remove the background from the copy:

1. Display **Slide 8** ("More Off-Campus Excursions" with the photo of the Sydney Opera House), click the photo to select it, and then, on the ribbon, click the **Home** tab, if necessary. The photo on Slide 8 is a photo of the Sydney Opera House in Sydney, Australia.
2. In the Clipboard group, click the **Copy button arrow**, and then click **Duplicate**. The photo is duplicated on the slide, and the duplicate is selected.
3. Point to the selected duplicate photo so that the pointer changes to the move pointer, and then drag it left to position it to the left of the original photo. The duplicate photo is on top of the bulleted list and extends beyond the slide border.

4. With the duplicate photo selected, click the **Picture Tools Format** tab on the ribbon.

5. In the Adjust group, click the **Remove Background** button. The areas of the photograph marked for removal are colored purple. A sizing box appears around the general area of the photograph that will be retained, and a new tab, the Background Removal tab, appears on the ribbon and is the active tab. See Figure 3-20. You can adjust the area of the photograph that is retained by dragging the sizing handles on the sizing box.

Figure 3-20 Photograph after clicking the Remove Background button

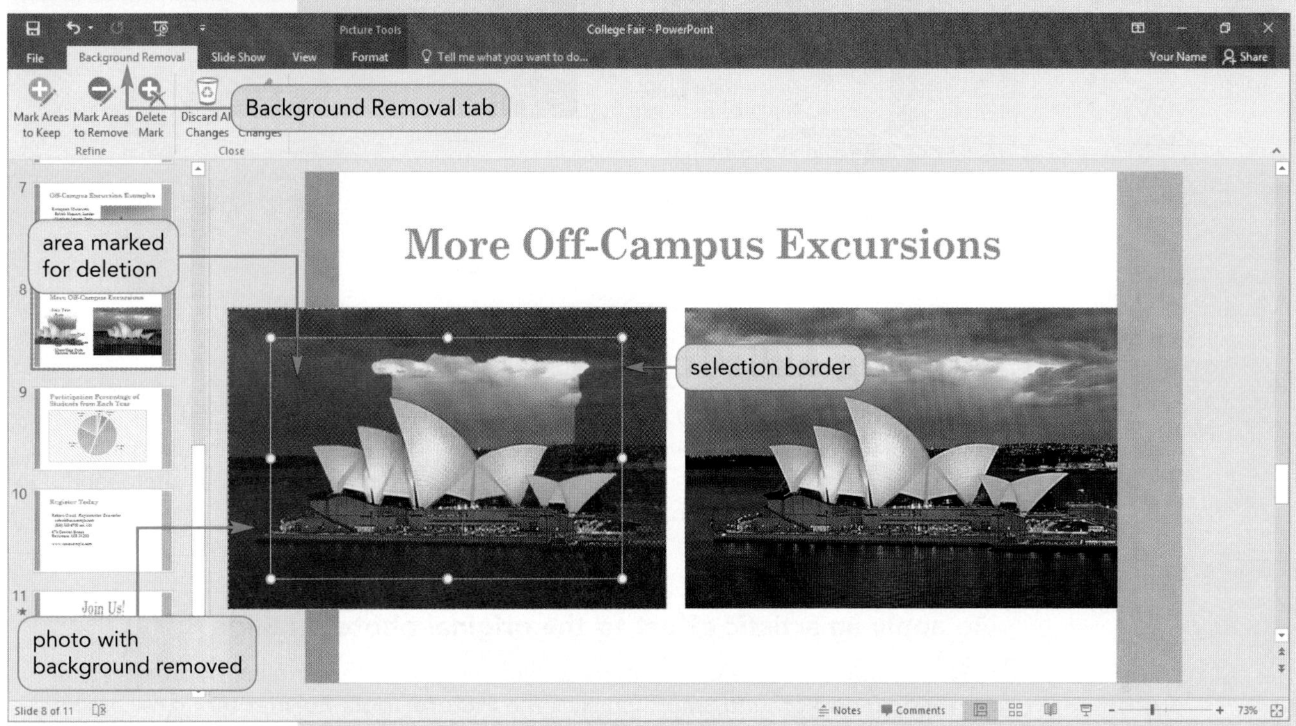

Courtesy of S. Scott Zimmerman; © iStock.com/Noppasin Wongchum; © iStock.com/Christopher Futcher

TIP

If the background of a photo is all one color, you can click the Color button in the Adjust group on the Picture Tools Format tab, click Set Transparent Color, and then click the color you want to make transparent.

6. Drag the top-middle sizing handle down to just above the tallest point of the opera house. Now only the opera house will be retained, and all of the sky and water will be removed.

   Trouble? If any of the background of the photo is colored normally, click the Mark Areas to Remove button in the Refine group on the Background Removal tab, and then drag through the area that should be removed.

7. On the Background Removal tab, in the Close group, click the **Keep Changes** button. The changes you made are applied to the photograph, and the Background Removal tab is removed from the ribbon. See Figure 3-21.

Figure 3-21 Duplicate photo with background removed

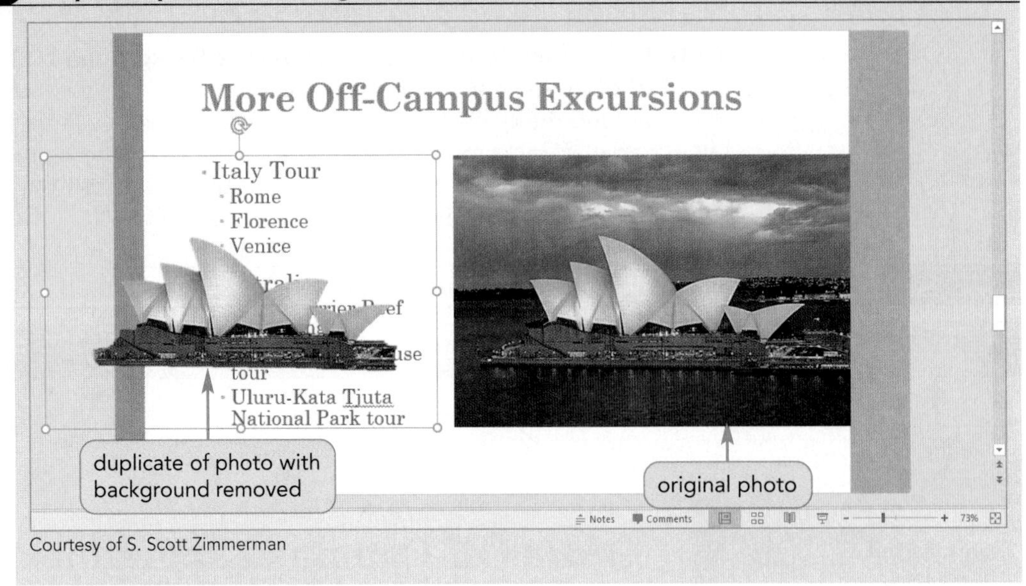

Courtesy of S. Scott Zimmerman

Applying Artistic Effects to Photos

You can apply artistic effects to photos to make them look like they are drawings, paintings, black-and-white line drawings, and so on. To make the opera house stand out in the photo, Robert wants you to apply an artistic effect to the original photo, and then place the photo with the background removed on top of it.

To apply an artistic effect to the original photo on Slide 8:

1. On Slide 8 ("More Off-Campus Excursions"), click the original photo with the visible background, and then click the **Picture Tools Format** tab, if necessary.
2. In the Adjust group, click the **Artistic Effects** button. See Figure 3-22.

Figure 3-22 Artistic Effects menu

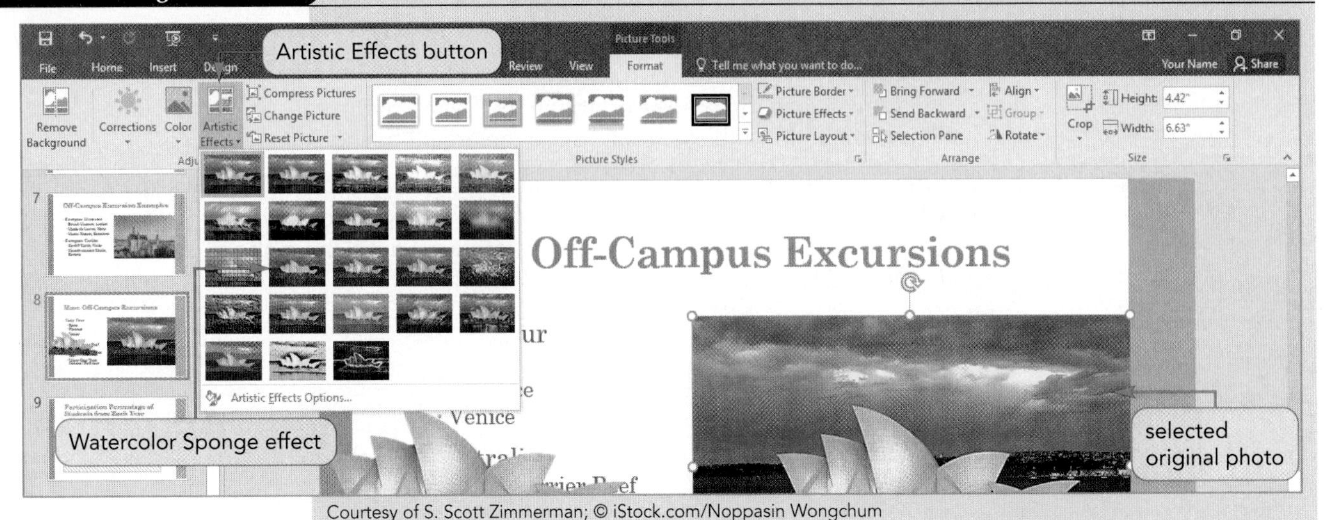

Courtesy of S. Scott Zimmerman; © iStock.com/Noppasin Wongchum

3. Click the **Watercolor Sponge** effect in the third row. The watercolor sponge effect is applied to the photo. Now you will place the photo with the background removed on top of the photo with the artistic effect.
4. Drag the photo with the background removed and position it directly on top of the opera house in the photo with the artistic effect applied. See Figure 3-23.

Figure 3-23 Final photo on Slide 8

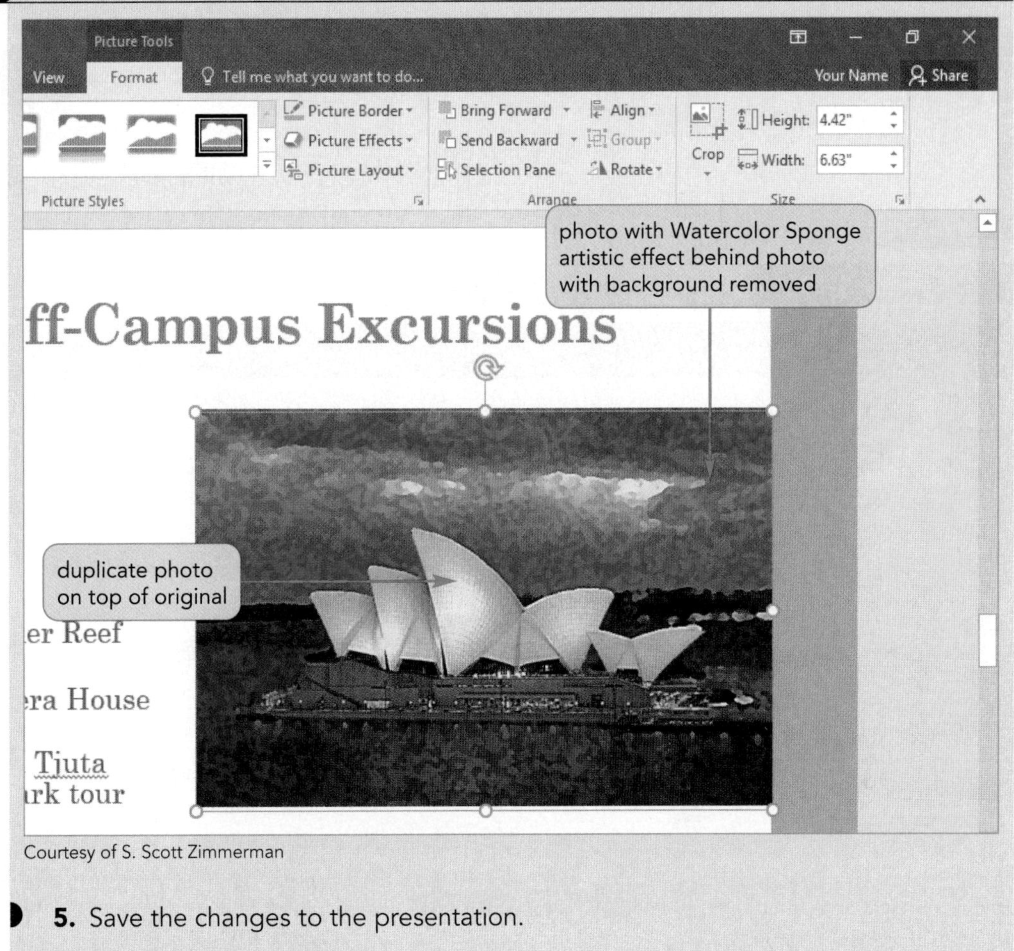

Courtesy of S. Scott Zimmerman

5. Save the changes to the presentation.

Creating a Custom Shape

You have learned how to insert and format shapes on slides. In PowerPoint you can also create a custom shape by merging two or more shapes. Then you can position and format the custom shape as you would any other shape.

ISC advertises that it offers three main advantages: rigorous curricula, cultural immersion, and individual support. To illustrate this three-pronged approach, Robert wants to use a graphic, but none of the built-in shapes or SmartArt diagrams matches the idea he has in mind. He asks you to create a custom shape similar to the one shown in Figure 3-24 to illustrate this concept.

Figure 3-24 **Robert's sketch of the shape for Slide 2**

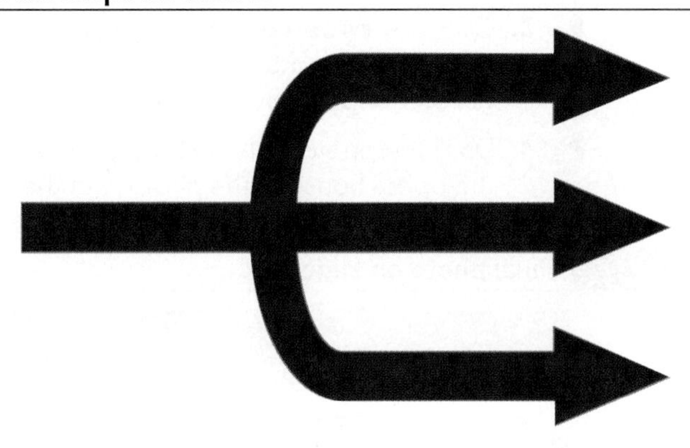

To create the custom shape for Robert, you will merge several shapes. Robert already placed three of these shapes on Slide 2. See Figure 3-25.

Figure 3-25 **Slide 2 with three shapes**

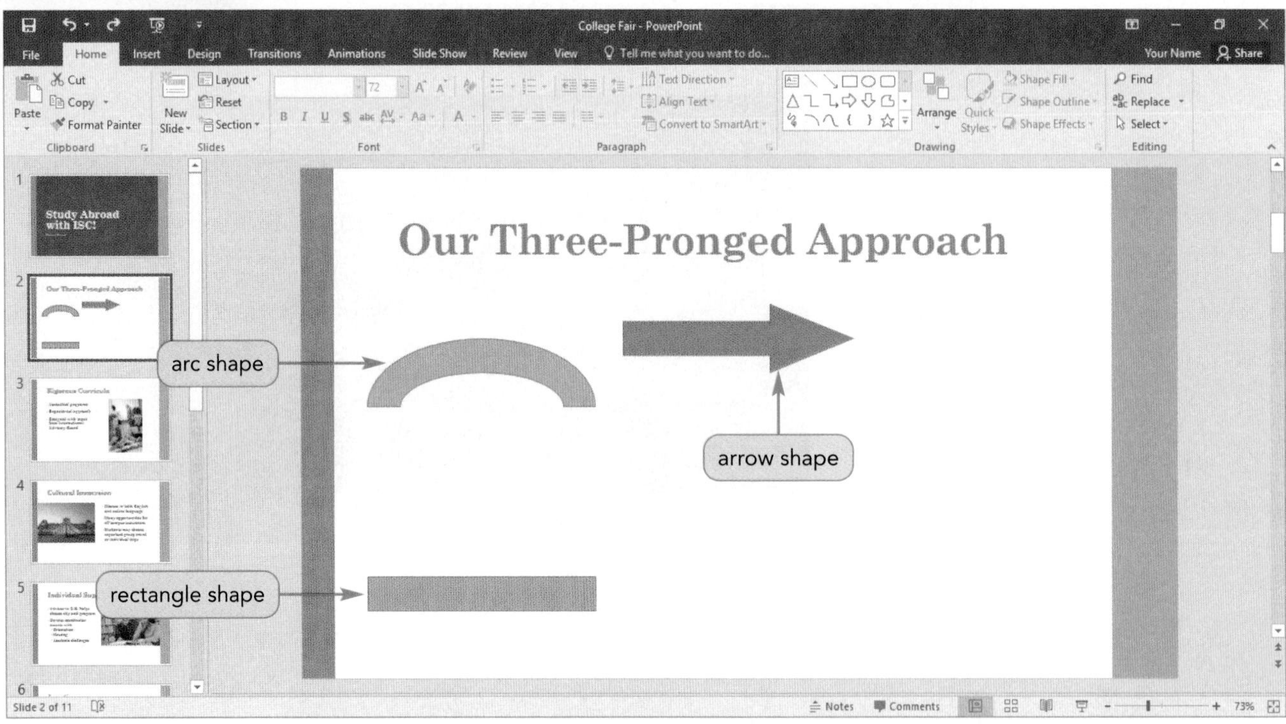

© iStock.com/sturti; © iStock.com/vichie81; © iStock.com/Susan Chiang

The first thing you need to do is duplicate the arrow shape twice to create the three prongs. Then you need to align the three arrow shapes.

TIP

You can also click the Align button in the Arrange group on the Format tab, and then click one of the alignment commands.

To align the three arrow shapes on Slide 2:

1. Display **Slide 2** ("Our Three-Pronged Approach"), and then duplicate the arrow shape twice.
2. Drag one of the duplicate arrows down until the smart guides indicate the bottom point of the arrow head is aligned with the top edge of the rectangle shape and so that its left and right ends are aligned with those of the original arrow.

3. Drag the other duplicate arrow so it is halfway between the top and bottom arrow, until the smart guides indicate that its left and right ends are aligned with those of the top and bottom arrows and so that there is the same amount of space between the top and middle arrow and between the middle and bottom arrow, as shown in Figure 3-26.

Figure 3-26 Smart guides showing alignment of arrow shapes

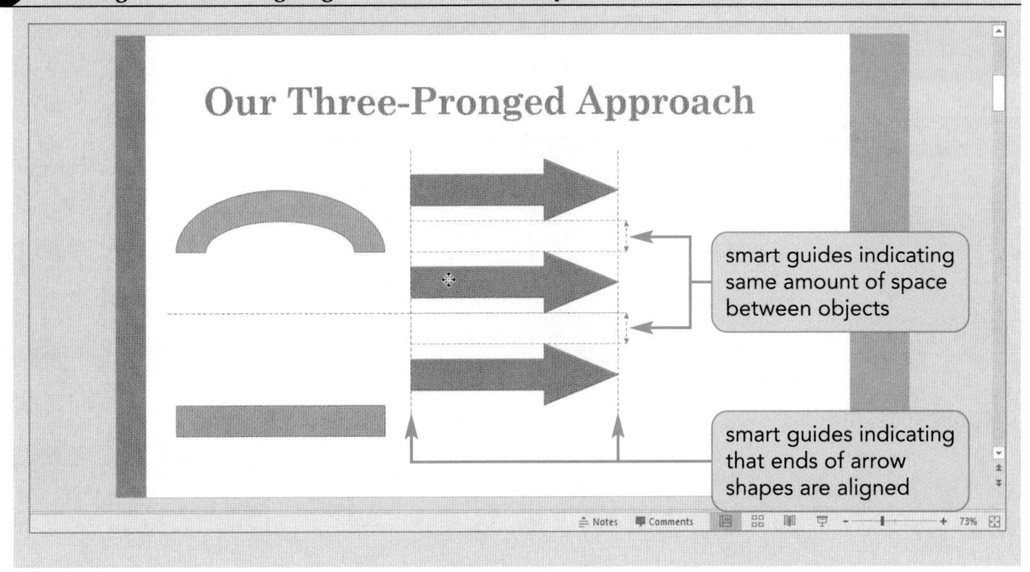

To create a custom shape, you need to use the commands on the Merge Shapes menu in the Insert Shapes group on the Drawing Tools Format tab. Each command has a different effect on selected shapes:

- **Union**—Combines selected shapes without removing any portions
- **Combine**—Combines selected shapes and removes the sections of the shapes that overlap
- **Fragment**—Separates overlapping portions of shapes into separate shapes
- **Intersect**—Combines selected shapes and removes everything except the sections that overlap
- **Subtract**—Removes the second shape selected, including any part of the first shape that is overlapped by the second shape

When you merge shapes, you place one shape on top of or touching another, and then you select the shapes. When you use the Union, Combine, Fragment, or Intersect command, the shape you select first determines the format of the merged shape. For example, if you select a red shape first and a blue shape second, and then you unite, combine, fragment, or intersect them, the merged shape will be red. When you use the Subtract command, the shape you select second is the shape that is removed.

You'll position the shapes and then merge them using the Union command.

To position the shapes and then merge them:

1. Click the **arc** shape to select it.
2. On the Home tab, in the Drawing group, click the **Arrange** button, point to **Rotate**, and then click **Rotate Left 90 degrees**.
3. Drag the arc shape and position it so that its ends touch the left end of the top arrow and bottom arrow shapes, making sure the shapes touch.
4. Drag the rectangle shape to position it so that its right end touches the end of the middle arrow. See Figure 3-27.

Make sure the arc and arrow shape are touching or the shapes won't merge when you use the Union command.

Figure 3-27 Shapes arranged to form new shape

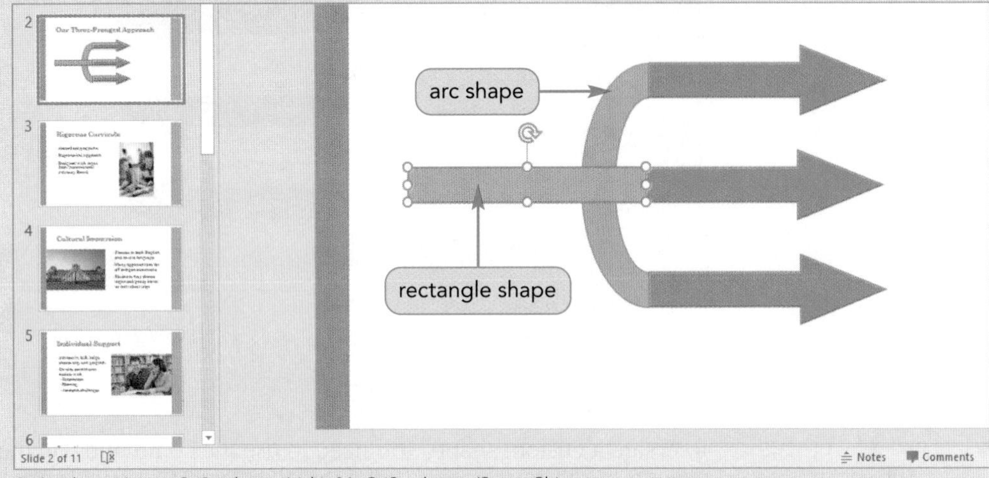

5. On the ribbon, click the **Drawing Tools Format** tab. In the Insert Shapes group, the Merge Shapes button is gray and unavailable. At least two shapes need to be selected to use the commands on the Merge Shapes menu.
6. Press and hold the **Shift** key, and then click the middle arrow. The rectangle and the middle arrow shape are now selected, and the Merge Shapes button is now available.
7. In the Insert Shapes group, click the **Merge Shapes** button, and then click **Union**. The two shapes are merged into a new shape formatted the same tan color as the rectangle shape because you selected the rectangle shape first.
8. Click the **arc** shape, press and hold the **Shift** key, click each of the arrow shapes including the merged shape, and then release the **Shift** key.
9. In the Insert Shapes group, click the **Merge Shapes** button, and then click **Union**. The four shapes are merged into a blue shape.

Applying Advanced Formatting to Shapes

You know that you can fill a shape with a solid color or with a picture. You can also fill a shape with a texture—a pattern that gives a tactile quality to the shape, such as crumpled paper or marble—or with a gradient. You'll change the fill of the custom shape to a texture.

To change the shape fill to a texture:

1. Make sure the custom shape is selected, and then click the **Drawing Tools Format** tab, if necessary.
2. In the Shape Styles group, click the **Shape Fill button arrow**, and then point to **Texture**. The Texture submenu opens. See Figure 3-28.

Figure 3-28 Texture submenu on Shape Fill menu

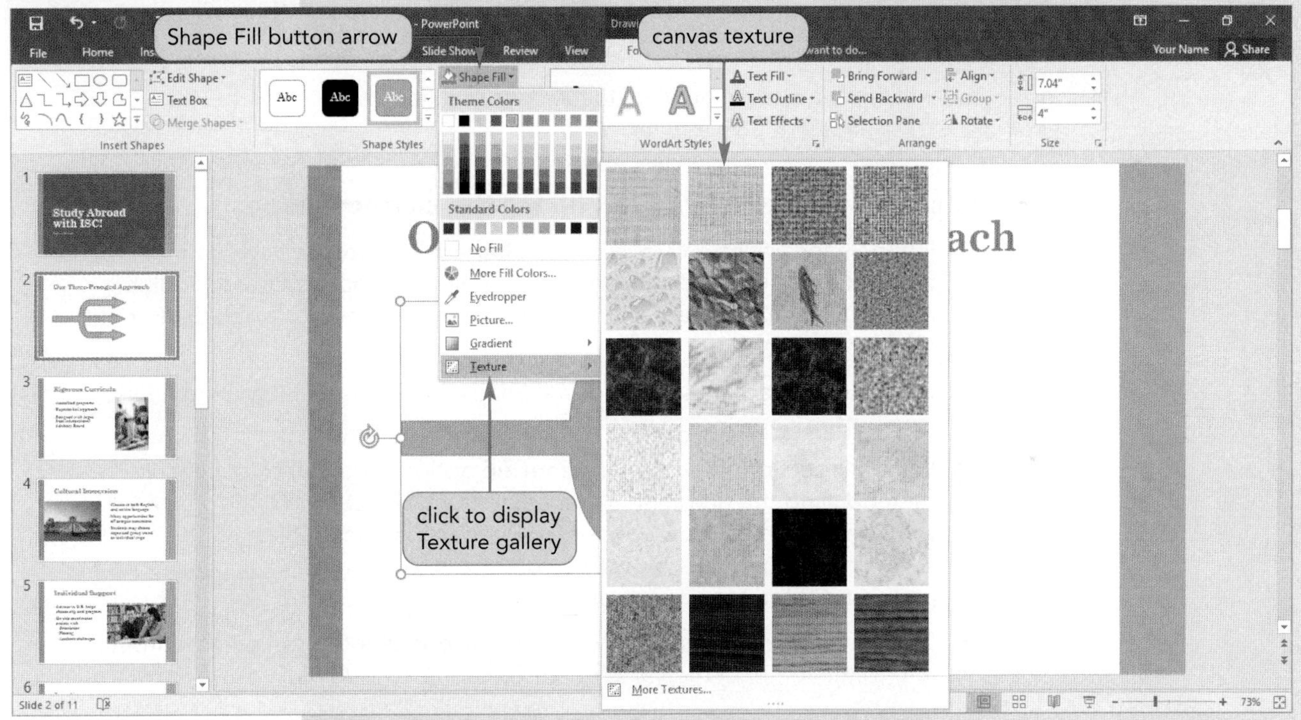

© iStock.com/sturti; © iStock.com/vichie81; © iStock.com/Susan Chiang

3. Click the **Canvas** texture, which is the second texture in the first row. The custom shape is filled with a texture resembling canvas. Robert doesn't like any of the textures as a fill for the shape. He asks you to remove the texture.
4. In the Shapes Styles group, click the **Shape Fill button arrow**, and then click **No Fill**. The texture is removed from the custom shape, and only the outline of the custom shape remains.

The texture did not achieve the effect Robert wanted for the shape. He now asks you to use a gradient to simulate the look of metal or silver. You can apply gradients on the Shape Fill menu that use shades of the Accent 1 color in the theme color palette. You can also create a custom gradient using the options in the Format Shape task pane. To create a custom gradient, you select the colors to use, specify the position in the shape where the color will change, and specify the direction of the gradient in the shape.

Refer to the Session 3.2 Visual Overview for more information about using the Format Shape task pane to create a custom gradient.

REFERENCE

Creating a Custom Gradient in a Shape

- Select the shape.
- Click the Drawing Tools Format tab.
- In the Shape Styles group, click the Shape Fill button arrow, point to Gradient, and then click More Gradients to open the Format Shape task pane.
- In the Format Shape task pane, on the Shape Options tab with the Fill & Line button selected, click the Gradient fill option button.
- On the Gradient stops slider, click a tab, drag it to the desired position on the slider, click the Color button, and then select a color.
- Repeat the above step for each tab.
- Click the Type arrow, and then click the type of gradient you want to use.
- Click the Direction button, and then click the direction of the gradient.

You will apply a custom gradient to the custom shape now.

To create a custom gradient fill for the custom shape:

1. In the Shape Styles group, click the **Shape Fill button arrow**, and then point to **Gradient**. The gradients on the submenu use shades of the Ice Blue, Accent 1 color. To create a custom gradient, you need to open the Format Shape task pane.
2. Click **More Gradients**. The Format Shape task pane opens with the Fill & Line button selected on the Shape Options tab.
3. In the Fill section, click the **Gradient fill** option button. The commands for modifying the gradient fill appear in the task pane, and the shape fills with shades of light blue. Under Gradient stops, the first tab on the slider is selected, and its value in the Position box is 0%. You will change the position and color of the second tab on the slider.
4. On the Gradient stops slider, drag the **Stop 2 of 4** tab (second tab from the left) to the left until the value in the Position box is **40%**.

   Trouble? If you can't position the slider exactly, click the Stop 2 of 4 tab, type 40 in the Position box, and then press the Enter key.

5. With the Stop 2 of 4 tab selected, click the **Color** button. The color palette opens.

   TIP: Click the Add gradient stop button to add another gradient stop to the slider; click the Remove gradient stop button to remove the selected gradient stop from the slider.

6. Click the **White, Background 1, Darker 5%** color. Next you need to change the color of the third tab.
7. Click the **Stop 3 of 4** tab, click the **Color** button, and then click the **White, Background 1, Darker 50%** color.
8. Click the **Stop 4 of 4** tab, click the **Color** button, and then click the **Gray-50%, Accent 6, Lighter 60%** color.

   Next you will change the direction of the gradient. Above the Gradient stops slider, in the Type box, Linear is selected. This means that the shading will vary linearly—that is, top to bottom, side to side, or diagonally. You will change the direction to a diagonal.

9. Click the **Direction** button. A gallery of gradient options opens.
10. Click the **Linear Diagonal – Top Right to Bottom Left** direction. The shading in the shape changes so it varies diagonally. See Figure 3-29.

Figure 3-29 **Custom shape with gradient fill**

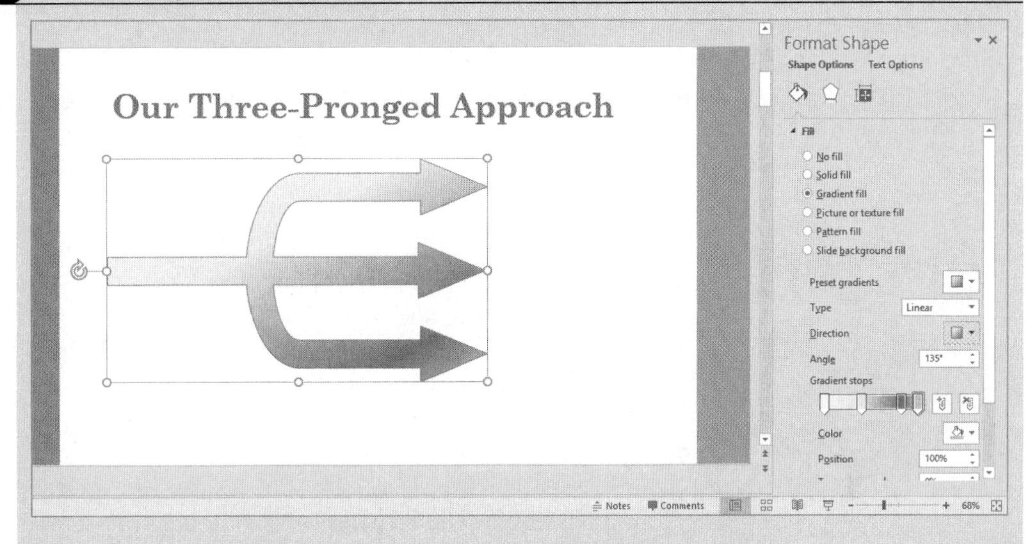

11. In the Format Shape task pane, click the **Close** button.

Although the gradient shading helped, the shape looks flat and doesn't really look metallic. To finish formatting the shape, you need to apply a bevel effect, which will give the edges a three-dimensional, rounded look.

To add a bevel effect to the custom shape:

1. On the ribbon, click the **Drawing Tools Format** tab, if necessary.
2. In the Shape Styles group, click the **Shape Effects** button. The menu that opens lets you choose from a variety of effects you can apply to shapes.
3. Point to **Bevel**, and then click the **Circle** bevel. The shape has a bevel effect.

TIP

To save a custom shape as a picture file so that you can use it in other files, right-click it, and then click Save as Picture on the shortcut menu.

Now you need to complete the slide by adding text boxes that list the three elements of the ISC approach. You will position the custom shape, and then place a text box next to each prong.

To add text boxes to Slide 2:

1. Drag the shape so its left edge aligns with the left edge of the title text box.
2. On the ribbon, click the **Insert** tab, and then in the Text group, click the **Text Box** button.
3. To the right of the shape's top arrow, drag to draw a text box approximately 2 inches wide, and then type **Rigorous Curricula**.

4. Change the font size of the text in the text box to **32** points. The text now appears on two lines in the text box.

   Trouble? If the text did not adjust to appear on two lines in the text box, drag the right-middle sizing handle to the left until it does.

5. Drag the text box to position it so that the top of the text box is aligned with the top of the shape and the left edge of the text box is aligned with the right edge of the shape.
6. Duplicate the text box, and then position the duplicate to the right of the shape's middle arrow, aligning the left and right edges with the left and right edges of the top text box and aligning the middle of the text box with the middle of the shape.
7. Duplicate the second text box. A third text box appears.
8. Point to the third text box so that the pointer changes to , press and hold the mouse button, and then, if necessary, drag the third text box to the right of the shape's bottom arrow, aligning the left and right edges with the left and right edges of the other two text boxes and so that there is the same amount of space between each text box.
9. In the text box to the right of the middle arrow, replace the text with **Cultural Immersion**, and then in the text box to the right of the bottom arrow, replace the text with **Individual Support**. Compare your screen to Figure 3-30, and make any adjustments if necessary.

Figure 3-30 Text boxes next to custom shape with beveled edge

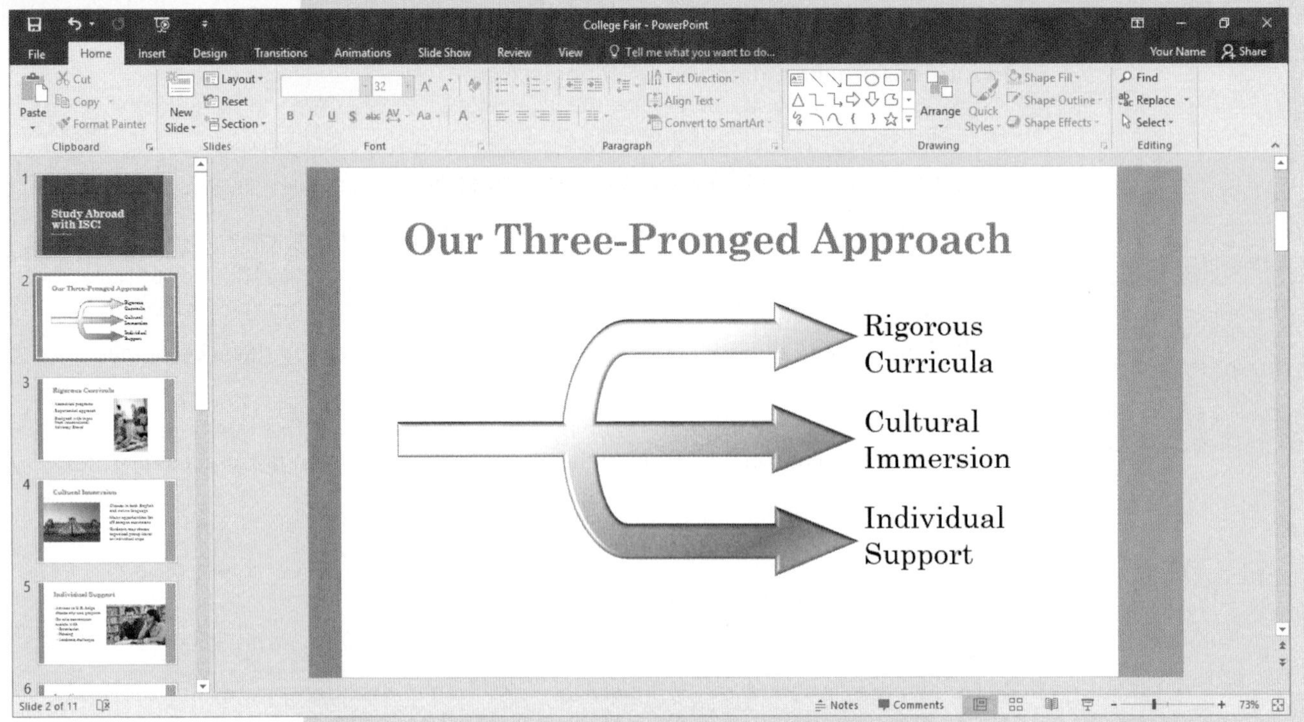

© iStock.com/sturti; © iStock.com/vichie81; © iStock.com/Susan Chiang

10. Save the changes to the presentation.

INSIGHT

Using the Format Shape and Format Picture Task Panes

Many options are available to you in the Format Shape and Format Picture task panes. Most of the commands are available on the Drawing Tools and Picture Tools Format tabs on the ribbon, but you can refine their effects in the task panes. For example, you can fill a shape with a color and then use a command in the Format Shape task pane to make the fill color partially transparent so you can see objects behind the shape. Because these task panes are so useful, you can access them in a variety of ways. Once a picture or shape is selected, you can do one of the following to open the corresponding task pane:

- Click any of the Dialog Box Launchers on the Drawing Tools or Picture Tools Format tab.
- Right-click a shape or picture, and then click Format Shape or Format Picture on the shortcut menu.
- Click a command at the bottom of a menu, such as the More Gradients command at the bottom of the Gradients submenu on the Fill Color menu or the Picture Corrections Options command at the bottom of the Corrections menu.

Making Presentations Accessible

People with physical impairments or disabilities can use computers because of technology that makes them accessible. For example, people who cannot use their arms or hands instead can use foot, head, or eye movements to control the pointer. One of the most common assistive technologies is the screen reader. The screen reader identifies objects on the screen and produces an audio of the text.

Graphics and tables cause problems for users of screen readers unless they have **alternative text**, often shortened to **alt text**, which is text added to an object that describes the object. For example, the alt text for a SmartArt graphic might describe the intent of the graphic. When a screen reader encounters an object that has alt text, it announces that an object is on the slide, and then it reads the alt text.

Adding Alt Text

You can add alt text for any object on a PowerPoint slide. Many screen readers can read the text in title text boxes and bulleted lists, so you usually do not need to add alt text for those objects. Most screen readers cannot read the text in SmartArt, in text boxes you draw, or in other shapes, so you will add alt text to the SmartArt diagram and the text box on Slide 6.

To add alt text for the SmartArt graphic:

1. Display **Slide 6** ("Locations").
2. Right-click the white area near any of the shapes in the SmartArt graphic to select the entire graphic.
3. On the shortcut menu, click **Format Object**. The Format Shape task pane opens with the Shape Options tab selected.
4. In the task pane, click the **Size & Properties** button, and then click **Text Box** to collapse that section, if necessary.

Make sure you select the entire SmartArt object and not just one shape. If you right-click a shape, the alt text will be applied only for that individual shape.

5. In the task pane, click **Alt Text** to expand the Alt Text section. A Title box and a Description box appear below the Alt Text section heading. See Figure 3-31.

Figure 3-31 Alt Text section in the Format Shape task pane

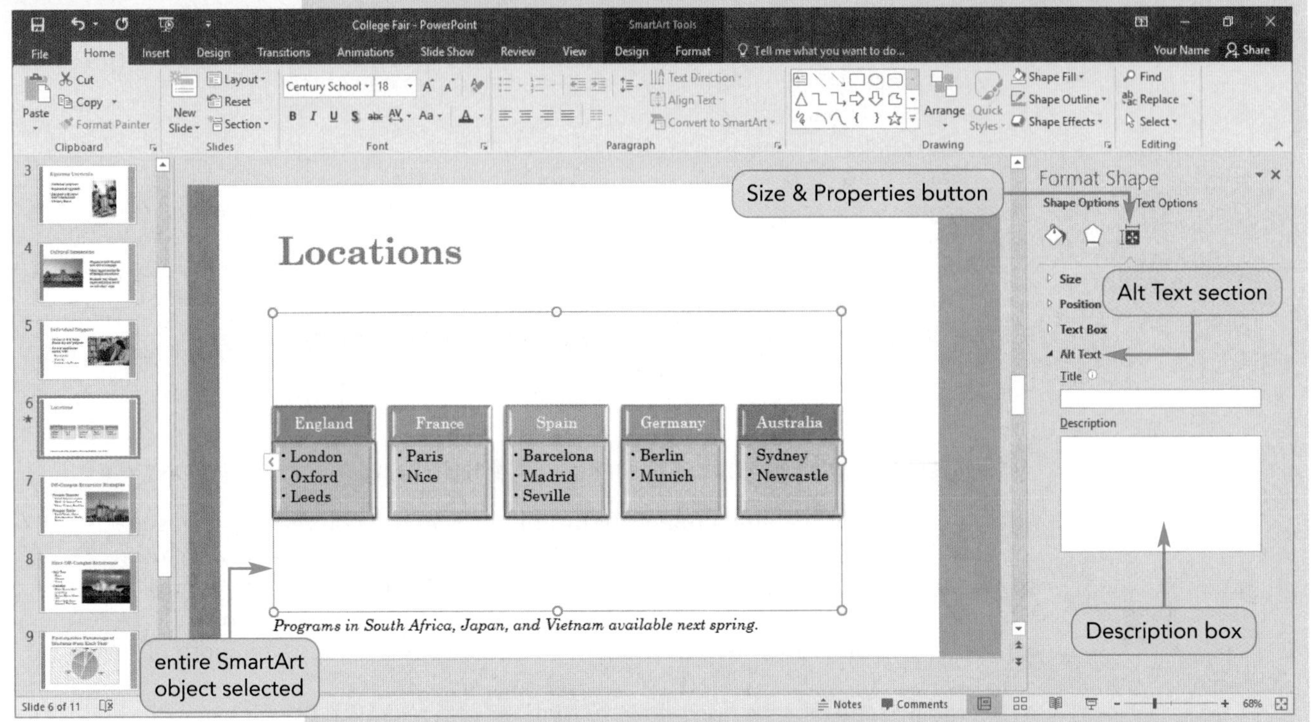

6. Click in the **Description** box, and then type **SmartArt graphic listing the ISC program countries and cities. The countries are England, France, Spain, Germany, and Australia.** (including the last period). This is the text a screen reader would read. (Note that in this case, if you were creating this slide for a real-life presentation, you should also add the city names to the Alt text.)
7. On Slide 6, click the text box at the bottom of the slide to select it. The Format Shape task pane changes to show an empty Description box. Now you will type alt text for the text box.
8. In the Format Shape task pane, click in the **Description** box, and then type **Note indicating that programs in South Africa, Japan, and Vietnam will be available next spring.** (including the period).

You also need to add alt text to the chart on Slide 9. To do this, you need to make sure that the chart area is selected and not just one element in the chart; otherwise the Alt Text commands will not be available in the task pane.

To select the chart area and add alt text to the chart on Slide 9:

1. Display **Slide 9** ("Participation Percentage of Students from Each Year"), and then click the chart.
2. On the ribbon, click the **Chart Tools Format** tab.
3. In the Current Selection group, click the **Chart Elements arrow** (the arrow on the top box in the group), and then click **Chart Area**, if necessary. Now the alt text will be added to the entire chart. In the task pane, the title is now Format Chart Area.
4. In the task pane, click the **Size & Properties** button. In the Alt Text section, the Description box is empty.
5. In the task pane, click in the **Description** box, and then type **Pie chart illustrating that 47% of students in the program are in their 3rd year, 26% are in their 4th year, 18% are in their 5th year, and a small percentage are in their 1st or 2nd year.** (including the period).
6. Close the Format Chart Area task pane.

Robert will add alt text for the rest of the graphics in the presentation later. Next, you need to make sure that the objects on slides will be identified in the correct order for screen readers.

Checking the Order Objects Will Be Read by a Screen Reader

When a person uses a screen reader to access a presentation, the screen reader selects and describes the elements on the slides in the order they were added. In PowerPoint, most screen readers first explain that a slide is displayed. After the user signals to the screen reader that he is ready for the next piece of information (for example, by pressing the Tab key), the reader identifies the first object on the slide. For most slides, this means that the first object is the title text box. The second object is usually the content placeholder on the slide. To check the order in which a screen reader will describe objects on a slide, you can use the Tab key or open the Selection pane. You'll check the order of objects on Slide 8.

To identify the order of objects on Slide 8:

1. Display **Slide 8** ("More Off-Campus Excursions"), and then click a blank area on the slide. The slide is active, but nothing on the slide is selected.
2. Press the **Tab** key. The title text box is selected.
3. Press the **Tab** key again. The bulleted list text box is selected next.
4. Press the **Tab** key. The photo is selected. However, remember that there are two photos here, one placed on top of the other. To see which one is selected, you can use the Selection pane.
5. On the Home tab, in the Editing group, click the **Select** button, and then click **Selection Pane**. The Selection pane opens. See Figure 3-32.

Figure 3-32 Selection pane listing objects on Slide 8

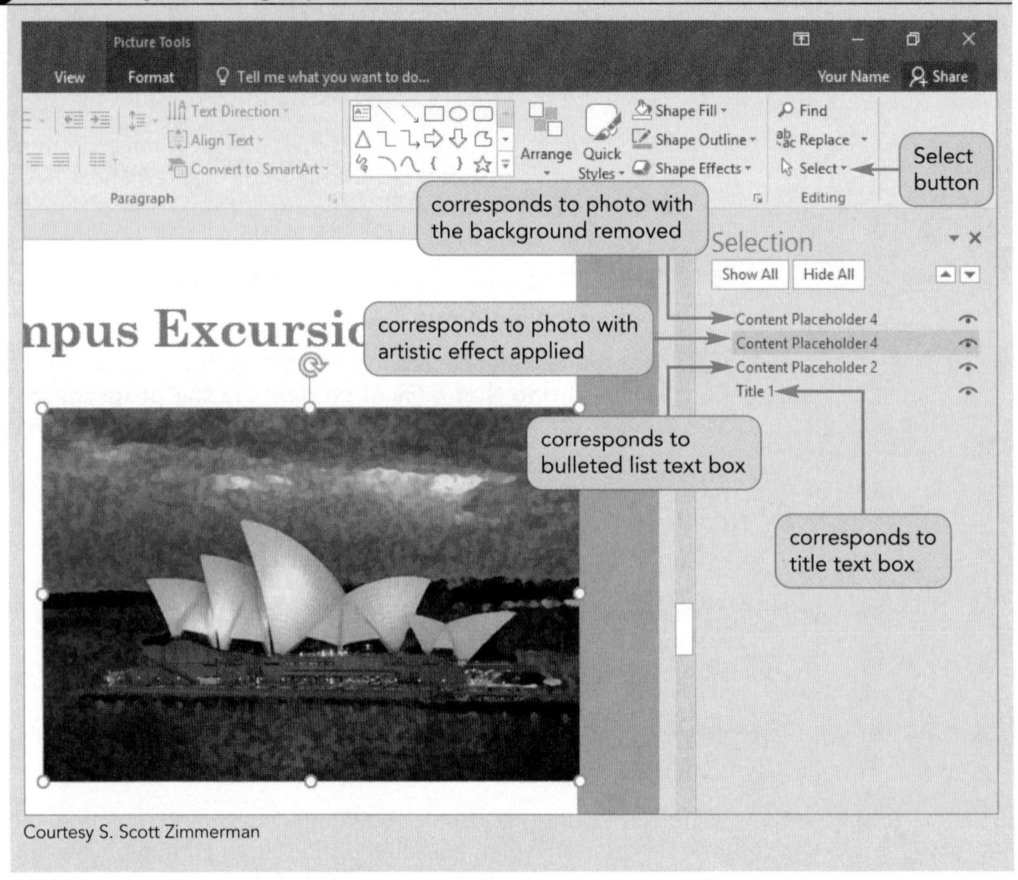

Courtesy S. Scott Zimmerman

In the Selection pane, the first object added to the slide appears at the bottom of the list, and the last object added appears at the top of the list. (The blue bar on the right side of the slide and the gray bar on the left side of the slide aren't listed in the Selection pane because they are part of the slide background.)

INSIGHT

Reordering Objects in the Selection Pane

If an object is listed in the wrong order in the Selection pane—for example, if the content placeholder was identified first and the title second—you could change this in the Selection pane. To do this, click the object you want to move, and then at the top of the pane, click the Bring Forward ▲ or Send Backward ▼ buttons to move the selected object up or down in the list.

Renaming Objects in the Selection Pane

In the Selection pane for Slide 8, there are two objects with the same name. This is because you duplicated the photo, so the name in the Selection pane was duplicated as well. To make it clearer which items on slides are listed in the Selection pane, you can rename each object in the list.

To rename objects in the Selection pane:

1. On the slide, click the photo to select it, if necessary, and then drag left so that the version of the photo with the background removed is to the left of the version of the photo with the artistic effect applied. In the Selection pane, the top Content Placeholder 4 is selected.
2. In the Selection pane, click the **selected Content Placeholder 4**. An orange border appears around the selected item. The insertion point appears in the selected text.
3. Press the **Delete** and **Backspace** keys as needed to delete "Content Placeholder 4," type **Photo with background removed**, and then press the **Enter** key. The name is changed in the Selection pane.
4. In the pane, click **Content Placeholder 4**, click it again, delete the text "Content Placeholder 4," type **Photo with artistic effect**, and then press the **Enter** key.
5. Drag the photo with the background removed back on top of the photo with the artistic effect applied.
6. Close the Selection pane.
7. Display **Slide 1** (the title slide), replace Robert's name in the subtitle with your name, and then save and close the presentation.

PROSKILLS

Decision Making: Selecting the Right Tool for the Job

Many programs with advanced capabilities for editing and correcting photos and other programs for drawing complex shapes are available. Although the tools provided in PowerPoint for accomplishing these tasks are useful, if you need to do more than make simple photo corrections or create a simple shape, consider using a program with more advanced features, or choose to hire someone with skills in graphic design to help you.

You have created and saved a custom shape and used advanced formatting techniques for shapes and photos in the presentation. Robert is pleased with the presentation. With the alt text you've added, he is also confident that users of screen readers will be able to understand the slide containing the SmartArt and the text box and the slide containing the chart.

REVIEW

Session 3.2 Quick Check

1. What are the five types of corrections you can make to photos in PowerPoint?
2. What happens when you use the Remove Background command?
3. What are artistic effects?
4. What happens when you merge shapes?
5. How do you create a custom gradient?
6. What is alt text?

PRACTICE

Review Assignments

Data Files needed for the Review Assignments: Employee.m4a, RA.pptx

Sara Allen is the human resources director at International Study Crossroads (ISC). Each year, she needs to hire resident advisors (RAs) for the program. The company requires one RA for every 50 students. Sara plans to attend career fairs at local colleges in Maryland, Washington, D.C., Virginia, Delaware, and southern Pennsylvania, and she asks you to help her create a presentation she can use to recruit new RAs. Complete the following:

1. Open the presentation **RA**, located in the PowerPoint3 > Review folder included with your Data Files, add your name as the Slide 1 subtitle, and then save it as **ISC RAs** to the location where you are storing your files.
2. On Slide 8 ("Interested in Applying?"), create a SmartArt diagram using the Circle Process layout, which is a Process type diagram. From left to right, replace the placeholder text in the shapes with **Fill out application**, **Submit information for CORI check**, and **Schedule drug test**.
3. Add a new first-level shape as the rightmost shape to the SmartArt diagram, and then replace the placeholder text in it with **Schedule interview**. Move the "Schedule interview" shape so it is the second shape in the diagram.
4. Change the style of the SmartArt diagram to the Powder style, and then change the color to Colorful – Accent Colors.
5. On Slide 9 (the last slide), add the audio clip **Employee**, located in the PowerPoint3 > Review folder. Set it to play automatically, and hide the icon during the slide show. Position the icon in the lower-right corner of the slide at the bottom of the orange bar.
6. On Slide 7 ("Number of Students by Country in 2016"), add a pie chart. In cells A2 through A6, type **England**, **France**, **Spain**, **Germany**, and **Australia**. In cell B1, type **2016**. In cells B2 through B6, type **14990**, **7233**, **9107**, **12997**, and **2673**.
7. Apply Layout 4 to the chart.
8. Click one of the data labels that was added, and then change the font color to Black, Text 1 and the font size to 16 points.
9. Change the position of the data labels to the Outside End option.
10. On Slide 5 ("Qualifications"), add a text box approximately 2 inches wide and one-half inch high. Type ***Criminal Offender Record Information**. Change the format of the text box so the text doesn't wrap and so that the left margin is zero.
11. Align the left edge of the text box with the left edge of the bulleted list text box, and align its top edge with the bottom edge of the picture and the bulleted list.
12. On Slide 9, insert a WordArt text box using the Fill - Orange, Accent 3, Sharp Bevel style. Replace the placeholder text with **Submit Your**, press the Enter key, type **Application**, press the Enter key, and then type **Today!**
13. Change the fill color of the WordArt text to Dark Red, Accent 1, and then change the font size of the text to 66 points. Add the Perspective Diagonal Upper Left shadow effect. (*Hint*: Use the Text Effects button in the WordArt Styles group on the Drawing Tools Format tab.)
14. Position the WordArt text box so it is entered horizontally and vertically on the slide. (*Hint*: Use the Align command in the Arrange group on the Drawing Tools Format tab.)
15. On Slide 5 ("Qualifications"), remove the background of the photo.
16. On Slide 6 ("Mandatory Training Dates"), change the color tone of the photo to Temperature: 7200K.
17. On Slide 3 ("What to Expect"), change the saturation of the photo to 66%.
18. On Slide 4 ("Locations"), sharpen the photo by 50%, and then change the contrast to 30%. Then apply the Pencil Sketch artistic effect to the photo.

19. On Slide 2, drag the gray doughnut shape on top of the large circle. Position the doughnut shape near the top right of the large circle so that smart guides appear indicating that the top and right of the two shapes are aligned. Subtract the doughnut shape from the larger circle by selecting the shape you want to keep—the large circle—first, and then selecting the shape you want to subtract—the gray doughnut shape—before using the Subtract command.
20. Drag the small yellow circle on top of the solid orange circle that was created in the merged shape. Position the yellow circle near the top right of the solid circle in the merged shape without overlapping the edges of the circles, and then subtract the yellow circle from the merged shape. The final shape should look like Figure 3-33.

Figure 3-33 Merged shape

21. On Slide 2, create a text box approximately 2 inches wide and 1 inch high. Type **ISC** in the text box. Deselect the Wrap text in shape option, if necessary. Change the font to Impact, and the font size to 48 points.
22. Drag the text box to the center of the white circle created when you subtracted the yellow circle in the merged shape. Select the merged shape first, and then select the text box. Use the Union command to combine the shapes.
23. Fill the merged shape with the From Bottom Left Corner gradient under Dark Variations on the Gradient submenu on the Shape Fill menu. Then customize the gradient by changing the position of the Stop 2 of 3 tab to 40% and changing the color of the Stop 3 of 3 tab to Dark Red, Accent 1, Lighter 80%.
24. Copy the merged shape. Display Slide 1 (the title slide), and then paste the copied shape to the slide. Resize the merged shape so that it is 1.4 inches square, and then position the shape to the left of "International Study Crossroads" so that its left edge is aligned with the left edge of the slide title text box and so that its top is aligned with the top of the "International Study Crossroads" text box. Delete Slide 2.
25. On Slide 6 ("Number of Students by Country in 2016"), add the following as alt text to the chart: **Pie chart showing the number of students in the program who went to each of the five countries.**
26. On Slide 7 ("Interested in Applying?"), add the following as alt text to the SmartArt shape: **SmartArt diagram listing four steps required to apply to be an RA.**
27. On Slide 7, edit the Content Placeholder 2 name in the Selection Pane to **SmartArt**.
28. Save and close the presentation.

APPLY

Case Problem 1

Data Files needed for this Case Problem: PT.pptx, Recovery.m4a

PT PLUS Ben and Helen Acosta, both physical therapists, opened their practice PT PLUS in Searcy, Arkansas, seven years ago. They have a state-of-the-art facility and equipment including a pool for aquatic therapy, and they have built a good reputation among local doctors and hospitals because patients referred to them have faster recovery times than average. They are preparing a bid for a local semi-pro football team to be the exclusive providers of physical therapy to the team members. As part of their bid, Helen prepared a PowerPoint presentation and asked you to finish it for her. Complete the following steps:

1. Open the presentation **PT**, located in the PowerPoint3 > Case1 folder included with your Data Files, add your name as the subtitle, and then save the presentation as **PT PLUS** to the location where you are storing your files.
2. On Slide 2 ("The PT PLUS Difference"), add a text box, and type ***American Board of Physical Therapy Specialties**. Turn off the Wrap text option, change the right margin to 0, and then right-align the text in the text box. Position the text box so that its right edge is aligned with the right edge of the title and bulleted list text boxes and its top edge is aligned with the bottom edge of the bulleted list text box.
3. On Slide 3 ("State of the Art Facility"), change the brightness of the photo on the left to -10% and the contrast to 30%.
4. On Slide 3, sharpen the photo on the right by 25%, change its saturation to 200%, and then change its tone to a temperature of 5900 K.
5. On Slide 4 ("Recovery Time Examples in Weeks"), add a clustered column chart in the content placeholder. Enter the date shown in Figure 3-34 in the spreadsheet to create the chart.

Figure 3-34 **Data for Slide 4**

	Industry Average	PT PLUS
Meniscus tear	8	5
Rotator cuff injuries	35	26
Achilles tendon rupture	24	18

6. Drag the small blue box in the lower-right corner of cell D5 up and to the left so that the blue border surrounds cells B2 through C4 and the data in column D and row 5 is removed from the chart.
7. Change the style of the chart to Style 2, and then change the colors of the chart to the Color 3 palette. (*Hint*: Use the Chart Styles button next to the chart.)
8. Move the legend so it appears below the chart, and then change the font size of the text in the legend to 16 points. Change the font size of the labels on the x-axis to 14 points, and then change the font size of the data labels to 16 points. (*Hint*: To modify all the data labels, select the data label above one color column and modify it, and then select the data label above a column of the other color and modify it.)
9. Remove the chart title.
10. On Slide 4, insert the audio clip **Recovery**, located in the PowerPoint3 > Case1 folder. Hide the icon during a slide show, and set it to play automatically. Position the sound icon centered below the chart.
11. Add the following alt text for the chart: **Chart showing that recovery times for certain injuries is faster at PT PLUS than the industry average.**
12. Save and close the presentation.

CHALLENGE

Case Problem 2

Data Files needed for this Case Problem: Elder.pptx

Keystone State Elder Services Shaina Brown is the director of Keystone State Elder Services, a company that provides in-home services for elderly and disabled people in Youngstown, Ohio, and surrounding cities so that they can continue to live at home rather than in a nursing home. Shaina travels to senior centers, churches, and other locations to explain the services her company provides. She started creating a PowerPoint presentation and asked you to help complete it by creating a logo based on her design, correcting photos, and adding SmartArt. Complete the following steps:

1. Open the file named **Elder**, located in the PowerPoint3 > Case2 folder included with your Data Files, add your name as the subtitle on Slide 1, and then save it as **Elder Services** to the location where you are storing your files.
2. On Slide 2, duplicate the red filled square shape three times. These are the four squares behind the center square in Figure 3-35. Arrange them as shown in Figure 3-35 so that there is about one-quarter inch of space between each square. Merge the four squares using the Union command.

Figure 3-35 **Logo for Keystone State Elder Services**

3. Apply the From Center Gradient style in the Light Variations set of gradient styles to the square. Customize this gradient by changing the Stop 1 of 3 tab to the Red, Accent 1 color, changing the Stop 2 of 3 tab to the Red, Accent 1, Darker 50% color, and changing the Stop 3 of 3 tab to Red, Accent 1, Lighter 40% color and changing its position to 80%. Then change the gradient Type to Linear and the direction to Linear Down.
4. Create a text box, type **KS**, press the Enter key, and then type **ES**. Turn off the Wrap text option if necessary, change the font to Copperplate Gothic Bold, change the font size to 40 points, and then use the Center button in the Paragraph group on the Home tab to center the text in the box. Change the size of the text box to 1.5″ square. Fill the text box shape with the White, Background 1 color. Apply the Preset 5 shape effect to this square (located on the Presets submenu on the Shape Effects menu).
5. Position the text box so it is centered over the custom shape, using the smart guides to assist you.

Explore 6. Group the custom shape and the text box. (*Hint*: Use the appropriate command on the Drawing Tools Format tab.)

Explore 7. Save the final grouped shape as a picture named **Logo** to the location where you are storing your files. (*Hint*: Right-click the shape.)

8. Delete Slide 2, and then insert the picture **Logo** on Slide 1 (the title slide). Resize it, maintaining the aspect ratio, so that it is approximately 2.6 inches by 2.6 inches (it may not be perfectly square). Position it to the left of the title so that it is bottom-aligned with the title text box and so that there is an equal amount of space between the logo and the slide title and the logo and the left side of the slide.
9. Add **Company logo** as alt text for the logo.
10. On Slide 2 ("Our Services"), change the saturation of the photo to 66%, and then change the tone to a temperature of 7200K.
11. On Slide 3 ("What We Do"), change the contrast of the photo to -20%, and sharpen it by 50%.
12. Add **Photo of a smiling woman at a keyboard** as alt text for the picture.
13. On Slide 4 ("How to Set Up Services"), insert a SmartArt diagram using the Sub-Step Process layout (in the Process category). Type the following as first-level items in the diagram:

    Schedule Services

    Set Up Assessment Appointment

    Answer Interview Questions

    Call Elder Line
14. Delete the second-level placeholders in the diagram. (*Hint*: Use the text pane.)

Explore 15. Reverse the order of the boxes in the diagram. (*Hint*: Use a command in the Create Graphic group on the SmartArt Tools Design tab.)

16. Change the style of the SmartArt diagram to the Cartoon style.
17. Add **SmartArt diagram listing the four steps to take to receive services.** as alt text for the SmartArt diagram.
18. On Slide 5 ("We Are Here for You"), insert the **Logo** file you created in the content placeholder on the left, and add **Company logo** as alt text for the logo on Slide 5.
19. Save and close the presentation.

CHALLENGE

Case Problem 3

Data Files needed for this Case Problem: Books.jpg, Tutoring.pptx

Total Learning Tutoring Total Learning Tutoring (TLT), in Durham, North Carolina, offers tutoring services for students of all ages who need extra help to keep up with their classwork or who want to learn additional material not offered in their classes. They also offer SAT and ACT test prep courses. Over the past three years, the popularity of their test prep courses has exploded. In addition, the number of students who enroll in ACT test prep courses instead of SAT test prep has increased significantly. Tom Shaughnessy, the owner of TLT, wants to expand and asks you to help him create a PowerPoint presentation that he can use when he talks to potential investors. Complete the following steps:

1. Open the presentation **Tutoring**, located in the PowerPoint3 > Case3 folder included with your Data Files, add your name as the subtitle, and then save the presentation as **Total Learning Tutoring** to the location where you are storing your files.
2. On Slide 1 (the title slide), apply the Photocopy artistic effect to the photo.
3. On Slide 2 ("Our Services"), insert the photo **Books**, located in the PowerPoint 3 > Case3 folder, in the content placeholder to the left of the bulleted list. Resize it, maintaining the aspect ratio, so it is 3.5" high. Position it so that its left edge is aligned with the left edge of the slide and so it is aligned with the middle of the bulleted list text box.

Explore 4. On Slide 2, make the background of the photo transparent. (*Hint*: Use the appropriate command on the Color menu on the Picture Tools Format tab.)

5. On Slide 2, increase the saturation of the photo to 200%, and then sharpen it by 25%.

6. On Slide 2, insert a text box below the bulleted list. Type ***for original SAT score between 300 and 1150 or an original ACT score between 13 and 29** in the text box. Change the font size of the text in the text box to 14 points, and italicize it. Turn off the Wrap text option, change the left and right margins of the text box to 0 inches, and then resize the text box so it just fits the text inside it. Position the text box so its left edge is aligned with the left edge of the bulleted list text box and its top edge is aligned with the bottom of the bulleted list text box.
7. On Slide 3 ("Tremendous Growth in Just Three Years"), change the contrast of the photo by -30%.
8. On Slide 4 ("SAT and ACT Prep Course Enrollment"), insert a clustered column chart using the data shown in Figure 3-36.

Figure 3-36 **Data for Slide 4**

	SAT Prep	ACT Prep
2014	201	87
2015	587	334
2016	922	885

9. In the spreadsheet, drag the small blue selection handle in the lower-right corner of cell D5 up one row and left one column to exclude the Series 3 column of data and the Category 4 row of data.
10. Change the style of the chart to Style 4.
11. Remove the chart title and the legend.
12. **Explore** Add the data table, and remove the data labels. (*Hint*: Use the CHART ELEMENTS menu.)
13. Change the font color of the text in the data table to Black, Text 2, and the font size to 14 points.
14. Add **Column chart showing that SAT and ACT Prep course enrollment has increased over the past three years.** as alt text for the chart.
15. Change the colors used in the chart to the Color 4 palette. (*Hint*: Use the Chart Styles button next to the chart.)
16. **Explore** Animate the chart with the entrance animation Appear. Modify the animation so that the chart grid animates first, then the three data markers for the SAT Prep data series one at a time, then the three data markers for the ACT Prep data series one at a time. Finally, modify the start timing of the chart grid animation so it animates with the previous action.
17. On Slide 5 ("Proposed Test Prep Course Expansion"), change the color tone of the photo to a temperature of 7200 K.
18. On Slide 7, format the text "Thank You!" as WordArt using the Gradient Fill – Brown, Accent 4, Outline – Accent 4 style. Center the WordArt in the text box, and then change the font size to 60 points.
19. Save and close the presentation.

RESEARCH

Case Problem 4

Data Files needed for this Case Problem: Bullying.pptx

Partners Counseling Patricia Burrell is one of the owners of Partners Counseling in Middletown, Connecticut. Partners Counseling is a group of therapists who specialize in providing therapy to children. Patricia has been hired by several school districts to talk to teachers and school support staff about ways they can identify and stop bullying. She asks you to help her create her presentation by researching statistics about bullying and ways to identify and prevent bullying. Complete the following steps:

1. Research bullying online. For example, look for statistics about the number of children who are bullied, suggested ways others can help, and ways to identify bullying. While you are researching the topic, look for information that can be presented in a chart or in a SmartArt graphic. Make sure you note the webpage addresses of the pages that contain the information you are going to use because you will need to include that on your slides.
2. Open the presentation **Bullying**, located in the PowerPoint3 > Case4 folder included with your data files. Add your name as the subtitle, and then save the presentation as **Stop Bullying** to the location where you are saving your files.
3. Based on your research, on Slide 3, create a chart that shows statistics about bullying, and then add a slide title that describes the data in the chart. On Slide 4 ("How to Help"), insert SmartArt containing suggestions for how to stop bullying. On Slide 5, add any additional information you think is helpful, such as describing a list of things that adults should not do, suggestions on how to stop bullying when it happens, or descriptions of times when the police should be called.
4. On Slide 2 ("What Is Bullying?"), change the tone of the photo to a temperature of 5900 K. On Slide 5, sharpen the photo by 50%.
5. On each slide that contains information from a webpage, include a text box at the bottom of the slide that contains **Data from** followed by the name of the website and the name of the webpage followed by the webpage address in parentheses.
6. Add appropriate transitions and animations.
7. Check the spelling in your presentation and proof it carefully.
8. Save and close the presentation.

MODULE 4

Advanced Animations and Distributing Presentations

Creating an Advanced Presentation for Agricultural Development

POWERPOINT

OBJECTIVES

Session 4.1
- Use guides to place objects
- Add more than one animation to an object
- Set animation triggers
- Use a picture as the slide background
- Create and edit hyperlinks
- Add action buttons
- Create a custom color palette

Session 4.2
- Create a self-running presentation
- Rehearse slide timings
- Record slide timings and narration
- Set options to allow viewers to override timings
- Inspect a presentation for private information
- Save a presentation in other formats

Case | *Division of Agricultural Development*

Brian Meyers works in the Division of Agricultural Development in the New Hampshire Department of Agriculture, Markets & Food. Over the past few years, small family-owned farms have contacted his office requesting suggestions and assistance in expanding and extending their cash flow into the fall and early winter seasons. In response, Brian will begin presenting on this topic at agricultural fairs and tradeshows across the state, and he wants your help in finishing the presentation he has created.

In this module, you will enhance Brian's presentation by adding multiple animations to objects and setting triggers for animations. You'll also add a picture as the slide background, create links, and create a self-running presentation including narration. Finally, you'll save the presentation in other formats for distribution.

STARTING DATA FILES

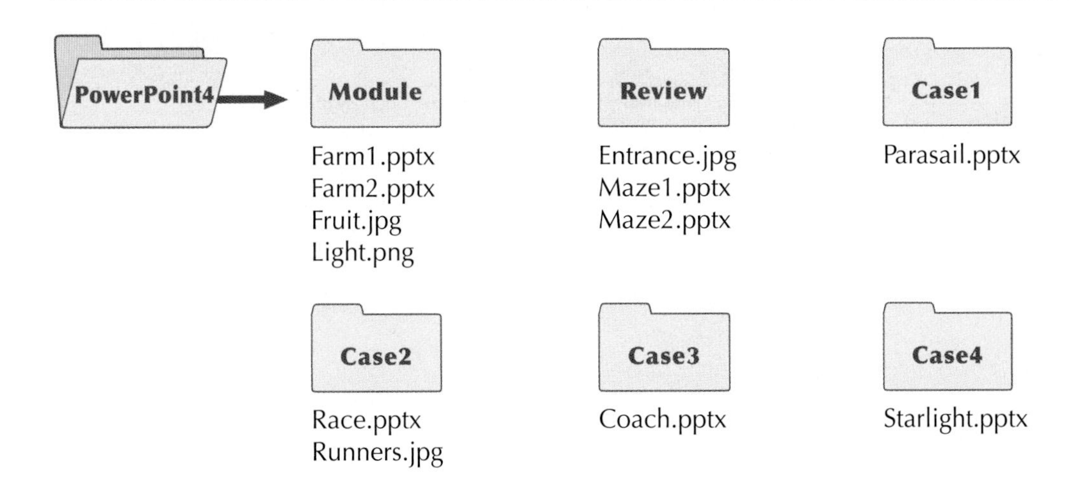

Session 4.1 Visual Overview:

If the second animation applied to an object is set to With Previous or After Previous, the animation sequence icons are stacked on top of one another.

To add a second animation to an object, click the Add Animation button in the Advanced Animation group on the Animations tab.

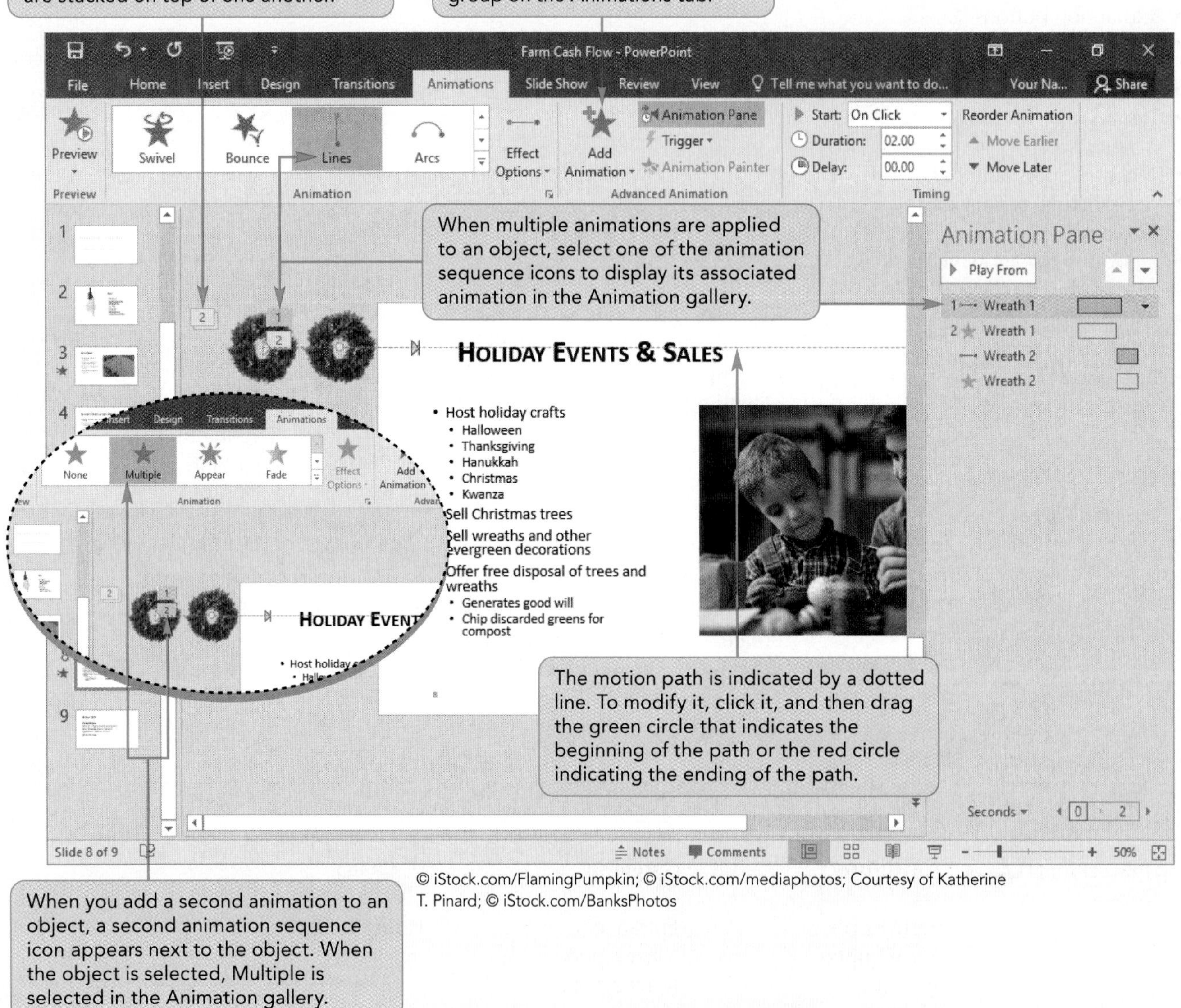

© iStock.com/FlamingPumpkin; © iStock.com/mediaphotos; Courtesy of Katherine T. Pinard; © iStock.com/BanksPhotos

Understanding Advanced Animations

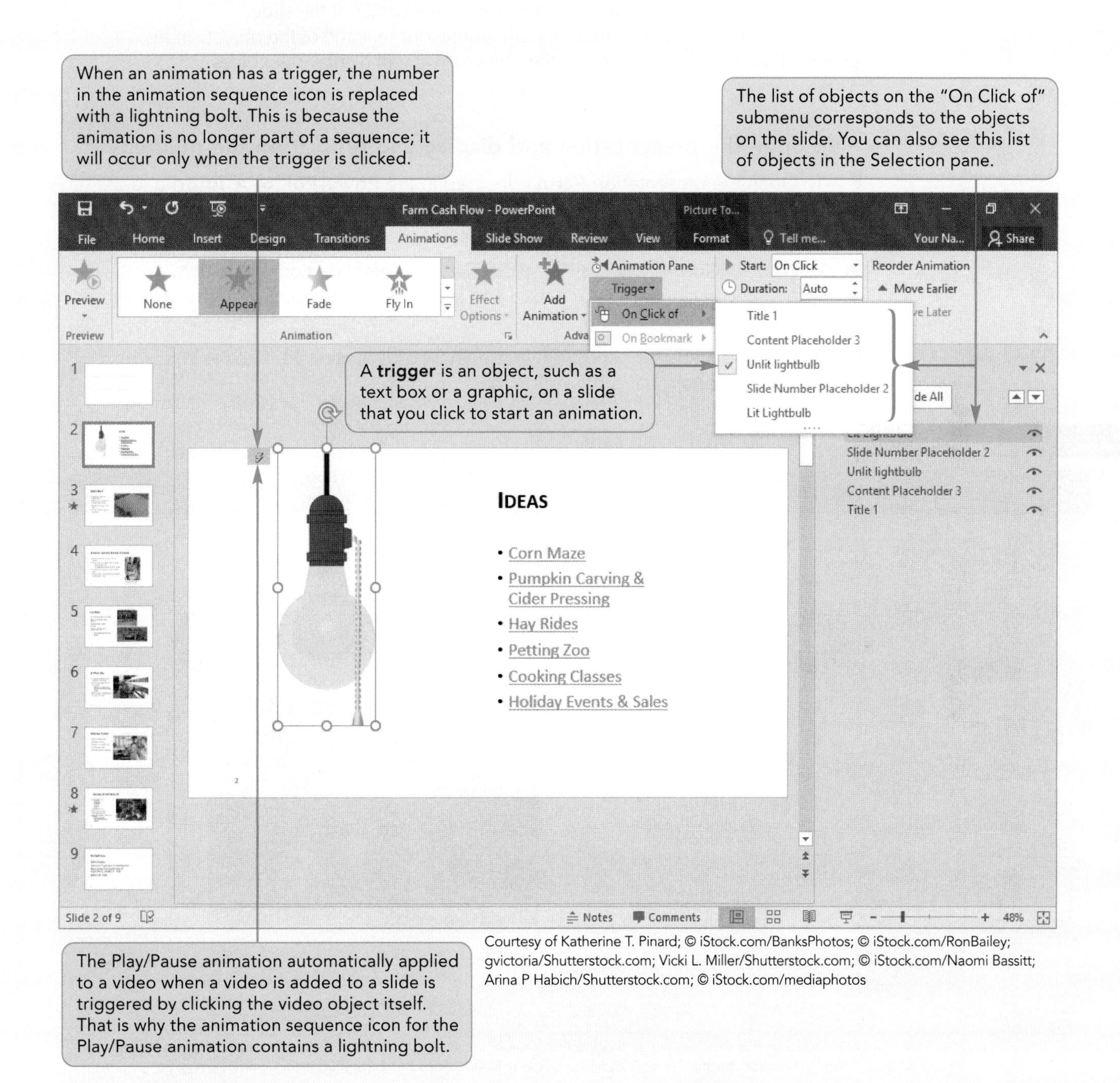

Courtesy of Katherine T. Pinard; © iStock.com/BanksPhotos; © iStock.com/RonBailey; gvictoria/Shutterstock.com; Vicki L. Miller/Shutterstock.com; © iStock.com/Naomi Bassitt; Arina P Habich/Shutterstock.com; © iStock.com/mediaphotos

Using Guides

You are already familiar with using smart guides, which are the dashed red lines that appear when you drag objects on a slide, to help you align objects. **Guides** are dashed vertical and horizontal lines that you can display and position on the slide in any location to help you place objects. When you drag a guide to reposition it, a ScreenTip appears, indicating the distance in inches from the center of the slide.

Brian wants you to apply motion path animations to some of the objects in his presentation. To help you position the objects, you will display the guides.

To open the presentation and display and reposition the guides:

1. Open the presentation **Farm1**, located in the **PowerPoint4 > Tutorial** folder included with your Data Files, and then save it as **Farm Cash Flow** to the location where you are saving your files.
2. Display **Slide 8** ("Holiday Events & Sales"). This slide contains a title, a bulleted list, an image of a man and a young boy working on crafts, and two small Christmas wreaths.
3. Click the **View** tab, and then in the Show group, click the **Guides** check box. The guides appear on the slide. See Figure 4-1.

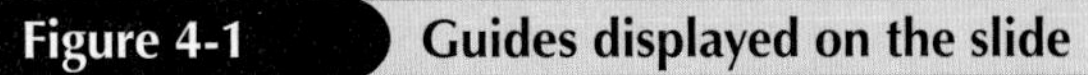

Figure 4-1 Guides displayed on the slide

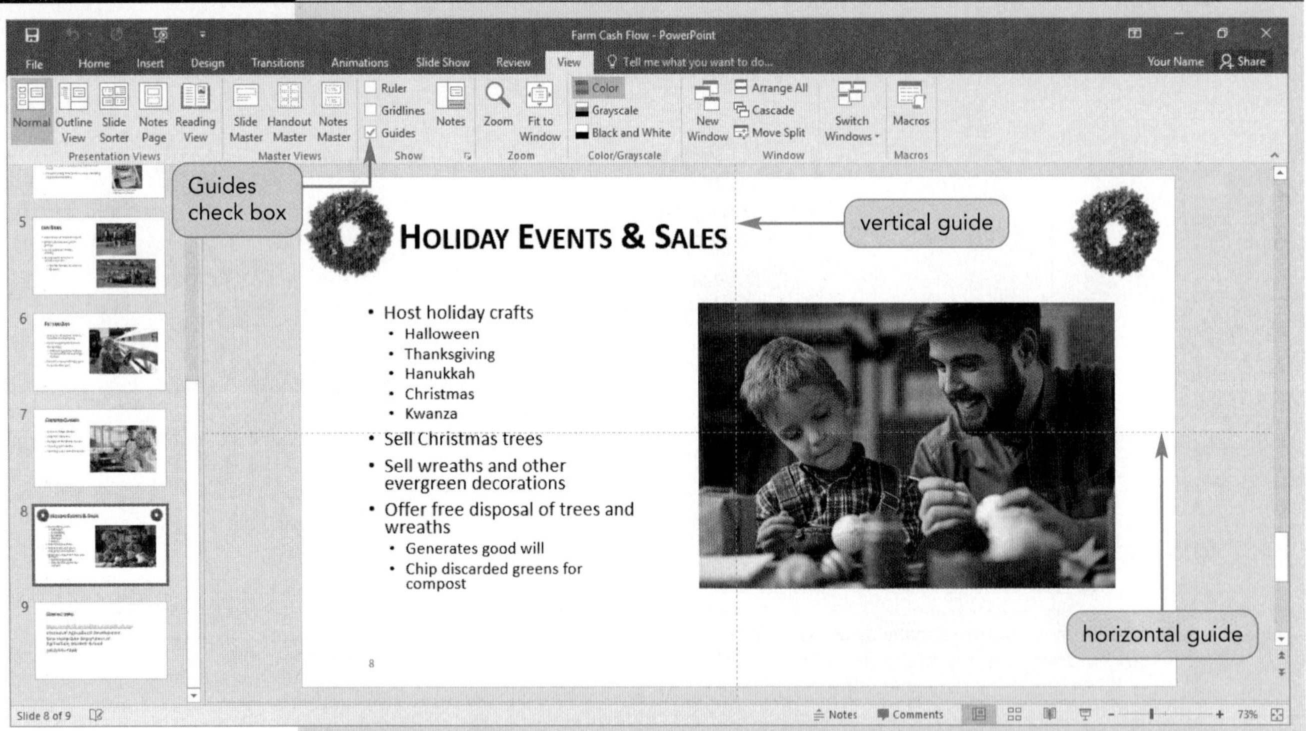

© iStock.com/FlamingPumpkin; © iStock.com/mediaphotos; © iStock.com/RonBailey; gvictoria/Shutterstock.com; Vicki L. Miller/Shutterstock.com; © iStock.com/Naomi Bassitt; Arina P Habich/Shutterstock.com

4. In a blank area of the slide, position the pointer on top of the horizontal guide so that the pointer changes to ⇕, and then press and hold the mouse button. The pointer disappears and a ScreenTip appears in its place displaying 0.00. This indicates that the horizontal guide is in the middle of the slide.

   Trouble? If the pointer doesn't change, you are pointing to the bulleted list text box or the photo. Repeat Step 4, this time positioning the pointer on top of the guide in a blank area of the slide.

5. Drag the guide up until the ScreenTip displays 2.92, and then release the mouse button. The horizontal guide now intersects the middle of the wreaths at the top of the slide. Next, you will create a second vertical guide.
6. Position the pointer on top of the vertical guide so that the pointer changes to ⇔, press and hold the **Ctrl** key, press and hold the mouse button, and then start dragging the guide to the right. A second vertical guide is created and moves right with the mouse pointer.
7. Continue dragging to the right until the ScreenTip displays **6.42**, release the mouse button, and then release the Ctrl key. The vertical guide you created is aligned with the right side of the wreath in the upper-right corner of the slide.
8. Drag the original vertical guide to the right until its ScreenTip displays 5.08 and it is aligned with the left side of the wreath. The guides are now positioned for your use in applying animations to the wreaths on the slide.

Adding More Than One Animation to an Object

You know how to apply an animation to an object and how to specify how the animation starts, its duration, and its speed. An object can have more than one animation applied to it. For example, you might apply an entrance animation to an object by having it fly into a slide, and then once the object is on the slide, you might want to animate it a second time to further emphasize a bullet point on the slide, or to show a relationship between the object and another object on the slide.

On Slide 8 in the presentation, Brian created list ideas for events that farm owners can conduct during the fall and winter holiday season. Brian wants you to add animations to the photos of wreaths on Slide 8 to add interest. He wants the wreaths to roll onto the slide.

To add a motion path animation to an object on Slide 8:

1. Click the wreath in the upper-right corner of the slide, and then on the ribbon, click the **Animations** tab.
2. In the Animation group, click the **More** button, scroll down to locate the Motion Paths section, and then click the **Lines** animation. The animation previews and the wreath moves down the slide. After the preview, the path appears below the wreath, and a faint image of the wreath appears at the end of the path. At the beginning of the path, the green circle indicates the path's starting point, and at the end of the path, the red circle indicates the path's ending point. See Figure 4-2.

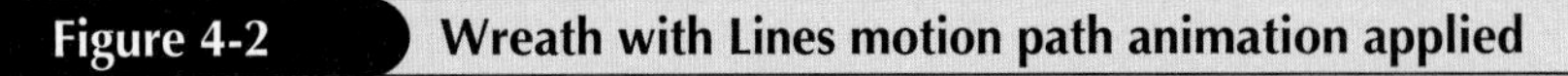

Figure 4-2 Wreath with Lines motion path animation applied

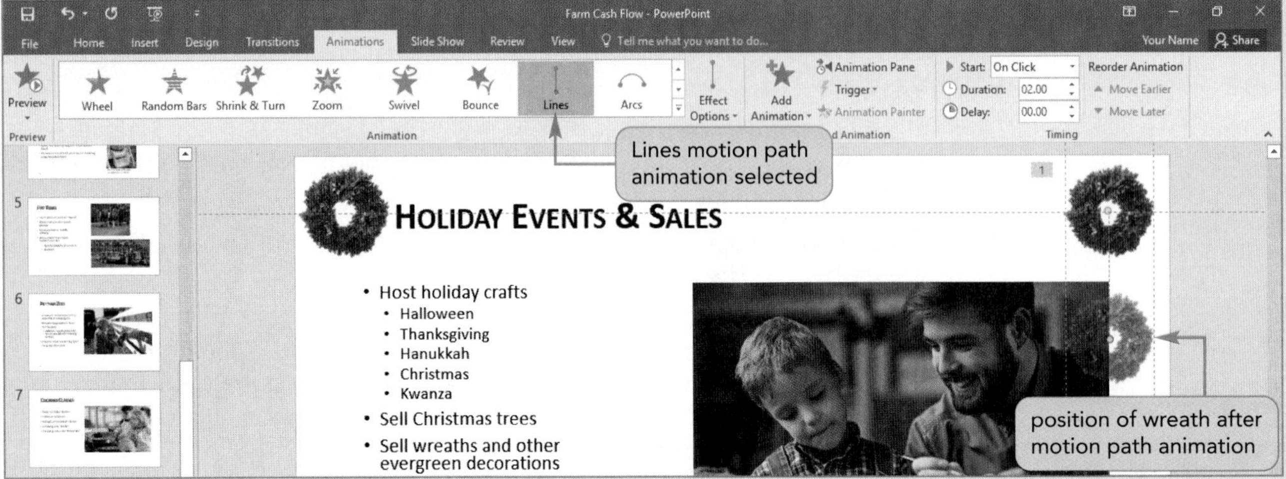

© iStock.com/FlamingPumpkin; © iStock.com/mediaphotos; © iStock.com/RonBailey; gvictoria/Shutterstock.com; Vicki L. Miller/Shutterstock.com; © iStock.com/Naomi Bassitt; Arina P Habich/Shutterstock.com

To have the wreath roll onto the slide, you need to position it in the area next to the slide. The area outside of the slide is part of the PowerPoint workspace, but anything positioned in this area will not be visible in any view except Normal view.

You will position the wreath to the left of the slide, and then change the direction of the Lines animation so that the wreath moves to the right instead of down. Then you will adjust the ending point of the motion path so that the wreath ends up in the upper-right corner of the slide when the animation is finished.

To move the wreath off the slide and modify the motion path animation:

1. Drag the wreath from the upper-right corner of the slide to the left until it is completely off of the slide, keeping its center aligned with the horizontal guide and the wreath in the upper-left corner. After you release the mouse button, the slide shifts to the right so there is some extra space to the left of the slide. See Figure 4-3.

Figure 4-3 Wreath positioned to the left of Slide 8

© iStock.com/FlamingPumpkin; © iStock.com/mediaphotos; © iStock.com/RonBailey; © iStock.com/Naomi Bassitt

2. In the Animation group, click the **Effect Options** button, and then click **Right**. The motion path changes to a horizontal line, the wreath moves right, and the circles at the beginning and end of the motion path change to arrows. You need to reposition the end point of the motion path so that the wreath ends up in the upper-right corner of the slide after the animation is finished. First you need to select the motion path.
3. Point to the motion path so that the pointer changes to the move pointer, and then click the motion path. The arrows on the ends of the motion path change to circles, and a faint copy of the image appears at the end of the motion path. Now you can drag the start and end points to new locations.

   Trouble? If you have trouble selecting the motion path, click the green or red arrow at the beginning or end of the path.
4. Position the pointer on top of the red circle so that it changes to the resize pointer, and then press and hold the **Shift** key. Pressing the Shift key while you adjust the motion path keeps the path a straight line.
5. Press and hold the mouse button. The pointer changes to +.
6. Drag the red circle to the right until the faint image of the wreath is in the upper-right corner of the slide between the two vertical guides, release the mouse button, and then release the Shift key. See Figure 4-4.

   Trouble? If the path moves so it is slanted, you released the Shift key before you released the mouse button. If you haven't released the mouse button yet, press and hold the Shift key, position the wreath, release the mouse button, and then release the Shift key. If you have released the mouse button, click the Undo button on the Quick Access Toolbar, and then repeat Steps 4 through 6.

Figure 4-4 Modified Lines motion path animation

© iStock.com/FlamingPumpkin; © iStock.com/mediaphotos; © iStock.com/RonBailey; gvictoria/Shutterstock.com; Vicki L. Miller/Shutterstock.com; © iStock.com/Naomi Bassitt

Brian wants the wreath to look like it is rolling onto the slide. To accomplish this effect you need to add a second animation to the wreath. To add a second animation to an object, you must use the Add Animation button in the Advanced Animation group on the Animations tab. If you try to add a second animation to an object by clicking an animation in the gallery in the Animation group, you will simply replace the animation already applied to the object.

Make sure you do not click another animation in the Animation group.

To add a second animation to the wreath on Slide 8:

1. Click the wreath positioned to the left of the slide to select it, and then click the **Animations** tab, if necessary.
2. In the Advanced Animation group, click the **Add Animation** button.

   The same gallery of animations that appears in the Animation group appears.
3. In the Emphasis section of the gallery, click the **Spin** animation. The Spin animation previews, but you can't see it because the wreath is not on the slide. When the preview finishes, the slide shifts right again. Next to the wreath that is positioned to the left of the slide, a second animation sequence icon appears and is selected. In the Animation group, the Spin animation is selected, which means that animation sequence icon 2 corresponds to the Spin animation. You can preview both animations.
4. Click the **Preview** button. The wreath moves right onto the slide and stops in the upper-right corner, and then spins once in a clockwise direction.

To make the wreath look like it is rolling onto the slide, you need to change the start timing of the Spin animation so it happens at the same time as the Lines animation—in other words, set its start timing to With Previous. Because two animations are applied to the object, you need to make sure that the correct animation sequence icon is selected and the correct animation is selected in the Animation group on the Animations tab before you make any changes.

To modify the start timing of the second animation applied to the wreath:

1. Click the wreath with the animations applied to it. In the Animation gallery, Multiple is selected. This indicates that more than one animation is applied to the selected object.
2. Click the **2** animation sequence icon to select it. In the Animation gallery, Spin is selected. This is the animation that corresponds to the selected animation sequence icon.
3. In the Timing group, click the **Start** arrow, and then click **With Previous**. The two animation sequence icons are stacked on top of the other and they are both selected.
4. In the Preview group, click the **Preview** button. Because the Line motion path and the Spin animation happen at the same time, the wreath appears to roll onto the slide.

Next, you need to apply the same animations to the wreath that is positioned in the upper-left corner of the slide. You can follow the same steps you took when you applied the animations to the first wreath, or you can copy the animations and then modify them. You will copy the animations.

To copy and modify the animations:

1. Click the wreath that has the animations applied to it so that Multiple is selected in the Animation group, and then in the Advanced Animation group, click the **Animation Painter** button.

2. Click the wreath that is in the upper-left corner of the slide. The animations are copied and previewed. Now you need to move the wreath in the upper-left corner of the slide off of the slide and then adjust its motion path.
3. In the status bar, click the **Zoom Out** button [−] twice to change the zoom percentage to 60%.
4. Drag the wreath in the upper-left corner of the slide off of the slide and position it to the left of the other wreath so that it is horizontally aligned with the other wreath and so that the vertical smart guide appears between the two wreaths. Now you need to change the end position of the motion path so that the leftmost wreath stops in the upper-left corner of the slide.
5. In the center of the leftmost wreath, point to the green arrow that indicates the beginning of the motion path applied to that wreath so that the pointer changes to [pointer], and then click the green arrow. The motion path is selected and the arrows on either end change to circles.
6. Press and hold the **Shift** key, drag the red circle that indicates the end of the motion path to the left until the faint image of the wreath is in the upper-left corner of the slide between the slide title and the left edge of the slide, release the mouse button, and then release the Shift key.
7. Click a blank area of the slide to deselect the wreath, and then in the Preview group, click the **Preview** button. The first wreath rolls onto the slide and stops in the upper-right corner, then the second wreath rolls onto the slide and stops in the upper-left corner. You are finished using the guides so you can hide them.
8. Click the **View** tab, and then in the Show group, click the **Guides** check box. The guides no longer appear on the screen.

When previewing the slide, you might have noticed that when the first wreath rolled onto the slide, it seemed to slide part of the way instead of roll completely across the slide. And when the second wreath rolled onto the slide, it continued rolling after it was in position in the upper-right corner of the slide. You can adjust the Spin animation so the effect causes the wreaths to appear as if they are rolling into position and then stop. In this instance, the easiest way to do this is using the Animation Pane.

Using the Animation Pane

When multiple animations are applied to an object and the start timing of one of the animations is set to With Previous or After Previous, you can't select only one of the animation sequence icons because they are stacked on top of one another. To see a list of all the animations on a slide, you can open the Animation Pane. You'll examine the animations on Slide 8 in the Animation Pane.

To examine the animations on Slide 8 in the Animation Pane:

1. Click the **Animations** tab, and then in the Advanced Animation group, click the **Animation Pane** button. The Animation Pane opens. See Figure 4-5.

Figure 4-5 **Animation Pane listing the animations on Slide 8**

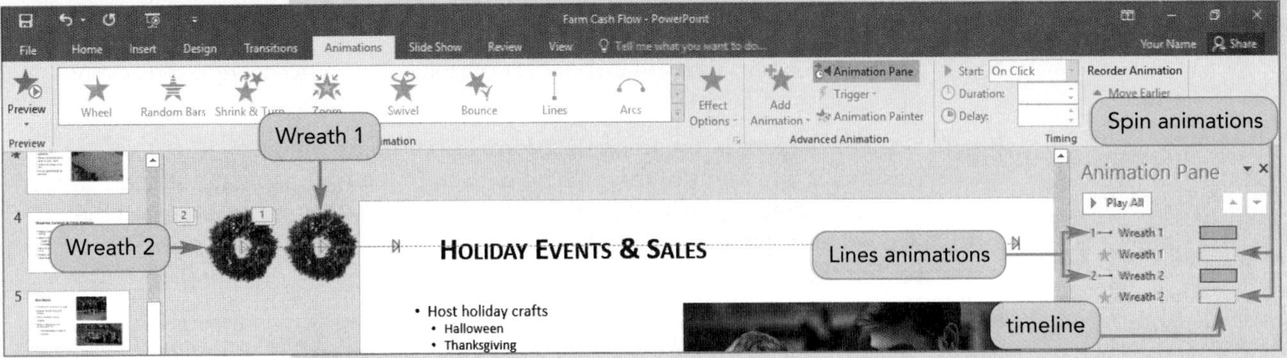

© iStock.com/FlamingPumpkin; © iStock.com/mediaphotos; © iStock.com/BanksPhotos; gvictoria/Shutterstock.com; Vicki L. Miller/Shutterstock.com

2. In the Animation Pane, point to the first animation in the list, Wreath 1. A ScreenTip appears, identifying the start timing (On Click), the animation (Right), and the full name of the object (Wreath 1). This is the Lines animation applied to the wreath that ends up in the upper-right corner of the slide. The horizontal line to the left of the object name indicates that this is a motion path animation, and the number 1 to the left of the object name is the same number that appears in the animation sequence icon for this animation.
3. In the Animation Pane, point to the second animation in the list, the second Wreath 1. This is the Spin animation applied to the wreath that ends up in the upper-right corner of the slide. There is no number to the left of this animation because this animation occurs automatically (With Previous), not when the slide show is advanced (On Click). The yellow star to the left of the object name indicates that this is an emphasis animation. (Entrance animations are indicated with a green star, and exit animations are indicated with a red star.)
4. To the right of the first animation in the list, Wreath 1, point to the blue rectangle so that the pointer changes to ↔. The rectangle indicates the length of the animation. The ScreenTip identifies the start time as 0s (zero seconds), which means it starts immediately after the slide show is advanced. The animation takes two seconds to complete so the ending time in the ScreenTip is 2s.
5. In the Animation Pane, click the **Close** button ☒.

TIP

The entrance animation Appear and the exit animation Disappear have no length so an arrow appears in the Animation Pane instead of a rectangle and the ScreenTip displays only a start time.

You will use the Animation Pane to select the Spin animation applied to each wreath so that you can modify them. To make the rolling effect appear more realistic, you will change the number of revolutions each wreath makes.

To select the Spin animations in the Animation Pane and modify them:

1. Click the **1** animation sequence icon. Because two animation sequence icons are stacked on top of one another, the Animation Pane opens automatically. In the Animation Pane, the two animations applied to the first wreath that animates are selected. In the Animation group on the Animations tab, Multiple is selected.
2. In the Animation Pane, click the **Wreath 1 Spin** animation (the second animation in the list). On the Animations tab, in the Animation group, the Spin animation is selected.

3. In the Animation group, click the **Effect Options** button. In the Amount section, Full Spin is selected. Because this wreath needs to travel all the way across the slide, two spins would look better.
4. On the Effect Options menu, click **Two Spins**. The menu closes. As the animation previews (which you can't see because the wreath is not on the slide), only the Wreath 1 Spin animation is shown in the Animation Pane, and a vertical line moves across the pane.
5. Press and hold the **Shift** key, click the **Wreath 1 Lines** animation in the Animation Pane, and then release the Shift key. The button at the top of the Animation Pane changes to the Play Selected button.
6. Click the **Play Selected** button. The two selected animations preview, with the wreath rolling onto the slide, spinning twice, and stopping in the upper-right corner.
7. In the Animation Pane, click the **Wreath 2 Spin** animation (the last animation in the list).
8. On the Animations tab, in the Animation group, click the **Effect Options** button, and then click **Half Spin**.
9. In the Animation Pane, click the **Wreath 1 Lines** animation, and then at the top of the pane, click the **Play From** button. The four animations preview.

The first wreath that animates continues to roll after it is in position. To fix this problem, you will slightly speed up the Spin animation applied to it by shortening its duration. The second wreath that animates seems to roll more slowly than the first wreath. To fix this, you will speed up both of the animations that are applied to the second wreath that animates (the wreath that ends up in the upper-left corner of the slide).

To modify the duration of animations:

1. In the Animation Pane, click the **Wreath 1 Spin** animation.
2. On the Animations tab, in the Timing group, click in the **Duration** box, type **1.75**, and then press the **Enter** key.
3. In the Animation Pane, click the **Wreath 2 Lines** animation.
4. On the Animations tab, in the Timing group, click in the Duration box, type **1**, and then press the **Enter** key.
5. Change the duration of the **Wreath 2 Spin** animation to **1.00** second. You will preview the modified animations in Slide Show view.
6. On the status bar, click the **Slide Show** button, and then press the **spacebar**. The first wreath rolls onto the slide and no longer has an extra spin at the end.
7. Press the **spacebar** again. The second wreath rolls on faster than before.
8. Press the **Esc** key to end the slide show and return to Normal view.

Brian wants the wreaths to roll onto the slide automatically after the slide transitions onto the screen during a slide show. In order for this to happen, the start timing of the Lines animations needs to be set to After Previous.

To change the start timing of the Lines animations:

1. In the Animation Pane, click the **Wreath 1 Lines** animation. An arrow appears to the right of the blue rectangle.
2. Click the **arrow** to the right of the blue rectangle. A menu appears. The first three commands are the same commands that appear when you click the Start arrow in the Timing group on the Animations tab. See Figure 4-6.

Figure 4-6 Menu for the selected Wreath 1 Lines animation

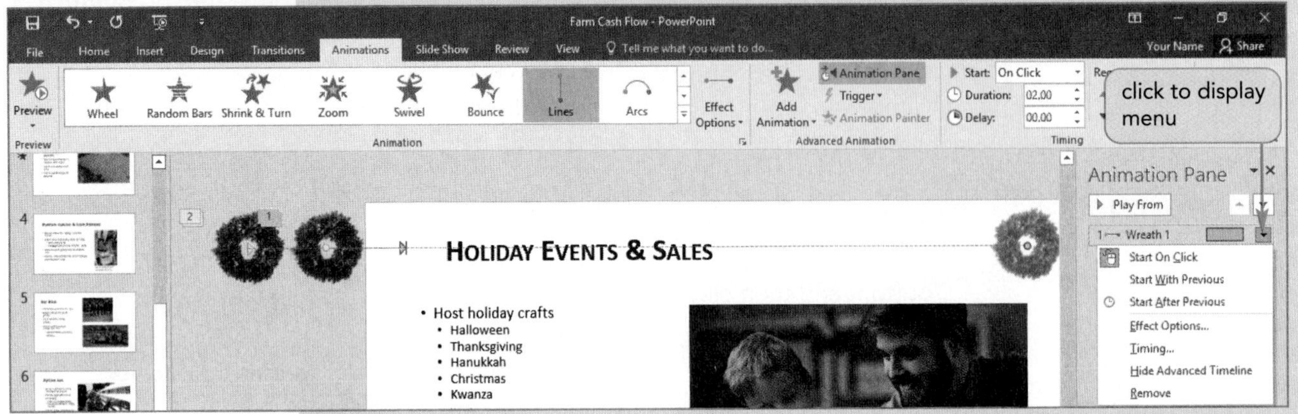

3. Click **Start After Previous**. Now the first wreath will roll onto the slide after the slide transitions. Notice that the number 1 that had been next to the animation changes to zero.
4. Click the **Wreath 2 Lines** animation, click the arrow that appears, and then click **Start After Previous**. The blue and yellow rectangles next to the Wreath 2 animations shift right to indicate that they won't start until after the previous animations finish. See Figure 4-7.

Figure 4-7 Modified timeline in the Animation Pane

5. Point to the blue rectangle to the right of the Wreath 2 Lines animation. The ScreenTip indicates that the animation will start two seconds after the slide show is advanced and will end three seconds after the slide show was advanced. Now preview the animations in Slide Show view.

6. On the status bar, click the **Slide Show** button. Slide 8 appears in Slide Show view, the first wreath rolls onto the slide, and then the second wreath rolls on.
7. Press the **Esc** key to end the slide show.
8. On the Animations tab, in the Advanced Animation group, click the **Animation Pane** button. The Animation Pane closes.
9. On the status bar, click the **Fit slide to current window** button. The slide increases in size.
10. Save the presentation.

Setting Animation Triggers

You would use a trigger for an animation that you want to be able to choose when it occurs while giving the presentation. Refer to the Session 4.1 Visual Overview for more information about triggers.

Brian created an overview slide listing his suggestions for increasing the cash flow for farms in the fall and early winter months. He included a graphic of an unlit lightbulb on the slide, and he wants to be able to click it during his presentation and have it change so it looks like he turned the light on. To do this, you need to insert a graphic of the lightbulb turned on and then apply an entrance animation to the lit bulb so that it appears when the unlit bulb is clicked; in other words, you need to make the unlit bulb a trigger for that entrance animation.

To set a trigger for an animation on Slide 2:

1. Display **Slide 2** ("Ideas"), and then, on the ribbon, click the **Home** tab. Slide 2 contains a title, a lightbulb graphic, and a bulleted list.
2. In the Editing group, click the **Select** button, and then click **Selection Pane**. The Selection pane opens.
3. On the slide, click the lightbulb. In the Selection pane, Content Placeholder 4 is selected.
4. In the Selection pane, click **Content Placeholder 4**, drag across **Content Placeholder 4** to select the text, type **Unlit Lightbulb**, and then press the **Enter** key.
5. Insert the picture **Light**, located in the PowerPoint 4 > Module folder. The same lightbulb graphic is added to the slide, but this one looks like the lightbulb is turned on. In the Selection pane, Picture 4 is added to the top of the list.
6. In the Selection pane, click **Picture 4**, drag across **Picture 4** to select the text, type **Lit Lightbulb**, and then press the **Enter** key.
7. On the slide, drag the lit version of the lightbulb graphic directly on top of the unlit version, using the smart guides to make sure the two graphics are perfectly aligned.
8. Click the **Animations** tab, and then in the Animation group, click the **Appear** entrance animation. The Appear animation is applied to the lit lightbulb. Now you need to make the unlit lightbulb the trigger for this animation.

TIP

To remove a trigger, select the animated object, click the Trigger button, and then click the checked object on the menu.

9. In the Advanced Animation group, click the **Trigger** button, and then point to **On Click of**. The same list of objects that appears in the Selection pane appears on the submenu.
10. Click **Unlit Lightbulb**. The animation sequence icon next to the light changes to a lightning bolt.
11. In the Selection pane, click the **Close** button.

Next you need to test the trigger. You'll view Slide 2 in Slide Show view and click the unlit lightbulb to make sure the lit bulb appears.

To test the animation trigger in Slide Show view:

1. On the status bar, click the **Slide Show** button. Slide 2 appears in Slide Show view displaying the slide title, the bulleted list, and the unlit version of the lightbulb graphic.
2. Click the lightbulb. The lightbulb appears to turn on, as the lit version of the lightbulb graphic appears on top of the unlit version.

   Trouble? If Slide 3 ("Corn Maze") appears instead of the lit bulb appearing on Slide 2, you clicked the slide area instead of clicking the lightbulb. Press the Backspace key to redisplay Slide 2, and then click the lightbulb graphic.
3. Press the **Esc** key to end the presentation, and then save the presentation.

Changing the Slide Background

The background of a slide can be as important as the foreground when you are creating a presentation with a strong visual impact. To change the background, you use the Format Background pane. When you change the background, you are essentially changing the fill of the background. The commands are the same as the commands you use when you change the fill of a shape. For example, you can change the color, add a gradient or a pattern, or fill it with a texture or a picture.

REFERENCE

Modify the Slide Background

- On the ribbon, click the Design tab, and then in the Customize group, click the Format Background button to open the Format Background pane with the Fill button selected and the Fill section expanded.
- Click one of the fill option buttons to select the type of fill you want to use.
- Use the option buttons, menus, and sliders that appear to customize the selected fill option.
- To apply the background to all the slides in the presentation, click the Apply to All button.

Brian wants you to add color to the slide background. You will do this now.

To fill the slide background with a gradient color:

1. Click the **Design** tab, and then in the Customize group, click the **Format Background** button. The Format Background pane opens. See Figure 4-8. This pane has only one button—the Fill button—and one section of commands—the Fill section. It contains the same commands as the Fill section in the Format Shape pane. The Solid fill option button is selected, indicating that the current background has a solid fill.

Figure 4-8 **Format Background pane**

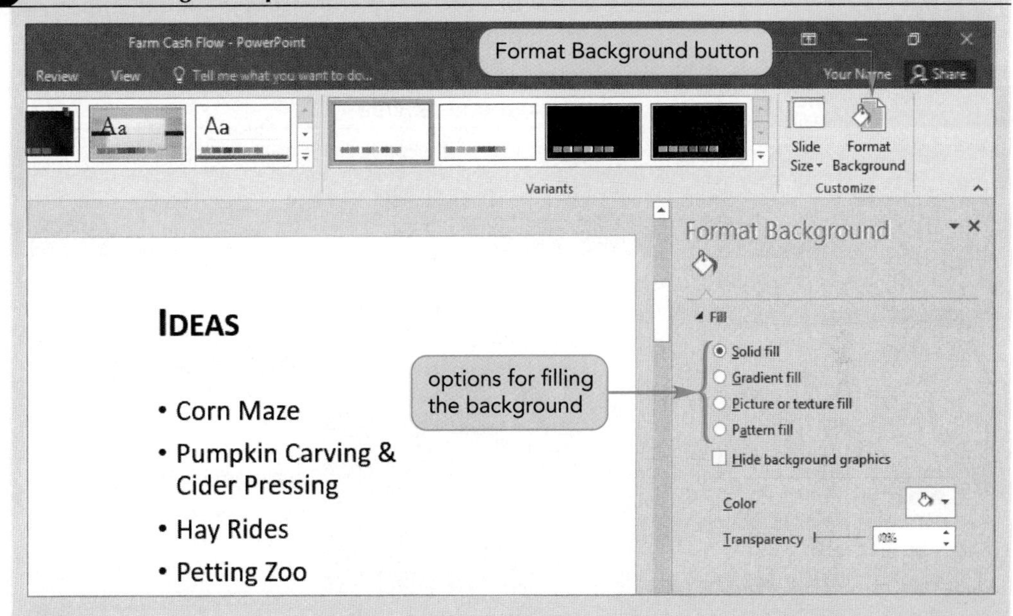

2. In the pane, click the **Color** button, and then click the **Olive Green, Accent 3** color. The slide background changes to the color you selected. This is too dark.
3. Click the **Gradient fill** option button. The slide is filled with a gradient of the color, and options for modifying the gradient fill appear in the Format Background pane.
4. Click the **Preset gradients** button, and then click the **Light Gradient – Accent 3** gradient. The gradient on the slide background changes so it is lighter at the top of the slide.
5. Click the **Type** arrow, and then click **Shade from title**. The gradient changes so that the darker shading is added along the top and sides of the slide.
6. At the bottom of the Format Background pane, click the **Apply to All** button. The gradient background is applied to all the slides in the presentation.

Brian wants the title slide to have a different background than the rest of the slides. You can display one image of a picture as the slide background, or you can tile it, which means to make the picture appear as repeating images across the slide. When you set an image to tile across the background, you can make the tiles smaller so that more tiles appear on the background.

You'll add a picture of fruit in bins at a fruit stand as the slide background of Slide 1, and then you will make it appear as tiles in the background for Slide 1.

To tile a picture in the background of Slide 1:

1. Display **Slide 1** (the title slide), and then in the Format Background pane, click the **Picture or texture fill** option button. The default texture is applied to the current slide background and the pane changes to include commands for inserting pictures.
2. In the Insert picture from section of the pane, click the **File** button. The Insert Picture dialog box opens.
3. Navigate to the **PowerPoint 4 > Module** folder, click **Fruit**, and then click the **Insert** button. The picture of fruit in a bin at a fruit stand fills the slide background of Slide 1. See Figure 4-9.

Figure 4-9 Picture in background of Slide 1

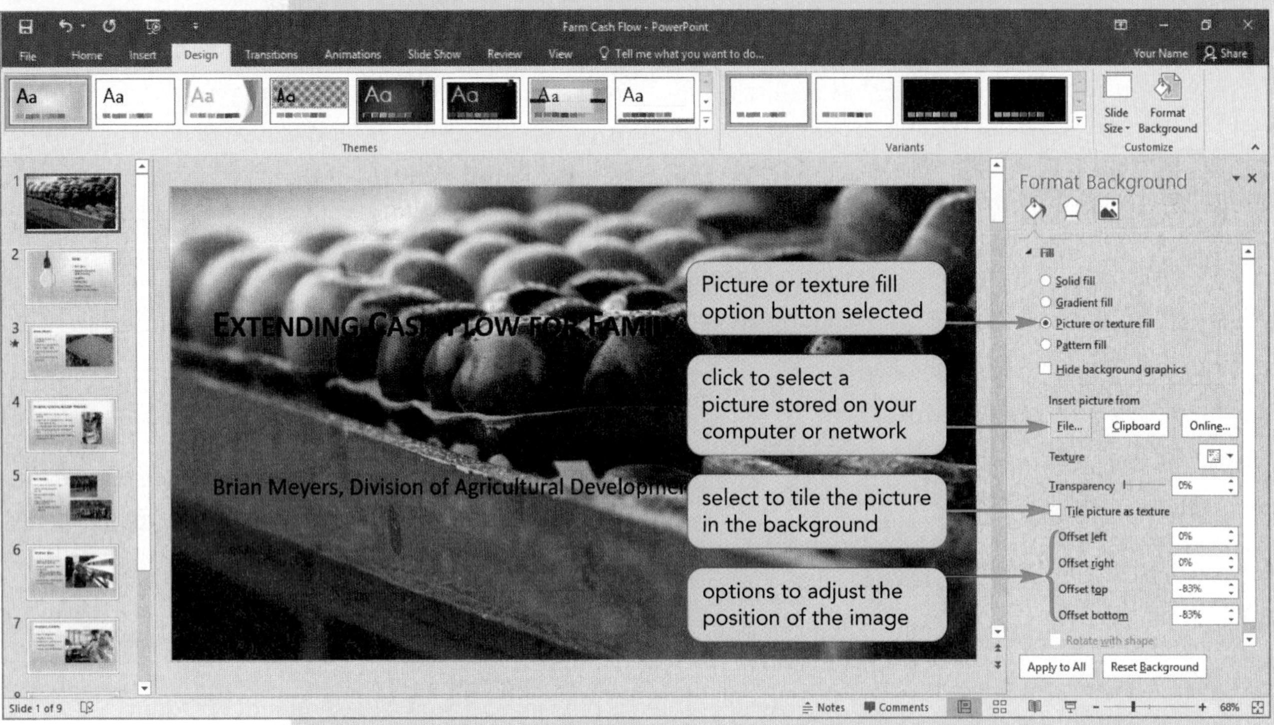

© iStock.com/cgering; Courtesy of Katherine T. Pinard; © iStock.com/BanksPhotos; © iStock.com/RonBailey; gvictoria/Shutterstock.com; Vicki L. Miller/Shutterstock.com; © iStock.com/Naomi Bassitt; Arina P Habich/Shutterstock.com

4. In the pane, click the **Tile picture as texture** check box to select it. The picture changes to a series of tiles on the slide. You want rows of tiles to appear.
5. Click in the **Scale X** box, delete the value in it, type **20**, and then press the **Enter** key. The tiles are resized narrower. To maintain the aspect ratio, you need to reduce the height of the tiles to the same percentage.
6. Click in the **Scale Y** box, delete the value in it, type **20**, and then press the **Enter** key. The tiles are resized vertically by the same amount that they were resized horizontally.
7. Scroll to the bottom of the Format Background pane, click the **Mirror type** arrow, and then click **Horizontal**. Each tile is duplicated and the duplicates are flipped horizontally to create mirror images. See Figure 4-10.

TIP

To adjust the position of the photo, use the offset options in the pane.

Figure 4-10 Picture tiled in background of Slide 1 with a mirror effect

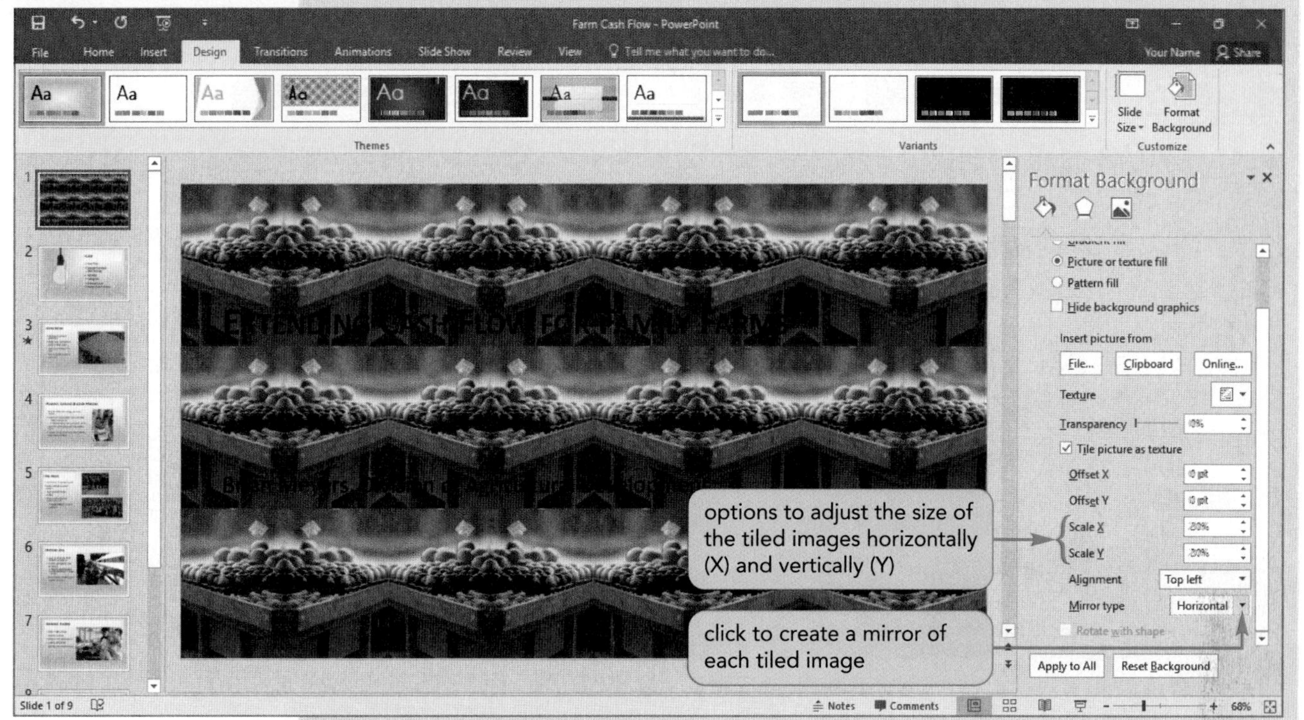

© iStock.com/cgering; Courtesy of Katherine T. Pinard; © iStock.com/BanksPhotos; © iStock.com/RonBailey; gvictoria/Shutterstock.com; Vicki L. Miller/Shutterstock.com; © iStock.com/Naomi Bassitt; Arina P Habich/Shutterstock.com

The text on the slide is hard to see with the dark photo background.

8. Click the **title text**, press and hold the **Shift** key, and then click the **subtitle text**. The two text boxes on Slide 1 are selected. Note that the pane changed to the Format Shape pane.
9. Click the **Home** tab, in the Font group, click the **Font Color button arrow**, and then click the **White, Background 1, Darker 5%** color.

The text is still a little hard to see on the picture background. You could adjust the brightness and the contrast of the photo, or you could make the photo more transparent. You'll adjust the transparency of the photo now.

TIP

To view a presentation in black-and-white or grayscale, click the View tab, and then in the Color/Grayscale group, click the Grayscale button or the Black and White button.

To change the transparency of the background picture:

1. Click the **Design** tab, and then in the Customize group, click the **Format Background** button. The Format Background pane reappears.
2. In the pane, drag the **Transparency** slider to the right until the value in the Transparency box is 20%. Compare your screen to Figure 4-11.

   Trouble? If you can't position the slider so that 20% appears in the Transparency box, click the up or down arrows in the Transparency box as needed to change the value.

Figure 4-11 **Tiled picture in slide background with transparency adjusted**

© iStock.com/cgering; Courtesy of Katherine T. Pinard; © iStock.com/BanksPhotos; © iStock.com/RonBailey; gvictoria/Shutterstock.com; Vicki L. Miller/Shutterstock.com; © iStock.com/Naomi Bassitt; Arina P Habich/Shutterstock.com

3. In the Format Background pane, click the **Close** button ☒.
4. Save the presentation.

INSIGHT

Hiding Background Graphics

Some themes include graphics as part of the slide background. If you need to print slides with graphics in the background in black and white or grayscale, you might want to remove those graphics before printing the slides because the graphics could make the text difficult to read. To hide graphics in the background, select the Hide background graphics check box in the Format Background pane. Note that selecting this option will not hide anything you use as a fill for the background, such as the picture you added as the background in this module.

Creating and Editing Hyperlinks

If you've visited webpages on the Internet, you have clicked hyperlinks (or links) to "jump to"—or display—other webpages or files. In PowerPoint, a link on a slide accomplishes the same thing. You can convert any text or object on a slide to a link to another slide in the same presentation, a different file, or a webpage. A link can be customized to do several other actions as well.

To create a link, you use the Hyperlink button or the Action button in the Links group on the Insert tab. You can use either button to create most types of links; however the Action Settings dialog box allows you to also create a link to start a program and a few other advanced activities. In addition, when you use the Action button, you can create a link that responds when you simply point to it rather than click it.

Creating and Editing Text Links

As you know, when you type a webpage or an email address, it is automatically converted to a link. You can convert any text on a slide to a link. Text links are usually underlined and a different color than the rest of the text on a slide. After you click a text link during a slide show, the link changes to another color to indicate that it has been clicked, or followed.

Slide 9 contains Brian's email address formatted as a link. You can edit this link so that the text displayed on the slide is Brian's name instead of the email address.

To change the text displayed for a link:

1. Display **Slide 9** ("Contact Info"), and then click anywhere in the email address link on the slide.
2. Click the **Insert** tab, and then in the Links group, click the **Hyperlink** button. The Edit Hyperlink dialog box opens. In the Link to list on the left, the E-mail Address option is selected. The email address, preceded by the "mailto" instruction, appears in the E-mail address box. In addition, the email address that appears on the slide is in the Text to display box at the top of the dialog box. See Figure 4-12.

Figure 4-12 Edit Hyperlink dialog box for a link to an email address

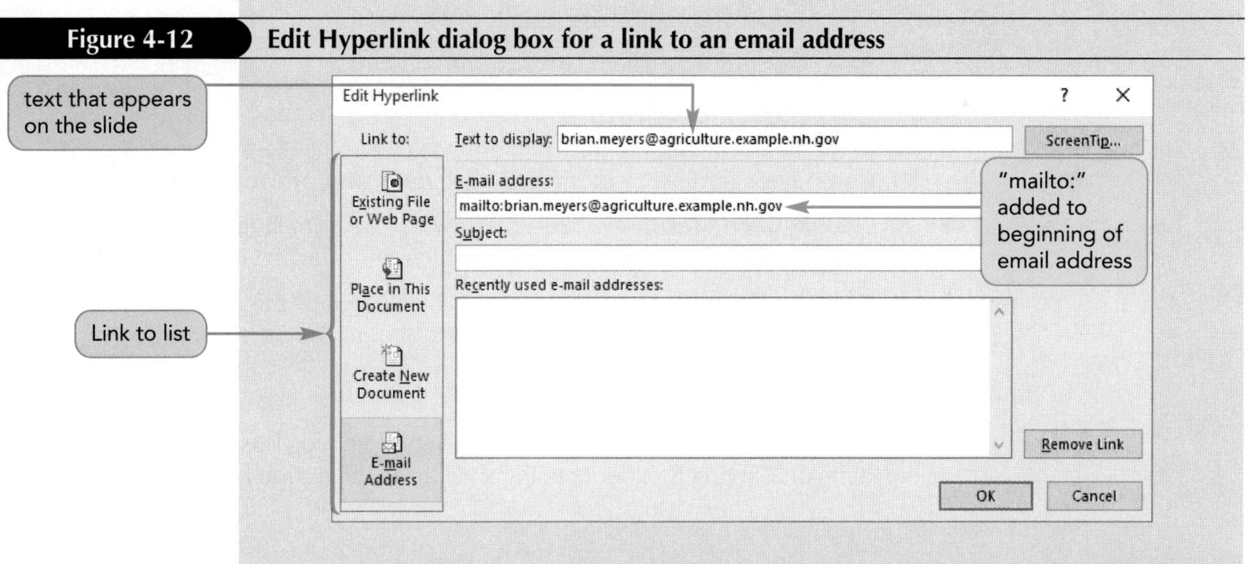

3. Click in the Text to display box, delete all the text, and then type **Brian Meyers**.
4. Click the **OK** button. The dialog box closes, and the email address on Slide 9 changes to the text you typed in the Edit Hyperlink dialog box, Brian Meyers.

Slide 2 in Brian's presentation is an overview slide. Each bulleted item on this slide names another slide in the presentation. Brian wants you to convert each bulleted item to a hyperlink that links to the related slide. One way to create hyperlinks is to use the Insert Hyperlink dialog box.

To create a hyperlink using the Insert Hyperlink dialog box:

1. Display **Slide 2** ("Ideas"), and then click the first bullet symbol. The text of the first bulleted item—"Corn Maze"—is selected.
2. Click the **Insert** tab, if necessary, and then in the Links group, click the **Hyperlink** button. The Insert Hyperlink dialog box opens. In the Link to list on the left, the E-mail Address option is selected. You need to identify the file or location to which you want to link. In this case, you're going to link to a slide in the current presentation.
3. In the Link to list on the left, click **Place in This Document**. The dialog box changes to show the Select a place in this document box, listing all the slides in the presentation. See Figure 4-13.

Figure 4-13 Insert Hyperlink dialog box displaying slides in this presentation

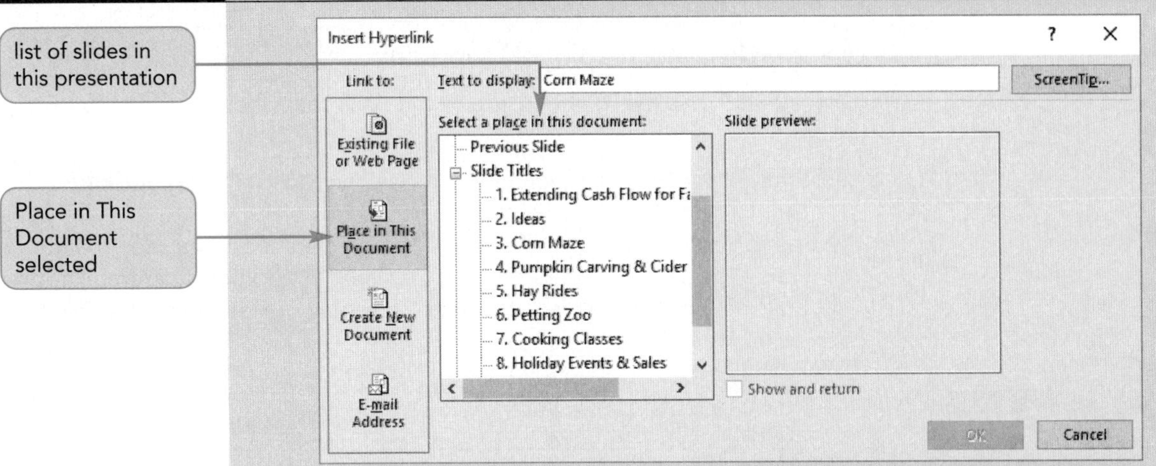

4. In the Select a place in this document list, scroll up to the top of the list. Commands for linking to the first, last, next, and previous slides are listed.
5. Click **3. Corn Maze**. The Slide preview on the right side of the dialog box displays Slide 3. This is the slide to which the selected text will be linked.
6. Click the **OK** button, and then click a blank area of the slide to deselect the text. The text of the first bullet is now a hyperlink and is formatted in yellow and underlined.

You can also create a link using the Action Settings dialog box. You'll create the link to the Pumpkin Carving & Cider Pressing slide using the Action button on the Insert tab.

To create a hyperlink using the Action Settings dialog box:

1. Click the second bullet in the list. The text of the second bulleted item, Pumpkin Carving & Cider Pressing, is selected.
2. On the Insert tab, in the Links group, click the **Action** button. The Action Settings dialog box opens with the Mouse Click tab selected. See Figure 4-14.

Figure 4-14 Action Settings dialog box

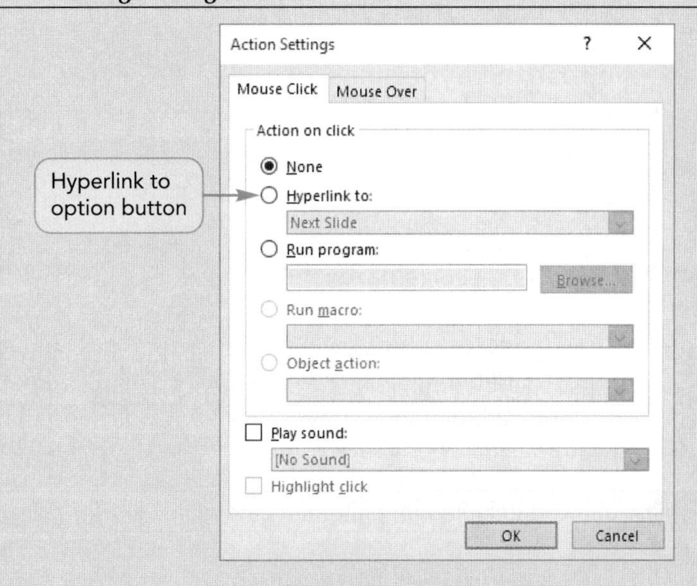

TIP

Click the Mouse Over tab to create a link that you only need to point to in order to display the linked slide or file.

3. In the Action on click section, click the **Hyperlink to** option button. The Hyperlink to box becomes available.
4. Click the **Hyperlink to** arrow. The commands on the list allow you to create hyperlinks to the same things you can link to using the Insert Hyperlink dialog box. You want to link to a specific slide in the current presentation.
5. Click **Slide**. The Hyperlink to Slide dialog box opens listing all the slides in the presentation. See Figure 4-15.

Figure 4-15 Hyperlink to Slide dialog box

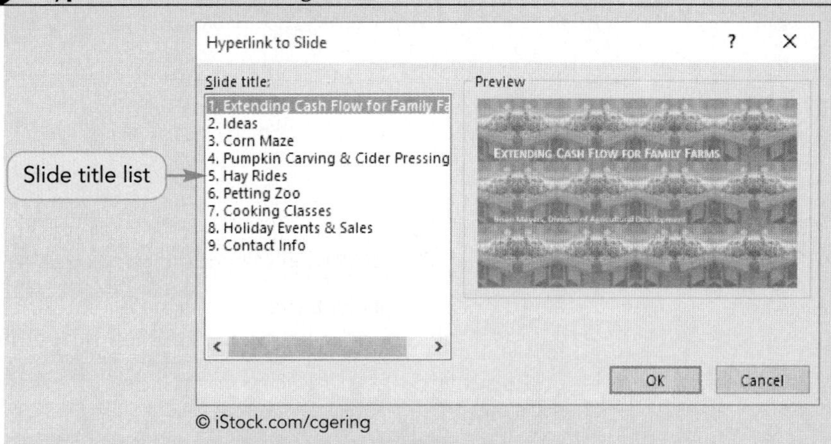

© iStock.com/cgering

6. Click **4. Pumpkin Carving & Cider Pressing**, and then click the **OK** button. The Hyperlink to Slide dialog box closes and "Pumpkin Carving & Cider Pressing" appears in the Hyperlink to box.
7. Click the **OK** button. The dialog box closes and the second bulleted item is formatted as a link.
8. Change the next four bulleted items to links to Slides 5, 6, 7, and 8 respectively, using either the Hyperlink or the Action button.

Now you need to test the links you created. Links are not active in Normal view, so you will switch to Slide Show view.

To test the hyperlinks:

1. With Slide 2 ("Ideas") displayed, click a blank area of the slide to deselect the text box, if necessary.
2. On the status bar, click the **Slide Show** button. Slide 2 appears in Slide Show view.
3. Click the **Corn Maze** hyperlink. Slide 3 ("Corn Maze") appears in Slide Show view.
4. Right-click anywhere on the slide, and then on the shortcut menu, click **Last Viewed**. Slide 2 ("Ideas") appears in Slide Show view. The link text in the first bulleted item is now brown, indicating that the link had been clicked, or was followed. See Figure 4-16.

Figure 4-16 **Followed link on Slide 2 in Slide Show view**

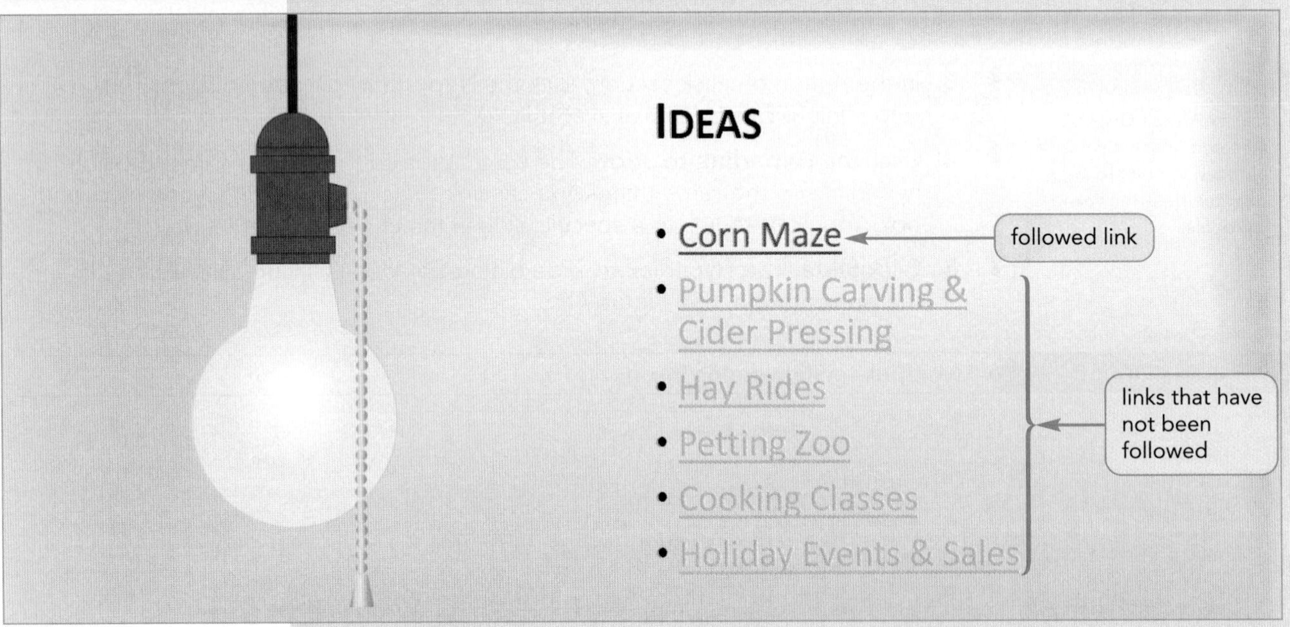

Courtesy of Katherine T. Pinard

5. Click each of the other links to verify that they link to the correct slides, using the Last Viewed command on the shortcut menu to return to Slide 2 each time.
6. Press the **Esc** key to end the slide show. Slide 2 appears in Normal view. The links are now all brown. They changed color because they have been clicked—followed—during a slide show. They will reset to the yellow color when you close and reopen the presentation.

   Trouble? If Slide 2 is not displayed, you did not return to Slide 2 in the Slide Show after clicking the last link. Display Slide 2.

   Trouble? If the links on Slide 2 are not brown, display any other slide, and then redisplay Slide 2.

Creating Object Links

You can also convert objects into links. Object hyperlinks are visually indistinguishable from objects that are not hyperlinks, except that when you move the mouse pointer over the object in Slide Show, Presenter, or Reading view, the pointer changes to a hand pointer. Object links do not change in appearance after they have been clicked.

Although Brian can use commands on the shortcut menu in Slide Show view to return to Slide 2 after clicking a link to another slide, it would be easier for him to navigate during the slide show if you added a link to Slide 2 on each slide. You'll do this now by adding a shape that you format as a link on Slides 3 through 8.

To create a shape and format it as a link:

1. Display **Slide 3** ("Corn Maze").
2. On the Insert tab, in the Illustrations group, click the **Shapes** button, and then in the Rectangles group, click the **Rounded Rectangle** shape.
3. Click below the picture of the corn maze to insert the shape, resize it so it is one-half inch high and 1.2 inches wide, and then using the smart guides that appear, position it so that the shape's right edge is aligned with the right side of the photo and its center is aligned with the slide number.
4. With the shape selected, type **Ideas**, and then change the font size to **24** points and make the text bold.
5. On the ribbon, click the **Drawing Tools Format** tab.
6. In the Shape Styles group, click the **More** button, and then in the Presets section, click the **Transparent, Colored Outline – Olive Green, Accent 3** style. See Figure 4-17.

Figure 4-17 **Ideas shape on Slide 3**

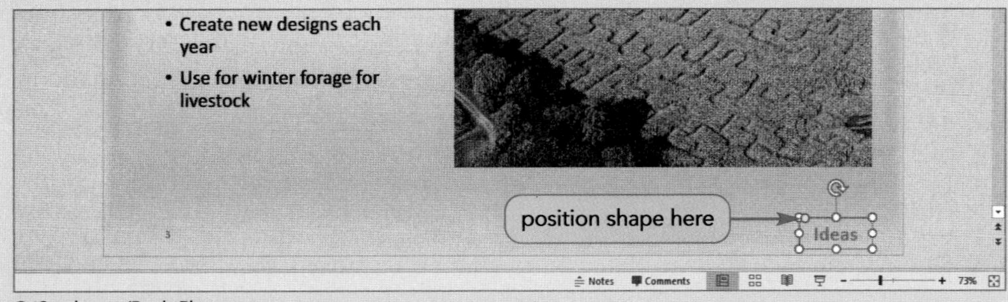

© iStock.com/BanksPhotos

7. On the ribbon, click the **Insert** tab.
8. With the shape selected, in the Links group, click the **Hyperlink** button. The Insert Hyperlink dialog box opens. Because Slide 2 is the previous slide, you could select the Previous Slide location instead of clicking the slide number. However, you will be copying this link to other slides, so you will link specifically to Slide 2.
9. With Place in This Document selected in the Link to list, click **2. Ideas** in the Select a place in this document list, and then click the **OK** button. The shape does not look any different now that it is a link. You want the same link to appear on Slides 4 through 7. You can insert a shape on each slide and format it as a link, or you can copy the shape on Slide 3 and paste it on each slide.
10. With the **Ideas** shape selected, click the **Home** tab, and then in the Clipboard group, click the **Copy** button.

11. Display **Slide 4** ("Pumpkin Carving & Cider Pressing"), and then in the Clipboard group, click the **Paste** button. A copy of the Ideas link appears in the lower-right corner of the slide—the same position it was in on Slide 3.
12. Paste the Ideas link on Slide 5 ("Hay Rides"), Slide 6 ("Petting Zoo"), Slide 7 ("Cooking Classes"), and Slide 8 ("Holiday Events & Sales").

You need to test the Ideas links. Again, you must switch to Slide Show view to do this.

To test the Ideas shape links:

1. Display **Slide 2** ("Ideas"), and then on the status bar, click the **Slide Show** button.
2. Click the **Corn Maze** hyperlink. Slide 3 ("Corn Maze") appears in Slide Show view.
3. In the lower-right corner of the slide, click the **Ideas** shape. Slide 2 ("Ideas") appears on the screen.
4. On Slide 2 ("Ideas"), click each of the other links to display those slides, and then click the Ideas shape on each of those slides to return to Slide 2.
5. Press the **Esc** key to end the slide show and return to Slide 2 in Normal view.

Inserting Action Buttons

Finally, you want to add a link on Slide 2 that links to the last slide in the presentation, Slide 9 ("Contact Info"). Brian did not add a bulleted item in the overview on Slide 2 for Slide 9 because, as the final slide, it is meant to display only as the presentation is concluding. You will use an action button to do this. An action button is a shape that, when inserted, causes the Action Settings dialog box to be opened automatically, ready for you to specify the link. Some action buttons are preset to link to the first, last, next, or previous slides.

To insert an action button on Slide 2:

1. With Slide 2 ("Ideas") displayed, on the ribbon, click the **Insert** tab.
2. In the Illustrations group, click the **Shapes** button, scroll to the bottom of the gallery, and then in the Action Buttons section, click the **Action Button: End** shape.
3. Click below the bulleted list. The action button is inserted and the Action Settings dialog box opens. The Hyperlink to option button is selected, and Last Slide appears in the Hyperlink to box.
4. Click the **OK** button.
5. On the Drawing Tools Format tab, in the Shape Styles group, click the **More** button, scroll down, and then click the **Semitransparent – Olive Green, Accent 3, No Outline** style in the Presets section.
6. Resize the action button so it is one-half inch high and one inch wide, position it in the lower-right corner of the slide so it is in about the same position as the Ideas shape on the other slides, and then click a blank area of the slide to deselect the button. Compare your screen to Figure 4-18.

Figure 4-18 Action button on Slide 2

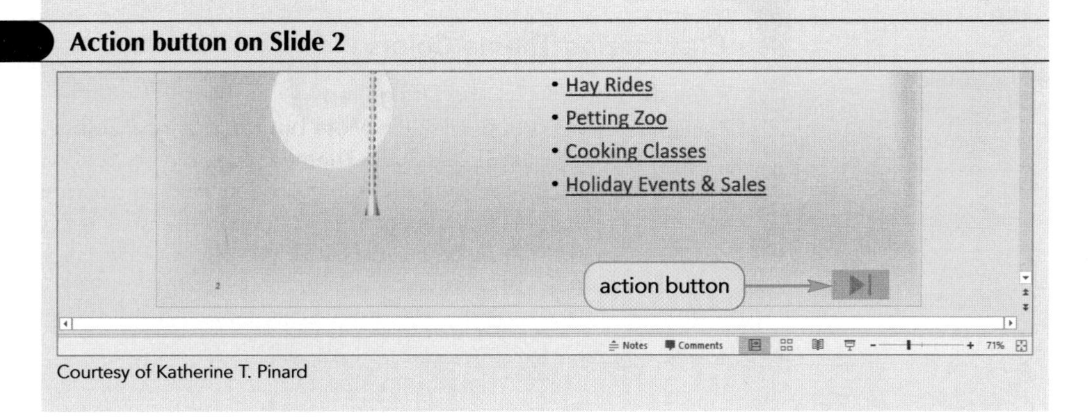

Courtesy of Katherine T. Pinard

Now you need to test the new link. Once again, you will switch to Slide Show view.

To test the shape link in Slide Show view:

1. On the status bar, click the **Slide Show** button. Slide 2 ("Ideas") appears in Slide Show view.
2. Click the action button. Slide 9 ("Contact Info") appears.
3. Press the **Esc** key to end the slide show. Slide 9 appears in Normal view.
4. Save the presentation.

INSIGHT

Linking to Another File

You can create a link to another file so that when you click the link during a slide show, the other file opens. The other file can be any file type; it doesn't need to be a PowerPoint file. To create a link to another file, open the Insert Hyperlink dialog box, click Existing File or Web Page in the Link to list, and then click the Browse for File button. To change the link destination of an action button to another file, open the Action Settings dialog box, click the Hyperlink to option button, click the Hyperlink to arrow, and then click Other PowerPoint Presentation or Other File. For either type of link, a dialog box opens in which you can navigate to the location of the file.

When you create a link to another file, the linked file is not included within the PowerPoint file; only the original path and filename to the files on the computer where you created the links are stored in the presentation. Therefore, if you need to show the presentation on another computer, you must copy the linked files as well as the PowerPoint presentation file to the other computer, and then you need to edit the path to the linked file so that PowerPoint can find the file in its new location. To update the path for a text or graphic link, right-click it, and then click Edit Hyperlink on the shortcut menu to open the Edit Hyperlink dialog box. To edit the path of a file linked to an action button, right-click the action button, and then click Hyperlink to open the Action Settings dialog box.

Customizing Theme Colors

As you know, each theme has its own color palette. In addition, you can switch to one of several built-in color palettes. However, sometimes, you might want to customize a palette. You can do so by changing one or all of the theme colors in a palette.

REFERENCE

Customizing Theme Colors

- On the ribbon, click the Design tab.
- In the Variants group, click the More button, point to Colors, and then click Customize Colors to open the Create New Theme Colors dialog box.
- Click the button next to the theme color you want to customize.
- Click a color in the Theme Colors section or in the Standard Colors section of the palette, or click More Colors, click a color in the Colors dialog box, and then click the OK button.
- Replace the name in the Name box with a meaningful name for the custom palette.
- Click the Save button.

In the Farm Cash Flow presentation, the color of the unfollowed text links is a little light on the colored slide background. To fix that, you will customize the link color in the color palette.

To create custom theme colors:

1. Make sure Slide 9 ("Contact Info") is displayed, and then on the ribbon, click the **Design** tab.
2. In the Variants group, click the **More** button, and then point to **Colors**. A menu of color palettes opens. See Figure 4-19. If you wanted to change the entire color palette, you could select one of these options. However, you want to change only the color of text links.

Figure 4-19 Color palettes on Colors submenu

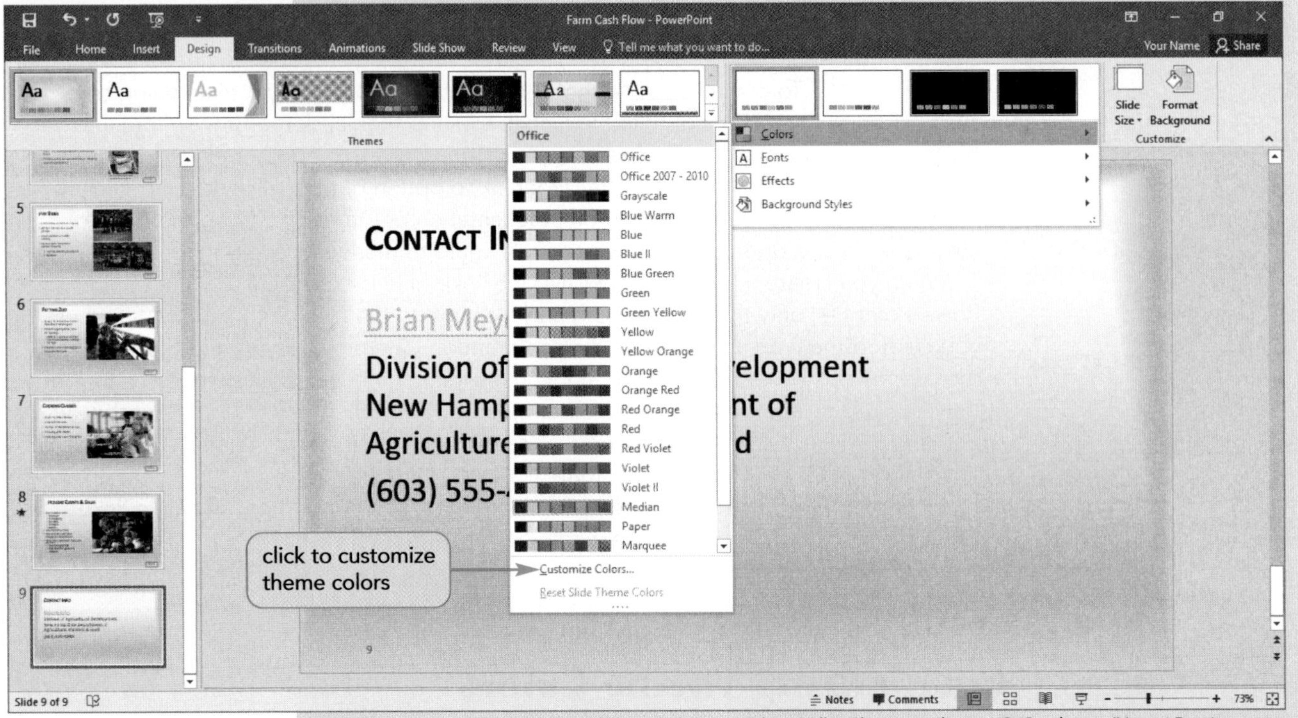

3. At the bottom of the menu, click **Customize Colors**. The Create New Theme Colors dialog box opens. See Figure 4-20. You want to change the color of hyperlinks to a darker shade.

Figure 4-20 Create New Theme Colors dialog box

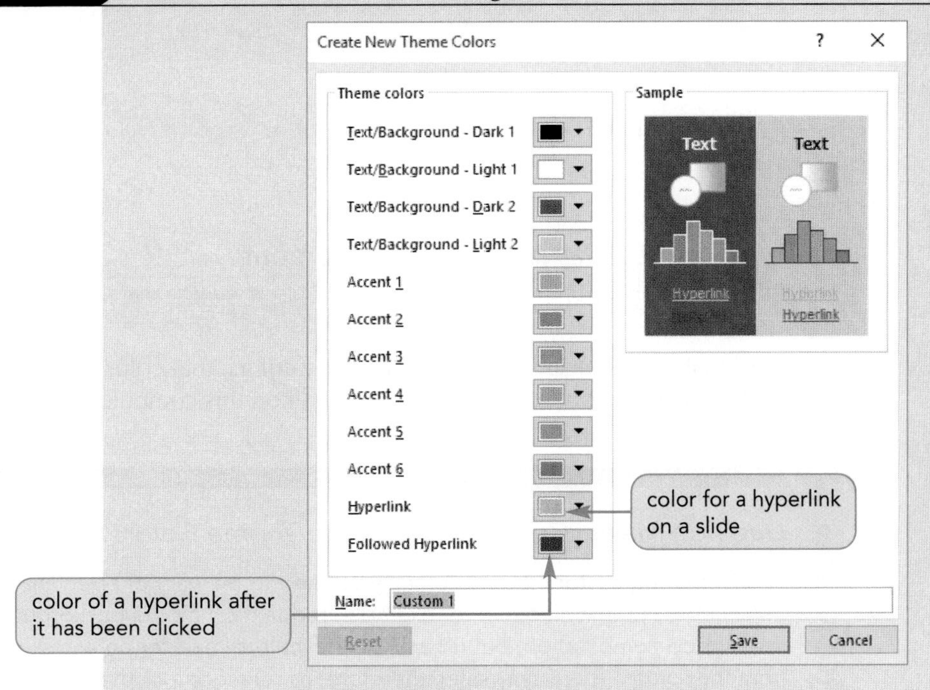

4. Click the **Hyperlink** button to display the complete Theme Colors and Standard Colors palettes.
5. In the Theme Colors section, point to the second to last color in the first row. The ScreenTip identifies this as Gold, Hyperlink. This is the current color for text hyperlinks.
6. Click the **Gold, Hyperlink, Darker 25%** color (second to last color in the column). The Hyperlink color is now the darker gold color you selected, and the top Hyperlink text in the Sample panel in the dialog box is now also darker.

TIP

Never place dark text on a dark background or light text on a light background.

7. Click in the **Name** box, delete the text "Custom 1," and then type **Custom Link Color**.
8. Click the **Save** button. The dialog box closes and the custom color is applied to the presentation. As you can see on Slide 9, the link is now the darker gold color you chose for unfollowed links. See Figure 4-21.

Figure 4-21 New link color on Slide 9

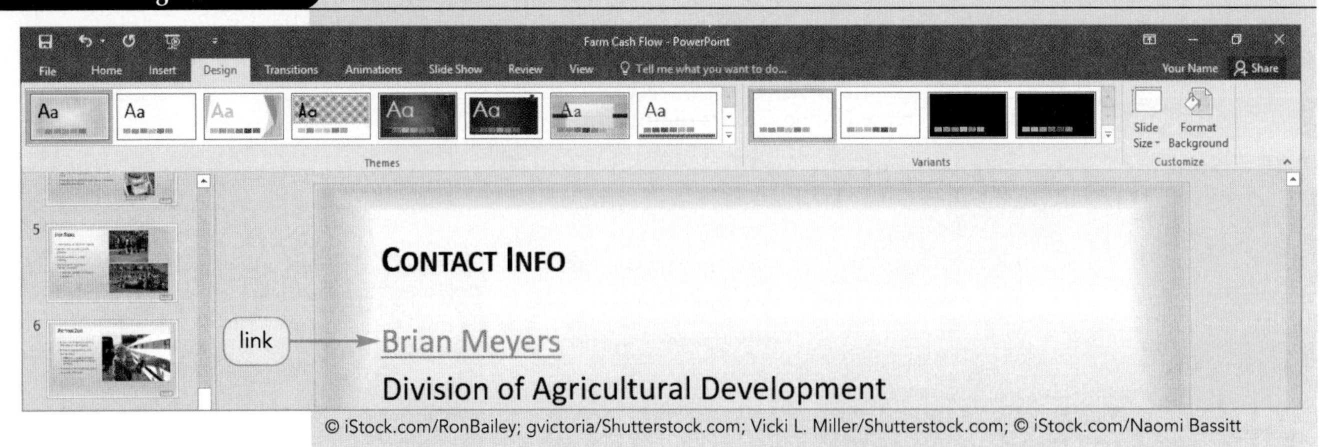

Now that you have saved the custom theme colors, that color palette is available to apply to any presentation that you create or edit on this computer.

PROSKILLS

Decision Making: Choosing Custom Theme Colors

When creating custom theme colors, you need to be wary of selecting colors that don't match or make text illegible; for example, red text on a blue background might seem like a good combination, but it's actually difficult to read for an audience at a distance from the screen. It's usually safer, therefore, to select one of the built-in theme color sets and stick with it or make only minor modifications. If you do create a new set of theme colors, select colors that go well together and that maximize the legibility of your slides.

Deleting Custom Theme Colors

When you save a custom theme color palette, the palette is saved to the computer. If you've applied the custom palette to a presentation, that color palette will stay applied to that presentation even if you delete the custom palette from the computer. You'll delete the custom theme color palette you created from the computer you are using.

To delete the custom color palette:

1. On the Design tab, in the Variants group, click the **More** button, and then point to **Colors**. The Custom Link Color palette you created appears at the top of the Colors submenu. If you had not given it a different name, it would be listed with the default name—Custom 1—which had appeared in the Create New Theme Colors dialog box.
2. Right-click the **Custom Link Color** palette, and then click **Delete**. A dialog box opens, asking if you want to delete these theme colors.
3. Click the **Yes** button to delete the custom theme colors. You can confirm that the color palette was deleted from your computer.
4. In the Variants group, click the **More** button, and then point to **Colors**. The Custom Link Color palette no longer appears on the Colors submenu.
5. Click a blank area of the slide to close the menu without making a selection.

6. Display **Slide 1** (the title slide), and then replace Brian Meyers' name in the slide subtitle with your name.
7. Save and close the presentation.

Brian is happy with the modifications you've made to the presentation so far. You applied two animations to pictures and modified motion path animations. You changed the slide background by filling all the slide backgrounds with a gradient and filling the title slide background with a tiled picture that you made somewhat transparent. You converted text and a shape to links and added an action button. Finally, you changed the color of linked text so that it can be more easily distinguished on the slides.

In the next session, you will create a self-running presentation by setting slide timings. You will then record a narration to accompany the self-running presentation. You also will save the presentation in other formats so it can be more easily distributed.

REVIEW

Session 4.1 Quick Check

1. What happens if you try to add a second animation by using the Animation gallery instead of the Add Animation button?
2. What is a trigger?
3. Name the five types of fill you can add to a slide background.
4. What items on a slide can be a link?
5. What is an action button?
6. What view(s) do you need to be in to test links?

Session 4.2 Visual Overview:

To set automatic timings manually, select the After check box. During a slide show, the slides will advance automatically after the time displayed in the After box.

When the On Mouse Click check box is selected, the slide show can be advanced by clicking the slide, even if there are saved slide timings. If the On Mouse Click check box is deselected, the slide show cannot be advanced by clicking a slide, although users can still use the keyboard or click links to display other slides.

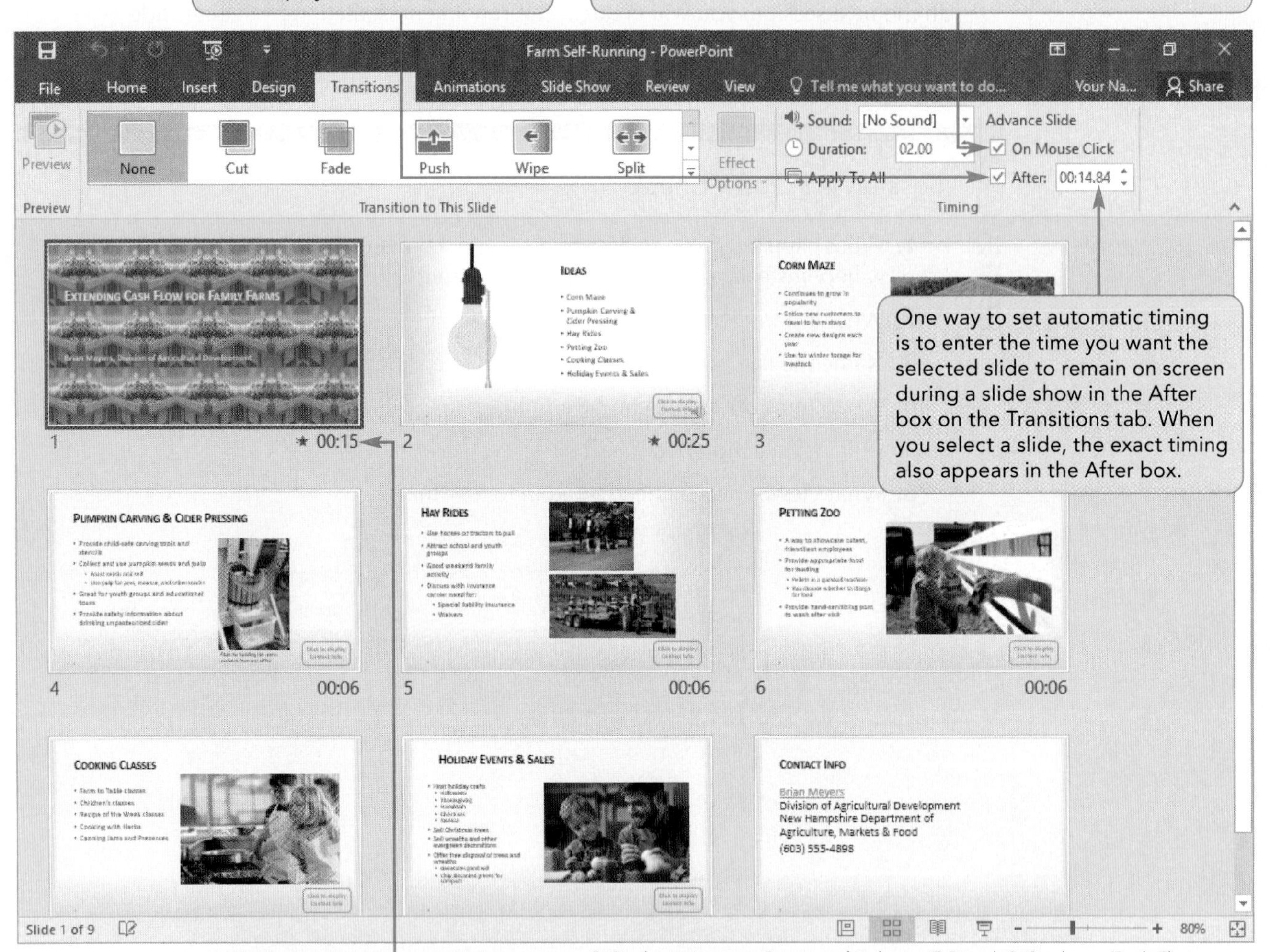

One way to set automatic timing is to enter the time you want the selected slide to remain on screen during a slide show in the After box on the Transitions tab. When you select a slide, the exact timing also appears in the After box.

Automatic timings indicate how many seconds a slide will stay on the screen before transitioning to the next slide during a slide show.

Automatic Slide Timings

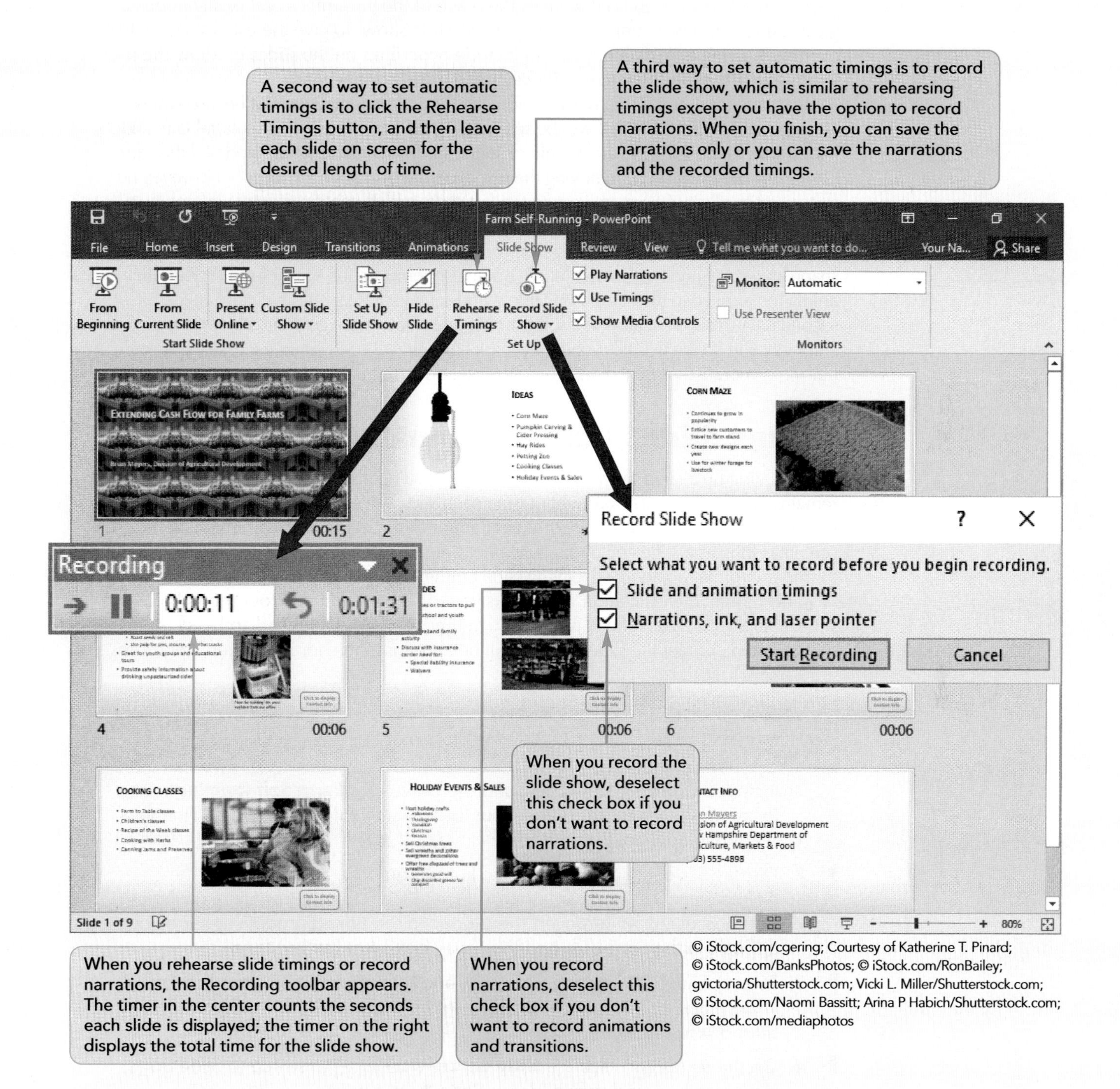

© iStock.com/cgering; Courtesy of Katherine T. Pinard; © iStock.com/BanksPhotos; © iStock.com/RonBailey; gvictoria/Shutterstock.com; Vicki L. Miller/Shutterstock.com; © iStock.com/Naomi Bassitt; Arina P Habich/Shutterstock.com; © iStock.com/mediaphotos

Understanding Self-Running Presentations

A self-running presentation advances without a presenter or viewer doing anything. Self-running presentations include settings that specify the amount of time that each slide is displayed as well as the time at which animations occur. Some self-running presentations include audio that takes the place of the presenter's oral explanations or gives the viewer instructions for watching the slide show. To give the user more control over his viewing experience, you can include hyperlinks on the slides or allow the user to advance the slide show manually using the mouse or keyboard.

Brian intends to use the Farm Cash Flow file for oral presentations, but he also wants to create a version of the file that will be self-running on a computer at agricultural fairs and tradeshows for people who are unable to attend his presentation. Brian modified the Farm Cash Flow presentation by removing the text hyperlinks on Slide 2 ("Ideas"). However, he does want to allow viewers to jump to the last slide, which contains contact information, if they want to skip some of the slides. So he replaced the action button on Slide 2 and the Ideas shape on Slides 3 ("Corn Maze") through 8 ("Holiday Events & Sales") with a new shape linked to Slide 9 ("Contact Info"). Brian also removed the trigger from the entrance animation applied to the lit bulb on Slide 2 and set it to appear automatically after a one-second delay. This is because in a self-running presentation, trigger animations do not occur automatically, so the lit bulb would never appear unless the viewer knew to click the unlit bulb. This modified presentation can now be set up as a self-running presentation.

Setting Slide Timings Manually

When setting up a slide show to be self-running, you need to specify how long each slide remains on the screen. The amount of time each slide stays on the screen might vary for different slides—a slide with only three bullet points might not need to remain on the screen as long as a slide containing six bullet points. See the Session 4.2 Visual Overview for more information about specifying slide timings.

In his modified presentation, Brian asks you to set the timings to four seconds per slide. Four seconds, of course, is not enough time for a viewer to read and understand the slide content, but the slide timings will be kept short here for instructional purposes.

To open the modified presentation and set slide timings:

1. Open the presentation **Farm2**, located in the **PowerPoint4 > Module** included with your Data Files, and then save it as **Farm Self-Running** to the location where you are saving your files. First you'll examine the animations that Brian applied.
2. Display **Slide 2** ("Ideas"), click the lit bulb graphic, and then click the **Animations** tab. The animation sequence icon does not contain a lightning bolt because Brian removed the trigger. In the timing group, After Previous appears in the Start box, and the Delay box is set for 1 second.
3. Display **Slide 7** ("Cooking Classes"), and then click the bulleted list. The Wipe entrance animation is applied to the list, and On Click appears in the Start box in the Timing group.
4. On the status bar, click the **Slide Sorter** button to switch to Slide Sorter view, scroll up, and then click the **Slide 1** thumbnail.
5. Press and hold the **Shift** key, scroll down, and then click the **Slide 9** ("Contact Info") thumbnail. All the slides are selected.
6. On the ribbon, click the **Transitions** tab. In the Timing group, the On Mouse Click check box is selected in the Advance Slide section. This means that the viewer can take an action to advance the slide show.

7. In the Timing group, click the **After** check box. The check box is selected, and 00:00 appears below each slide thumbnail. See Figure 4-22.

Figure 4-22 Transitions tab with After box selected

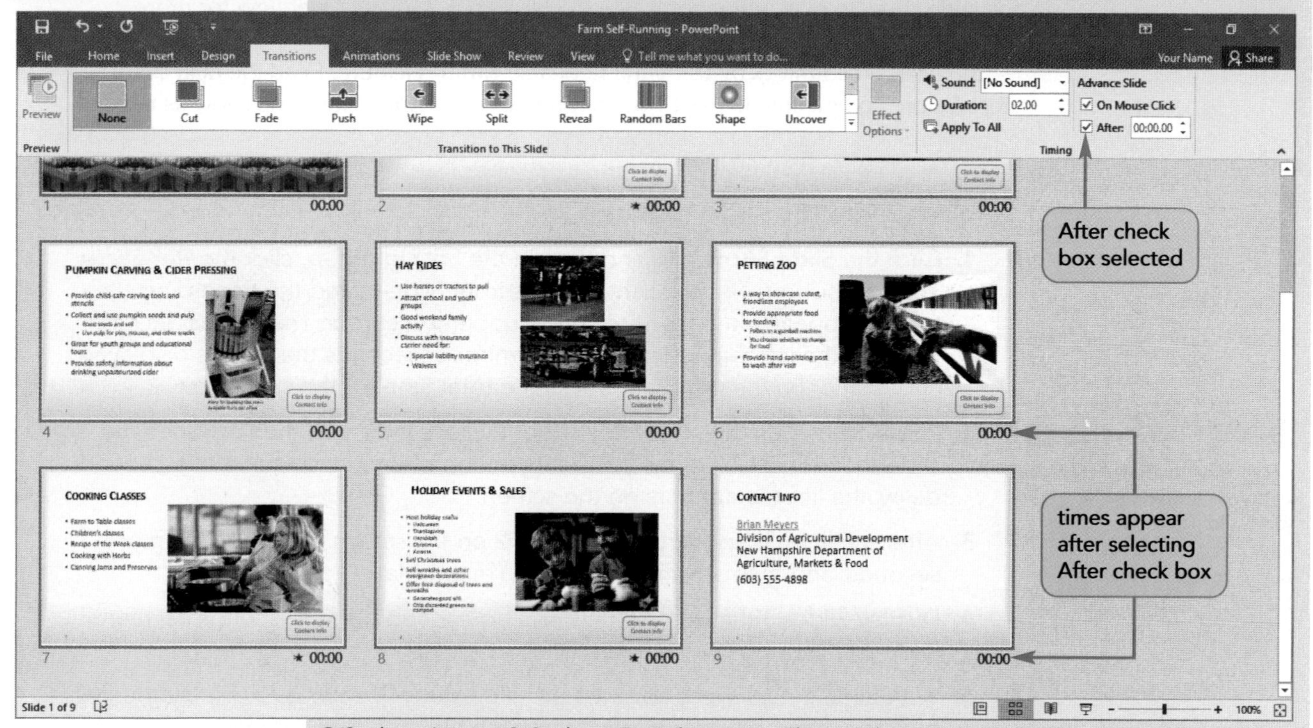

TIP

If you want to remove slide timings, select all the slides in Slide Sorter view, click the Transitions tab, and then click the After check box in the Timing group to deselect it.

8. In the Timing group, click the **After up arrow** four times to change the time to four seconds per slide. Under each slide thumbnail, the time changes to 00:04.
9. On the Quick Access Toolbar, click the **Start From Beginning** button. Watch as Slide 1 appears, then after four seconds, Slide 2 ("Ideas") appears. After one second, the lit bulb appears, and then three seconds later Slide 3 ("Corn Maze") appears.
10. Immediately click the mouse button. Slide 4 ("Pumpkin Carving & Cider Pressing") appears. You are able to advance the slide show by clicking the mouse button because you left the On Mouse Click check box on the Transitions tab selected.
11. Watch as the slide show advances through the rest of the slides. When Slide 7 ("Cooking Classes") appears, the animations occur automatically, even though they are set to start On Click. This is because the automatic timing overrides the On Click start setting.
12. When the black slide that indicates the end of the slide show appears, press the **spacebar**. The presentation appears in Slide Sorter view.

You could prevent viewers from advancing the slide show by clicking the mouse button by deselecting the On Mouse Click check box in the Timing group on the Transitions tab. Note, however, that the viewer will still be able to advance the slide show using the keyboard. If you do deselect the On Mouse Click check box, the viewer will still be able to click links and right-click the slide to display the shortcut menu.

Rehearsing Timings

Instead of guessing how much time each slide needs to remain displayed, you can ensure you have the right slide timing for each slide by rehearsing the slide show and then saving the slide timings. When you rehearse a slide show, the amount of time each slide is displayed during the slide show is recorded, as well as when you advance the slide show to play animations. See the Session 4.2 Visual Overview for more information about rehearsing presentations.

You'll set slide timings by using the Rehearse Timings feature. Read the next set of steps before completing them so you are prepared to advance the slide show as needed.

To rehearse the slide timings:

1. Click the **Slide Show** tab, and then in the Set Up group, click the **Rehearse Timings** button. The slide show starts from Slide 1, and the Recording toolbar appears on the screen in the upper-left corner. The toolbar includes a timer on the left that indicates the number of seconds the slide is displayed, and a timer on the right that tracks the total time for the slide show.
2. Leave Slide 1 on the screen for about five seconds, and then advance the slide show. Slide 2 ("Ideas") appears on the screen, and after a one-second delay, the lit bulb appears on the screen.
3. After the lit bulb appears, leave Slide 2 on the screen for about five more seconds, and then advance to Slide 3 ("Corn Maze").
4. Display Slides 3 through 6 ("Petting Zoo") for about five seconds each until Slide 7 ("Cooking Classes") appears.
5. With Slide 7 displayed, advance the slide show five times to display the five bulleted items, pausing briefly after each bulleted item appears, and then advance the slide show to display Slide 8 ("Holiday Events & Sales").
6. After the single wreath rolls onto the slide, wait five seconds, advance the slide show to display Slide 9, wait five seconds, and then advance the slide show once more. A dialog box opens asking if you want to save the timings.
7. Click the **Yes** button. The presentation appears in Slide Sorter view. The rehearsed time appears below each slide thumbnail. You can also see the timing assigned to the slides on the Transitions tab.
8. Click the **Transitions** tab, and then click the **Slide 1** thumbnail. In the Timing group, the recorded timing to the hundredth of a second for the selected slide appears in the After box. The rehearsed timing replaced the four-second slide timing you set previously.

TIP

Click the Pause Recording button on the Recording toolbar to pause the timer; click the Repeat button to restart the timer for the current slide.

After you rehearse a slide show, you should run it to evaluate the timings. If a slide stays on the screen for too much or too little time, stop the slide show, and then change that slide's time in the After box in the Timing group on the Transitions tab.

To play the slide show using the rehearsed slide timings:

1. On the Quick Access Toolbar, click the **Start From Beginning** button. The slide show starts and Slide 1 appears on the screen. The slide show advances to Slide 2 ("Ideas") automatically after the saved rehearsal timing for Slide 1 elapses. When Slide 7 ("Cooking Classes") appears, the animations occur automatically at the pace you rehearsed them.
2. When the final black slide appears, advance the slide show to end it.

Brian wants you to see what happens if the viewer tries to interact with the slide show and clicks one of the shapes that links to the last slide.

To interact with the self-running presentation:

1. Click the **Slide 2** thumbnail, and then on the status bar, click the **Slide Show** button. Slide 2 ("Ideas") appears in Slide Show view.
2. Move the mouse to display the pointer, and then in the lower-right corner, click the **Click to display Contact Info** shape. Slide 9 ("Contact Info") appears.
3. Press the **Backspace** key as many times as needed to display Slide 5 ("Hay Rides"). The slide show does not advance automatically to Slide 6.
4. Press the **spacebar**. Slide 6 ("Petting Zoo") appears, and the automatic timing is reactivated, so that after about five seconds, the next slide, Slide 7 ("Cooking Classes"), appears.
5. Right-click a blank area of the slide, and then on the shortcut menu, click **See All Slides**. The slides appear as thumbnails, similar to Slide Sorter view.
6. Click the **Slide 3** thumbnail. Slide 3 ("Corn Maze") appears in Slide Show view. After about five seconds, the slide show advances.
7. Press the **S** key. The slide show stops advancing automatically.
8. Press the **S** key again. The slide show resumes advancing automatically.
9. Press the **Esc** key to end the slide show.

TIP

You can also right-click a blank area of the screen, and then click Pause to stop the automatic slide advancement or click Resume to resume the automatic advancement.

Recording Narration and Timings

You can record narration to give viewers more information about your presentation's content. This is similar to what you did when you created a mix. When you use the Rehearse Timings command, only the amount of time a slide is displayed during the slide show and the time when animations occur are saved. If you want to record narration to play while a slide is displayed, you can use the Record Slide Show command. Using the Record Slide Show command is similar to the Rehearse Timings command, except you record narration while you rehearse the timing. When you record narration, the recorded audio for each slide is inserted on the slide as an audio object. Refer to the Session 4.2 Visual Overview for more information about recording narration.

If you add narration to a slide, you should not read the text on the slide—the viewers can read that for themselves. Your narration should provide additional information about the slides or instructions for the viewers as they watch the self-running presentation so that they know, for instance, that they can click action buttons to manually advance the presentation.

INSIGHT

Using the Record Sound Dialog Box

Another way to add narration is to click the Audio button in the Media group on the Insert tab, and then click Record Audio. To start recording, click the button with the red circle. When you are finished recording, click the button with the blue square.

REFERENCE

Recording Narration

- Click the Slide Show tab, click the Record Slide Show button arrow in the Set Up group, and then click Start Recording from Beginning or Start Recording from Current Slide.
- Speak into the microphone to record the narration for the current slide.
- Press the spacebar to go to the next slide (if desired), record the narration for that slide, and then continue, as desired, to other slides.
- End the slide show after recording the last narration; or continue displaying all the slides in the presentation for the appropriate amount of time, even if you do not add narration to each slide, and then end the slide show as you normally would.

Brian wants viewers to have some guidance in navigating through the presentation. You will record narration for Slides 1 and 2. You will also adjust the timing for these two slides to accommodate the accompanying narrations.

To record narration for Slides 1 and 2:

1. Make sure your computer is equipped with a microphone.

   Trouble? If your computer doesn't have a microphone, connect one, or check with your instructor or technical support person. If you can't connect a microphone, read the following steps but do not complete them.

2. On the ribbon, click the **Slide Show** tab.
3. In the Set Up group, click the **Record Slide Show button arrow**, and then click **Start Recording from Beginning**. The Record Slide Show dialog box opens. You want to record both narration and timings, so you will not change the default settings.

TIP

To start recording on a slide other than Slide 1, click the Record Slide Show button arrow in the Set Up group, and then click Start Recording from Current Slide.

4. Click the **Start Recording** button. The dialog box closes and the slide show starts from Slide 1. The Recording dialog box appears on the screen in the upper-left corner as it did when you rehearsed the slide timings.
5. Speak the following into the microphone: "**This presentation describes several ideas for increasing cash flow at your farm in the fall and early winter months. The presentation will advance automatically from one slide to the next.**"
6. Wait for a moment, press the **spacebar** to advance to Slide 2, wait for the light to "turn on," and then say into the microphone, "**To skip to the last slide, which contains contact information, click the button in the lower-right corner. To return to an earlier slide, click the right mouse button, click See All Slides, and then click the slide you want to view. To pause or resume the slide show, press S on the keyboard.**"
7. Wait five seconds, and then press the **Esc** key. The timer in the Recording toolbar stops, and then the newly recorded timings appear under the thumbnails for Slides 1 and 2 in Slide Sorter view.

   Trouble? If you advanced the slide show to Slide 4 instead of pressing the Esc key to end it, when Slide Sorter view appears again, double-click the Slide 3 thumbnail to display it in Normal view, click the Transitions tab, and then change the time in the After box to five seconds. Next, click the sound icon in the lower-right corner of Slide 3, and then press the Delete key to delete it. Return to Slide Sorter view.

TIP

To remove narration on a slide, delete the sound icon.

8. Double-click the **Slide 1** thumbnail to display it in Normal view, and then click the sound icon in the lower-right corner. This is the narration you recorded on Slide 1.
9. On the ribbon, click the **Audio Tools Playback** tab. In the Audio Options group, note that the start timing is set to Automatically, and the Hide During Show check box is selected.
10. On the Quick Access Toolbar, click the **Start From Beginning** button. The slide show starts, the recording that you made for Slide 1 plays, and then the slide show advances to Slide 2 a few seconds after the recorded time elapses. Five seconds after the recording on Slide 2 finishes playing, the slide show advances automatically to display Slide 3. The rest of the slides will continue to appear using the timings you set when you rehearsed the presentation.
11. Press the **Esc** key to end the slide show, and then save your changes.

Applying Kiosk Browsing

Brian wants you to set the presentation so that after the last slide appears, it will restart. He also doesn't want the viewer to be able to do anything other than click the links and press the Esc key to end the slide show. To do this, you'll set up the slide show to be browsed at a kiosk. If you apply kiosk browsing, every slide must have a link or timing assigned to it. Otherwise, after Slide 1 appears, and the viewer will be unable to advance the slide show.

To set up the presentation for browsing at a kiosk:

1. Click the **Slide Show** tab, and then in the Set Up group, click the **Set Up Slide Show** button. The Set Up Show dialog box opens. See Figure 4-23.

Figure 4-23 Set Up Show dialog box

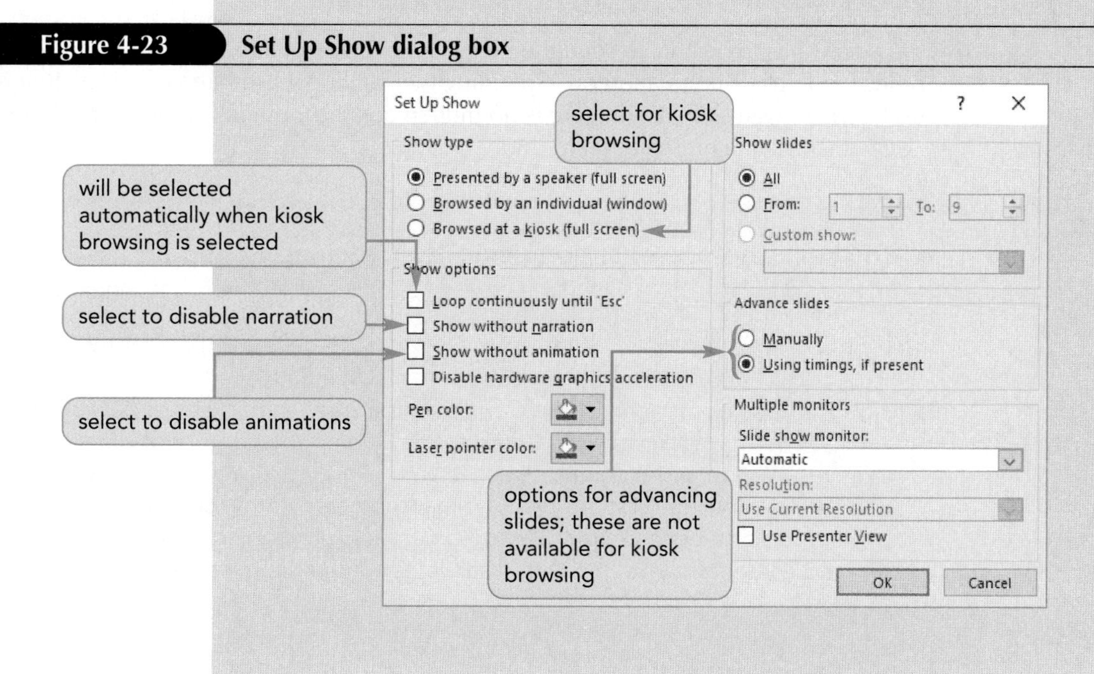

Note that the Advance slides section in the Set Up Show dialog box is similar to the options in the Timing group on the Transitions tab, but the options in this dialog box take precedence. For example, if the After check box is selected on the Transitions tab, but you select the Manually option button in this dialog box, the slide show will not advance automatically.

TIP

To change the resolution of the slide show, click the Slide show monitor arrow, click the monitor you are showing the slide show on, click the Resolution arrow, and then click the resolution you want to use.

2. In the Show type section, click the **Browsed at a kiosk (full screen)** option button. Under Show options, the Loop continuously until 'Esc' check box becomes selected. That option has also changed to light gray, indicating that you cannot deselect it. The options under Advance slides also cannot be changed now.
3. Click the **OK** button. The dialog box closes, and the presentation is set up for kiosk browsing.
4. Display **Slide 2** ("Ideas"), and then on the status bar, click the **Slide Show** button. Slide 2 appears in Slide Show view.
5. Click the **Click to display Contact Info** shape. Slide 9 ("Contact Info") appears.
6. Press the **spacebar**. The slide show does not advance, rather Slide 9 remains on the screen until the saved timing for Slide 9 elapses, and then the slide show automatically starts over with Slide 1.
7. After Slide 1 (the title slide) appears on the screen, press the **Esc** key to end the slide show.
8. Save the presentation.

Using the Document Inspector

The Document Inspector is a tool you can use to check a presentation for hidden data, such as the author's name and other personal information, objects that are in the presentation but are hidden or placed in the area next to a slide instead of on the slide, and speaker notes.

Brian wants to be able to send the presentation to small farmers who call into his office looking for information on expanding their selling season and offerings. Before doing so, he wants to ensure there is no hidden data he wouldn't want to distribute. You will check the presentation for hidden data.

To check the presentation using the Document Inspector:

1. With Slide 1 (the title slide) displayed, on the status bar, click the **Notes** button. Notice that there is a note on this slide that Brian added before he gave you the presentation to work with.
2. On the ribbon, click the **File** tab. The Info screen in Backstage view appears. On the right, file properties are listed, including the number of slides in the presentation and the author name. On the left, next to the Check for Issues button, a bulleted list informs you that the presentation contains document properties that you might want to delete, off-slide objects, presentation notes, and content that people with disabilities are unable to read. See Figure 4-24.

Figure 4-24 Info screen in Backstage view

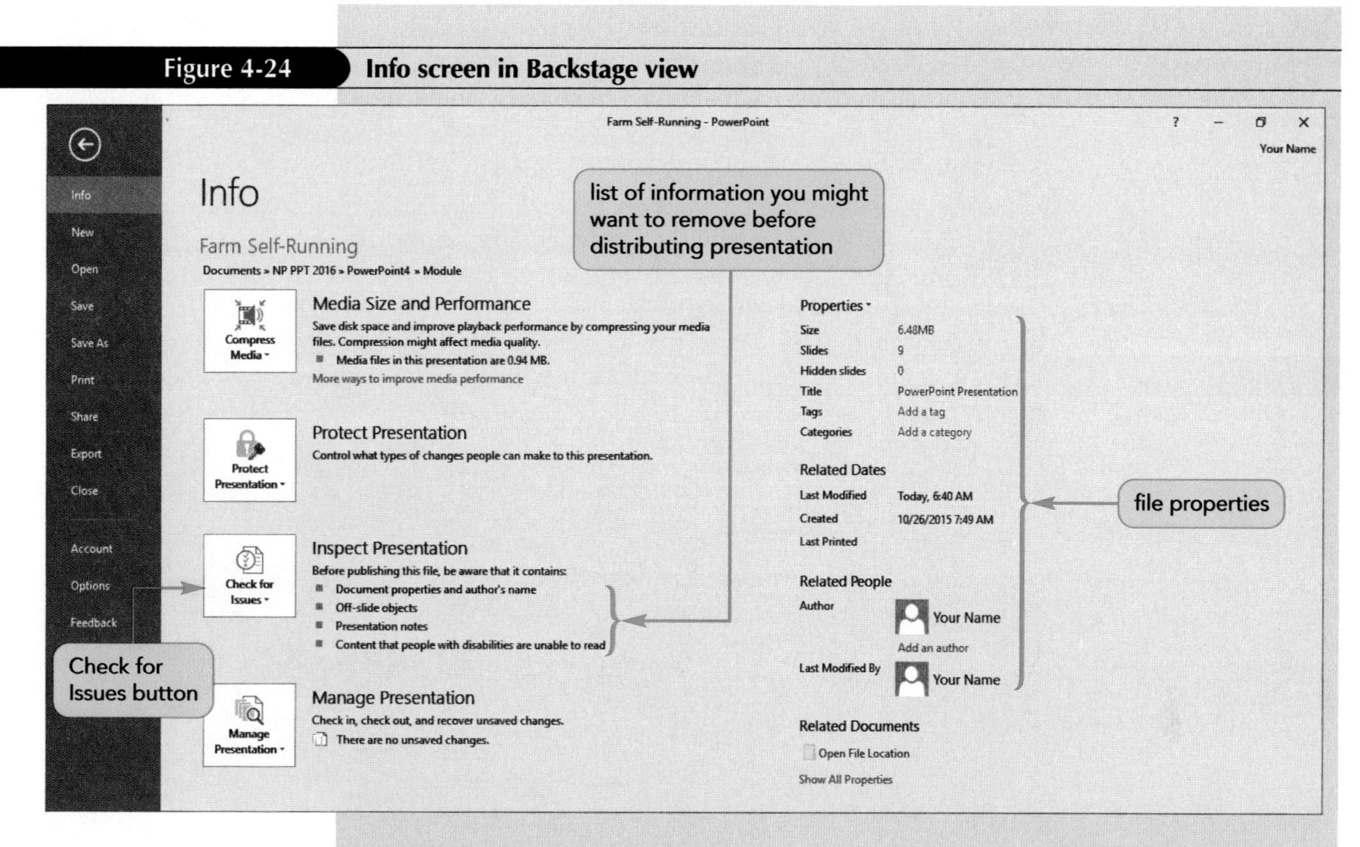

3. Click the **Check for Issues** button, and then click **Inspect Document**. The Document Inspector dialog box opens. All of the visible check boxes are selected. See Figure 4-25.

   Trouble? If a dialog box opens telling you that you need to save the presentation first, click the Yes button to save the presentation.

Figure 4-25 Document Inspector dialog box

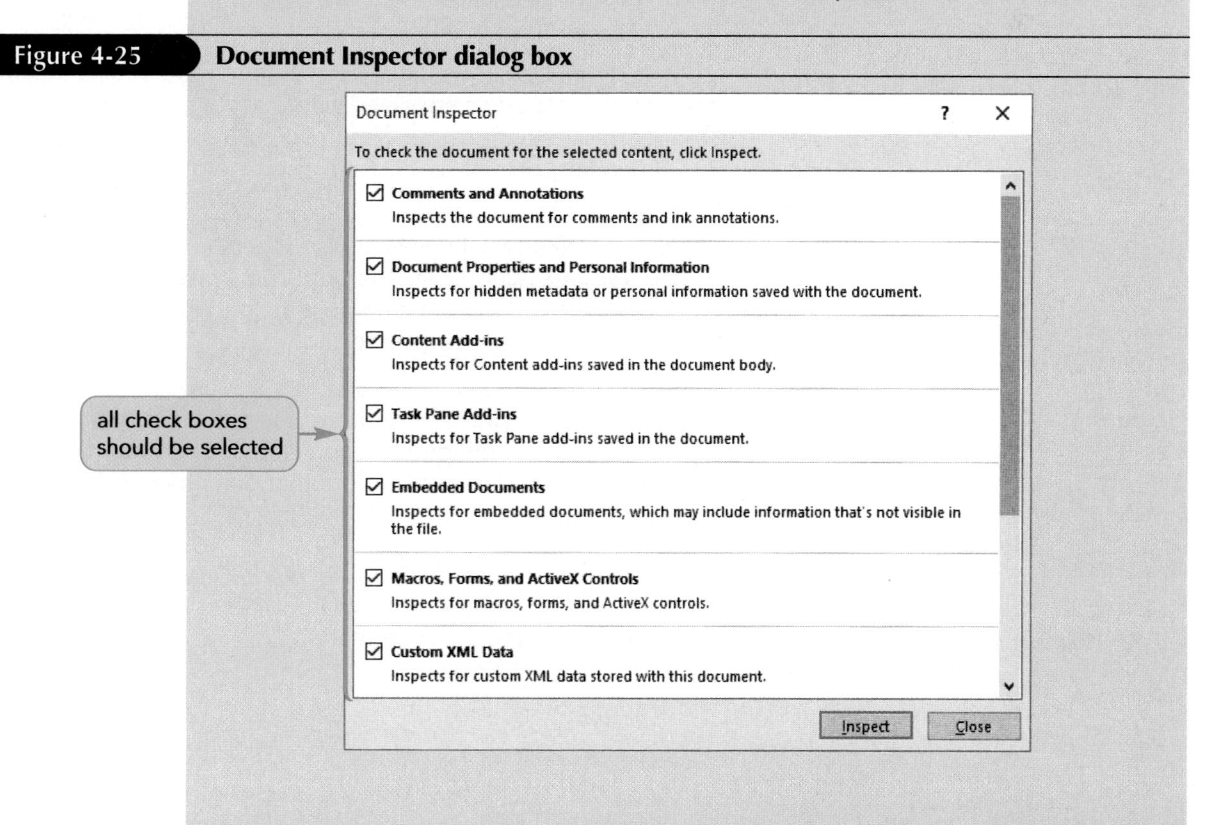

4. Scroll down to the bottom of the list. The Off-Slide Content check box is not selected. Notice that it says that objects that are off-slide that have an animation applied to them will not be flagged, so the wreath that is positioned next to Slide 8 will not be listed as a problem.
5. Click the **Off-Slide Content** check box to select it, and then click the **Inspect** button. After a moment, the Document Inspector dialog box displays the results. Potential problems have a red exclamation point and a Remove All button next to them. See Figure 4-26.

Figure 4-26 Document Inspector dialog box after inspecting the presentation

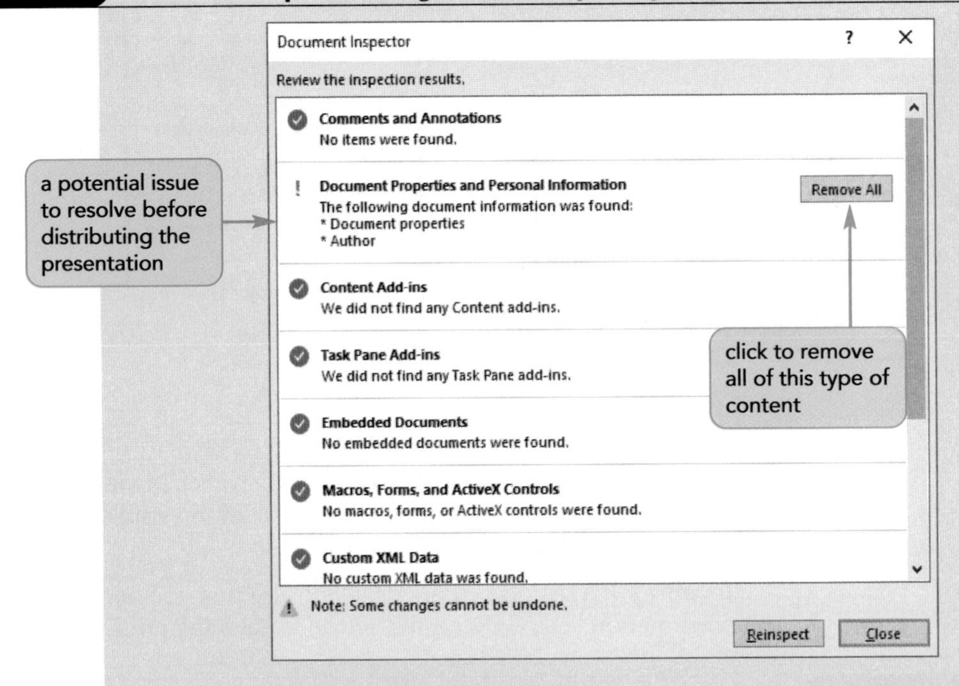

Brian doesn't mind that he is identified as the author of the presentation or that other document properties are saved with the file, so you will not remove the document properties and personal information. You should, however, scroll the Document Inspector dialog to make sure no other potential problems are identified.

6. In the dialog box, scroll down if necessary, and then next to Presentation Notes, click the **Remove All** button. The button disappears, a blue checkmark replaces the red exclamation point next to Presentation Notes, and a message appears in that section telling you that all items were successfully removed.
7. In the dialog box, click the **Close** button, and then, if necessary, click the **Back** button to return to the presentation with Slide 1 (the title slide) displayed in Normal view. The speaker note that Brian had added is no longer in the Notes pane.
8. On the status bar, click the **Notes** button to close the Notes pane.
9. On **Slide 1** (the title slide), replace Brian's name in the subtitle with your name, and then save the changes to the presentation.

Save the changes now because next you will be saving the presentation in a different format.

Packaging a Presentation for CD

Brian will present the slide show at various conventions and exhibitions around New Hampshire. He plans to bring his own laptop, but he knows it's a good idea to have backups. One way to back up a presentation is to use the Package a Presentation for CD feature. This puts all the fonts and linked files and anything else needed to burn and run the presentation on a CD or DVD or in a folder that you can put on a USB drive.

To package the presentation for CD:

1. Click the **File** tab, and then in the navigation bar, click **Export**. The Export screen appears in Backstage view.
2. Click **Package Presentation for CD**. The right side of the screen changes to display a description of this command.
3. Click the **Package for CD** button. The Package for CD dialog box opens. See Figure 4-27.

Figure 4-27 Package for CD dialog box

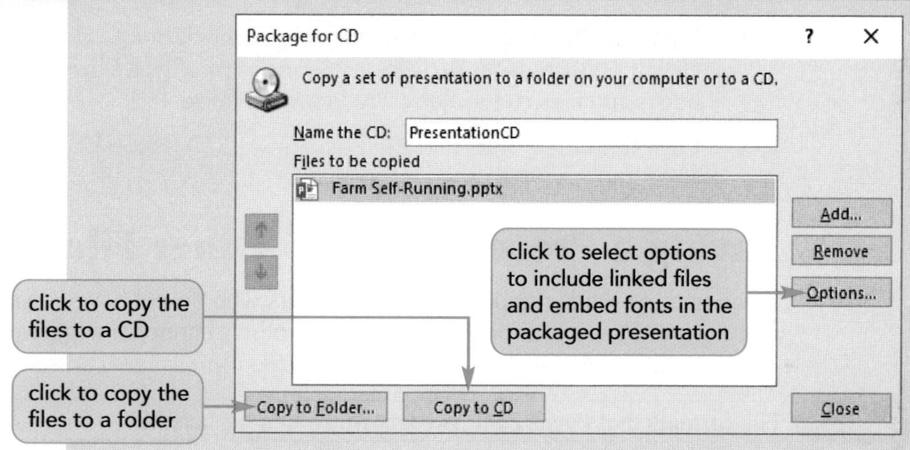

4. Click the **Options** button. The Options dialog box opens. See Figure 4-28.

Figure 4-28 Options dialog box when packaging a presentation for CD

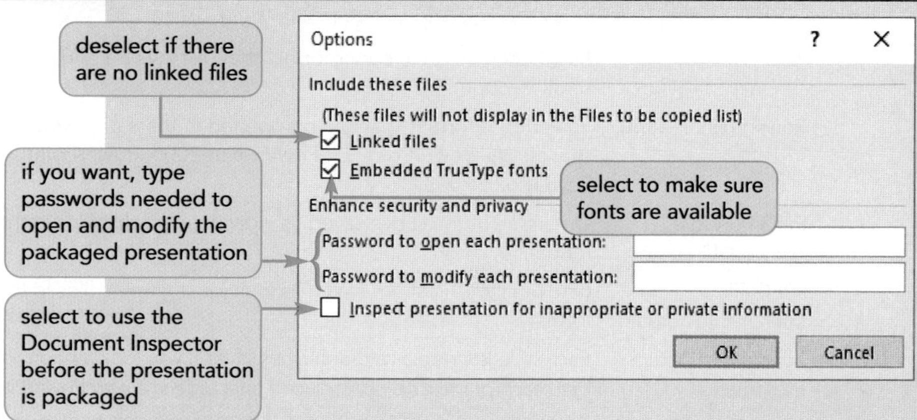

You will keep the Embedded TrueType fonts check box selected to ensure that you will have the fonts used in the presentation available if you run the packaged presentation on another computer. If your presentation contained

links to any other files, you would keep the Linked files check box selected to include those files in the package. However, the presentation file does not contain any linked files, so you will deselect that check box.

5. Click the **Linked files** check box to deselect it.
6. Click the **OK** button. The Package for CD dialog box is visible again.
7. Click the **Copy to Folder** button. The Copy to Folder dialog box opens. The default name for the folder you will create to hold the files of the packaged presentation—PresentationCD—appears in the Folder name box.

   Trouble? If you are copying your presentation to a CD, click the Cancel button to close this dialog box, insert a blank CD in the CD drive, click the Copy to CD button, click the No button when the dialog box opens asking if you want to copy the same files to another CD, and then skip to Step 10.

8. Click in the **Folder name** box, delete the text, and then type **Farm Presentation**.
9. Click the **Browse** button to open the Choose Location dialog box, navigate to the folder where you are storing your files, and then click the **Select** button. You return to the Copy to Folder dialog box.
10. Click the **Open folder when complete** check box to deselect it, and then click the **OK** button. A dialog box opens briefly as PowerPoint copies all the necessary files to the Farm Presentation folder.
11. Click the **Close** button in the Package for CD dialog box.

Saving a Presentation in Other File Formats

If you need to send your presentation to others who do not have PowerPoint 2016, or if you want to save your presentation so that others cannot change it, you can save it in other formats. Figure 4-29 lists several of the file formats you can save a presentation in.

Figure 4-29 **File formats that PowerPoint presentations can be saved in**

File Format	Description
PDF	Portable Document File format, a file format that can be opened on any make or model of computer, as long as a free PDF reader program is installed, such as the Reader app included with Windows 10.
XPS	Microsoft electronic paper format that displays the slides as a list that you can scroll through.
PowerPoint 97-2003	PowerPoint format that can be opened in the earlier versions of PowerPoint, specifically, PowerPoint 97, PowerPoint 2000, PowerPoint 2002, and PowerPoint 2003.
PNG Portable Network Graphics	One or all of the slides saved as individual graphic files in the PNG graphic format.
JPEG File Interchange Format	One or all of the slides saved as individual graphic files in the JPG graphic format.
PowerPoint Picture Presentation	Each slide is saved as a graphic object (as if you took a photo of each slide) and then each graphic object is placed on a slide in a new PowerPoint presentation.
PowerPoint Show	PowerPoint format that automatically opens in Slide Show view if you double-click the file in a File Explorer window.
OpenDocument Presentation	OpenDocument format, a free format that can be read by other presentation programs.
Outline/RTF	The text of the presentation is saved in a Word document.

INSIGHT

Checking a Presentation for Compatibility with Earlier Versions of PowerPoint

If you want to save a presentation in a format compatible with earlier versions of PowerPoint, you should first use the Compatibility Checker to identify features in the presentation that are incompatible with earlier versions of PowerPoint so that you can decide whether to modify the presentation. To do this, click the File tab, and then on the Info screen in Backstage view, click the Check for Issues button, and then click Check Compatibility.

Because the PDF format can be opened on any make or model of computer, it is a good format to choose if you don't know whether the people to whom you distribute the presentation have PowerPoint available. In addition, recipients cannot edit the presentation when it is saved as a PDF. When you save a presentation as a PDF, you can choose the number of slides to include on each page, similar to choosing the number of slides per handout when you print handouts.

Brian wants to be able to email the presentation to small farmers when they contact him for information about expanding their season or services. To ensure that the presentation can be opened and viewed by anyone, regardless of the type of computer they have and the programs they have access to, he asks you to save the presentation in the PDF format. You will save the presentation in the PDF format as a handout with all nine slides on a page.

TIP

You can save a presentation in different file types using the options on the Export screen in Backstage view.

To publish the presentation in PDF format:

1. Click the **File** tab to open Backstage view, and then click **Export** in the navigation bar. The Export screen appears with Create PDF/XPS Document selected.
2. Click the **Create PDF/XPS** button. Backstage view closes, and the Publish as PDF or XPS dialog box opens with PDF listed in the Save as type box. See Figure 4-30.

   Trouble? If XPS appears in the Save as type box instead of PDF, click the Save as type arrow, and then click PDF.

Figure 4-30 Publish as PDF or XPS dialog box

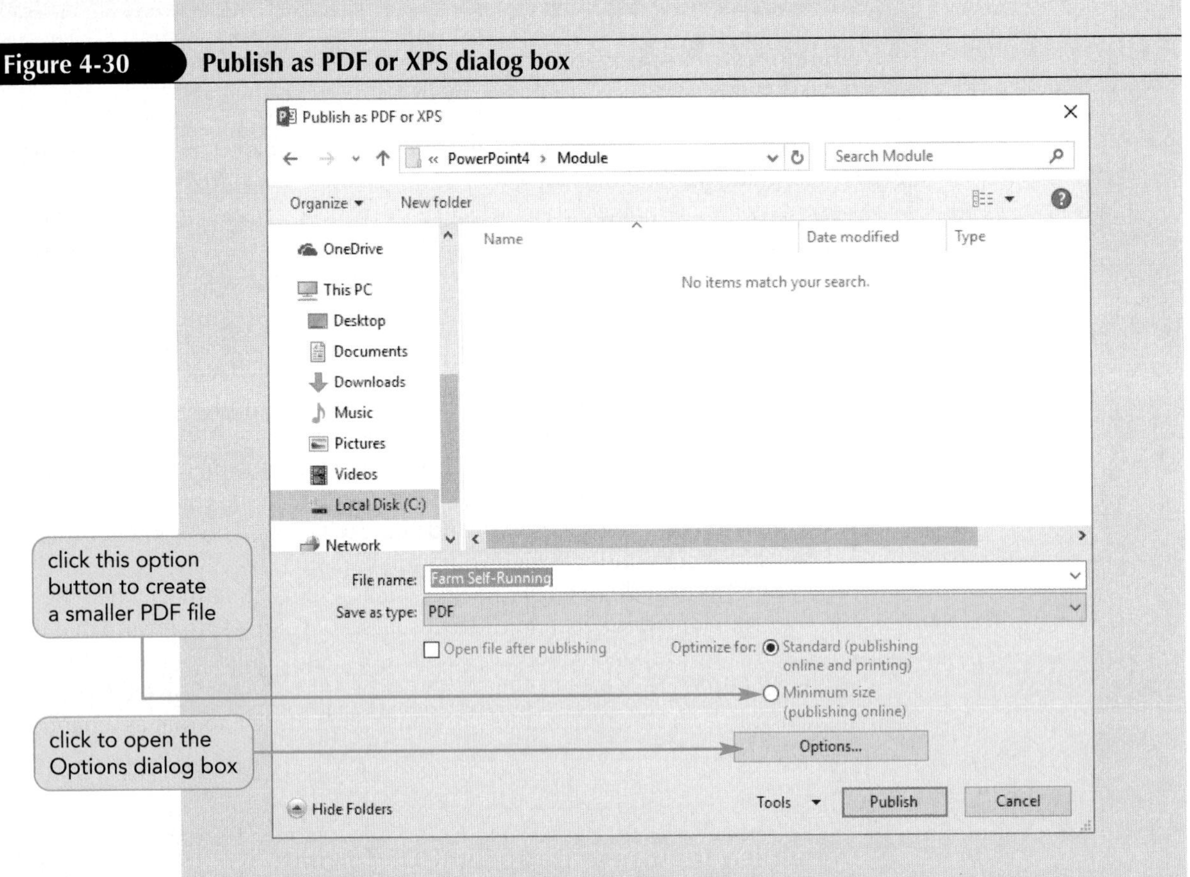

3. Navigate to the location where you are storing your files, if necessary, and then change the filename to **Farm PDF**. You want to create a smaller file size suitable for attaching to an email message.
4. Click the **Minimum size (publishing online)** option button. Now you need to set the option to save it as a handout.
5. Click the **Options** button. The Options dialog box opens. See Figure 4-31.

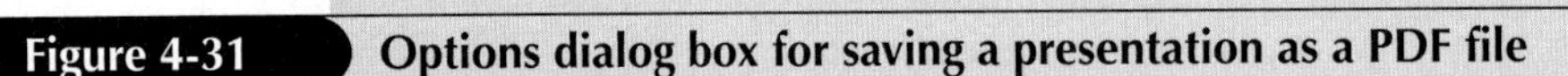

Figure 4-31 Options dialog box for saving a presentation as a PDF file

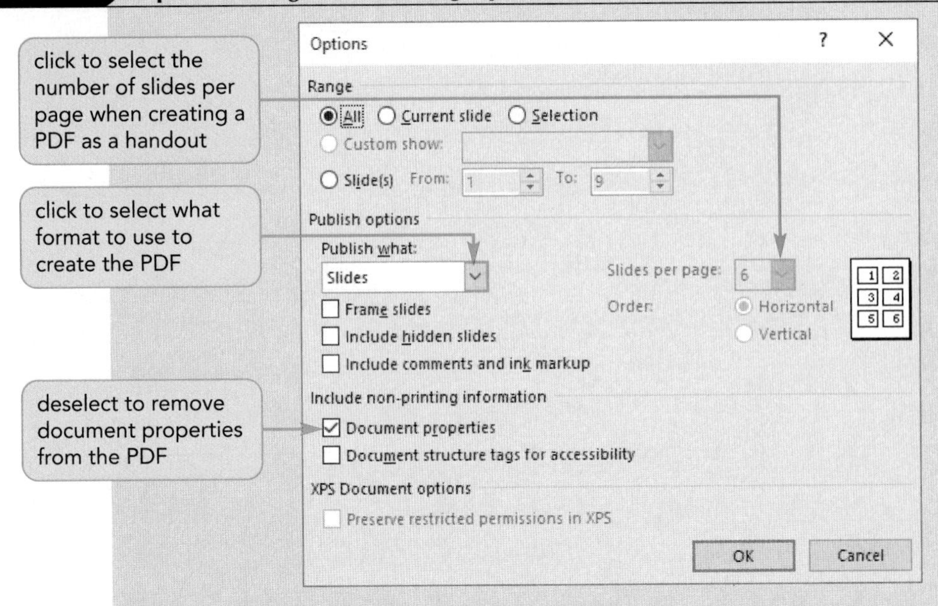

6. In the Publish options section, click the **Publish what** arrow, and then click **Handouts**.
7. In the Publish options section, click the **Slides per page** arrow, and then click **9**. Brian doesn't want the document properties to be included.
8. In the Include non-printing information section, click the **Document properties** check box to deselect it.
9. Click the **OK** button.
10. In the Publish as PDF or XPS dialog box, click the **Open file after publishing** check box to deselect it, if necessary.
11. Click the **Publish** button. A dialog box briefly appears as the presentation is saved in PDF format.

INSIGHT

Saving a Presentation as a Video

You can create a video of your presentation that can be viewed the same way you view any digital video, in an app such as the Movies & TV app included with Windows 10. On the Export screen in Backstage view, click Create a Video. Click the Presentation Quality box to select the video quality you want. Click the box below the box listing the quality to choose whether to use recorded timings and narrations. Then, in the Seconds spent on each slide box, set the number of seconds you want each slide to be displayed if you are not using timings and narrations or for any slides that do not have a saved time. Click the Create Video button to open the Save As dialog box. The MPEG-4 Video file type appears by default in the Save as type box, however, you can change that by clicking the Save as type arrow and then clicking Windows Media Video.

You have finished the Farm Self-Running presentation and ensured that Brian has the presentation in the formats he needs.

REVIEW

Session 4.2 Quick Check

1. How do you change the amount of time a slide stays on the screen during Slide Show view in a self-running presentation?
2. Do links work in a self-running presentation?
3. How do you prevent viewers from using normal methods of advancing the slide show in a self-running presentation?
4. What does the Document Inspector reveal?
5. Why would you package a presentation to a CD?
6. What does the Compatibility Checker reveal?

PRACTICE

Review Assignments

Data Files needed for the Review Assignments: Entrance.jpg, Maze1.pptx; Maze2.pptx

Some small farmers have asked Brian Meyers for suggestions on how to create a corn maze. Specifically, farmers have asked about how to design and build the maze, how to monitor customers in the maze, how to advertise the attraction, and how to set ticket prices. Brian created a presentation that he plans to use when he describes building a corn maze, and he wants your help to finish it. Complete the following steps:

1. Open the file **Maze1**, located in the PowerPoint4 > Review folder included with your Data Files, add your name as the subtitle, and then save the presentation as **Maze Suggestions** to the location where you are saving your files.
2. On Slide 2, display the guides, and then reposition the horizontal guide at 0.42 inches below the middle and the vertical guide at 2.17 inches to the right of center.
3. On Slide 2, position the maze to the left of the slide, keeping its top aligned with the bottom of the title text placeholder. Apply the Lines motion path animation with the Right effect. Adjust the ending of the lines motion path so that the center of the maze is on the intersection of the guides.
4. Add the Spin emphasis animation to the maze. Change its start timing to With Previous, and then change its duration to 1.75 seconds.
5. Change the start timing of the Lines animation to After Previous, and then view Slides 2 and 3 in Slide Show view to ensure that that the motion path applied to the maze on Slide 2 ends at the correct point on the slide so that that when Slide 3 transitions onto the screen it appears seamless.
6. Hide the guides.
7. On Slide 8 ("Pricing"), add the Zoom entrance animation to the text box containing the green dollar sign. Set the Zoom animation to occur when the viewer clicks the title text box.
8. Add a gradient fill to the background of all the slides in the presentation. Change the color of the Stop 1 of 4 tab to Gold, Accent 4, Darker 25%. (Note that after you apply this color, the name of the color changes to Dark Yellow, Accent 4, Darker 25%.) Change the color of the other three tabs to White, Background 1, Darker 5%. Change the Direction to Linear Right, and then change the position of the Stop 2 of 4 tab to 11%.
9. Add the photo **Entrance**, located in the PowerPoint4 > Review folder included with your Data Files, to the background of Slide 1 (the title slide). Tile the picture as texture, and then change the scale to 18% in both directions. Apply the vertical mirror effect.
10. Change the transparency of the photo background on Slide 1 to 50%.
11. On Slide 3 ("Plan"), format each of the bulleted items to links to the corresponding slides.
12. On Slide 4 ("Design and Build"), insert the Octagon shape, and then type **Plan** in the shape. Change the font size to 20 points. Resize the shape so it is 0.5 inches high and 0.9 inches wide. Apply the Intense Effect – Gold, Accent 4 shape style, and then position the shape in the lower-right corner of the slide so there is about one-eighth of an inch between the shape and the right side of the slide and between the shape and the bottom of the slide.
13. Format the Plan shape as a link to the previous slide.
14. Copy the Plan shape on Slide 4 ("Design and Build") to Slide 5 ("Operation"). Edit the link so that it links to Slide 3 ("Plan"), and then copy the Plan shape on Slide 5 to Slides 6 ("Overlooks"), 7 ("Marketing and Insurance"), and 8 ("Pricing").
15. On Slide 3 ("Plan"), insert the End action button to link to the last slide. Format the action button with the Colored Outline – Gold, Accent 4 shape style. Resize the action button so it is one-half inch square, and then position it so that its top is aligned with the bottom of the maze and there is about the same amount of space between its right side and the edge of the slide and between its bottom and the bottom of the slide.
16. Change the color palette so that links are Green, Accent 6, Darker 50%, and then delete the custom palette from your computer.

17. Save the presentation and close it.
18. Open the presentation **Maze2**, add your name as the subtitle, and then save it as **Maze Self-Running** to the location where you are saving your files.
19. Rehearse the timings, displaying the content of each slide for about five seconds, except Slide 2. Display Slide 2 only as long as it takes for the maze to slide onto the screen (one to two seconds) and then immediately display Slide 3. On Slide 3, after the path through the maze, the title, the bulleted list, and the TIPS shape appear, wait five seconds. On Slide 8, wait for the dollar sign to appear, and then wait five seconds.
20. Change the timing of Slide 9 to 10 seconds.
21. Display Slide 3 ("Plan"), and then start recording narration from the current slide. After the title, bulleted list, and TIPS shape appear on the screen, say, **"To skip to the last slide, which contains tips for running the corn maze attraction, click the button in the lower-right corner."** Wait five seconds, and then press the Esc key.
22. Set up the show to be browsed at a kiosk.
23. Run the Document Inspector and then remove anything found, except do not remove the document properties and personal information.
24. Save the changes to the presentation, and then package the presentation to a folder stored in the location where you are saving your files without including linked files. Name the folder **Maze Presentation**, and do not open the folder when complete.
25. Save the presentation file as a PDF named **Maze PDF** in the location where you are saving your files. Use the Minimum size option, remove the document properties, and create a handout with nine slides per page.
26. Close the file.

APPLY

Case Problem 1

Data Files needed for this Case Problem: Parasail.pptx

Carolina Coast Parasailing Ellie Nowicki founded Carolina Coast Parasailing on Hilton Head Island, South Carolina, in 2009. To promote her business, Ellie created a presentation that she gives at travel conventions and tradeshows. She also wants to run it on a kiosk at the hotels on the island. She asked you to help her finish the presentation. Complete the following steps:

1. Open the file **Parasail**, located in the PowerPoint 4 > Case1 folder included with your Data Files, add your name as the subtitle on the title slide, and then save it as **Carolina Coast Parasailing** in the location where you are saving your files.
2. Add a gradient to the background of all the slides. Set the first gradient tab to the Black, Background 1 color and position it at 10%. Change the color of the rest of the gradient tabs to Dark Teal, Background 2 color. Change the position of the second gradient tab to 65%.
3. On Slide 2 ("Come Fly with Us!"), insert the Round Diagonal Corner Rectangle shape and resize it so it is 1.3 inches high and 3.7 inches wide. Fill the shape with the Gold, Accent 5 color, and then apply the Cool Slant bevel effect. Type **Click here to reserve your adventure!** in the shape, change the font size to 20 points, and format the text as bold.
4. On Slide 2, display the guides, and then drag the horizontal guide down to 2.58 inches below center. (Note that in this presentation, this creates a second horizontal guide.) Position the shape so its center is aligned with the bulleted list on the right and so its bottom edge is aligned with the horizontal guide you dragged.
5. On Slide 2, format the shape you drew as a link to the webpage **www.carolinacoastparasailing.example.com/reservations.**

6. Copy the shape you created on Slide 2 to Slide 6 ("Reserve Today!"). On Slide 6, resize the shape so it is two inches high and four inches wide and increase the font size to 32 points. Drag the vertical guide to the right to position it 5.50 inches to the right of center, and then position the shape so its bottom edge is aligned with the horizontal guide in the center of the slide and its right edge is aligned with the vertical guide you just dragged.
7. Customize the color palette so that links are the Teal, Text 2, Lighter 60% color, and then delete the custom palette from your computer.
8. On Slide 3 ("Prices"), drag the silhouette image of the boat towing a parasailer to the left of the slide, keeping it aligned with the bottom of the slide. Animate the image with the Lines motion path and the Right effect, adjusting the end position of the path so it is on top of the vertical guide in the center of the slide. Set this animation to occur automatically after the previous action.
9. On Slide 3, add a second Lines motion path animation with the Right effect to the image. Position the end point of the second motion path to the right of the slide so that the faint image of the graphic is all the way off of the slide. Then adjust the starting point of the second Lines motion path so it is on top of the vertical guide in the center of the slide. Change the start timing of this animation to After Previous with a delay of one second.
10. On Slide 3, apply the Bold Reveal emphasis animation to the text box that contains the text "Price includes." Move this animation earlier so that the first Lines animation applied to the boat occurs first, then the emphasis animation applied to the text box, and finally the second Lines animation applied to the boat. Set the emphasis animation to occur automatically after the previous action with a delay of one-half second.
11. On Slide 4 ("Safety"), drag the life preserver off the slide to the left, keeping the top of the object aligned with the top of the slide. Apply the Lines motion path animation with the Right effect. Adjust the end point of the motion path so it is on top of the vertical guide positioned 5.50 inches to the right of center. Change the duration of the animation to 2.25 seconds, and change the start timing to After Previous.
12. On Slide 4, add the Spin emphasis animation to the life preserver. Set the Spin animation to occur at the same time as the Lines animation.
13. Rehearse the timings. Leave Slide 1 (the title slide) and Slide 2 ("Come Fly with Us!") displayed for five seconds. After Slide 3 ("Prices") appears, wait for the boat to move onto the slide, then for the text in the text box on the right to change to bold, then for the boat to leave the slide, and then wait for five seconds. After Slide 4 ("Safety") appears, wait for the life preserver to appear on the slide, wait five seconds and then advance the slide show. Leave the last two slides displayed for about five seconds each.
14. Record the presentation from the beginning. After Slide 1 appears, say, **"Carolina Coast Parasailing, where the fun never stops!"** Wait five seconds, and then press the Esc key to end the slide show.
15. Change the timing of Slide 2 ("Come Fly with Us!") to 10 seconds.
16. Set the slide show to be browsed at a kiosk.
17. Run the Document Inspector to remove notes, and then save the changes to the presentation.
18. Package the presentation in a folder named **Parasailing Presentation** in the location where you are saving your files. Do not include linked files.
19. Save the presentation as a PDF named **Carolina Coast Parasailing PDF** in the location where you are saving your files. Use the Minimum size option, remove the document properties, and create a handout with six slides per page.
20. Close the presentation.

TROUBLESHOOT

Case Problem 2

Data Files needed for this Case Problem: Race.pptx, Runners.jpg

Road Race Management Fiona Spaulding works for Road Race Management, a company in Wilmington, Delaware, that organizes road races for organizations and cities or provides guidance so that they can organize the races themselves. Harborside Homeless Shelter recently asked Road Race Management for assistance in organizing a new, annual road race whose proceeds will benefit the shelter. Fiona prepared a PowerPoint presentation and asked you to help her complete it. Complete the following steps:

1. Open the presentation **Race**, located in the PowerPoint4 > Case2 folder included with your Data Files, add your name as the subtitle, and then save the presentation with the filename **Race Planning**.
2. Add the picture **Runners**, located in the PowerPoint4 > Case2 folder, as the slide background. Change the transparency to 80%, and apply this to all the slides.
3. On Slide 1 (the title slide), change the background's transparency to 25%.
4. **Troubleshoot** On Slide 1, evaluate the problem changing the background caused and make any adjustments needed to correct this.
5. On Slide 6 ("Registration"), format the "Running in the USA" subbullet so it is a link to **www.runningintheusa.com**; format the "Road Race Runner" subbullet so it is a link to **www.roadracerunner.com**; and format the subbullet "Runner's World" so it is a link to **www.runnersworld.com**.
6. **Troubleshoot** On Slide 6, evaluate the problem formatting the text as links caused and correct it.
7. On Slide 7 ("Budget Items"), display the guides. Position the horizontal guide 3.58 inches below the center.
8. Reposition the text box that contains "Try to find a corporate sponsor" so its bottom edge is aligned with the horizontal guide and so its center is aligned with the vertical guide.
9. Animate the text box that contains "Try to find a corporate sponsor" with the Grow & Turn entrance animation, and then make the medal the trigger for this animation.
10. Add the Wave emphasis animation to the text box that contains "Try to find a corporate sponsor." Set its start timing to After Previous. Move this animation later so that it appears after the Trigger animation in the Animation Pane.
11. On Slide 7, animate the left gray and red ribbon with the Wipe entrance animation and the From Top effect, and set its start timing so that it animates automatically after the previous action. Then animate the right gray and red ribbon with the Wipe entrance animation and the From Bottom effect, and set its start timing so that it animates automatically after the previous action.
12. On Slide 8 ("Get the Word Out"), start recording from the current slide and say, **"Although every planning step is important, if you don't let people know about your new race, you won't have any participants."** Press the Esc key to end the slide show.
13. On Slide 9 ("Contact Information"), change the background to the Tan, Background 2 color.
14. Change the color palette so that links are Aqua, Accent 5, Darker 50%, and then delete the custom palette from your computer.
15. Save the changes to the presentation, and then close it.

CHALLENGE

Case Problem 3

Data Files needed for this Case Problem: Coach.pptx

Kid Coach Mara Riggs and John Sunjata own Kid Coach, a company that runs sports clinics for children in Thousand Oaks, California. They periodically visit schools and parent groups to explain the programs they offer. Mara created a presentation that they can use during these visits. She asked you to help her finish the presentation. Complete the following steps:

1. Open the presentation **Coach**, located in the PowerPoint4 > Case3 folder included with your Data Files, add your name as the subtitle, and then save the presentation with the filename **Kid Coach**.
2. On Slide 1 (the title slide), change the slide background to a gradient fill. Change the color of the Stop 1 of 4 gradient tab to the Turquoise, Accent 1, Darker 50% color. Change the color of the Stop 4 of 4 gradient tab to the White, Background 1, Darker 5% color. Change the color of the Stop 3 of 4 gradient tab to the Turquoise, Accent 1, Lighter 80% color, and then change its position to 97%. Change the color of the Stop 2 of 4 gradient tab to the Turquoise, Accent 1, Lighter 40% color, and then change its position to 92%. Change the type to Rectangular and the direction to From Center, if necessary. Do not apply the background to all the slides.
3. On Slide 1, change the color of the title and subtitle text to White, Background 1, Darker 5%.
4. On Slide 3 ("Sports Offered"), format each of the images as a link to the appropriate slide.
5. On Slide 4 ("Baseball Softball"), drag the white baseball off of the slide to the left and position it below the bottom-left corner of the slide. Apply the Lines animation to the baseball with the Up effect. Change the start timing to After Previous and the duration to 1.50. Do the same thing to the yellow softball, except position it off of the slide above the upper-left corner of the slide and leave the Lines effect as Down.
6. Create a copy of the vertical guide and drag the copy to 3.50 inches to the right of center. Create a copy of the horizontal guide and drag the copy to 1.75 inches above center. Then create another copy of the horizontal guide and drag it to 1.50 inches below center.
7. On Slide 4, adjust the ending points of both motion paths so they are each a diagonal line that ends on top of the intersections of the guides above and below center with the baseball ending above center and the softball ending below center.
8. On Slide 5 ("Lacrosse Soccer"), apply the entrance animation Fade to the lacrosse stick, set the start timing to After Previous, and set a delay of one-half second.
9. On Slide 5, drag the center horizontal guide down so it is 2.92 inches below center. (It will be aligned with the bottom of the blue and gray rectangles.)

Explore 10. Change the color of the bottom horizontal guide to red. (*Hint*: Right-click the guide.)

11. Drag the soccer ball off of the slide to the left keeping the ball between the two horizontal guides. (*Hint*: Press and hold the Alt key to have the ball not snap to the grid as you position it.)
12. Apply the Lines motion path animation to the soccer ball, and change its effect to Right. Drag the ending point of this animation to the right until the right edge of the soccer ball is touching the left side of the gray bar on the right side of the slide. (*Hint*: Again, press and hold the Alt key if needed to position the ending point where you want it.)
13. On Slide 5, apply a second Lines animation to the soccer ball, and change its effect to Left. Position its starting point on top of the ending point of the first motion path, and then position its end point on top of the vertical guide at 3.50 inches to the right of center.
14. On Slide 5, change the duration of the two Lines animations to one second. Set the start timing of both Lines animations to After Previous.

Explore 15. On Slide 5, add a 0.75-second bounce effect to the Lines animation. (*Hint*: Click the Dialog Box Launcher in the Animation group on the Animations tab to open the Effect Options dialog box for the Lines animation.)

16. On Slide 6 ("Basketball Volleyball"), drag the basketball straight up so it is above the slide, and then apply the Lines motion path animation. Drag the end point of the motion path down so that the bottom of the basketball is touching the bottom horizontal guide. Change its start timing to After Previous and its duration to 1.50 seconds.
17. On Slide 6, drag the vertical guide that is in the center of the slide to the left until it is 0.13 inches to the left of center. Apply a second Lines motion path to the basketball with the Right effect, and change its start timing to After Previous and its duration to 0.75 seconds. Adjust the start point so it is aligned with the end point of the first Lines animation that you applied to the basketball. Adjust the end point of the second Lines animation so that the right side of the basketball is touching the vertical guide you just moved.
18. On Slide 6, add the Spin emphasis animation as the third animation applied to the basketball. Change its start timing to With Previous and its duration to 0.75 seconds.
19. On Slide 6, drag the volleyball off of the slide to the left. Apply the Arcs motion path animation with the Up effect to the volleyball. Drag the end point of the arc path so that the bottom of the faint image of the volleyball is aligned with the bottom horizontal guide and the ending point is on top of the vertical guide positioned at 3.50 inches to the right of center. Finally, drag the top-middle sizing handle of the arc animation up until the top of the rectangle that defines the arc object is aligned with the smart guide that appears above "Basketball" above the bulleted list on the left. Change the start timing to After Previous.
20. On Slide 7 ("FAQs"), apply the Appear entrance animation to each answer, and then set the corresponding question for each question to be the trigger for that animation.

Explore 21. On Slide 8 ("Registration"), record the following: **"Go to www.kidcoach.example.com to register."** (*Hint*: Use the Audio button in the Media group on the Insert tab.) Set the audio clip to play automatically and hide it during the slide show.

22. Save the changes to the presentation, and then use the Document Inspector to remove document properties and the author's name.

Explore 23. Save Slide 1 (the title slide) as a PNG Portable Network Graphics file named **Kid Coach Slide 1** in the location where you are saving your files.

24. Save the presentation as a handout PDF with nine slides per page named **Kid Coach PDF** to the location where you are saving your files. Use the minimum size for publishing.
25. Save the changes, and then close the file.

CHALLENGE

Case Problem 4

Data Files needed for this Case Problem: Starlight.pptx

Starlight Fundraising Matt Elliott is an account manager at Starlight Fundraising, a company in Boulder, Colorado, that runs fundraisers for schools and nonprofit organizations. Starlight offers a wide variety of products that people can sell. All fundraising companies give a percentage of the profits to the schools and organizations, but the percentage that Starlight returns to the groups is among the highest. One of Matt's jobs is to convince schools to allow Starlight to run their fundraisers. He asked you to help him prepare his presentation. Complete the following steps:

1. Open the presentation **Starlight**, located in the PowerPoint4 > Case4 folder included with your Data Files, add your name as the subtitle, and then save the presentation with the filename **Starlight Fundraising**.
2. Display the guides, and then drag the horizontal guide up to 2.00 inches above the center and the vertical guide right to 4.29 inches to the right of the center.
3. On Slide 1 (the title slide), drag the picture of the star that is to the right of the slide title off of the slide to the right, and position it so that it is top-aligned with the subtitle text box.
4. Apply the Lines motion path animation to the star with the Up effect.

5. Change the ending of the motion path so it is on top of the intersection of the guides, and then hide the guides. Change the duration of the Lines animation to 0.50 seconds.
6. Add the Grow/Shrink emphasis animation to the picture of the star. Change its duration to one second, and set it to occur automatically after the previous action.
7. **Explore** On Slide 1 only, add the 90% pattern to the slide background using the Foreground color Dark Blue, Text 2.
8. **Explore** On Slide 2, format each shape in the SmartArt as a link to the corresponding slide.
9. On Slide 2, add the End action button that links to the last slide. Resize it so it is 0.6 inches high and one inch wide. Apply the Semitransparent – Blue, Accent 1, No Outline shape style to the action button. Position the action button in the lower-left corner of the slide about one-eighth inch from the left and bottom edges of the slide.
10. On Slide 3 ("Large Variety of Items"), open the Selection pane to see that each picture is listed and that the bulleted list is actually five separate text boxes. Apply the Appear entrance animation to each of the five images. For each Appear animation, set a trigger so that when you click the corresponding text box, the image appears.
11. On Slide 3, insert a rounded rectangle, and then type **Overview** in the rectangle. Resize the rectangle so it is 0.6 inches high and 1.5 inches wide. Apply the Intense Effect – Blue, Accent 1 shape style, and then make the text bold. Position the Overview shape in the lower-left corner so there is about one-eighth of an inch between it and the left and bottom sides of the slide.
12. Format the Overview shape as a link to Slide 2 ("Overview"), and then copy this shape to Slide 4 ("High Percentage of Sales Returned to School") and Slide 5 ("Dedicated Support").
13. Use the Document Inspector to remove off-slide content. Save the changes to the presentation.
14. Use the Package Presentation for CD command to package the presentation to a folder named **Fundraising Presentation** in the location where you are storing your files, making sure to embed fonts and without including linked files.
15. **Explore** Save the presentation as an outline in the RTF format with the filename **Starlight Fundraising Outline**. (*Hint*: Use the Save as type box in the Save As dialog box.)
16. **Explore** Save the presentation in a format compatible with PowerPoint 97-2003 in the location where you are saving your files. Name the file **Starlight Fundraising Earlier Version**.
17. Close the presentation.

MODULE 5

Integrating PowerPoint with Other Programs

Creating a Presentation for a Rowing Convention

POWERPOINT

OBJECTIVES

Session 5.1
- Import a Word outline
- Reset slides
- Reuse slides from another presentation
- Work in Outline view
- Create sections in a presentation
- Move objects through layers on a slide
- Use the Effect Options dialog box to modify animations

Session 5.2
- Embed an Excel worksheet
- Link an Excel chart
- Format a chart with advanced options
- Embed a Word table
- Format a table with advanced options
- Annotate slides during a slide show
- Create handouts in Microsoft Word

Case | *Newburgh College Rowing Team*

Andrew Foreman has been the head coach of the rowing team at Newburgh College in Newburgh, New York, for the past 10 years. Although some coaches have a hard time attracting and retaining first-time rowers (called novices), Andrew consistently retains 90 percent of his novices. He has been asked to give a presentation describing his approach for coaching novices at an upcoming convention for rowing coaches.

In this module, you will import a Word outline to create slides and insert slides from another presentation. You will also divide a presentation into sections, layer objects on a slide, apply advanced animation effects, and embed and link objects created in other programs. Finally, you will annotate slides during a slide show and create handouts in Microsoft Word.

STARTING DATA FILES

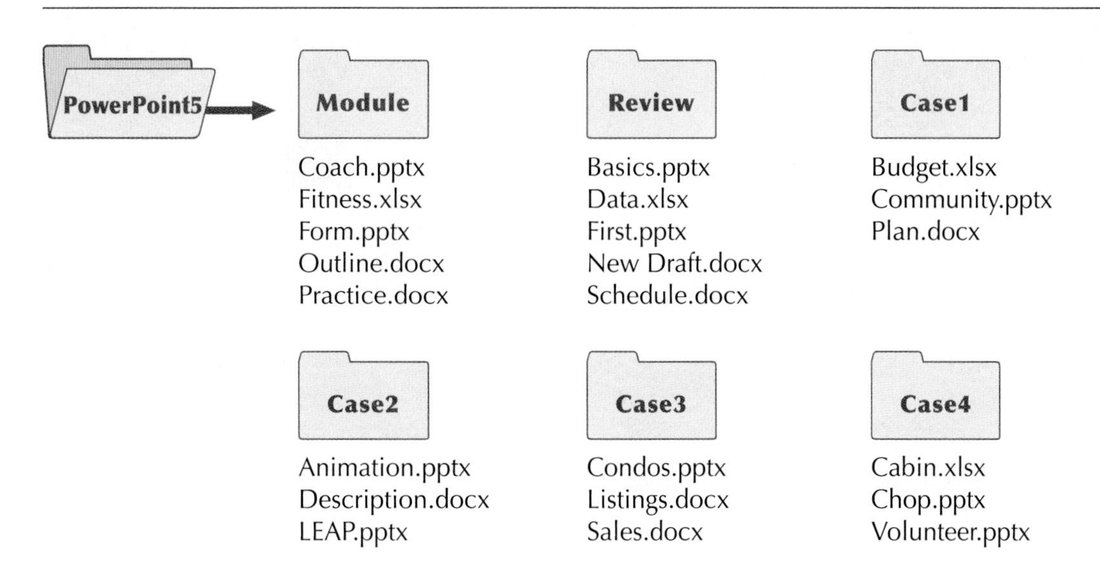

Session 5.1 Visual Overview:

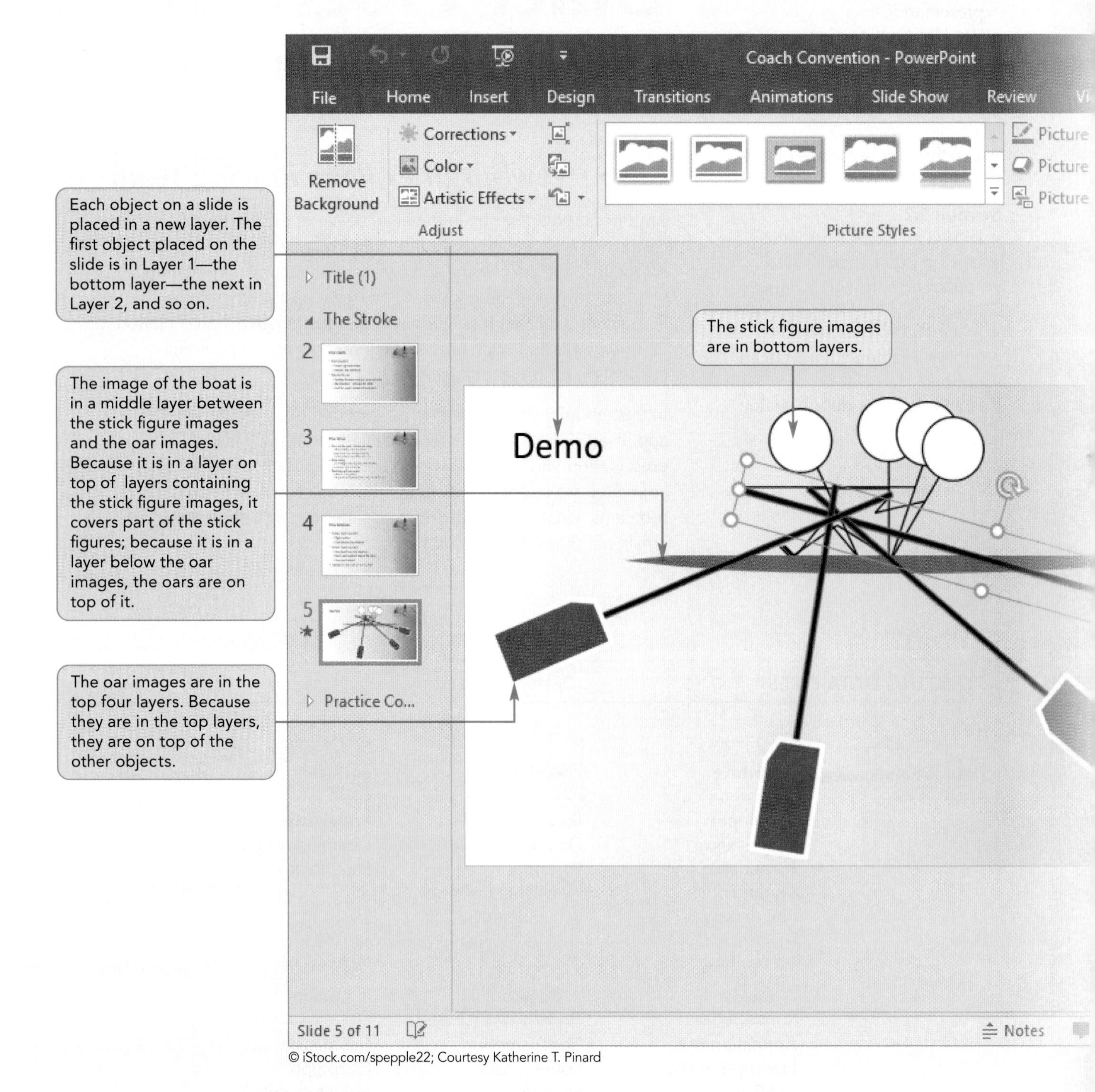

© iStock.com/spepple22; Courtesy Katherine T. Pinard

Understanding Layers

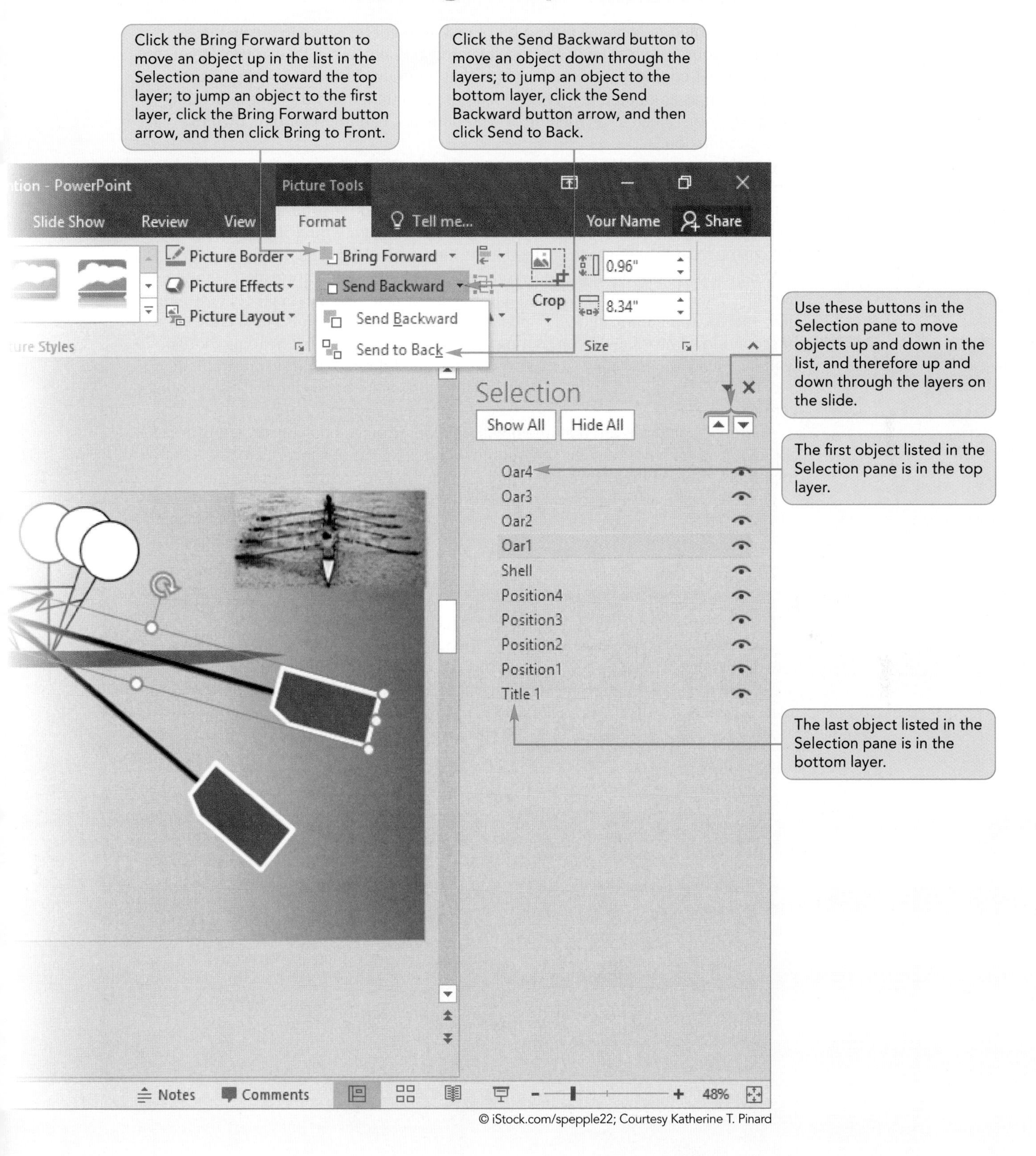

Creating a Presentation by Importing a Word Outline

If your presentation contains quite a bit of text, it might be easier to create the outline of your presentation in Microsoft Word, so that you can take advantage of the extensive text-editing features available in that program. Fortunately, if you create your presentation as an outline in a Word document and utilize Word's built-in heading styles, you don't need to retype it in PowerPoint; you can import it directly into your presentation.

In order to import a Word outline, the outline levels in the document need to be formatted with the Word Heading styles. For example, the first-level items in the outline need to be formatted with the Heading 1 style, the second-level items need to be formatted with the Heading 2 style, and so on. In Word, you do this by clicking the style name in the Styles group on the Home tab.

When you import the formatted Word outline, each heading formatted with the Heading 1 style in Word (also called a level-one or first-level heading) becomes a slide title; each heading formatted with the Heading 2 style in Word (also called a level-two or second-level heading) becomes a first-level bulleted item; each heading formatted with the Heading 3 style in Word (also called a level-three or third-level heading) becomes a second-level bulleted item—that is, a subitem below the first-level bulleted items—and so on.

Andrew created a Word document with text describing coaching suggestions. He applied heading styles to create an outline with text at various levels. He asks you to import his outline into a PowerPoint presentation that he created with a custom theme.

First you will examine the outline in Word.

To examine the Word outline:

1. Start Microsoft Word 2016, open the document **Outline**, located in the PowerPoint5 > Module folder included with your Data Files, and then scroll down a little so that "Timing" in the first line of the document is at the top of the document window. The document contains an outline, and the insertion point is in the first line. On the Home tab on the ribbon, in the Styles group, the Heading 1 style is selected. This heading will become a slide title. See Figure 5-1.

Figure 5-1 Outline in Word document

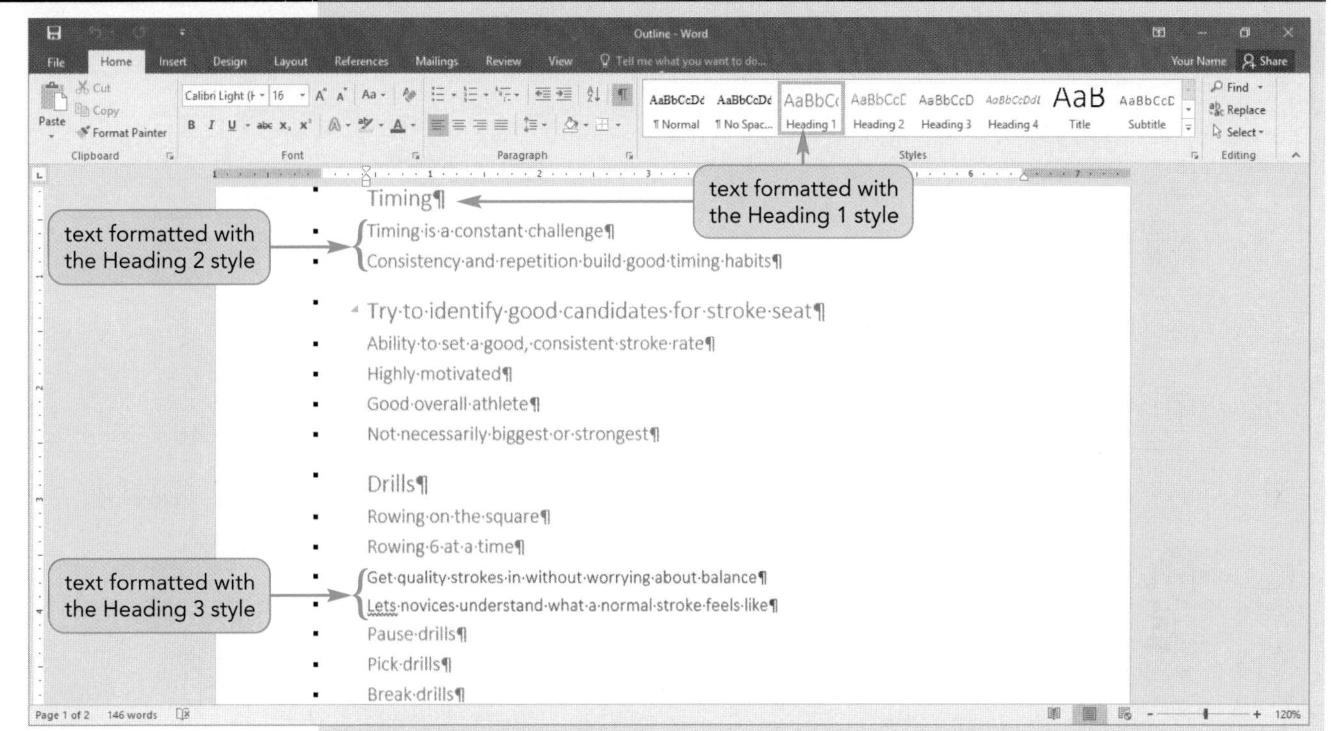

Trouble? If you don't see the dots to the left of each line and the paragraph marks at the end of each line, click the Show/Hide button ¶ in the Paragraph group on the Home tab.

2. Press the ↓ key. The insertion point moves down one line, and in the Styles group, the Heading 2 style is selected. This heading will become a first-level bullet on a slide.
3. Near the bottom of the screen, click anywhere in the line that starts "Get quality strokes." In the Styles group, the Heading 3 style is selected. This heading will become a second-level bullet on a slide.
4. Close the document.

Now you will import the outline into PowerPoint. You do this using a command on the New Slide button menu.

TIP

If imported content on a slide creates a bulleted list that is too long, use the Add or Remove Columns button in the Paragraph group on the Home tab to arrange text in multiple columns.

To import the Word outline into a presentation:

1. Open the presentation **Coach** from the PowerPoint5 > Module folder included with your Data Files, and then save the file with the filename **Coach Convention** to the location where you are saving your files. The presentation consists of only a title slide. See Figure 5-2.

Figure 5-2 Coach Convention presentation

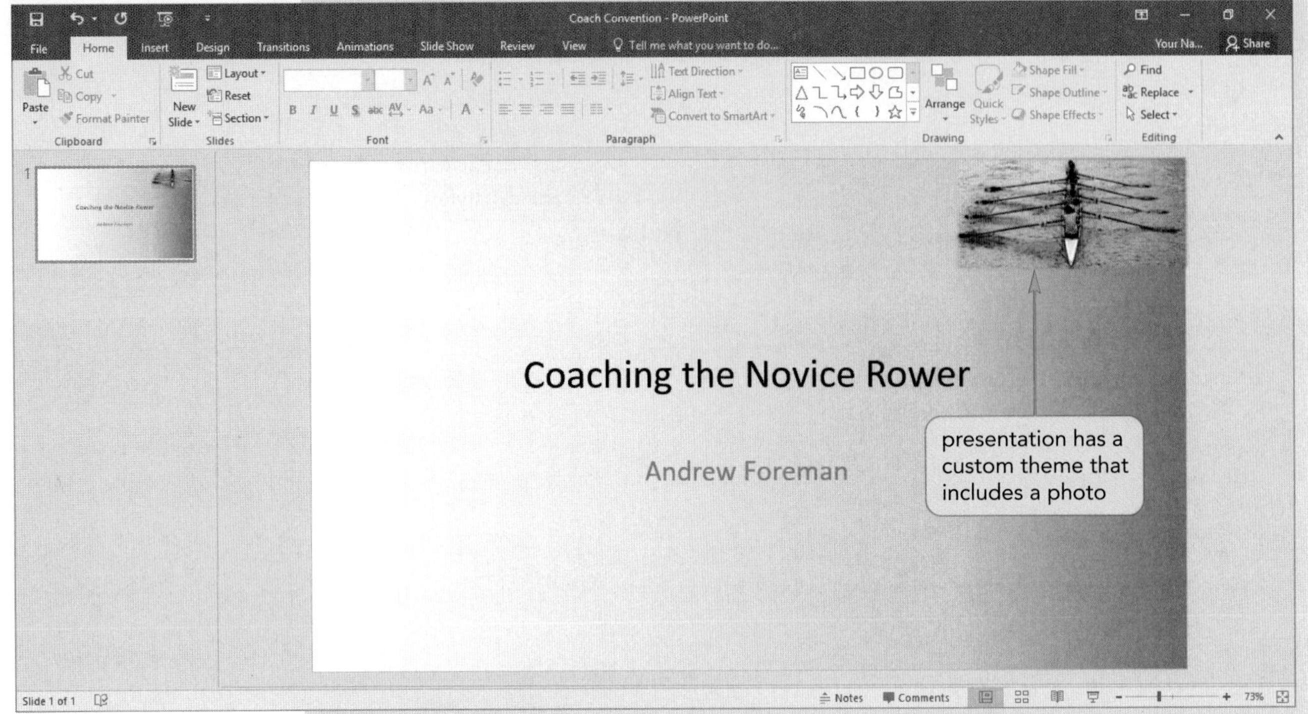

© iStock.com/spepple22

2. On the Home tab, in the Slides group, click the **New Slide button arrow**, and then click **Slides from Outline**. The Insert Outline dialog box opens.
3. Navigate to the PowerPoint5 > Module folder, click **Outline**, and then click the **Insert** button. The Word outline is inserted as new slides after the current slide in the PowerPoint presentation, with all the Heading 1 text becoming new slide titles. Slide 2 is displayed. See Figure 5-3.

Figure 5-3 Presentation with slides created from imported Word outline

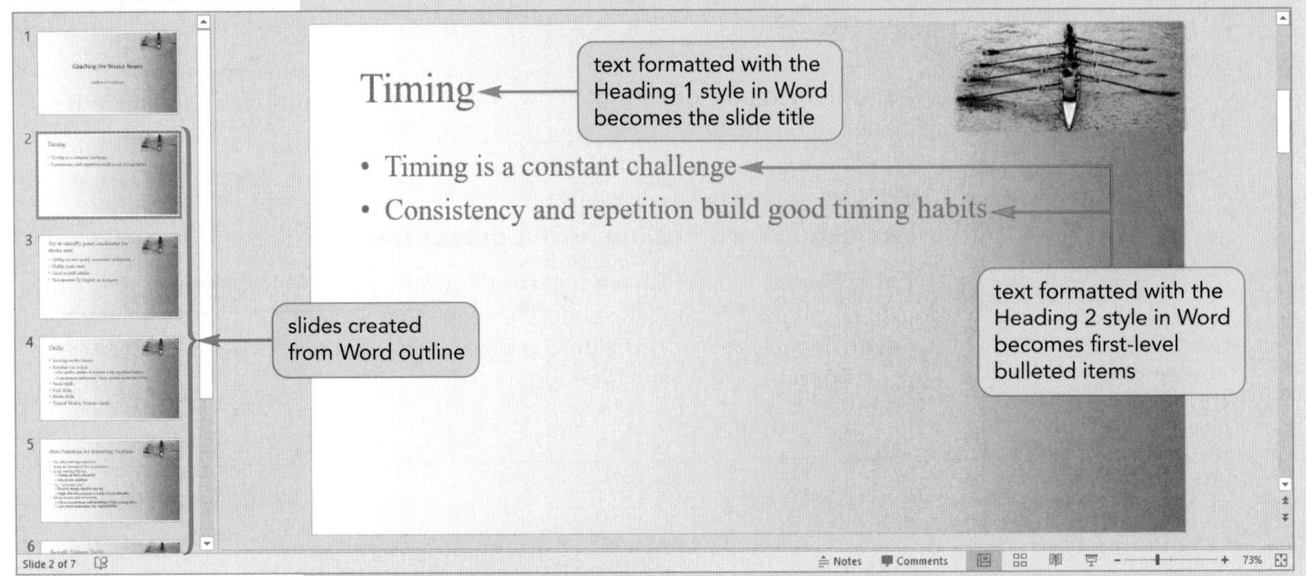

© iStock.com/spepple22

4. In the Slides group, click the **Layout** button. Notice that a new layout, Title and Text, was created and applied. This layout was applied to all of the slides created by importing the outline.
5. Press the **Esc** key to close the Layout menu.

Notice that the text of the slides created by importing the outline retained the fonts and text colors of the outline document rather than picking up those of the presentation theme. You can fix this by resetting the slides.

Resetting Slides

You can reset a slide any time that formatting is changed unexpectedly or isn't applied as you intended, or if placeholders are modified. To do this, you use the Reset button in the Slides group on the Home tab. When you reset slides, you reset every object on the slides, so if you reset slides that contain objects, you might need to reposition the objects or reapply styles. You'll reset the slides created when you imported the Word outline.

To reset the slides:

1. In the Slides pane, click the **Slide 2** thumbnail, if necessary.
2. In the Slides pane, scroll down to the bottom, press and hold the **Shift** key, and then click the **Slide 7** thumbnail.
3. On the Home tab, in the Slides group, click the **Reset** button. The slides are reset to match the presentation theme so the font changes to black Calibri. See Figure 5-4.

Figure 5-4 **Slides reset to presentation theme**

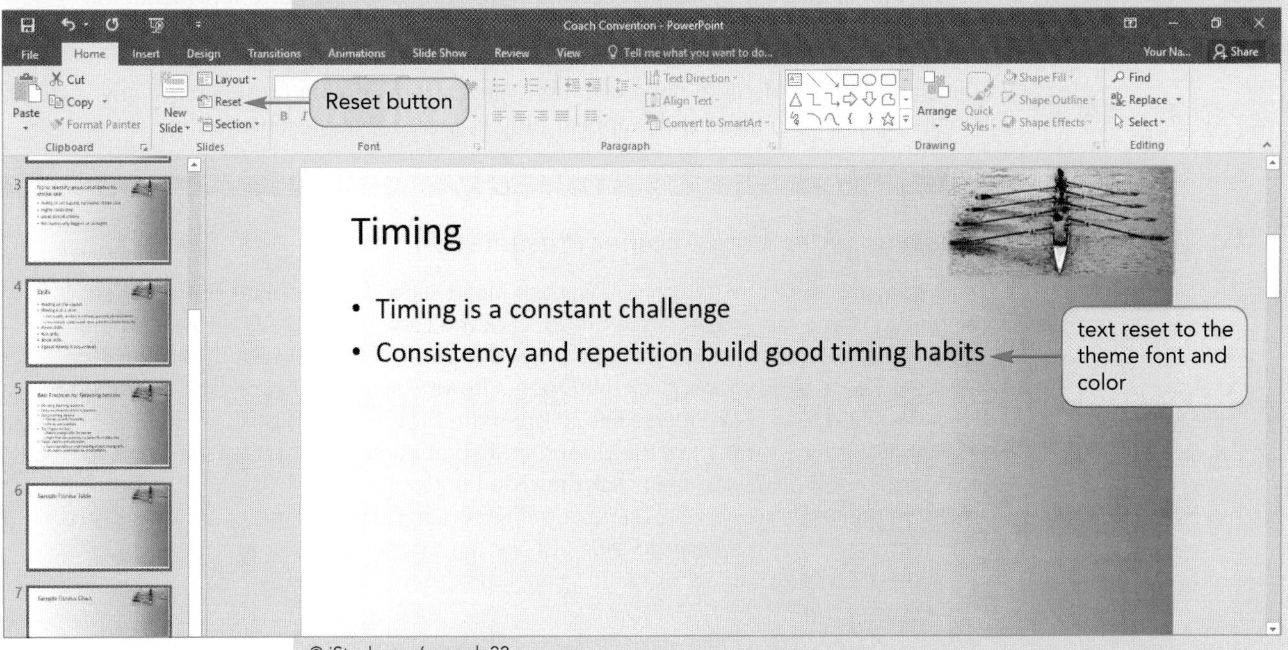

© iStock.com/spepple22

4. Save the changes to the presentation.

The imported Word outline is now in the PowerPoint presentation with the custom theme of the Coach Convention presentation applied. Because you imported the outline, the text is now part of PowerPoint and has no relationship with the Outline Word file.

INSIGHT

Changing Slide Size and Orientation

The default for PowerPoint presentations is to be formatted for wide screen displays at a ratio of 16 to 9. You can change this if you need to. To do this, click the Slide Size button in the Customize group on the Design tab. To change the slide size to a 4:3 ratio, click Standard (4:3) on the menu. To select other sizes or to create a custom size, click Custom Slide Size to open the Slide Size dialog box, and then select the size from the Slides sized for list. Slides in a presentation can be in landscape (wider than tall) or portrait (taller than wide) orientation. Handouts can also be formatted in either orientation. To change the orientation of slides or handouts, open the Slide Size dialog box. In the Orientation section of the dialog box, click the Portrait or Landscape option button in the Slides or Notes, Handouts, & Outline sections.

Inserting Slides from Another Presentation

TIP

To display two open presentations side by side, click the View tab, and then in the Window group, click the Arrange All button.

In addition to importing a Word outline, you can insert slides from another presentation. To do this, you can open the second presentation in Slide Sorter view and then use the familiar Copy command to copy a slide. In the presentation in which you want to paste the copied slide, switch to Slide Sorter view, click the location where you want to paste the copied slide, and then use the Paste command. You can paste the slide using the destination theme or the source formatting.

You can also use the Reuse Slides command. When you do this, you open the Reuse Slides pane, in which you can access the slides from another presentation or a slide library. Then you click the slides you want to insert. If the inserted slides have a different theme than the current presentation, the design of the current presentation will override the design of the inserted slides as long as the Keep source formatting check box at the bottom of the Reuse Slides pane is selected.

Like an imported outline, once you insert slides from another presentation, any changes you make to those slides appear only in the current presentation.

REFERENCE

Reusing Slides from Another Presentation

- Display the slide after which you want to insert slides from another presentation.
- On the Home tab, in the Slides group, click the New Slide button arrow, and then click Reuse Slides to display the Reuse Slides pane.
- In the Reuse Slides pane, click the Open a PowerPoint File link, or click the Browse button, and then click Browse File to open the Browse dialog box.
- Navigate to the location of the presentation that contains the slides you want to insert, click the file, and then click the Open button.
- In the Reuse Slides pane, make sure the Keep source formatting check box is not selected to force the inserted slides to use the theme in the current presentation, or click the Keep source formatting check box to retain the theme of the slides you want to import.
- In the Reuse Slides pane, click each slide that you want to insert into the current presentation.

Andrew asked his assistant coach, Shawna Cooper, to create slides that describe the proper form a rower should have. Shawna started but has not completed the slides yet. You will insert the slides that she created into the Coach Convention presentation and then help Andrew finish them.

To insert slides from another presentation:

1. Display **Slide 1** (the title slide). You want to insert the slides from Shawna's presentation after Slide 1.
2. On the Home tab, in the Slides group, click the **New Slide button arrow**, and then click **Reuse Slides**. The Reuse Slides pane opens. See Figure 5-5.

Figure 5-5 **Reuse Slides pane**

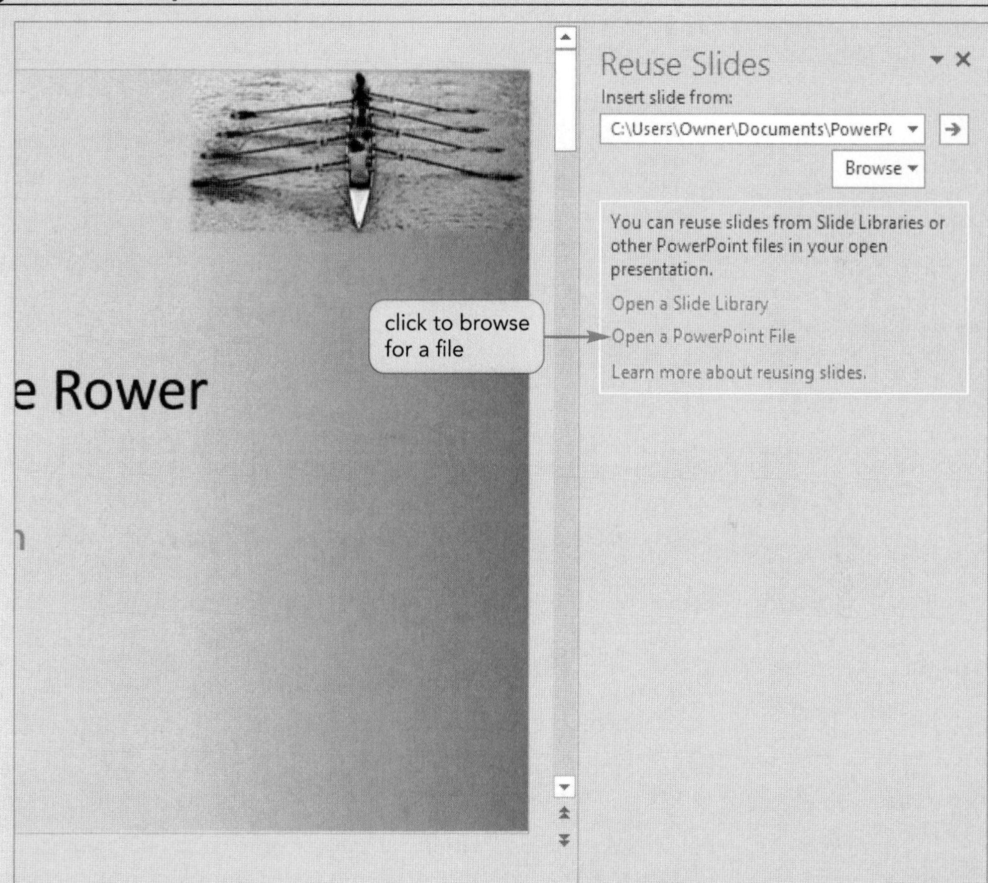

© iStock.com/spepple22

3. In the Reuse Slides pane, click the **Open a PowerPoint File** link. The Browse dialog box opens.
4. Navigate to the PowerPoint5 > Module folder, click **Form**, and then click the **Open** button. Thumbnails of the five slides in the Form presentation appear in the Reuse Slides pane. The theme applied to this presentation is different from the theme applied to the Coach Convention presentation. At the bottom of the pane, the Keep source formatting check box is unchecked. See Figure 5-6.

Figure 5-6 Reuse Slides pane with slides from another presentation

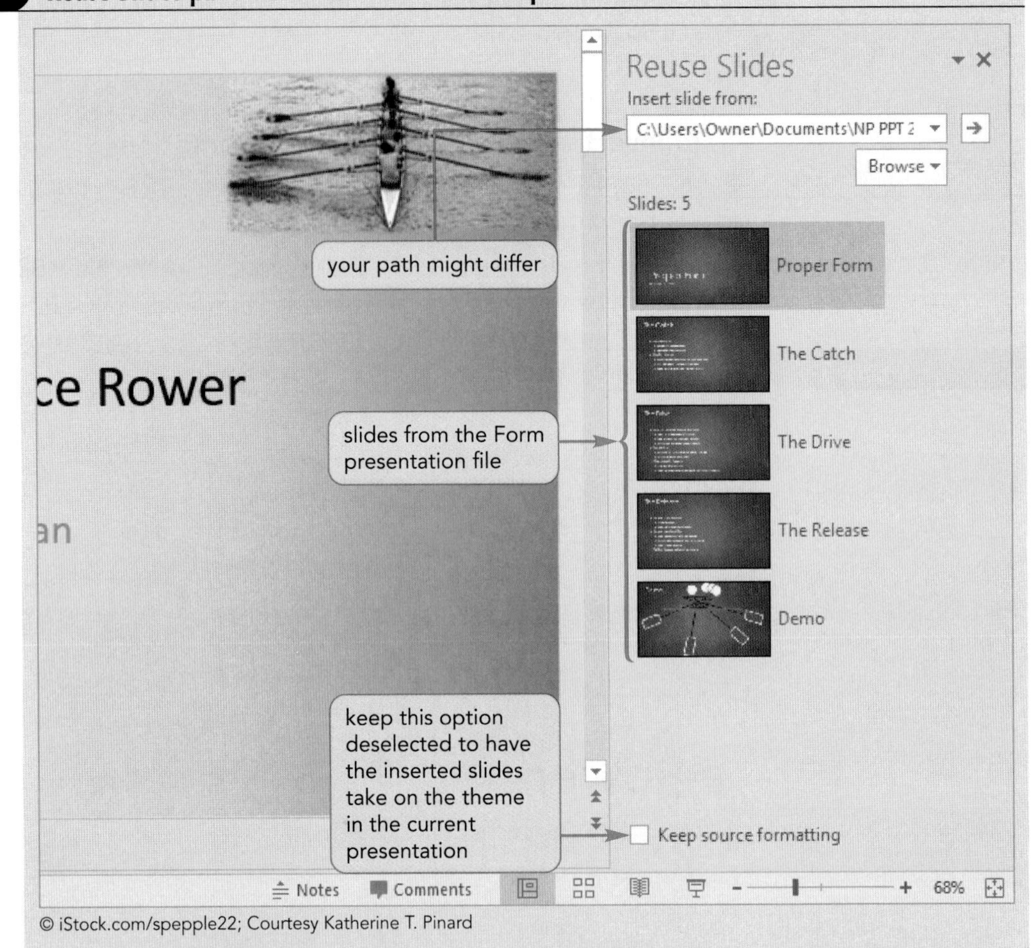

© iStock.com/spepple22; Courtesy Katherine T. Pinard

5. In the Reuse Slides pane, click the **The Catch**, which is the second slide. The slide is inserted into the Coach Convention presentation after the current slide (Slide 1). Because the Keep source formatting check box is unchecked, the theme used in the Coach Convention presentation is applied to the slide instead of the theme used in the Form presentation.
6. In the Reuse Slides task pane, click **The Drive**, click **The Release**, and then click **Demo**. The slides are added to the Coach Convention presentation.
7. In the Reuse Slides pane title bar, click the **Close** button ✕.
8. Save the changes to the presentation.

The four slides you inserted from the Form presentation are now Slides 2 through 5 in the Coach Convention presentation.

INSIGHT

Using Slides from a Slide Library

A **slide library** is a collection of slides saved as individual files on a SharePoint server. Slide libraries are often used in businesses so that coworkers can share slides that are commonly needed. To add slides to a slide library, click the File tab, click Share in the navigation pane, click Publish Slides, and then click the Publish Slides button. This opens the Publish Slides dialog box. Click the check boxes next to the slides you want to add to the slide library. To select the location of the slide library, click the Browse button, navigate to the location of the library, and then click the Select button. Finally, click the Publish button. To display slides in a slide library in the Reuse Slides pane, click the Open a Slide Library link, navigate to the location of the library, click the folder containing the library, and then click the Select button. Note that you must have access to a SharePoint server to add slides to or reuse slides from a slide library.

Working in Outline View

Outline view displays the outline of the presentation in the Outline pane, which appears in place of the Slides pane. In Outline view, the Slides pane, containing the slide thumbnails, is not visible. In the Outline pane, presentation text is arranged as in an ordinary outline. Slide titles are the top levels in the outline, and the slide content—that is, the bulleted lists—are indented below the slide titles.

You can use the Outline pane to see the outline of the entire presentation, move text around, and even change the order of slides. For example, you can move a bulleted item from one slide to another, change a subitem into a first-level item, or change a bulleted item into a slide title, creating a new slide.

Moving an item higher in the outline by, for example, changing a second-level bullet into a first-level bullet or changing a first-level bulleted item into a slide title, is called **promoting** the item. Moving an item lower in the outline by, for example, changing a slide title into a bulleted item on the previous slide or changing a first-level bullet into a second-level bullet, is called **demoting** the item.

The Coach Convention presentation has material from two sources, Andrew's outline and Shawna's presentation. The presentation needs some organizing. You will do this in the Outline pane in Outline view.

To modify the presentation outline in Outline view:

1. On the ribbon, click the **View** tab, and then in the Presentation Views group, click the **Outline View** button. The Outline pane, listing the outline of the presentation, replaces the Slides pane, and the Notes pane becomes visible as well. See Figure 5-7.

Figure 5-7 Outline pane in Outline view

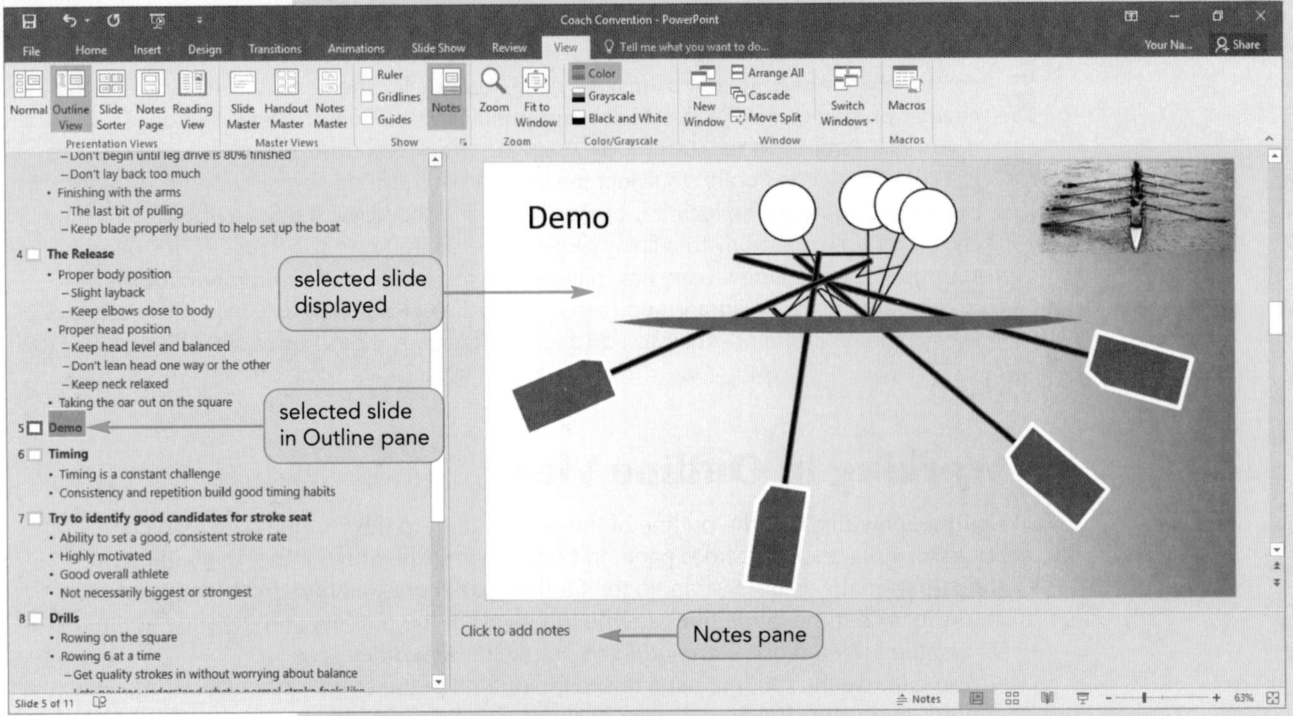

© iStock.com/spepple22; Courtesy Katherine T. Pinard

You need to demote the text on Slide 7 ("Try to identify good candidates for stroke seat") so it is part of Slide 6 ("Timing").

2. In the Outline pane, point to the **Slide 7** slide icon so that the pointer changes to , and then click the **Slide 7** slide icon . All the text on Slide 7 is selected in the Outline pane, and Slide 7 is displayed.

3. Press the **Tab** key. The selected text is demoted so that the slide title becomes the last first-level bullet on Slide 6, and the items that were first-level items on Slide 7 indent to become second-level items on Slide 6.

Now you need to promote one of the bulleted items on Slide 7 ("Drills") so it becomes a slide title.

4. Scroll to the bottom of the Outline pane, and then on Slide 7 ("Drills"), click the bullet next to "Typical Weekly Practice Goals."

5. On the ribbon, click the **Home** tab, and then in the Paragraph group, click the **Decrease List Level** button . "Typical Weekly Practice Goals" becomes the title for a new Slide 8.

Now you need to move Slide 9 ("Best Practices for Retaining Novices") so it appears after Slide 11 ("Sample Fitness Chart").

6. Point to the **Slide 9** slide icon so that the pointer changes to , press and hold the mouse button, and then drag the slide icon down so that the horizontal line indicating the position of the item you are dragging appears below Slide 11 as shown in Figure 5-8.

Figure 5-8 Dragging an item in the Outline pane

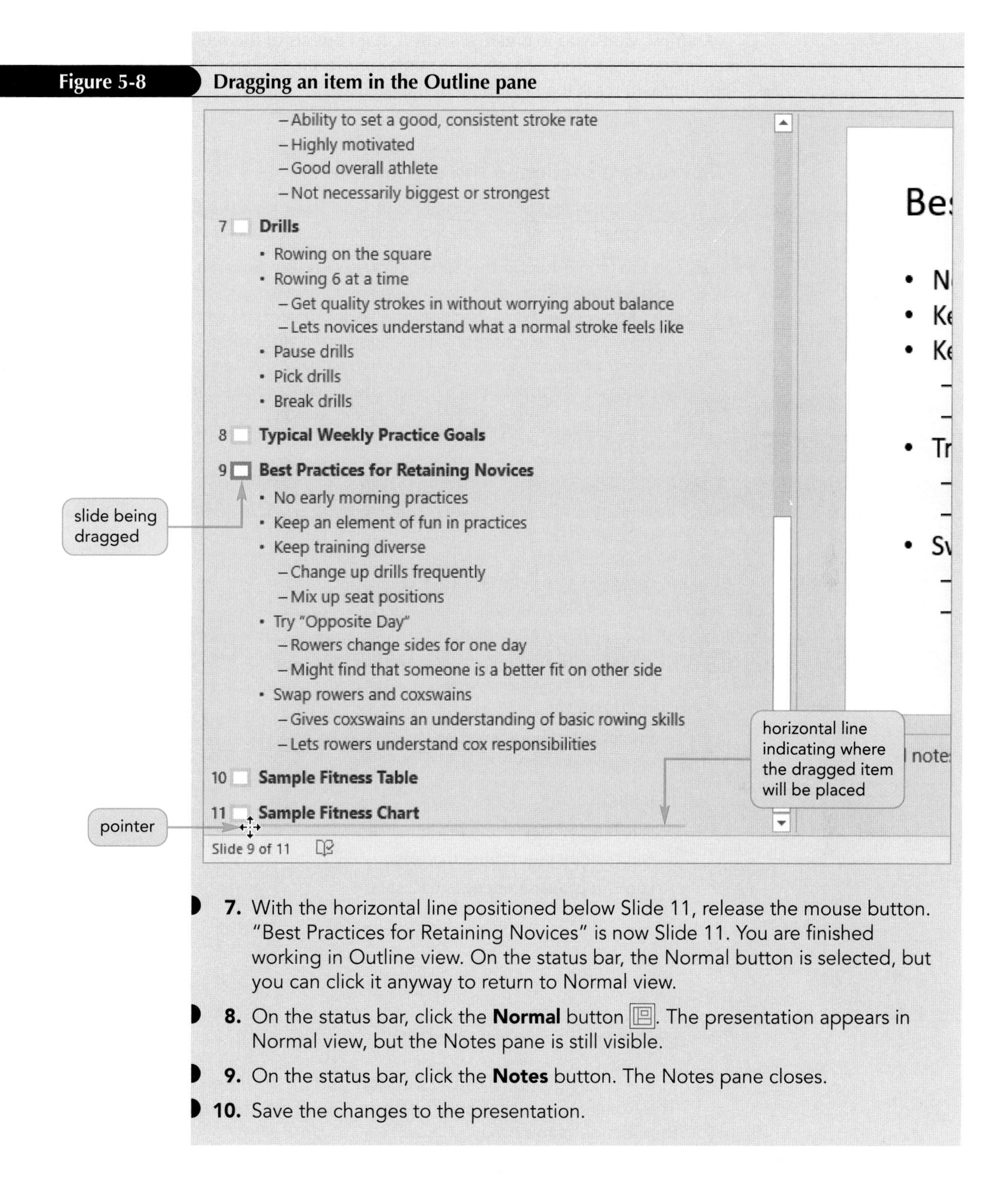

7. With the horizontal line positioned below Slide 11, release the mouse button. "Best Practices for Retaining Novices" is now Slide 11. You are finished working in Outline view. On the status bar, the Normal button is selected, but you can click it anyway to return to Normal view.
8. On the status bar, click the **Normal** button. The presentation appears in Normal view, but the Notes pane is still visible.
9. On the status bar, click the **Notes** button. The Notes pane closes.
10. Save the changes to the presentation.

Dividing a Presentation into Sections

If you are working with a long presentation, it can be helpful to divide it into sections. Presentation sections are designed to help the presentation creator work with and manage a presentation with many slides.

Andrew wants you to create a section that consists of the four slides that describe the rowing stroke from Shawna's presentation. To do this, you need to first select the slide that will mark the beginning of the section.

To create a section in the presentation:

1. Scroll to the top of the Slides pane, and then click the **Slide 2** ("The Catch") thumbnail. This will be the first slide in the section you will create.
2. On the Home tab, in the Slides group, click the **Section** button, and then click **Add Section**. The new section is created and is named "Untitled Section" in the Slides pane. Slide 2 and all the slides after it are selected. See Figure 5-9. When you create a section that starts with a slide after Slide 1, all the slides before it are placed in a different section, and this section is titled Default Section. At the top of the Slides pane, Slide 1 appears in the Default Section.

Figure 5-9 New section

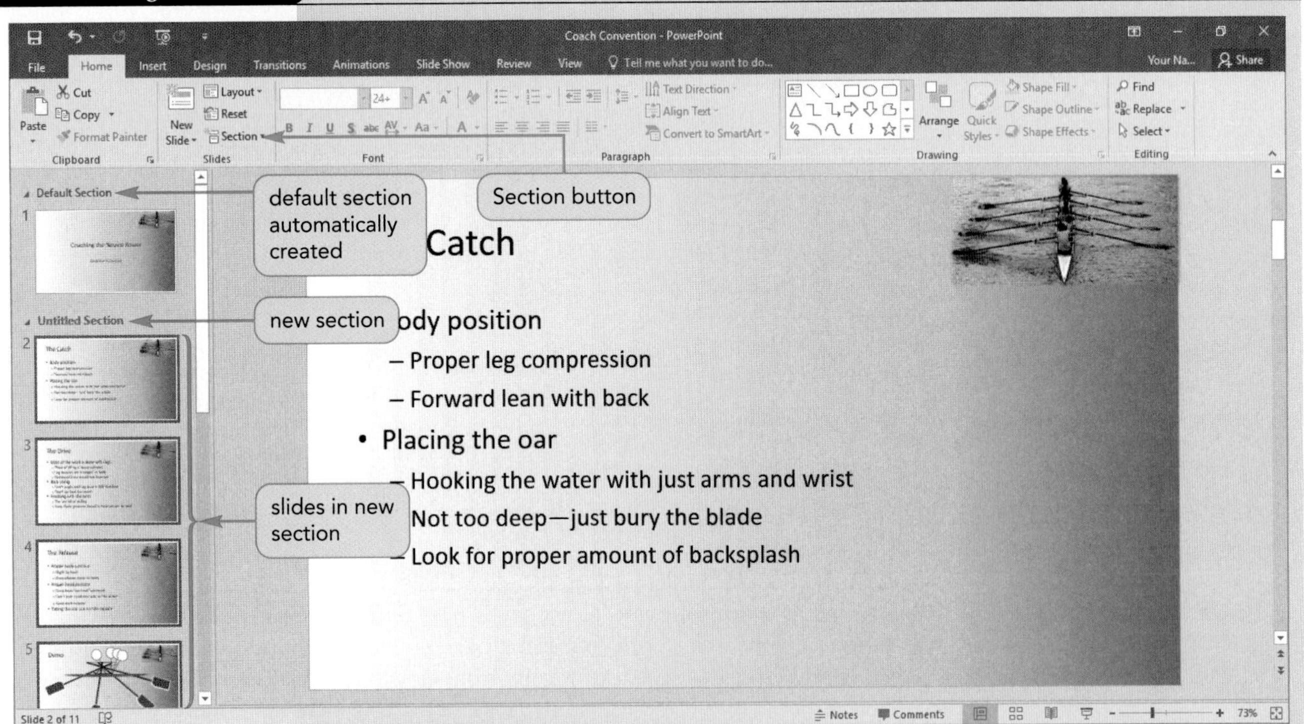

© iStock.com/spepple22; Courtesy Katherine T. Pinard

3. In the Slides group, click the **Section** button, and then click **Rename Section**. The Rename Section dialog box opens with the temporary name selected in the Section name box.
4. In the Section name box, type **The Stroke**, and then click the **Rename** button. The section is renamed.

TIP

If different people are responsible for different sections, consider naming each section with the name of the person responsible for that section.

The new section should include only the four slides that Shawna created. To fix this, you need to create another section that includes the last three slides in the presentation. Also, at the top of the Slides pane, the section name "Default Section" appears. That section includes only Slide 1. You will rename this section.

To create more sections in the presentation:

1. In the Slides pane, scroll down, and then click the **Slide 6** thumbnail.
2. Right-click the **Slide 6** thumbnail, and then on the shortcut menu, click **Add Section**.
3. In the Slides pane, right-click **Untitled Section**, and then on the shortcut menu, click **Rename Section** to open the Rename Section dialog box.
4. Type **Practice Concerns**, and then click the **Rename** button.
5. Scroll to the top of the Slides pane, and then rename the Default Section as **Title**.

TIP

You can also work with sections in Slide Sorter view.

Sections can be collapsed, allowing you to focus on one section of slides at a time. This is helpful when you are working on a presentation with many slides because you can collapse the sections containing slides you are not working on. You'll collapse the sections now.

To collapse sections:

1. In the Slides pane, next to the section name "Title," click the **Collapse Section** arrow. The section is collapsed, and the number 1 appears after the section name; this is the number of slides in the section.
2. In the Slides pane, next to the section name "The Stroke," click the **Collapse Section** arrow. The section collapses, and the number 4 appears after the section name.
3. Collapse the **Practice Concerns** sections. See Figure 5-10.

Figure 5-10 Collapsed sections in the Slides pane

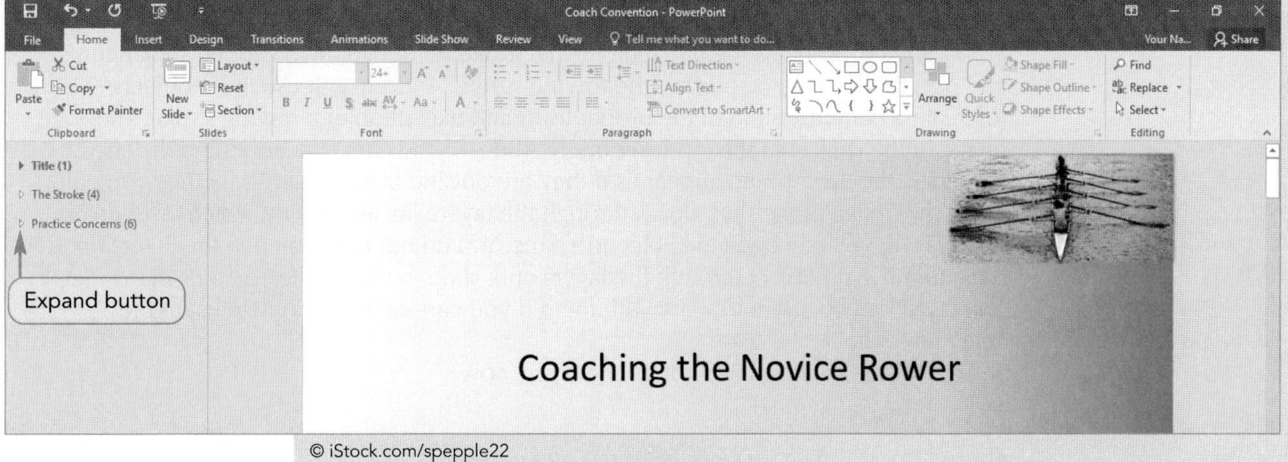

4. Save the changes to the presentation.

Problem Solving: Creating a Slide Show with Two Orientations

There may be times that the content of your presentation requires you to use a combination of portrait and landscape slide orientations. For example, suppose you are creating a presentation that contains some photos in portrait orientation and some in landscape orientation. In PowerPoint, you cannot create a single presentation file with slides in both orientations; rather, you need to create two presentations and create links between them. To do this, create one presentation using the default landscape orientation, create a second presentation and change the orientation to portrait, and then add the appropriate photos to each file. Decide which presentation will be the primary file; it should be the presentation that you want to use at the start of your presentation. Then, decide the order in which you want the photos to appear. When you want to display a slide using the orientation used in the other presentation, insert a hyperlink on the slide that will appear prior to displaying the slide with the other orientation. If you use the Hyperlink command, in the Insert Hyperlink dialog box, click Existing File or Web Page in the Link to list, click the file you want to link to, and then click the Bookmark button to open the Select Place in Document dialog box listing the slides in the presentation you selected. Click the slide you want to link to, and then click the OK buttons in the dialog boxes. If you need to, add a link in the second presentation back to the appropriate slide in the first presentation. You should store the two presentations in the same folder so that they will always be together.

Working with Layers

Every time you add an object to a slide, you add it in a new layer. As illustrated in the Session 5.1 Visual Overview, you can send objects to the back (bottom) of the layers on a slide, or you can bring an object to the front (top) of the layers. To change an object's layer, you use commands in the Arrange group on the Drawing Tools Format tab or on the Arrange button menu in the Drawing group on the Home tab, or you can move objects through layers using the Selection pane.

On Slide 5, which is the last slide in The Stroke section, Shawna added stick figures and oars to illustrate the parts of the rowing stroke. Andrew will use these objects to create a demonstration of the proper form and execution of a rowing stroke. The image of the shell is in the top layer on the slide, so the oars appear behind the shell. However, the oars should appear as if they are outside of the shell. To fix this, you will move the image of the shell down through the layers. To see exactly which layer an object is in, you can open the Selection pane. You do not need to open the Selection pane to move an object through the layers on a slide, but if a slide contains many objects, it can be easier to work with them if you can see the complete list in the Selection pane.

You will move the shell through the layers now.

To open the Selection pane and move the image of the shell through layers on Slide 5:

1. Expand **The Stroke** section, and then display **Slide 5** ("Demo").
2. Click the image of the boat (the shell), and then click the **Picture Tools Format** tab.

3. In the Arrange group, click the **Selection Pane** button. The Selection pane opens. Every object on the slide is listed in the pane, and Shawna renamed them so that Andrew can easily identify each object in the list. The Shell object is the first item in the list because it is in the top layer on the slide, and the Title 1 object is the last item in the list indicating it is in the bottom layer. See Figure 5-11.

Figure 5-11 Selection pane listing objects in layers

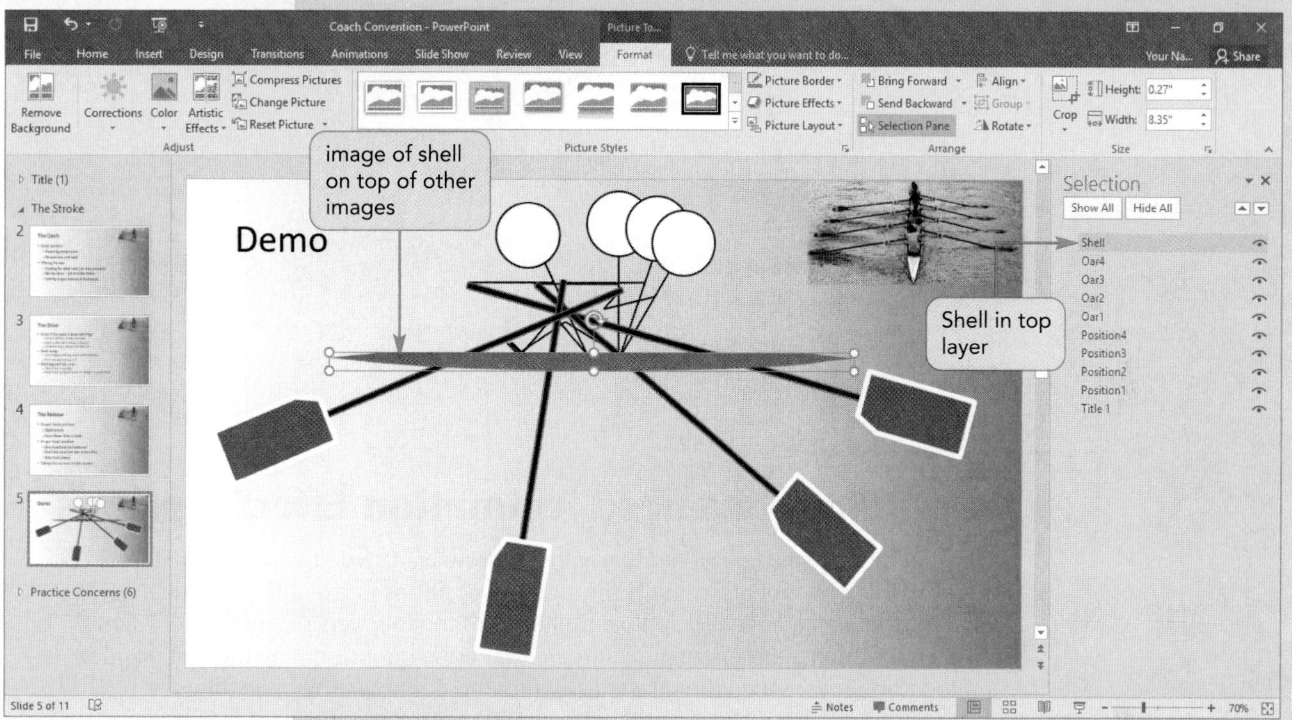

© iStock.com/spepple22; Courtesy Katherine T. Pinard

TIP

You can also click the Arrange button in the Drawing group on the Home tab, and then click Send to Back.

4. In the Arrange group, click the **Send Backward button arrow**, and then click **Send to Back**. The image of the shell moves to the bottom layer. In the Selection pane, Shell moves to the bottom of the list, and on the slide, the shell now looks like it is behind the oars and the stick figures. This is still incorrect because the shell should be in a layer on top of the stick figures.

5. On the Picture Tools Format tab, in the Arrange group, click the **Bring Forward** button. On the slide, nothing appears to change, but in the Selection pane, the selected object, Shell, moved up one place in the list.

6. At the top of the Selection pane, click the **Bring Forward** button four times. In the Selection pane, the selected object moves up four more positions so it is above the Position4 object and below the Oar1 object, and on the slide, the shell now appears on top of stick figures and behind the oars. See Figure 5-12.

Figure 5-12 **Shell positioned in correct layer**

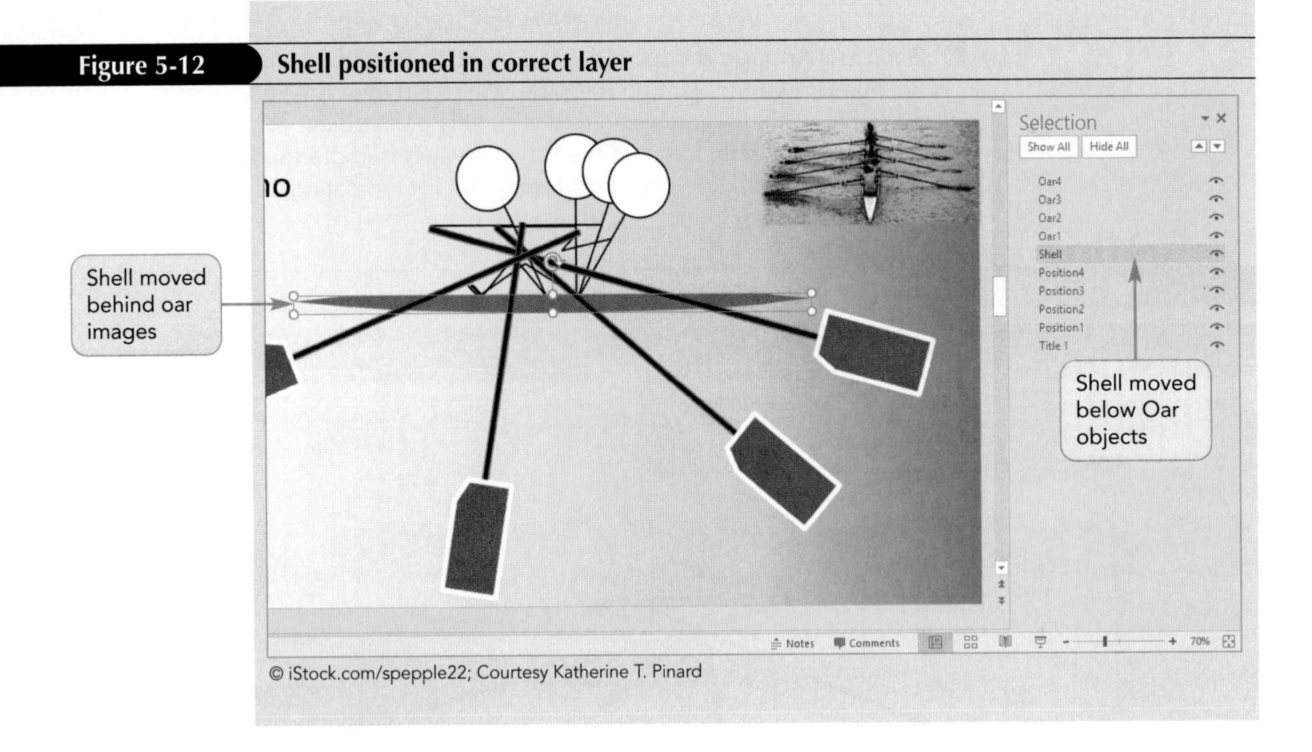

© iStock.com/spepple22; Courtesy Katherine T. Pinard

Modifying Advanced Animation Effect Options

Now that the objects are layered correctly, Andrew wants you to apply animations so the stick figure appears to move through the positions of executing a stroke. To accomplish this, you need to apply animations to the four versions of the stick figure and the oars so that the first stick figure and oar appear representing the first position and then disappear when the next stick figure and oar appear representing the second position, and so on. You could add exit animations to each object, or you can set the animated object to hide after the animation is finished or the next time you click the mouse. To do this, you need to use the Effect Options dialog box. The exact title and contents of this dialog box vary depending on the selected animation, but it always contains an Effect tab and a Timing tab. For entrance, exit, and emphasis animations, the title of the dialog box matches the name of the animation; for most motion path animations, the title of the dialog box matches the selected direction effect.

You will add animations to the images on Slide 5 now.

To apply animations and modify them using the Effect Options dialog box:

1. On the ribbon, click the **Home** tab.
2. In the Editing group, click the **Select** button, and then click **Select All**. All of the objects on the slide are selected, including the title text box. The title text box and the shell should not have an animation applied to them. See Figure 5-13.

Figure 5-13 All the objects on Slide 5 selected

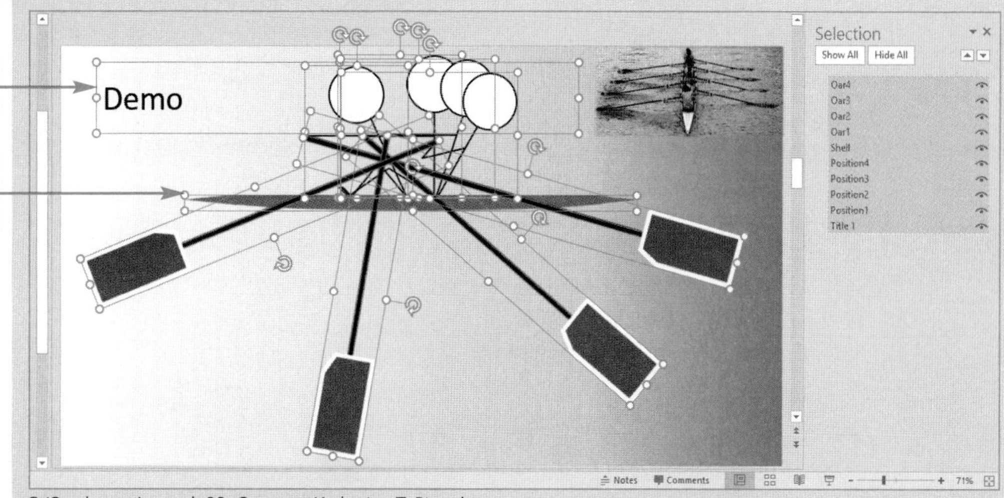

3. Press and hold the **Shift** key, point to the title text box on the slide so that the pointer changes to , and then click the title text box. The title text box is no longer selected.
4. While still holding the **Shift** key, click the image of the shell to deselect it, and then release the Shift key. The title text box and the shell are no longer selected, but all of the other images remain selected.

   Trouble? If one of the other images is deselected instead of the shell, press and hold the Shift key, click the deselected image to select it again, click the left end of the shell image to deselect the shell image, and then release the Shift key.
5. Click the **Animations** tab, and then in the Animation group, click the **Fade** entrance animation. The Fade animation is applied to all of the selected objects.
6. In the Timing group, in the Duration box, click the down arrow to change the duration to 0.25 seconds.
7. In the Animation group, click the **Dialog Box Launcher**. The Fade dialog box opens. This is the Effect Options dialog box for the Fade animation. See Figure 5-14.

Figure 5-14 **Effect Options dialog box titled "Fade"**

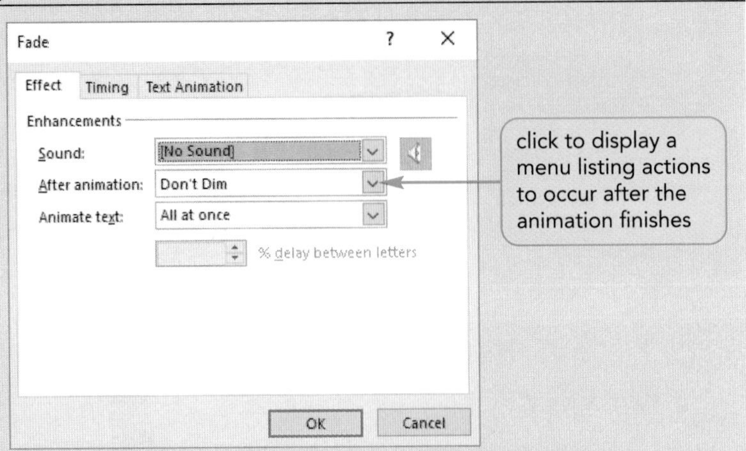

8. In the dialog box, click the **After animation** arrow. The menu that opens contains options for effects to happen after the animation completes. If the selected object is text, you can choose one of the colors to change the color of text after the animation completes. You want each object to disappear when you advance the slide show to display the next object.
9. Click **Hide on Next Mouse Click**, and then click the **OK** button.
10. On the status bar, click the **Slide Show** button. Slide 5 appears in Slide Show view. The title text box, the background photo, and the image of the shell appear.
11. Press the **spacebar**. All of the images appear on the slide.
12. Press the **spacebar** again. All of the images disappear.
13. Press the **Esc** key to end the slide show.

When you applied the animation to all of the objects at the same time, the first object in the list in the Animation Pane was set to start On Click, but the rest of the animations were set to With Previous. However, Andrew wants each stick figure and corresponding oar to appear when he advances the slide show. Also, the images representing the start of the stroke should be on the slide when the slide appears, so the start timing of these images should be set to With Previous. And the images representing the last part of the stroke should not disappear before the slide transitions, so the Hide on Mouse Click effect option should be removed. You need to modify the order and start timing of the animations so that they appear correctly. To make it easier to select specific animations, you will open the Animation Pane.

To modify the animations on Slide 5:

1. On the Animations tab, in the Advanced Animation group, click the **Animation Pane** button. The Animation Pane opens next to the Selection pane. See Figure 5-15. First, you need to reorder the animations so that the stick figure and oar representing the start of the stroke appear first, followed by the second position, and so on.

Figure 5-15 Animation Pane listing the animations on Slide 5

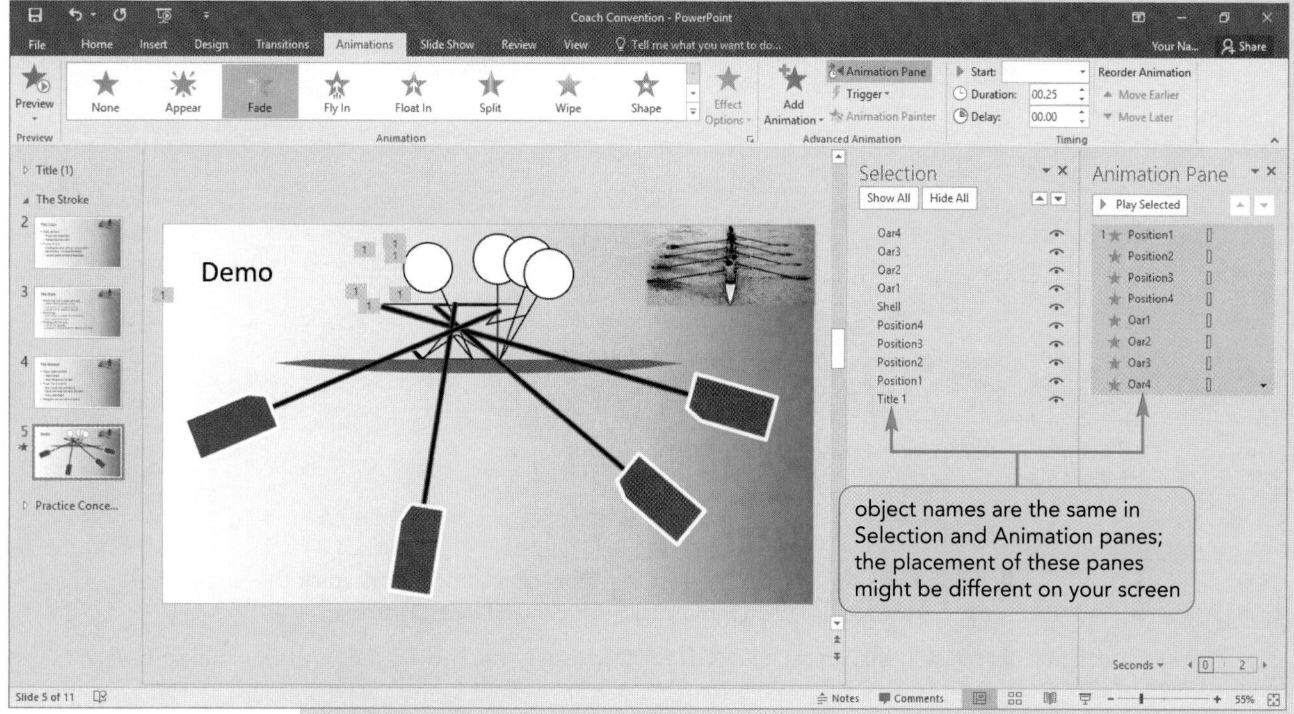

© iStock.com/spepple22; Courtesy Katherine T. Pinard

2. In the Animation Pane, click **Oar1**, and then on the Animations tab, in the Timing group, click the **Move Earlier** button three times. The Oar1 animation is now the second animation in the list.
3. Move the **Oar2** and **Oar3** animations up in the list so that the Oar2 animation is listed after the Position2 animation, and the Oar3 animation is listed after the Position3 animation. Next you will modify the animations applied to Position2, Position3, and Position4 so that they start On Click.
4. In the Animation Pane, click **Position2**, press and hold the **Ctrl** key, click **Position3**, click **Position4**, and then release the **Ctrl** key. The three animations are selected.
5. In the Timing group, click the **Start button arrow**, and then click **On Click**. Now you need to modify the animation applied to the Position1 object so that it appears when the slide transitions.
6. In the Animation Pane, click **Position1**.
7. In the Timing group, click the **Start button arrow**, and then click **With Previous**. Compare your screen to Figure 5-16. Finally, you need to modify the animations applied to Position4 and Oar4 so that they do not disappear before the slide transitions. You will remove the effect option you applied.

Figure 5-16 **Animation Pane after reordering animations and modifying start timings**

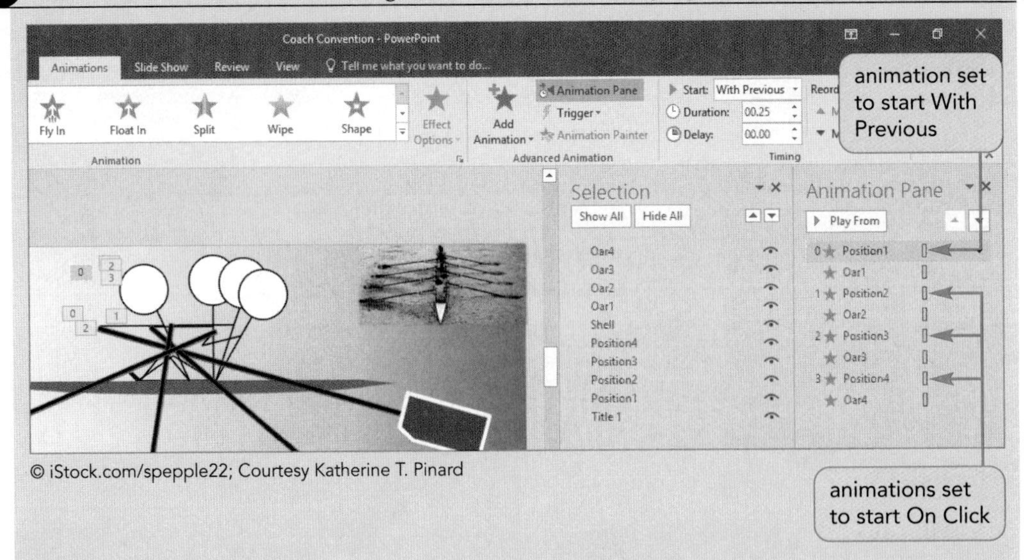

8. In the Animation Pane, select **Position4** and **Oar4**, click the arrow that appears next to Oar4, and then click **Effect Options**.
9. On the menu, click **Effect Options**. The Fade Effect Options dialog box opens.
10. In the dialog box, click the **After animation arrow**, and then click **Don't Dim**. This is the default option and means that nothing will happen after the animation completes.
11. Click the **OK** button. The dialog box closes.

Now you will see how the modified animations look in Slide Show view. Each stick figure and corresponding oar should appear one at a time, in the correct order, and disappear when the next set of images appears.

To view the animations on Slide 5 in Slide Show view:

1. On the status bar, click the **Slide Show** button. Slide 5 appears in Slide Show view, and the stick figure and oar illustrate the first position of the stroke.
2. Press the **spacebar**. The stick figure and oar illustrating the first position of the stroke disappear, and the stick figure and oar illustrating the second position of the stroke appear.
3. Press the **spacebar** two more times to view the final two positions of the stroke, and then press the **Esc** key to end the slide show.
4. Close the Animation and Selection panes, and then save the changes to the presentation.

You have created a presentation by importing an outline and inserting slides from another presentation. You modified the presentation outline in Outline view and divided the presentation into sections. You moved objects through layers and modified animation effects using the Effect Options dialog box. In the next session, you will insert and modify objects created in Excel and Word and format them using advanced options. You will also annotate slides during a slide show and create handouts in Microsoft Word.

REVIEW

Session 5.1 Quick Check

1. Describe how you use a Word outline to create slides in PowerPoint.
2. Describe how you insert slides from one presentation into another.
3. When you insert slides from one presentation into another, how do you apply the colors and other formatting from the destination presentation to the newly inserted slides?
4. What happens when you promote a first-level bulleted item in the Outline pane in Outline view?
5. How are layers created on a slide?
6. What is another way to cause an animated object to disappear after it animates without adding an Exit animation?

Session 5.2 Visual Overview:

source file (Word table)

When you import an object, you copy the object in the source file, and then paste it into the destination file; you can edit the object with the tools available in the destination program. There is no connection between the inserted object and its source file.

The program used to create the object is called the **source program**; the file that initially contains the object is called the **source file**.

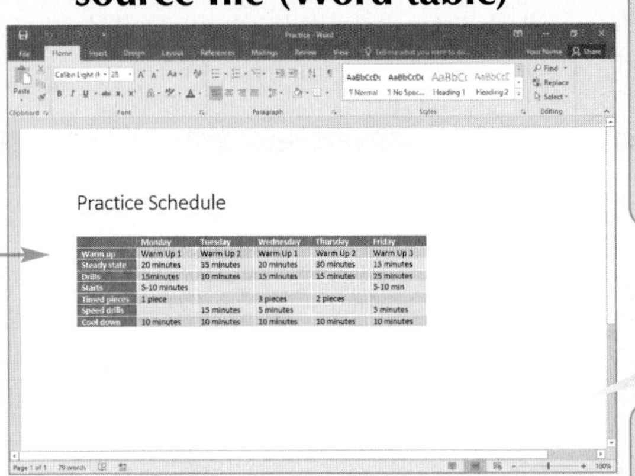

source file (Excel table)

When you **embed** an object, a copy of the object along with a one-way connection to the source program become part of the destination file, and you can edit the object using the source program's commands. Changes made do not appear in the source file.

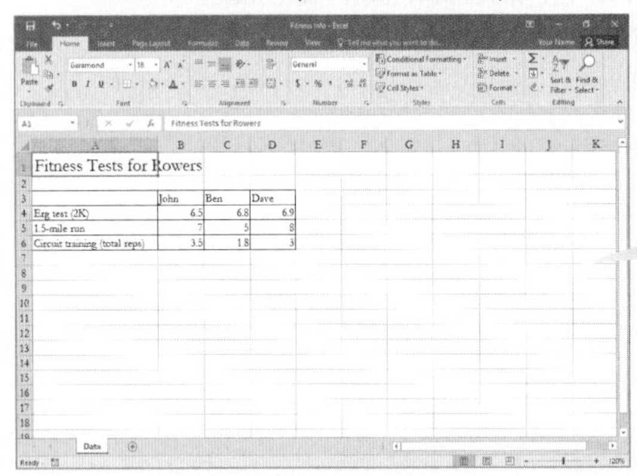

source program

You must have access to the source program to edit an embedded object; however, you do not need access to the source file.

source file (Excel chart)

When linking an object, you must have access to the source file if you want to make changes to the source object.

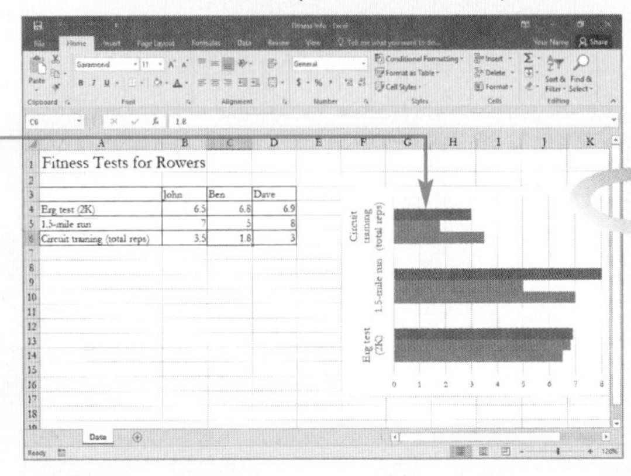

Importing, Embedding, and Linking

destination file (PowerPoint presentation)

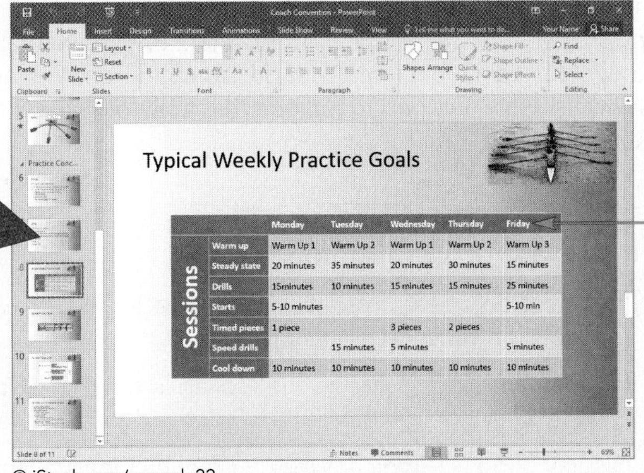

© iStock.com/spepple22

The program used to create the file where you want to insert the object is called the **destination program**; the file where you want to insert the object is called the **destination file**.

destination file (PowerPoint presentation)

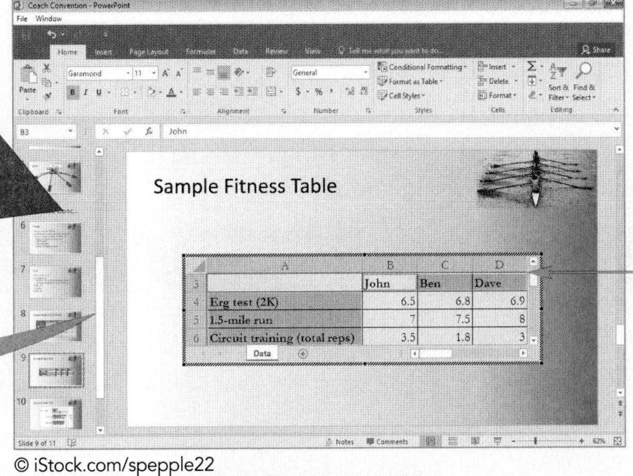

© iStock.com/spepple22

There is no connection between an embedded object and its source file; therefore, changes made to the object in the source file do not appear in the destination file.

When you **link** an object, a direct connection is created between the source and destination programs so that the object exists in only one place—the source file—but the link displays the object in the destination file as well.

destination file (PowerPoint presentation)

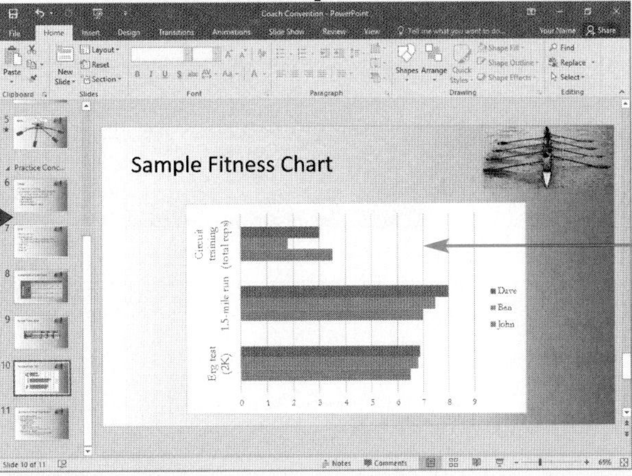

© iStock.com/spepple22

If you edit a linked object in the source file, the link ensures that the changes appear in the destination file.

Inserting a Word Table

You know how to use PowerPoint commands to create a table on a slide, but what if you've already created a table using Word? You don't need to re-create it in PowerPoint; instead, you can copy the table from the Word document and then paste it on a slide. Similar to importing a Word outline or inserting slides from another presentation, once you paste the table, the table becomes part of the PowerPoint file, and any changes you make to it will not affect the original table in the source file.

Andrew created a table in a Word document describing the weekly practice plan for his rowers. He wants you to include that table on Slide 8 in the Coach Convention presentation.

To insert a Word table on a slide:

1. If you took a break after the previous session, make sure the **Coach Convention** presentation is open.
2. If necessary, in the Slides pane, collapse the "Title" and "The Stroke" sections, and then expand the "Practice Concerns" section.
3. Display **Slide 8** ("Typical Weekly Practice Goals"), and then change the layout to **Title Only**.
4. Start Microsoft Word 2016, and then open the document **Practice**, located in the PowerPoint5 > Module folder included with your Data Files.
5. Point to the table so that the Table Select Handle appears in the top-left corner, and then click the **Table Select handle** to select the entire table. See Figure 5-17.

Figure 5-17 Selected table in Word document

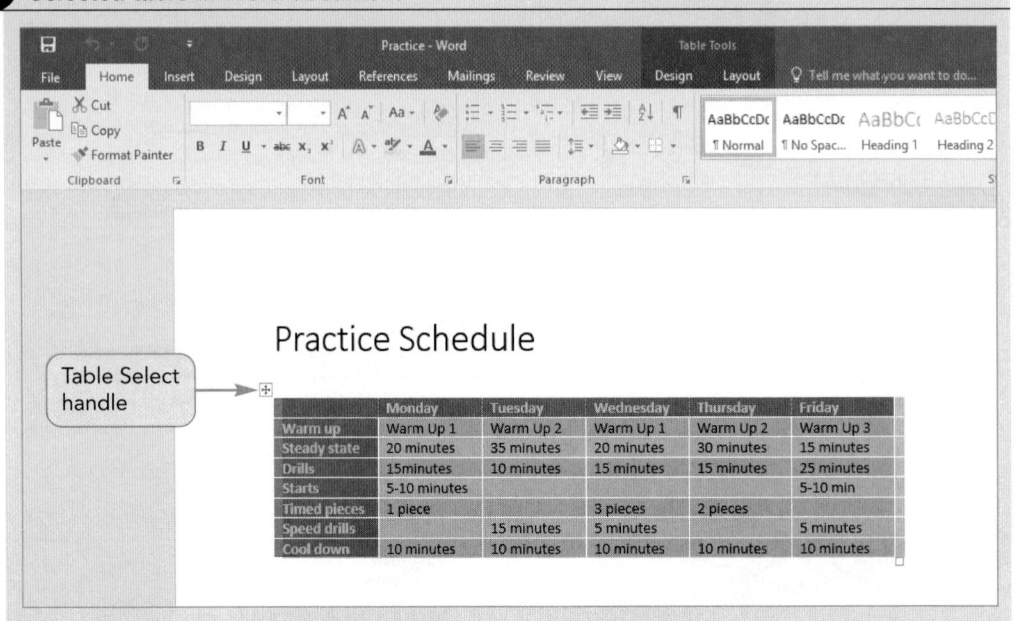

Practice Schedule

	Monday	Tuesday	Wednesday	Thursday	Friday
Warm up	Warm Up 1	Warm Up 2	Warm Up 1	Warm Up 2	Warm Up 3
Steady state	20 minutes	35 minutes	20 minutes	30 minutes	15 minutes
Drills	15minutes	10 minutes	15 minutes	15 minutes	25 minutes
Starts	5-10 minutes				5-10 min
Timed pieces	1 piece		3 pieces	2 pieces	
Speed drills		15 minutes	5 minutes		5 minutes
Cool down	10 minutes	10 minutes	10 minutes	10 minutes	10 minutes

TIP

To insert a Word file on a slide, click the Object button in the Text group on the Insert tab, click the Create from file option button, browse to the Word file, and then click the OK button.

6. On the Home tab, in the Clipboard group, click the **Copy** button.
7. On the Windows taskbar, click the **Coach Convention – PowerPoint** button to switch back to the Coach Convention presentation.
8. On the Home tab, in the Clipboard group, click the **Paste button arrow**, and then click the **Keep Source Formatting** button. The table is pasted on the slide as a PowerPoint table with the formatting from the source file (the Word file). You need to make the table larger.
9. On the ribbon, click the **Table Tools Layout** tab.
10. In the Table Size group, click in the **Height** box, type **4.2**, and then press the **Enter** key.
11. In the Table Size group, click in the **Width** box, type **9.5**, and then press the **Enter** key.
12. Make sure the entire table is still selected, and then on the ribbon, click the **Home** tab.
13. In the Font group, click the **Font Size arrow**, and then click **18**. The font size of the text in the table increases to 18 points.
14. Point to the table border so that the pointer changes to , and then drag the table to position it approximately in the center of the blank area of the slide.
15. On the Windows taskbar, click the **Practice – Word** button, and then close the document and exit Word. You return to the Coach Convention presentation.

Formatting Cells in Tables

Your previous work with tables focused on formatting and modifying a table's appearance and structure. You can also make formatting changes to individual cells. For example, you can merge cells, rotate text in cells, and change the width of borders.

When you merge cells, you combine two or more cells into one. You can merge cells in the same row, the same column, or the same rectangular block of rows and columns. Merging cells is especially useful when you need to enter large amounts of information into a single cell, or when you want to add a heading that spans more than one column. To merge cells, you use the Merge Cells button, which is located in the Merge group on the Table Tools Layout tab.

Andrew recommends practices be divided into seven sessions devoted to specific activities. Instead of adding the word "Session" to each label in the first column, you will merge cells to create one larger cell containing the label "Sessions."

To create a new first column and merge cells:

1. Click in the first column in the table, and then on the ribbon, click the **Table Tools Layout** tab.
2. In the Rows & Columns group, click the **Insert Left** button. A new first column is added to the table.
3. Click in the second cell in the new column to position the insertion point, press and hold the mouse button, and then drag down to select the rest of the cells in the column.
4. On the Table Tools Layout tab, in the Merge group, click the **Merge Cells** button. The seven selected cells are merged into one cell. See Figure 5-18.

Figure 5-18 Merged cell in imported table

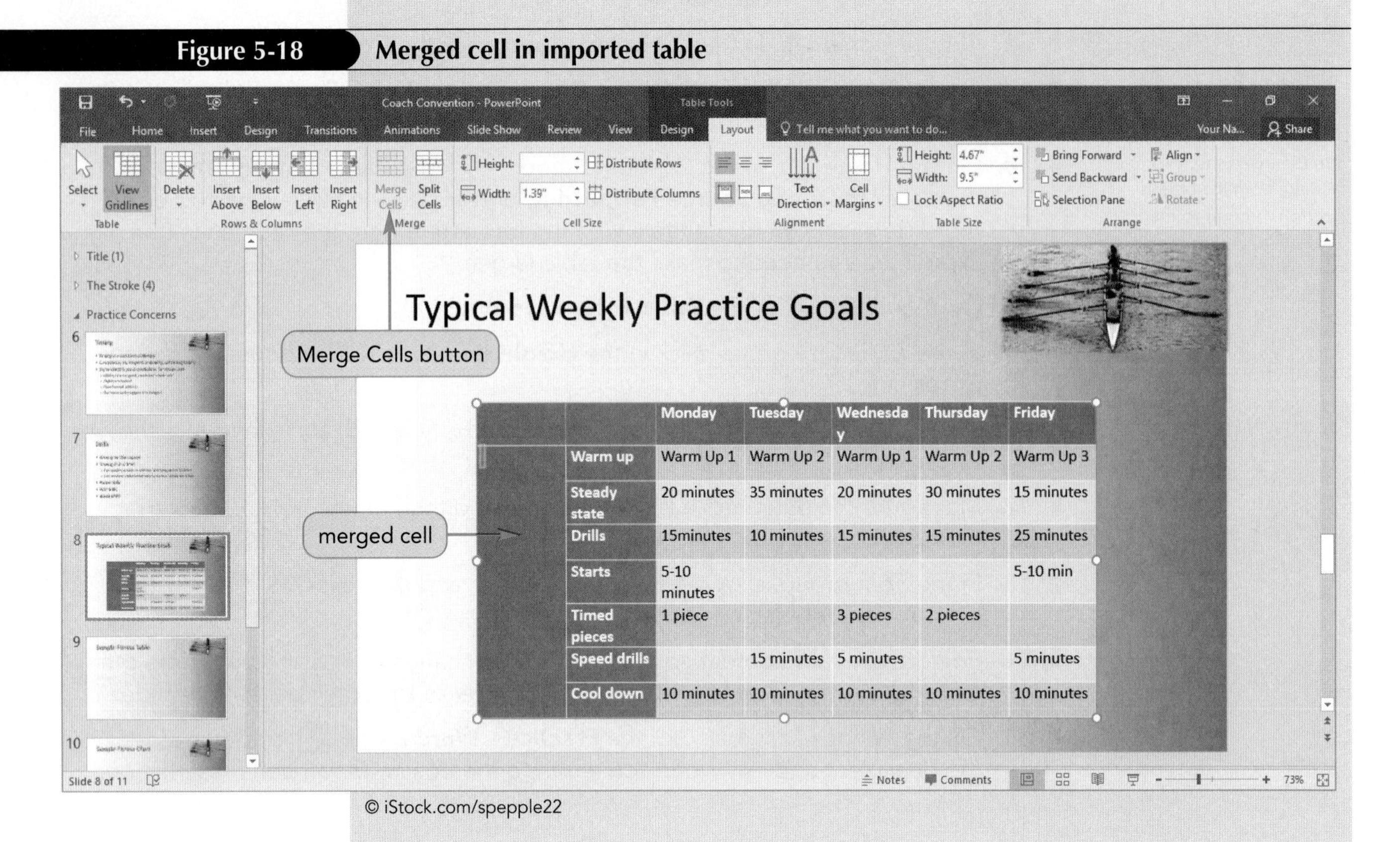

You can rotate text in a cell to read from the top to the bottom or from the bottom to the top. You will enter the label in the merged cell and then rotate it so it is read from bottom to top.

To enter, rotate, and format text in a cell:

1. Click in the merged cell, if necessary, and then type **Sessions**.
2. In the Alignment group, click the **Text Direction** button, and then click **Rotate all text 270°**. The text in the cell rotates so it reads sideways from the bottom up. See Figure 5-19.

Figure 5-19 Text rotated in merged cell

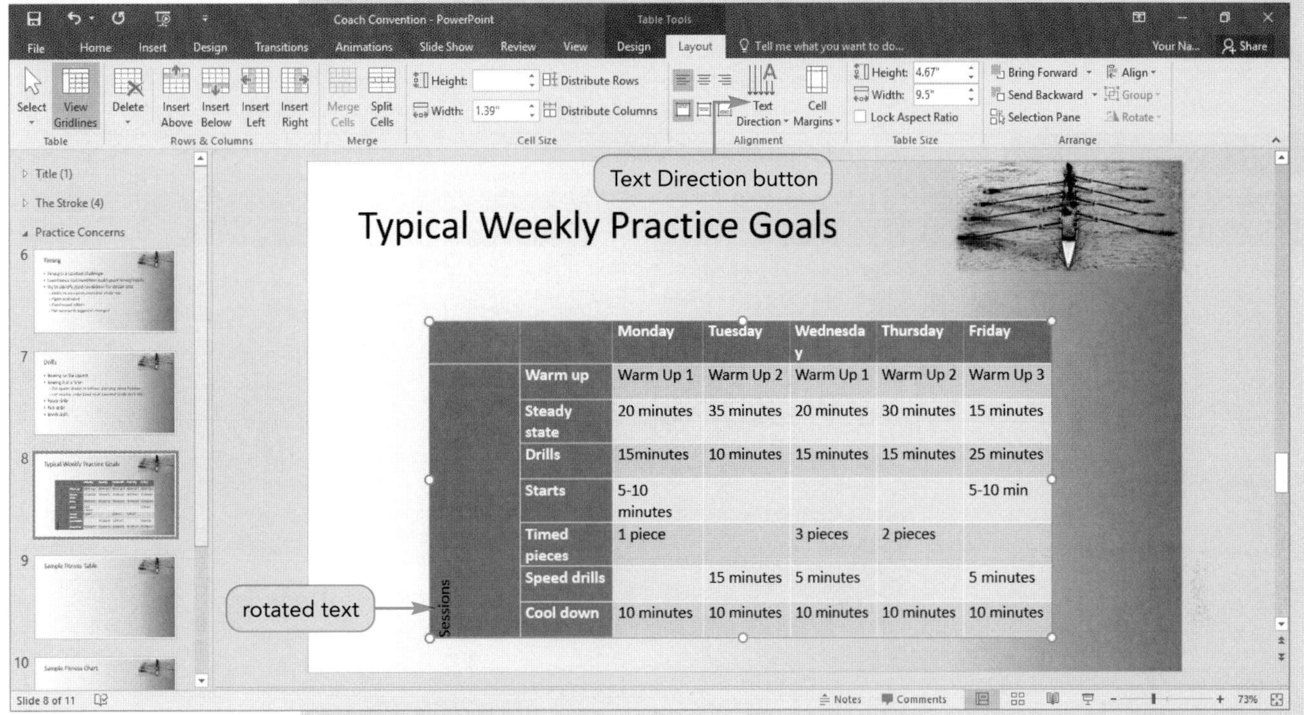

3. Double-click **Sessions**, click the **Home** tab, and then in the Font group, click the **Bold** button B. The text is small and hard to read.
4. In the Font group, click the **Font Size arrow**, and then click **44**.
5. In the Font group, click the **Font Color button arrow** A, and then click the **White, Background 1** color.

To finish formatting the table, you'll adjust the width of the columns and align the cell contents so the table elements are properly proportioned. Finally, you will format the text in the first column so it is center-aligned.

To resize columns and align the text in cells:

1. Click the **Table Tools Layout** tab.
2. In the Table group, click the **Select** button, and then click **Select Table**.
3. In the Cell Size group, click in the **Width** box, type **1.56**, and then press the **Enter** key. All the columns are resized to 1.56 inches wide.

   Trouble? If all of the columns resize so they are extremely narrow, click the Undo button on the Quick Access Toolbar. Then repeat Step 3, this time making sure you click in the Width box that is in the Cell Size group (not the Width box in the Table Size group).
4. In the Alignment group, click the **Center Vertically** button. The content of each cell in the table is centered vertically.
5. Click in the merged cell, and then change the width of this column to one inch.

6. In the Alignment group, click the **Center** button. The text in the merged cell is now centered both vertically and horizontally.
7. If necessary, reposition the table so that it is visually centered in the blank space on the slide. Compare your screen to Figure 5-20.

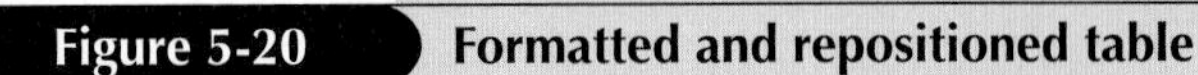

Figure 5-20 **Formatted and repositioned table**

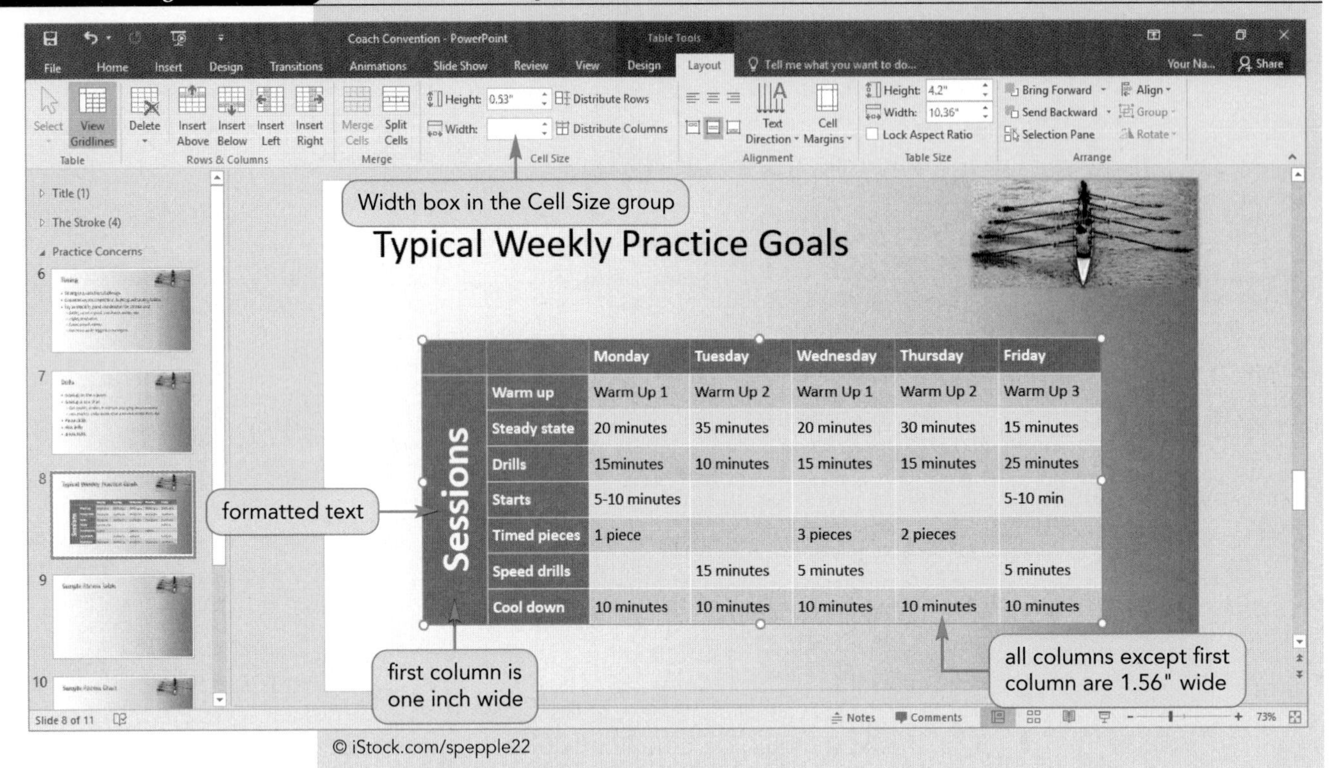

© iStock.com/spepple22

8. Save the changes to the presentation.

Inserting Excel Data and Objects

You can also insert objects from Excel workbooks and add them to slides. In addition to pasting an object from the Clipboard, you can embed or link it. Pasting, embedding, and linking all involve inserting an object from a source file into a destination file. The difference between them lies in where their respective objects are stored and which program's commands are used to modify the object. Refer to the Session 5.2 Visual Overview for more information about the differences between pasting, embedding, and linking.

If you do not need to access the source program commands from within the destination file, pasting an object is probably a better choice than embedding it. This is because when you embed an object, you insert a link to the source program as well as the object itself, and this increases the file size.

Embedding an Excel Worksheet

You can insert a worksheet created in Excel on a slide. When you do, you can choose to paste it as a table or a picture, embed it, or link it. To paste a worksheet as a table or a picture or to embed it, you use one of the buttons on the Paste menu. If you want to link the data in the worksheet, you need to click the Paste Special command on the Paste menu and then click the Paste link option button in the Paste Special dialog box that opens.

Andrew regularly has his rowers perform fitness tests. They are timed when they row two kilometers on a rowing machine called an ergometer (or erg, for short) and when they run one and a half miles, and the number of times they complete a circuit of exercises is counted. Andrew tracks this data in an Excel workbook. He also creates charts that he posts so that the rowers are motivated to try to improve their numbers. Andrew asked you to embed sample data from the workbook into Slide 9 of the presentation.

REFERENCE

Embedding an Excel Worksheet in a Slide

- Start Excel (the source program), open the file containing the worksheet you want to embed, and then select that worksheet's sheet tab.
- In the Excel worksheet, click and drag to select the cells you want to copy, and then on the Home tab, in the Clipboard group, click the Copy button.
- Switch to the PowerPoint presentation, and then display the slide in which you want to embed the copied cells.
- On the Home tab, in the Clipboard group, click the Paste button arrow, and then click the Embed button, or click the Paste button arrow, click Paste Special, make sure Microsoft Excel Worksheet Object is selected in the As list, and then click the OK button.

First, you will open the Excel workbook and then copy the cells containing the sample data to be embedded in Slide 9 of the Coach Convention presentation.

To embed Excel worksheet data in Slide 9:

1. Display **Slide 9** ("Sample Fitness Table"), and then change the layout to **Title Only**.
2. Start Microsoft Excel 2016, open the file **Fitness**, located in the PowerPoint5 > Module folder included with your Data Files, and then save the workbook as **Fitness Info** to the location where you are storing your files. See Figure 5-21.

Figure 5-21 Data worksheet in Fitness Info workbook

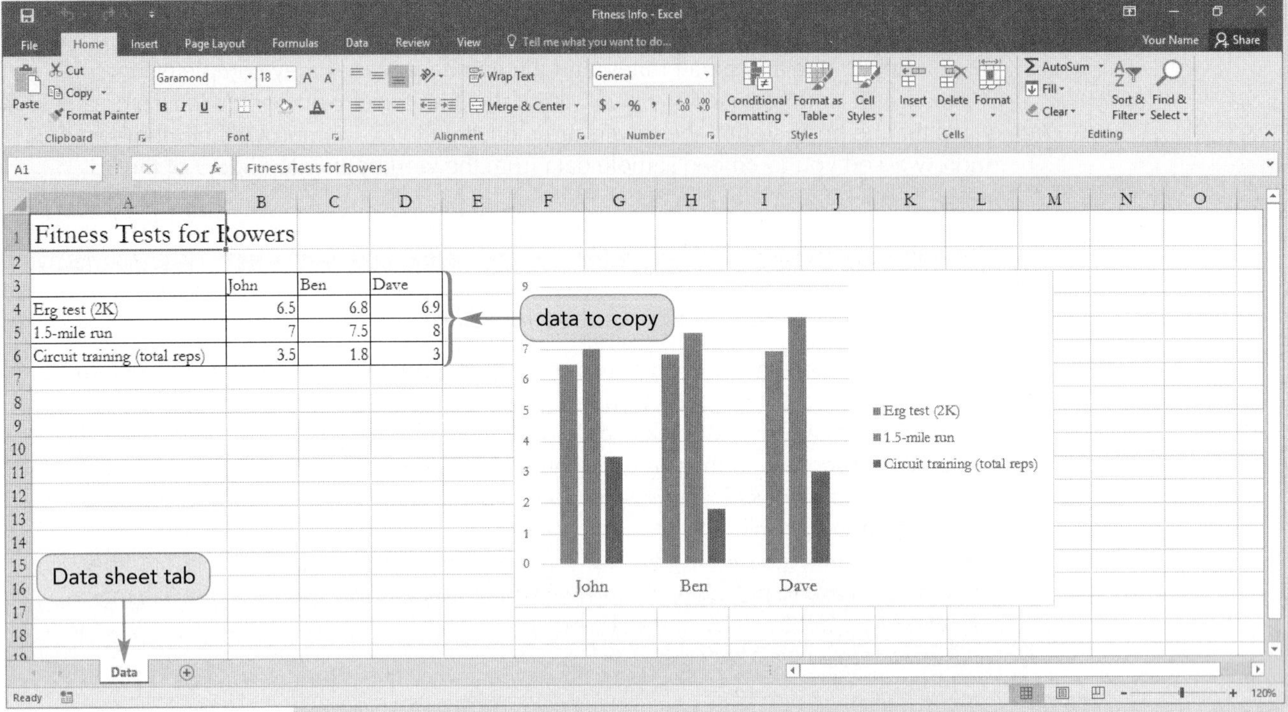

Trouble? If the worksheet is not at 120% zoom, use the Zoom slider on the right end of the status bar to change the zoom to 120%.

3. Point to cell **A3**, press and hold the mouse button, drag down to cell **D6**, and then release the mouse button. Cells A3 through D6 are selected.
4. On the Home tab, in the Clipboard group, click the **Copy** button.
5. On the Windows taskbar, click the **Coach Convention – PowerPoint** button to switch back to the Coach Convention presentation with Slide 9 displayed.

TIP

To create an embedded Excel worksheet from within PowerPoint, click the Insert tab, click the Table button in the Tables group, and then click Excel Spreadsheet.

6. On the Home tab, in the Clipboard group, click the **Paste button arrow**, and then click the **Embed** button. The worksheet is embedded in the slide.
7. On the ribbon, click the **Drawing Tools Format** tab, and then drag the corner sizing handles to resize the worksheet object so it is 2 inches high and about 9.09 inches wide.
8. Drag the table by its outside border until it appears centered in the blank area of the slide. See Figure 5-22.

Figure 5-22 **Excel data embedded in Slide 9**

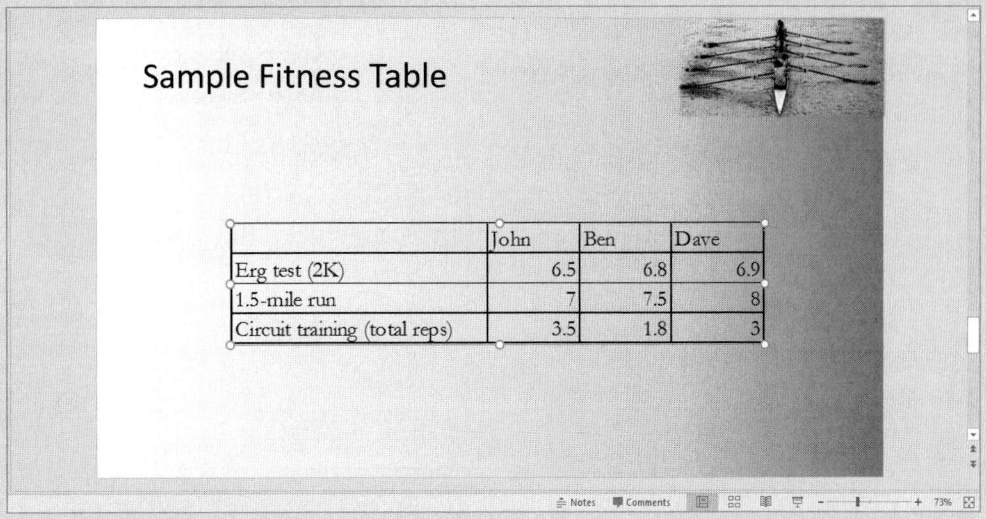

Sample Fitness Table

	John	Ben	Dave
Erg test (2K)	6.5	6.8	6.9
1.5-mile run	7	7.5	8
Circuit training (total reps)	3.5	1.8	3

© iStock.com/spepple22

To modify an embedded worksheet, you need to double-click the selected worksheet object to display the Excel tabs and commands on the ribbon in the PowerPoint window. You can then change the data or format it using the Excel commands on the ribbon.

Andrew thinks the data in the table is hard to read on the slide so he wants you to fill the cells with color. He also wants the column and row labels to be bold. You'll make these changes now.

To modify the embedded worksheet:

1. On Slide 9 ("Sample Fitness Table"), double-click the selected worksheet object. The ribbon changes to display the Excel tabs and commands. See Figure 5-23. Cells A3 through D6 are selected.

Figure 5-23 Embedded Excel object with Excel active

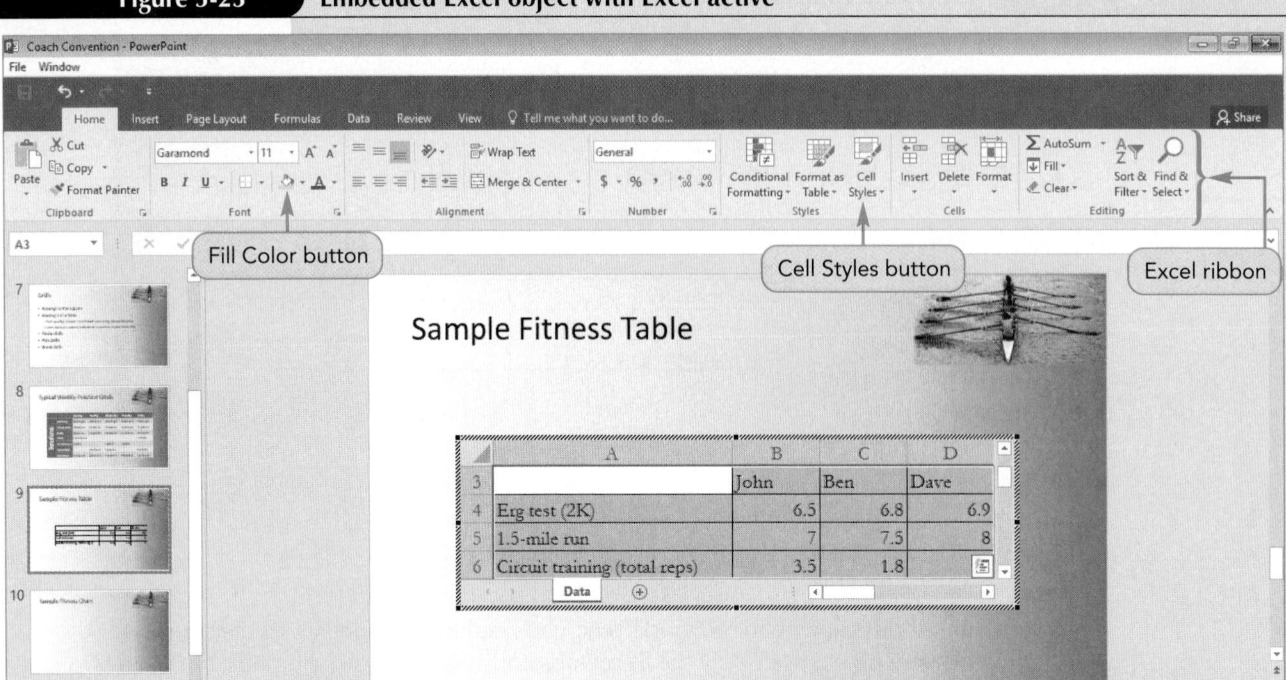

© iStock.com/spepple22

2. On the Home tab, in the Font group, click the **Fill Color button arrow**, and then click the **Gold, Accent 6, Lighter 80%** color. The selected cells are filled with the light gold color.
3. Point to cell **A4**, press and hold the mouse button, drag down to cell **A6**, and then release the mouse button. Cells A4 through A6 are selected.
4. Press and hold the **Ctrl** key, drag to select cells **B3** through **D3**, and then release the mouse button. Cells A4 through A6 and cells B3 through D3 are selected.
5. In the Styles group, click the **Cell Styles** button, and then click **Heading 4**. The selected cells are formatted with the Heading 4 style, which formats the text as bold.
6. Click a blank area of the slide. The presentation window minimizes, and the Excel window is the active window.
7. On the taskbar, click the **Coach Convention – PowerPoint** button. On Slide 9, the embedded object is still selected.

   Trouble? If the PowerPoint window does not appear, click the Coach Convention – PowerPoint button again.
8. Click a blank area of the slide again to deselect the object. See Figure 5-24.

Figure 5-24 Formatted data in embedded Excel workbook

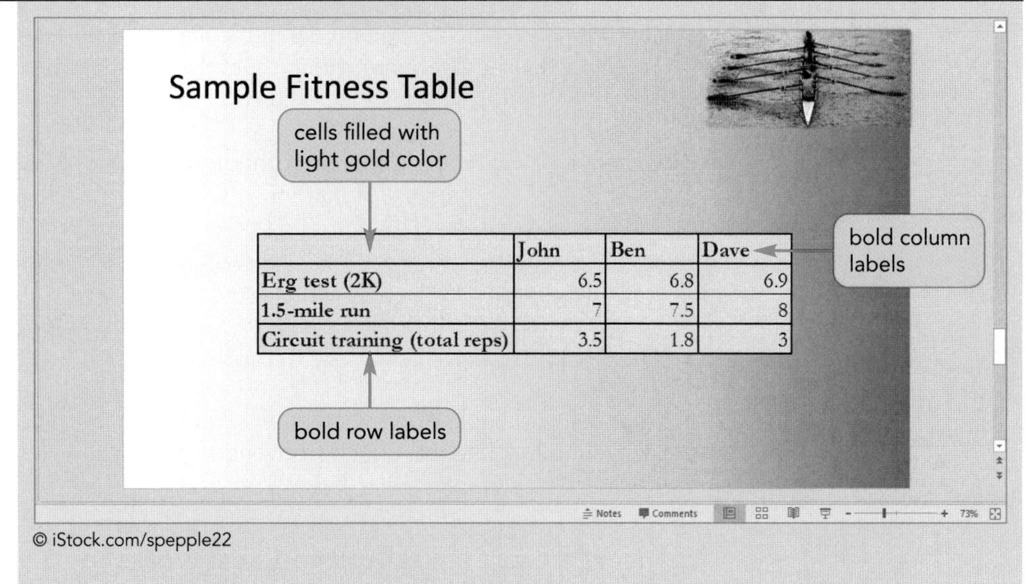

9. Save the changes to the presentation.

Keep in mind that the changes you made to the embedded object did not change the original worksheet in the Excel workbook because embedding maintains a connection only with the program that was used to create the object, not with the original object itself.

Linking an Excel Chart

If you need to include an Excel chart in your presentation that is based on data that might change, you can link the chart instead of embed it. For example, you might need to include a chart on a slide, but you know that the final data is not available yet or that the chart data will change over time. In this case, you should link the chart so that when the source file is updated, the linked chart in the destination file is updated and reflects the changes made to the source file.

To link a chart from an Excel workbook to a presentation, you need to use the Paste Special dialog box, which you open by clicking the Paste Special command on the Paste button menu. If you need to link only the underlying data of an Excel chart to a presentation, and you do not need the linked chart to visually match the source chart (in formatting and style), you can use either the Destination Theme and Link Data button or the Keep Source Formatting and Link Data button on the Paste menu instead of using the options in the Paste Special dialog box. When you link a chart or data using the Paste Special dialog box, you do not have the option to use the style of the destination file.

REFERENCE

Linking an Excel Chart to a Slide

- Start Excel (the source program), open the file containing the chart to be linked, and then select the sheet tab of the worksheet that contains the chart.
- Point to the chart to display the ScreenTip "Chart Area," and then click the chart to select it.
- On the Home tab, in the Clipboard group, click the Copy button.
- Switch to the PowerPoint presentation, and then display the slide to which you want to link the chart.
- On the Home tab, in the Clipboard group, click the Paste button arrow, click Paste Special to open the Paste Special dialog box, click the Paste link option button, and then click the OK button.

In the Excel workbook, Andrew created a column chart to illustrate the sample data. He wants you to link it to the Coach Convention presentation.

To insert a chart linked to the Excel worksheet:

1. Display **Slide 10** ("Sample Fitness Chart"), and then change the layout to **Title Only**.
2. On the taskbar, click the **Fitness Info – Excel** button. The Fitness Info workbook appears with the Data worksheet selected. The column chart on the Data worksheet was created from the sample data.
3. Point to the chart so that the ScreenTip "Chart Area" appears, and then click to select the chart.

   Trouble? If the ScreenTip displays something other than "Chart Area," move the pointer closer to the top or bottom edge of the chart.
4. On the Home tab, in the Clipboard group, click the **Copy** button.
5. On the taskbar, click the **Coach Convention – PowerPoint** button. The Coach Convention presentation appears with Slide 10 displayed.
6. In the Clipboard group, click the **Paste button arrow**, and then click **Paste Special**. The Paste Special dialog box opens. See Figure 5-25.

Figure 5-25 **Paste Special dialog box**

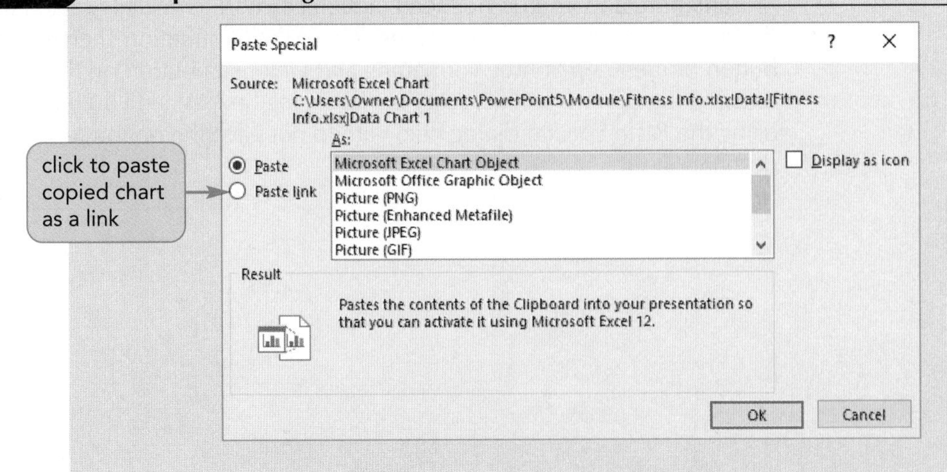

7. In the dialog box, click the **Paste link** option button. The As list changes to include only one object, a Microsoft Excel Chart Object.
8. Click the **OK** button. The chart is linked to Slide 10 using the source style.
9. On the ribbon, click the **Drawing Tools Format** tab, and then resize the chart so it is 5.3 inches high and about 8.86 inches wide, using the Shape Height and Shape Width boxes in the Size group on the Drawing Tools Format tab to help you.
10. Drag the chart to center it in the blank area of the slide. See Figure 5-26.

Figure 5-26 **Linked chart on Slide 10**

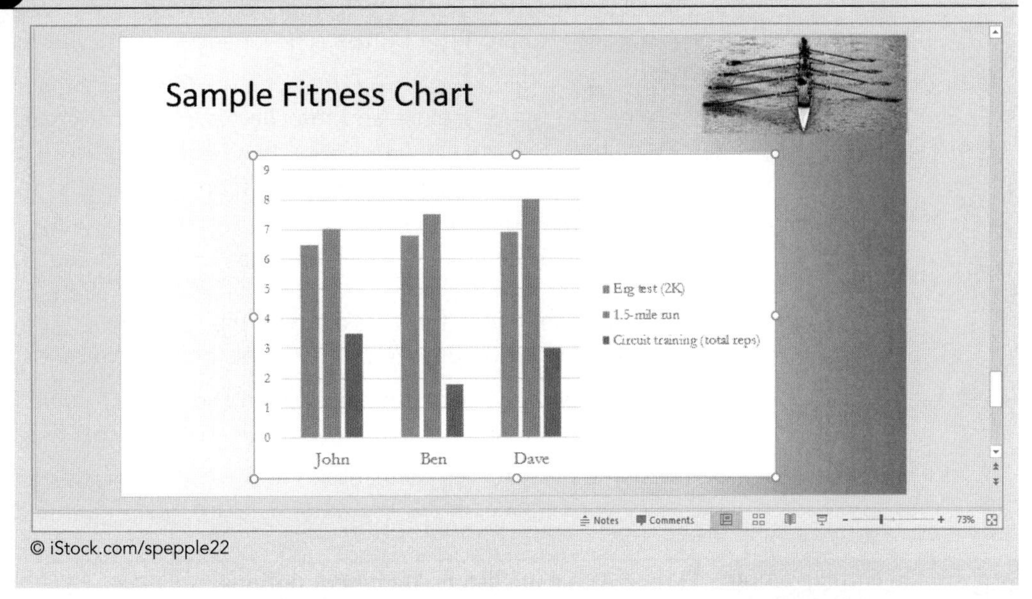

© iStock.com/spepple22

Andrew wants to make some changes to the chart. He wants to change the sample data for Ben's time for the run so there is a greater difference in this data for the three rowers. He asks you to make the changes in the Excel worksheet and then make sure the changes are reflected in the PowerPoint presentation.

To modify the linked chart:

1. On Slide 10 ("Sample Fitness Chart"), right-click the linked chart, on the shortcut menu, point to **Linked Worksheet Object**, and then click **Edit**. The Data worksheet in the Fitness Info workbook becomes active.
2. Click cell **C5**, type **5**, and then press the **Enter** key. The column in the chart that shows Ben's time for the run changes to reflect the new data.
3. Switch to the Coach Convention presentation, and notice that the chart has been updated on the slide.

   Trouble? If the chart on Slide 10 did not update, right-click the chart to select it, and then on the shortcut menu, click Update Link.

Andrew thinks that a bar chart would better illustrate the sample data he created, so he asks you to change the chart type to a bar chart. He also thinks that the data would be easier to understand if the rows and columns of data are plotted so that each bar or column in the chart represents the type of test, not a person's data. This representation will make it easier to compare how each rower did in each fitness test. To make any changes to the chart, including formatting changes, you will need to make them from the source file.

To change the chart type:

1. On Slide 10 ("Sample Fitness Chart"), right-click the chart, point to **Linked Worksheet Object**, and then click **Edit**. The Data worksheet in the Fitness Info workbook becomes active.
2. Point to the chart so that the ScreenTip "Chart Area" appears, and then click to select the chart.
3. Click the **Chart Tools Design** tab, and then, in the Type group, click the **Change Chart Type** button. The Change Chart Type dialog box opens.
4. In the navigation pane on the left, click **Bar**, and then click the **OK** button. The dialog box closes, and the chart is now a bar chart. Next you need to change how the rows and columns of source data are plotted on the chart.
5. On the Chart Tools Design tab, in the Data group, click the **Switch Row/Column** button. The chart changes so that the bars represent each column of data rather than each row of data. This means the legend identifying each bar color now contains the column labels Dave, Ben, and John, and the labels identifying the bars are now the row labels. Andrew thinks the chart will fit better on the slide if the labels on the vertical axis were rotated.
6. Double-click one of the labels on the vertical axis. The Format Axis pane opens with the Axis Options tab selected.
7. In the Format Axis pane, click the **Size & Properties button**. Alignment options appear in the Format Axis pane. See Figure 5-27.

Figure 5-27 Format Axis pane listing Alignment options

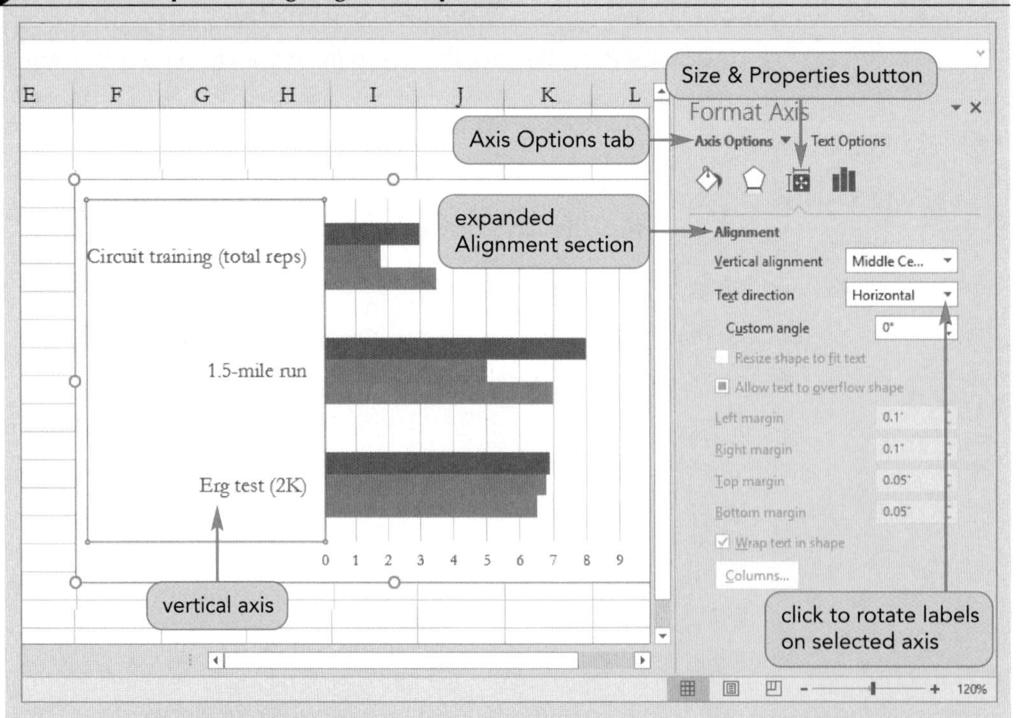

8. In the Format Axis pane, click the **Text direction button arrow**, and then click **Rotate all text 270°**. The labels on the vertical axis rotate so they read from bottom to top.
9. In the Format Axis pane, click the **Close** button, save the changes to the Excel workbook, and then close the workbook and exit Excel. You return to the Coach Convention presentation. All the changes you made to the chart are shown in the chart on Slide 10. See Figure 5-28.

Figure 5-28 Updated linked chart on Slide 10

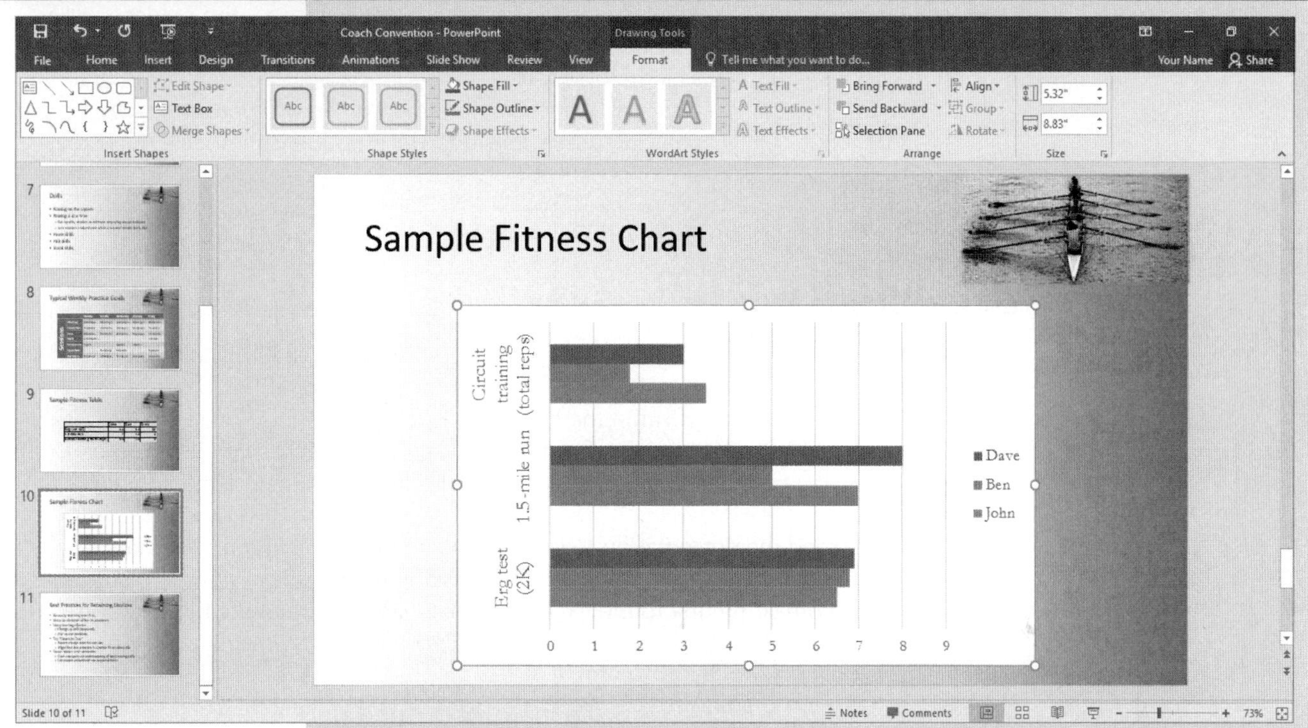

© iStock.com/spepple22

Trouble? If the changes were not applied to the chart on the slide, right-click the chart, and then on the shortcut menu, click Update Link.

10. Save the changes to the presentation.

You have now linked and edited an Excel chart in a PowerPoint presentation. Any additional changes made to the workbook will be reflected in the linked chart in the PowerPoint slide.

PROSKILLS

Decision Making: Comparing Paste, Embed, and Linking Options

Each method of including objects from another file has advantages and disadvantages. The advantage of pasting or embedding an object instead of linking it is that the source file and the destination file can be stored separately. You can make changes to the object in the destination file, and the source file will be unaffected. The disadvantage of pasting or embedding an object is that you do not have access to the source program from within the destination file to modify the object. Another disadvantage of embedding an object is that the destination file size is somewhat larger than it would be if the object were simply imported as a picture or text or linked.

The advantage of linking an object instead of embedding it is that the object remains identical in the source and destination files, and the destination file size does not increase as much as if the object were embedded. The disadvantage is that the source and destination files must be stored together. When you need to copy information from one program to another, consider which option is the best choice for your needs.

Breaking Links

When you link an object to a slide, you need to keep the source file in its original location so that the link can be maintained. If you move the source file, you need to identify the new location from within the PowerPoint file. You do this by using the Links dialog box, which you can open from the Info screen in Backstage view. You can also change how the object is updated—manually or automatically—from the Links dialog box.

If you plan to send the presentation to others, you should break all links so that when they open the file, they don't see a message asking them if they want to update the links. You will break the link to the Excel data that was used to create the chart on Slide 10.

To break the link to the Excel workbook:

1. On the ribbon, click the **File** tab. The Info screen appears in Backstage view.
2. In the Related Documents section, click **Edit Links to Files**. The Links dialog box opens. See Figure 5-29. The filename of the object and the path appear in the Links list. Because it is selected, this information also appears below the Links box next to "Source."

Figure 5-29 Links dialog box on the Info screen in Backstage view

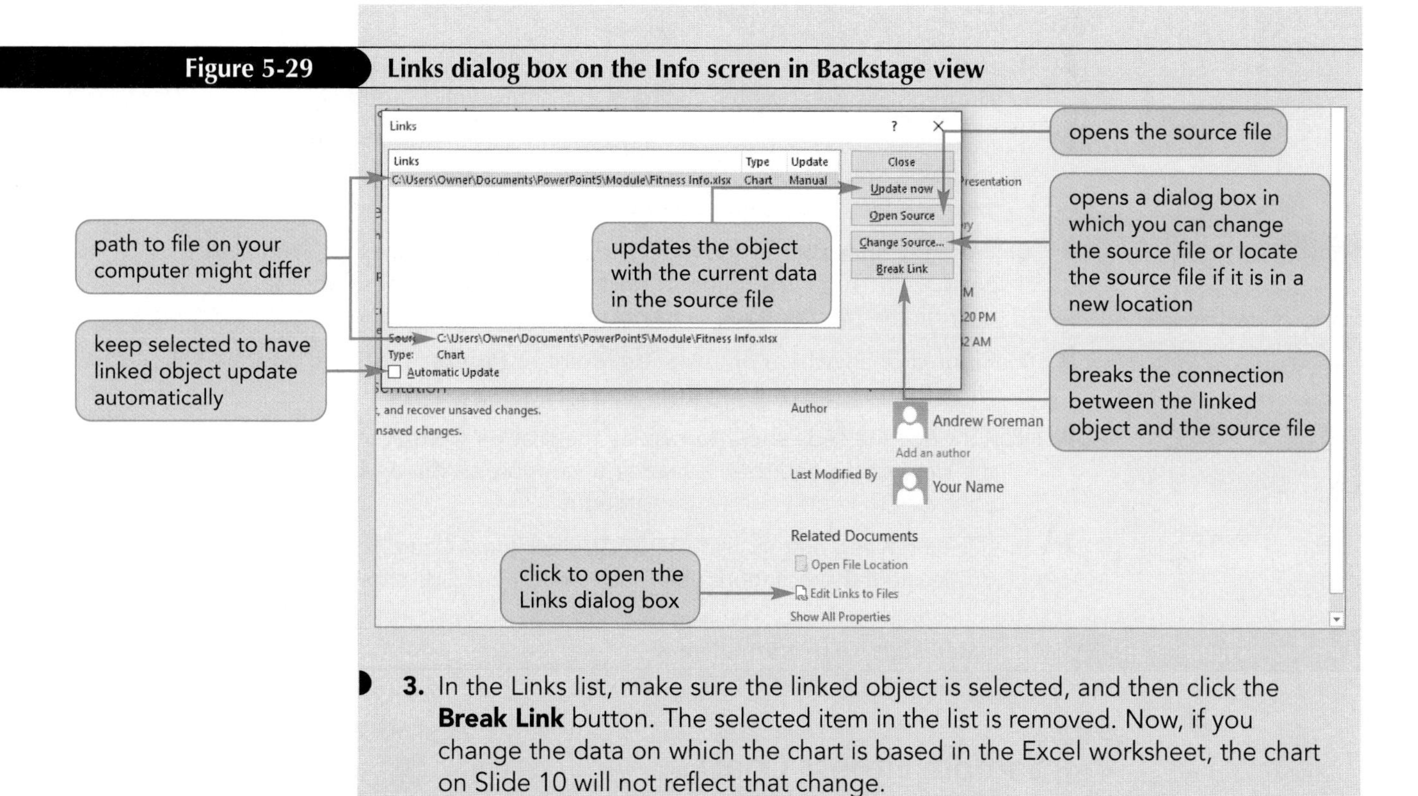

3. In the Links list, make sure the linked object is selected, and then click the **Break Link** button. The selected item in the list is removed. Now, if you change the data on which the chart is based in the Excel worksheet, the chart on Slide 10 will not reflect that change.
4. In the Links dialog box, click the **Close** button.
5. At the top of the navigation bar, click the **Back** button to close Backstage view.

Annotating Slides During a Slide Show

During a slide show, you can annotate—mark—the slides to emphasize a point. To do this, you change the pointer to a pen, which allows you to draw lines on a slide during a slide show, or to a highlighter, which allows you to highlight something on a slide during a slide show. For example, you might use the Pen to underline a word or phrase that you want to emphasize or to circle a graphic that you want to point out. You can change the ink color of the Pen or Highlighter you select. You can also select the Eraser tool to remove Pen or Highlighter lines that you draw.

After you go through a presentation and mark it, you have the choice of keeping the markings as graphic objects in the presentation or discarding them.

To use the Pen to mark slides during the slide show:

1. With Slide 10 ("Sample Fitness Chart") displayed, on the status bar, click the **Slide Show** button. Slide 10 appears in Slide Show view.
2. Right-click anywhere on the screen, point to **Pointer Options** on the shortcut menu, and then click **Pen**. The mouse pointer changes to a small, red dot.
3. Click and drag to draw an arrow pointing to the right end of the top green bar (the bar representing John's circuit training total reps). Next, you want to highlight John's name in the legend.

4. Right-click anywhere on the screen, point to **Pointer Options**, and then click **Highlighter**. The pointer changes to a small, yellow rectangle.
5. In the legend, click and drag across **John** and the green square in the legend to highlight it with yellow. When the Pen or the Highlighter is active, you cannot advance the slide show by clicking the mouse button.
6. Press the **spacebar** to move to Slide 11 ("Best Practices for Retaining Novices"). There is nothing on this slide that you want to annotate, so you'll change the pointer back to its normal shape.
7. Right-click anywhere on the slide, point to **Pointer Options**, and then click **Highlighter**. The pointer changes to its normal shape.
8. Advance the slide show to display the black slide that indicates the end of the slide show, and then advance once more. A dialog box opens asking if you want to keep your ink annotations.
9. Click the **Keep** button. Slide 10 ("Sample Fitness Chart") appears in Normal view displaying the annotations you made during the slide show. See Figure 5-30.

TIP

If you do not want a slide to be displayed during a slide show, in Normal or Slide Sorter view, select the slide thumbnail, and then on the Slide Show tab, in the Set Up group, click the Hide Slide button.

Figure 5-30 Annotated Slide 10 in Normal view

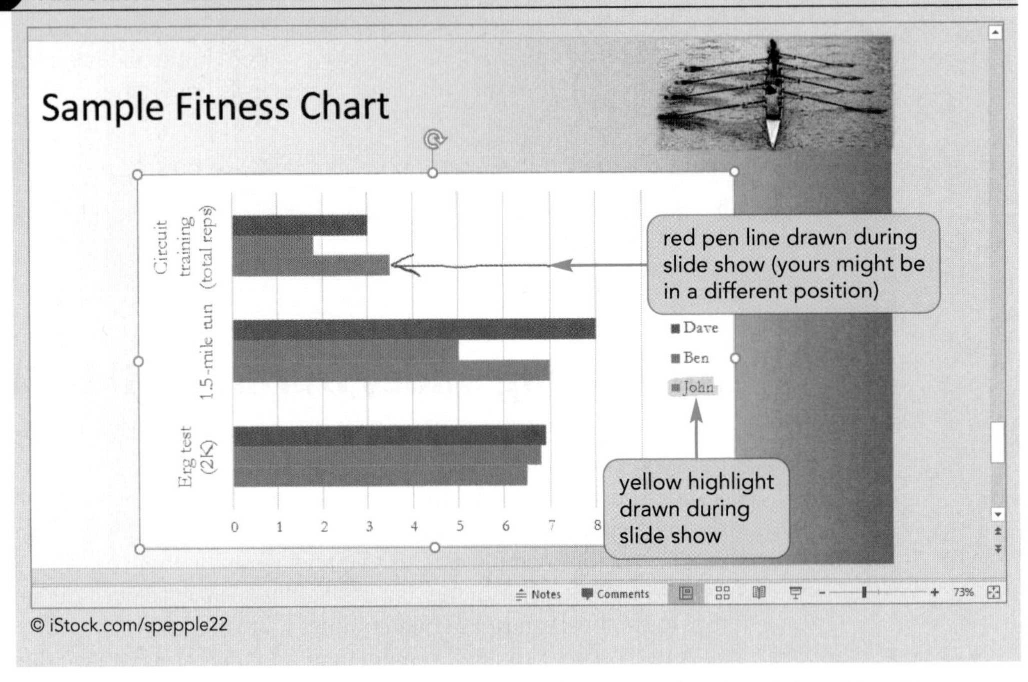

The marks you drew in Slide Show view can be manipulated or deleted just like any object on a slide. When you select an annotation on the slide, the Drawing Tools Format and Ink Tools Pens tabs appear on the ribbon. You can change the color and width of annotations, as well as move them through layers, align and rotate them, and change their overall size. The tools on the Ink Tools Pen tab are available only for touchscreens and screens that allow the use of a stylus to write.

You will delete the highlight mark on Slide 10.

To delete the annotation mark on Slide 10:

TIP

To erase an annotation in Slide Show view, right-click anywhere on the slide, point to Pointer Options, click Eraser, and then click the annotation.

1. On Slide 10 ("Sample Fitness Chart"), click the highlight mark in the legend that you drew during the slide show. The highlight mark is selected. On the ribbon, in addition to the Drawing Tools Format tab, the Ink Tools Pens tab appears as well.
2. Press the **Delete** key. The highlight is deleted.
3. In the Slides pane, collapse the "Practice Concerns" section, and then expand the "Title" section.
4. Display **Slide 1** (the title slide), and then change the name in the subtitle to your name.

Save the file now because you will be renaming it next.

5. Save the changes to the presentation.

INSIGHT

Using the Laser Pointer During a Slide Show

You can change the pointer into a red dot that looks like a laser pointer during a slide show so that you can point to objects or text on a slide during your presentation. To do this, right-click a slide during the slide show, point to Pointer Options on the shortcut menu, and then click Laser Pointer. As when you change the pointer to a Pen or Highlighter, you cannot click the mouse button to advance the slide show while the pointer is the Laser Pointer.

Creating Handouts by Exporting a Presentation to Word

You know how to print a presentation using the Handouts setting so that one or more slides are printed per page. You can also use Word to create handouts by exporting the slides to a new Word document. When you do this, you can choose from the following options:

- **Notes next to slides**—lists the speaker notes next to each slide; the number of slides per page depends on how many lines of speaker notes are on each slide
- **Blank lines next to slides**—adds blank lines next to each slide, three slides per page
- **Notes below slides**—lists the speaker notes below each slide; one slide per page
- **Blank lines below slides**—adds blank lines below each slide, one slide per page
- **Outline only**—lists the outline of the presentation as a bulleted list with first-level bulleted items at the same level as slide titles and second-level bulleted items indented

Andrew wants you to export the presentation to Word to create handouts displaying thumbnails of the slides with lines for notes to the right of each thumbnail. Slide 5 ("Demo") doesn't really need to be part of the handouts because the slide image next to the notes does not convey the same information as watching the animated images during a slide show. Also, slides containing multiple images can sometimes cause problems when you create handouts in Word, so Andrew asks you to save the presentation with a new name and then delete Slide 5 before you create the handouts.

To create handouts by exporting the presentation to Word:

1. Save the presentation as **Coach Convention for Handouts** to the location where you are saving your files.
2. Delete **Slide 5** ("Demo"), and then save the changes to the presentation.
3. On the ribbon, click the **File** tab to open Backstage view, and then in the navigation bar, click **Export**. The Export screen appears.
4. Click **Create Handouts**. The screen changes to display a description of creating handouts in Microsoft Word and a button for doing this. See Figure 5-31.

Make sure you save the changes after deleting Slide 5 or you might not be able to export the presentation as handouts.

Figure 5-31 Export screen in Backstage view with Create Handouts selected

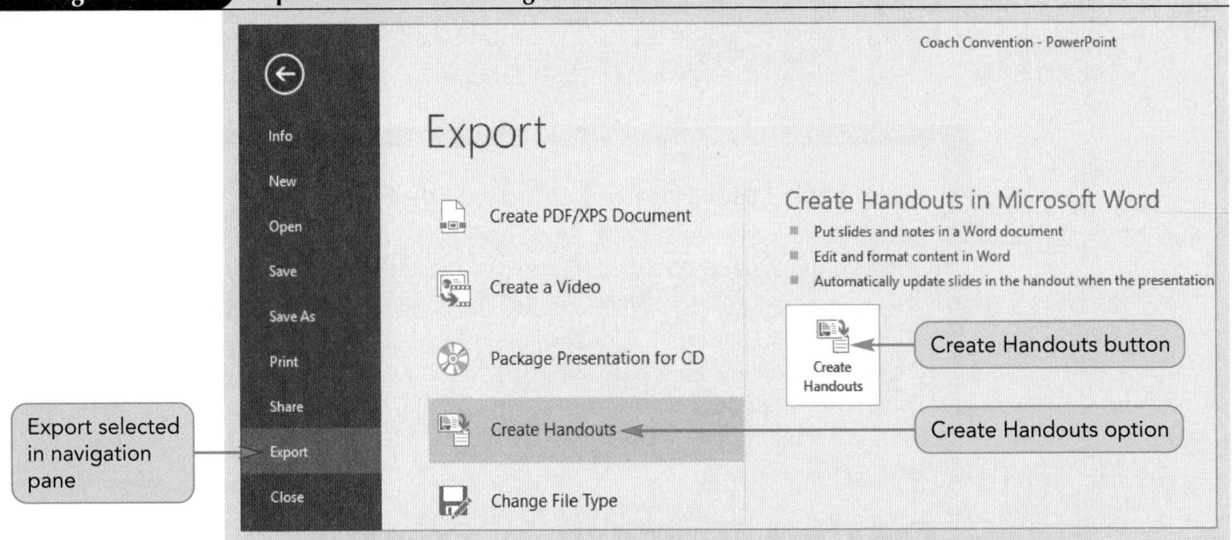

5. Click the **Create Handouts** button. Backstage view closes, and the Send to Microsoft Word dialog box opens. You can choose from five options for creating handouts, and you can choose to link the slides instead of simply exporting them. If you choose to link the handouts, when you modify the presentation, the change will be reflected in the handouts. See Figure 5-32.

Figure 5-32 Send to Microsoft Word dialog box

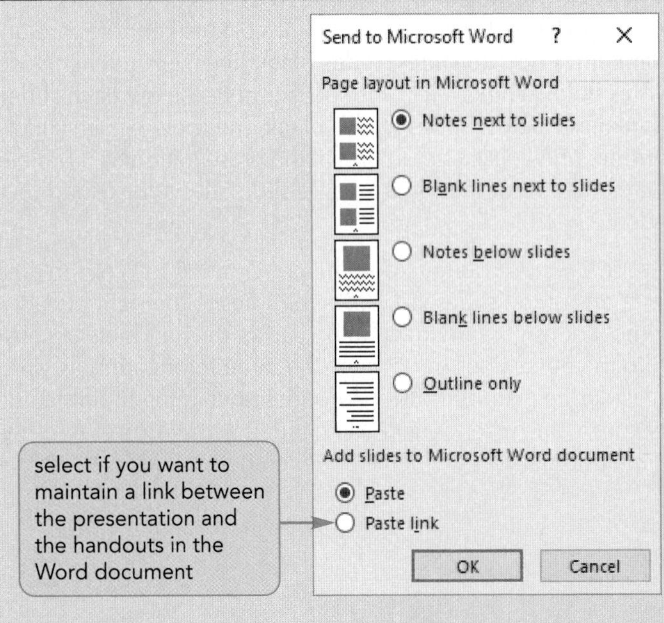

TIP

To export only the presentation outline to a document, click the Outline only option button in the Send to Microsoft Word dialog box.

6. Click the **Blank lines next to slides** option button, and then click the **OK** button. The dialog box closes, and a new Microsoft Word document is created. On the taskbar, a Microsoft Word button appears and starts blinking, indicating the document is being created. After the document is created, the button stops blinking. The time it takes for this to happen depends on the speed of your computer.
7. On the taskbar, click the **Document1 – Word** program button. The handouts appear in a Word document with thumbnails of three slides on each page and blank lines next to each slide thumbnail.

   Trouble? If the pointer blinks and changes to a blue circle, the document is still being created. Wait until the pointer is no longer a circle before continuing.
8. On the Quick Access Toolbar, click the **Save** button to open the Save As screen in Backstage view.
9. Click the **Browse** button to open the Save As dialog box, type **Coach Handouts** in the File name box, navigate to the location where you are storing your files, and then click the **Save** button. The file is saved.
10. Close the **Coach Handouts** document, and exit Word.
11. Close the **Coach Convention for Handouts** presentation.

REVIEW

Session 5.2 Quick Check

1. What does it mean to embed an object in a presentation?
2. If you modify the source file of a linked object, what happens to the linked object in the PowerPoint slide?
3. Why would you link an object instead of embed it?
4. If you link an Excel chart to a slide with one of the Paste Link buttons on the Paste menu, is the chart formatting linked as well?
5. How is an annotation that you created during a slide treated in Normal view?
6. Describe how to create handouts in Word.

PRACTICE

Review Assignments

Data Files needed for the Review Assignments: Basics.pptx, Data.xlsx, First.pptx, New Draft.docx, Schedule.docx

Andrew decided to create a presentation describing basic rules and procedures to new rowers at Newburgh College. He prepared an outline of part of the presentation, and assistant coach Shawna prepared slides describing basic terminology. He asked you to help create the final presentation. Complete the following steps:

1. Open the presentation **First**, located in the PowerPoint5 > Review folder, change the name in the subtitle to your name, and then save it as **First-Time Rower Orientation** in the location where you are storing your files.
2. After Slide 1, create slides from the outline in the Word file **New Draft**, located in the PowerPoint5 > Review folder. Reset the seven slides you create.
3. After Slide 1 in the First-Time Rower Orientation presentation, insert Slides 2 ("Don't step in the…") 3 ("Terminology"), 4 ("Types of Shells"), and 5 ("Identifying the R…") from the **Basics** presentation, located in the PowerPoint5 > Review folder, so they becomes Slides 2 through 5 in the First-Time Rowers Orientation presentation.
4. In Outline view, reorder the presentation by moving Slide 2 ("Don't step in the bottom of the boat!") so it becomes Slide 5, and then on Slide 10 ("Average 5K Erg Test Scores in Minutes"), promote the "Student Athlete" bulleted item and its subitems so that "Student Athlete" becomes a new Slide 11.
5. Create four sections in the presentation. The first should include Slide 1 and be named **Title**; the second should include Slides 2 through 5 and be named **Basics**; the third should include Slide 6 and be named **Safety**; and the fourth should include Slides 7 through 13 and be named **Routine and Expectations**.
6. On Slide 5 ("Don't step in the bottom of the boat!"), move the Foot2 object behind the Broken shell and Unbroken shell objects.
7. On Slide 5, view the animations on the slide in Slide Show view. Modify the motion path animation applied to the Foot1 object in the Effect Options dialog box by changing the Smooth end setting to 0 seconds, and then modify the motion path animation applied to the Foot2 object by changing the Smooth start setting to 0 seconds. View the animations again to see how this change affected the animation.
8. On Slide 8 ("2017-2018 Schedule"), change the layout to Title Only. Copy the table in the Word file **Schedule**, located in the PowerPoint5 > Review folder, to Slide 8 using the source formatting. Close the Schedule document and exit Word.
9. Resize the table so it is four inches high and 10.3 inches wide, and then change the font size of all the text in the table to 18 points.
10. Insert a new first column. In the new first column, merge the second through sixth cells, and then merge the seventh through eleventh cells. In the top merged cell, type **Fall**, and in the bottom merged cell type **Spring**.
11. Change the font size of the text in the merged cells to 36 points, and then rotate the text in the merged cells so it reads from the bottom of the cell up. Center the text in the merged cells both horizontally and vertically.
12. Resize the new first column so it is 0.75 inches wide, resize the second column so it is 5.75 inches wide, and then resize the third column so that it is 3.8 inches wide. Center the table vertically in the blank area of the slide, and align its left edge with the left edge of the title text box.
13. Open the Excel workbook **Data**, located in the PowerPoint5 > Review folder, and then save it as **Crew Data** in the location where you are saving your files.
14. On Slide 12 ("Average GPA"), change the layout to Title Only, and then embed cells A3 through F5 from the GPA worksheet in the Crew Data workbook on Slide 12. Resize the embedded object so it is 1.6 inches high and 11.52 inches wide, and then position it so its left edge is aligned with the left edge of the title text box and so it is centered in the space below the title and picture.

15. On Slide 12, fill cells A3 through F5 in the embedded workbook with Blue, Accent 1, Lighter 80% color. Format cells A4 through A5 and cells B3 through F3 with the Heading 4 cell style, and then change the font size of the text in these cells to 14 points.
16. On Slide 10 ("Average 5K Erg Test Scores in Minutes"), change the layout to Title Only, and then link the chart on the Erg Scores worksheet in the Crew Data workbook to Slide 10. Resize the linked chart so it is five inches high and 8.46 inches wide, and then center the chart in the blank area of the slide.
17. Update the data on which the chart is based by typing **7:25** in cell B7 (indicating that the Novice Women's average score in Week 8 is 7:25 minutes). Change the chart type of the chart in the Excel workbook to Clustered Bar, and then switch the columns and the rows. Save the changes to the Crew Data workbook, and then exit Excel.
18. Break the link between the First-Time Rower Orientation presentation and the Crew Data workbook.
19. Display Slide 6 ("Safety") in Slide Show view, circle the "Report all injuries" bulleted item using the red Pen, and then end the slide show, keeping the annotation.
20. Create handouts in a Word document using the Outline only option. Save the Word document as **Rower Handouts** in the location where you are storing your files. Close the Rower Handouts file and exit Word.
21. Save the changes to the First-Time Rower Orientation presentation.

APPLY

Case Problem 1

Data Files needed for this Case Problem: Budget.xlsx, Community.pptx, Plan.docx

Community Table Igor Karman and Karen Sawicki recently founded Community Table in Ypsilanti, Michigan. Community Table is a joint effort by local religious and civic groups to provide meals in a comfortable, welcoming atmosphere for people in need. The goal is to provide family-style dining rather than a soup kitchen buffet line. They have asked you to help them create the presentation. Complete the following steps:

1. Open the presentation **Community**, located in the PowerPoint5 > Case1 folder included with your data files, replace the names in the subtitle with your name, and then save the file as **Community Table** in the location where you are storing your files.
2. Create additional slides after Slide 1 from the outline contained in Word file **Plan**, located in the PowerPoint5 > Case1 folder. Reset the 12 newly created slides.
3. On Slide 2 ("Mission Statement"), change the bulleted list to an unnumbered list, resize the text in the unnumbered list so it is 36 points, and then vertically center the unnumbered list in the text box. (*Hint*: Use the Align Text button in the Paragraph group on the Home tab.)
4. Demote all the text on Slide 4 ("Create partnerships") so "Create partnerships" becomes a first-level bulleted item on Slide 3 ("Building the Team").
5. Demote all the text on Slide 6 ("Equipment") so "Equipment" becomes a first-level bulleted item on Slide 5 ("Supplies"), and then move the "Equipment" bulleted item and its subitems up so the "Equipment" bulleted item is the second first-level bulleted item in the bulleted list on Slide 5.
6. Start Excel, open the **Budget** workbook, located in the PowerPoint5 > Case1 folder, and then save it as **Projected Budget**.
7. On the Budget worksheet in the Projected Budget workbook, copy the Projected Monthly Expenses column chart. Switch to the Community Table presentation, display Slide 7 ("Monthly Expenses"), change the layout to Title Only, and then link the copied chart to Slide 7.
8. Edit the chart source file by changing the value in cell B8 to **-140**, and then change the chart type in the source file to a pie chart.
9. On Slide 7, resize the chart so it is five inches high and 8.37 inches wide, and then center it in the space below the slide title.

10. Break the link between the Community Table presentation and the Projected Budget workbook.
11. On the Budget worksheet in the Projected Budget workbook, copy cells A17 through B30. Switch to the Community Table presentation, display Slide 8 ("Annual Estimated Income"), and then change the layout to Title Only. Embed the copied data on Slide 8, resize the Excel object so it is five inches high and 6.47 inches wide, and then position it so it is centered in the blank area on the slide.
12. Format cells A18 through B24 in the embedded workbook so that black border lines appear between all the cells. (*Hint*: Click the Borders button arrow in the Font group on the Home tab, and then click Borders and Shading. Make sure you add borders only between all the cells, not on the outside edges of the selected range of cells.) Save the Projected Budget workbook, and close Excel.
13. In the presentation, create the following sections:
    - **Intro**, which includes Slides 1 and 2
    - **Organization**, which includes Slides 3 through 5
    - **Finances**, which includes Slides 6 through 8
    - **Menu & Operations**, which includes Slides 9 and 10
    - **Advertise**, which includes Slide 11
14. Save the changes to the presentation.
15. Create handouts in Word using the Outline only option. Save this file as **Community Table Handouts** in the location where you are saving your files. Close the Community Table Handouts file, and exit Word.

APPLY

Case Problem 2

Data Files needed for this Case Problem: Animation.pptx, Description.docx, LEAP.pptx

LEAP Alternative High School James Greer is the principal of LEAP, an alternative high school in Pike County, Kentucky. He is periodically asked to describe the school to parent groups, civic groups, and school boards. He created an outline of a presentation in Word, and he created a slide with an animation on it that he wants to include in his presentation. He asked you to help him finish the PowerPoint presentation. Complete the following steps:

1. Open the presentation **LEAP**, located in the PowerPoint5 > Case2 folder included with your data files, replace "James Greer" with your name in the subtitle, and then save the file as **LEAP Presentation** to the location where you are saving your files.
2. Create new slides from the outline in the Word file **Description**, located in the PowerPoint 5 > Case2 folder. Reset the five new slides you added.
3. In Outline view, promote the last first-level bulleted item on Slide 6 ("Orientation") so that "Eligibility Requirements" is the title of a new Slide 7.
4. Move Slide 7 ("Eligibility Requirements") so that it becomes Slide 5.
5. Reuse Slide 2 from the **Animation** presentation file, located in the PowerPoint5 > Case2 folder. Insert this slide as Slide 3 in the LEAP Presentation file.
6. Watch the animation on Slide 3. Then reorder the objects on Slide 3 so that the SUCCESS object appears on top of the OBSTACLES object instead of behind it. Watch the animation again.
7. Create a new section named **Introduction** that contains Slides 1 through 3. Create a new section named **Students** that contains Slides 4 and 5. Create a new section named **Program** that contains Slides 6 through 8.
8. Display Slide 2 ("LEAP") in Slide Show view, and then highlight the first letter of each first-level bulleted item with yellow. End the slide show, and keep the annotations.
9. Create handouts in Word using the Blank lines below slides option. Save the Word document as **LEAP Handouts**. Exit Word.
10. Save the changes to the presentation.

TROUBLESHOOT

Case Problem 3

Data Files need for this Case Problem: Condos.pptx, Listings.docx, Sales.docx

Union Street Condominiums Kelly Osmanski is a realtor contracted by Union Street Condos in Nashville, Tennessee, to sell and rent condo units. She asked you to help her create a presentation she can use at the upcoming Nashville Home Show. She created an outline in Word and prepared a title slide using a template from Office.com. She also created a table describing the listings. Complete the following steps:

1. Open the presentation **Condos**, located in the PowerPoint5 > Case3 folder included with your Data Files, replace the name in the subtitle with your name, and then save it as **Union St Condos** in the location where you are storing your files.
2. Create additional slides after Slide 2 ("Attractive Rooms") in the presentation using the outline contained in the Word document **Sales**, located in the PowerPoint5 > Case3 folder.
3. **Troubleshoot** Evaluate the problem with the new slides and fix it.
4. **Troubleshoot** On Slide 4 ("Amenities"), the last bulleted item ("Current Listings") is supposed to be a slide title on the slide after Slide 4 ("Amenities"). Fix this problem.
5. Move Slide 2 ("Attractive Rooms") so it becomes Slide 3.
6. Create sections named **Title** that includes Slide 1, **Property** that includes Slides 2 through 4, **Listings** that includes Slide 5, and **Contact** that includes Slide 6.
7. On Slide 3 ("Attractive Rooms"), modify the Fly In animation applied to the title text by changing the effect option so the text flies in one letter at a time with a delay of 15% between the letters. (*Hint*: Use the Effect Options dialog box.)
8. **Troubleshoot** On Slide 3, examine the four pictures and animations on Slide 3, and watch the animations in Slide Show view. One image is never visible. Fix this problem.
9. Start Word, and open the file named **Listings**, located in the PowerPoint5 > Case3 folder. Copy the table in the Word document, and then exit Word. In the Union St Condos presentation, change the layout of Slide 5 ("Current Listings") to Title Only, and then paste the table on Slide 5 ("Current Listings") using the destination styles.
10. On Slide 5, add a new first column to the table, and then change the width of the first column to 0.7 inches.
11. On Slide 5, in the first column, merge the cells in the second, third, and fourth rows, and then merge the cells in the fifth through eighth rows. Type **For Sale** in the top merged cell, and then type **Rentals** in the bottom merged cell.
12. Rotate the text in the merged cells so the text reads from the bottom to the top.
13. Change the width of the second column to 5.2 inches, change the width of the third column to 1.7 inches, and then change the width of the last column to 1.3 inches. Change the height of all the rows to 0.5 inches. Change the size of all the text in the table to 20 points, and then change the size of the text in the merged cells to 28 points and make it bold.
14. Change the vertical alignment of all the text in all the cells so that it is centered, and then change the horizontal alignment of the text in the two merged cells in the first column so it is centered.
15. Position the table so its left edge is aligned with the left edge of the title text box and so it is centered in the blank area of the slide.
16. View the slide show. On Slide 2 ("Beautiful Living in Downtown Nashville"), draw a red arrow pointing to "Ryman Auditorium." On Slide 4 ("Amenities"), highlight "Rooftop garden" in yellow. When the slide show is finished, keep the annotations.
17. Save the changes to the presentation.

CHALLENGE

Case Problem 4

Data Files needed for this Case Problem: Cabin.xlsx, Chop.pptx, Volunteer.pptx

Flathead Lake Experience Camp Cy Zirnkilton is a volunteer on the Activities and Program committees for Flathead Lake Experience Camp, an overnight camp in Bigfork, Montana. Flathead Lake Experience Camp provides overnight camping for nonprofit youth groups. Because many of the cabins have wood-burning stoves, the camp recently decided to allow groups to rent the camp for weekends during the winter. Cy was chosen to organize a weekend volunteer effort during which the volunteers would chop firewood for the winter camp guests to use to heat their cabins. Cy plans to promote the weekend at upcoming committee meetings, and he asked you to help him create the presentation. Complete the following steps:

1. Open the presentation **Chop**, located in the PowerPoint5 > Case4 folder included with your Data Files, replace the name in the subtitle with your name, and then save it as **Chop Weekend** in the location where you are storing your files.
2. Reuse Slides 2 ("What Is It?") through 6 ("Don't Worry—We'll…") from the PowerPoint file **Volunteer**, located in the PowerPoint5 > Case4 folder by adding them after Slide 2 ("Why Shop When You Can Chop?") so that they become Slides 3 through 7 in the Chop Weekend presentation.
3. In Outline view, demote Slide 6 ("Log handling equipment") so "Log handling equipment" becomes a first-level bulleted item on Slide 5 ("Additional Equipment Needed"). Move Slide 7 ("Cabin Data") so it becomes Slide 4, and then move Slide 8 ("Equipment Needed") so it becomes Slide 6.
4. Create sections named **Introduction** that includes Slides 1 through 4, **Description** that includes Slides 5 through 7, and **Meals** that includes Slide 8.
5. On Slide 6 ("Equipment Needed"), add the Grow/Shrink animation to the Chainsaw, Truck, Splitter, and Wood objects, and then reorder these animations so that each Grow/Shrink animation occurs after the motion path animation already applied to each of the objects. Set the start timing of the Grow/Shrink animations to With Previous, and change the duration to 0.75 seconds.
6. On Slide 6, change the delay of the Grow/Shrink animation applied to the Chainsaw and Wood objects to 1.25 seconds, and change the delay of the Grow/Shrink animation applied to the Truck and Splitter objects to 0.75 seconds.
7. **Explore** On Slide 6, change the Size setting of the Grow/Shrink animations to 38%.
8. **Explore** On Slide 6, add the Camera sound to the Appear entrance animations applied to the Chainsaw, Truck, Splitter, and Wood objects, and add the Arrow sound to the Zoom entrance animations applied to the Plus 1, Plus 2, and Equal objects.
9. On Slide 6, move the Wood and Splitter objects in front of the Plus 2 and Plus 1 objects.
10. Start Excel, open the file **Cabin**, located in the PowerPoint5 > Case4 folder, and then save it as **Cabin Data** in the location where you are saving your files.
11. **Explore** Link cells A4 through C11 on the Sheet1 worksheet in the Excel file Cabin Data to Slide 4 ("Cabin Data"). In the Cabin Data file, apply the Accent 6 cell style to cells A4 through C11, add bold formatting to cells A4 through C4, and then change the content of cell B8 to **20**.
12. Save the changes to Cabin Data, and then exit Excel.
13. On Slide 4, resize the linked object so it is 4.4 inches high and 7.08 inches wide, and then center it in the blank area on the slide.
14. Break the link between the Chop Weekend presentation and the Cabin Data file.
15. Display Slide 2 in Slide Show view.
16. **Explore** Draw a green circle around the third bulleted item ("Ignore Black Friday chaos"), and then keep the annotations.
17. Create handouts in Word using the Outline only option. Save the Word document as **Chopping Weekend Outline** in the location where you are saving your files, and then exit Word.
18. Save the changes to the Chop Weekend presentation.

MODULE 6

Customizing Presentations and the PowerPoint Environment

Creating a Presentation for a Race Track

POWERPOINT

OBJECTIVES

Session 6.1

- Compare presentations, and accept or reject changes
- Add, reply to, and delete comments
- Change theme fonts
- Change theme colors
- Modify elements on the Slide Master
- Modify the style of lists
- Create a custom layout

Session 6.2

- Save a presentation as a template
- Create a custom show
- Modify file properties
- Encrypt a presentation
- Mark a presentation as final
- Present a presentation online

Case | *Checkered Flag Speedway*

Chris Stern is the promotions director at Checkered Flag Speedway in Culpeper, Virginia. In addition to hosting stock car racing events, the race track also hosts a variety of other events, including a program called "Racing Experience," which lets patrons drive race cars around the track. He wants to create a presentation that describes the various events. He created a few introductory slides and several slides that describe the Racing Experience program. He will add more slides later to describe the other events the track hosts. He asks you to help him as he works on the presentation.

In this module, you will compare two presentations and work with comments. You will modify a theme and the slide master, and you will create a custom layout. Then you will save the presentation as a template. You will also create a custom show and modify file properties. Finally, you will encrypt a presentation, mark it as final, and then learn how to present the presentation online.

STARTING DATA FILES

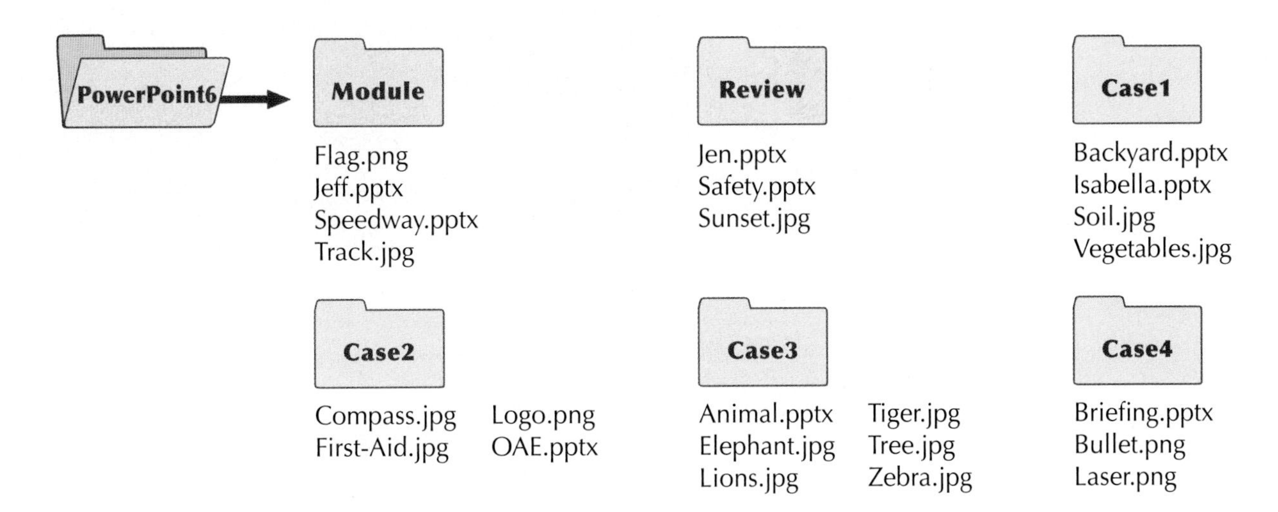

Session 6.1 Visual Overview:

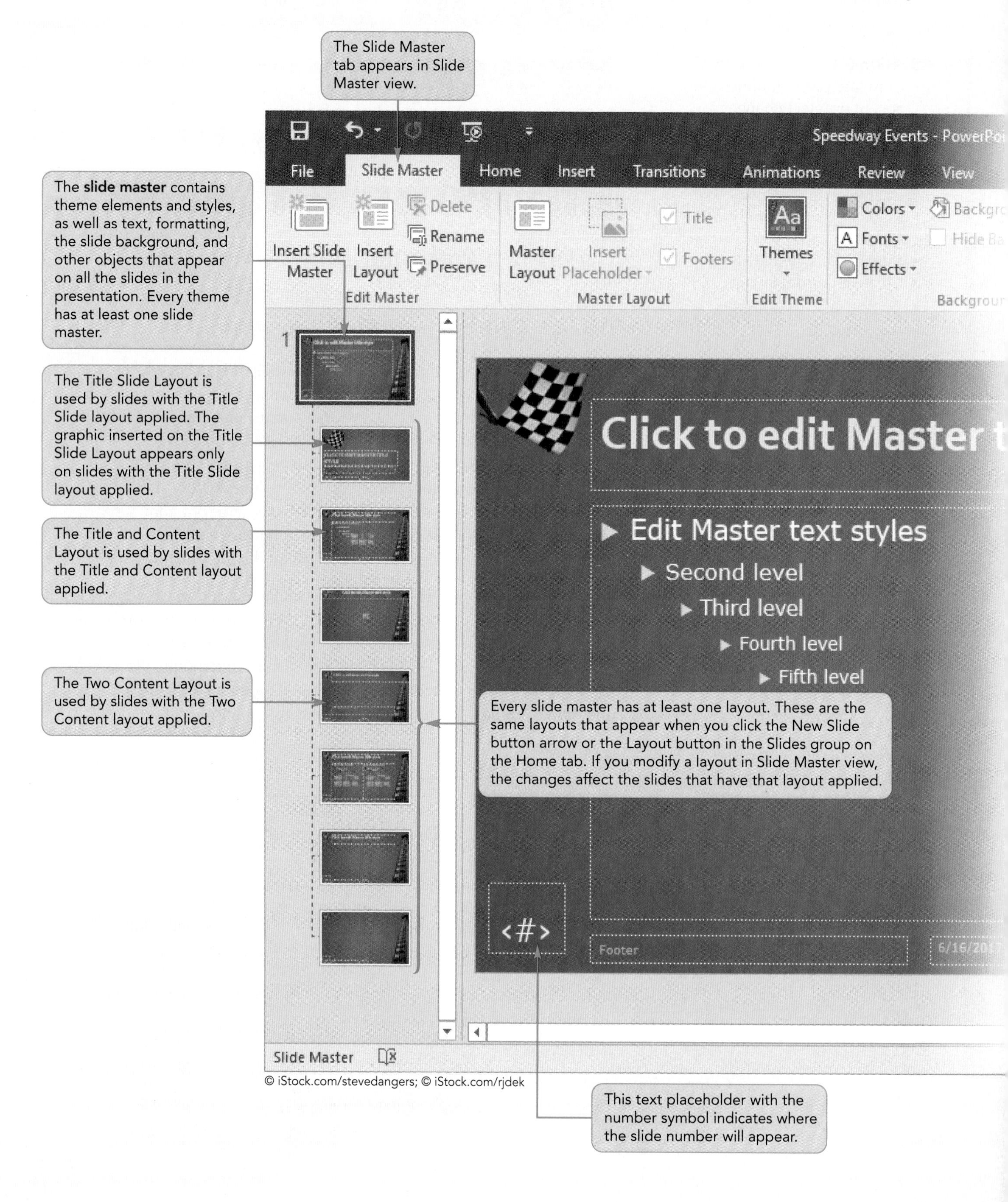

© iStock.com/stevedangers; © iStock.com/rjdek

Slide Master View

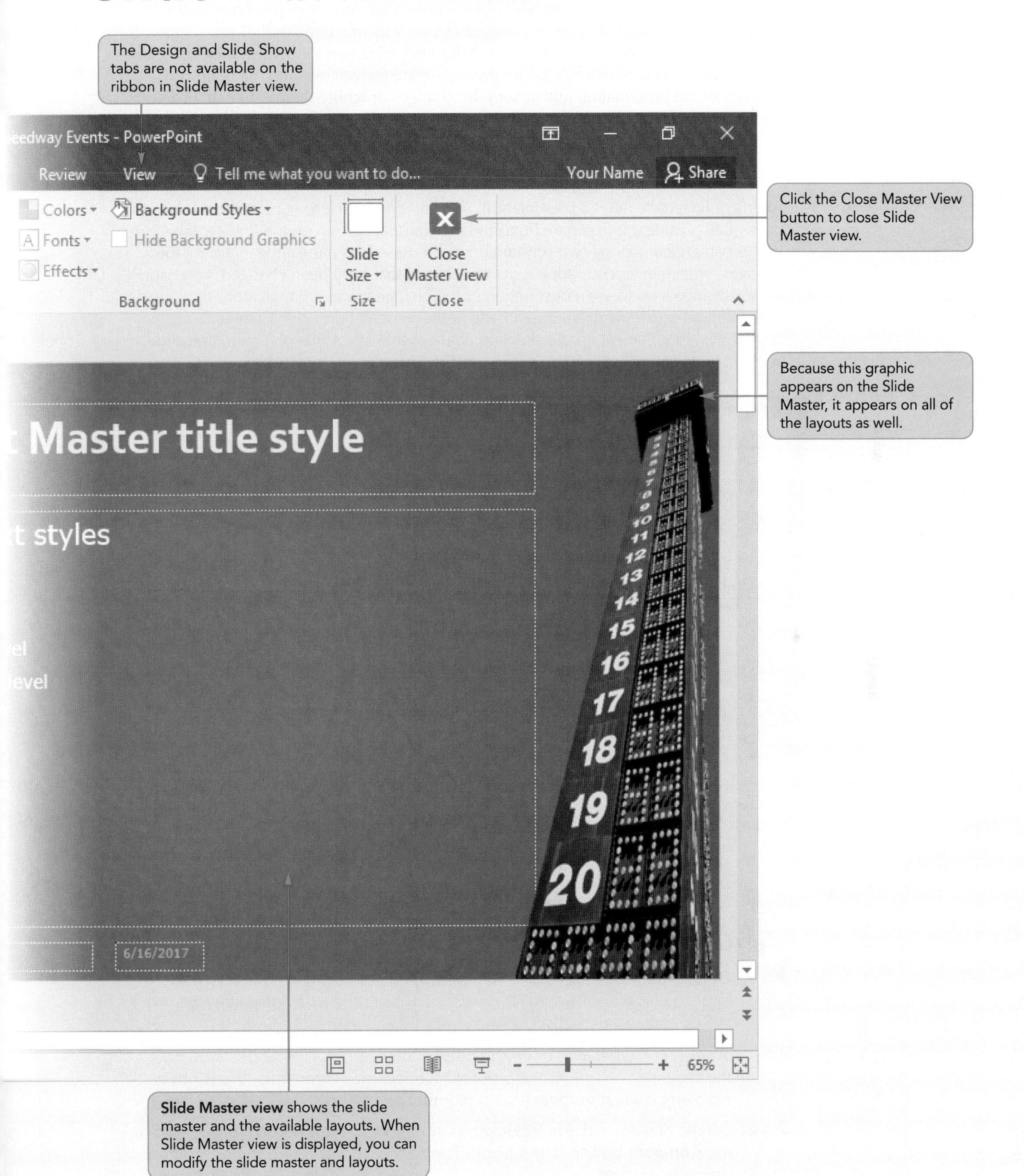

Sharing and Collaborating with Others

It is a good idea to ask others to review your presentations before you finalize and present them. Another set of eyes can spot errors or inconsistencies that you might otherwise miss. When you send a presentation to colleagues for review, they can make changes and add comments. You can then compare the original and the reviewed versions of the presentation and accept the changes or ignore them. You can also add comments and reply to or delete existing comments in a presentation.

Comparing Presentations

After a colleague reviews a presentation, you can compare it to your original presentation using the Compare button in the Compare group on the Review tab. While you are comparing two presentations, the Revisions pane appears listing the changes, and change icons appear next to objects that have been changed; you can click a change icon to see a description of the change made. Change icons that appear in the Slides pane indicate changes made at the presentation level. Change icons that appear next to an object on the slide are changes that affect that object on that slide. You can view each change and decide whether to accept it or reject it.

REFERENCE

Comparing Presentations

- On the Review tab, in the Compare group, click the Compare button to open the Choose File to Merge with Current Presentation dialog box.
- Navigate to the location containing the presentation with which you want to compare, click it, and then click the Merge button.
- In the box describing the first change, click the check box to select it to see the change.
- To keep the change, keep the check box selected; to reject the change, click the check box to deselect it.
- In the Compare group, click the Next button to display the next change in the presentation.
- After reviewing all the changes in the presentation, in the Compare group, click the End Review button.
- In the dialog box that opens asking if you are sure you want to end the review, click the Yes button.

Chris created his presentation and then sent it to Jeff Wilson, the operations manager, and asked him to review it. Jeff made a few changes and then sent it back to Chris. Chris asks you to compare his original presentation with the reviewed presentation.

To compare the original presentation with the reviewed presentation:

1. Open the presentation **Speedway**, located in the **PowerPoint6 > Module** folder included with your Data Files, and then save it as **Speedway Events** in the location where you are storing your files.

   Trouble? If, when you open the presentation, a message appears below the slide indicating that the presentation includes comments, this is not a problem; it will disappear after a moment.

2. On the ribbon, click the **Review** tab, and then in the Compare group, click the **Compare** button. The Choose File to Merge with Current Presentation dialog box opens.

3. Navigate to the **PowerPoint6 > Module** folder, click **Jeff**, and then click the **Merge** button. The Revisions pane opens with the DETAILS tab selected. A description of the first difference between the two presentations appears in a box next to a change icon in the Slides pane. See Figure 6-1.

Figure 6-1 Slide 1 after using the Compare command

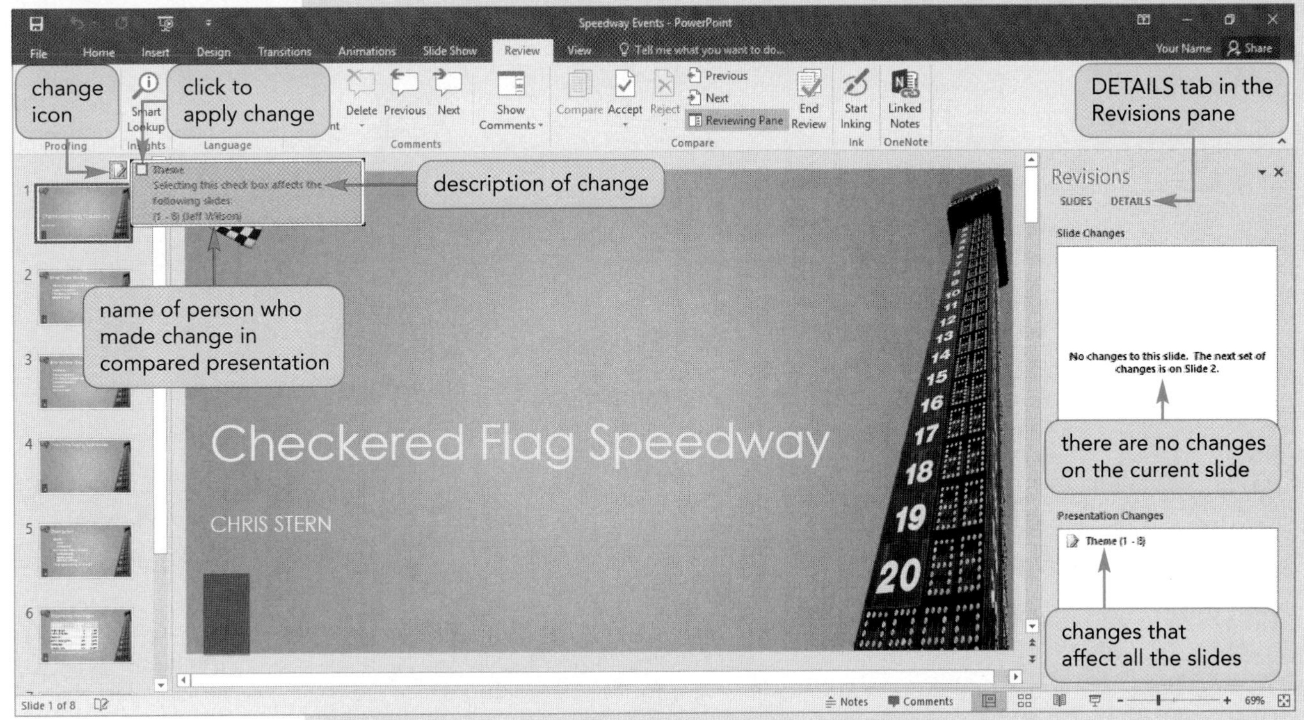

© iStock.com/stevedangers; © iStock.com/rjdek

Trouble? If the Comments pane opens, click the Close button in the Comments pane to close it.

Trouble? If the box containing the description of the Theme change does not appear, click the change icon at the top of the Slides pane.

In the Slide Changes section of the Revisions pane, the message that no changes were made to this slide appears. However, in the Presentation Changes section, Theme (1 - 8) appears, indicating that the person who reviewed the presentation made a change that affected the theme. This corresponds to the change icon and description at the top of the Slides pane.

4. In the Slides pane, in the change box, click the check box next to Theme to select it. The change is applied to the presentation, and the theme is changed. Chris does not want to make this change.

TIP

You can also click the Reject button in the Compare group on the Review tab to reject a selected change.

5. In the change box, click the check box next to Theme again to deselect it. The theme change is removed from the presentation.

6. In the Compare group, click the **Next** button. Slide 7 ("Requirements") appears in the Slide pane with a change box that indicates the content placeholder was changed. This change is listed in the Slide Changes section of the Revisions pane because the change affects this slide only. See Figure 6-2.

Figure 6-2 Slide 7 with a change noted

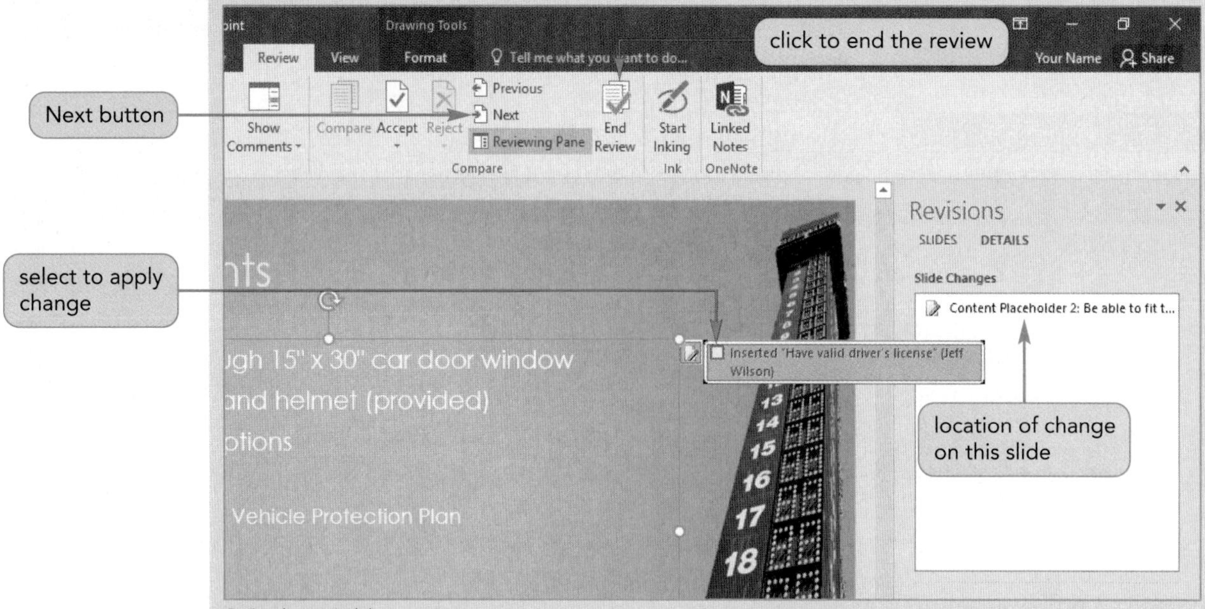

Next button

select to apply change

click to end the review

location of change on this slide

© iStock.com/rjdek

7. In the change box, click the check box next to "Inserted." "Have valid driver's license" is added as the first bulleted item. Chris likes this change so you will keep the check box selected.
8. In the Compare group, click the **Next** button. A dialog box opens, telling you that was the last change in the presentation and asking if you want to continue reviewing from the beginning. Because Slide 1 was displayed when you used the Compare command, you don't need to continue from the beginning.
9. Click the **Cancel** button. You are finished reviewing the merged changes. In order to accept all the changes you selected, reject the changes you did not select, and remove the change icons, you need to end the review.
10. In the Compare group, click the **End Review** button. A dialog box opens, asking if you are sure you want to end the review and warning that any unapplied changes will be discarded.
11. Click the **Yes** button. The dialog box and the Revisions pane close, and the change icons disappear.

Working with Comments

When a colleague reviews a presentation, he or she can add comments to ask a question or make a suggestion. You can also add comments to direct others' attention to something on a slide or reply to a comment that someone else has placed on a slide.

If you are signed in to Office with a Microsoft account, when you insert a comment in a presentation, the comment is labeled with your Microsoft account username, as shown in the upper-right corner of the PowerPoint window. If you are not signed in to Office with a Microsoft account, comments are labeled with the name in the User name box on the General tab in the PowerPoint Options dialog box. You can change the username in the PowerPoint Options dialog box by clicking the File tab and then clicking Options in the navigation bar of Backstage view.

You will insert a comment labeled with your username.

To insert a comment on Slide 5:

1. Display **Slide 5** ("Description").
2. On the Review tab, in the Comments group, click the **New Comment** button. The Comments pane appears with a box labeled with your username. A comment balloon appears in the top-left corner of the slide. See Figure 6-3.

Figure 6-3 New comment added to Slide 5

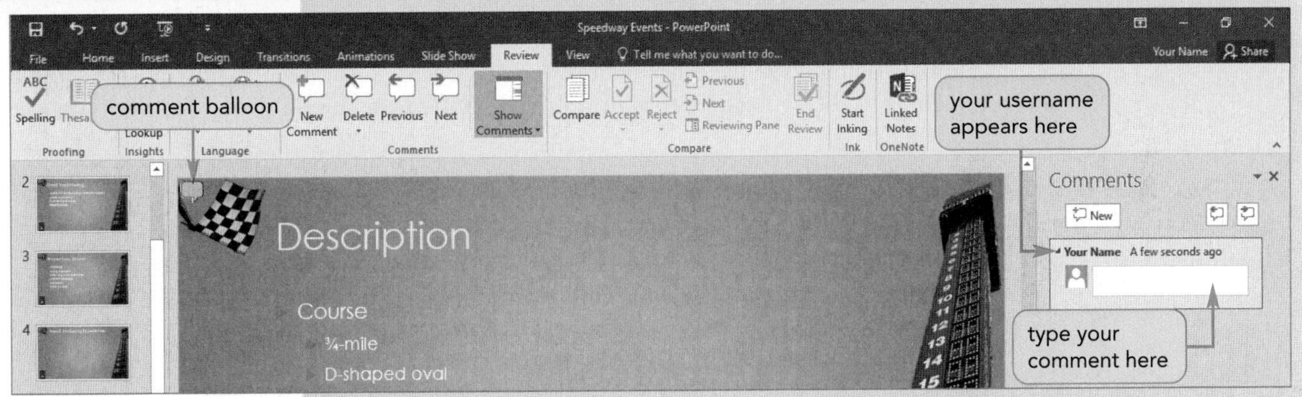

© iStock.com/stevedangers; © iStock.com/rjdek

3. In the box in the Comments pane, type **Add that the corners are banked 18 degrees?**.
4. On Slide 5, drag the comment balloon to position it to the right of the word "Course" in the bulleted list.
5. Display **Slide 1** (the title slide). The Comments pane changes to indicate that there are comments on other slides.

TIP

If you are not signed in with a Microsoft account, change the username by clicking the File tab, clicking Options, and then in the User name box in the PowerPoint Options dialog box, type your name.

Chris inserted a comment on Slide 2 ("Small Track Racing"). Instead of making the change the comment suggests, you will reply to his comment.

To reply to a comment:

1. On the Review tab, in the Comments group, click the **Next** button. Slide 2 ("Small Track Racing") appears, displaying a comment that Chris had inserted. A Reply box appears below the comment in the Comments pane.
2. Click in the **Reply** box, and then type **I agree.** (including the period).
3. Click in a blank area of the Comments pane. The reply is labeled with your username. On the slide, a second comment balloon appears on top of the first balloon. See Figure 6-4.

TIP

You can also click a comment balloon to open the Comments pane.

Figure 6-4 Reply to comment on Slide 2

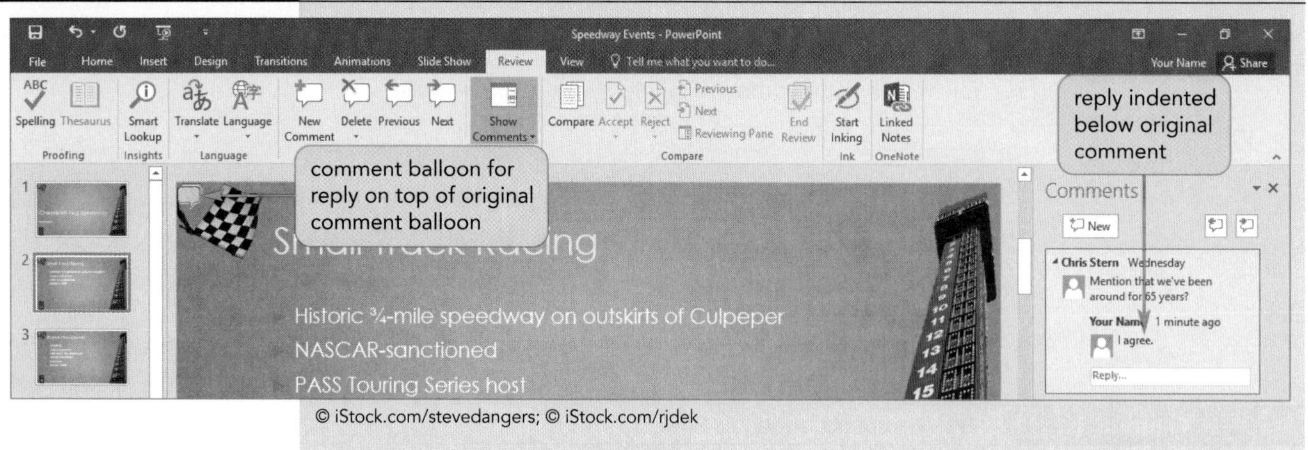

© iStock.com/stevedangers; © iStock.com/rjdek

You will use the Next button in the Comments group to see if there are any additional comments in the presentation. You can decide what to do based upon a comment, and then you can delete the comment when you are finished, if appropriate.

To review and delete comments in the presentation:

1. In the Comments pane, click the **Next** button. Your reply to Chris's comment is selected.
2. In the Comments pane, click the **Next** button. Slide 3 ("Events Year-Round") appears, and Chris's comment appears in the Comments pane.
3. Read the comment in the Comments pane. Chris asked if the racing series should be added below the Pro Racing bulleted item.
4. In the bulleted list, click after the item "Pro Racing," press the **Enter** key, press the **Tab** key, type **NASCAR-sanctioned racing**, press the **Enter** key, type **PASS tour**, press the **Enter** key, and then type **Whelen Modified tour**. Now that you've made the change, you can delete Chris's comment.
5. In the Comments pane, point to Chris Stern's comment. A border appears around the comment, and a Delete button appears. See Figure 6-5.

TIP

To hide comments, click the Show Comments button arrow in the Comments group on the Review tab, and then click Show Markup to deselect it.

Figure 6-5 Delete button on comment on Slide 3

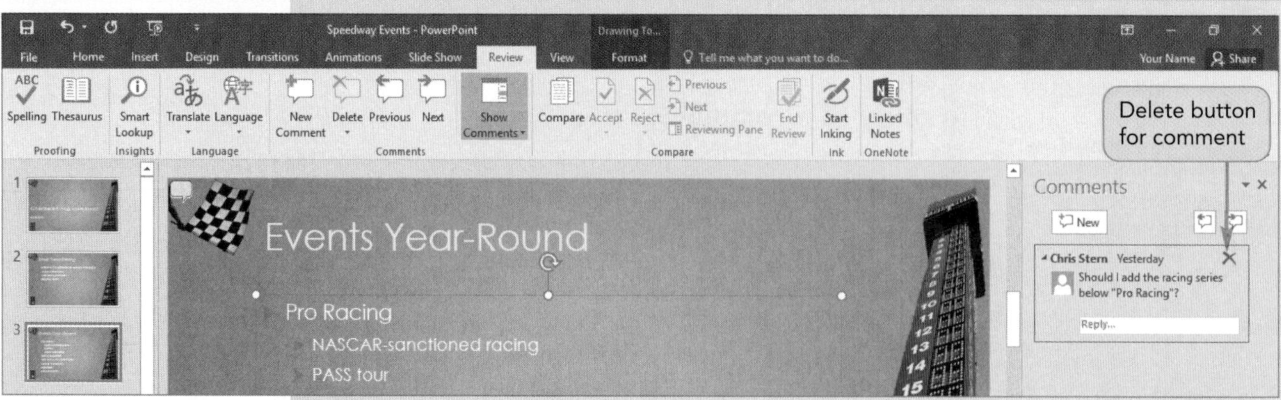

© iStock.com/stevedangers; © iStock.com/rjdek

6. Click the **Delete** button ☒. The comment is deleted.
7. On the Review tab, in the Comments group, click the **Next** button. Slide 5 (Description") appears. This is the slide to which you added a comment earlier.
8. In the Comments group, click the **Next** button. A dialog box opens, asking if you want to continue from the beginning of the presentation.
9. Click the **Continue** button. Slide 2 ("Small Track Racing") appears, and Chris's comment and your reply are in the Comments pane. You have seen all of the comments in the presentation.
10. In the Comments pane, click the **Close** button ☒.
11. Save the changes to the presentation.

Modifying Themes

The built-in themes and variants provide many choices for customizing the design of a presentation. However, if you don't like the specific colors or fonts that come with a theme, you can easily change them.

Changing Theme Fonts

Recall that theme fonts are two coordinating fonts or font styles, one for the titles (or headings) and one for text in content placeholders and other text elements on a slide. To change the theme fonts, you click the Fonts button in the Themes group on the Design tab and then select the coordinating set of fonts from another theme. You can also create a set of custom theme fonts using the Customize Fonts command.

Chris created the custom Speedway theme that is applied to the presentation, but he decided he doesn't like the fonts. He would like you to change the theme fonts.

TIP

To change the theme effects, click the More button in the Variants group, and then point to Effects.

To change the theme fonts:

1. On the ribbon, click the **Design** tab.
2. In the Variants group, click the **More** button, and then point to **Fonts**. The gallery of theme fonts opens. See Figure 6-6.

Figure 6-6 Fonts menu listing gallery of theme fonts

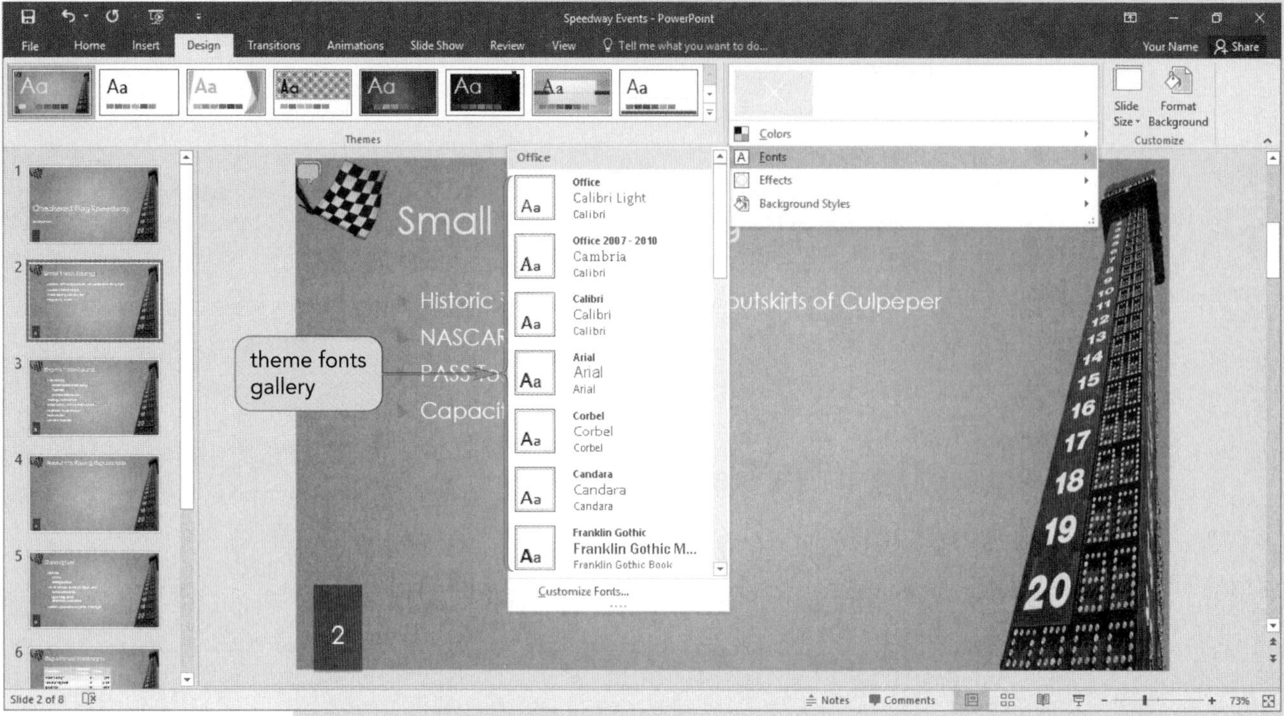

© iStock.com/stevedangers; © iStock.com/rjdek

3. Scroll to the bottom of the list, and then click **Consolas-Verdana**. The font of the slide titles change to Consolas, and the font of the lists change to Verdana.
4. In the Variants group, click the **More** button, point to **Fonts**, and then click **Customize Fonts**. The Create New Theme Fonts dialog box opens. See Figure 6-7.

Figure 6-7 Create New Theme Fonts dialog box

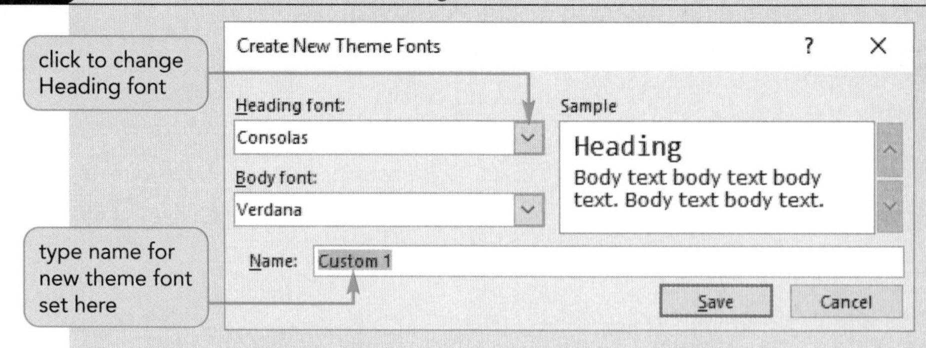

5. Click the **Heading font** arrow, scroll down the alphabetical list, and then click **Corbel**.
6. Click in the **Name** box, delete the text in the box, and then type **Speedway Fonts**.
7. Click the **Save** button. Now the custom set of fonts will appear at the top of the Fonts gallery.

Chris likes the new fonts you chose.

When you save a set of custom theme fonts, the set is saved to the computer, and it can be applied to any presentation opened on the computer. If you've applied the custom theme font set to a presentation, that set of custom theme fonts will still be applied to that presentation even if you delete the custom set from the computer's hard drive.

You'll delete the custom theme font set you created from the computer you are using.

To delete the custom theme fonts from the computer:

1. In the Variants group, click the **More** button, and then point to **Fonts**. The custom theme font set you created appears at the top of the menu. See Figure 6-8.

Figure 6-8 **Custom theme font set in the theme fonts gallery**

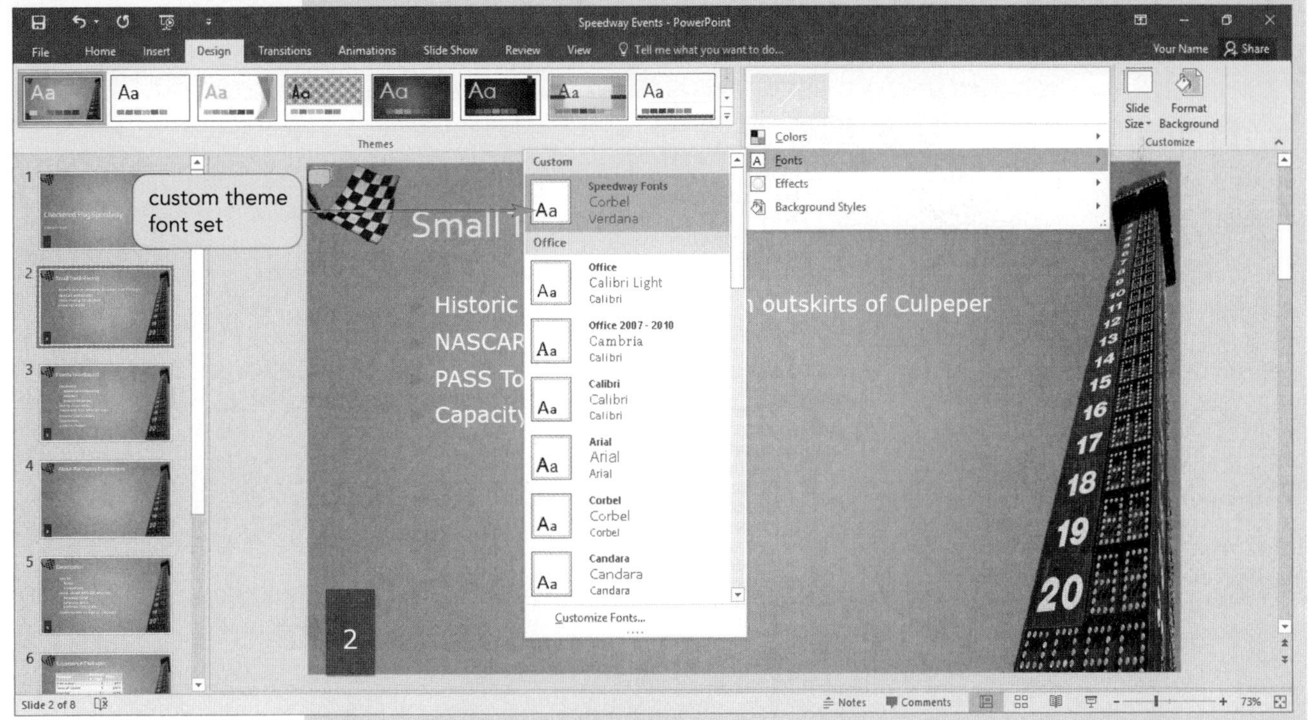

2. Right-click **Speedway Fonts** on the menu, and then on the shortcut menu, click **Delete**. A dialog box opens, asking if you want to delete these theme fonts.
3. Click the **Yes** button. The custom theme font set is deleted from the computer. It is still part of the current presentation's theme. You can verify this by looking at the font list on the Home tab.
4. Click the **Home** tab, and then click in the title text box on Slide 2. In the Font box in the Font group, the font is still Corbel (Headings).

Changing Theme Colors

Each PowerPoint theme has a palette of 12 theme colors associated with it. You can choose another palette of theme colors.

Chris chose the Grayscale color palette when he created his presentation. He decided he wants the presentation to be more colorful. He asks you to apply a different color palette.

To change the theme colors in the presentation:

1. On the ribbon, click the **Design** tab.
2. In the Variants group, click the **More** button, and then point to **Colors**. The gallery of theme colors opens. See Figure 6-9. The Grayscale color palette is selected.

Figure 6-9 Colors menu displaying gallery of color palettes

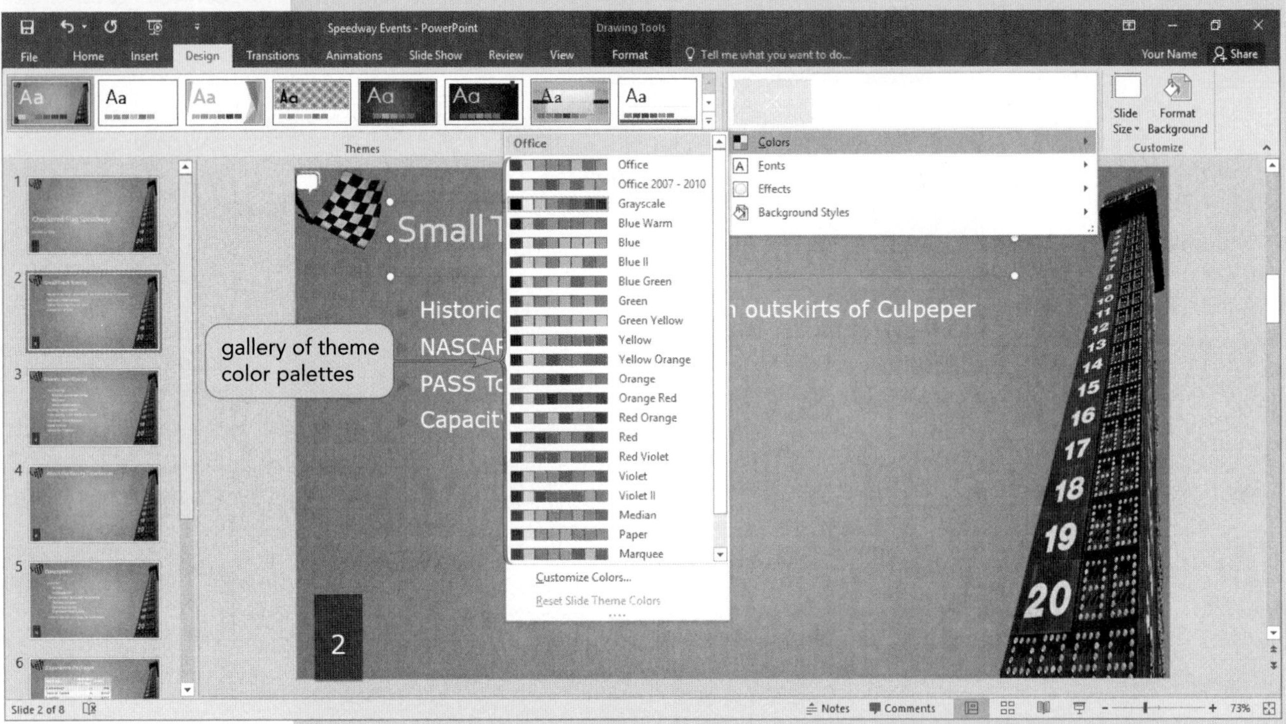

© iStock.com/stevedangers; © iStock.com/rjdek

TIP

To save your changes to the theme as a custom theme, click the More button in the Themes group on the Design tab, and then click Save Current Theme.

3. At the bottom of the list, click the **Marquee** palette. The Marquee palette is applied to the presentation, changing the slide background color and the color of the rectangle in the lower-left corner of each slide.
4. Save the changes to the presentation.

As you know, you can click Customize Colors on the Colors submenu to create a custom color palette. You should be wary of doing this without some knowledge of how colors work together. Usually, dark font colors work well on a light background, and light font colors are readable on a dark background. However, not all colors are complementary, and some combinations can be visually jarring or illegible. For example, avoid red text on a blue background or blue text on a green background (and vice versa) unless the shades of those colors are in strong contrast. These combinations might look fine up close on your computer monitor, but they are almost totally illegible to an audience watching your presentation on a screen in a darkened room. Also avoid using red/green combinations, which color-blind people find illegible.

Problem Solving: Should You Create Your Own Theme?

PowerPoint comes with professionally designed themes, theme colors, and theme fonts. The various combinations give you hundreds of designs from which to choose. If you decide you need to create a custom theme, you can start "from scratch" and assign every theme color and create your own combination of fonts. But unless you are a graphic designer, consider starting with a theme or theme colors that most closely match the colors you want to use, and then selectively customize some of the colors, fonts, or styles. By creating a theme this way, you can take advantage of the professional designs available in PowerPoint to create your own custom look.

Working in Slide Master View

Slide masters ensure that all the slides in the presentation have a similar appearance and contain the same elements. All presentations contain at least one slide master and one layout. Most themes include multiple layouts. To work with slide masters, you need to switch to Slide Master view. Refer to the Session 6.1 Visual Overview for more information about slide masters.

Chris wants you to make several changes to the look of the slides in the presentation. Because he wants the changes to be applied to all of the slides in the presentation, you will modify the slide master. First, you need to switch to Slide Master view and examine the slide master and its layouts.

To switch to Slide Master view:

1. On the ribbon, click the **View** tab, and then in the Master Views group, click the **Slide Master** button. The view changes to Slide Master view, and a new tab, the Slide Master tab, appears on the ribbon to the left of the Home tab. In place of the slide thumbnails in the Slides pane, the layout thumbnails appear.
2. In the Slides pane, point to the selected layout thumbnail. The ScreenTip identifies this layout as the Title and Content Layout and indicates that it is used by Slides 2–3 and 5–8. In addition to placeholders for the title and content, there are placeholders for the slide number, date, and footer. There are also three graphics on the slide—a checkered flag in the top-left corner, a picture of the pole along the right side that indicates which driver is in the lead, and an orange rectangle behind the slide number placeholder in the bottom-left corner.
3. On the slide, click the photo of the checkered flag. The picture is not selected. This is because this photo is not placed directly on this layout. Instead, it is placed on the slide master.
4. Click the photo of the pole that indicates the leader, and then click the orange rectangle behind the slide number placeholder. Notice that clicking these images does not select them, because they are not placed directly on this layout.

5. Scroll to the top of the Slides pane, and then point to the top thumbnail, which is larger than the other thumbnails. This is the slide master, and it is named for the theme applied to the presentation—in this case, it is the Speedway Slide Master, as indicated by the ScreenTip—because the theme applied to the presentation is a custom theme named "Speedway." The ScreenTip also indicates that it is used by slides 1–8, which are all the slides in the presentation.
6. Click the **Speedway Slide Master** thumbnail, and then click the photo of the checkered flag. The photo is selected.
7. Click the photo of the pole that indicates the leader, and then click the orange rectangle. These photos are also selected when you click them. Because these images are on the Slide Master, they appear on all the layouts.

You can apply more than one theme to a presentation. To apply a theme to only one slide or selected slides, right-click it in the Themes group on the Design tab, and then click Apply to Selected Slides. Usually, this is not a good idea; presentations should have a cohesive look. However, if you want each section of a presentation to have a different look—for example, if your presentation is about different music styles, and several slides are about each style—you might want to use a different theme for each section. When multiple themes are applied to a presentation, each theme has a slide master and its associated layouts.

Modifying the Slide Master

TIP

You can change slide backgrounds to a gradient by clicking the Background Styles button in the Background group on the Slide Master tab or by clicking the More button in the Variants group on the Design tab and then pointing to Background Styles.

You can modify a slide master in many ways. For example, you can change the size and style of text in the placeholders, add or delete graphics, change the slide background, and change the style of lists. Changes you make to the slide master affect all of the slides in the presentation. For example, if you modify the font, font size, or font style on the slide master, or if you add an image or an animation to the slide master, it will appear on all the slides in the presentation. Changes you make to a layout in Slide Master view appear only on slides with that layout applied.

The first thing Chris wants you to do is format the slide titles so they are all bold. You will make this change to the slide master.

To modify the slide master:

1. On the Speedway Slide Master, click the border of the title text placeholder.

TIP

If you change the font on the slide master or on a layout, that font will be applied to the slides, overriding the theme font.

2. On the ribbon, click the **Home** tab, and then in the Font group, click the **Bold** button B. The text in the title text placeholder on the slide master becomes bold.

   Trouble? If nothing happened when you clicked the Bold button, the title text placeholder is active but not selected. Click directly on the border of the title text placeholder, and then repeat Step 2.

3. On the slide, click the orange rectangle behind the slide number placeholder, and then press the **Delete** key. The orange rectangle graphic is removed from the slide master.

   Because you changed the slide master, these two changes should affect all of the layouts, but you should check each one to make sure because sometimes changes made to the slide master do not get applied to all of the layouts.

4. In the Slides pane, click the **Title Slide Layout** thumbnail, click the **Title and Content Layout** thumbnail, and then click the **Section Header Layout** thumbnail (the next three thumbnails below the Speedway Slide Master thumbnail). Although the orange rectangle was deleted from each layout, the placeholder text in the title text placeholder on the Section Header Layout slide is not bold.
5. On the Section Header Layout slide, click the title text placeholder border, and then in the Font group, click the **Bold** button **B**.
6. Click the next two layout thumbnails to see that the title text on each is bold, and then click the last layout thumbnail, which is the Blank Layout. The Blank Layout does not have a title text placeholder.

Modifying Individual Layouts

Changes you make to the slide master are applied to all of the layouts associated with the slide master and, consequently, to all the slides in the presentation. You can also modify individual layouts. When you do this, only the individual layout—and, therefore, only slides that have that layout applied—are affected.

Chris wants the presentation title to be all uppercase. To have this happen even if someone types the title normally, you will format the title text placeholder on the Title Slide layout to be all uppercase letters. Chris also wants you to add a larger version of the photo of the checkered flag to the Title Slide Layout. He also does not want the other images on the slide master to appear on the Title Slide Layout. You will modify the layouts now.

To modify individual layouts:

1. In the Slides pane, point to the second thumbnail. The ScreenTip identifies this as the Title Slide Layout and indicates that it is used by Slide 1.
2. Click the **Title Slide Layout** thumbnail, and then on the slide, click the title text placeholder border.
3. On the Home tab, in the Font group, click the **Dialog Box Launcher**. The Font dialog box opens with the Font tab selected. See Figure 6-10.

Figure 6-10 **Font dialog box**

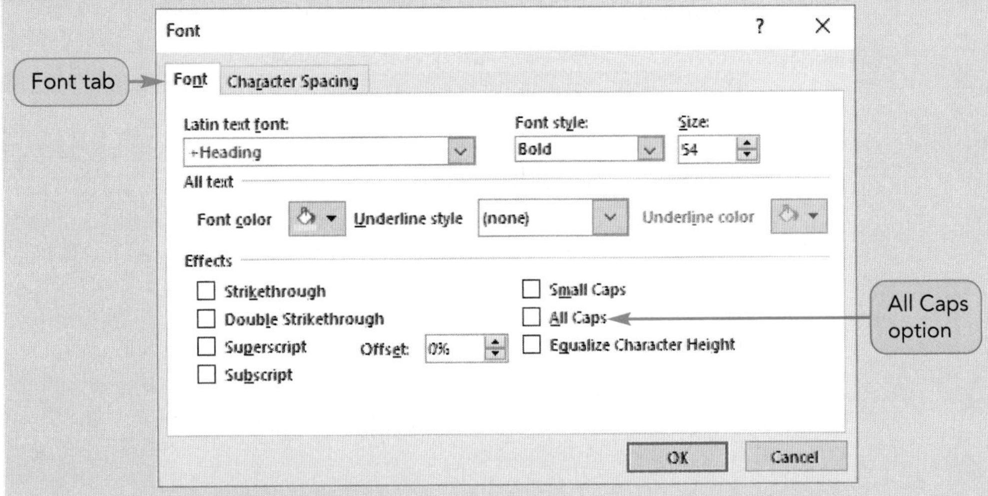

TIP

You can also modify Handout and Notes masters. Click the appropriate button in the Master Views group on the View tab.

4. Click the **All Caps** check box, and then click the **OK** button. The text in the title text placeholder on the Title Slide layout is all uppercase. Next, you will hide the images on the slide master on this layout.
5. Click the **Slide Master** tab, and then in the Background group, click the **Hide Background Graphics** check box to select it. The graphics that are on the slide master no longer appear on the Title Slide Layout. Finally, you will add the larger version of the flag image to this slide layout.
6. Insert the picture **Flag**, located in the **PowerPoint6 > Module** folder, resize it (maintaining the aspect ratio) so that it is three inches high, and then align its left and top edges with the left and top edges of the slide. See Figure 6-11.

Figure 6-11 **Title Slide layout after changes**

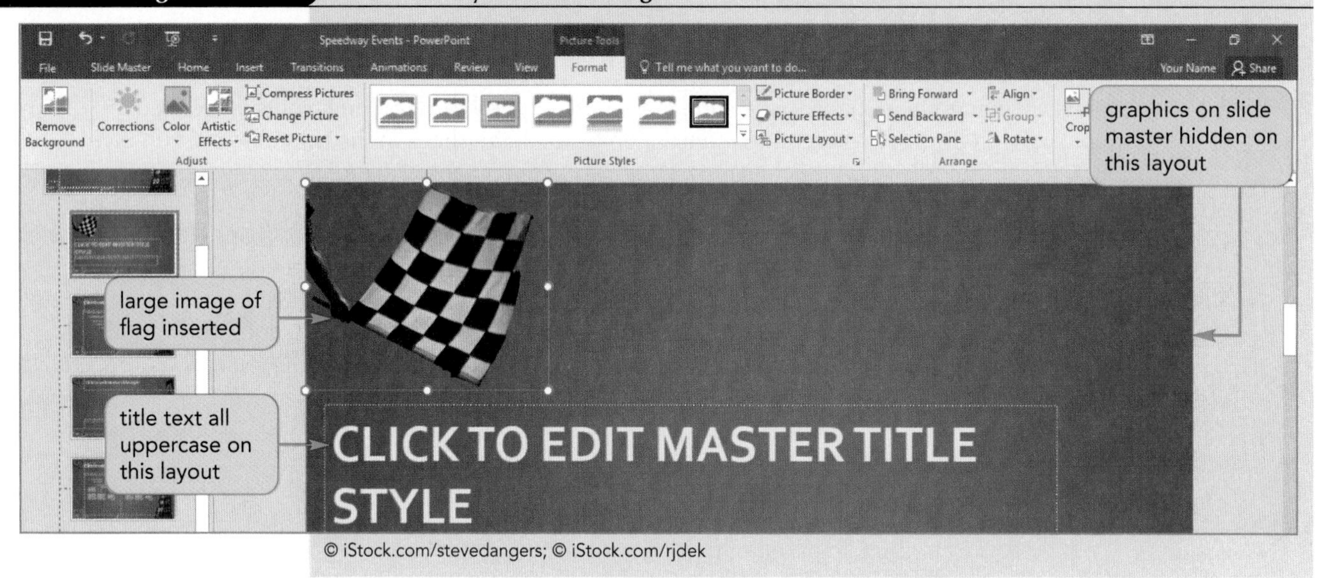

© iStock.com/stevedangers; © iStock.com/rjdek

Modifying the Style of Lists

You can modify the style of lists in many ways. For example, you can change the bullet symbol, size, and color or change the font used for numbers in a numbered list. Good presentation design dictates list styles should be consistent across all slides in a presentation. Therefore, when modifying the style of lists in a presentation, you should make these formatting changes to the slide master, ensuring that the changes appear on all slide layouts.

REFERENCE

Modifying the Bullet Symbol

- Select the content text box.
- On the Home tab, in the Paragraph group, click the Bullets button arrow, and then click Bullets and Numbering to open the Bulleted tab in the Bullets and Numbering dialog box.
- To change the bullet symbol, click the Customize button to open the Symbol dialog box, click the new symbol, and then click the OK button.
- To change the size of the bullet symbol, adjust the value in the Size box.
- To change the color of the bullet symbol, click the Color button, and then click a color.
- Click the OK button.

Chris would like you to change the color of the bullet symbol used in the Speedway Events presentation to a light blue. You'll make this change on the slide master.

To modify the bullet style on the slide master:

1. In the Slides pane, click the **Speedway Slide Master** thumbnail.
2. On the slide, click the border of the content placeholder. Now the change you make to the bullet symbol will affect all bullet levels.
3. Click the **Home** tab, and then in the Paragraph group, click the **Bullets button arrow**. The Bullets gallery opens. See Figure 6-12. You can select one of the styles in the gallery or open a dialog box where you can customize your bullets.

Figure 6-12 **Bullets gallery**

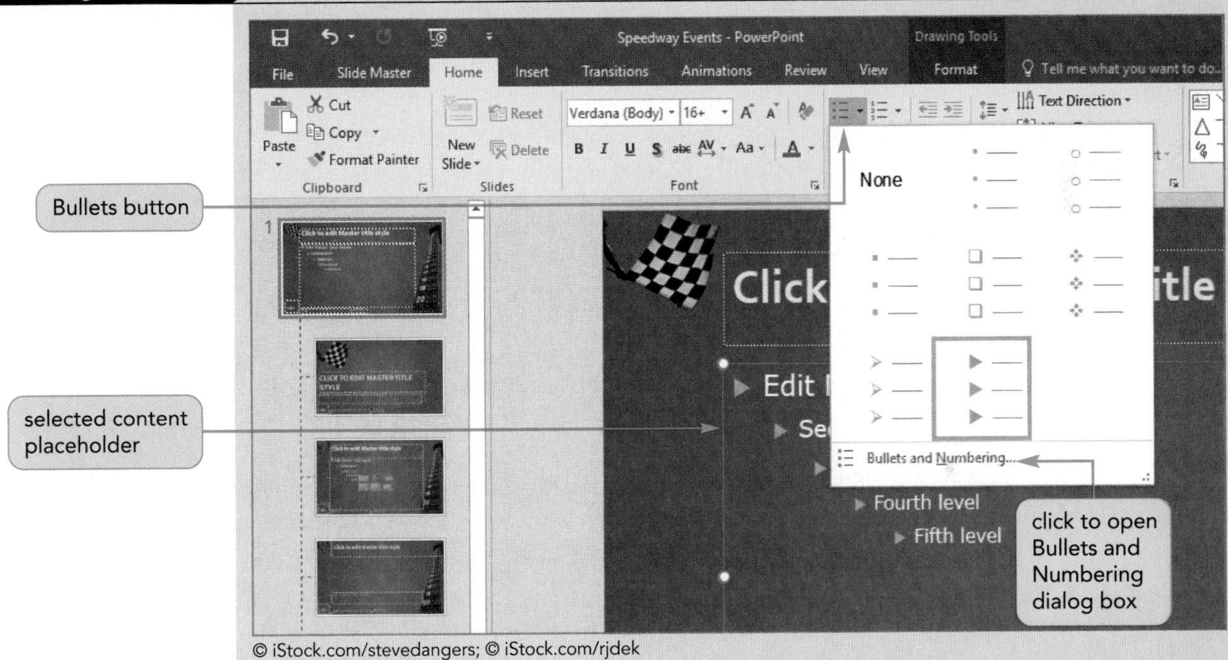

© iStock.com/stevedangers; © iStock.com/rjdek

4. Click **Bullets and Numbering**. The Bullets and Numbering dialog box opens with the Bulleted tab selected. See Figure 6-13.

Figure 6-13 **Bulleted tab in the Bullets and Numbering dialog box**

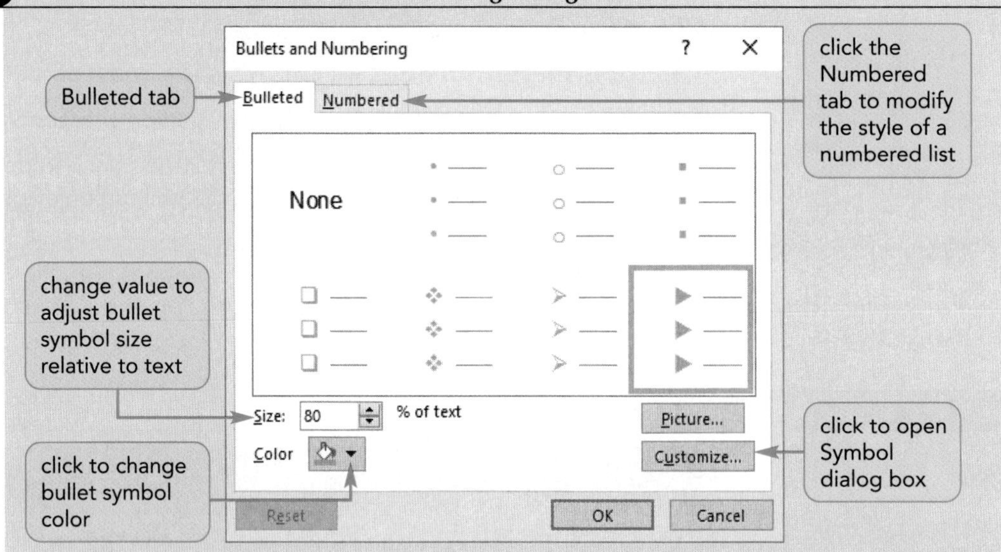

5. Click the **Color** button, and then click the **Aqua, Accent 1, Lighter 80%** color.
6. Click the **OK** button. The bullet symbols in the content placeholder change to the color you selected. Now you will examine the changes you made to the slide master and the Title Slide layout in Normal view.
7. On the ribbon, click the **Slide Master** tab, and then in the Close group, click the **Close Master View** button. The Presentation appears in Normal view with Slide 2 ("Small Track Racing") displayed. The title is bold, the orange rectangle behind the slide number is no longer on the slide, and in the content placeholder, the bullet symbols are the color you chose. These changes correspond to the changes you made to the slide master. See Figure 6-14.

Figure 6-14 Slide master changes reflected on Slide 3

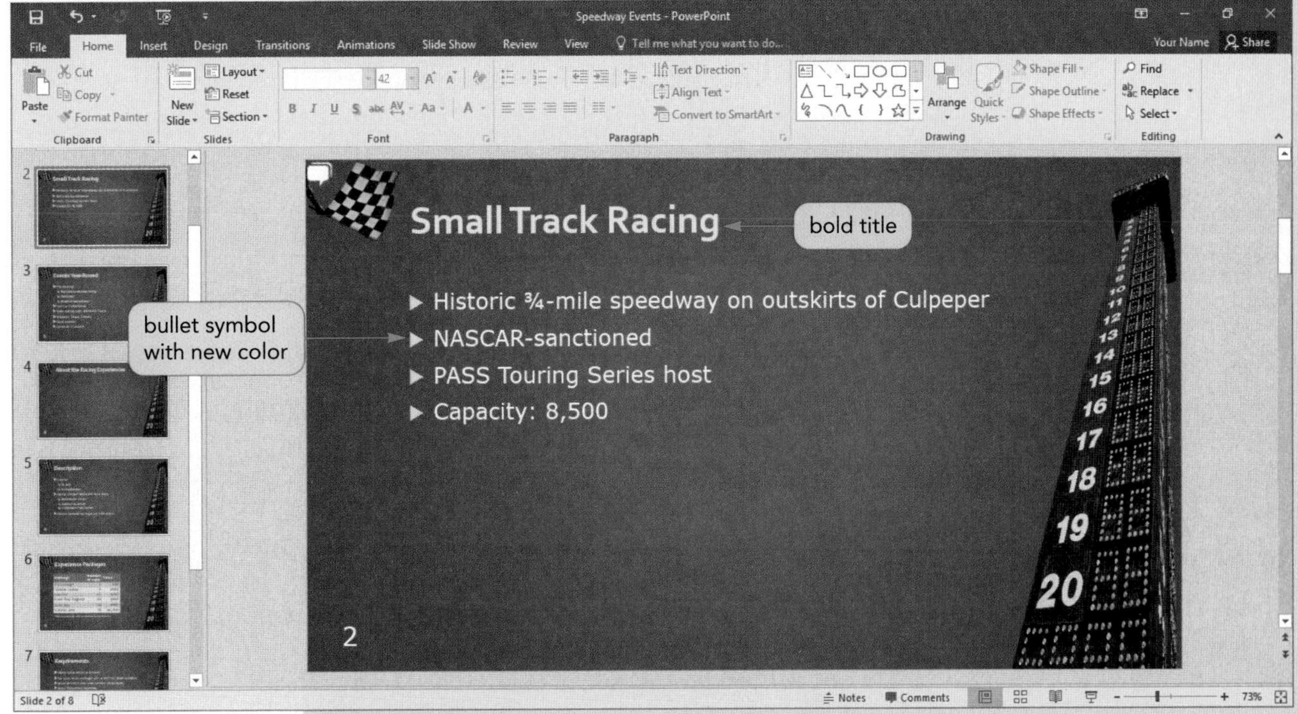

© iStock.com/stevedangers; © iStock.com/rjdek

8. Display **Slide 1** (the title slide). The title text is bold, corresponding to the change you made on the slide master. The title is also all uppercase, the images on the slide master do not appear, and the larger photo of the flag that you inserted appears. These changes correspond to the changes you made to the Title Slide layout.
9. Save the changes to the presentation.

Creating a Custom Layout

If the theme you are using does not contain a layout that suits your needs, you can create a new layout. You do this in Slide Master view. After you create a new layout, it will be listed on the New Slide and Layout menus in the Slides group on the Home tab.

In the Speedway Events presentation, Slides 5 through 8 are about the race track's "Racing Experience" program, which gives people an opportunity to drive race cars on the track. Chris wants to add a section header slide that is filled with a photo before these slides. Note that a slide with a section header layout applied is not the same as creating sections in the presentation. When you create sections in a presentation file, the sections are visible only to people who work with the file; they are not visible to an audience when you present the slide show. Slides with a section header layout *are* visible to an audience during a slide show and indicate to the audience that the upcoming slides are going to contain content somewhat different from the previous slides.

Chris wants you to create a custom section header layout for the presentation. He can then reuse this custom layout to be the section header for slides he will insert later about the other events that the race track hosts. The layout will have a picture placeholder that is the same size as the slide. Chris could have you add a picture as the background to the new layout, but he wants to be able to change the picture depending on the presentation content.

To create a custom layout:

1. Switch to Slide Master view, and then in the Slides pane, click the **Title and Content Layout** thumbnail.
2. On the Slide Master tab, in the Edit Master group, click the **Insert Layout** button. A new layout is inserted below the Title and Content Layout. See Figure 6-15.

Figure 6-15 New layout added in Slide Master view

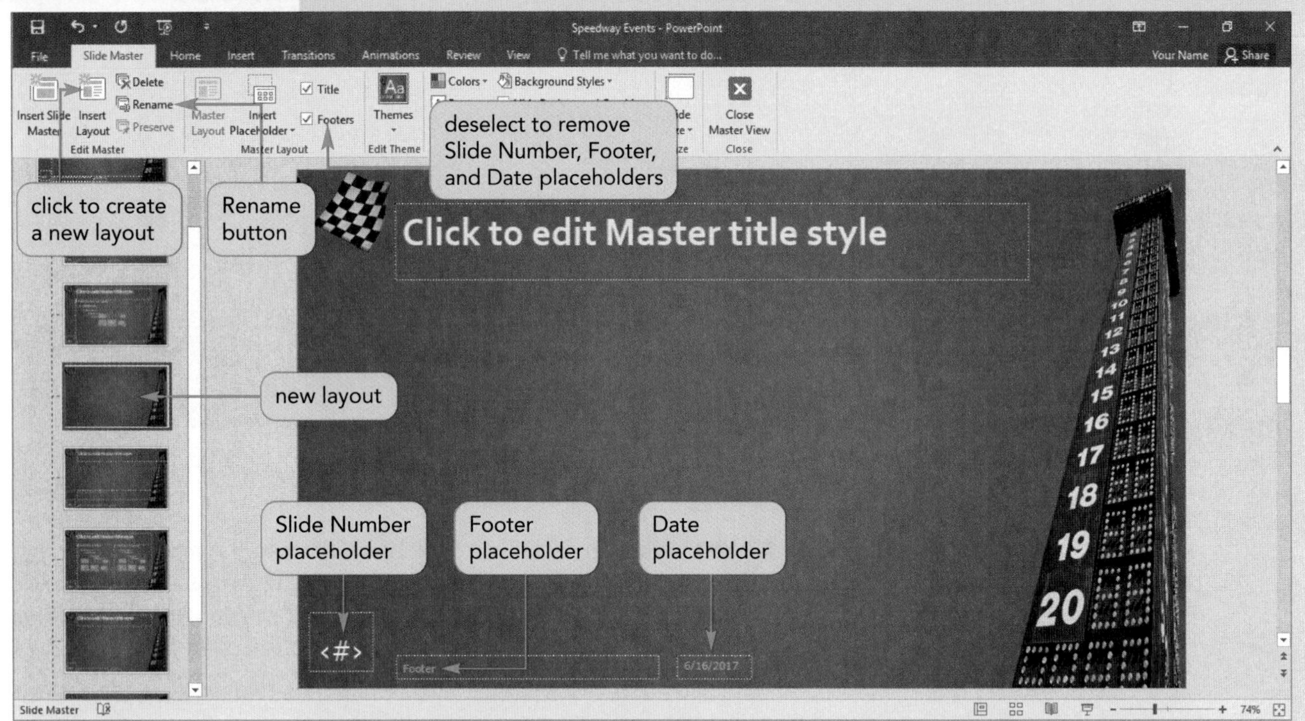

© iStock.com/stevedangers; © iStock.com/rjdek

The new layout contains the photos of the checkered flag and the pole that indicates the leader that are on the slide master. The new layout also includes placeholders for the slide title and the slide number, date, and footer. You can remove the placeholders by deleting the placeholder boxes or by deselecting the Footers check box in the Master Layout group.

3. In the Master Layout group, click the **Insert Placeholder button arrow**. A gallery of placeholders opens. See Figure 6-16.

Figure 6-16 Placeholder gallery

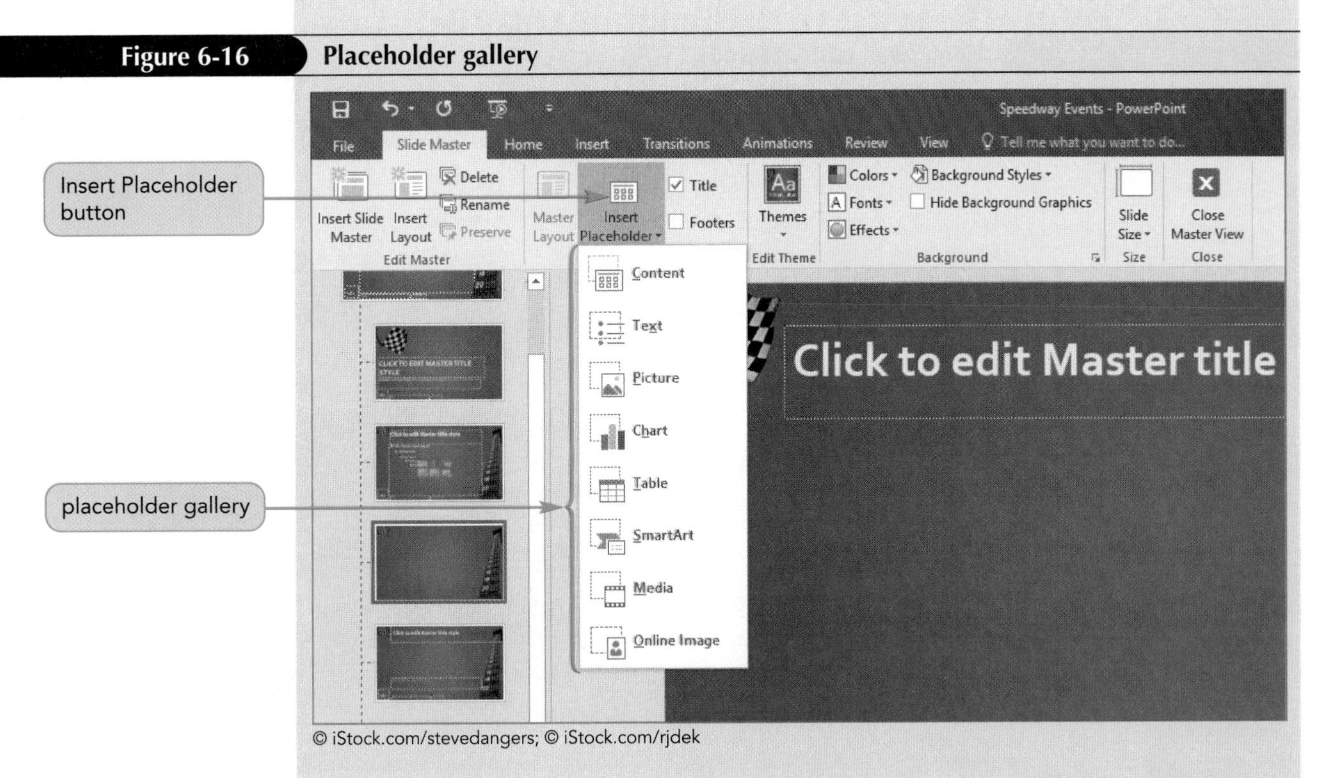

© iStock.com/stevedangers; © iStock.com/rjdek

4. Click **Picture**. The pointer changes to +.
5. Drag to draw a placeholder on the slide that is the same height and width as the slide. On the Drawing Tools Format tab, in the Size group, the measurement in the Shape Height box should be 7.5", and the measurement in the Shape Width box should be 13.33". The picture placeholder is in the layer on top of the title text placeholder.
6. With the picture placeholder selected, in the Arrange group, click the **Send Backward** button. Now you can modify the title text placeholder.
7. Drag the title text placeholder so that its left and top borders are aligned with the left and top edges of the slide, and then drag the right-middle sizing handle to the right so that the title text placeholder is as wide as the slide.
8. Click the **Home** tab, and then in the Paragraph group, click the **Center** button. The title text is centered in the placeholder. See Figure 6-17.

Figure 6-17 Completed custom layout

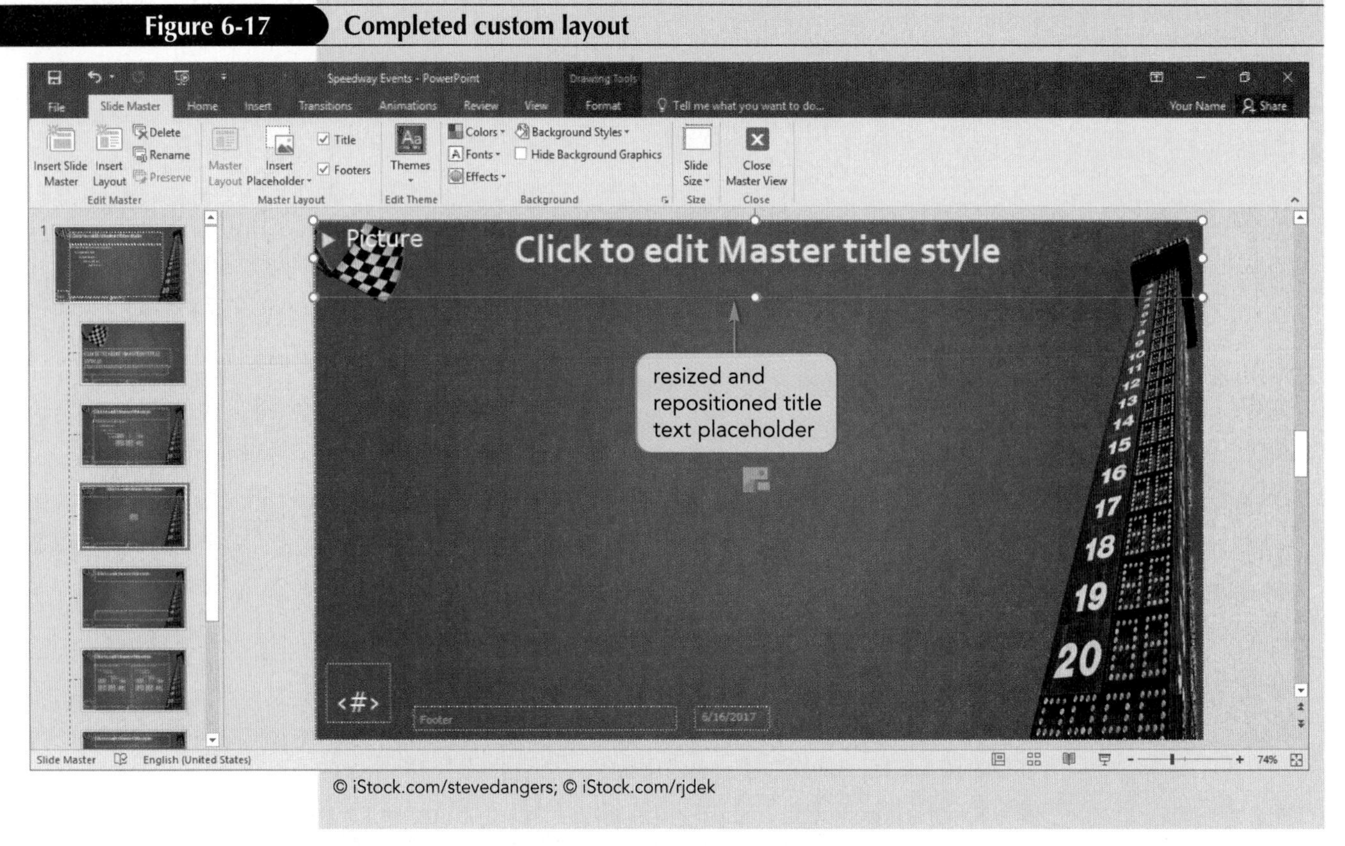

Now that you have created the custom layout, you will give it a meaningful name.

To rename the custom layout:

1. Make sure the custom layout is selected in the Slides pane, and then click the **Slide Master** tab.
2. In the Edit Master group, click the **Rename** button. The Rename Layout dialog box opens.
3. In the Layout name box, delete the text, and then type **Picture Section Header**.
4. Click the **Rename** button. You're finished working with the Slide Master.
5. On the Slide Master tab, in the Close group, click the **Close Master View** button.

Next, you will apply the custom Picture Section Header layout to Slide 4 in the presentation. Slide 4 currently has the Section Header layout applied.

To apply the custom layout:

1. Display **Slide 4** ("About the Racing Experiences").
2. On the Home tab, in the Slides group, click the **Layout** button. The layout you created, Picture Section Header, appears in the top row of the layout gallery. See Figure 6-18.

Figure 6-18 Layout gallery including custom layout

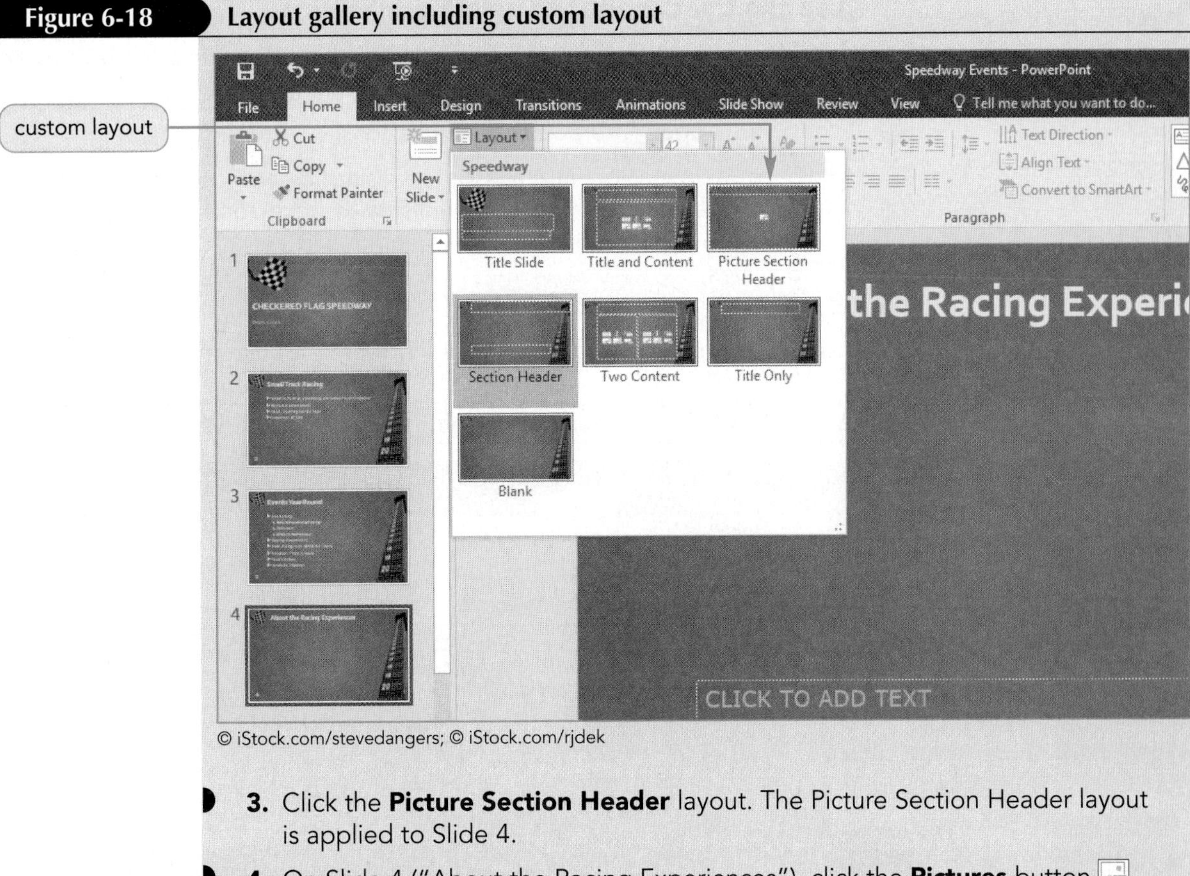

© iStock.com/stevedangers; © iStock.com/rjdek

3. Click the **Picture Section Header** layout. The Picture Section Header layout is applied to Slide 4.
4. On Slide 4 ("About the Racing Experiences"), click the **Pictures** button. The Insert Picture dialog box opens.
5. Navigate to the **PowerPoint6 > Module** folder, and then double-click the photo **Track** to insert this picture on the slide. The title text is difficult to see against the picture background.
6. Click the title text, and then click the title text box border.
7. On the Home tab, in the Font group, click the **Font Color button arrow**, and then click the **White, Text 1** color.

The title text placeholder is still hard to see on the picture. To fix this, you will fill the title text box with a color from the photo.

Fill a Shape with a Gradient of a Color Used on the Slide

To fill a shape with a color used on a slide, you click Eyedropper on the Shape Fill menu, and then click an area of the slide. The shape is then filled with the exact color that you clicked. When you point to a color using the Eyedropper tool, a ScreenTip appears listing a general name for the color, such as Red, Gold, or Black, and the color's RGB values. RGB stands for Red, Green, and Blue. Every color is made up of some combination of these three colors on a scale of 0 through 255. For example, pure red has a Red value of 255 and Green and Blue values of 0, but one shade of orange has a Red value of 229, a Green value of 128, and a Blue value of 27.

You'll change the fill of the title text box on Slide 4.

TIP

If you select the Eyedropper tool and then decide you don't want to use it, press the Esc key.

To use the Eyedropper to select a fill color:

1. With the title text placeholder selected, click the **Drawing Tools Format** tab.
2. In the Shape Styles group, click the **Shape Fill button arrow**, and then click the **Eyedropper**. The pointer changes to [eyedropper pointer].
3. Point to various colors in the photo, pausing to allow the ScreenTips to appear. When you point to a color, a small square appears showing that color. When you pause, a ScreenTip appears listing the color name and the RGB values.
4. In the lower-left corner of the title text box, point to the dark gray cloud as shown in Figure 6-19. It's fine if your RGB values do not match the figure exactly.

Figure 6-19 **Eyedropper tool showing ScreenTip identifying color on slide**

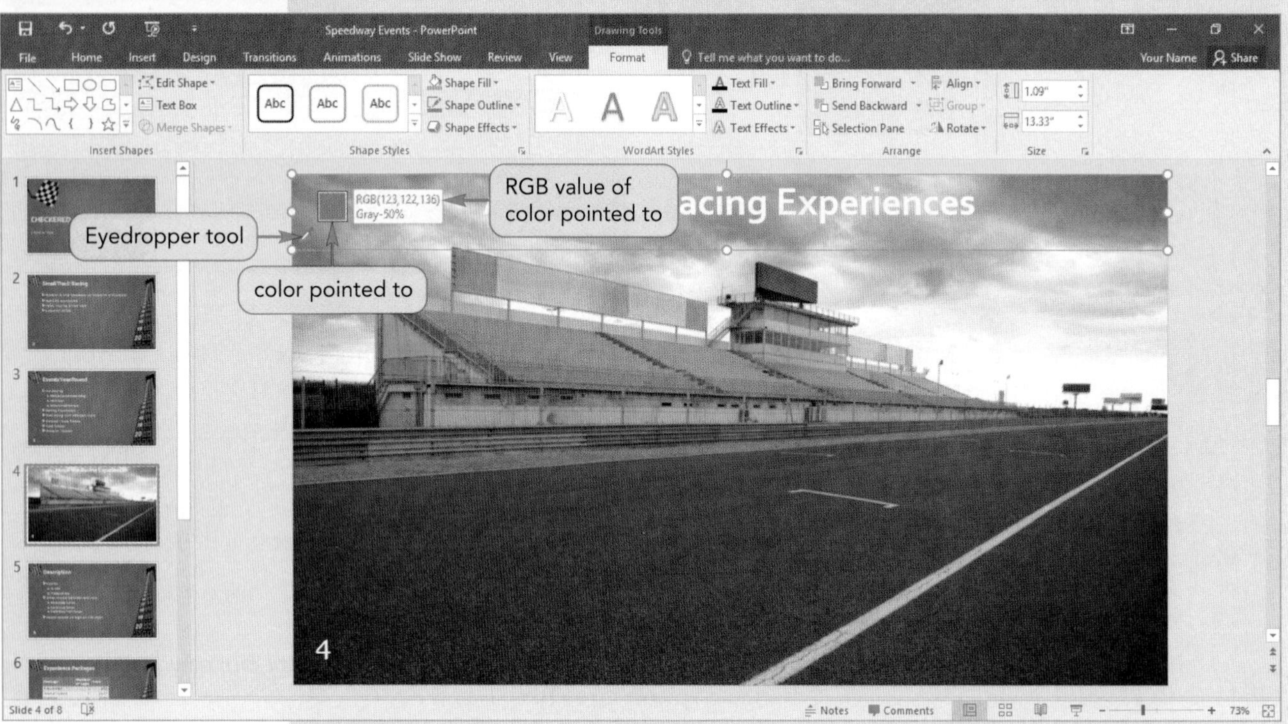

© iStock.com/cipango27; © iStock.com/stevedangers; © iStock.com/rjdek

5. When the pointer is positioned as shown in Figure 6-19, click. The fill of the title text box changes to the color you clicked.

Now the sky in the photo behind the title text box is no longer visible. To fix this, you will make the fill semitransparent so you can see the picture behind it.

To change the fill transparency of the title text box:

1. In the Shape Styles group, click the **Dialog Box Launcher**. The Format Shape pane opens with the Shape Options tab selected and the Fill & Line button selected.

   Trouble? If the Fill & Line button is not selected, click it.

2. Click **Fill** to expand the Fill commands. See Figure 6-20.

Figure 6-20 Format Shape pane after selecting a color fill

© iStock.com/cipango27

Trouble? If the Fill commands are already expanded, skip Step 2.

3. Drag the **Transparency** slider to the right until the value in the Transparency box is 50%.

Now you can see the photo behind the title text, but the gray bar is distracting. If you use a gradient to fill the placeholder shape and vary the transparency of the gradient stops from 100%—not transparent at all—to 0%—completely transparent, you will be able to see the photo and read the text, and you don't notice that the title text box has a fill. You will use the same gray color that you selected with the Eyedropper tool, but the color at the top of the text box will be completely opaque—not transparent at all—and the color at the bottom of the text box will be completely transparent.

To change the fill to a gradient of transparencies:

1. In the Format Shape pane, click the **Gradient fill** option button. The title text box is filled with a gradient. In the Type box, Linear is selected.
2. Click the **Direction** button, and then click the **Linear Down** style. Now the options set for the first gradient stop will affect the top of shape, and the options set for the last gradient stop will affect the bottom of the shape.

   The first stop on the Gradient stops slider is selected. You want to change the color of this gradient stop to the gray color from the photo.
3. Click the **Color** button. Below the Standard Colors row, a Recent Colors row appears. The gray color you selected in the previous set of steps appears in the Recent Colors row. See Figure 6-21.

Figure 6-21 **Color palette showing recently selected color**

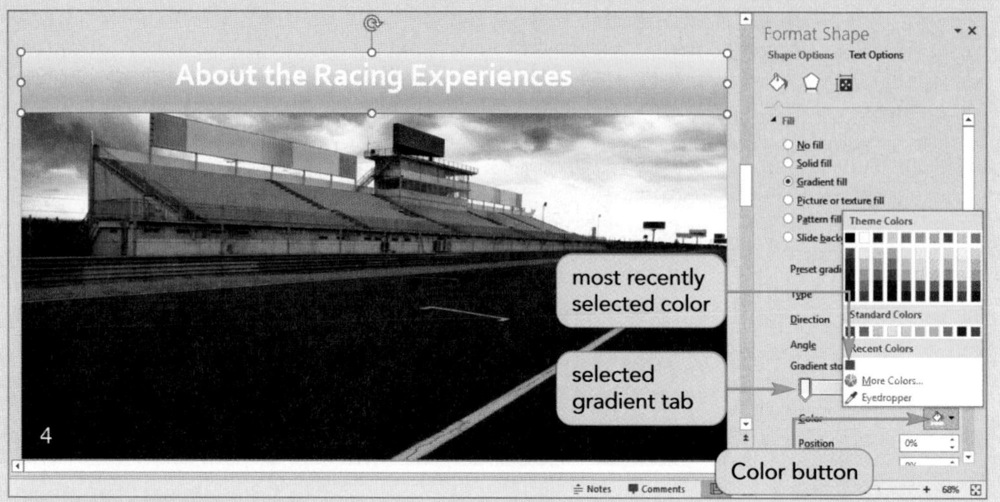

© iStock.com/cipango27

Trouble? If there is more than one color below the Recent Colors label, the most recently selected color—the gray color you selected in the previous set of steps—is the first color in the row.

4. In the Recent Colors section, click the **Gray** color. Now you need to change the rightmost gradient stop to the same gray color.
5. Click the rightmost gradient stop, click the **Color** button, and then in the Recent Colors section, click the **Gray** color. You only need one of the middle two gradient stops.
6. Click one of the middle two gradient stops, and then to the right of the stops, click the **Remove gradient stop** button.
7. Click the remaining middle gradient stop, change its color to the **Gray** color under Recent Colors in the color palette, and then change its position to **65%**. Next, you need to change the transparency of the middle and the rightmost stops.
8. Scroll to the bottom of the Format Shape pane to display the Transparency options. The middle gradient stop is selected, and the Transparency setting is 0%. See Figure 6-22.

Figure 6-22 Transparency option for gradient stops in Format Shape pane

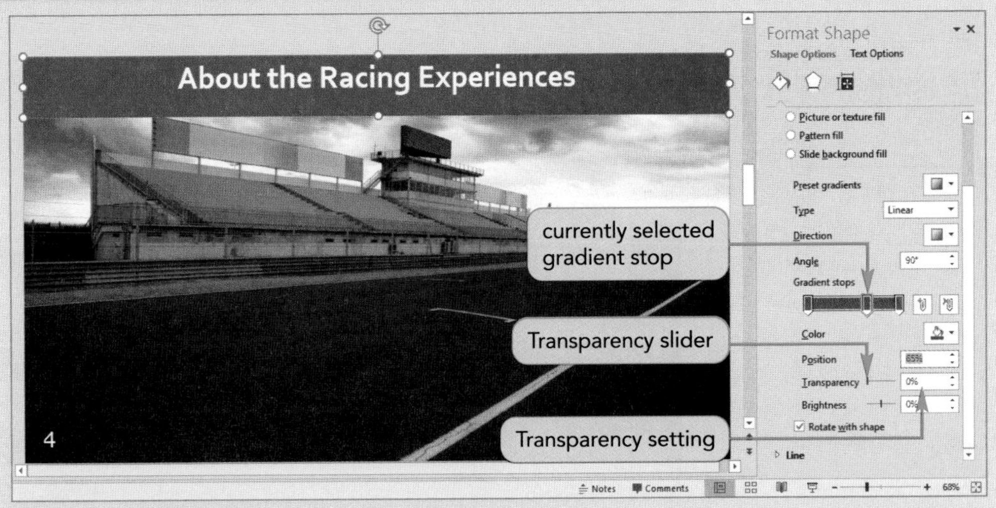

9. Drag the **Transparency** slider to the right until the value in the Transparency box is **50%**.
10. Click the rightmost gradient stop, and then drag the **Transparency** slider all the way to the right to set the value in the Transparency box to **100%**. The left edge of the text is still a little hard to read against the clouds, so you will extend the part of the fill that is opaque a little way down.
11. Drag the leftmost gradient stop to the right until the value in the Position box is **15%**. See Figure 6-23.

Figure 6-23 Final gradient for the title text box

opaque fill stops around here

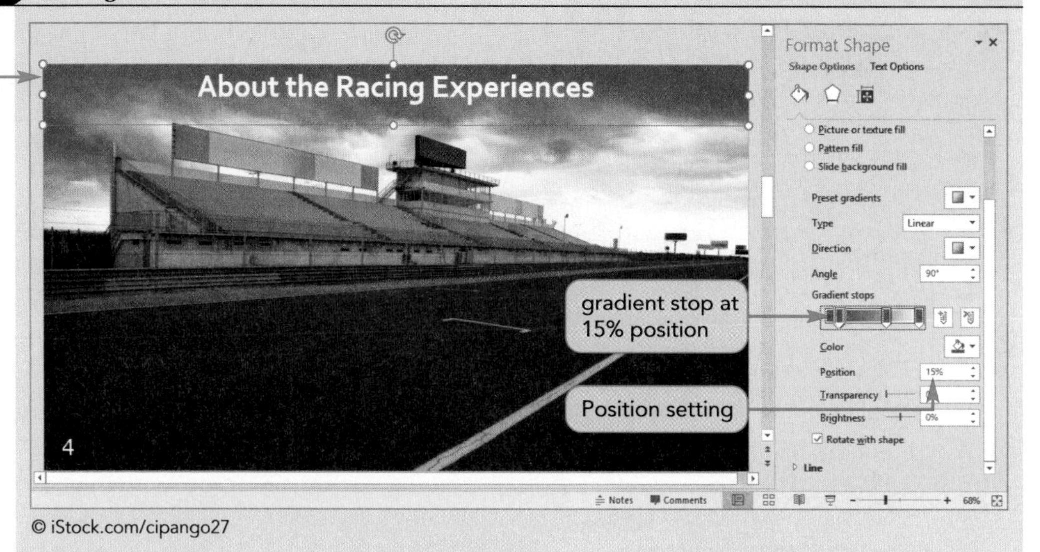

© iStock.com/cipango27

12. Close the Format Shape pane, and then save the changes to the presentation.

INSIGHT

Creating a Photo Album

PowerPoint includes a built-in Photo Album command, which allows you to create a photo album with one, two, or four pictures per slide, and optionally, with titles and captions. The advantage of this feature is that you can insert a large number of photographs all at once into the presentation, without needing to insert each picture individually. To create this type of photo album, you click the Insert tab, and then, in the Images group, click the Photo Album button to open the Photo Album dialog box. To add a photo, click the File/Disk button, select the photo or photos you want to add from the Insert New Pictures dialog box, and then click the Insert button. To modify a photo, click the check box next to it in the Pictures in album list, and then click one of the Rotate buttons to rotate the picture 90 degrees, and click one of the Brightness or Contrast buttons to make the image brighter or darker or to increase or decrease the contrast. To add text boxes below each photo for captions, click the Captions below ALL pictures check box.

To change the layout of the slides, click the Picture layout arrow, and then click a layout. Note that when you do this, you are not actually changing the layout of the slides. All of the options on the Picture layout menu that do not include a title place the slides on the Blank layout from the Office theme; all of the options that include a title place the slides on the Title Only layout from the Office theme.

In this session, you compared presentations and worked with comments. You also modified the theme by changing the theme fonts and color palette, and you modified the slide master by changing the formatting on the slide master and on individual layouts, by changing the bullet style, and by creating a custom layout. In the next session, you will save the presentation as a template, create a custom show, modify file properties, encrypt the presentation, and mark it as final.

REVIEW

Session 6.1 Quick Check

1. How do you accept a change when comparing two presentations?
2. What name appears above a comment in the Comments pane?
3. How do you create a new theme font set?
4. What is a slide master?
5. How do you change size and color of the bullet symbol used in a presentation?
6. Describe how to create a new layout.
7. Describe how to add a placeholder to a layout.

Session 6.2 Visual Overview:

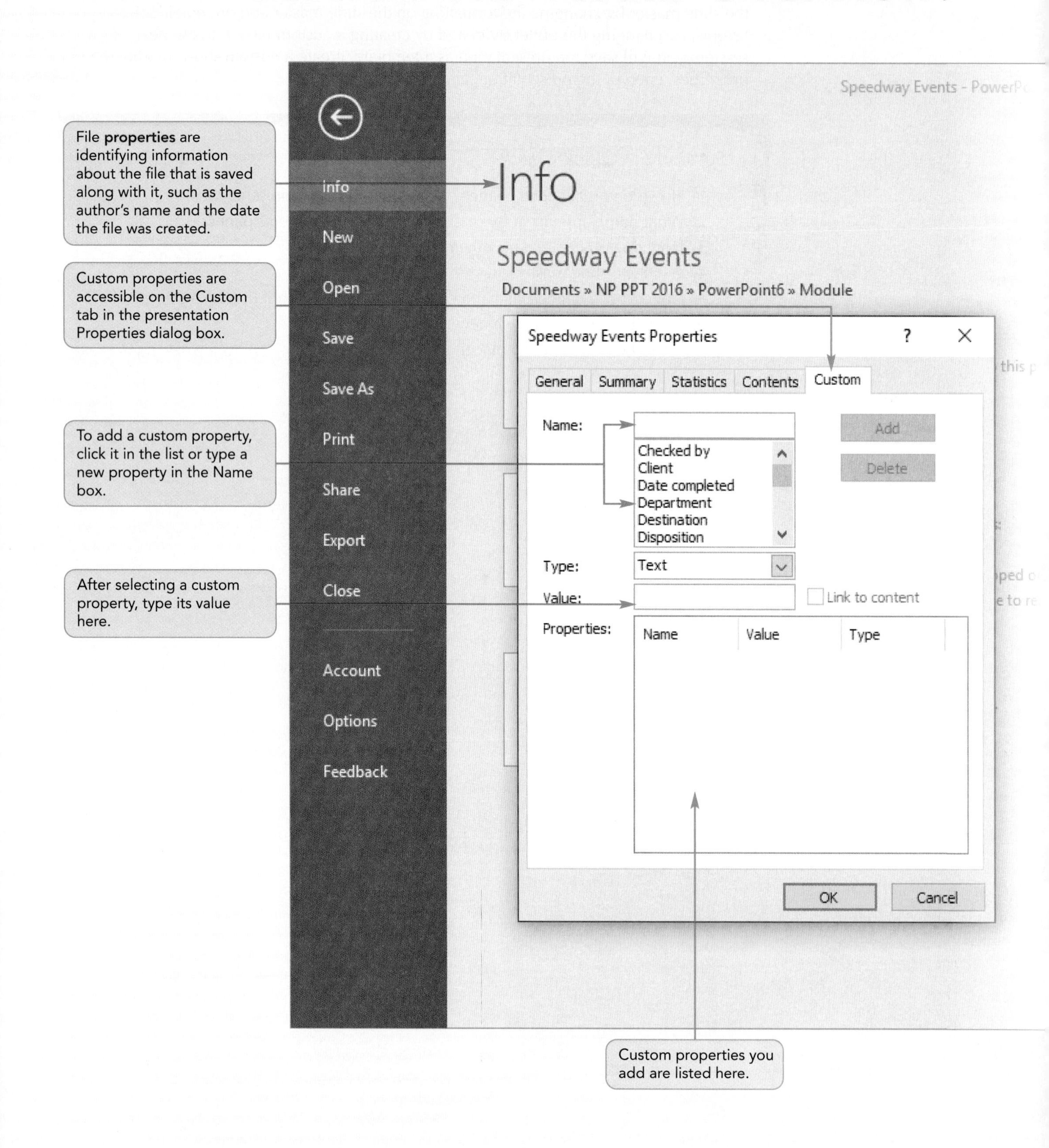

File Properties

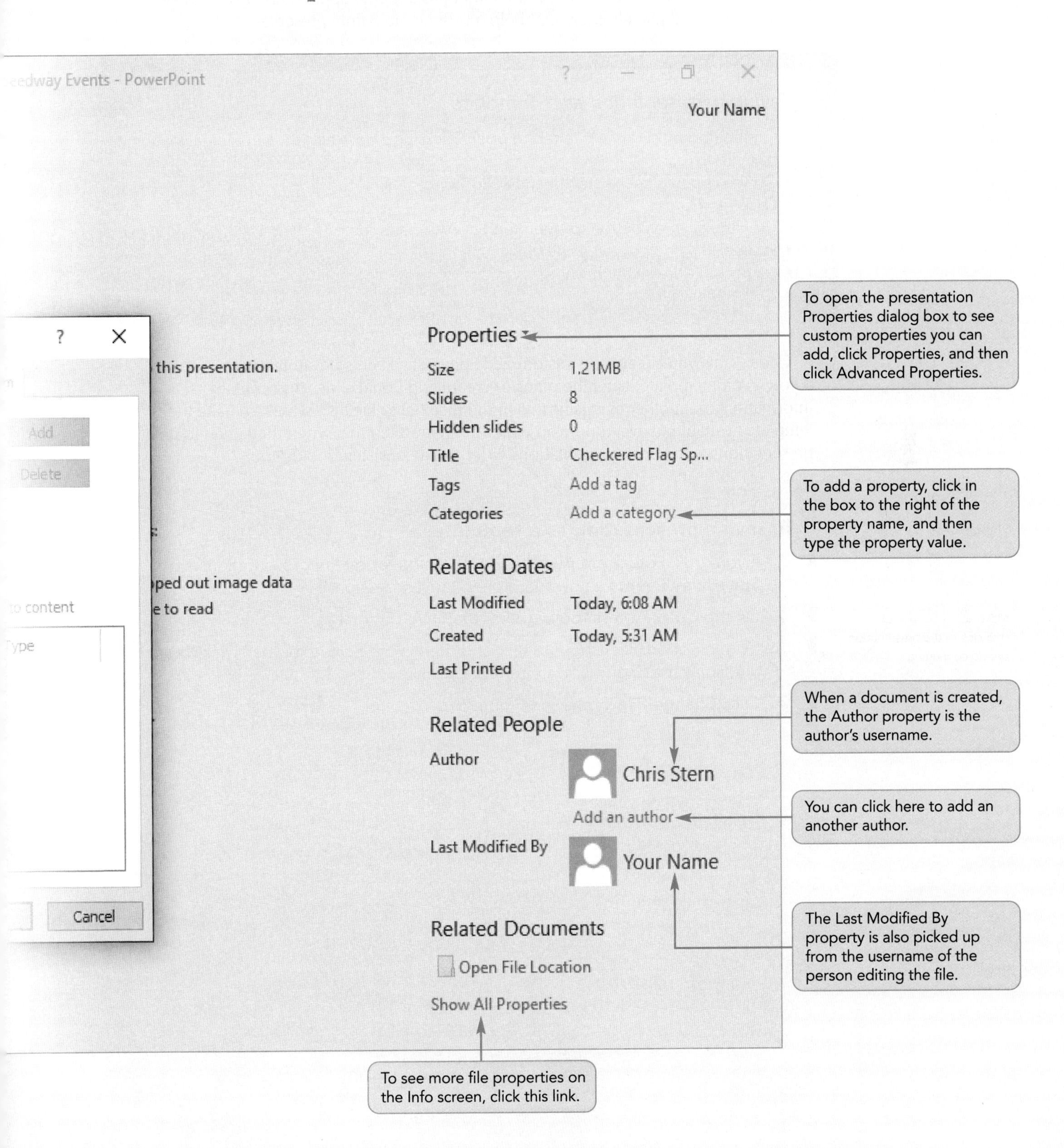

Saving a Presentation as a Template

Recall that a template is a PowerPoint file that has a theme applied and also contains text, graphics, and placeholders that help a user create a final presentation.

REFERENCE

Saving a Presentation as a Template

- On the ribbon, click the File tab to open Backstage view, and then in the navigation bar, click Export.
- On the Export screen, click Change File Type.
- Click Template.
- Click the Save As button to open the Save As dialog box.
- In the File name box, type the filename.
- Navigate to the location where you want to save the template.
- Click the Save button.

Chris wants you to save the customized Speedway Events presentation as a PowerPoint template. Later, he plans to create additional slides that contain information about other events hosted at the race track. He also wants to make the template available to everyone who works at the track so that when they need to create presentations, everyone's presentations will have a consistent look.

To save a presentation as a template:

1. If you took a break after the previous session, open the presentation **Speedway Events** you worked on in the last session.
2. On the Quick Access toolbar, click the **Save** button.

   Make sure you save the changes to the presentation before continuing.
3. On the ribbon, click the **File** tab, and then in the navigation bar, click **Export** to display the Export screen in Backstage view.
4. Click **Change File Type**. See Figure 6-24.

Figure 6-24 Export screen in Backstage view

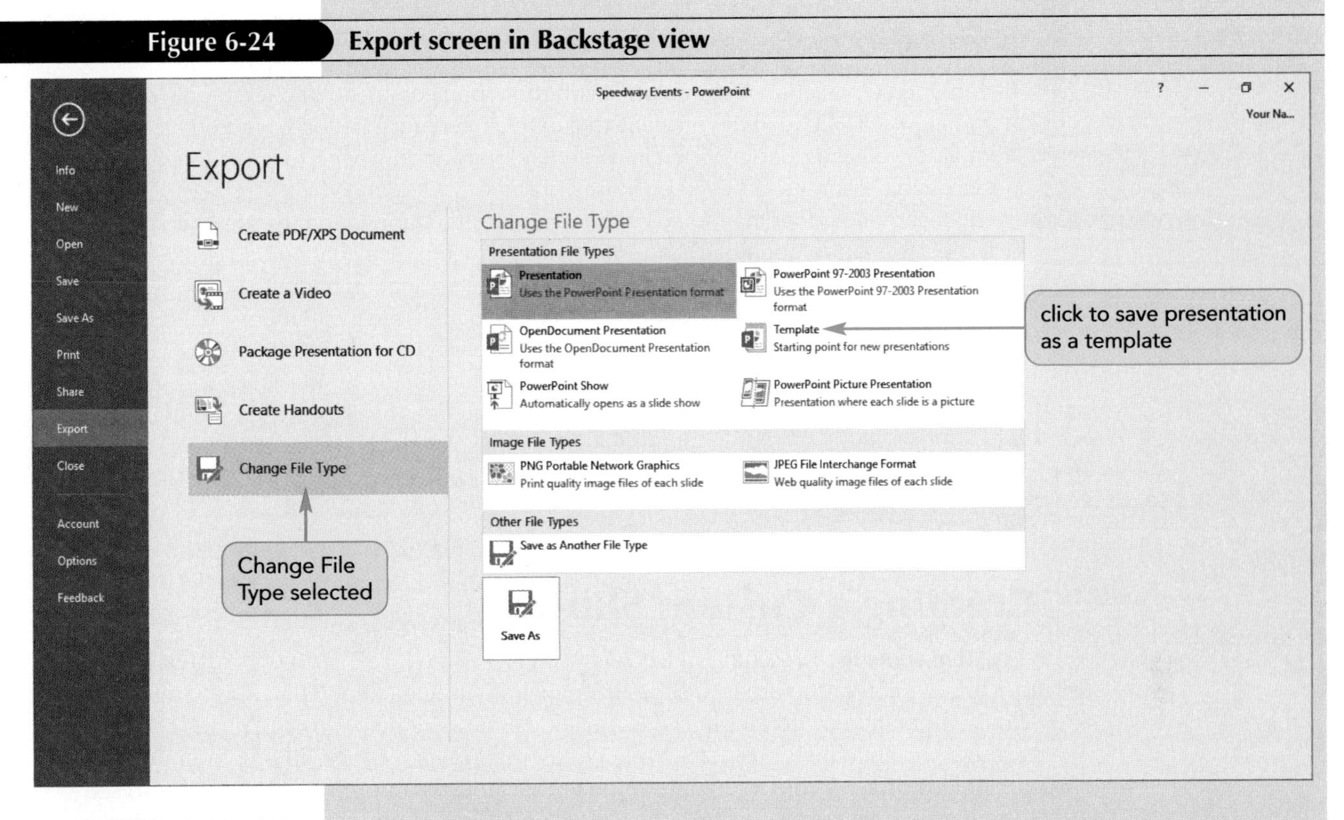

TIP

To embed fonts when saving, click the File tab, click Options, click Save in the PowerPoint Options dialog box, and then select the Embed fonts in file check box.

5. In the Presentation File Types section, click **Template**, and then click the **Save As** button. The Save As dialog box opens with PowerPoint Template in the Save as type box.
6. In the File name box, type **Speedway Template**.
7. Navigate to the location where you are storing your files, and then click the **Save** button. Chris wants you to save only the title slide, and he will add additional template content later.
8. In the Slides pane, select Slides 2 through 8.
9. Press the **Delete** key. The slides are deleted.
10. On Slide 1, replace "Chris Stern" in the subtitle with your name, save the changes to the template, and then close the template.

INSIGHT

Creating a New Presentation Based on a Custom Template

If you open a presentation template using the Open command in Backstage view, the template itself will open. If you want to create a new presentation based on a custom template, you can double-click it in a File Explorer window or store it in a location that is accessible from the New screen in Backstage view.

To locate the folder that contains the templates that appear on the New screen, click the File tab to open Backstage view, and then in the navigation bar, click Options to open the PowerPoint Options dialog box. In the navigation bar in the dialog box, click Save. In the Save presentations section, the path in the Default personal templates location is the location where templates that appear on the New screen need to be stored. You can change this location to any folder on your computer or network. A shared network folder is often used to make templates available throughout an organization. To access templates in this folder, display the New screen in Backstage view, and then just above the templates on the New screen, click PERSONAL.

Creating a Custom Show

A **custom show** is a presentation in which selected slides are included in a version of the presentation or the order of slides is changed without actually deleting or moving slides within the PowerPoint file. Custom slide shows are helpful if you need to quickly create a presentation for a specific audience or if you know you will be presenting to an audience that needs to see only some of the slides in a presentation or needs to see the slides in a different order. Custom slide shows are also useful if you will be using the same slide in multiple custom shows and you need to make a change to the slide; you only need to change it once, and the updated slide will appear in all the custom shows in which it is included.

REFERENCE

Creating a Custom Show

- On the Slide Show tab, in the Start Slide Show group, click the Custom Slide Show button, and then click Custom Shows to open the Custom Shows dialog box.
- Click the New button to open the Define Custom Show dialog box.
- In the Slide show name box, type the name of the custom show.
- In the Slides in presentation box, click the check boxes next to the slides you want to add to the custom show, and then click the Add button to add those slides to the Slides in custom show box.
- To reorder slides in the custom show, select a slide in the Slides in custom show box, and then click the Up or Down arrow.
- Click the OK button, and then click the Close button.

After Chris adds more slides about other events at the race track, he wants to create custom shows that include only the slides about the particular event. For now, he asks you to create a custom show in the Speedway Events presentation that contains only the five slides about the Racing Experience program.

To create a custom show in the Speedway Events presentation:

1. Open the **Speedway Events** presentation, and then on the ribbon, click the **Slide Show** tab.
2. In the Start Slide Show group, click the **Custom Slide Show** button, and then click **Custom Shows**. The Custom Shows dialog box opens.
3. Click the **New** button. The Define Custom Show dialog box opens. See Figure 6-25.

Figure 6-25 Define Custom Show dialog box

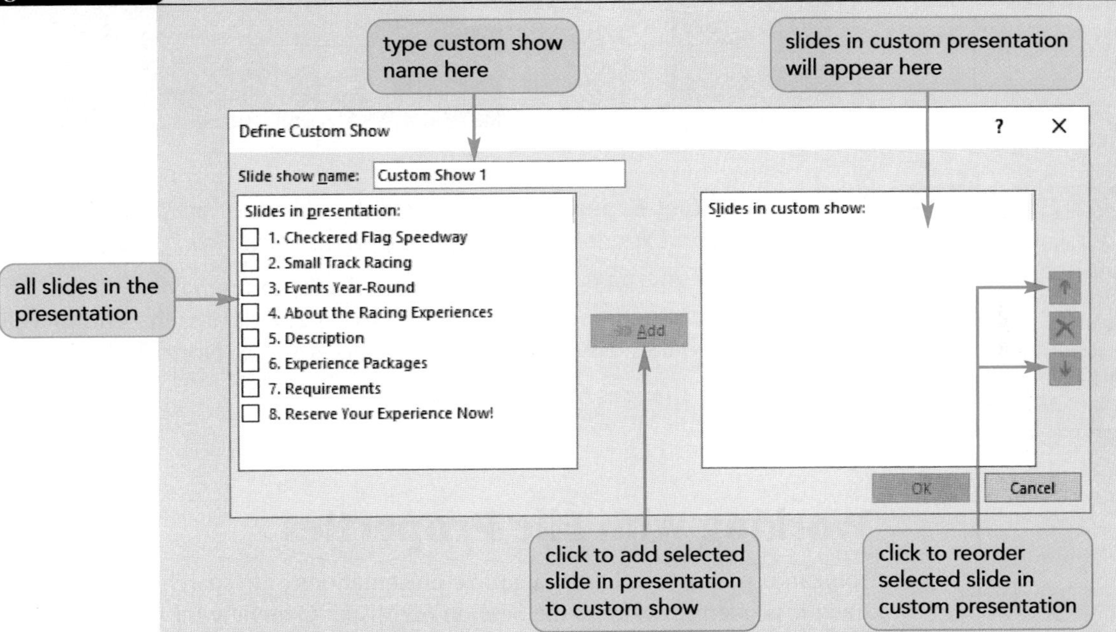

4. In the Slide show name box, delete the text, and then type **Racing Experience**. Next, you'll select the slides that you want to use in the custom show.
5. In the Slides in presentation box on the left, click the check boxes next to **4. About the Racing Experiences**, **5. Description**, **6. Experience Packages**, **7. Requirements**, and **8. Reserve Your Experience Now!**.
6. Click the **Add** button. The selected slides on the left are added to the Slides in custom show box on the right.
7. Click the **OK** button. The custom show you created is added to the list in the Custom Shows dialog box.
8. Click the **Close** button in the dialog box.

To run the custom show, you can click the Show button in the Custom Shows dialog box, or you can run it from Normal, Slide Show, or Presenter view.

To run a custom show:

1. On the Slide Show tab, in the Start Slide Show group, click the **Custom Slide Show** button. The menu now includes the custom show you created. See Figure 6-26.

Figure 6-26 Custom Slide Show menu listing a custom show

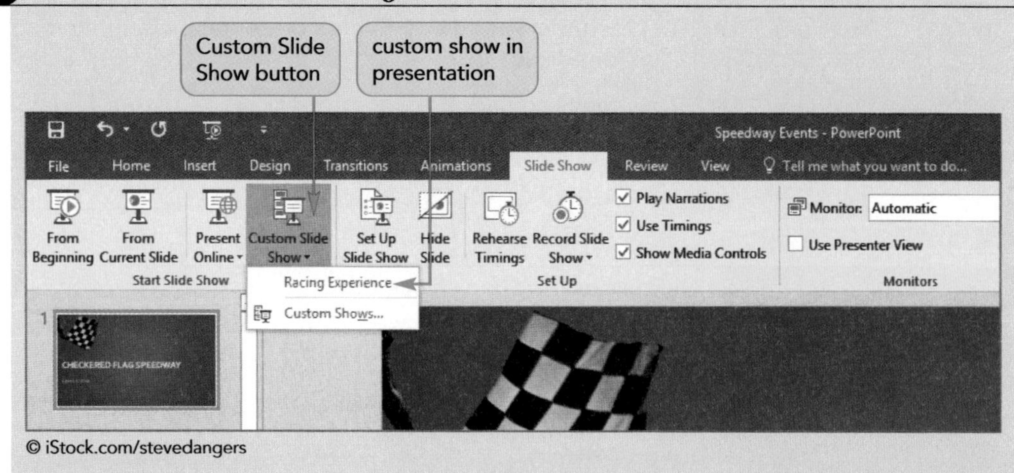

© iStock.com/stevedangers

TIP

You can also start the slide show by right-clicking anywhere on a slide in Slide Show view, pointing to Custom Show on the shortcut menu, and then clicking the custom presentation.

2. Click **Racing Experience**. The first slide in the custom show, Slide 4 ("About the Racing Experiences"), appears in Slide Show view.
3. Advance the slide show five times to display the remaining slides in the custom presentation and the black slide that indicates the end of a slide show, and then advance it once more to return to Normal view.
4. Save the changes to the presentation.

Working with File Properties

You can use file properties to organize presentations or to search for files that have specific properties. Refer to the Session 6.2 Visual Overview for more information on file properties. To view or modify properties, you need to display the Info screen in Backstage view.

Chris wants you to modify the Author property by adding yourself as an author and in the Status property, indicating that this presentation is not yet final.

To modify file properties:

1. On the ribbon, click the **File** tab. The Info screen in Backstage view appears. The document properties are listed on the right side of the screen. See Figure 6-27.

Figure 6-27 Properties on Info screen in Backstage view

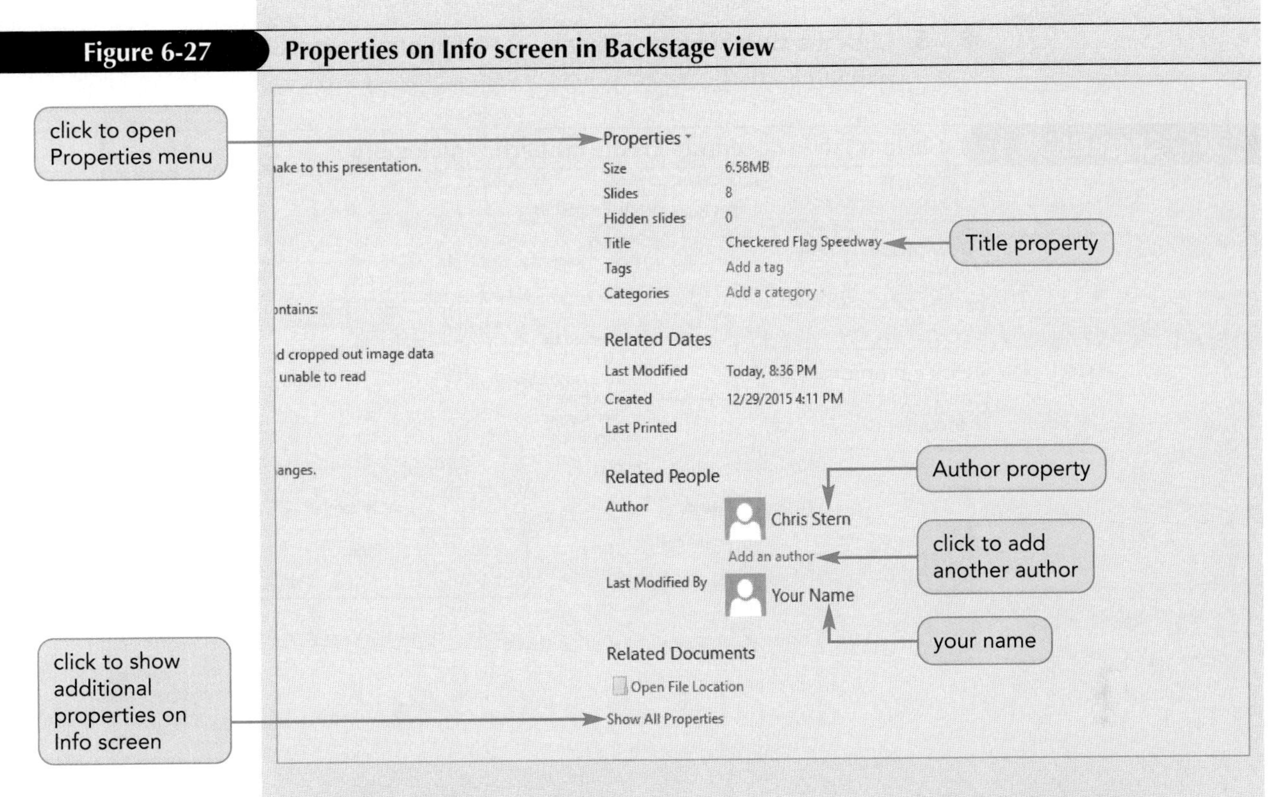

Because Chris created the original document, his name is listed as the Author. Because you have saved the file after making changes, your name (or the name in the User name box on your computer) appears in the Last Modified By box. You'll add yourself as an author.

2. In the Related People section, click **Add an author**, type your name in the box that appears, and then click a blank area of the screen.

   Trouble? If you pressed the Enter key after typing your name and a dialog box opens, click a blank area of the screen.

3. Scroll down, and then at the bottom of the Properties list, click the **Show All Properties** link. The Properties list expands to include all of the document properties.

4. Next to Status, click **Add text**, type **Draft**, and then click a blank area of the screen.

Chris also wants you to add the Checked by property so that you can list the names of people who have reviewed the presentation. The Checked by property is not listed on the Info screen. To add this property to the file, you need to open the Properties dialog box for the presentation, and then add the property on the Custom tab. Even after you add a custom property, however, the custom property will not appear on the Info screen.

To add a custom file property:

1. At the top of the list of document properties, click the **Properties** button, and then click **Advanced Properties**. The Speedway Events Properties dialog box opens.

2. If necessary, click the **Summary** tab. The Author box shows your name next to Chris's name.

3. Click the **Custom** tab. This tab lists additional properties you can add. See Figure 6-28.

Figure 6-28 Custom tab in Speedway Events Properties dialog box

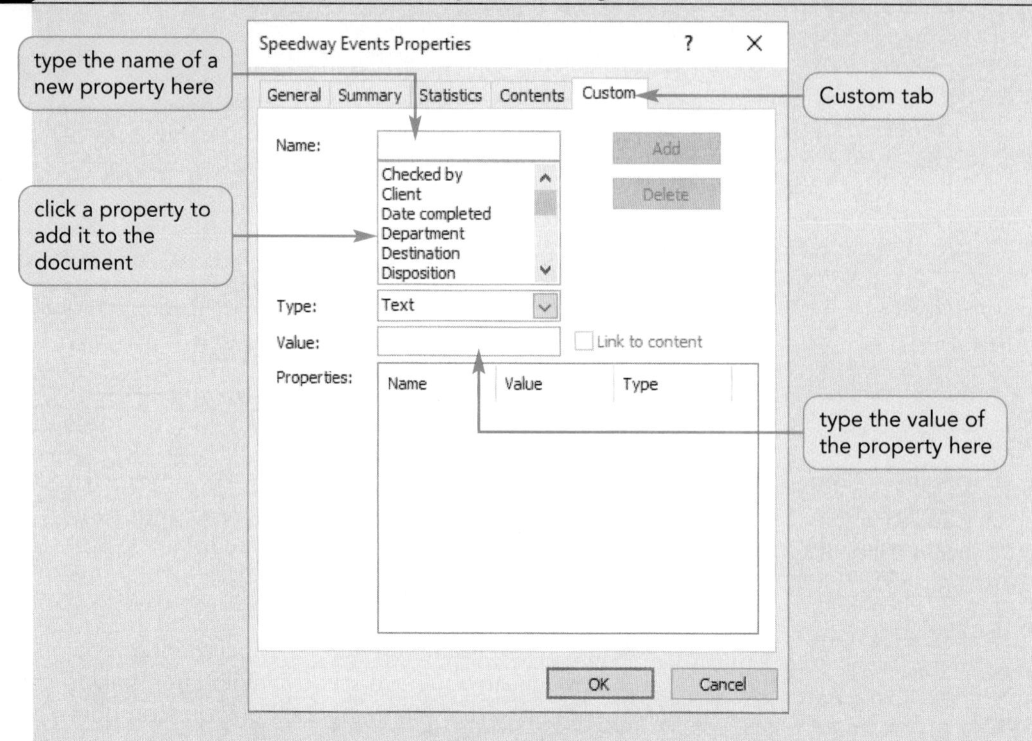

TIP

To create a new property, type its name in the Name box, type a value in the Value box, and then click the Add button.

4. In the Name list, click **Checked by**. "Checked by" appears in the Name box above the list.
5. Click in the **Value** box, type **Jeff Wilson**, and then click the **Add** button. "Checked by" and the value you gave it appear in the Properties list below the Value box.
6. Click the **OK** button.
7. In the navigation bar, click **Save**. The changes to the presentation are saved, and Backstage view closes.

INSIGHT

Customizing PowerPoint

In PowerPoint, you can customize the ribbon and the Quick Access Toolbar to suit your working style or your needs for creating a particular presentation. To customize the Quick Access Toolbar, you can add or remove buttons and change its location in the window. You customize the ribbon by creating a new group on an existing tab or creating a new tab with new groups and then adding buttons to the new groups. To customize these elements, click the File tab, and then click Options to open the PowerPoint Options dialog box. To customize the Quick Access Toolbar, click Quick Access Toolbar in the navigation bar; to customize the ribbon, click Customize Ribbon in the navigation bar. In both cases, the right side of the dialog box changes to show two lists. On the left is an alphabetical list of commands. On the right, the current buttons on the Quick Access Toolbar or the current tabs and groups on the ribbon are listed. The list of commands on the left are Popular Commands; to see all the commands in PowerPoint, click the Choose commands from arrow, and then click All Commands. To add a command to the Quick Access Toolbar or to the selected group on the ribbon, click the command in the list on the left, and then click the Add button. To customize the ribbon, you must create a new group first. Select the tab on which you want to create the new group (or click the New Tab button to create a new tab), and then click the New Group button.

To move the Quick Access Toolbar so it appears below the ribbon, click the Customize Quick Access Toolbar button to the right of the Quick Access Toolbar, and then click Show Below the Ribbon.

Checking for Accessibility Issues

You already know how to add alt text to objects so that people who use screen readers will understand what is on each slide. You also know how to open the Selection pane and verify the order in which objects on a slide will be identified. You can use the Check Accessibility command to help you identify possible problems on slides that might prevent a presentation from being completely accessible. The Accessibility Checker classifies potential problems into three categories—errors, warnings, and tips. An error is content that is difficult-to-impossible for people with disabilities to access. Content that is flagged with a warning is content that sometimes makes it difficult for people with disabilities to access. And content flagged with a tip isn't necessarily impossible for people with disabilities to access, but it could possibly be organized in a way that would make it easier to access.

You will use the Accessibility Checker to see if you need to add alt text or change the order of objects on the slides.

To use the Accessibility Checker:

1. Display **Slide 1** (the title slide) if necessary, and then click the **File** tab. The Info screen appears in Backstage view.
2. Click the **Check for Issues** button, and then click **Check Accessibility**. Backstage view closes, and the Accessibility Checker pane opens. See Figure 6-29. You can examine the issues identified by the Accessibility Checker.

Figure 6-29 Accessibility Checker pane listing potential issues

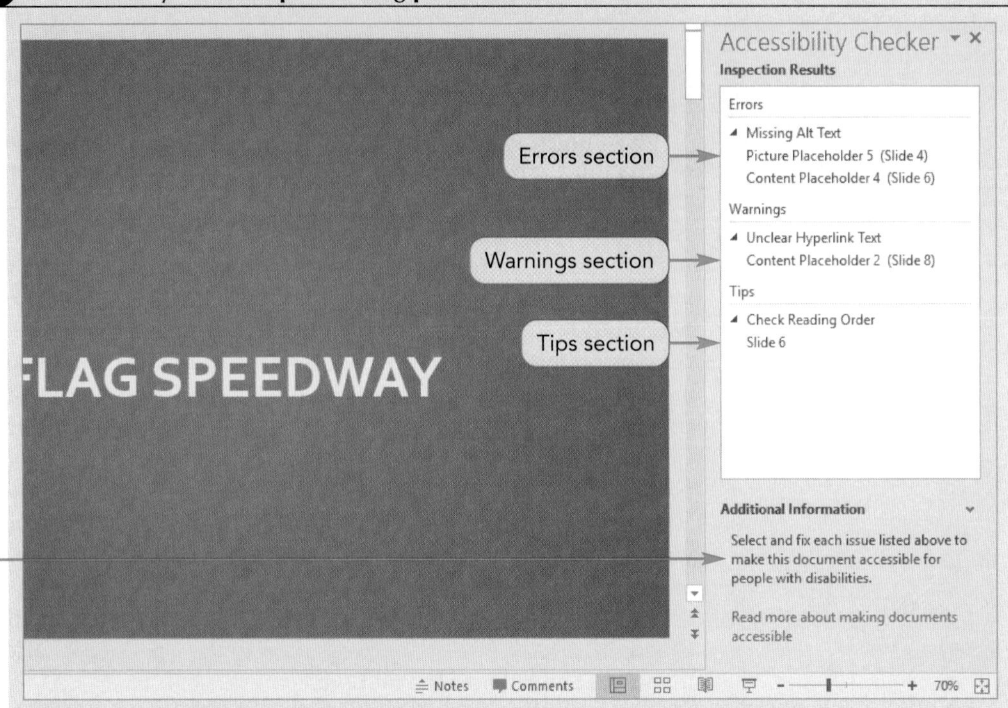

3. In the Errors section, click **Picture Placeholder 5 (Slide 4)**. Slide 4 is displayed, and the Additional Information at the bottom of the pane changes to describe the problem. The background picture on Slide 4 is missing alt text.
4. In the Errors section, click **Content Placeholder 4 (Slide 6)**. Slide 6 is displayed, and the table is selected on the slide. The table also does not have alt text.
5. In the Warnings section, click **Content Placeholder 2 (Slide 8)**. Slide 8 is displayed, and the Additional Information section in the pane changes to describe the problem with the unclear hyperlink text. You cannot add alt text to text, only to objects. To resolve an unclear hyperlink, you can open the Edit Hyperlink dialog box and change the text to display a description of the web page or document to which you are linking; or you can add text to the slide that describes the link. For example, you could change the text to display for the link on Slide 8 to "Checkered Flag Speedway Website."
6. In the Tips section in the Accessibility Checker pane, click **Slide 6**. Slide 6 is displayed. The objects on this slide might not be read by a screen reader in the order you want, so you need to check the order of the objects on the slide.
7. On the ribbon, click the **Home** tab.
8. In the Editing group, click the **Select** button, and then click **Selection Pane**. The Selection Pane opens. Remember that the objects on the slide will be identified in the reverse order that they are listed in the Selection Pane—in other words, from the bottom layer to the top layer. In this case, the title will be identified first, then the table, then the slide number, and finally, the text box that contains the footnote for Ride-Along in the table. It would be better if the footnote is identified immediately after the table.
9. In the Selection Pane, click **TextBox5**, and then click the **Send Backward** button at the top of the pane, and then close the Selection Pane.

10. In the Accessibility Checker pane, click the **Close** button [X].
11. Save the changes to the presentation.

You will let Chris know about the objects that need alt text and suggest that he change the displayed text for the link on Slide 8 so it is clear.

Encrypting a Presentation

To **encrypt** a file is to modify it to make the information unreadable to unauthorized people. When you encrypt a PowerPoint file, you assign a password to the file. The only way to open the file is by entering the password. When you create passwords, keep in mind that they are case sensitive; this means that "PASSWORD" is different from "password." Also, you must remember your password. This might seem obvious, but if you forget the password you assign to a file, you won't be able to open it.

REFERENCE

Encrypting a Presentation

- On the ribbon, click the File tab to open the Info screen in Backstage view.
- Click the Protect Presentation button, and then click Encrypt with Password.
- In the Encrypt Document dialog box, type a password in the Password box, and then click the OK button to open the Confirm Password dialog box.
- Retype the password in the Reenter password box.
- Click the OK button.

Chris wants you to encrypt the Speedway Events file so that it can be opened only by people with whom he has shared the password.

To encrypt the presentation with a password:

1. On the ribbon, click the **File** tab to open the Info screen in Backstage view.
2. Click the **Protect Presentation** button. A menu opens listing options for protecting the presentation. See Figure 6-30.

Figure 6-30 Protect Presentation menu on Info screen

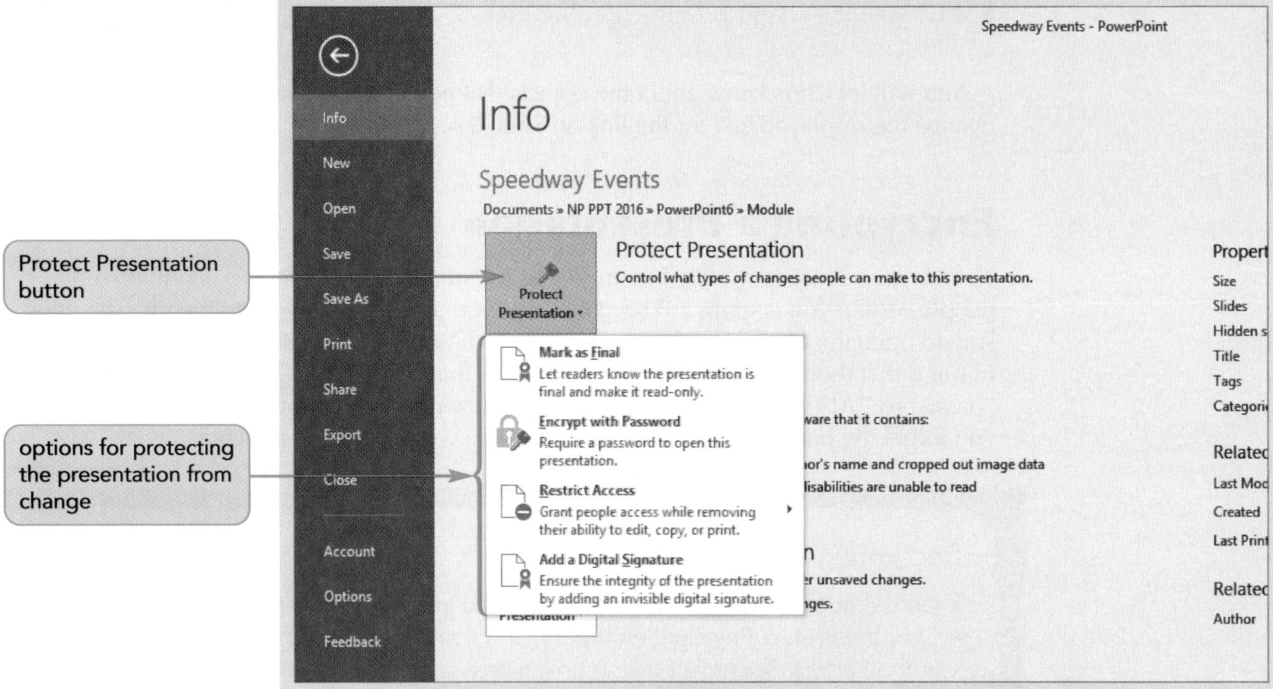

Protect Presentation button

options for protecting the presentation from change

TIP

To remove the password, delete the password in the Encrypt Document dialog box, and then click the OK button.

3. Click **Encrypt with Password**. The Encrypt Document dialog box opens. Here you'll type a password.
4. Type **Speedway**. The characters you type appear as black dots to prevent anyone from reading the password over your shoulder.
5. Click the **OK** button. The dialog box changes to the Confirm Password dialog box.
6. Type **Speedway** again to verify the password, and then click the **OK** button. The Protect Presentation section heading and the Protect Presentation button are yellow to indicate that a protection has been set, and the message in the Protect Presentation section explains that a password is required to open the presentation. See Figure 6-31.

Figure 6-31 Info screen after encrypting file

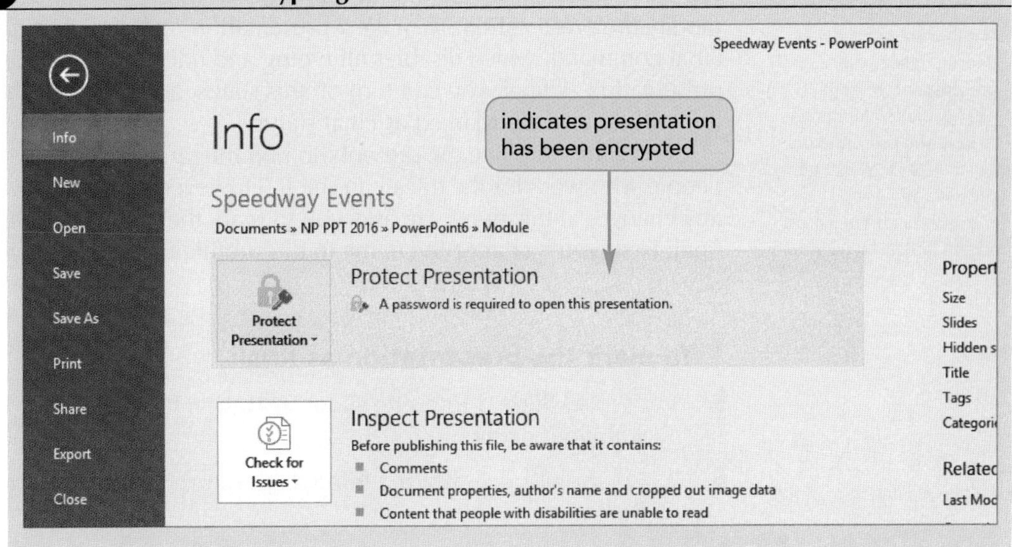

7. Save the changes to the presentation.

Now, when you save the file, it will be in an encrypted format, so that it can't be opened except by someone who knows the password. (Normally, you would use a stronger password than "Speedway," but for the purpose here, you'll keep it simple and easy to remember.)

PROSKILLS

Decision Making: Creating Strong Passwords You Can Easily Remember

In a world where sharing digital information electronically is an everyday occurrence, a password used to encrypt a presentation is just one more password to remember. When deciding on a password, you should consider a strong password that consists of at least eight characters using a combination of uppercase and lowercase letters, numbers, and symbols. However, this type of password can be difficult to remember, especially if you have to remember multiple passwords. Some people use the same password for everything. This is not a good idea because if someone ever discovered your password, they would have access to all of the data or information protected by that password. Instead, you should come up with a plan for creating passwords. For example, you could choose a short word that you can easily remember for one part of the password. The second part of the password could be the name of the file, website, or account, but instead of typing it directly, type it backwards, or use the characters in the row above or below the characters that would spell out the name. Or you could split the name of the site and put your short word in the middle of the name. Other possibilities are to combine your standard short word and the site or account name, but replace certain letters with symbols—for example, replace every letter "E" with "#," or memorize a short phrase from a poem or story and use it with some of the substitutions described above. Establishing a process for creating a password means that you will be able to create strong passwords for all of your accounts that you can easily remember.

Marking the Presentation as Final

TIP

Another way to allow people to see your presentation without being able to change it is to save the presentation as a PDF or as a picture presentation using commands on the Export screen in Backstage view.

You can make a presentation **read-only**, which means that others can read but cannot modify the presentation. To make a presentation read-only, you use the Mark as Final command, which disables all typing and editing commands. After you mark a presentation as final, you can turn off this status, and then edit the presentation, but this will remove the Marked as Final status.

Chris wants to place the presentation on the race track's network so that other people who work for the track can see it. However, he doesn't want anyone to make any changes at this point. He asks you to mark the Speedway Events presentation as final. First, you'll change the name in the subtitle text box to your own name.

To mark the presentation as final:

1. Display **Slide 1** (the title slide), and then replace "Chris Stern" in the subtitle with your name.
2. On the ribbon, click the **File** tab to return to the Info screen in Backstage view.
3. Click the **Protect Presentation** button, and then click **Mark as Final**. A dialog box opens stating that the presentation will be marked as final and then saved.
4. Click the **OK** button. The dialog box and Backstage view close, and another dialog box opens telling you that the document has been marked as final.

   Trouble? If the dialog box stating that the document has been marked as final does not appear, a previous user clicked the Don't show this message again check box in that dialog box. Skip Step 5.
5. Click the **OK** button. The ribbon is collapsed, a yellow MARKED AS FINAL bar appears below the collapsed ribbon, the Marked as Final icon appears in the status bar, and "Read-Only" appears in the title bar. See Figure 6-32.

Figure 6-32 Presentation marked as final

© iStock.com/stevedangers; © iStock.com/rjdek; © iStock.com/cipango27

Now if you want to modify the presentation, you must remove the editing restriction by clicking the Edit Anyway button in the yellow MARKED AS FINAL bar.

INSIGHT

Adding a Digital Signature and Restricting Access

A **digital signature** is an electronic attachment, which is not visible in the file, that verifies the authenticity of the author or the version of the file by comparing the digital signature to a digital certificate. A **digital certificate** is a code attached to a file that verifies the identity of the creator of the file. When you digitally sign a document, the file is automatically marked as final to protect it from changes. If anyone removes the Marked as Final status so that you can make changes to the document, the signature is marked as invalid because it is no longer the same document the signatory signed. You can obtain a digital certificate from a certification authority.

To add a digital signature to a file, click the Protect Presentation button on the Info screen in Backstage view, and then click Add a Digital Signature. If the Get a Digital ID dialog box opens indicating that you don't have a digital ID and asking if you would like to get one from a Microsoft Partner, that means no digital certificate is stored on the computer you are using. If you click the Yes button, your browser starts, and a webpage opens, listing certificate authorities from whom you can purchase a digital certificate.

If you or your company has access to a Rights Management Server or you are using Office 365 with RMS Online, you can restrict access to a presentation so that others can read it but not make any changes to it or copy or print it. To do this, click the Protect Presentation button, and then use the Restrict Access command.

Presenting Online

You can run a slide show over the Internet so that anyone with a browser and the URL (the address for a webpage on the Internet) for the presentation can watch it while you present. When you present online, you send the presentation to a special Microsoft server that is made available for this purpose. (If you have access to a SharePoint server, you can send the presentation to that server instead.) A unique web address is created, and you can send this web address to anyone you choose. Then, while you run your presentation on your computer in Slide Show view, your remote audience members can view it on their computers in a web browser at the same time. Note that viewers will not be able to hear you unless you also set up a conference call. This is different from posting an Office mix. When you post a mix, anyone who has a link to it can view it at any time. When you present online, viewers need to click the link and watch the presentation while you are presenting.

In order to present online, you need a Microsoft account (or access to a SharePoint server), and you need to be connected to the Internet. If you don't have a Microsoft account, you can get one by clicking the Sign in link in the upper-right corner of the PowerPoint window or by going to www.live.com. Once you have a Microsoft account, you can connect to the Microsoft server from within your PowerPoint presentation to create the unique web address for your presentation and start presenting online.

To present a slide show online, click the Slide Show tab, and then in the Start Slide Show group, click the Present Online button to open the Present Online dialog box, as shown in Figure 6-33.

Figure 6-33 **Present Online dialog box**

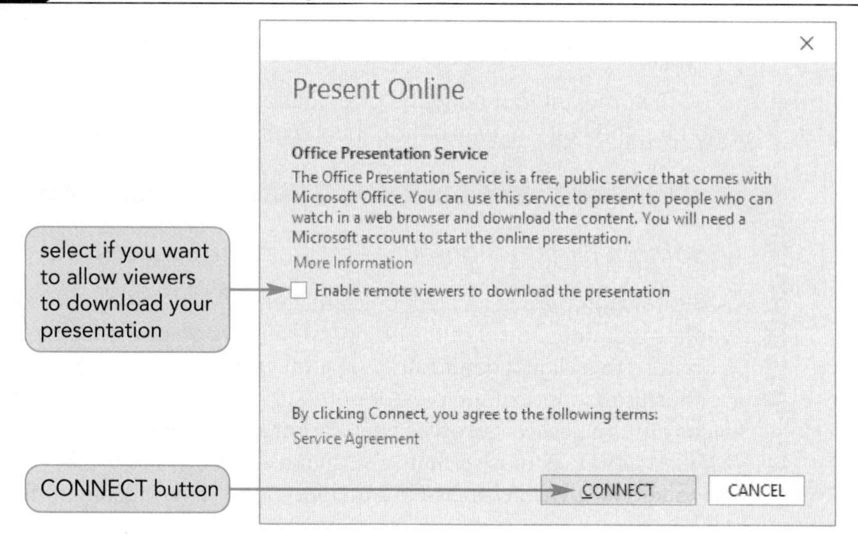

Click the CONNECT button. If you are signed into your Microsoft account in Office, the dialog box changes to display the link to your presentation on the Microsoft server and a new tab—the Present Online tab—appears on the ribbon, as shown in Figure 6-34. If you are not signed in to your Microsoft account, you will need to sign in before the link is created.

Figure 6-34 **Present Online dialog box after web address is created**

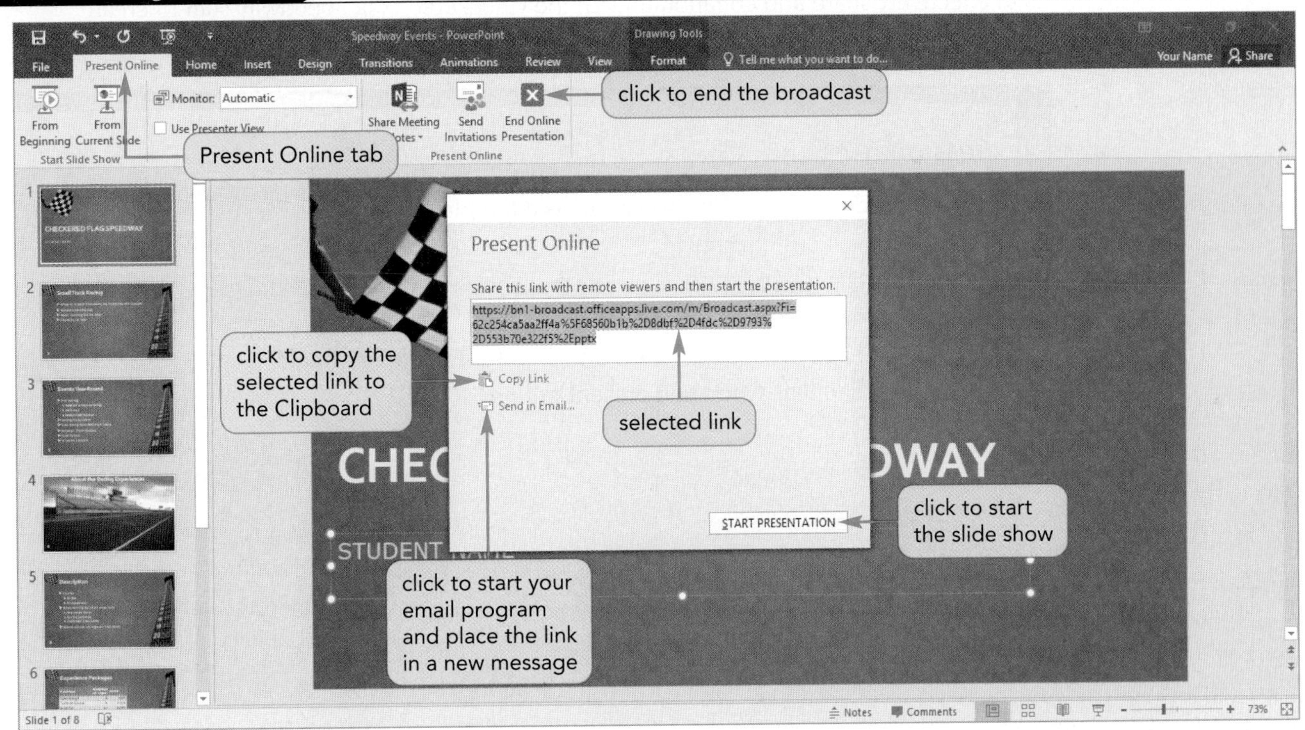

To invite people to watch your presentation, you need to send them the link. You can copy the link and send it to people via email, Facebook, or whichever your preferred method of communicating over the Internet is, or you can click Send in Email to open your email program and automatically include the link in the message. If you need to retrieve this link again after you close this dialog box, you can click the Send Invitations button in the Present Online group on the Present Online tab.

To start the online slide show, click the Start Presentation button in the Present Online dialog box, or click one of the buttons in the Start Slide Show group on the Present Online tab. The presentation appears in Slide Show view on your computer (although you can switch to Presenter view if you prefer). Anyone watching the presentation online will see the first slide in his or her browser window. You can advance through the slide show as you normally would, and viewers will see the slides on their screens. Note that no matter what transition you see in Slide Show or Presenter view on your computer, viewers watching online might see a different transition. In addition, not all animations will animate correctly. Therefore, if you plan to present online, you should preview the presentation in your own browser first and make sure the transitions and animations are acceptable.

To end the online slide show and disconnect from the Microsoft server, click the End Online Presentation button in the Present Online group on the Present Online tab. In the dialog box that opens warning you that everyone watching the online presentation will be disconnected, click the End Online Presentation button.

Note that if you needed to sign into your Microsoft account in order to present online, you are now signed into that account in Office. To sign out, click your username in the upper-right corner of the PowerPoint window, and then click Account settings to open the Account screen in Backstage view. Below your username, click Sign out.

You have finished working on Chris's presentation. He has the versions he needs to effectively share and collaborate with the Checkered Flag Speedway staff to create consistent presentations to meet multiple purposes.

REVIEW

Session 6.2 Quick Check

1. How do you save a presentation as a template?
2. What is a custom show?
3. What is a file property?
4. What is an encrypted presentation?
5. What happens to a presentation when it is marked as final?
6. What happens when you present online?

PRACTICE

Review Assignments

Data Files needed for the Review Assignments: Jen.pptx, Safety.pptx, Sunset.jpg

People who purchase a Racing Experience package need to attend a safety orientation before they drive on the track. Jeff, the operations manager, usually gives the orientation. He created a PowerPoint presentation that others can use as a guideline in case he is not able to give the orientation lecture. He started with the custom theme that Chris, the promotions director, created, but he made a few changes that he sent to Chris. Chris had his assistant, Jen Randall, make a few changes and send the presentation back to Jeff. Jeff asks you to help him complete the presentation. Complete the following steps:

1. Open the file **Safety**, located in the PowerPoint6 > Review folder included with your Data Files. On Slide 1, add your name as the subtitle, and then save the file as **Safety Orientation** in the location where you are saving your files.
2. Compare the Safety Orientation presentation with the file **Jen**, located in the PowerPoint6 > Review folder. Do not accept the theme change, do not accept the change that says that Jen deleted your name on Slide 1, accept the change on Slide 3 ("Passing"), and then end the review.
3. On Slide 3 ("Passing"), read the comment from Jeff, and then type the following as a reply: **The text box Jen added at the bottom of the slide addresses this.**
4. On Slide 1 (the title slide), insert the following as a new comment: **I think a red background would be better.**
5. On Slide 7 ("Insurance"), read Jeff's comment. Insert the following as the first bulleted item in the bulleted list: **$69 additional fee** and then delete Jeff's comment.
6. Change the theme fonts to a theme font set that uses Century Gothic for the Headings font, and then customize the theme font set so that Body text uses the Corbel font. Save the custom theme font set with the default name.
7. Delete the custom theme font set from the computer.
8. Change the theme color palette to the Orange Red palette.
9. Modify the Speedway2 Slide Master by modifying the format of the text in the title text box so it is bold.
10. Continue modifying the Speedway2 Slide Master by changing the color of the bullet symbols in the content placeholder to White, Background 1, and change the size of the bullets to 120% of the text.
11. Create a new layout after the Title Slide Layout.
12. Hide the background graphics on the new layout.
13. In the new layout, below the title text placeholder, add a Picture placeholder that is the same height as the slide (7.5" high) and is 8.2" wide. Use the Align Center command to center it on the slide, and then move it to the bottom layer.
14. Resize the title text placeholder so it is the same width as the picture placeholder you inserted (8.2"). Position the title text placeholder so its top edge is aligned with the top edge of the slide and so its left and right edges are aligned with the left and right edges of the picture placeholder. Change the size of the text in the title text placeholder to 54 points and center it in the title text placeholder.
15. Rename the custom layout **Title Slide Alternate**.
16. Change the layout of Slide 1 (the title slide) to Title Slide Alternate. In the Picture placeholder, insert the photo **Sunset**, located in the PowerPoint6 > Review folder.
17. On Slide 1, select the text box containing your name, and then remove the bullet symbol. Resize the text box so your name just fits in it on one line, and then position it in the bottom-right corner, so its right and bottom edges are aligned with the right and bottom edges of the slide.

18. On Slide 1, fill the title text placeholder with a Dark Blue color that has an RGB value approximately 46, 78, 117 from the area of the photo just above and to the left of the letter "S" in "Safety." Change the fill to a gradient that uses two gradient stops that both use the Blue color you selected from the photo. Change the type of the gradient to Linear, and then change the direction to Linear Down. Change the transparency of the rightmost gradient stop, positioned at the 100% mark, to 100%. If necessary, change the transparency of the leftmost gradient stop to 0%. Reposition the leftmost gradient stop at the 40% position.
19. Save the changes to the presentation.
20. Save the presentation as a template named **Safety Template** in the location where you are saving your files. Delete Slides 2 through 7, delete the comment on Slide 1, save the changes, and then close the template. Reopen the **Safety Orientation** presentation.
21. Create a custom show named **Rules** that contains Slide 3 ("Passing") and Slide 5 ("Flags").
22. Add **Revised** as the Status property. Add the custom property Editor with your name as the value of that property.
23. Check the presentation for accessibility issues. On the two slides that are flagged to check the reading order, change the order so that the text box would be read before the slide number.
24. Encrypt the presentation with the password **Safety**, and then mark the presentation as final.

APPLY

Case Problem 1

Data Files needed for this Case Problem: Backyard.pptx, Isabella.pptx, Soil.jpg, Vegetables.jpg

Backyard Farmer for Hire Isabella Delgado founded Backyard Farmer for Hire in Pittsburgh, Pennsylvania, in 2015. She and her staff design and plant vegetable and herb gardens for people at their homes. They plant directly in the ground if that's what the client wants, but they recommend and specialize in creating raised beds. They also create container gardens for small spaces. Clients can then choose to maintain and harvest their gardens, or they can have Isabella and her staff return on a weekly basis to do this. Isabella rented a booth at the upcoming Pittsburgh home and garden show, and she wants a PowerPoint presentation to be running on a computer in her booth. She asks you to help her complete the presentation. Complete the following:

1. Open the file **Backyard.pptx**, located in the PowerPoint > Case1 folder included with your Data Files, add your name as the subtitle, and then save the file as **Backyard Farmer** in the location where you are saving your files.
2. Compare the presentation with the file **Isabella.pptx**, located in the PowerPoint6 > Case1 folder. Do not accept the change on Slide 1, and then accept the change on Slide 6.
3. Read the comment from Isabella on Slide 1 (the title slide), and then delete it.
4. Change the theme fonts so the font used for the headings is Calisto MT, and then delete the custom font set. Change the theme colors to Green.
5. On the Office Theme Slide Master, change the size of the bullet symbols in the content placeholder to 120% of the text.
6. On the Office Theme Slide Master, insert the picture **Soil**, located in the PowerPoint > Case1 folder. Position it so it is aligned with the left edge of the slide.
7. Duplicate the Soil picture, and position the duplicate picture so it is right-aligned with the right edge of the slide.
8. Move the two Soil pictures to the bottom layers.
9. Insert a rectangle shape that is the same height as the slide (7.5") and that is as wide as the title text and content placeholders (11.23"). Position the rectangle in the center of the slide so it is on top of the placeholders. Fill the rectangle with the White, Background 1 color. Move the rectangle to the layer behind the placeholders and in front of the two Soil pictures.

10. On the Title Slide Layout, insert the picture **Vegetables**, located in the PowerPoint6 > Case1 folder. Resize the picture of vegetables so it is the same size as the white rectangle you drew. Send the picture to the bottom layer on the layout.
11. On the Title Slide Layout, change the fill of the title text placeholder to the Lavender color with an RGB value of about 225, 214, 219 below the "t" in "to." Change the fill to a gradient using three gradient stops with the color of all three gradient stops set to the Lavender color you filled the text box with. Change the type to Rectangular and the direction to From Center. Position the first gradient stop at the 60% position with 40% transparency. Position the second gradient stop at the 70% position with 50% transparency. Position the third gradient stop at the 100% position with 100% transparency.
12. Create a custom show named **Locations** consisting of Slides 1 and 5.
13. Add **Draft** as the Status property.
14. Add the custom property Purpose with the value **New Clients**.
15. Check the presentation for accessibility issues. On the slide listed under Check Reading Order, adjust the reading order so that the text box is identified before Content Placeholder 4.
16. Encrypt the presentation using the password **Backyard**.
17. Mark the presentation as final.

CREATE

Case Problem 2

Data Files needed for this Case Problem: Compass.jpg, First-Aid.jpg, Logo.png, OAE.pptx

OAE Stores Seth Wilder manages OAE in Mankato, Minnesota. OAE, which stands for Outdoor Adventures and Equipment, is a retail store that sells equipment for outdoor recreational activities, such as camping, fishing, and hiking. OAE also runs Discovery School, where customers can learn skills and techniques for outdoor activities. Seth wants to create a presentation that describes the classes at Discovery School. He created slides that describe two of the courses, and he plans to create the rest of the slides later. He asked you to help him design the slide master. Refer to Figure 6-35 as you complete the following:

1. Open the presentation **OAE**, located in the PowerPoint6 > Case2 folder included with your data files, add your name as the subtitle, and then save the file as **OAE Stores** in the location where you are saving your files.
2. Refer to Figure 6-35, and make the changes listed in the figure. All needed files are located in the PowerPoint6 > Case2 folder.
3. Delete the custom theme font set you created.
4. Add **Discovery School** as the Categories property.
5. Add **Seth Wilder** as the Checked by custom property.
6. Save the changes to the presentation.
7. Save the presentation as a template named **OAE Template**. Delete Slides 2 through 5, and then save and close the presentation.
8. Reopen the **OAE Stores** file, and then encrypt the presentation with the password **OAE**.
9. Mark the presentation as final.

Figure 6-35 OAE Stores presentation slides

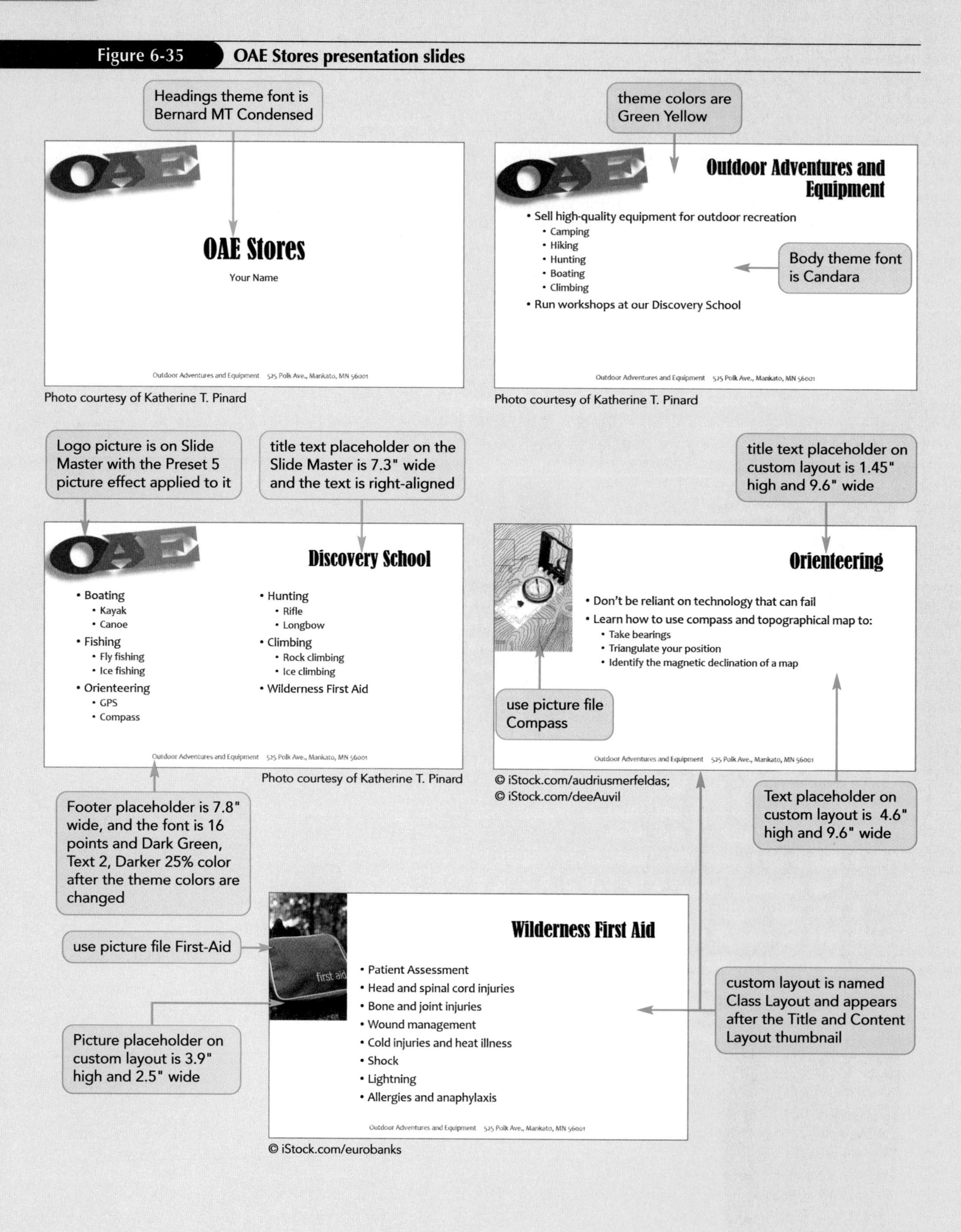

© iStock.com/eurobanks

E

F

G

H

I